Bond Markets

Fabozzi, *Bond Markets, Analysis and Strategies, 5e*

Money and Capital Markets

Fabozzi/Modigliani, *Capital Markets: Institutions and Instruments, 3e*

Financial Markets and Institutions

Fabozzi/Modigliani/Ferri/Jones, *Foundations of Financial Markets and Institutions, 3e*
Van Horne, *Financial Market Rates and Flows, 6e*

Financial Research Methods

Seiler, *Performing Financial Studies: A Methodological Cookbook*

Entrepreneurial Finance

Cornwall/Vang/Hartman, *Entrepreneurial Financial Management*

International Finance

Click/Coval, *The Theory and Practice of International Financial Management*

Risk Management

Dorfman, *Introduction to Risk Management and Insurance, 8e*

Commercial Banking

Sinkey, *Commercial Bank Financial Management, 6e*

Personal Finance

Keown, *Personal Finance: Turning Money into Wealth, UPDATED, 3e*
Winger/Frasca, *Personal Finance: An Integrated Planning Approach, 6e*

Capital Budgeting

Shapiro, *Capital Budgeting*

Financial Economics

Bodie/Merton, *Finance*

For more information on Finance titles from Prentice Hall, visit us at: www.prenhall.com/finance.

FIFTH EDITION

FUNDAMENTALS OF FUTURES AND OPTIONS MARKETS

John C. Hull

Maple Financial Group Professor of Derivatives and Risk Management
Director, Bonham Center for Finance
Joseph L. Rotman School of Management
University of Toronto

PEARSON EDUCATION INTERNATIONAL

Senior Acquisitions Editor: Jackie Aaron
Editorial Director: Jeff Shelstad
Managing Editor (Editorial): Gladys Soto
Assistant Editor: Francesca Calogero
Executive Marketing Manager: Debbie Clare
Marketing Assistant: Nicole Macchiarelli
Managing Editor (Production): Cynthia Regan
Production Editor: Denise Culhane
Production Manager: Arnold Vila
Manufacturing Buyer: Diane Peirano
Design Director: Maria Lange
Cover Design: The Lehigh Press, Inc.
Composition/Full-Service Project Management: The Geometric Press
Printer/Binder: Hamilton Printing Company
Typeface: 10/12pt Times

Credits and acknowledgments borrowed from other sources and reproduced, with permission, in this textbook appear on appropriate page within text.

Pearson Education LTD.
Pearson Education Singapore, Pte. Ltd
Pearson Education, Canada, Ltd
Pearson Education–Japan
Pearson Education Australia PTY, Limited
Pearson Education North Asia Ltd
Pearson Educaciœn de Mexico, S.A. de C.V.
Pearson Education Malaysia, Pte. Ltd
Pearson Education Upper Saddle River, New Jersey

10 9 8 7 6 5 4 3 2 1
ISBN 0-13-127394-9

To
My Students

Contents

BUSINESS SNAPSHOTS

Preface

I was originally persuaded to write this book by colleagues who liked my other book *Options, Futures, and Other Derivatives*, but found the material a little too advanced for their students. *Fundamentals of Futures and Options Markets* covers much of the same ground as *Options, Futures, and Other Derivatives*, but in a way that readers who have had limited training in mathematics find easier to understand. One important difference between the two books is that there is no calculus in the present book. *Fundamentals* is suitable for undergraduate and graduate elective courses offered by business, economics, and other faculties. In addition, many practitioners who want to improve their understanding of futures and options markets will find the book useful.

Instructors can use this book in many different ways. Some may choose to cover only the first eleven chapters, finishing with binomial trees. For those who want to do more, there are many different sequences in which the material in Chapters 12 to 23 can be covered. From Chapter 16 onward, each chapter has been designed so that it is independent of the others and can be included in or omitted from a course without causing problems. I would recommend finishing a course with Chapter 23, which students always find interesting and entertaining.

What's New in This Edition

1. There is a new chapter on credit derivatives (Chapter 21).
2. The opening six chapters have been replaced by seven chapters that cover forward, futures, and swap contracts in a more student-friendly way. The chapter on hedging using futures has been moved to Chapter 3. Chapter 4 is now devoted to understanding how interest rates are calculated and used. Chapter 5 covers the determination of futures and forward prices. Chapter 6 deals with interest rate futures and Chapter 7 covers swaps.
3. Forty descriptions of real-world situations and interesting issues, referred to as *Business Snapshots*, illustrate points being made in the text.
4. There is a new release of DerivaGem (version 1.51), which includes Excel functions and examples of how they can be used.
5. The sequencing of Chapters 15 to 18 has been changed to better meet the needs of students and instructors.
6. The "Introduction to Binomial Trees" chapter has been extended to provide a more complete coverage of binomial trees in one place relatively early in the book.
7. For readers unfamiliar with the exponential and logarithm functions, an explanatory appendix has been added to Chapter 4.

8. The *Solutions Manual* has been expanded to become a *Solutions Manual and Study Guide*
9. There have been two changes to the mathematical notation. Here, K is used instead of X for an option's strike price, and δt, δx, etc., have been replaced by Δt, Δx, etc. (This reverses a change made in the last edition, where I was trying to avoid overworking Δ, but found that the change was not popular!)
10. New end-of-chapter problems have been added.

The book (including end-of-chapter references) has been fully updated. Many changes have been made to improve the presentation of material.

Software

DerivaGem version 1.51 is included with this book. This consists of two Excel applications: the *Options Calculator* and the *Applications Builder*. The Options Calculator consists of the software in the previous release (with minor improvements including the unlocking of worksheets). The Applications Builder consists of a number of Excel functions from which users can build their own applications. It includes a number of sample applications and enables students to explore the properties of options and numerical procedures more easily. It also allows more interesting assignments to be designed.

The software is described more fully at the end of the book. Updates to the software can be downloaded from my website:

http://www.rotman.utoronto.ca/~hull

Slides

Several hundred PowerPoint slides are available from my website. Instructors adopting the book for their courses are welcome to adapt the slides to meet their own needs.

Answers to End-of-Chapter Problems

At the end of each chapter (except the last) there are seven quiz questions that students can use to provide a quick test of their understanding of the key concepts. The answers to these are given at the end of the book. There are also over 270 Questions and Problems at the ends of chapters. Answers to these and advice for readers on how each chapter of the book should be studied are in the *Solutions Manual and Study Guide* (ISBN 0-13-144570-7), which is published by Prentice Hall. In addition, there are about one hundred Assignment Questions at the ends of chapters. Solutions to these are in the *Instructor's Manual*, which is available from Prentice Hall only to adopting instructors.

Acknowledgments

Many people have played a part in the production of this book. Academics, students, and practitioners who have made excellent and useful suggestions over the years include Farhang Aslani, Emilio Barone, Giovanni Barone-Adesi, George Blazenko, Laurence Booth, Phelim Boyle, Peter Carr, Don Chance, J. P. Chateau, Brian Donaldson, Jerome Duncan, Steinar Ekern, Robert Eldridge, David Fowler, Louis Gagnon, Mark Garman, Dajiang Guo, Bernie Hildebrandt, Jim Hilliard, Basil Kalymon, Patrick Kearney, Cheng-kun Kuo, Elizabeth Maynes, Eddie Mizzi, Izzy Nelken, Paul Potvin, Richard Rendleman, Gordon Roberts, Edward Robbins, Chris Robinson, John Rumsey,

Klaus Schurger, Eduardo Schwartz, Michael Selby, Piet Sercu, Yochanan Shachmurove, Bill Shao, Stuart Turnbull, Yisong Tian, Ton Vorst, George Wang, Zhanshun Wei, Bob Whaley, Alan White, Qunfeng Yang, and Jozef Zemek. Rebecca Sun provided excellent research assistance.

I would particularly like to thank Alan White. Alan is a colleague at the University of Toronto with whom I have been carrying out joint research in options and futures for over twenty years. We have spent many hours discussing different issues concerning options and futures markets. Many of the new ideas in this book, and many of the new ways used to explain old ideas, are as much Alan's as mine. Alan has done most of the development work on the DerivaGem software.

Special thanks are due to my editor at Prentice Hall, Jackie Aaron, for her support, enthusiasm, advice, and encouragement. I am also grateful to Scott Barr, Leah Jewell, Paul Donnelly, and Maureen Riopelle, who at different times in the past have played key roles in the development of the book.

I welcome comments on the book from readers. My e-mail address is:

hull@rotman.utoronto.ca

John Hull
University of Toronto

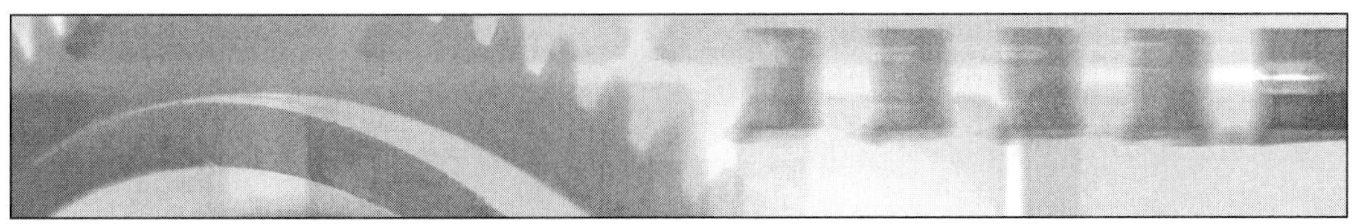

CHAPTER 1 Introduction

In recent years derivatives markets have become increasingly important in the world of finance and investments. We have now reached the stage where it is essential for all finance professionals to understand how these markets work, how they can be used, and what determines prices in them. This book addresses these issues.

In this opening chapter we take a first look at futures, forward, and options markets. We examine their history and provide an overview of how they are used by hedgers, by speculators, and by arbitrageurs.

1.1 FUTURES CONTRACTS

A *futures contract* is an agreement to buy or sell an asset at a certain time in the future for a certain price. There are many exchanges throughout the world trading futures contracts. The two largest futures exchanges in the United States are the Chicago Board of Trade (www.cbot.com) and the Chicago Mercantile Exchange (www.cme.com). Two of the largest exchanges in Europe are the London International Financial Futures and Options Exchange (www.liffe.com) and Eurex (www.eurexchange.com). Other large exchanges include Bolsa de Mercadorias y Futuros (www.bmf.com.br) in São Paulo, the Tokyo International Financial Futures Exchange (www.tiffe.or.jp), the Singapore International Monetary Exchange (www.simex.com.sg), and the Sydney Futures Exchange (www.sfe.com.au). For a more complete list, see the table at the end of this book.

Futures exchanges provide a mechanism for people who want to buy or sell assets in the future to trade with each other. In March an investor in New York might contact a broker with instructions to buy 5,000 bushels of corn for July delivery. The broker would immediately communicate the client's instructions to the Chicago Board of Trade. At about the same time, another investor in Kansas might instruct a broker to sell 5,000 bushels of corn for July delivery. These instructions would also be passed on to the Chicago Board of Trade. A price would be determined and the deal would be done.

The investor in New York who agreed to buy has what is termed a *long futures position*; the investor in Kansas who agreed to sell has what is termed a *short futures*

Figure 1.1 A futures contract (assuming it is held to maturity)

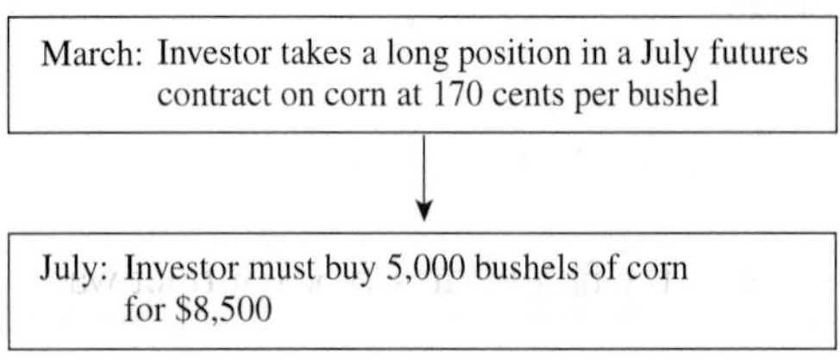

position. The price is known as the *futures price*. We will suppose the price is 170 cents per bushel. This price, like any other price, is determined by the laws of supply and demand. If at a particular time more people wish to sell July corn than to buy July corn, the price goes down. New buyers will then enter the market so that a balance between buyers and sellers is maintained. If more people wish to buy July corn than to sell July corn, the price goes up—for similar reasons.

Issues such as margin requirements, daily settlement procedures, trading practices, commissions, bid–offer spreads, and the role of the exchange clearinghouse will be discussed in Chapter 2. For the time being, we can assume that the end result of the events just described is that the investor in New York has agreed to buy 5,000 bushels of corn for 170 cents per bushel in July and the investor in Kansas has agreed to sell 5,000 bushels of corn for 170 cents per bushel in July. Both sides have entered into a binding contract. The contract is illustrated in Figure 1.1.

1.2 HISTORY OF FUTURES MARKETS

Futures markets can be traced back to the Middle Ages. They were originally developed to meet the needs of farmers and merchants. Consider the position of a farmer in April of a certain year who will harvest a known amount of grain in June. There is uncertainty about the price the farmer will receive for the grain. In years of scarcity it might be possible to obtain relatively high prices—particularly if the farmer is not in a hurry to sell. On the other hand, in years of oversupply the grain might have to be disposed of at fire-sale prices. The farmer and the farmer's family are clearly exposed to a great deal of risk.

Consider next a company that has an ongoing requirement for grain. The company is also exposed to price risk. In some years an oversupply situation may create favorable prices; in other years scarcity may cause the prices to be exorbitant. It clearly makes sense for the farmer and the company to get together in April (or even earlier) and agree on a price for the farmer's production of grain in June. In other words, it makes sense for them to negotiate a type of futures contract. The contract provides a way for each side to eliminate the risk it faces because of the uncertain future price of grain.

We might ask what happens to the company's requirements for grain during the rest of the year. Once the harvest season is over, the grain must be stored until the next season. In undertaking this storage, the company does not bear any price risk, but does incur the costs of storage. If the farmer or some other person stores the grain, the company and the storer both face risks associated with the future grain price, and again there is a clear role for futures contracts.

The Chicago Board of Trade

The Chicago Board of Trade was established in 1848 to bring farmers and merchants together. Initially its main task was to standardize the quantities and qualities of the grains that were traded. Within a few years the first futures-type contract was developed. It was known as a *to-arrive contract*. Speculators soon became interested in the contract and found trading the contract to be an attractive alternative to trading the grain itself. The Chicago Board of Trade now offers futures contracts on many different underlying assets, including corn, oats, soybeans, soybean meal, soybean oil, wheat, Treasury bonds, and Treasury notes.

The Chicago Mercantile Exchange

In 1874 the Chicago Produce Exchange was established, providing a market for butter, eggs, poultry, and other perishable agricultural products. In 1898 the butter and egg dealers withdrew from the exchange to form the Chicago Butter and Egg Board. In 1919, this was renamed the Chicago Mercantile Exchange (CME) and was reorganized for futures trading. Since then, the exchange has provided a futures market for many commodities, including pork bellies (1961), live cattle (1964), live hogs (1966), and feeder cattle (1971). In 1982 it introduced a futures contract on the Standard & Poor's (S&P) 500 Stock Index.

The Chicago Mercantile Exchange started futures trading in foreign currencies in 1972. The currency futures traded now include the British pound, the Canadian dollar, the Japanese yen, the Swiss franc, the Australian dollar, the Mexican peso, the Brazilian real, the South African rand, the New Zealand dollar, the Russian rouble, and the euro. The Chicago Mercantile Exchange also trades the very popular Eurodollar futures contract.

Electronic Trading

Traditionally futures contracts have been traded using what is known as the *open-outcry system*. This involves traders physically meeting on the floor of the exchange and using a complicated set of hand signals to indicate the trades they would like to carry out. In the example we considered earlier, one floor trader would represent the investor in New York who wanted to buy July corn and another floor trader would represent the investor in Kansas who wanted to sell July corn. Exchanges are increasingly replacing the open outcry system by *electronic trading*. This involves traders entering their required trades at a keyboard and a computer being used to match buyers and sellers. The open-outcry system has its advocates, but as time passes exchanges are increasingly using electronic trading.

1.3 THE OVER-THE-COUNTER MARKET

Not all trading is done on exchanges. What is known as the *over-the-counter* or OTC market is an important alternative to exchanges. It is a telephone- and computer-linked network of dealers, who do not physically meet. Trades are done over the phone. One side to the transaction is usually a trader working for a financial institution. The other side is likely to be either a trader working for another financial institution or a corporate treasurer or a fund manager. Financial institutions often act as market makers for the more commonly traded instruments. This means that they are always prepared to quote both a bid price (a price at which they are prepared to buy) and an offer price (a price at which they are prepared to sell).

Telephone conversations in the over-the-counter market are usually taped. If there is a dispute about what was agreed, the tapes are replayed to resolve the issue. Trades in the over-the-counter market are typically much larger than trades in the exchange-traded market. A key advantage of the over-the-counter market is that the terms of a contract do not have to be those specified by an exchange. Market participants are free to negotiate any mutually attractive deal. A disadvantage is that there is usually some credit risk in an over-the-counter trade (that is, there is a small risk that the contract will not be honored). As we shall see in the next chapter, exchanges have organized themselves to eliminate virtually all credit risk.

Both the over-the-counter and the exchange-traded market for derivatives are huge. Although the statistics that are collected for the two markets are not exactly comparable, it is clear that the over-the-counter market is much larger than the exchange-traded market. The Bank for International Settlements (www.bis.org) started collecting statistics on the markets in 1998. Figure 1.2 compares (a) the estimated total principal amounts underlying transactions that were outstanding in the over-the counter markets between 1998 and 2003 and (b) the estimated total value of the assets underlying exchange-traded contracts during the same period. Using these measures, by June 2003, the over-the-counter market had grown to \$169.7 trillion (approximately four times the world gross domestic product) and the exchange-traded market had grown to \$38.2 trillion.

In interpreting these numbers we should bear in mind that the principal underlying

Figure 1.2 Size of over-the-counter and exchange-traded derivatives markets

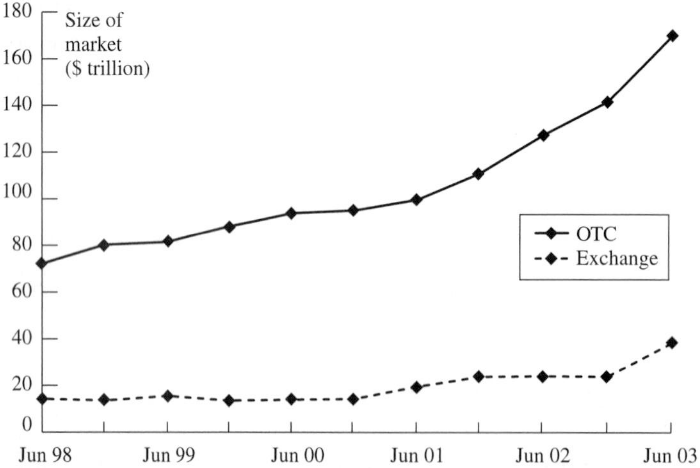

an over-the-counter transaction is not the same as its value. An example of an over-the-counter contract as is an agreement to buy 100 million U.S. dollars with British pounds at a predetermined exchange rate in one year. The total principal amount underlying this transaction is $100 million. However, the value of the contract might be only $500,000. The Bank for International Settlements estimates the gross market value of all OTC contracts outstanding in June 2003 to be $7.9 trillion.[1]

1.4 FORWARD CONTRACTS

A forward contract is similar to a futures contracts in that it is an agreement to buy or sell an asset at a certain time in the future for a certain price. But, whereas futures contracts are traded on exchanges, forward contracts trade in the over-the-counter market.

Forward contracts on foreign exchange are very popular. Most large banks employ both spot traders and forward traders. Spot traders are trading a foreign currency for almost immediate delivery. Forward traders are trading for delivery at a future time. Table 1.1 provides the quotes on the exchange rate between the British pound (GBP) and the U.S. dollar (USD) that might be made by a large international bank on June 3, 2003. The quote is for the number of USD per GBP. The first row indicates that the bank is prepared to buy GBP (also known as sterling) in the spot market (i.e., for virtually immediate delivery) at the rate of $1.6281 per GBP and sell sterling in the spot market at $1.6285 per GBP. The second row indicates that the bank is prepared to buy sterling in one month at $1.6248 per GBP and sell sterling in one month at $1.6253 per GBP; the third row indicates that it is prepared to buy sterling in three months at $1.6187 per GBP and sell sterling in three months at $1.6192 per GBP; and so on.

The quotes are for very large transactions. (As anyone who has traveled abroad knows, retail customers face much larger spreads between bid and offer quotes than those in Table 1.1.) After examining the quotes in Table 1.1, a large corporation might agree to sell £100 million in six months for $160.94 million to the bank as part of its hedging program.

There is a relationship between the forward price of a foreign currency, the spot price

Table 1.1 Spot and forward quotes for the USD/GBP exchange rate, June 3, 2003 (GBP = British pound; USD = U.S. dollar; quote is number of USD per GBP)

	Bid	*Offer*
Spot	1.6281	1.6285
1-month forward	1.6248	1.6253
3-month forward	1.6187	1.6192
6-month forward	1.6094	1.6100

[1] A contract that is worth $2 million to one side and –$2 million to the other side would be counted as having a gross market value of $2 million.

of the foreign currency, domestic interest rates and foreign interest rates. This is explained in Chapter 5.

1.5 OPTIONS CONTRACTS

There are two basic types of options: calls and puts. A *call option* gives the holder the right to buy an asset by a certain date for a certain price. A *put option* gives the holder the right to sell an asset by a certain date for a certain price. The price in the contract is known as the *exercise price* or the *strike price*; the date in the contract is known as the *expiration date* or the *maturity date*. A *European option* can be exercised only on the maturity date; an *American option* can be exercised at any time during its life.

It should be emphasized that an option gives the holder the right to do something. The holder does not have to exercise this right. This fact distinguishes options from futures (or forward) contracts. The holder of a long futures contract is committed to buying an asset at a certain price at a certain time in the future. By contrast, the holder of a call option has a choice as to whether to buy the asset at a certain price at a certain time in the future. It costs nothing (except for margin requirements, which will be discussed in Chapter 2) to enter into a futures contract. By contrast, an investor must pay an up-front price, known as the *option premium*, for an options contract.

The largest exchange in the world for trading stock options is the Chicago Board Options Exchange (CBOE; www.cboe.com). Table 1.2 gives the closing prices of some of the American options trading on Intel on May 29, 2003. The option strike prices are \$20 and \$22.50. The maturities are June 2003, July 2003, and October 2003. The June options have an expiration date on June 21, 2003; the July options have an expiration date on July 19, 2003; the October options have an expiration date on October 18, 2003. Intel's stock price at the close of trading on May 29, 2003, was 20.83.

Suppose an investor instructs a broker to buy one October call option contract on Intel with a strike price of \$22.50. The broker will relay these instructions to a trader at the CBOE. This trader will then find another trader who wants to sell one July call contract on Intel with a strike price of \$22.50, and a price will be agreed. We assume that the price is \$1.15, as indicated in Table 1.2. This is the price for an option to buy one share. In the United States, one stock option contract is a contract to buy or sell 100 shares. Therefore, the investor must arrange for \$115 to be remitted to the exchange through the broker. The exchange will then arrange for this amount to be passed on to the party on the other side of the transaction.

Table 1.2 Prices of options on Intel, May 29, 2003; stock price = \$20.83

Strike price (\$)	*Calls*			*Puts*		
	June	*July*	*Oct.*	*June*	*July*	*Oct.*
20.00	1.25	1.60	2.40	0.45	0.85	1.50
22.50	0.20	0.45	1.15	1.85	2.20	2.85

Figure 1.3 Net profit per share from (a) purchasing a contract consisting of 100 Intel October call options with a strike price of $22.50 and (b) purchasing a contract consisting of 100 Intel July put options with a strike price of $20.00

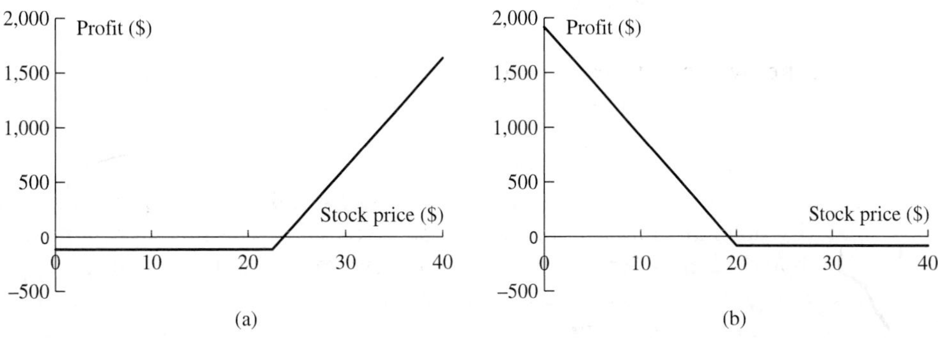

In our example the investor has obtained at a cost of $115 the right to buy 100 Intel shares for $22.50 each. The party on the other side of the transaction has received $115 and has agreed to sell 100 Intel shares for $22.50 per share if the investor chooses to exercise the option. If the price of Intel does not rise above $22.50 before October 18, 2003, the option is not exercised and the investor loses $115. But if the Intel share price does well and the option is exercised when it is $30, the investor is able to buy 100 shares at $22.50 per share when they are worth $30 per share. This leads to a gain of $750, or $635 when the initial cost of the options are taken into account.

An alternative trade for the investor would be the purchase of one July put option contract with a strike price of $20. From Table 1.2 we see that this would cost 100×0.85 or $85. The investor would obtain at a cost of $85 the right sell 100 Intel shares for $20 per share prior to July 19, 2003. If the Intel share price stays above $20 the option is not exercised and the investor loses $85. But if the investor exercises when the stock price is $15, the investor makes a gain of $500 by buying 100 Intel shares at $15 and selling them for $20. The net profit after the cost of the options is taken into account is $415.

The options trading on the CBOE are American. If we assume for simplicity that they are European so that they can be exercised only at maturity, the investor's profit as a function of the final stock price is shown in Figure 1.3.

Further details about the operation of options markets and how prices such as those in Table 1.2 are determined by traders are given in later chapters. At this stage we note that there are four types of participants in options markets:

1. Buyers of calls
2. Sellers of calls
3. Buyers of puts
4. Sellers of puts

Buyers are referred to as having *long positions*; sellers are referred to as having *short positions*. Selling an option is also known as *writing the option*.

1.6 HISTORY OF OPTIONS MARKETS

The first trading in puts and calls began in Europe and in the United States as early as the eighteenth century. In the early years the market got a bad name because of certain corrupt practices. One of these involved brokers being given options on a certain stock as an inducement for them to recommend the stock to their clients.

Put and Call Brokers and Dealers Association

In the early 1900s a group of firms set up the Put and Call Brokers and Dealers Association. The aim of this association was to provide a mechanism for bringing buyers and sellers together. Investors who wanted to buy an option would contact one of the member firms. This firm would attempt to find a seller or writer of the option from either its own clients or those of other member firms. If no seller could be found, the firm would undertake to write the option itself in return for what was deemed to be an appropriate price.

The options market of the Put and Call Brokers and Dealers Association suffered from two deficiencies. First, there was no secondary market. The buyer of an option did not have the right to sell it to another party prior to expiration. Second, there was no mechanism to guarantee that the writer of the option would honor the contract. If the writer did not live up to the agreement when the option was exercised, the buyer had to resort to costly lawsuits.

The Formation of Options Exchanges

In April 1973 the Chicago Board of Trade set up a new exchange, the Chicago Board Options Exchange, specifically for the purpose of trading stock options. Since then options markets have become increasingly popular with investors. The American Stock Exchange (www.amex.com) and the Philadelphia Stock Exchange (www.phlx.com) began trading options in 1975. The Pacific Exchange (www.pacificex.com) did the same in 1976. By the early 1980s the volume of trading had grown so rapidly that the number of shares underlying the option contracts traded each day exceeded the daily volume of shares traded on the New York Stock Exchange.

In the 1980s markets developed in the United States for options in foreign exchange, options on stock indices, and options on futures contracts. The Philadelphia Stock Exchange is the premier exchange for trading foreign exchange options. The Chicago Board Options Exchange trades options on the S&P 100 stock index (OEX), the S&P 500 stock index (SPX), the Nasdaq 100 Index (NDX), and the Dow Jones Industrial Average (DJX). Most exchanges offering futures contracts now also offer options on these contracts. Thus, the Chicago Board of Trade offers options on corn futures, the Chicago Mercantile Exchange offers options on live cattle futures, and so on. Options exchanges now exist all over the world. (See the table at the end of this book.)

The Over-the-Counter Market for Options

The over-the-counter market for options has grown very rapidly since the early 1980s and is now bigger than the exchange-traded market. One advantage of options traded in the over-the-counter market is that they can be tailored to meet the particular needs of a corporate treasurer or fund manager. For example, a corporate treasurer who wants a European call option to buy 1.6 million British pounds at an exchange rate of 1.5125 may not find exactly the right product trading on an exchange. However, it is likely that many investment banks would be pleased to provide a quote for an over-the-counter contract that meets the treasurer's precise needs.

1.7 TYPES OF TRADERS

Futures, forward, and options markets have been outstandingly successful. The main reason is that they have attracted many different types of traders and have a great deal of liquidity. When an investor wants to take one side of a contract, there is usually no problem in finding someone that is prepared to take the other side.

Three broad categories of traders can be identified: hedgers, speculators, and arbitrageurs. Hedgers use futures, forwards, and options to reduce the risk that they face from potential future movements in a market variable. Speculators use them to bet on the future direction of a market variable. Arbitrageurs take offsetting positions in two or more instruments to lock in a profit. In the next few sections, we consider the activities of each type of trader in more detail.

1.8 HEDGERS

In this section we illustrate how hedgers can reduce their risks with forward contracts and options.

An Example of Hedging Using Forward Contracts

Suppose that it is June 3, 2003, and ImportCo, a company based in the United States, knows that it will have to pay £10 million on September 3, 2003, for goods it has purchased from a British supplier. The USD/GBP exchange rate quotes made by a financial institution are shown in Table 1.1. ImportCo could hedge its foreign exchange risk by buying pounds (GBP) from the financial institution in the three-month forward market at 1.6192. This would have the effect of fixing the price to be paid to the British exporter at $16,192,000.

Consider next another U.S. company, which we will refer to as ExportCo, that is exporting goods to the United Kingdom and on June 3, 2003, knows that it will receive £30 million three months later. ExportCo can hedge its foreign exchange risk by selling £30 million in the three-month forward market at an exchange rate of 1.6187. This would have the effect of locking in the U.S. dollars to be realized for the sterling at $48,561,000.

Trading Note 1.1 summarizes the hedging strategies open to ImportCo and ExportCo. Note that a company might do better if it chooses not to hedge than if it chooses to hedge. Alternatively, might do worse. Consider ImportCo. If the exchange rate is 1.5000 on September 3 and the company has not hedged, the £10 million that it has to pay will cost $15,000,000, which is less than $16,192,000. On the other hand, if the exchange rate is 1.7000, the £10 million will cost $17,000,000—and the company will wish it had hedged! The position of ExportCo if it does not hedge is the reverse. If

Trading Note 1.1 Hedging with forward contracts

It is June 3, 2003. ImportCo must pay £10 million on September 3, 2003, for goods purchased from Britain. Using the quotes in Table 1.1, it buys £10 million in the three-month forward market to lock in an exchange rate of 1.6192 for the sterling it will pay.

ExportCo will receive £30 million on September 3, 2003, from a customer in Britain. Using quotes in Table 1.1 it sells £30 million in the three-month forward market to lock in an exchange rate of 1.6187 for the sterling it will receive.

the exchange rate in September proves to be less than 1.6187, the company will wish it had hedged; if the rate is greater than 1.6187, it will be pleased it has not done so.

This example illustrates a key aspect of hedging. The cost of, or price received for, the underlying asset is ensured. However, there is no assurance that the outcome with hedging will be better than the outcome without hedging.

An Example of Hedging Using Options

Options can also be used for hedging. Consider an investor who in May 2003 owns 1,000 Microsoft shares. The current share price is $28 per share. The investor is concerned about a possible share price decline in the next two months and wants protection. The investor could buy 10 July put option contracts on Microsoft on the Chicago Board Options Exchange with a strike price of $27.50. This would give the investor the right to sell a total of 1,000 shares for a price of $27.50. If the quoted option price is $1, each option contract would cost 100 × $1 = $100, and the total cost of the hedging strategy would be 10 × $100 = $1,000.

This strategy is summarized in Trading Note 1.2. The strategy costs $1,000 but guarantees that the shares can be sold for at least $27.50 per share during the life of the option. If the market price of Microsoft falls below $27.50, the options can be exercised so that $27,500 is realized for the entire holding. When the cost of the options is taken into account, the amount realized is $26,500. If the market price stays above $27.50, the options are not exercised and expire worthless. However, in this case the value of the holding is always above $27,500 (or above $26,500 when the cost of the options is taken into account). Figure 1.4 shows the net value of the portfolio (after

Trading Note 1.2 Hedging with options

It is May, 2003. An investor owns 1,000 Microsoft shares and wants protection against a possible decline in the share price over the next two months. Market quotes:

Current Microsoft share price: $28
Microsoft July 27.50 put: $1

Trading Strategy
The investor buys 10 put option contracts for a total cost of $1,000. This gives the investor the right to sell 1,000 shares for $27.50 per share during the next two months.

Figure 1.4 Value of Microsoft holding in two months with and without hedging

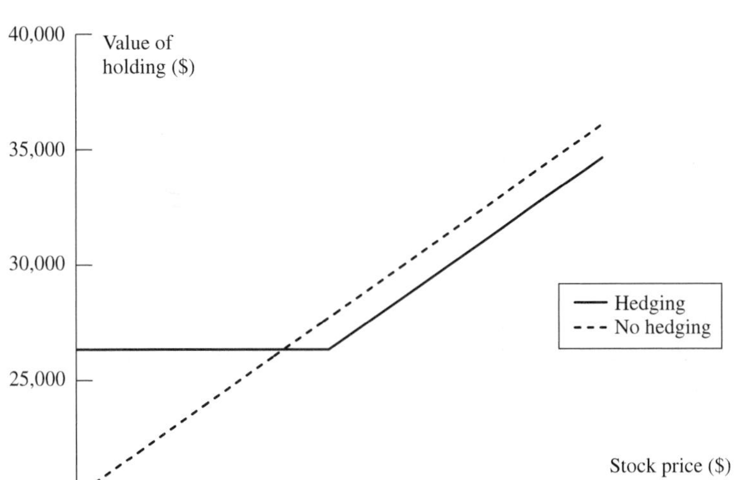

taking the cost of the options into account) as a function of Microsoft's stock price in two months. The dotted line shows the value of the portfolio assuming no hedging.

A Comparison

There is a fundamental difference between the use of forward contracts and options for hedging. Forward contracts are designed to neutralize risk by fixing the price that the hedger will pay or receive for the underlying asset. Option contracts, by contrast, provide insurance. They offer a way for investors to protect themselves against adverse price movements in the future while still allowing them to benefit from favorable price movements. Unlike forwards, options involve the payment of an up-front fee.

1.9 SPECULATORS

We now move on to consider how futures and options markets can be used by speculators. Whereas hedgers want to avoid an exposure to adverse movements in the price of an asset, speculators wish to take a position in the market. Either they are betting that the price of the asset will go up or they are betting that it will go down.

An Example of Speculation Using Futures

Consider a U.S. speculator who in February thinks that the British pound will strengthen relative to the U.S. dollar over the next two months and is prepared to back that hunch to the tune of £250,000. One thing the speculator can do is purchase £250,000 in the spot market in the hope that the sterling can be sold later at higher price. (The sterling once purchased would be kept in an interest-bearing account.)

Table 1.3 Speculation using spot and futures contracts. One futures contract is on £62,500

	February Trade	
	Buy £250,000 *Spot price = 1.6470*	*Buy 4 futures contracts* *Futures price = 1.6410*
Investment	\$411,750	\$20,000
Profit if April spot = 1.7000	\$13,250	\$14,750
Profit if April spot = 1.6000	−\$11,750	−\$10,250

Another possibility is to take a long position in four CME April futures contracts on sterling. (Each futures contract is for the purchase of £62,500.) Table 1.3 summarizes the two alternatives on the assumption that the current exchange rate is 1.6470 dollars per pound and the April futures price is 1.6410 dollars per pound. If the exchange rate turns out to be 1.7000 dollars per pound in April, the futures contract alternative enables the speculator to realize a profit of $(1.7000 - 1.6410) \times 250{,}000 = \$14{,}750$. The spot market alternative leads to 250,000 units of an asset being purchased for \$1.6470 in February and sold for \$1.7000 in April, so that a profit of $(1.7000 - 1.6470) \times 250{,}000 = \$13{,}250$ is made. If the exchange rate falls to 1.6000 dollars per pound, the futures contract gives rise to a $(1.6410 - 1.6000) \times 250{,}000 = \$10{,}250$ loss, whereas the spot market alternative gives rise to a loss of $(1.6470 - 1.6000) \times 250{,}000 = \$11{,}750$. The alternatives appear to give rise to slightly different profits and losses. But these calculations do not reflect the interest that is earned or paid. As shown in Chapter 5, when the interest earned in sterling and the interest paid in dollars are taken into account, the profit or loss from the two alternatives is the same.

What then is the difference between the two alternatives? The first alternative of buying sterling requires an up-front investment of \$411,750. By contrast, the second alternative requires only a small amount of cash—perhaps \$20,000—to be deposited by the speculator in what is termed a margin account. The futures market allows the speculator to obtain leverage. With a relatively small initial outlay, the investor is able to take a large speculative position.

An Example of Speculation Using Options

Options can also be used for speculation. Suppose that it is October and a speculator considers that Amazon.com is likely to increase in value over the next two months. The stock price is currently \$20, and a two-month call option with a \$22.50 strike price is currently selling for \$1. Table 1.4 illustrates two possible alternatives assuming that the speculator is willing to invest \$2,000. One alternative is to the purchase of 100 shares. Another involves the purchase of 2,000 call options (i.e., 20 call option contracts). Suppose that the speculator's hunch is correct and the price of Amazon.com's shares rises to \$27 by December. The first alternative of buying the stock yields a profit of

$$100 \times (\$27 - \$20) = \$700$$

Table 1.4 Comparison of profits (losses) from two alternative strategies for using $2,000 to speculate on Amazon.com stock in October

	December stock price	
Investor's strategy	*$15*	*$27*
Buy 100 shares	($500)	$700
Buy 2000 call options	($2,000)	$7,000

However, the second alternative is far more profitable. A call option on Amazon.com with a strike price of $22.50 gives a payoff of $4.50, because it enables something worth $27 to be bought for $22.50. The total payoff from the 2,000 options that are purchased under the second alternative is

$$2{,}000 \times \$4.50 = \$9{,}000$$

Subtracting the original cost of the options yields a net profit of

$$\$9{,}000 - \$2{,}000 = \$7{,}000$$

The options strategy is, therefore, ten times more profitable than the strategy of buying the stock.

Options also give rise to a greater potential loss. Suppose the stock price falls to $15 by December. The first alternative of buying stock yields a loss of

$$100 \times (\$20 - \$15) = \$500$$

Figure 1.5 Profit or loss from two alternative strategies for speculating on Amazon.com's stock price

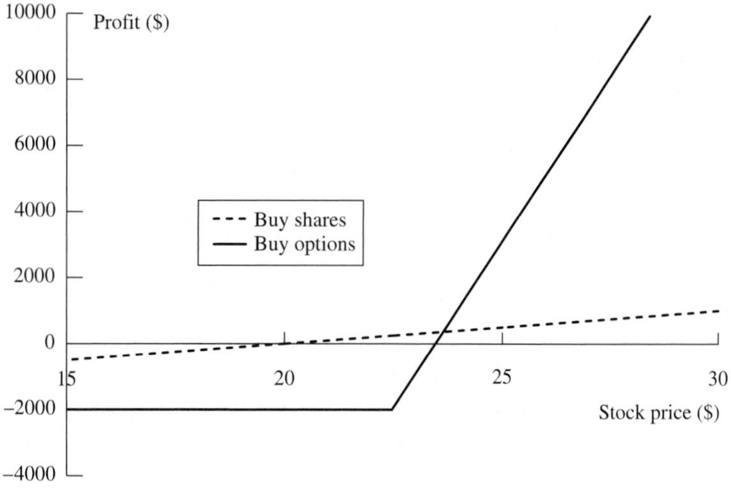

Because the call options expire without being exercised, the options strategy would lead to a loss of \$2,000—the original amount paid for the options. Figure 1.5 shows the profit or loss from the two strategies as a function of the price of Amazon.com in two months.

Options like futures provide a form of leverage. For a given investment, the use of options magnifies the financial consequences. Good outcomes become very good, while bad outcomes become very bad!

A Comparison

Futures and options are similar instruments for speculators in that they both provide a way in which a type of leverage can be obtained. However, there is an important difference between the two. When a speculator uses futures the potential loss as well as the potential gain is very large. When options are used, no matter how bad things get, the speculator's loss is limited to the amount paid for the options.

1.10 ARBITRAGEURS

Arbitrageurs are a third important group of participants in futures, forward, and options markets. Arbitrage involves locking in a riskless profit by simultaneously entering into transactions in two or more markets. In later chapters we will see how arbitrage is sometimes possible when the futures price of an asset gets out of line with its spot price. We will also examine how arbitrage can be used in options markets. This section illustrates the concept of arbitrage with a very simple example.

Consider a stock that is traded on both the New York Stock Exchange (www.nyse.com) and the London Stock Exchange (www.stockex.co.uk). Suppose that the stock price is \$172 in New York and £100 in London at a time when the exchange rate is \$1.7500 per pound. An arbitrageur could simultaneously buy 100 shares of the stock in New York and sell them in London to obtain a risk-free profit of

$$100 \times [(\$1.75 \times 100) - \$172]$$

or \$300 in the absence of transactions costs. The strategy is summarized in Trading Note 1.3. Transactions costs would probably eliminate the profit for a small investor. However, a large investment bank faces very low transactions costs in both the stock market and the foreign exchange market. It would find the arbitrage opportunity very attractive and would try to take as much advantage of it as possible.

Arbitrage opportunities such as the one just described cannot last for long. As arbitrageurs buy the stock in New York, the forces of supply and demand will cause the dollar price to rise. Similarly, as they sell the stock in London, the sterling price will be driven down. Very quickly the two prices will become equivalent at the current exchange rate. Indeed, the existence of profit-hungry arbitrageurs makes it unlikely that a major disparity between the sterling price and the dollar price could ever exist in the first place. Generalizing from this example, we can say that the very existence of arbitrageurs means that in practice only very small arbitrage opportunities are observed in the prices that are quoted in most financial markets. In this book most of the arguments concerning futures prices, forward prices, and the values of option contracts will be based on the assumption that there are no arbitrage opportunities.

Trading Note 1.3 An arbitrage opportunity

A stock is traded on both the New York Stock Exchange and the London Stock Exchange. The following quotes have been obtained:

New York Stock Exchange: \$172 per share
London Stock Exchange: £100 per share
Value of £1: \$1.7500

The Trader's Arbitrage Strategy

1. Buy 100 shares in New York.
2. Sell the shares in London.
3. Convert the sale proceeds from pounds to dollars.

The Profit

$$100 \times [(\$1.75 \times 100) - \$172] = \$300$$

1.11 DANGERS

Derivatives are very versatile instruments. As we have seen they can be used for hedging, for speculation, and for arbitrage. It is this very versatility that can cause problems. Sometimes traders who have a mandate to hedge risks or follow an arbitrage strategy become (consciously or unconsciously) speculators. The results can be disastrous. One example of this is provided by the activities of Nick Leeson at Barings Bank (see Business Snapshot 1.1).[2]

To avoid the type of problems Barings encountered it is very important for both financial and nonfinancial corporations to set up controls to ensure that derivatives are being used for their intended purpose. Risk limits should be set and the activities of traders should be monitored daily to ensure that the risk limits are adhered to.

SUMMARY

In this chapter we have taken a first look at futures, forward, and options markets. Futures and forward contracts are agreements to buy or sell an asset at a certain time in the future for a certain price. Futures contracts are traded on an exchange whereas forward contracts are traded in the over-the-counter market. There are two types of options: calls and puts. A call option gives the holder the right to buy an asset by a certain date for a certain price. A put option gives the holder the right to sell an asset by a certain date for a certain price. Options trade on both exchanges and in the over-the-counter market.

Futures, forwards, and options have been very successful innovations. Three main types of participants in the markets can be identified: hedgers, speculators, and arbitrageurs. Hedgers are in the position of facing risk associated with the price of an asset. They use futures, forward, or option contracts to reduce or eliminate this risk. Speculators wish to bet on future movements in the price of an asset. Futures,

[2] The movie *Rogue Trader* provides a good dramatization of the failure of Barings Bank.

Business Snapshot 1.1 The Barings Bank Disaster

Derivatives are very versatile instruments. They can be used for hedging, speculation, and arbitrage. One of the risks faced by a company that trades derivatives is that an employee who has a mandate to hedge or to look for arbitrage opportunities may become a speculator.

Nick Leeson, an employee of Barings Bank in the Singapore office in 1995, had a mandate to look for arbitrage opportunities between the Nikkei 225 futures prices on the Singapore exchange and the Osaka exchange. Over time Leeson moved from being an arbitrageur to being a speculator without anyone in the Barings London head office fully understanding that he had changed the way he was using derivatives. He began to make losses, which he was able to hide. He then began to take bigger speculative positions in an attempt to recover the losses, but only succeeded in making the losses worse.

By the time Leeson was found out, his total loss was close to one billion dollars. As a result, Barings—a bank that had been in existence for 200 years—was wiped out. One of the lessons from Barings is that it is important to define unambiguous risk limits for traders and then monitor what they do carefully to make sure that the limits are adhered to.

forward, and option contracts can give them extra leverage; that is, the contracts can increase both the potential gains and potential losses in a speculative investment. Arbitrageurs are in business to take advantage of a discrepancy between prices in two different markets. If, for example, they see the futures price of an asset getting out of line with the spot price, they will take offsetting positions in the two markets to lock in a profit.

FURTHER READING

Chancellor, E. *Devil Take the Hindmost—A History of Financial Speculation*. New York: Farra Straus Giroux, 1999.

Merton, R. C. "Finance Theory and Future Trends: The Shift to Integration," *Risk*, 12, 7 (July 1999): 48–51.

Miller, M. H. "Financial Innovation: Achievements and Prospects," *Journal of Applied Corporate Finance*, 4 (Winter 1992): 4–11.

Rawnsley, J. H. *Total Risk: Nick Leeson and the Fall of Barings Bank*. New York: Harper Collins, 1995.

Zhang, P. G. *Barings Bankruptcy and Financial Derivatives*. Singapore: World Scientific, 1995.

Quiz (Answers at End of Book)

1.1. What is the difference between a long futures position and a short futures position?

1.2. Explain carefully the difference between (a) hedging, (b) speculation, and (c) arbitrage.

1.3. What is the difference between (a) entering into a long futures contract when the futures price is \$50 and (b) taking a long position in a call option with a strike price of \$50?

1.4. An investor enters into a short forward contract to sell 100,000 British pounds for U.S. dollars at an exchange rate of 1.5000 U.S. dollars per pound. How much does the investor gain or lose if the exchange rate at the end of the contract is (a) 1.4900 and (b) 1.5200?

1.5. Suppose that you write a put contract with a strike price of \$40 and an expiration date in three months. The current stock price is \$41 and one put option contract is on 100 shares. What have you committed yourself to? How much could you gain or lose?

1.6. You would like to speculate on a rise in the price of a certain stock. The current stock price is \$29 and a three-month call with a strike price of \$30 costs \$2.90. You have \$5,800 to invest. Identify two alternative strategies. Briefly outline the advantages and disadvantages of each.

1.7. What is the difference between the over-the-counter market and the exchange-traded market? What are the bid and offer quotes of a market maker in the over-the-counter market?

Questions and Problems (Answers in Solutions Manual/Study Guide)

1.8. Suppose you own 5,000 shares that are worth \$25 each. How can put options be used to provide you with insurance against a decline in the value of your holding over the next four months?

1.9. A stock when it is first issued provides funds for a company. Is the same true of an exchange-traded stock option? Discuss.

1.10. Explain why a futures contract can be used for either speculation or hedging.

1.11. A cattle farmer expects to have 120,000 pounds of live cattle to sell in three months. The live-cattle futures contract on the Chicago Mercantile Exchange is for the delivery of 40,000 pounds of cattle. How can the farmer use the contract for hedging? From the farmer's viewpoint, what are the pros and cons of hedging?

1.12. It is now July 2004. A mining company has just discovered a small deposit of gold. It will take six months to construct the mine. The gold will then be extracted on a more or less continuous basis for one year. Futures contracts on gold are available on the New York Commodity Exchange. There are delivery months every two months from August 2004 to December 2005. Each contract is for the delivery of 100 ounces. Discuss how the mining company might use futures markets for hedging.

1.13. Suppose that a March call option on a stock with a strike price of \$50 costs \$2.50 and is held until March. Under what circumstances will the holder of the option make a gain? Under what circumstances will the option be exercised? Draw a diagram showing how the profit on a long position in the option depends on the stock price at the maturity of the option.

1.14. Suppose that a June put option on a stock with a strike price of \$60 costs \$4 and is held until June. Under what circumstances will the holder of the option make a gain? Under what circumstances will the option be exercised? Draw a diagram showing how the profit on a long position in the option depends on the stock price at the maturity of the option.

1.15. An investor writes a September call option with a strike price of \$20. It is now May, the stock price is \$18 and the option price is \$2. Describe the investor's cash flows if the option is held until September and the stock price is \$25 at this time.

1.16. An investor writes a December put option with a strike price of \$30. The price of the option is \$4. Under what circumstances does the investor make a gain?

1.17. The Chicago Board of Trade offers a futures contract on long-term Treasury bonds. Characterize the investors likely to use this contract.

1.18. An airline executive has argued: "There is no point in our using oil futures. There is just as much chance that the price of oil in the future will be less than the futures price as there is that it will be greater than this price." Discuss the executive's viewpoint.

1.19. "Options and futures are zero-sum games." What do you think is meant by this statement?

1.20. A trader enters into a short forward contract on 100 million yen. The forward exchange rate is \$0.0080 per yen. How much does the trader gain or lose if the exchange rate at the end of the contract is (a) \$0.0074 per yen; (b) \$0.0091 per yen?

1.21. A trader enters into a short cotton futures contract when the futures price is 50 cents per pound. The contract is for the delivery of 50,000 pounds. How much does the trader gain or lose if the cotton price at the end of the contract is (a) 48.20 cents per pound; (b) 51.30 cents per pound?

1.22. A company knows that it is due to receive a certain amount of a foreign currency in four months. What type of option contract is appropriate for hedging?

1.23. A United States company expects to have to pay 1 million Canadian dollars in six months. Explain how the exchange rate risk can be hedged using (a) a forward contract; (b) an option.

Assignment Questions

1.24. The price of gold is currently \$500 per ounce. Forward contracts are available to buy or sell gold at \$700 for delivery in one year. An arbitrageur can borrow money at 10% per annum. What should the arbitrageur do? Assume that the cost of storing gold is zero and that gold provides no income.

1.25. Discuss how foreign currency options can be used for hedging in the situation described in Trading Note 1.1 so that (a) ImportCo is guaranteed that its exchange rate will be less than 1.6300, and (b) ExportCo is guaranteed that its exchange rate will be at least 1.5900.

1.26. The current price of a stock is \$94, and three-month call options with a strike price of \$95 currently sell for \$4.70. An investor who feels that the price of the stock will increase is trying to decide between buying 100 shares and buying 2,000 call options (20 contracts). Both strategies involve an investment of \$9,400. What advice would you give? How high does the stock price have to rise for the option strategy to be more profitable?

1.27. On May 29, 2003, an investor owns 100 Intel shares. As indicated in Table 1.2 the share price is 20.83 and an October put option with a strike price 200 costs 1.50. The investor is comparing two alternatives to limit downside risk. The first involves buying one October put option contract with a strike price of 20. The second involves instructing a broker to sell the 100 shares as soon as Intel's price reaches 20. Discuss the advantages and disadvantages of the two strategies.

1.28. A trader buys a European call option and sells a European put option. The options have the same underlying asset, strike price, and maturity. Describe the trader's position. Under what circumstances does the price of the call equal the price of the put?

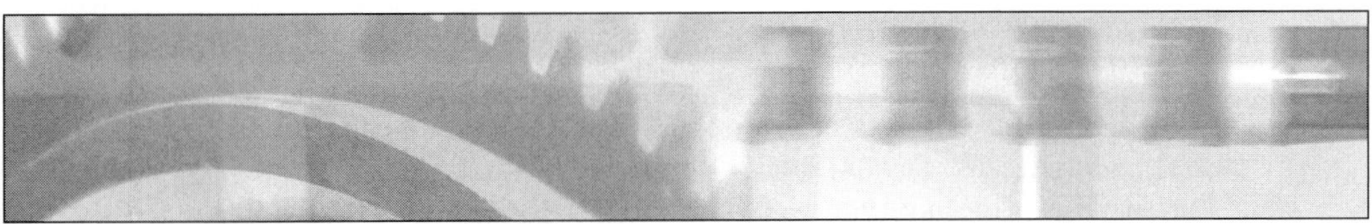

CHAPTER 2 Mechanics of Futures Markets

In Chapter 1 we explained that both futures and forward contracts are agreements to buy or sell an asset at a future time for a certain price. Futures contracts are traded on an organized exchange, and the contract terms are standardized by that exchange. By contrast, forward contracts are private agreements between two financial institutions or between a financial institution and one of its corporate clients.

This chapter covers the details of how futures markets work. We examine issues such as the specification of contracts, the operation of margin accounts, the organization of exchanges, the regulation of markets, the way in which quotes are made, and the treatment of futures transactions for accounting and tax purposes. We compare futures contracts with forward contracts and explain the difference between the payoffs realized from them.

2.1 OPENING AND CLOSING FUTURES POSITIONS

A futures contract is an agreement to buy or sell an asset for a certain price at a certain time in the future. A contract is usually referred to by its delivery month. Thus an investor could instruct a broker to buy one October oil futures contract. There is a period of time during the delivery month (often the whole month) when delivery can be made. Trading in the contract usually ceases some time during the delivery period. The party with the short position chooses when delivery is made.

The reader may be surprised to learn that the vast majority of the futures contracts that are initiated do not lead to delivery. The reason is that most investors choose to close out their positions prior to the delivery period specified in the contract. Making or taking delivery under the terms of a futures contract is often inconvenient and in some instances quite expensive. This is true even for a hedger who wants to buy or sell the asset underlying the futures contract. Such a hedger usually prefers to close out the futures position and then buy or sell the asset in the usual way.

Closing a position involves entering into an opposite trade to the original one that opened the position. For example, an investor who buys five July corn futures contracts on May 6 can close out the position on June 20 by selling (i.e., shorting) five July corn futures contracts. An investor who sells (i.e., shorts) five July contracts on May 6 can close out the position on June 20 by buying five July contracts. In each case, the investor's total gain or loss is determined by the change in the futures price between May 6 and June 20.

Delivery is so unusual that traders sometimes forget how the delivery process works (see Business Snapshot 2.1). Nevertheless we will spend part of this chapter reviewing the delivery arrangements in futures contracts. This is because it is the possibility of final delivery that ties the futures price to the spot price.[1]

2.2 THE SPECIFICATION OF A FUTURES CONTRACT

The major exchanges that trade futures contracts are listed at the end of this book. When developing a new contract, the exchange must specify in some detail the exact nature of the agreement between the two parties. In particular, it must specify the asset, the contract size (exactly how much of the asset will be delivered under one contract), where delivery will be made, and when delivery will be made.

Sometimes alternatives are specified for the grade of the asset that will be delivered or for the delivery locations. As a general rule, it is the party with the short position (the party that has agreed to sell the asset) that chooses what will happen when alternatives are specified by the exchange. When the party with the short position is ready to deliver, it files a *notice of intention to deliver* with the exchange. This notice indicates selections it has made with respect to the grade of asset that will be delivered and the delivery location.

The Asset

When the asset is a commodity, there may be quite a variation in the quality of what is available in the marketplace. When the asset is specified, it is therefore important that the exchange stipulate the grade or grades of the commodity that are acceptable. The New York Cotton Exchange has specified the asset in its orange juice futures contract as

> U.S. Grade A, with Brix value of not less than 57 degrees, having a Brix value to acid ratio of not less than 13 to 1 nor more than 19 to 1, with factors of color and flavor each scoring 37 points or higher and 19 for defects, with a minimum score 94.

The Chicago Mercantile Exchange in its random-length lumber futures contract has specified that

> each delivery unit shall consist of nominal 2×4s of random lengths from 8 feet to 20 feet, grade-stamped Construction and Standard, Standard and Better, or #1 and #2; however, in no case may the quantity of Standard grade or #2 exceed 50%. Each delivery unit shall be manufactured in California, Idaho, Montana, Nevada, Oregon, Washington, Wyoming, or Alberta or British Columbia, Canada, and contain lumber produced from grade-stamped Alpine fir, Englemann spruce, hem-fir, lodgepole pine, and/or spruce pine fir.

For some commodities a range of grades can be delivered, but the price received depends the grade chosen. For example, in the Chicago Board of Trade corn futures

[1] As mentioned in Chapter 1, the spot price is the price for almost immediate delivery.

Business Snapshot 2.1 The unanticipated delivery of a futures contract

This story (which may well be apocryphal) was told to the author of this book by a senior executive of a financial institution. It concerns a new employee of the financial institution who had not previously worked in the financial sector. One of the clients of the financial institution regularly entered into a long futures contract on live cattle for hedging purposes and issued instructions to close out the position on the last day of trading. (Live cattle futures contracts trade on the Chicago Mercantile Exchange and each contract is on 40,000 pounds of cattle.) The new employee was given responsibility for handling the account.

When the time came to close out a contract, the employee noted that the client was long one contract and instructed a trader at the exchange to go long (not short) one contract. The result of this mistake was that the financial institution ended up with a long position in two live cattle futures contracts. By the time the mistake was spotted, trading in the contract had ceased.

The financial institution (not the client) was responsible for the mistake. As a result it started to look into the details of the delivery arrangements for live cattle futures contracts—something it had never done before. Under the terms of the contract, cattle could be delivered by the party with the short position to a number of different locations in the United States during the delivery month. Because it was long, the financial institution could do nothing but wait for a party with a short position to issue a *notice of intention to deliver* to the exchange and for the exchange to assign that notice to the financial institution.

It eventually received a notice from the exchange and found that it would receive live cattle at a location 2,000 miles away the following Tuesday. The new employee was despatched to the location to handle things. It turned out that the location had a cattle auction every Tuesday. The party with the short position that was making delivery bought cattle at the auction and then immediately delivered them. Unfortunately the cattle could not be resold until the next cattle auction the following Tuesday. The employee was therefore faced with the problem of making arrangements for the cattle to be housed and fed for a week. This was a great start to a first job in the financial sector!

contract, the standard grade is "No. 2 Yellow", but substitutions are allowed with the price being adjusted in a way established by the exchange.

The financial assets in futures contracts are generally well defined and unambiguous. For example, there is no need to specify the grade of a Japanese yen. However, there are some interesting features of the Treasury bond and Treasury note futures contracts traded on the Chicago Board of Trade. The underlying asset in the Treasury bond contract is any long-term U.S. Treasury bond that has a maturity of greater than 15 years and is not callable within 15 years. In the Treasury note futures contract, the underlying asset is any long-term Treasury note with a maturity of no less than 6.5 years and no more than 10 years from the date of delivery. In both cases, the exchange has a formula for adjusting the price received according to the coupon and maturity date of the bond delivered. This is discussed in Chapter 6.

The Contract Size

The contract size specifies the amount of the asset that has to be delivered under one contract. This is an important decision for the exchange. If the contract size is too large, many investors who wish to hedge relatively small exposures or who wish to take relatively small speculative positions will be unable to use the exchange. On the other hand, if the contract size is too small, trading may be expensive as there is a cost associated with each contract traded.

The correct size for a contract clearly depends on the likely user. Whereas the value of what is delivered under a futures contract on an agricultural product might be $10,000 to $20,000, it is much higher for some financial futures. For example, under the Treasury bond futures contract traded on the Chicago Board of Trade, instruments with a face value of $100,000 are delivered.

In some cases exchanges have introduced "mini" contracts to attract smaller investors. For example, the CME's Mini Nasdaq 100 contract is on 20 times the Nasdaq 100 index whereas the regular contract is on 100 times the index.

Delivery Arrangements

The place where delivery will be made must be specified by the exchange. This is particularly important for commodities that involve significant transportation costs. In the case of the Chicago Mercantile Exchange's random-length lumber contract, the delivery location is specified as

> on track and shall either be unitized in double-door boxcars or, at no additional cost to the buyer, each unit shall be individually paper-wrapped and loaded on flatcars. Par delivery of hem-fir in California, Idaho, Montana, Nevada, Oregon, and Washington, and in the province of British Columbia.

When alternative delivery locations are specified, the price received by the party with the short position is sometimes adjusted according to the location chosen by that party. For example, in the case of the corn futures contract traded by the Chicago Board of Trade, delivery can be made at Chicago, Burns Harbor, Toledo, or St. Louis. However, deliveries at Toledo and St. Louis are made at a discount of 4 cents per bushel from the Chicago contract price.

Delivery Months

A futures contract is referred to by its delivery month. The exchange must specify the precise period during the month when delivery can be made. For many futures contracts, the delivery period is the whole month.

The delivery months vary from contract to contract and are chosen by the exchange to meet the needs of market participants. For example, corn futures traded on the Chicago Board of Trade have delivery months of March, May, July, September, and December. At any given time, contracts trade for the closest delivery month and a number of subsequent delivery months. The exchange specifies when trading in a particular month's contract will begin. The exchange also specifies the last day on which trading can take place for a given contract. Trading generally ceases a few days before the last day on which delivery can be made.

Price Quotes

The futures price is quoted in a way that is convenient and easy to understand. For example, crude oil futures prices on the New York Mercantile Exchange are quoted in dollars per barrel to two decimal places (i.e., to the nearest cent). Treasury bond and Treasury note futures prices on the Chicago Board of Trade are quoted in dollars and thirty-seconds of a dollar. The minimum price movement that can occur in trading is consistent with the way in which the price is quoted. Thus, it is $0.01 per barrel for the oil futures and one thirty-second of a dollar for the Treasury bond and Treasury note futures.

Price Limits and Position Limits

For most contracts, daily price movement limits are specified by the exchange. If the price moves down by an amount equal to the daily price limit, the contract is said to be *limit down*. If it moves up by the limit, it is said to be *limit up*. A *limit move* is a move in either direction equal to the daily price limit. Normally, trading ceases for the day once the contract is limit up or limit down. However, in some instances the exchange has the authority to step in and change the limits.

The purpose of daily price limits is to prevent large price movements from occurring because of speculative excesses. However, limits can become an artificial barrier to trading when the price of the underlying commodity is advancing or declining rapidly. Whether price limits are, on balance, good for futures markets is controversial.

Position limits are the maximum number of contracts that a speculator may hold. The purpose of the limits is to prevent speculators from exercising undue influence on the market.

2.3 CONVERGENCE OF FUTURES PRICE TO SPOT PRICE

As the delivery month of a futures contract is approached, the futures price converges to the spot price of the underlying asset. When the delivery period is reached, the futures price equals, or is very close to the spot price.

To see why this is so, we first suppose that the futures price is above the spot price during the delivery period. Traders then have a clear arbitrage opportunity:

1. Short a futures contract
2. Buy the asset
3. Make delivery

These steps are certain to lead to a profit equal to the amount by which the futures price exceeds the spot price. As traders exploit this arbitrage opportunity, the futures price will fall. Suppose next that the futures price is below the spot price during the delivery period. Companies interested in acquiring the asset will find it attractive to enter into a long futures contract and then wait for delivery to be made. As they do so, the futures price will tend to rise.

The result is that the futures price is very close to the spot price during the delivery period. Figure 2.1 illustrates the convergence of the futures price to the spot price. In Figure 2.1a the futures price is above the spot price prior to the delivery month, and in

Figure 2.1 Relationship between futures price and spot price as the delivery month is approached: (a) futures price above spot price; (b) futures price below spot price

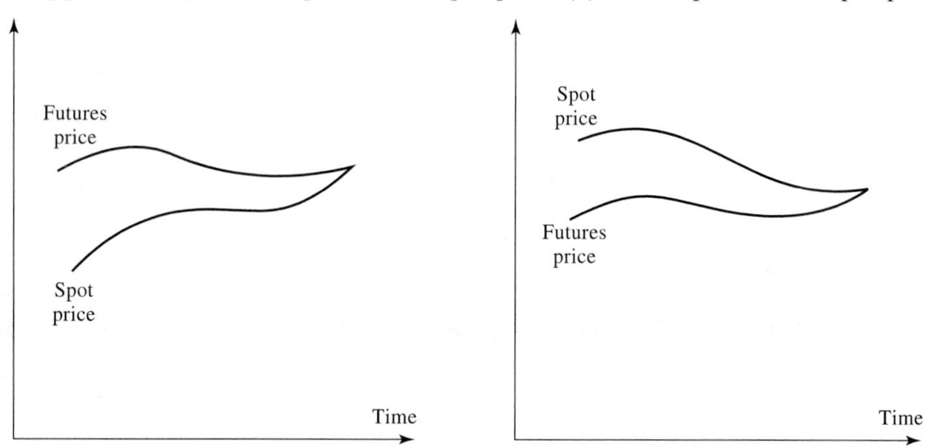

Figure 2.1b the futures price is below the spot price prior to the delivery month. The circumstances under which these two patterns are observed are discussed in Chapter 5.

2.4 THE OPERATION OF MARGINS

If two investors get in touch with each other directly and agree to trade an asset in the future for a certain price, there are obvious risks. One of the investors may regret the deal and try to back out. Alternatively, the investor simply may not have the financial resources to honor the agreement. One of the key roles of the exchange is to organize trading so that contract defaults are avoided. This is where margins come in.

Marking to Market

To illustrate how margins work, we consider an investor who contacts his or her broker on Thursday, June 5 to buy two December gold futures contracts on the New York Commodity Exchange (COMEX). We suppose that the current futures price is \$400 per ounce. Because the contract size is 100 ounces, the investor has contracted to buy a total of 200 ounces at this price. The broker will require the investor to deposit funds in a *margin account*. The amount that must be deposited at the time the contract is entered into is known as the *initial margin*. We suppose this is \$2,000 per contract, or \$4,000 in total. At the end of each trading day, the margin account is adjusted to reflect the investor's gain or loss. This practice is referred to as *marking to market* the account.

Suppose, for example, that by the end of June 5 the futures price has dropped from \$400 to \$397. The investor has a loss of \$600 (= 200 × \$3), because the 200 ounces of December gold, which the investor contracted to buy at \$400, can now be sold for only \$397. The balance in the margin account would therefore be reduced by \$600 to \$3,400. Similarly, if the price of December gold rose to \$403 by the end of the first day, the balance in the margin account would be increased by $600 to $4,600. A trade is first marked to market at the close of the day on which it takes place. It is then marked to market at the close of trading on each subsequent day.

Note that marking to market is not merely an arrangement between broker and client. When there is a decrease in the futures price so that the margin account of an investor with a long position is reduced by $600, the investor's broker has to pay the exchange $600 and the exchange passes the money on to the broker of an investor with a short position. Similarly, when there is an increase in the futures price, brokers for parties with short positions pay money to the exchange and brokers for parties with long positions receive money from the exchange. Later we will examine in more detail the mechanism by which this happens.

The investor is entitled to withdraw any balance in the margin account in excess of the initial margin. To ensure that the balance in the margin account never becomes negative, a *maintenance margin*, which is somewhat lower than the initial margin, is set. If the balance in the margin account falls below the maintenance margin, the investor receives a margin call and is expected to top up the margin account to the initial margin

Table 2.1 Operation of margins for a long position in two gold futures contracts. The initial margin is $2,000 per contract, or $4,000 in total, and the maintenance margin is $1,500 per contract, or $3,000 in total. The contract is entered into on June 5 at $400 and closed out on June 26 at $392.30. The numbers in the second column, except the first and the last, represent the futures prices at the close of trading

Day	*Futures price ($)*	*Daily gain (loss) ($)*	*Cumulative gain (loss) ($)*	*Margin account balance ($)*	*Margin call ($)*
	400.00			4,000	
June 5	397.00	(600)	(600)	3,400	
June 6	396.10	(180)	(780)	3,220	
June 9	398.20	420	(360)	3,640	
June 10	397.10	(220)	(580)	3,420	
June 11	396.70	(80)	(660)	3,340	
June 12	395.40	(260)	(920)	3,080	
June 13	393.30	(420)	(1,340)	2,660	1,340
June 16	393.60	60	(1,280)	4,060	
June 17	391.80	(360)	(1,640)	3,700	
June 18	392.70	180	(1,460)	3,880	
June 19	387.00	(1,140)	(2,600)	2,740	1,260
June 20	387.00	0	(2,600)	4,000	
June 23	388.10	220	(2,380)	4,220	
June 24	388.70	120	(2,260)	4,340	
June 25	391.00	460	(1,800)	4,800	
June 26	392.30	260	(1,540)	5,060	

level the next day. The extra funds deposited are known as a *variation margin*. If the investor does not provide the variation margin, the broker closes out the position by selling the contract. In the case of the investor considered earlier, closing out the position would involve neutralizing the existing contract by selling 200 ounces of gold for delivery in December.

Table 2.1 illustrates the operation of the margin account for one possible sequence of futures prices in the case of the investor considered earlier. The maintenance margin is assumed for the purpose of the illustration to be $1,500 per contract, or $3,000 in total. On June 13 the balance in the margin account falls $340 below the maintenance margin level. This drop triggers a margin call from the broker for additional $1,340. Table 2.1 assumes that the investor does in fact provide this margin by the close of trading on June 16. On June 19 the balance in the margin account again falls below the maintenance margin level, and a margin call for $1,260 is sent out. The investor provides this margin by the close of trading on June 20. On June 26 the investor decides to close out the position by selling two contracts. The futures price on that day is $392.30, and the investor has a cumulative loss of $1,540. Note that the investor has excess margin on June 16, 23, 24, and 25. Table 2.1 assumes that the excess is not withdrawn.

Further Details

Many brokers allow an investor to earn interest on the balance in a margin account. The balance in the account does not, therefore, represent a true cost, providing the interest rate is competitive with what could be earned elsewhere. To satisfy the initial margin requirements (but not subsequent margin calls), an investor can sometimes deposit securities with the broker. Treasury bills are usually accepted in lieu of cash at about 90% of their face value. Shares are also sometimes accepted in lieu of cash—but at about 50% of their market value.

The effect of the marking to market is that a futures contract is settled daily rather than all at the end of its life. At the end of each day, the investor's gain (loss) is added to (subtracted from) the margin account, bringing the value of the contract back to zero. A futures contract is in effect closed out and rewritten at a new price each day.

Minimum levels for initial and maintenance margins are set by the exchange. Individual brokers may require greater margins from their clients than those specified by the exchange. However, they cannot require lower margins than those specified by the exchange. Margin levels are determined by the variability of the price of the underlying asset. The higher this variability, the higher the margin levels. The maintenance margin is usually about 75% of the initial margin.

Margin requirements may depend on the objectives of the trader. A bona fide hedger, such as a company that produces the commodity on which the futures contract is written, is often subject to lower margin requirements than a speculator. The reason is that there is deemed to be less risk of default. Day trades and spread transactions often give rise to lower margin requirements than do hedge transactions. In a *day trade* the trader announces to the broker an intent to close out the position in the same day. In a *spread transaction* the trader simultaneously takes a long position in a contract on an asset for one maturity month and a short position in a contract on the same asset for another maturity month.

Note that margin requirements are the same on short futures positions as they are on long futures positions. It is just as easy to take a short futures position as it is to take a long one. The spot market does not have this symmetry. Taking a long position in the spot market involves buying the asset for immediate delivery and presents no problems. Taking a short position involves selling an asset that you do not own. This is a more complex transaction that may or may not be possible in a particular market. It is discussed further in Chapter 5.

The Clearinghouse and Clearing Margins

The *exchange clearinghouse* is an adjunct of the exchange and acts as an intermediary in futures transactions. It guarantees the performance of the parties to each transaction. The clearinghouse has a number of members, who must post funds with the exchange. Brokers who are not members themselves must channel their business through a member. The main task of the clearinghouse is to keep track of all the transactions that take place during a day so that it can calculate the net position of each of its members.

Just as an investor is required to maintain a margin account with a broker, a clearinghouse member is required to maintain a margin account with the clearinghouse. This is known as a *clearing margin*. The margin accounts for clearinghouse members are adjusted for gains and losses at the end of each trading day in the same way as are the margin accounts of investors. However, in the case of the clearinghouse member, there is an original margin, but no maintenance margin. Every day the account balance for each contract must be maintained at an amount equal to the original margin times the number of contracts outstanding. Thus, depending on transactions during the day and price movements, the clearinghouse member may have to add funds to its margin account at the end of the day. Alternatively, it may find it can remove funds from the account at this time. Brokers who are not clearinghouse members must maintain a margin account with a clearinghouse member.

In determining clearing margins, the exchange clearinghouse calculates the number of contracts outstanding on either a gross or a net basis. The *gross basis* simply adds the total of all long positions entered into by clients to the total of all the short positions entered into by clients. The net basis allows these to be offset against each other. Suppose a clearinghouse member has two clients: one with a long position in 20 contracts, the other with a short position in 15 contracts. Gross margining would calculate the clearing margin on the basis of 35 contracts; net margining would calculate the clearing margin on the basis of 5 contracts. Most exchanges currently use net margining.

Credit Risk

The whole purpose of the margining system is ensure that traders do not walk away from their commitments. Overall the system has been very successful. Investors entering into contracts at major exchanges have always had their contracts honored. Futures exchanges were tested on October 19, 1987, when the S&P 500 index declined by over 20% and investors with long positions in S&P futures found they had negative margin balances. Some of the investors walked away from their positions (even though they were legally obligated to make good on their contracts). As a result some brokers went bankrupt because, without their clients' money, they were unable to meet margin calls on contracts they entered into on behalf of their clients. However, everyone who had a short futures position on the S&P 500 got paid off.

Business Snapshot 2.2 Long-Term Capital Management's big loss

Long-Term Capital Management (LTCM), a hedge fund formed in the mid-1990s, always collateralized its transactions. The hedge fund's investment strategy was known as convergence arbitrage. A very simple example of what it might do is the following. It would find two bonds, X and Y, issued by the same company that promised the same payoffs, with X being less liquid (i.e., less actively traded) than Y. The market always places a value on liquidity. As a result the price of X would be less than the price of Y. LTCM would buy X, short Y, and wait, expecting the prices of the two bonds to converge at some future time.

When interest rates increased, the company expected both bonds to move down in price by about the same amount so that the collateral it paid on bond X would be about the same as that it received on bond Y. Similarly, when interest rates decreased LTCM expected both bonds to move up in price by about the same amount so that the collateral it received on bond X would be about the same as the collateral it paid on bond Y. It therefore expected that there would be no significant outflow of funds as a result of its collateralization agreements.

In August 1998, Russia defaulted on its debt and this led to what is termed a "flight to quality" in capital markets. One result was that investors valued liquid instruments more highly than usual and the spreads between the prices of the liquid and illiquid instruments in LTCM's portfolio increased dramatically. The prices of the bonds LTCM had bought went down and the prices of those it had shorted increased. It was required to post collateral on both. The company was highly levered and unable to make the payments required under the collateralization agreements. The result was that positions had to be closed out and there was a total loss of about $4 billion. If the company had been less highly levered, it would probably have been able to survive the flight to quality and could have waited for the prices of the liquid and illiquid bonds to become closer to each other.

Collateralization in OTC Markets

Credit risk has traditionally been a feature of the over-the-counter markets. There is always a chance that the party on the other side of an over-the-counter trade will default. It is interesting that, in an attempt to reduce credit risk, the over-the-counter market is now imitating the margining system adopted by exchanges with a procedure known as *collateralization*.

Consider two participants in the over-the-counter market, company A and company B, with an outstanding over-the-counter contract. Under a collateralization agreement they would value the contract each day using a pre-agreed valuation methodology. If from one day to the next the value of the contract to company A increased, company B would be required to pay collateral equal to this increase and company A would receive collateral equal to the increase. Similarly, if the value of the contract to company A decreased, company A would be required to pay collateral equal to the decrease and company B would receive collateral equal to the decrease.

Collateralization significantly reduces the credit risk in over-the-counter contracts. Collateralization agreements were used by a hedge fund, Long-Term Capital Management (LTCM) in the 1990s. They allowed LTCM to be highly levered. The contracts did provide credit risk protection, but as described in Business Snapshot 2.2 the high leverage left the hedge fund vulnerable to other risks.

2.5 NEWSPAPER QUOTES

Many newspapers carry futures prices. Table 2.2 shows the prices for commodities as they appeared in the *Wall Street Journal* of Thursday, February 5, 2004. The prices refer to the trading that took place on the previous day (i.e., Wednesday, February 4, 2004). The prices for index futures, currency futures, and interest-rate futures are given in Chapters 3, 5, and 6, respectively.

The asset underlying the futures contract, the exchange that the contract is traded on, the contract size, and how the price is quoted are all shown at the top of each section in Table 2.2. The first asset is corn, traded on the Chicago Board of Trade. The contract size is 5,000 bushels, and the price is quoted in cents per bushel. The months in which particular contracts are traded are shown in the first column. Corn contracts with maturities in March 2004, May 2004, July 2004, September 2004, December 2004, March 2005, and December 2005 were traded on February 4, 2004.

Prices

The first three numbers in each row show the opening price, the highest price achieved in trading during the day, and the lowest price achieved in trading during the day. The opening price is representative of the prices at which contracts were trading immediately after the opening bell. For March 2004 corn on February 4, 2004, the opening price was 273.25 cents per bushel and, during the day, the price traded between 269.25 and 274.75 cents.

Settlement Price

The fourth number is the *settlement price*. This is the price used for calculating daily gains and losses and margin requirements. It is usually calculated as the average of the prices at which the contract traded immediately before the bell signaling the end of trading for the day. The fifth number is the change in the settlement price from the previous day. For the March 2004 corn futures contract, the settlement price was 270.25 cents on February 4, 2004, down 2.75 cents from February 3, 2004.

In the case of the March 2004 futures, an investor with a long position in one contract would find his or her margin account balance reduced by \$137.50 (= 5,000 × 2.75 cents) between February 3, 2004, and February 4, 2004. Similarly, an investor with a short position in one contract would find that the margin balance increased by \$137.50 between these two dates.

Lifetime Highs and Lows

The sixth and seventh numbers show the highest futures price and the lowest futures price achieved in the trading of the particular contract over its lifetime. The March 2004 corn contract had traded for well over a year on February 4, 2004. During this period the highest and lowest prices achieved were 281.50 cents and 219.00 cents.

Table 2.2 Commodity futures quotes from the *Wall Street Journal*, February 5, 2004. (Columns show month, open, high, low, settle, change, lifetime high, lifetime low, and open interest, respectively.)

Exchange Abbreviations

For commodity futures and futures options

CBT-Chicago Board of Trade;
CME-Chicago Mercantile Exchange;
CSCE-Coffee, Sugar & Cocoa Exchange, New York;
CMX-COMEX (Div. of New York Mercantile Exchange);
EUREX-European Exchange;
FINEX-Financial Exchange (Div. of New York Cotton Exchange);
IPE-International Petroleum Exchange;
KC-Kansas City Board of Trade;
LIFFE-London International Financial Futures Exchange;
MATIF-Marche a Terme International de France;
ME-Montreal Exchange;
MPLS-Minneapolis Grain Exchange;
NQLX-NQLX (unit of Euronext.liffe)
NYCE-New York Cotton Exchange;
NYFE-New York Futures Exchange (Sub. of New York Cotton Exchange);
NYM-New York Mercantile Exchange;
ONE-OneChicago
SFE-Sydney Futures Exchange;
SGX-Singapore Exchange Ltd.;

Futures prices reflect day and overnight trading
Open interest reflects previous day's trading

Wednesday, February 4, 2004

Grain and Oilseed Futures

Corn (CBT)-5,000 bu.; cents per bu.

	OPEN	HIGH	LOW	SETTLE	CHG	LIFETIME HIGH	LIFETIME LOW	OPEN INT
Mar	273.25	274.75	269.25	270.25	-2.75	281.50	219.00	292,145
May	278.00	279.75	274.00	275.25	-2.75	285.75	224.50	130,369
July	280.50	282.50	277.00	278.25	-2.25	288.50	227.75	79,647
Sept	274.50	276.00	272.50	272.50	-2.75	283.00	229.75	14,330
Dec	270.75	273.00	268.50	270.00	-.75	278.75	232.50	105,132
Mr05	274.25	276.00	272.25	273.50	-1.00	281.50	239.00	7,662
Dec	252.50	252.75	252.50	252.75	-.25	258.00	235.00	1,364

Est vol 54,315; vol Tue 81,306; open int 632,256, +1,555.

Oats (CBT)-5,000 bu.; cents per bu.

	OPEN	HIGH	LOW	SETTLE	CHG	LIFETIME HIGH	LIFETIME LOW	OPEN INT
Mar	156.25	156.25	153.00	153.00	-3.00	164.75	131.00	4,361
May	158.50	158.50	155.75	155.75	-3.25	163.75	135.00	1,403

Est vol 543; vol Tue 1,134; open int 6,487, +277.

Soybeans (CBT)-5,000 bu.; cents per bu.

	OPEN	HIGH	LOW	SETTLE	CHG	LIFETIME HIGH	LIFETIME LOW	OPEN INT
Mar	803.00	813.00	802.00	805.75	3.25	855.00	508.00	110,983
May	805.00	811.50	804.00	805.75	1.25	853.50	515.50	83,539
July	795.50	799.50	791.50	792.00	-3.00	842.00	520.00	37,181
Aug	765.50	770.00	760.00	760.50	-5.25	804.00	521.00	8,682
Sept	714.00	714.00	705.00	706.50	-5.50	748.00	528.00	4,033
Nov	643.50	646.50	635.00	636.50	-8.25	678.00	483.00	22,489
Ja05	643.00	643.00	638.00	638.00	-7.00	678.00	573.00	440

Est vol 51,149; vol Tue 69,055; open int 267,713, -1,819.

Soybean Meal (CBT)-100 tons; $ per ton.

	OPEN	HIGH	LOW	SETTLE	CHG	LIFETIME HIGH	LIFETIME LOW	OPEN INT
Mar	246.80	249.80	246.50	247.00	.20	268.80	152.50	46,742
May	247.00	249.80	246.40	246.50	-.40	268.20	153.00	59,488
July	243.40	245.50	242.30	242.40	-1.00	263.20	152.50	32,077
Aug	234.80	235.50	232.80	233.00	-1.10	251.20	154.00	11,892
Sept	221.00	222.00	218.80	219.30	-.90	234.50	154.00	9,574
Oct	192.50	192.50	189.00	190.00	-1.40	206.00	150.50	7,015
Dec	189.00	189.00	185.50	185.60	-2.60	202.50	150.00	15,868
Ja05	188.00	188.00	185.50	185.80	-2.40	203.00	161.50	882

Est vol 20,000; vol Tue 33,272; open int 184,147, -2,396.

Soybean Oil (CBT)-60,000 lbs.; cents per lb.

	OPEN	HIGH	LOW	SETTLE	CHG	LIFETIME HIGH	LIFETIME LOW	OPEN INT
Mar	29.86	30.13	29.75	29.86	...	30.37	19.00	70,068
May	29.75	30.02	29.66	29.76	.04	30.19	19.01	64,391
July	29.80	29.80	29.40	29.45	-.02	29.87	19.01	41,093
Aug	29.08	29.15	28.85	28.90	-.05	29.20	19.05	5,103
Sept	28.25	28.25	27.95	28.00	-.02	28.35	19.01	6,754
Oct	26.90	27.00	26.80	26.90	-.15	27.10	19.00	5,429
Dec	25.90	25.90	25.75	25.78	-.19	26.30	18.98	10,994

Est vol 17,571; vol Tue 33,871; open int 204,766, +2,177.

Rough Rice (CBT)-2,000 cwt.; cents per cwt.

	OPEN	HIGH	LOW	SETTLE	CHG	LIFETIME HIGH	LIFETIME LOW	OPEN INT
Mar	776.00	784.50	770.00	773.00	-1.00	925.00	680.00	5,418
July	816.00	816.00	809.00	809.00	-1.00	939.00	761.00	541

Est vol 409; vol Tue 973; open int 7,275, -63.

Wheat (CBT)-5,000 bu.; cents per bu.

	OPEN	HIGH	LOW	SETTLE	CHG	LIFETIME HIGH	LIFETIME LOW	OPEN INT
Mar	380.50	382.00	375.25	376.00	-4.50	421.50	301.50	75,392
May	386.75	387.00	381.00	382.50	-4.25	413.00	290.00	28,178
July	381.00	381.50	377.00	377.25	-4.25	404.00	298.00	25,753
Sept	382.00	383.50	381.00	381.50	-3.50	402.00	326.00	1,803
Dec	391.50	392.00	388.50	390.50	-3.50	410.00	330.00	3,219

Est vol 18,516; vol Tue 24,710; open int 134,517, +36.

Wheat (KC)-5,000 bu.; cents per bu.

	OPEN	HIGH	LOW	SETTLE	CHG	LIFETIME HIGH	LIFETIME LOW	OPEN INT
Mar	386.00	387.50	380.00	380.50	-7.00	416.00	314.00	35,068
May	385.75	387.00	379.00	380.50	-6.75	412.00	315.00	14,006
July	383.50	384.00	380.00	380.50	-4.75	408.00	313.00	11,690
Sept	384.50	386.00	383.50	386.00	-2.00	405.00	330.50	1,938
Dec	392.50	393.50	390.00	390.00	-5.50	408.50	341.00	1,273

Est vol 19,427; vol Tue 10,017; open int 63,983, -463.

Wheat (MPLS)-5,000 bu.; cents per bu.

	OPEN	HIGH	LOW	SETTLE	CHG	LIFETIME HIGH	LIFETIME LOW	OPEN INT
Mar	412.00	413.25	409.00	411.00	-2.50	423.75	343.75	13,938
May	407.00	407.25	401.50	402.25	-4.75	420.00	349.50	7,993
July	400.00	400.00	395.00	395.00	-5.50	411.00	352.00	4,185
Sept	396.50	396.50	391.50	391.50	-5.50	403.00	346.00	4,898
Dec	400.00	401.00	395.75	396.00	-5.00	408.00	355.00	1,037

Est vol 7,695; vol Tue 6,203; open int 32,066, -868.

Livestock Futures

Cattle-Feeder (CME)-50,000 lbs.; cents per lb.

	OPEN	HIGH	LOW	SETTLE	CHG	LIFETIME HIGH	LIFETIME LOW	OPEN INT
Mar	83.70	83.80	82.22	82.22	-1.50	97.45	77.50	5,192
Apr	85.30	85.40	83.92	83.92	-1.50	94.90	78.30	2,260
May	85.85	85.85	84.35	84.35	-1.50	93.90	79.10	3,739
Aug	88.10	88.20	86.77	86.77	-1.50	93.25	81.60	2,316
Sept	87.75	87.75	87.00	87.00	-1.50	92.00	81.70	297
Oct	88.25	88.25	87.00	87.00	-1.50	92.00	81.95	317

Est vol 1,472; vol Tue 1,739; open int 14,199, +22.

Cattle-Live (CME)-40,000 lbs.; cents per lb.

	OPEN	HIGH	LOW	SETTLE	CHG	LIFETIME HIGH	LIFETIME LOW	OPEN INT
Feb	76.30	76.45	74.82	74.82	-1.50	94.95	71.00	18,526
Apr	72.87	73.05	71.37	71.37	-1.50	85.55	68.60	42,771
June	69.95	70.15	68.42	68.42	-1.50	78.75	66.50	15,578
Aug	72.45	72.55	70.95	70.95	-1.50	77.20	68.00	8,444
Oct	75.50	75.55	74.02	74.20	-1.32	78.80	69.50	10,518
Dec	77.07	77.15	75.65	76.12	-1.02	78.90	72.00	3,520

Est vol 16,156; vol Tue 10,727; open int 100,345, +316.

Hogs-Lean (CME)-40,000 lbs.; cents per lb.

	OPEN	HIGH	LOW	SETTLE	CHG	LIFETIME HIGH	LIFETIME LOW	OPEN INT
Feb	59.80	59.97	58.97	59.42	.50	63.00	50.75	5,560
Apr	59.67	60.00	58.70	58.87	-.47	62.40	53.55	28,654
May	60.55	60.85	60.30	60.65	-.05	63.90	55.90	1,621
June	65.00	65.10	64.05	64.60	-.15	67.10	58.40	8,907
July	61.70	61.80	61.25	61.47	-.02	63.85	56.90	2,289
Aug	59.70	59.80	59.25	59.65	.10	61.37	55.00	1,521
Oct	52.50	52.85	52.25	52.25	-.35	54.65	49.00	919
Dec	52.40	53.15	52.25	52.37	-.12	53.97	49.00	522

Est vol 10,289; vol Tue 8,924; open int 50,055, -1,609.

Pork Bellies (CME)-40,000 lbs.; cents per lb.

	OPEN	HIGH	LOW	SETTLE	CHG	LIFETIME HIGH	LIFETIME LOW	OPEN INT
Feb	86.30	87.67	86.30	87.30	1.17	93.40	76.40	831
Mar	87.30	88.25	87.30	88.02	1.30	93.15	76.90	879
May	89.05	89.50	88.75	89.50	1.67	94.15	79.40	385

Est vol 669; vol Tue 883; open int 2,270, -26.

Food and Fiber Futures

Lumber (CME)-110,000 bd. ft., $ per 1,000 bd. ft.

	OPEN	HIGH	LOW	SETTLE	CHG	LIFETIME HIGH	LIFETIME LOW	OPEN INT
Mar	334.20	344.50	334.00	344.50	10.00	365.00	256.20	2,408
May	336.60	346.60	336.60	346.60	10.00	357.50	263.10	686
July	337.90	344.00	335.10	343.20	6.80	354.90	282.00	233

Est vol 889; vol Tue 286; open int 3,368, -22.

Milk (CME)-200,000 lbs., cents per lb.

	OPEN	HIGH	LOW	SETTLE	CHG	LIFETIME HIGH	LIFETIME LOW	OPEN INT
Feb	11.74	11.75	11.72	11.75	.05	11.90	10.95	2,554
Mar	12.20	12.26	12.20	12.20	.05	12.35	11.05	2,525
Apr	12.65	12.75	12.60	12.73	.13	12.75	11.00	1,988
May	12.88	13.00	12.87	12.95	.13	13.00	11.00	1,948
June	13.13	13.26	13.12	13.26	.16	13.32	11.41	1,761
July	13.74	13.95	13.72	13.86	.12	13.95	11.60	1,676
Aug	14.18	14.25	14.13	14.20	.02	14.28	11.65	1,723
Sept	14.55	14.75	14.55	14.65	.05	14.75	12.10	1,900
Oct	13.94	14.15	13.89	14.05	.11	14.15	11.89	1,513
Nov	12.95	13.20	12.95	13.20	.25	13.30	11.39	1,169
Dec	12.40	12.45	12.40	12.45	.05	12.50	11.30	809

Est vol 1,437; vol Tue 842; open int 19,736, +289.

Cocoa (CSCE)-10 metric tons; $ per ton.

	OPEN	HIGH	LOW	SETTLE	CHG	LIFETIME HIGH	LIFETIME LOW	OPEN INT
Mar	1,606	1,615	1,578	1,581	−19	2,358	1,250	22,360
May	1,596	1,599	1,565	1,569	−21	2,265	1,345	13,766
July	1,595	1,596	1,572	1,564	−23	2,307	1,350	12,922
Sept	1,590	1,590	1,562	1,563	−24	2,402	1,370	8,710

Est vol 9,057; vol Tue 9,675; open int 87,295, −1,218.

Coffee (CSCE)-37,500 lbs.; cents per lb.

	OPEN	HIGH	LOW	SETTLE	CHG	LIFETIME HIGH	LIFETIME LOW	OPEN INT
Mar	73.75	74.00	71.60	72.60	−2.05	83.00	59.65	59,048
May	75.60	75.80	73.70	74.65	−1.95	82.00	61.75	26,054
July	77.00	77.70	75.70	76.45	−1.95	82.50	63.90	8,737
Sept	78.40	79.20	77.40	78.15	−1.90	83.45	65.75	7,837
Dec	80.15	81.25	80.15	80.75	−1.90	85.95	68.50	4,577
Mr05	83.40	83.70	83.40	83.30	−1.85	87.90	71.00	2,948

Est vol 32,220; vol Tue 15,761; open int 109,783, +1,170.

Sugar-World (CSCE)-112,000 lbs.; cents per lb.

	OPEN	HIGH	LOW	SETTLE	CHG	LIFETIME HIGH	LIFETIME LOW	OPEN INT
Mar	5.74	5.77	5.66	5.68	−.07	7.65	5.50	131,494
May	5.94	5.97	5.87	5.88	−.07	7.32	5.54	50,135
July	5.97	6.00	5.92	5.93	−.06	6.95	5.50	37,213
Oct	6.09	6.10	6.02	6.03	−.06	6.88	5.55	25,822
Mr05	6.33	6.33	6.27	6.28	−.04	6.82	6.24	11,411
May	6.32	6.33	6.30	6.30	−.03	6.57	6.20	4,813
July	6.28	6.29	6.28	6.25	−.03	6.42	6.15	2,901

Est vol 23,839; vol Tue 32,525; open int 265,575, −1,048.

Sugar-Domestic (CSCE)-112,000 lbs.; cents per lb.

	OPEN	HIGH	LOW	SETTLE	CHG	LIFETIME HIGH	LIFETIME LOW	OPEN INT
Mar	20.35	20.40	20.35	20.40	.04	22.02	20.20	884
May	20.35	20.35	20.35	20.35	...	22.07	20.15	3,835
July	20.50	20.50	20.50	20.50	...	22.10	20.25	3,280
Sept	20.74	20.74	20.74	20.74	−.01	22.07	20.63	3,087
Nov	21.05	21.05	21.05	21.05	...	21.70	20.94	855
Ja05	20.80	20.80	20.80	20.80	...	21.40	20.80	285

Est vol 43; vol Tue 203; open int 12,510, −112.

Cotton (NYCE)-50,000 lbs.; cents per lb.

	OPEN	HIGH	LOW	SETTLE	CHG	LIFETIME HIGH	LIFETIME LOW	OPEN INT
Mar	69.10	69.90	68.70	69.25	.35	86.00	45.60	43,633
May	71.20	71.95	70.75	71.27	.44	86.00	51.50	27,184
July	72.35	73.00	71.80	72.30	.35	85.50	56.75	8,924
Dec	68.00	68.25	67.50	67.75	.05	71.00	59.00	6,330

Est vol 12,611; vol Tue 21,022; open int 88,074, +239.

Orange Juice (NYCE)-15,000 lbs.; cents per lb.

	OPEN	HIGH	LOW	SETTLE	CHG	LIFETIME HIGH	LIFETIME LOW	OPEN INT
Mar	61.20	62.00	60.80	61.65	.25	103.50	60.60	25,803
May	64.50	64.70	64.00	64.45	.25	105.00	63.50	7,488
July	67.20	67.30	66.50	67.05	.35	106.00	66.40	1,518
Sept	69.40	70.00	69.40	69.40	.20	86.80	69.25	774
Nov	71.30	71.30	71.30	71.90	−.10	91.50	71.30	491

Est vol 1,846; vol Tue 1,259; open int 36,251, −123.

Metal Futures

Copper-High (CMX)-25,000 lbs.; cents per lb.

	OPEN	HIGH	LOW	SETTLE	CHG	LIFETIME HIGH	LIFETIME LOW	OPEN INT
Feb	116.90	117.30	116.90	117.35	0.60	117.30	67.20	1,033
Mar	116.85	117.55	116.50	117.45	0.60	117.55	69.75	65,863
Apr	116.55	116.90	116.55	117.10	0.60	116.90	71.95	941
May	116.05	116.70	115.95	116.55	0.45	116.70	70.90	8,263
June	116.00	116.15	115.75	115.95	0.40	116.15	73.50	724
July	115.00	115.45	115.00	115.30	0.35	115.45	70.90	6,549
Aug	114.30	114.70	114.30	114.70	0.40	114.70	73.65	486
Sept	113.90	114.00	113.90	114.05	0.40	114.00	70.95	2,211
Oct	113.25	113.25	113.25	113.45	0.40	113.25	74.00	388
Nov	112.55	112.70	112.45	112.85	0.40	112.70	79.00	287
Dec	111.85	112.35	111.60	112.20	0.35	112.35	74.20	4,135
Mr05	110.55	110.55	110.50	110.40	0.25	110.55	74.40	322

Est vol 11,000; vol Tue 8,170; open int 91,868, −170.

Gold (CMX)-100 troy oz.; $ per troy oz.

	OPEN	HIGH	LOW	SETTLE	CHG	LIFETIME HIGH	LIFETIME LOW	OPEN INT
Feb	399.80	401.30	398.50	401.00	1.80	431.50	322.00	5,090
Apr	400.70	401.80	399.40	401.70	1.80	432.30	320.00	143,464
June	401.40	403.00	400.50	402.70	1.80	432.00	287.00	29,868
Aug	403.10	403.10	402.00	403.70	1.80	431.30	324.70	8,621
Dec	404.10	405.50	403.00	405.50	1.70	434.50	290.00	22,312

Est vol 40,000; vol Tue 40,608; open int 236,512, −4,897.

Platinum (NYM)-50 troy oz.; $ per troy oz.

	OPEN	HIGH	LOW	SETTLE	CHG	LIFETIME HIGH	LIFETIME LOW	OPEN INT
Apr	824.00	824.00	812.00	820.60	−5.70	868.00	677.00	6,816
July	...	...	...	810.60	−5.70	852.00	801.00	292

Est vol 602; vol Tue 808; open int 7,126, −95.

Silver (CMX)-5,000 troy oz.; cnts per troy oz.

	OPEN	HIGH	LOW	SETTLE	CHG	LIFETIME HIGH	LIFETIME LOW	OPEN INT
Feb	611.5	611.5	611.5	614.5	2.4	611.5	611.5	240
Mar	613.0	618.5	607.0	614.8	2.5	679.5	437.0	78,208
May	614.5	620.0	608.5	616.2	2.6	681.0	445.0	7,153
July	616.5	621.0	611.0	617.4	2.6	673.0	436.0	5,063
Dec	618.5	623.0	613.0	619.9	2.6	677.0	440.0	12,458
Dc05	627.0	627.0	627.0	624.6	3.9	675.0	436.0	1,564

Est vol 16,000; vol Tue 15,059; open int 107,432, −482.

Petroleum Futures

Crude Oil, Light Sweet (NYM)-1,000 bbls.; $ per bbl.

	OPEN	HIGH	LOW	SETTLE	CHG	LIFETIME HIGH	LIFETIME LOW	OPEN INT
Mar	34.09	34.45	32.95	33.10	−1.00	35.25	20.35	196,160
Apr	32.82	33.25	31.85	31.99	−0.83	34.50	20.35	91,932
May	32.11	32.20	31.25	31.32	−0.72	33.85	20.35	42,864
June	31.55	31.65	30.80	30.84	−0.63	33.25	20.53	39,700
July	31.00	31.10	30.40	30.37	−0.60	32.60	20.86	29,920
Aug	30.57	30.60	30.10	29.93	−0.58	32.15	20.84	19,040
Sept	30.21	30.21	29.65	29.58	−0.56	31.61	20.82	26,690
Oct	29.93	29.93	29.93	29.33	−0.54	31.20	23.75	17,830
Nov	29.59	29.70	29.59	29.11	−0.53	30.85	24.75	14,370
Dec	29.60	29.60	29.00	28.92	−0.52	30.69	16.35	51,129
Ja05	29.00	29.00	29.00	28.67	−0.50	30.33	23.25	15,606
Feb	28.75	28.75	28.75	28.48	−0.49	30.07	23.85	5,061
June	28.24	28.24	28.24	27.79	−0.45	29.05	22.40	10,556
Dec	27.42	27.52	27.20	27.03	−0.39	28.31	17.00	25,454
Dc06	26.77	26.77	26.60	26.38	−0.39	27.65	19.10	16,726
Dc07	26.45	26.50	26.40	26.18	−0.34	27.35	19.50	9,971
Dc08	26.50	26.50	26.50	26.18	−0.34	27.15	19.75	7,354

Est vol 225,976; vol Tue 219,163; open int 663,890, +1,691.

Heating Oil No. 2 (NYM)-42,000 gal.; $ per gal.

	OPEN	HIGH	LOW	SETTLE	CHG	LIFETIME HIGH	LIFETIME LOW	OPEN INT
Mar	.9142	.9280	.8830	.8897	−.0245	1.0129	.6370	64,063
Apr	.8770	.8840	.8505	.8586	−.0166	.9417	.6275	22,296
May	.8436	.8436	.8200	.8251	−.0151	.8881	.6140	10,010
June	.8174	.8185	.7950	.8016	−.0136	.8581	.6354	11,337
July	.7800	.7910	.7800	.7896	−.0131	.8380	.6415	7,713
Aug	.7925	.7925	.7750	.7876	−.0126	.8373	.6455	5,437
Oct	.8050	.8050	.8050	.7986	−.0121	.8425	.6655	1,466
Nov	.8100	.8100	.8100	.8046	−.0121	.8480	.6820	1,548
Dec	.8175	.8175	.8100	.8106	−.0121	.8540	.6937	10,047

Est vol 66,129; vol Tue 49,216; open int 141,064, +3,503.

Gasoline-NY Unleaded (NYM)-42,000 gal.; $ per gal.

	OPEN	HIGH	LOW	SETTLE	CHG	LIFETIME HIGH	LIFETIME LOW	OPEN INT
Mar	1.0015	1.0150	.9740	.9857	−.0158	1.0410	.7325	67,894
Apr	1.0475	1.0530	1.0190	1.0305	−.0124	1.0800	.7975	27,871
May	1.0310	1.0310	1.0130	1.0150	−.0119	1.0655	.8080	13,375
June	1.0050	1.0100	.9920	.9895	−.0109	1.0410	.8070	6,390
July	.9550	.9650	.9550	.9615	−.0104	1.0100	.9300	3,617
Sept	.9090	.9090	.9050	.8940	−.0089	.9380	.8530	5,260

Est vol 46,056; vol Tue 48,469; open int 131,831, +2,200.

Natural Gas (NYM)-10,000 MMBtu.; $ per MMBtu

	OPEN	HIGH	LOW	SETTLE	CHG	LIFETIME HIGH	LIFETIME LOW	OPEN INT
Mar	5.670	5.790	5.560	5.654	.003	7.500	3.150	51,734
Apr	5.350	5.420	5.280	5.340	.015	6.010	2.970	23,196
May	5.180	5.270	5.180	5.210	.020	5.668	3.030	25,805
June	5.220	5.260	5.190	5.210	.020	5.612	3.010	19,336
July	5.230	5.274	5.200	5.235	.020	5.622	3.040	17,676
Aug	5.260	5.294	5.220	5.250	.020	5.624	3.120	13,402
Sept	5.220	5.265	5.180	5.218	.020	5.640	3.100	13,093
Oct	5.230	5.240	5.200	5.225	.017	5.580	3.100	14,742
Nov	5.430	5.460	5.400	5.423	.017	5.735	3.270	10,289
Dec	5.610	5.660	5.580	5.613	.015	5.912	3.460	12,860
Ja05	5.745	5.800	5.710	5.750	.015	6.027	3.520	9,971
Feb	5.710	5.720	5.680	5.710	.015	5.991	3.400	9,752
Mar	5.570	5.570	5.505	5.540	.020	5.740	3.640	8,955
May	4.880	4.880	4.880	4.900	.020	5.000	3.500	4,187
June	4.920	4.920	4.920	4.925	.020	5.020	3.530	4,518
July	4.950	4.950	4.950	4.961	.020	5.050	3.560	10,788
Aug	4.950	4.950	4.950	4.971	.020	5.065	3.230	5,319
Dec	5.290	5.290	5.290	5.311	.015	5.400	3.960	4,389

Est vol 46,926; vol Tue 45,710; open int 307,861, −1,771.

Brent Crude (IPE)-1,000 net bbls.; $ per bbl.

	OPEN	HIGH	LOW	SETTLE	CHG	LIFETIME HIGH	LIFETIME LOW	OPEN INT
Mar	29.52	29.80	28.85	28.88	−0.62	32.10	23.00	81,701
Apr	29.28	29.53	28.62	28.66	−0.63	31.54	22.95	82,264
May	29.10	29.34	28.45	28.48	−0.66	31.18	21.97	22,069
June	28.88	29.07	28.25	28.29	−0.65	30.83	23.45	27,498
July	28.69	28.83	28.29	28.08	−0.65	30.55	23.65	10,450
Aug	28.10	28.51	28.10	27.87	−0.64	30.20	24.00	9,032
Sept	28.25	28.29	27.88	27.65	−0.64	29.77	24.40	11,307
Oct	27.94	28.08	27.94	27.45	−0.63	39.45	20.90	5,806
Nov	27.73	27.88	27.73	27.27	−0.61	38.85	24.15	5,352
Dec	27.65	27.70	27.17	27.10	−0.59	38.83	25.32	24,112
Ja05	27.44	27.45	27.35	26.88	−0.57	28.70	22.43	3,611
Dec	26.00	26.00	25.90	25.65	−0.34	26.90	21.91	20,253
Dc06	25.30	25.30	25.30	25.05	−0.29	26.05	24.10	3,400

Est vol 113,000; vol Tue 113,278; open int 321,427, −3,267.

Source: Reprinted by permission of Dow Jones, Inc., via Copyright Clearance Center, Inc.,

Open Interest and Volume of Trading

The final column in Table 2.2 shows the *open interest* for each contract. This is the total number of contracts outstanding. The open interest is the number of long positions or, equivalently, the number of short positions. Because of the problems in compiling the data, the open-interest information is one trading day older than the price information. Thus, in the *Wall Street Journal* of February 5, 2004, the open interest is for the close of trading on February 3, 2004. For the March 2004 corn futures contract, the open interest was 292,145 contracts.

At the end of each section, Table 2.2 shows the estimated volume of trading in contracts of all maturities on February 4, 2004, and the actual volume of trading in these contracts on February 3, 2004. It also shows the total open interest for all contracts on February 3, 2004, and the change in this open interest from the previous trading day. For all corn futures contracts, the estimated trading volume was 54,315 contracts on February 4, 2004, and the actual trading volume was 81,306 contracts on February 4, 2004. The open interest for all corn futures contracts was 632,256 on February 3, 2004, up 1,555 from the previous trading day.

Sometimes the volume of trading in a day is greater than the open interest at the end of the day. This is indicative of a large number of day trades.

Patterns of Futures Prices

A number of different patterns of futures prices can be picked out from Table 2.2. Figure 2.2 shows the pattern of (settlement) futures prices for the gold contract trading on the New York Commodity Exchange and the Brent crude oil contract trading on the International Petroleum Exchange. The futures price of gold increases as the time to maturity increases. This is known as a normal market. By contrast, the futures price of crude oil is a decreasing function of maturity. This is known as an *inverted market*. Other commodities show mixed patterns. For example, the futures price of heating oil first decreases, then increases with maturity.

Figure 2.2 Settlement futures price as a function of time to maturity on February 4, 2004, for (a) gold and (b) Brent crude oil

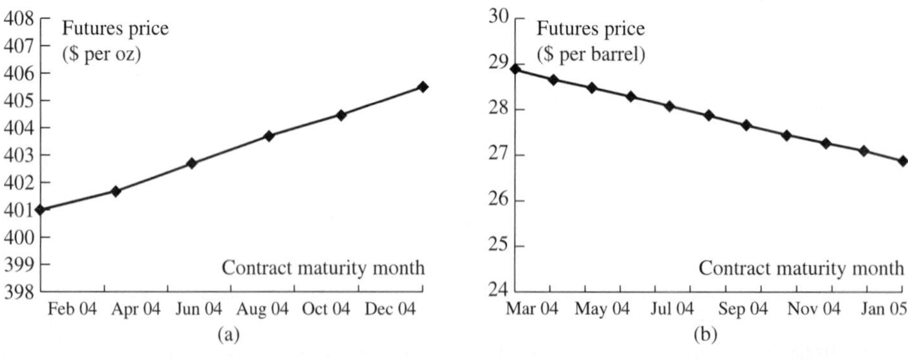

2.6 DELIVERY

As mentioned earlier in this chapter, very few of the futures contracts that are entered into lead to delivery of the underlying asset. Most are closed out early. Nevertheless, it is the possibility of eventual delivery that determines the futures price. An understanding of delivery procedures is therefore important.

The period during which delivery can be made is defined by the exchange and varies from contract to contract. The decision on when to deliver is made by the party with the short position, whom we shall refer to as investor A. When investor A decides to deliver, investor A's broker issues a notice of intention to deliver to the exchange clearinghouse. This notice states how many contracts will be delivered and, in the case of commodities, also specifies where delivery will be made and what grade will be delivered. The exchange then chooses a party with a long position to accept delivery.

Suppose that investor B was the party on the other side of investor A's futures contract when it was entered into. It is important to realize that there is no reason to expect that it will be investor B who takes delivery. Investor B may well have closed out his or her position by trading with investor C, investor C may have closed out his or her position by trading with investor D, and so on. The usual rule chosen by the exchange is to pass the notice of intention to deliver on to the party with the oldest outstanding long position. Parties with long positions must accept delivery notices. However, if the notices are transferable, long investors have a short period of time, usually half an hour, to find another party with a long position that is prepared to accept the notice from them.

In the case of a commodity, taking delivery usually means accepting a warehouse receipt in return for immediate payment. The party taking delivery is then responsible for all warehousing costs. In the case of livestock futures, there may be costs associated with feeding and looking after the animals. In the case of financial futures, delivery is usually made by wire transfer. For all contracts the price paid is usually based on the settlement price immediately preceding the date of the notice of intention to deliver. Where appropriate, this price is adjusted for grade, location of delivery, and so on. The whole delivery procedure from the issuance of the notice of intention to deliver to the delivery itself generally takes two to three days.

There are three critical days for a contract. These are the first notice day, the last notice day, and the last trading day. The *first notice day* is the first day on which a notice of intention to make delivery can be submitted to the exchange. The *last notice day* is the last such day. The *last trading day* is generally a few days before the last notice day. To avoid the risk of having to take delivery, an investor with a long position should close out his or her contracts prior to the first notice day.

Cash Settlement

Some financial futures, such as those on stock indices, are settled in cash because it is inconvenient or impossible to deliver the underlying asset. In the case of the futures contract on the S&P 500, for example, delivering the underlying asset would involve delivering a portfolio of 500 stocks. When a contract is settled in cash there is a final settlement price and all contracts are declared closed. The final settlement price is set equal to the spot price of the underlying asset at either the opening or close of trading on a particular day. For example, in the S&P 500 futures contract trading on the Chicago Mercantile Exchange, the final settlement is the opening price of the index on the third Friday of the delivery month.

2.7 TYPES OF TRADERS AND TYPES OF ORDERS

There are two main types of traders executing trades: commission brokers and locals. *Commission brokers* are following the instructions of their clients and charge a commission for doing so; *locals* are trading on their own account.

Individuals taking positions, whether locals or the clients of commission brokers, can be categorized as hedgers, speculators, or arbitrageurs, as discussed in Chapter 1. Speculators can be classified as scalpers, day traders, or position traders. Scalpers are watching for very short term trends and attempt to profit from small changes in the contract price. They usually hold their positions for only a few minutes. *Day traders* hold their positions for less than one trading day. They are unwilling to take the risk that adverse news will occur overnight. *Position traders* hold their positions for much longer periods of time. They hope to make significant profits from major movements in the markets.

Orders

The simplest type of order placed with a broker is a *market order*. It is a request that a trade be carried out immediately at the best price available in the market. However, there are many other types of orders. We will consider those that are more commonly used.

A *limit order* specifies a particular price. The order can be executed only at this price or at one more favorable to the investor. Thus, if the limit price is $30 for an investor wanting to take a long position, the order will be executed only at a price of $30 or less. There is, of course, no guarantee that the order will be executed at all, because the limit price may never be reached.

A *stop order* or *stop-loss order* also specifies a particular price. The order is executed at the best available price once a bid or offer is made at that particular price or a less-favorable price. Suppose a stop order to sell at $30 is issued when the market price is $35. It becomes an order to sell when and if the price falls to $30. In effect, a stop order becomes a market order as soon as the specified price has been hit. The purpose of a stop order is usually to close out a position if unfavorable price movements take place. It limits the loss that can be incurred.

A *stop–limit order* is a combination of a stop order and a limit order. The order becomes a limit order as soon as a bid or offer is made at a price equal to or less favorable than the stop price. Two prices must be specified in a stop–limit order: the stop price and the limit price. Suppose that, at the time the market price is $35, a stop–limit order to buy is issued with a stop price of $40 and a limit price of $41. As soon as there is a bid or offer at $40, the stop–limit becomes a limit order at $41. If the stop price and the limit price are the same, the order is sometimes called a *stop-and-limit order*.

A *market-if-touched order* (MIT) is executed at the best available price after a trade occurs at a specified price or at a price more favorable than the specified price. In effect, an MIT becomes a market order once the specified price has been hit. An MIT is also known as a *board order*. Consider an investor who has a long position in a futures contract and is issuing instructions that would lead to closing out the contract. A stop order is designed to place a limit on the loss that can occur in the event of unfavorable price movements. By contrast, a market-if-touched order is designed to ensure that profits are taken if sufficiently favorable price movements occur.

A *discretionary order* or *market-not-held order* is traded as a market order except that execution may be delayed at the broker's discretion in an attempt to get a better price.

Some orders specify time conditions. Unless otherwise stated, an order is a day order and expires at the end of the trading day. A *time-of-day order* specifies a particular period of time during the day when the order can be executed. An *open order* or a *good-till-canceled order* is in effect until executed or until the end of trading in the particular contract. A *fill-or-kill order*, as its name implies, must be executed immediately on receipt or not at all.

2.8 REGULATION

Futures markets in the United States are currently regulated federally by the Commodity Futures Trading Commission (CFTC; www.cftc.gov), which was established in 1974. This body is responsible for licensing futures exchanges and approving contracts. All new contracts and changes to existing contracts must be approved by the CFTC. To be approved, the contract must have some useful economic purpose. Usually this means that it must serve the needs of hedgers as well as speculators.

The CFTC looks after the public interest. It is responsible for ensuring that prices are communicated to the public and that futures traders report their outstanding positions if they are above certain levels. The CFTC also licenses all individuals who offer their services to the public in futures trading. The backgrounds of these individuals are investigated, and there are minimum capital requirements. The CFTC deals with complaints brought by the public and ensures that disciplinary action is taken against individuals when appropriate. It has the authority to force exchanges to take disciplinary action against members who are in violation of exchange rules.

With the formation of the National Futures Association (NFA; www.nfa.futures.org) in 1982, some of responsibilities of the CFTC were shifted to the futures industry itself. The NFA is an organization of individuals who participate in the futures industry. Its objective is to prevent fraud and to ensure that the market operates in the best interests of the general public. The NFA requires its members to pass an exam. It is authorized to monitor trading and take disciplinary action when appropriate. The agency has set up an efficient system for arbitrating disputes between individuals and its members.

From time to time other bodies such as the Securities and Exchange Commission (SEC; www.sec.gov), the Federal Reserve Board (www.federalreserve.gov), and the U.S. Treasury Department (www.treas.gov) have claimed jurisdictional rights over some aspects of futures trading. These bodies are concerned with the effects of futures trading on the spot markets for securities such as stocks, Treasury bills, and Treasury bonds. The SEC currently has an effective veto over the approval of new stock or bond index futures contracts. However, the basic responsibility for all futures and options on futures rests with the CFTC.

Trading Irregularities

Most of the time futures markets operate efficiently and in the public interest. However, from time to time trading irregularities do come to light. One type of trading irregularity occurs when an investor group tries to "corner the market".[2] The investor group takes a huge long futures position and also tries to exercise some control over the supply of the underlying commodity. As the maturity of the futures contracts is approached, the investor group does not close out its position, so that the number of outstanding futures contracts may exceed the amount of the commodity available for delivery. The holders of short positions realize that they will find it difficult to deliver and become desperate to close out their positions. The result is a large rise in both futures and spot prices. Regulators usually deal with this type of abuse of the market by increasing margin requirements or imposing stricter position limits or prohibiting trades that increase a speculator's open position or requiring market participants to close out their positions.

Other types of trading irregularities can involve the traders on the floor of the exchange. These received some publicity early in 1989 when it was announced that the FBI had carried out a two-year investigation, using undercover agents, of trading on the Chicago Board of Trade and the Chicago Mercantile Exchange. The investigation was initiated because of complaints filed by a large agricultural concern. The alleged offenses included overcharging customers, not paying customers the full proceeds of sales, and traders using their knowledge of customer orders to trade first for themselves. (The latter is known as *front running*.)

2.9 ACCOUNTING AND TAX

The full details of the accounting and tax treatment of futures contracts are beyond the scope of this book. A trader who wants detailed information on this should consult experts. In this section we provide some general background information.

Accounting

Accounting standards require changes in the market value of a futures contract to be recognized when they occur unless the contract qualifies as a hedge. If the contract does qualify as a hedge, then gains or losses are generally recognized for accounting purposes in the same period in which the gains or losses from the item being hedged are recognized. The latter treatment is referred to as *hedge accounting*.

Consider a company that with a December year end. In September 2004 it takes a long position in a March 2005 corn futures contract and closes out the position at the end of February 2005. Suppose that the futures prices are 250 cents per bushel when the contract is entered into, 270 cents per bushel at the end of 2004, and 280 cents per bushel when the contract is closed out. The contract is for the delivery of 5,000 bushels. If the contract does not qualify as a hedge, the gains for accounting

[2] Possibly the best known example of this involves the activities of the Hunt brothers in the silver market in 1979–80. Between the middle of 1979 and the beginning of 1980, their activities led to a price rise from $9 per ounce to $50 per ounce.

> **Trading Note 2.1** Accounting treatment of a futures transaction
>
> September 2004: Company takes a long position in one March 2005 futures contract to buy 5,000 bushels of corn. Futures price is 250 cents per bushel.
> End of 2004: Futures price is 270 cents per bushel.
> February 2005: The contract is closed out. Futures price is 280 cents per bushel.
>
> *If contract is not a hedge*:
> Accounting profit in 2004 = 5,000 × 20 cents = \$1,000.
> Accounting profit in 2005 = 5,000 × 10 cents = \$500.
>
> *If contract is hedging a purchase of corn in 2005*:
> Accounting profit in 2004 = \$0.
> Accounting profit in 2005 = 5,000 × 30 cents = \$1,500.

purposes are

$$5{,}000 \times (2.70 - 2.50) = \$1{,}000$$

in 2004 and

$$5{,}000 \times (2.80 - 2.70) = \$500$$

in 2005. If the company is hedging the purchase of 5,000 bushels of corn in February 2005 so that the contract qualifies for hedge accounting, the entire gain of $1,500 is realized in 2005 for accounting purposes.

This example is shown in Trading Note 2.1. The treatment of hedging gains and losses is sensible. If the company is hedging the purchase of 5,000 bushels of corn in February 2005, the effect of the futures contract is to ensure that the price paid is close to 150 cents per bushel. The accounting treatment reflects that this price is paid in 2005. The 2004 accounts for the company are unaffected by the futures transaction.

In June 1998, the Financial Accounting Standards Board issued FASB Statement No. 133, Accounting for Derivative Instruments and Hedging Activities (FAS 133). FAS 133 applies to all types of derivatives (including futures, forwards, swaps, and options). It requires all derivatives to be included on the balance sheet at fair market value.[3] It increases disclosure requirements. It also gives companies far less latitude than previously in using hedge accounting. For hedge accounting to be used, the hedging instrument must be highly effective in offsetting exposures and an assessment of this effectiveness is required every three months. A similar standard IAS 39 has now been issued by the International Accounting Standards Board.

Tax

Under the U.S. tax rules, two key issues are the nature of a taxable gain or loss and the timing of the recognition of the gain or loss. Gains or losses are either classified as capital gains/losses or as part of ordinary income.

For a corporate taxpayer, capital gains are taxed at the same rate as ordinary income, and the ability to deduct losses is restricted. Capital losses are deductible only to the extent of capital gains. A corporation may carry back a capital loss for three years and carry it forward for up to five years. For a noncorporate taxpayer, short-

[3] Previously the attraction of derivatives in some situations was that they were "off-balance-sheet" items.

term capital gains are taxed at the same rate as ordinary income, but long-term capital gains are taxed at a lower rate than ordinary income. (Long-term capital gains are gains from the sale of a capital asset held for longer than one year; short term capital gains are the gains from the sale of a capital asset held one year or less.) The Taxpayer Relief Act of 1997 widened the rate differential between ordinary income and long-term capital gains. For a noncorporate taxpayer, capital losses are deductible to the extent of capital gains plus ordinary income up to $3,000 and can be carried forward indefinitely.

Generally, positions in futures contracts are treated as if they are closed out on the last day of the tax year. For the noncorporate taxpayer this gives rise to capital gains and losses. These are treated as if the are 60% long term and 40% short term without regard to the holding period. This is referred to as the "60/40" rule. A noncorporate taxpayer may elect to carry back for three years any net losses from the 60/40 rule to offset any gains recognized under the rule in the previous three years.

Hedging transactions are exempt from this rule. The definition of a hedge transaction for tax purposes is different from that for accounting purposes. The tax regulations define a hedging transaction as a transaction entered into in the normal course of business primarily for one of the following reasons:

1. To reduce the risk of price changes or currency fluctuations with respect to property that is held or to be held by the taxpayer for the purposes of producing ordinary income.
2. To reduce the risk of price or interest rate changes or currency fluctuations with respect to borrowings made by the taxpayer.

Within 35 days of entering into a hedging transaction it must be formally identified as a hedge. Gains or losses from hedging transactions are treated as ordinary income. The timing of the recognition of gains or losses from hedging transactions generally matches the timing of the recognition of income or deduction from the hedged items.

Special rules apply to foreign currency futures transactions. A taxpayer can make a binding election to treat gains and losses from all futures contracts in all foreign currencies as ordinary income, regardless of whether the contracts are entered into for hedging or speculative purposes. If a taxpayer does not make this election, foreign currencies futures transactions are treated in the same way as other futures transactions.

2.10 FORWARD vs. FUTURES CONTRACTS

As explained in Chapter 1, forward contracts are similar to futures contracts in that they are agreements to buy or sell an asset at a certain time in the future for a certain price. Whereas futures contracts are traded on an exchange, forward contracts are traded in the over-the-counter market. They are typically entered into by two financial institutions or by a financial institution and one of its corporate clients.

One of the parties to a forward contract assumes a *long position* and agrees to buy the asset on a certain specified date for a certain price. The other party assumes a *short position* and agrees to sell the asset on the same date for the same price. Forward contracts do not have to conform to the standards of a particular exchange. The

Table 2.3 Comparison of forward and futures contracts

Forward	*Futures*
Private contract between two parties	Traded on an exchange
Not standardized	Standardized contract
Usually one specified delivery date	Range of delivery dates
Settled at end of contract	Settled daily
Delivery or final cash settlement usually takes place	Contract is usually closed out prior to maturity
Some credit risk	Virtually no credit risk

contract delivery date can be any date mutually convenient to the two parties. Usually, in forward contracts a single delivery date is specified, whereas in futures contracts there is a range of possible delivery dates.

Unlike futures contracts, forward contracts are not marked to market daily. The two parties contract to settle up on the specified delivery date. Whereas most futures contracts are closed out prior to delivery, most forward contracts do lead to delivery of the physical asset or to final settlement in cash. Table 2.3 summarizes the main differences between forward and futures contracts.

Profits from Forward and Futures Contracts

Suppose that the sterling exchange rate for a 90-day forward contract is 1.6000 dollars per pound and that this rate is also the futures price for a contract that will be delivered in exactly 90 days. Under the forward contract, the whole gain or loss is realized at the end of the life of the contract. Under the futures contract, the gain or loss is realized day by day because of the daily settlement procedures. Figure 2.3 shows the net profit as a function of the exchange rate for 90-day long and short forward or futures positions on £1 million.

Figure 2.3 Profit from (a) long and (b) short forward or futures position on £1 million

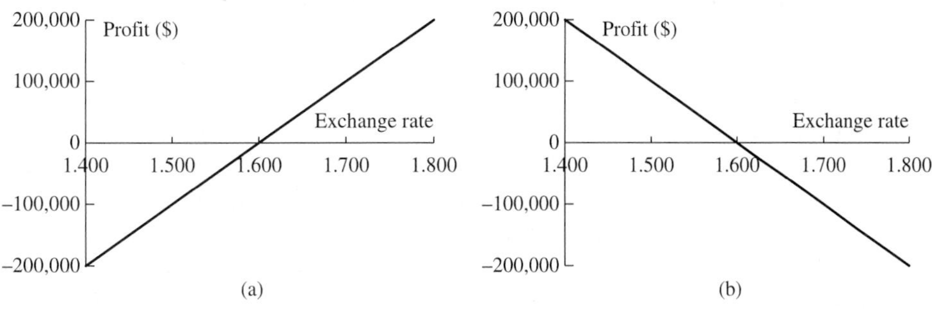

Trading Note 2.2 Futures vs. forwards

Investor A takes a long position in a 90-day forward contract on £1 million. The forward price is 1.6000 dollars per pound. Investor B takes a long position in 90-day futures contracts on £1 million. The futures price is also 1.6000 dollars per pound. At the end of the 90 days, the exchange rate proves to be 1.8000.

Outcome
Investors A and B each make a total gain equal to

$$(1.8000 - 1.6000) \times 1{,}000{,}000 = \$200{,}000$$

Investor A's gain is made entirely on the 90th day. Investor B's gain is realized day by day over the 90-day period. On some days investor B may realize a loss, whereas on other days he or she will realize a gain.

Suppose that investor A is long £1 million in a 90-day forward contract, and investor B is long £1 million in 90-day futures contracts. (Each futures contract is for the purchase or sale of £62,500, so investor B has purchased a total of 16 contracts.) Assume that the spot exchange rate in 90 days proves to be 1.8000 dollars per pound. Investor A makes a gain of $200,000 on the 90th day. Investor B makes the same gain—but spread out over the 90-day period. On some days investor B may realize a loss, whereas on other days he or she makes a gain. However, in total, when losses are netted against gains, there is a gain of $200,000 over the 90-day period. This scenario is summarized in Trading Note 2.2.

Foreign Exchange Quotes

Both forward and futures contracts trade actively on foreign currencies. However, there is a difference in the way exchange rates are quoted in the two markets. Futures prices are always quoted as the number of U.S. dollars per unit of the foreign currency or as the number of U.S. cents per unit of the foreign currency. Forward prices are always quoted in the same way as spot prices. This means that for the British pound, the euro, the Australian dollar, and the New Zealand dollar, the forward quotes show the number of U.S. dollars per unit of the foreign currency and are directly comparable with futures quotes. For other major currencies, forward quotes show the number of units of the foreign currency per U.S. dollar (USD). Consider the Canadian dollar (CAD). A futures price quote of 0.7050 USD per CAD corresponds to a forward price quote of 1.4184 CAD per USD (1.4184 = 1/0.7050).

SUMMARY

A very high proportion of the futures contracts that are traded do not lead to the delivery of the underlying asset. They are closed out before the delivery period is reached. However, it is the possibility of final delivery that drives the determination of the futures price. For each futures contract, there is a range of days during which delivery can be made and a well-defined delivery procedure. Some contracts, such as those on stock indices, are settled in cash rather than by delivery of the underlying asset.

The specification of contracts is an important activity for a futures exchange. The two sides to any contract must know what can be delivered, where delivery can take place, and when delivery can take place. They also need to know details on the trading hours, how prices will be quoted, maximum daily price movements, and so on. New contracts must be approved by the Commodity Futures Trading Commission before trading starts.

Margins are an important aspect of futures markets. An investor keeps a margin account with his or her broker. The account is adjusted daily to reflect gains or losses, and from time to time the broker may require the account to be topped up if adverse price movements have taken place. The broker either must be a clearinghouse member or must maintain a margin account with a clearinghouse member. Each clearinghouse member maintains a margin account with the exchange clearinghouse. The balance in the account is adjusted daily to reflect gains and losses on the business for which the clearinghouse member is responsible.

Information on futures prices is collected in a systematic way at exchanges and relayed within a matter of seconds to investors throughout the world. Many daily newspapers such as the *Wall Street Journal* carry a summary of the previous day's trading.

Forward contracts differ from futures contracts in a number of ways. Forward contracts are private arrangements between two parties, whereas futures contracts are traded on exchanges. There is generally a single delivery date in a forward contract, whereas futures contracts frequently involve a range of such dates. Because they are not traded on exchanges, forward contracts need not be standardized. A forward contract is not usually settled until the end of its life, and most contracts do in fact lead to delivery of the underlying asset or a cash settlement at this time.

In the next few chapters we will examine in more detail the ways in which forward and futures contracts can be used for hedging. We will also look at how forward and futures prices are determined.

FURTHER READING

Duffie, D. *Futures Markets*. Upper Saddle River, NJ: Prentice Hall, 1989.

Gastineau, G. L., D. J. Smith, and R. Todd. *Risk Management, Derivatives, and Financial Analysis under SFAS No. 133*. The Research Foundation of AIMR and Blackwell Series in Finance, 2001.

Jorion, P. "Risk Management Lessons from Long-Term Capital Management," *European Financial Management*, 6, 3 (September 2000): 277–300.

Kawaller, I. G. and P. D. Koch. "Meeting the Highly Effective Expectation Criterion for Hedge Accounting," *Journal of Derivatives*, 7, 4 (Summer 2000): 79–87.

Lowenstein, R. *When Genius Failed: The Rise and Fall of Long-Term Capital Management*. New York: Random House, 2000.

Warwick, B., F. J. Jones, and R. J. Teweles. *The Futures Game*. 3rd edn. New York: McGraw-Hill, 1998.

Quiz (Answers at End of Book)

2.1. Distinguish between the terms *open interest* and *trading volume*.

2.2. What is the difference between a *local* and a *commission broker*?

2.3. Suppose that you enter into a short futures contract to sell July silver for \$5.20 per ounce on the New York Commodity Exchange. The size of the contract is 5,000 ounces. The initial margin is \$4,000, and the maintenance margin is \$3,000. What change in the futures price will lead to a margin call? What happens if you do not meet the margin call?

2.4. Suppose that in September 2004 you take a long position in a contract on May 2005 crude oil futures. You close out your position in March 2005. The futures price (per barrel) is \$18.30 when you enter into your contract, \$20.50 when you close out your position, and \$19.10 at the end of December 2004. One contract is for the delivery of 1,000 barrels. What is your total profit? When is it realized? How is it taxed if you are (a) a hedger and (b) a speculator? Assume that you have a December 31 year-end.

2.5. What does a stop order to sell at \$2 mean? When might it be used? What does a limit order to sell at \$2 mean? When might it be used?

2.6. What is the difference between the operation of the margin accounts administered by a clearinghouse and those administered by a broker?

2.7. What differences exist in the way prices are quoted in the foreign exchange futures market, the foreign exchange spot market, and the foreign exchange forward market?

Questions and Problems (Answers in Solutions Manual/Study Guide)

2.8. The party with a short position in a futures contract sometimes has options as to the precise asset that will be delivered, where delivery will take place, when delivery will take place, and so on. Do these options increase or decrease the futures price? Explain your reasoning.

2.9. What are the most important aspects of the design of a new futures contract?

2.10. Explain how margins protect investors against the possibility of default.

2.11. An investor enters into two long July futures contracts on orange juice. Each contract is for the delivery of 15,000 pounds. The current futures price is 160 cents per pound, the initial margin is \$6,000 per contract, and the maintenance margin is \$4,500 per contract. What price change would lead to a margin call? Under what circumstances could \$2,000 be withdrawn from the margin account?

2.12. Show that, if the futures price of a commodity is greater than the spot price during the delivery period, there is an arbitrage opportunity. Does an arbitrage opportunity exist if the futures price is less than the spot price? Explain your answer.

2.13. Explain the difference between a market-if-touched order and a stop order.

2.14. Explain what a stop-limit order to sell at 20.30 with a limit of 20.10 means.

2.15. At the end of one day a clearinghouse member is long 100 contracts, and the settlement price is \$50,000 per contract. The original margin is \$2,000 per contract. On the following day the member becomes responsible for clearing an additional 20 long contracts, entered into at a price of \$51,000 per contract. The settlement price at the end of this day is \$50,200. How much does the member have to add to its margin account with the exchange clearinghouse?

2.16. On July 1, 2004, a U.S. company enters into a forward contract to buy 10 million British pounds on January 1, 2005. On September 1, 2004, it enters into a forward contract to sell 10 million British pounds on January 1, 2005. Describe the profit or loss the company will make in dollars as a function of the forward exchange rates on July 1, 2004, and September 1, 2004.

2.17. The forward price on the Swiss franc for delivery in 45 days is quoted as 1.8204. The futures price for a contract that will be delivered in 45 days is 0.5479. Explain these two quotes. Which is more favorable for an investor wanting to sell Swiss francs?

2.18. Suppose you call your broker and issue instructions to sell one July hogs contract. Describe what happens.

2.19. "Speculation in futures markets is pure gambling. It is not in the public interest to allow speculators to trade on a futures exchange." Discuss this viewpoint.

2.20. Identify the contracts with the highest open interest in Table 2.2. Consider each of the following sections separately: grains and oilseeds, livestock, food and fiber, metals, and petroleum.

2.21. What do you think would happen if an exchange started trading a contract in which the quality of the underlying asset was incompletely specified?

2.22. "When a futures contract is traded on the floor of the exchange, it may be the case that the open interest increases by one, stays the same, or decreases by one." Explain this statement.

2.23. Suppose that on October 24, 2004, you take a short position in an April 2005 live-cattle futures contract. You close out your position on January 21, 2005. The futures price (per pound) is 61.20 cents when you enter into the contract, 58.30 cents when you close out your position, and 58.80 cents at the end of December 2004. One contract is for the delivery of 40,000 pounds of cattle. What is your total profit? How is it taxed if you are (a) a hedger and (b) a speculator?

Assignment Questions

2.24. A company enters into a short futures contract to sell 5,000 bushels of wheat for 250 cents per bushel. The initial margin is \$3,000 and the maintenance margin is \$2,000. What price change would lead to a margin call? Under what circumstances could \$1,500 be withdrawn from the margin account?

2.25. Suppose that there are no storage costs for corn and the interest rate for borrowing or lending is 5% per annum. How could you make money on February 4, 2004, by trading March 2004 and May 2004 contracts? Use Table 2.2.

2.26. What position is equivalent to a long forward contract to buy an asset at K on a certain date and a put option to sell it for K on that date.

2.27. The author's website (`www.rotman.utoronto.ca/~hull/data`) contains daily closing prices for the December 2001 crude oil futures contract and the December 2001 gold futures contract. (Both contracts are traded on NYMEX.) You are required to download the data and answer the following:

a. How high do the maintenance margin levels for oil and gold have to be set so that there is a 1% chance that an investor with a balance slightly above the maintenence margin level on a particular day has a negative balance two days later (i.e. one day after a margin call). How high do they have to be for a 0.1% chance. Assume daily price changes are normally distributed with mean zero.
b. Imagine an investor who starts with a long position in the oil contract at the beginning of the period covered by the data and keeps the contract for the whole of the period of time covered by the data. Margin balances in excess of the initial margin are withdrawn. Use the maintenance margin you calculated in part (a) for a 1% risk level and assume that the maintenance margin is 75% of the initial margin. Calculate the number of margin calls and the number of times the investor has a negative margin balance and therefore an incentive to walk away. Assume that all margin calls are met in your calculations. Repeat the calculations for an investor who starts with a short position in the gold contract.

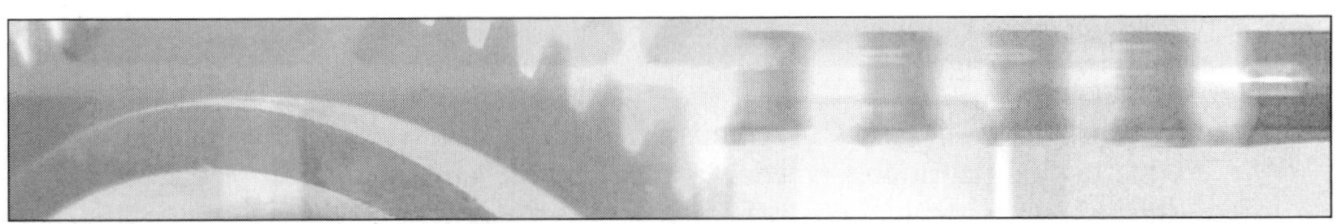

CHAPTER 3 Hedging Strategies Using Futures

Many of the participants in futures markets are hedgers. Their aim is to use futures markets to reduce a particular risk they face. This risk might relate to the price of oil, a foreign exchange rate, the level of the stock market, or some other variable. A *perfect hedge* is one that completely eliminates the risk. Perfect hedges are rare. For the most part, therefore, a study of hedging using futures contracts is a study of the ways in which hedges can be constructed so that they perform as close to perfect as possible.

In this chapter we consider a number of general issues associated with the way hedges are set up. When is a short futures position appropriate? When is a long futures position appropriate? Which futures contract should be used? What is the optimal size of the futures position for reducing risk? At this stage, we restrict our attention to what might be termed *hedge-and-forget* strategies. We assume that no attempt is made to adjust the hedge once it has been put in place. The hedger simply takes a futures position at the beginning of the life of the hedge and closes out the position at the end of the life of the hedge. In Chapter 15 we will examine dynamic hedging strategies in which the hedge is monitored closely and frequent adjustments are made.

Throughout this chapter we will treat futures contracts as forward contracts; that is, we will ignore daily settlement. This means that we can ignore the time value of money in most situations because all cash flows occur at the time the hedge is closed out.

3.1 BASIC PRINCIPLES

When an individual or company chooses to use futures markets to hedge a risk, the objective is usually to take a position that neutralizes the risk as far as possible. Consider a company that knows it will gain \$10,000 for each 1 cent increase in the price of a commodity over the next three months and lose \$10,000 for each 1 cent decrease in the price during the same period. To hedge, the company's treasurer should take a short futures position that is designed to offset this risk. The futures position should lead to a loss of \$10,000 for each 1 cent increase in the price of the commodity over the three months and a gain of \$10,000 for each 1 cent decrease in the price during this period. If the price of the commodity goes down, the gain on the futures position offsets the loss on the rest of the company's business. If the price of the commodity goes up, the loss on the futures position is offset by the gain on the rest of the company's business.

Short Hedges

A *short hedge* is a hedge, such as the one just described, that involves a short position in futures contracts. A short hedge is appropriate when the hedger already owns an asset and expects to sell it at some time in the future. For example, a short hedge could be used by a farmer who owns some hogs and knows that they will be ready for sale at the local market in two months. A short hedge can also be used when an asset is not owned right now but will be owned at some time in the future. Consider, for example, a U.S. exporter who knows that he or she will receive euros in three months. The exporter will realize a gain if the euro increases in value relative to the U.S. dollar and will sustain a loss if the euro decreases in value relative to the U.S. dollar. A short futures position leads to a loss if the euro increases in value and a gain if it decreases in value. It has the effect of offsetting the exporter's risk.

To provide a more detailed illustration of the operation of a short hedge in a specific situation, we assume that it is May 15 today and that an oil producer has just negotiated a contract to sell 1 million barrels of crude oil. It has been agreed that the price that will apply in the contract is the market price on August 15. The oil producer is therefore in the position where it will gain \$10,000 for each 1 cent increase in the price of oil over the next three months and lose \$10,000 for each 1 cent decrease in the price during this period. Suppose that the spot price on May 15 is \$19 per barrel and the August crude oil futures price on the New York Mercantile Exchange (NYMEX) is \$18.75 per barrel. Because each futures contract on NYMEX is for the delivery of 1,000 barrels, the company can hedge its exposure by shorting 1,000 August futures contracts. If the oil producer closes out its position on August 15, the effect of the strategy should be to lock in a price close to \$18.75 per barrel. This example is summarized in Trading Note 3.1

To illustrate what might happen, suppose that the spot price on August 15 proves to be \$17.50 per barrel. The company realizes \$17.5 million for the oil under its sales contract. Because August is the delivery month for the futures contract, the futures price on August 15 should be very close to the spot price of \$17.50 on that date. The

Trading Note 3.1 A short hedge

It is May 15. An oil producer has negotiated a contract to sell 1 million barrels of crude oil. The price in the sales contract is the spot price on August 15. Quotes:
Spot price of crude oil: \$19.00 per barrel
August oil futures price: \$18.75 per barrel

Hedging Strategy
May 15: Short 1,000 August futures contracts on crude oil.
August 15: Close out futures position.

Result
The company ensures that it will receive a price close to \$18.75 per barrel.

company therefore gains approximately

$$\$18.75 - \$17.50 = \$1.25$$

per barrel, or \$1.25 million in total from the short futures position. The total amount realized from both the futures position and the sales contract is therefore approximately \$18.75 per barrel, or \$18.75 million in total.

For an alternative outcome, suppose that the price of oil on August 15 proves to be \$19.50 per barrel. The company realizes \$19.50 for the oil and loses approximately

$$\$19.50 - \$18.75 = \$0.75$$

per barrel on the short futures position. Again, the total amount realized is approximately \$18.75 million. It is easy to see that in all cases the company ends up with approximately \$18.75 million.

Long Hedges

Hedges that involve taking a long position in a futures contract are known as *long hedges*. A long hedge is appropriate when a company knows it will have to purchase a certain asset in the future and wants to lock in a price now.

Suppose that it is now January 15. A copper fabricator knows it will require 100,000 pounds of copper on May 15 to meet a certain contract. The spot price of copper is 140 cents per pound, and the May futures price is 120 cents per pound. The fabricator can hedge its position by taking a long position in four May futures contracts on the COMEX division of NYMEX and closing its position on May 15. Each contract is for the delivery of 25,000 pounds of copper. The strategy has the effect of locking in the price of the required copper at close to 120 cents per pound.

This example is summarized in Trading Note 3.2. Suppose that the price of copper on May 15 proves to be 125 cents per pound. Because May is the delivery month for the futures contract, this should be very close to the futures price. The fabricator therefore gains approximately

$$100{,}000 \times (\$1.25 - \$1.20) = \$5{,}000$$

on the futures contracts. It pays $100{,}000 \times \$1.25 = \$125{,}000$ for the copper, making the total cost approximately $\$125{,}000 - \$5{,}000 = \$120{,}000$. For an alternative outcome,

Trading Note 3.2 A long hedge

It is January 15. A copper fabricator knows it will require 100,000 pounds of copper on May 15 to meet a certain contract. The spot price of copper is 140 cents per pound and the May futures price is 120 cents per pound.

Hedging Strategy

January 15: Take a long position in four May futures contracts on copper.

May 15: Close out the position.

Result

The company ensures that its cost will be close to 120 cents per pound.

suppose the futures price is 105 cents per pound on May 15. The fabricator then loses approximately

$$100{,}000 \times (\$1.20 - \$1.05) = \$15{,}000$$

on the futures contract and pays $100{,}000 \times \$1.05 = \$105{,}000$ for the copper. Again, the total cost is approximately $120,000, or 120 cents per pound.

Note that it is better for the company to use futures contracts than to buy the copper on January 15 in the spot market. If it does the latter, it will pay 140 cents per pound instead of 120 cents per pound and will incur both interest costs and storage costs. For a company using copper on a regular basis, this disadvantage would be offset by the convenience of having the copper on hand.[1] However, for a company that knows it will not require the copper until May 15, the futures contract alternative is likely to be preferred.

Long hedges can be used to manage an existing short position. Consider an investor who has shorted a certain stock. (See Section 5.2 for a discussion of shorting.) Part of the risk faced by the investor is related to the performance of the stock market as a whole. The investor can neutralize this risk with a long position in index futures contracts. This type of hedging strategy is discussed further later in the chapter.

In both the example in Trading Note 3.2 and that in Trading Note 3.1, we assume that the futures position is closed out in the delivery month. The hedge has the same basic effect if delivery is allowed to happen. However, making or taking delivery can be costly and inconvenient. For this reason, delivery is not usually made even when the hedger keeps the futures contract until the delivery month. As will be discussed later, hedgers with long positions usually avoid any possibility of having to take delivery by closing out their positions before the delivery period.

We have also assumed in the two examples that a futures contract is the same as a forward contract. In practice, marking to market does have a small effect on the performance of a hedge. As explained in Chapter 2, it means that the payoff from the futures contract is realized day by day throughout the life of the hedge rather than all at the end.

3.2 ARGUMENTS FOR AND AGAINST HEDGING

The arguments in favor of hedging are so obvious that they hardly need to be stated. Most companies are in the business of manufacturing, or retailing or wholesaling, or providing a service. They have no particular skills or expertise in predicting variables such as interest rates, exchange rates, and commodity prices. It makes sense for them to hedge the risks associated with these variables as they arise. The companies can then focus on their main activities—for which presumably they do have particular skills and expertise. By hedging, they avoid unpleasant surprises such as sharp rises in the price of a commodity.

In practice, many risks are left unhedged. In the rest of this section we will explore some of the reasons.

[1] See Chapter 5 for a discussion of convenience yields.

Hedging and Shareholders

One argument sometimes put forward is that the shareholders can, if they wish, do the hedging themselves. They do not need the company to do it for them. This argument is, however, open to question. It assumes that shareholders have as much information about the risks faced by a company as does the company's management. In most instances, this is not the case. The argument also ignores commissions and other transactions costs. These are less expensive per dollar of hedging for large transactions than for small transactions. Hedging is therefore likely to be less expensive when carried out by the company than when it is carried out by individual shareholders. Indeed, the size of futures contracts makes hedging by individual shareholders impossible in many situations.

One thing that shareholders can do far more easily than a corporation is diversify risk. A shareholder with a well-diversified portfolio may be immune to many of the risks faced by a corporation. For example, in addition to holding shares in a company that uses copper, a well-diversified shareholder may hold shares in a copper producer, so that there is very little overall exposure to the price of copper. If companies are acting in the best interests of well-diversified shareholders, it can be argued that hedging is unnecessary in many situations. However, the extent to which managers are in practice influenced by this type of argument is open to question.

Hedging and Competitors

If hedging is not the norm in a certain industry, it may not make sense for one particular company to choose to be different from all others. Competitive pressures within the industry may be such that the prices of the goods and services produced by the industry fluctuate to reflect raw material costs, interest rates, exchange rates, and so on. A company that does not hedge can expect its profit margins to be roughly constant. However, a company that does hedge can expect its profit margins to fluctuate!

To illustrate this point, consider two manufacturers of gold jewelry, SafeandSure Company and TakeaChance Company. We assume that most companies in the industry do not hedge against movements in the price of gold and that TakeaChance Company is no exception. However, SafeandSure Company has decided to be different from its competitors and to use futures contracts to hedge its purchase of gold over the next 18 months. If the price of gold goes up, economic pressures will tend to lead to a corresponding increase in the wholesale price of the jewelry, so that TakeaChance Company's profit margin is unaffected. In contrast, SafeandSure Company's profit margin will increase after the effects of the hedge have been taken into account. If the price of gold goes down, economic pressures will tend to lead to a corresponding decrease in the wholesale price of the jewelry. Again, TakeaChance Company's profit margin is unaffected. However, SafeandSure Company's profit margin goes down. In extreme conditions, SafeandSure Company's profit margin could become negative as a result of the "hedging" carried out! The situation is summarized in Table 3.1.

This example emphasizes the importance of looking at the big picture when hedging. All the implications of price changes on a company's profitability should be taken into account in the design of a hedging strategy to protect against the price changes.

Table 3.1 Danger in hedging when competitors do not hedge

Change in gold price	*Effect on Price of gold jewelry*	*Effect on Profits of TakeaChance Co.*	*Effect on Profits of SafeandSure Co.*
Increase	Increase	None	Increase
Decrease	Decrease	None	Decrease

Other Considerations

It is important to realize that a hedge using futures contracts can result in a decrease or an increase in a company's profits relative to its position with no hedging. In the example depicted in Table 3.1, if the price of oil goes down, the company loses money on its sale of 1 million barrels of oil, and the futures position leads to an offsetting gain. The treasurer can be congratulated for having had the foresight to put the hedge in place. Clearly, the company is better off than it would be with no hedging. Other executives in the organization, it is hoped, will appreciate the contribution made by the treasurer. If the price of oil goes up, the company gains from its sale of the oil, and the futures position leads to an offsetting loss. The company is in a worse position than it would have been in with no hedging. Although the hedging decision was perfectly logical, the treasurer may in practice have a difficult time justifying it. Suppose that the price of oil is $21.75 on August 15 in Trading Note 3.1, so that the company loses $3 per barrel on the futures contract. We can imagine a conversation such as the following between the treasurer and the president:

PRESIDENT: This is terrible. We've lost $3 million in the futures market in the space of three months. How could it happen? I want a full explanation.

TREASURER: The purpose of the futures contracts was to hedge our exposure to the price of oil—not to make a profit. Don't forget that we made about $3 million from the favorable effect of the oil price increases on our business.

PRESIDENT: What's that got to do with it? That's like saying that we do not need to worry when our sales are down in California because they are up in New York.

TREASURER: If the price of oil had gone down...

PRESIDENT: I don't care what would have happened if the price of oil had gone down. The fact is that it went up. I really do not know what you were doing playing the futures markets like this. Our shareholders will expect us to have done particularly well this quarter. I'm going to have to explain to them that your actions reduced profits by $3 million. I'm afraid this is going to mean no bonus for you this year.

TREASURER: That's unfair. I was only...

PRESIDENT: Unfair! You are lucky not to be fired. You lost $3 million.

TREASURER: It all depends how you look at it...

Business Snapshot 3.1 Hedging by gold mining companies

It is natural for a gold mining company to consider hedging against changes in the price of gold. Typically it takes several years to extract all the gold from a mine. Once a gold mining company decides to go ahead with production at a particular mine, it has a big exposure to the price of gold. Indeed a mine that looks profitable at the outset could become unprofitable if the price of gold plunges.

Some gold mining companies do not hedge and make this clear to potential shareholders. Their view is that many investors buy gold stocks because they want to benefit when the price of gold increases and are prepared to accept the risk of a loss from a decrease in the price of gold. Other companies choose to hedge (and explain this to potential shareholders). They estimate the number of ounces they will produce each month for the next few years and sell all or part of this production forward to an investment bank. (Typically their trades are too large for futures markets.)

It is interesting to examine how investment banks hedge their risk when they enter into forward contracts with gold mining companies. The central banks of many countries hold large amounts of gold. After it has entered into a forward contract to buy gold from a gold mining company, an investment bank borrows gold from a central bank and sells it for the current market price. At the end of the life of the forward contract it buys gold from the gold mining company under the terms of the forward contract and uses it to repay the central bank. The central bank charges a fee (perhaps 1.5% per annum) known as the gold lease rate for lending its gold in this way.

It is easy to see why many treasurers are reluctant to hedge! Hedging reduces risk for the company. However, it may increase risks for the treasurer if others do not fully understand what is being done. The only real solution to this problem involves ensuring that all senior executives within the organization fully understand the nature of hedging before a hedging program is put in place. Ideally, hedging strategies are set by a company's board of directors and are clearly communicated to both the company's management and the shareholders. (See Business Snapshot 3.1 for a discussion of hedging by gold mining companies.)

3.3 BASIS RISK

The hedges in the examples considered so far have been almost too good to be true. The hedger was able to identify the precise date in the future when an asset would be bought or sold. The hedger was then able to use futures contracts to remove almost all the risk arising from the price of the asset on that date. In practice, hedging is often not quite as straightforward. Some of the reasons are as follows:

1. The asset whose price is to be hedged may not be exactly the same as the asset underlying the futures contract.
2. The hedger may not be certain of the exact date the asset will be bought or sold.
3. The hedge may require the futures contract to be closed out before its delivery month.

Figure 3.1 Variation of basis over time

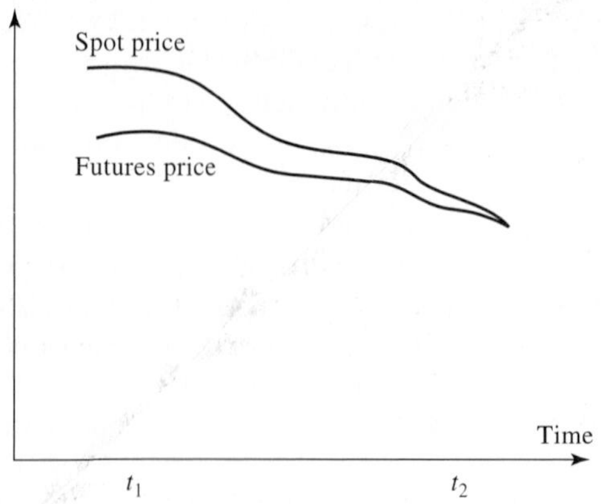

These problems give rise to what is termed *basis risk*. This concept will now be explained.

The Basis

The *basis* in a hedging situation is as follows:[2]

$$\text{Basis} = \text{Spot price of asset to be hedged} - \text{Futures price of contract used}$$

If the asset to be hedged and the asset underlying the futures contract are the same, the basis should be zero at the expiration of the futures contract. Prior to expiration, the basis may be positive or negative. The spot price is should equal the futures price for a very short maturity contract. From Table 2.2 and Figure 2.2 we see that the basis is positive for some assets (e.g., gold) and negative for others (e.g., Brent crude oil).

When the spot price increases by more than the futures price, the basis increases. This is referred to as a *strengthening of the basis*. When the futures price increases by more than the spot price, the basis declines. This is referred to as a *weakening of the basis*. Figure 3.1 illustrates how a basis might change over time in a situation where the basis is positive prior to expiration of the futures contract.

To examine the nature of basis risk, we will use the following notation:

S_1: Spot price at time t_1
S_2: Spot price at time t_2
F_1: Futures price at time t_1
F_2: Futures price at time t_2
b_1: Basis at time t_1
b_2: Basis at time t_2

[2] This is the usual definition. However, the alternative definition

$$\text{Basis} = \text{Futures price} - \text{Spot price}$$

is sometimes used, particularly when the futures contract is on a financial asset.

We will assume that a hedge is put in place at time t_1 and closed out at time t_2. As an example, we will consider the case where the spot and futures prices at the time the hedge is initiated are \$2.50 and \$2.20, respectively, and that at the time the hedge is closed out they are \$2.00 and \$1.90, respectively. This means that $S_1 = 2.50$, $F_1 = 2.20$, $S_2 = 2.00$, and $F_2 = 1.90$. From the definition of the basis,

$$b_1 = S_1 - F_1 \quad \text{and} \quad b_2 = S_2 - F_2$$

and, in our example, $b_1 = 0.30$ and $b_2 = 0.10$.

Consider first the situation of a hedger who knows that the asset will be sold at time t_2 and takes a short futures position at time t_1. The price realized for the asset is S_2 and the profit on the futures position is $F_1 - F_2$. The effective price obtained for the asset with hedging is therefore

$$S_2 + F_1 - F_2 = F_1 + b_2$$

In our example, this is \$2.30. The value of F_1 is known at time t_1. If b_2 were also known at this time, a perfect hedge would result. The hedging risk is the uncertainty associated with b_2 and is known as *basis risk*. Consider next a situation where a company knows it will buy the asset at time t_2 and initiates a long hedge at time t_1. The price paid for the asset is S_2 and the loss on the hedge is $F_1 - F_2$. The effective price paid with hedging is therefore

$$S_2 + F_1 - F_2 = F_1 + b_2$$

This is the same expression as before and is \$2.30 in the example. The value of F_1 is known at time t_1, and the term b_2 represents basis risk.

Note that basis risk can lead to an improvement or a worsening of a hedger's position. Consider a short hedge. If the basis strengthens unexpectedly, the hedger's position improves; if the basis weakens unexpectedly, the hedger's position worsens. For a long hedge, the reverse holds. If the basis strengthens unexpectedly, the hedger's position worsens; if the basis weakens unexpectedly, the hedger's position improves.

The asset that gives rise to the hedger's exposure is sometimes different from the asset underlying the hedge. The basis risk is then usually greater. Define S_2^* as the price of the asset underlying the futures contract at time t_2. As before, S_2 is the price of the asset being hedged at time t_2. By hedging, a company ensures that the price that will be paid (or received) for the asset is

$$S_2 + F_1 - F_2$$

This can be written as

$$F_1 + (S_2^* - F_2) + (S_2 - S_2^*)$$

The terms $S_2^* - F_2$ and $S_2 - S_2^*$ represent the two components of the basis. The $S_2^* - F_2$ term is the basis that would exist if the asset being hedged were the same as the asset underlying the futures contract. The $S_2 - S_2^*$ term is the basis arising from the difference between the two assets.

Choice of Contract

One key factor affecting basis risk is the choice of the futures contract to be used for hedging. This choice has two components:

1. The choice of the asset underlying the futures contract
2. The choice of the delivery month

If the asset being hedged exactly matches an asset underlying a futures contract, the first choice is generally fairly easy. In other circumstances, it is necessary to carry out a careful analysis to determine which of the available futures contracts has futures prices that are most closely correlated with the price of the asset being hedged.

The choice of delivery month can be influenced by several factors. In the examples earlier in this chapter, we assumed that when the expiration of the hedge corresponds to a delivery month, the contract with that delivery month is chosen. In fact, a contract with a later delivery month is usually chosen in these circumstances. The reason is that futures prices are in some instances quite erratic during the delivery month. Also, a long hedger runs the risk of having to take delivery of the physical asset if the contract is held during the delivery month. Taking delivery can be expensive and inconvenient.

In general, basis risk increases as the time difference between the hedge expiration and the delivery month increases. A good rule of thumb is therefore to choose a delivery month that is as close as possible to, but later than, the expiration of the hedge. Suppose delivery months are March, June, September, and December for a particular contract. For hedge expirations in December, January, and February, the March contract will be chosen; for hedge expirations in March, April, and May, the June contract will be chosen; and so on. This rule of thumb assumes that there is sufficient liquidity in all contracts to meet the hedger's requirements. In practice, liquidity tends to be greatest in short maturity futures contracts. The hedger may therefore, in some situations, be inclined to use short maturity contracts and roll them forward. This strategy is discussed later in the chapter.

Illustrations

We now illustrate some of the points made so far in this section. Suppose it is March 1. A U.S. company expects to receive 50 million Japanese yen at the end of July. Yen futures contracts on the Chicago Mercantile Exchange have delivery months of March, June, September, and December. One contract is for the delivery of 12.5 million yen.

Trading Note 3.3 Basis risk in a short hedge

It is March 1. A U.S. company expects to receive 50 million Japanese yen at the end of July. The September futures price for the yen is currently 0.7800 cents per yen.

Strategy

1. Short four September yen futures contracts on March 1 at a futures price of 0.7800.
2. Close out the contract when the yen arrive at the end of July.

The Outcome

Spot price at end of July = 0.7200
September futures price at end of July = 0.7250
Basis at end of July = −0.0050

Alternative Ways of Calculating Net Exchange Rate after Hedging

Spot price in July + Gain on futures = 0.7200 + 0.0550 = 0.7750
Futures price in March + Basis in June = 0.7800 − 0.0050 = 0.7750

Trading Note 3.4 Basis risk in a long hedge

It is June 8. A company knows that it will need to purchase 20,000 barrels of crude oil some time in October or November. The current December oil futures price is \$18.00 per barrel.

Strategy

1. Take a long position in 20 NYM December oil futures contracts on June 8 at a futures price of \$18
2. Close out the contract when ready to purchase the oil.

The Outcome

Company is ready to purchase oil on November 10

Spot price on Nov 10 = \$20.00

December futures price on Nov 10 = \$19.10

Basis on Nov 10 = \$0.90

Alternative Ways of Calculating Net Cost of Oil after Hedging

Spot price on Nov 10 + Gain on Futures = \$20.00 − \$1.10 = \$18.90

Futures Price on June 8 + Basis on Nov 10 = \$18.00 + \$0.90 = \$18.90

The criteria mentioned earlier for the choice of a contract suggest that the September contract be chosen for hedging purposes.

This example is summarized in Trading Note 3.3. The company shorts four September yen futures contracts on March 1. When the yen are received at the end of July, the company closes out its position. The basis risk arises from uncertainty about the difference between the futures price and the spot price at this time. We suppose that the futures price on March 1 in cents per yen is 0.7800 and that the spot and futures prices when the contract is closed out are 0.7200 and 0.7250, respectively. The basis is −0.0050, and the gain from the futures contracts is 0.0550. The effective price obtained in cents per yen is the spot price plus the gain on the futures:

$$0.7200 + 0.0550 = 0.7750$$

This can also be written as the initial futures price plus the basis:

$$0.7800 - 0.0050 = 0.7750$$

The company receives a total of 50×0.00775 million dollars, or \$387,500.

Our next example is summarized in Trading Note 3.4. We suppose it is June 8, and a company knows that it will need to purchase 20,000 barrels of crude oil at some time in October or November. Oil futures contracts are currently traded for delivery every month on NYMEX, and the contract size is 1,000 barrels. Following the criteria indicated, the company decides to use the December contract for hedging. On June 8 it takes a long position in 20 December contracts. At that time, the futures price is \$18.00 per barrel. The company finds that it is ready to purchase the crude oil on November 10. It therefore closes out its futures contract on that date. The basis risk arises from uncertainty as to what the basis will be on the day the contract is closed out. We suppose that the spot price and futures price on November 10 are \$20.00 per barrel and \$19.10 per barrel, respectively. The basis is therefore \$0.90, and the effective price paid is \$18.90 per barrel, or \$378,000 in total.

3.4 CROSS HEDGING

In the examples in Trading Notes 3.1 to 3.4, the asset underlying the futures contract has been the same as the asset whose price is being hedged. *Cross hedging* occurs when the two assets are different. Consider, for example, an airline that is concerned about the future price of jet fuel. Because there is no futures contract on jet fuel, it might choose to use heating oil futures contracts to hedge its exposure.

The *hedge ratio* is the ratio of the size of the position taken in futures contracts to the size of the exposure. When the asset underlying the futures contract is the same as the asset being hedged it is natural to use a hedge ratio of 1.0. This is the hedge ratio we have used in the examples considered so far. In Trading Note 3.4, for example, the hedger's exposure was on 20,000 barrels of oil, and futures contracts were entered into for the delivery of exactly this amount of oil.

When cross hedging is used, setting the hedge ratio equal to 1.0 is not always optimal. The hedger should choose a value for the hedge ratio that minimizes the variance of the value of the hedged position. We now consider how the hedger can do this.

Calculating the Minimum Variance Hedge Ratio

We will use the following notation:

- ΔS: Change in spot price, S, during a period of time equal to the life of the hedge
- ΔF: Change in futures price, F, during a period of time equal to the life of the hedge
- σ_S: Standard deviation of ΔS
- σ_F: Standard deviation of ΔF
- ρ: Coefficient of correlation between ΔS and ΔF
- h^*: Hedge ratio that minimizes the variance of the hedger's position

Figure 3.2 Dependence of variance of hedger's position on hedge ratio

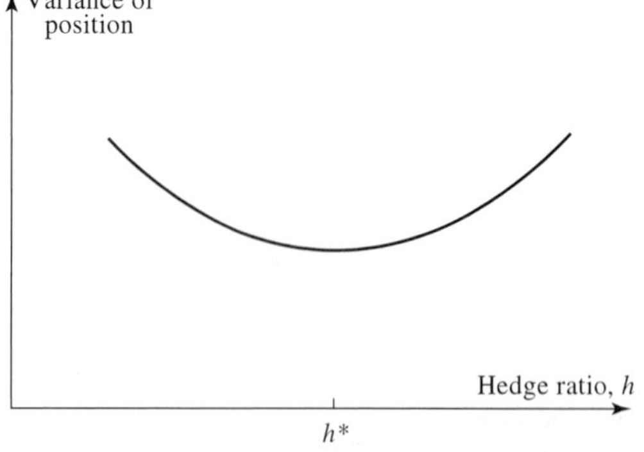

Figure 3.3 Regression of change in spot price against change in futures price

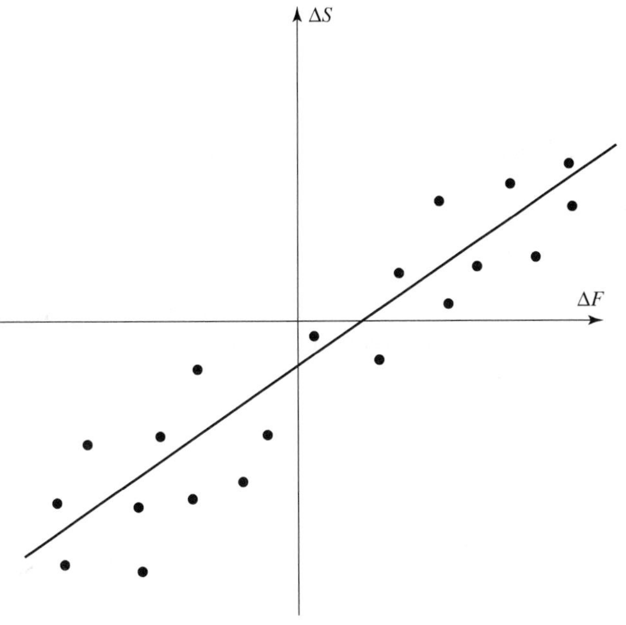

In the Appendix at the end of this chapter, we show that

$$h^* = \rho \frac{\sigma_S}{\sigma_F} \tag{3.1}$$

The optimal hedge ratio is the product of the coefficient of correlation between ΔS and ΔF and the ratio of the standard deviation of ΔS to the standard deviation of ΔF. Figure 3.2 shows how the variance of the value of the hedger's position depends on the hedge ratio chosen.

If $\rho = 1$ and $\sigma_F = \sigma_S$, the hedge ratio, h^*, is 1.0. This result is to be expected, because in this case the futures price mirrors the spot price perfectly. If $\rho = 1$ and $\sigma_F = 2\sigma_S$, the hedge ratio h^* is 0.5. This result is also as expected, because in this case the futures price always changes by twice as much as the spot price.

The optimal hedge ratio, h^*, is the slope of the best-fit line when ΔS is regressed against ΔF, as indicated in Figure 3.3. This is intuitively reasonable, because we require h^* to correspond to the ratio of changes in ΔS to changes in ΔF. The *hedge effectiveness* can be defined as the proportion of the variance that is eliminated by hedging. This is the R^2 from the regression of ΔS against ΔF and equals ρ^2, or

$$h^{*2} \frac{\sigma_F^2}{\sigma_S^2}$$

The parameters ρ, σ_F, and σ_S in equation (3.1) are usually estimated from historical data on ΔS and ΔF. (The implicit assumption is that the future will in some sense be like the past.) A number of equal nonoverlapping time intervals are chosen, and the values of ΔS and ΔF for each of the intervals are observed. Ideally, the length of each time interval is the same as the length of the time interval for which the hedge is in effect. In practice, this sometimes severely limits the number of observations that are available, and a shorter time interval is used.

Optimal Number of Contracts

Define variables as follows:

N_A: Size of position being hedged (units)

Q_F: Size of one futures contract (units)

N^*: Optimal number of futures contracts for hedging

The futures contracts used should have a face value of $h^* N_A$. The number of futures contracts required is therefore given by

$$N^* = \frac{h^* N_A}{Q_F} \tag{3.2}$$

Example

An airline expects to purchase two million gallons of jet fuel in one month and decides to use heating oil futures for hedging.[3] We suppose that Table 3.2 gives, for 15 successive months, data on the change, ΔS, in the jet fuel price

Table 3.2 Data to calculate minimum variance hedge ratio when heating oil futures contract is used to hedge purchase of jet fuel

Month i	*Change in futures price per gallon* $(= x_i)$	*Change in fuel price per gallon* $(= y_i)$
1	0.021	0.029
2	0.035	0.020
3	−0.046	−0.044
4	0.001	0.008
5	0.044	0.026
6	−0.029	−0.019
7	−0.026	−0.010
8	−0.029	−0.007
9	0.048	0.043
10	−0.006	0.011
11	−0.036	−0.036
12	−0.011	−0.018
13	0.019	0.009
14	−0.027	−0.032
15	0.029	0.023

[3] For an account of how Delta Airlines using heating oil to hedge its future purchases of jet fuel, see A. Ness, "Delta Wins on Fuel," *Risk*, June 2001: 8.

per gallon and the corresponding change, ΔF, in the futures price for the contract on heating oil that would be used for hedging price changes during the month. The number of observations, which we will denote by n, is 15. We will denote the ith observations on ΔF and ΔS by x_i and y_i, respectively. From Table 3.2,

$$\sum x_i = -0.013 \qquad \sum x_i^2 = 0.0138$$
$$\sum y_i = 0.003 \qquad \sum y_i^2 = 0.0097$$
$$\sum x_i y_i = 0.0107$$

Standard formulas from statistics give the estimate of σ_F as

$$\sqrt{\frac{\sum x_i^2}{n-1} - \frac{(\sum x_i)^2}{n(n-1)}} = 0.0313$$

The estimate of σ_S is

$$\sqrt{\frac{\sum y_i^2}{n-1} - \frac{(\sum y_i)^2}{n(n-1)}} = 0.0263$$

The estimate of ρ is

$$\frac{n\sum x_i y_i - \sum x_i \sum y_i}{\sqrt{[n\sum x_i^2 - (\sum x_i)^2][n\sum y_i^2 - (\sum y_i)^2]}} = 0.928$$

From equation (3.1), the minimum variance hedge ratio, h^*, is therefore

$$0.928 \times \frac{0.0263}{0.0313} = 0.78$$

Each heating oil contract traded on NYMEX is on 42,000 gallons of heating oil. From equation (3.2), the optimal number of contracts is

$$\frac{0.78 \times 2{,}000{,}000}{42{,}000} = 37.14$$

or, rounding to the nearest whole number, 37.

3.5 STOCK INDEX FUTURES

We now move on to consider stock index futures and how they are used to hedge or manage exposures to equity prices.

A *stock index* tracks changes in the value of a hypothetical portfolio of stocks. The weight of a stock in the portfolio equals the proportion of the portfolio invested in the stock. The percentage increase in the stock index over a small interval of time is set equal to the percentage increase in the value of the hypothetical portfolio. Dividends are usually not included in the calculation, so that the index tracks the capital gain/loss from investing in the portfolio.[4]

[4] An exception to this is a *total return index*. This is calculated by assuming that dividends on the hypothetical portfolio are reinvested in the portfolio.

If the hypothetical portfolio of stocks remains fixed, the weights assigned to individual stocks in the portfolio do not remain fixed. When the price of one particular stock in the portfolio rises more sharply than others, more weight is automatically given to that stock. Some indices are constructed from a hypothetical portfolio consisting of one of each of a number of stocks. The weights assigned to the stocks are then proportional to their market prices, with adjustments being made when there are stock splits. Other indices are constructed so that weights are proportional to market capitalization (stock price $\times$ number of shares outstanding). The underlying portfolio is then automatically adjusted to reflect stock splits, stock dividends, and new equity issues.

Table 3.3 Index futures quotes from *Wall Street Journal*, February 5, 2004: Columns show month, open, high, low, settle, change, lifetime high, lifetime low, and open interest, respectively

Index Futures

DJ Industrial Average (CBT)-$10 x index

Mar	10446	10507	10418	10440	-38	10687	8580	36,831
June	...	...	...	10419	-38	10475	9000	581

Est vol 11,816; vol Tue 182; open int 37,455, -65.
Idx prl: Hi 10524.22; Lo 10447.18; Close 10470.74, -34.44.

Mini DJ Industrial Average (CBT)-$5 x index

Mar	10446	10506	10417	10440	-38	10687	9069	46,175

Vol Wed 70,499; open int 48,145, -1,739.

DJ-AIG Commodity Index (CBT)-$100 x index

Feb	...	...	...	439.3	-3.5	456.2	452.1	2,351

Est vol 1,150; vol Tue 220; open int 2,571, unch.
Idx prl: Hi 139.159; Lo 137.163; Close 137.350, -1.171.

S&P 500 Index (CME)-$250 x index

Mar	113290	113360	112300	112390	-910	123950	77700	585,763
June	112620	113100	112250	112290	-910	115350	78000	21,212

Est vol 46,110; vol Tue 45,600; open int 610,710, +107.
Idx prl: Hi 1136.03; Lo 1124.74; Close 1126.52, -9.51.

Mini S&P 500 (CME)-$50 x index

Mar	113300	113350	112200	112400	-900	115500	98650	539,366

Vol Wed 595,531; open int 550,820, -18,936.

S&P Midcap 400 (CME)-$500 x index

Mar	584.50	586.00	580.30	580.80	-6.00	603.25	559.75	15,879

Est vol 582; vol Tue 672; open int 15,880, -98.
Idx prl: Hi 587.39; Lo 580.91; Close 581.63, -5.76.

Nasdaq 100 (CME)-$100 x index

Mar	148850	148850	146200	146300	-2400	150900	146200	72,861

Est vol 14,295; vol Tue 9,985; open int 72,918, -246.
Idx prl: Hi 1482.35; Lo 1461.01; Close 1462.61, -29.24.

Mini Nasdaq 100 (CME)-$20 x index

Mar	1488.0	1489.0	1461.5	1463.0	-24.0	1563.0	1307.0	249,320

Vol Wed 257,039; open int 250,794, +4,618.

GSCI (CME)-$250 x nearby index

Feb	264.50	266.10	258.50	258.50	-5.50	274.50	251.50	14,534

Est vol 243; vol Tue 104; open int 14,901, +31.
Idx prl: Hi 265.61; Lo 258.87; Close 259.53, -4.02.

TRAKRS Long-Short Tech (CME)-$1 x index

July	40.30	40.30	39.82	39.82	-1.40	45.25	19.76	410,834

Est vol 87; vol Tue 150; open int 410,834, +150.
Idx prl: Hi 40.03; Lo 38.16; Close 38.56, -1.47.

Russell 2000 (CME)-$500 x index

Mar	576.50	576.50	563.50	563.75	-14.40	585.75	557.50	22,953

Est vol 3,572; vol Tue 969; open int 22,953, -42.
Idx prl: Hi 579.15; Lo 564.03; Close 564.03, -15.12.

Russell 1000 (NYFE)-$500 x index

Mar	...	...	...	601.00	-5.05	618.00	603.00	77,631

Est vol 79; vol Tue 66; open int 77,631, -72.
Idx prl: Hi 607.34; Lo 601.23; close 602.10, -5.24.

NYSE Composite Index (NYFE)-$50 x index

Mar	...	...	...	6509.50	-57.00	6556.00	6115.00	1,260

Est vol 0; vol Tue 0; open int 1,260, unch.
Idx prl: Hi 6574.76; Lo 6520.91; Close 6526.10, -48.72.

U.S. Dollar Index (FINEX)-$1,000 x index

Mar	87.04	87.30	86.92	87.02	.04	103.18	85.10	16,414
June	...	...	...	87.43	.04	88.37	85.71	2,116

Est vol 2,500; vol Tue 2,272; open int 18,543, +610.
Idx prl: Hi 87.10; Lo 86.70; open int 86.84, +.05.

Nikkei 225 Stock Average (CME)-$5 x index

Mar	10400.	10510.	10360.	10380.	-265	11155.	7670.	30,555

Est vol 3,558; vol Tue 2,468; open int 30,730, +33.
Index: Hi 10627.26; Lo 10418.77; Close 10447.25, -194.67.

Share Price Index (SFE)-AUD 25 x index

Mar	3257.0	3267.0	3250.0	3254.0	-2.0	3346.0	2700.0	160,822
June	3264.0	3278.0	3264.0	3266.0	-2.0	3350.0	2700.0	3,931

Est vol 10,928; vol Tue 10,169; open int 167,890, +2,133.
Index: Hi 3273.5; Lo 3263.6; Close 3265.6, +1.3.

CAC-40 Stock Index (MATIF)-€10 x index

Feb	3626.0	3632.5	3603.0	3614.0	-29.5	3729.5	3531.5	346,178
Mar	3630.0	3634.5	3610.5	3620.0	-29.5	3734.5	2885.0	130,956
June	3563.5	3563.5	3562.5	3560.5	-29.0	3651.5	3282.0	8,810

Est vol 77,301; vol Tue 76,586; open int 489,860, +19,063.
Index: Hi 3625.38; Lo 3602.94; Close 3607.57, -30.64.

Xetra DAX (EUREX)-€25 x index

Mar	4050.0	4056.0	4018.0	4029.5	-31.0	4190.0	3237.5	286,286
June	4065.0	4074.5	4042.5	4050.5	-31.0	4210.0	3251.0	10,167
Sept	4086.5	4096.0	4064.0	4072.0	-31.5	4231.0	3961.0	2,874

Vol Wed 113,473; open int 299,327, -1,522.
Index: Hi 4050.08; Lo 4008.80; Close 4028.37, -29.14.

FTSE 100 Index (LIFFE)-£10 x index

Mar	4340.0	4386.5	4339.5	4376.0	10.0	4509.5	3895.5	426,561
June	4352.0	4385.5	4352.0	4384.5	9.5	4514.0	4019.5	17,929
Sept	4372.5	4374.5	4372.5	4394.5	10.0	4526.5	4288.5	10,192

Vol Wed 59,473; open int 462,529, +1,934.
Index: Hi 4409.30; Lo 4369.10; Close 4398.50, +7.90.

DJ Euro STOXX 50 Index (EUREX)-€10 x index

Mar	2834.0	2841.0	2820.0	2821.0	-27.0	2921.0	2376.0	1,226,828
June	2797.0	2800.0	2785.0	2783.0	-27.0	2883.0	2364.0	88,041
Sept	2796.0	2796.0	2787.0	2782.0	-27.0	2881.0	2709.0	14,454

Vol Wed 384,795; open int 1,329,323, -2,788.
Index: Hi 2839.55; Lo 2816.18; Close 2819.92, -21.34.

DJ STOXX 50 Index (EUREX)-€10 x index

Mar	2675.0	2689.0	2671.0	2674.0	-14.0	2757.0	2393.0	39,662
June	...	...	...	2653.0	-14.0	...	...	640

Vol Wed 1,895; open int 40,302, +513.
Index: Hi 2698.24; Lo 2681.59; Close 2689.82, -5.23.

Source: Reprinted by permission of Dow Jones, Inc., via Copyright Clearance Center, Inc., © 2004 Dow Jones & Company, Inc. All Rights Reserved Worldwide.

Stock Indices

Table 3.3 shows futures prices for contracts on a number of different stock indices as they were reported in the *Wall Street Journal* of February 5, 2004. The prices refer to the close of trading on February 4, 2004.

The *Dow Jones Industrial Average* is based on a portfolio consisting of 30 blue-chip stocks in the United States. The weights given to the stocks are proportional to their prices. The Chicago Board of Trade trades two contracts on the index. One is on $10 times the index. The other (the Mini DJ Industrial Average) is on $5 times the index.

The *Standard & Poor's 500* (S&P 500) *Index* is based on a portfolio of 500 different stocks: 400 industrials, 40 utilities, 20 transportation companies, and 40 financial institutions. The weights of the stocks in the portfolio at any given time are proportional to their market capitalizations. This index accounts for 80% of the market capitalization of all the stocks listed on the New York Stock Exchange. The Chicago Mercantile Exchange (CME) trades two contracts on the S&P 500. One is on $250 times the index; the other (the Mini S&P 500 contract) is on $50 times the index. The *Standard & Poor's MidCap 400 Index* is similar to the S&P 500, but based on a portfolio of 400 stocks that have somewhat lower market capitalizations.

The *Nasdaq 100* is based on 100 stocks using the National Association of Securities Dealers Automatic Quotations Service. The CME trades two contracts. One is on $100 times the index; the other (the Mini Nasdaq 100 contract) is on $20 times the index.

The *Russell 2000 Index* is an index of the prices of 2000 small capitalization stocks in the United States. The *Russell 1000 Index* is an index of the prices of the 1000 largest capitalization stocks in the United States. The *NYSE Composite Index* is an index of all stocks trading on the New York Stock Exchange. The *U.S. Dollar Index* is a trade-weighted index of the values of six foreign currencies (the euro, yen, pound, Canadian dollar, Swedish krona, and Swiss franc). The *Nikkei 225 Stock Average* is based on a portfolio of 225 of the largest stocks trading on the Tokyo Stock Exchange. Stocks are weighted according to their prices. One futures contract (traded on the CME) is on $5 times the index.

The *Share Price Index* is the All Ordinaries Share Price Index, a broadly based index of Australian stocks. The *CAC-40 Index* is based on 40 large stocks trading in France. The *Xetra DAX Index* is based on 30 stocks trading in Germany. The *FT-SE 100 Index* is based on a portfolio of 100 major U.K. stocks listed on the London Stock Exchange. The *DJ Euro Stoxx 50 Index* and the *DJ Stoxx 50 Index* are two different indices of blue chip European stocks compiled by Dow Jones and its European partners. The futures contracts on these indices trade on Eurex and are on 10 times the values of the indices measured in euros.

The other indices shown in Table 3.3 are not stock indices. The DJ-AIG commodity index and the GSCI index futures contract are designed to track commodity prices. The TRAKRS long–short tech index is an unusual index designed to reflect the performance of a portfolio that is long individual technology stocks and short financial instruments representing technology sectors.

As we mentioned in Chapter 2, futures contracts on stock indices are settled in cash, not by delivery of the underlying asset. All contracts are marked to market to either the opening price or the closing price of the index on the last trading day, and the positions are then deemed to be closed. For example, contracts on the S&P 500 are closed out at the opening price of the S&P 500 index on the third Friday of the delivery month.

Hedging an Equity Portfolio

Stock index futures can be used to hedge an equity portfolio. Define:

P: Current value of the portfolio

A: Current value of the stocks underlying one futures contract

If the portfolio mirrors the index, a hedge ratio of 1.0 is clearly appropriate, and equation (3.2) shows that the number of futures contracts that should be shorted is

$$N^* = \frac{P}{A} \tag{3.3}$$

Suppose, for example, that a portfolio worth \$1 million mirrors the S&P 500. The current value of the index is 1,000, and each futures contract is on \$250 times the index. In this case, $P = 1{,}000{,}000$ and $A = 250{,}000$, so that four contracts should be shorted to hedge the portfolio.

When the portfolio does not exactly mirror the index, we can use the parameter beta (β) from the capital asset pricing model to determine the appropriate hedge ratio. Beta is the slope of the best-fit line obtained when excess return on the portfolio over the risk-free rate is regressed against the excess return of the market over the risk-free rate. When $\beta = 1.0$, the return on the portfolio tends to mirror the return on the market; when $\beta = 2.0$, the excess return on the portfolio tends to be twice as great as the excess return on the market; when $\beta = 0.5$, it tends to be half as great; and so on.

A portfolio with a β of 2.0 is twice as sensitive to market movements as a portfolio with a beta 1.0. It is therefore necessary to use twice as many contracts to hedge the portfolio. Similarly, a portfolio with a beta of 0.5 is half as sensitive to market movements as a portfolio with a beta of 1.0 and we should use half as many contracts to hedge it. In general, we adjust equation (3.3) for a portfolio with a beta different from 1.0 as follows:

$$N^* = \beta\frac{P}{A} \tag{3.4}$$

This formula assumes that the maturity of the futures contract is close to the maturity of the hedge and ignores the daily settlement of the futures contract.[5]

We show that this formula gives good results by means of an example. Consider the following situation:

Value of S&P 500 index = 1,000

Value of portfolio = \$5,000,000

Risk-free interest rate = 4% per annum

Dividend yield on index = 1% per annum

Beta of portfolio = 1.5

[5] A small adjustment known as *tailing the hedge* can be used to take account of the daily settlement when a futures contract is used for hedging. For a discussion of this, see D. Duffie, *Futures Markets*, Upper Saddle River, NJ: Prentice Hall, 1989; R. Rendleman, "A Reconciliation of Potentially Conflicting Approaches to Hedging with Futures," *Advances in Futures and Options Research* 6 (1993), 81–92.

We assume that a futures contract on the S&P 500 with four months to maturity is used to hedge the value of the portfolio over the next three months and that the current futures price of this contract is 1,010. One futures contract is for delivery of \$250 times the index. It follows that $A = 250 \times 1{,}000 = 250{,}000$ and, from equation (3.4), the number of futures contracts that should be shorted to hedge the portfolio is

$$1.5 \times \frac{5{,}000{,}000}{250{,}000} = 30$$

Suppose the index turns out to be 900 in three months and the futures price is 902. The gain from the short futures position is then

$$30 \times (1{,}010 - 902) \times 250 = \$810{,}000$$

The loss on the index is 10%. The index pays a dividend of 1% per annum, or 0.25% per three months. When dividends are taken into account, an investor in the index would therefore earn −9.75% in the three-month period. The risk-free interest rate is approximately 1% per three months. Because the portfolio has a β of 1.5,

$$\begin{aligned}&\text{Expected return on portfolio} - \text{Risk-free interest rate}\\ &\qquad = 1.5 \times (\text{Return on index} - \text{Risk-free interest rate})\end{aligned}$$

It follows that the expected return (%) on the portfolio during the three months is

$$1.0 + [1.5 \times (-9.75 - 1.0)] = -15.125$$

The expected value of the portfolio (inclusive of dividends) at the end of the three months is therefore

$$\$5{,}000{,}000 \times (1 - 0.15125) = \$4{,}243{,}750$$

It follows that the expected value of the hedger's position, including the gain on the hedge, is

$$\$4{,}243{,}750 + \$810{,}000 = \$5{,}053{,}750$$

Table 3.4 summarizes these calculations together with similar calculations for other values of the index at maturity. It can be seen that the total value of the hedger's position in three months is almost independent of the value of the index.

The only thing we have not covered in this example is the relationship between futures prices and spot prices. We will see in Chapter 5 that the 1,010 assumed for the futures price today is roughly what we would expect given the interest rate and dividend we are assuming. The same is true of the futures prices in three months shown in Table 3.4.[6]

Reasons for Hedging an Equity Portfolio

Table 3.4 shows that the hedging scheme results in a value for the hedger's position at the end of the three months being about 1% higher than at the beginning of the three

[6] The calculations in Table 3.4 assume that the dividend yield on the index is predictable, the risk-free interest rate remains constant, and the return on the index over the three-month period is perfectly correlated with the return on the portfolio. In practice, these assumptions do not hold perfectly, and the hedge works rather less well than is indicated by Table 3.4.

Table 3.4 Performance of stock index hedge

Value of index in three months:	900	950	1,000	1,050	1,100
Futures price of index today:	1,010	1,010	1,010	1,010	1,010
Futures price of index in three months:	902	952	1,003	1,053	1,103
Gain on futures position ($000):	810,000	435,000	52,500	−322,500	−697,500
Return on market:	−9.750%	−4.750%	0.250%	5.250%	10.250%
Return on portfolio:	−15.125%	−7.625%	−0.125%	7.375%	14.875%
Portfolio value in three months (including dividends):	4,243,750	4,618,750	4,993,750	5,368,750	5,743,750
Total value of position in three months:	5,053,750	5,053,750	5,046,250	5,046,250	5,046,250

months. There is no surprise here. The risk-free rate is 4% per annum or 1% per three months. The hedge results in the investor's position growing at the risk-free rate.

It is natural to ask why the hedger should go to the trouble of using futures contracts. To earn the risk-free interest rate, the hedger can simply sell the portfolio and invest the proceeds in risk-free instruments such as Treasury bills.

One answer to this question is that hedging can be justified if the hedger feels that the stocks in the portfolio have been chosen well. In these circumstances, the hedger might be very uncertain about the performance of the market as a whole, but confident that the stocks in the portfolio will outperform the market (after appropriate adjustments have been made for the beta of the portfolio). A hedge using index futures removes the risk arising from market moves and leaves the hedger exposed only to the performance of the portfolio relative to the market. Another reason for hedging may be that the hedger is planning to hold a portfolio for a long period of time and requires short-term protection in an uncertain market situation. The alternative strategy of selling the portfolio and buying it back later might involve unacceptably high transaction costs.

Changing the Beta of a Portfolio

In the example in Table 3.4, the beta of the hedger's portfolio is reduced to zero. Sometimes futures contracts are used to change the beta of a portfolio to some value other than zero. Continuing with our earlier example:

$$\text{Value of S\&P 500 index} = 1{,}000$$

$$\text{Value of portfolio} = \$5{,}000{,}000$$

$$\text{Beta of portfolio} = 1.5$$

Because each contract is on $250 times the index, $A = 250{,}000$. To completely hedge the portfolio, equation (3.2) shows that the number of contracts shorted should be

$$1.5 \times \frac{5{,}000{,}000}{250{,}000} = 30$$

To reduce the beta of the portfolio from 1.5 to 0.75, the number of contracts shorted should be 15 rather than 30; to increase the beta of the portfolio to 2.0, a long position in 10 contracts should be taken; and so on. In general, to change the beta of the portfolio from β to β^*, where $\beta > \beta^*$, a short position in

$$(\beta - \beta^*)\frac{P}{A}$$

contracts is required. When $\beta < \beta^*$, a long position in

$$(\beta^* - \beta)\frac{P}{A}$$

contracts is required.

Exposure to the Price of an Individual Stock

Some exchanges do trade futures contracts on selected individual stocks, but in most cases a position in an individual stock can only be hedged using a stock index futures contract.

Hedging an exposure to the price of an individual stock using index futures contracts is similar to hedging a stock portfolio. The number of index futures contracts that the hedger should short into is given by $\beta P/A$, where β is the beta of the stock, P is the total value of the shares owned, and A is the current value of the stocks underlying one index futures contract. Note that although the number of contracts entered into is calculated in the same way as it is when a portfolio of stocks is being hedged, the performance of the hedge is considerably worse. The hedge provides protection only against the risk arising from market movements, and this risk is a relatively small proportion of the total risk in the price movements of individual stocks. The hedge is appropriate when an investor feels that the stock will outperform the market but is unsure about the performance of the market. It can also be used by an investment bank that has underwritten a new issue of the stock and wants protection against moves in the market as a whole.

Consider an investor who in June holds 20,000 IBM shares, each worth \$100. The investor feels that the market will be very volatile over the next month but that IBM has a good chance of outperforming the market. The investor decides to use the August futures contract on the S&P 500 to hedge the position during the one-month period. The β of IBM is estimated at 1.1. The current level of the index is 900, and the current futures price for the August contract on the S&P 500 is 908. Each contract is for delivery of \$250 times the index. In this case, $P = 20{,}000 \times 100 = 2{,}000{,}000$ and $A = 900 \times 250 = 225{,}000$. The number of contracts that should be shorted is therefore

$$1.1 \times \frac{2{,}000{,}000}{225{,}000} = 9.78$$

Rounding to the nearest integer, the hedger shorts 10 contracts, closing out the position one month later. Suppose IBM rises to \$125 during the month, and the futures price of the S&P 500 rises to 1080. The investor gains $20{,}000 \times (\$125 - \$100) = \$500{,}000$ on IBM, while losing $10 \times 250 \times (1080 - 908) = \$430{,}000$ on the futures contracts.

In this example, the hedge offsets a gain on the underlying asset with a loss on the futures contracts. The offset might seem to be counterproductive. However, it cannot be emphasized often enough that the purpose of a hedge is to reduce risk. A hedge tends to make unfavorable outcomes less unfavorable and favorable outcomes less favorable.

3.6 ROLLING THE HEDGE FORWARD

Sometimes the expiration date of the hedge is later than the delivery dates of all the futures contracts that can be used. The hedger must then roll the hedge forward by closing out one futures contract and taking the same position in a futures contract with a later delivery date. Hedges can be rolled forward many times. Consider a company that wishes to use a short hedge to reduce the risk associated with the price to be received for an asset at time T. If there are futures contracts 1, 2, 3, ..., n (not all necessarily in existence at the present time) with progressively later delivery dates, the company can use the following strategy:

Time t_1: Short futures contract 1

Time t_2: Close out futures contract 1
Short futures contract 2

Time t_3: Close out futures contract 2
Short futures contract 3

⋮

Time t_n: Close out futures contract $n - 1$
Short futures contract n

Time T: Close out futures contract n

Suppose that in April 2004 a company realizes that it will have 100,000 barrels of oil to sell in June 2005 and decides to hedge its risk with a hedge ratio of 1.0. The current spot price is \$19. Although futures contracts are traded with maturities stretching several years into the future, we suppose that only the first six delivery months have sufficient liquidity to meet the company's needs. The company therefore shorts 100 October 2004 contracts. In September 2004 it rolls the hedge forward into the March 2005 contract. In February 2005 it rolls the hedge forward again into the July 2005 contract.

One possible outcome is shown in Table 3.5. The October 2004 contract is shorted

Table 3.5 Data for the example on rolling oil hedge forward

Date	*Apr. 2004*	*Sept. 2004*	*Feb. 2005*	*June 2005*
Oct. 2004 futures price	18.20	17.40		
Mar. 2005 futures price		17.00	16.50	
July 2005 futures price			16.30	15.90
Spot price	19.00			16.00

> **Business Snapshot 3.2 Metallgesellschaft: Hedging gone awry**
>
> Sometimes rolling hedges forward can lead to cash flow pressures. This problem was illustrated dramatically by the activities of a German company, Metallgesellschaft (MG), in the early 1990s.
>
> MG sold a huge volume of 5- to 10-year heating oil and gasoline fixed-price supply contracts to its customers at 6 to 8 cents above market prices. It hedged its exposure with long positions in short-dated futures contracts that were rolled forward. As it turned out, the price of oil fell and there were margin calls on the futures positions. Considerable short-term cash flow pressures were placed on MG. The members of MG who devised the hedging strategy argued that these short-term cash outflows were offset by positive cash flows that would ultimately be realized on the long-term fixed-price contracts. However, the company's senior management and its bankers became concerned about the huge cash drain. As a result, the company closed out all the hedge positions and agreed with its customers that the fixed-price contracts would be abandoned. The outcome was a loss to MG of \$1.33 billion.

at \$18.20 per barrel and closed out at \$17.40 per barrel for a profit of \$0.80 per barrel; the March 2005 contract is shorted at \$17.00 per barrel and closed out at \$16.50 per barrel for a profit of \$0.50 per barrel. The July 2005 contract is shorted at \$16.30 per barrel and closed out at \$15.90 per barrel for a profit of \$0.40 per barrel. The final spot price is \$16.

The dollar gain per barrel of oil from the short futures contracts is

$$(18.20 - 17.40) + (17.00 - 16.50) + (16.30 - 15.90) = 1.70$$

The oil price declined from \$19 to \$16. Receiving only \$1.70 per barrel compensation for a price decline of \$3.00 may appear unsatisfactory. However, we cannot expect total compensation for a price decline when futures prices are below spot prices. The best we can hope for is to lock in the futures price that would apply to a June 2005 contract if it were actively traded.

The marking to market of futures contracts can cause a mismatch between the timing of the cash flows on hedge and the timing of the cash flows from the position being hedged. In situations where the hedge is rolled forward so that it lasts a long time this can lead to serious problems (see Business Snapshot 3.2).

SUMMARY

This chapter has discussed various ways in which a company can take a position in futures contracts to offset an exposure to the price of an asset. If the exposure is such that the company gains when the price of the asset increases and loses when the price of the asset decreases, a short hedge is appropriate. If the exposure is the other way round (i.e., the company gains when the price of the asset decreases and loses when the price of the asset increases), a long hedge is appropriate.

Hedging is a way of reducing risk. As such, it should be welcomed by most executives.

In reality, there are a number of theoretical and practical reasons why companies do not hedge. On a theoretical level, we can argue that shareholders, by holding well-diversified portfolios, can eliminate many of the risks faced by a company. They do not require the company to hedge these risks. On a practical level, a company may find that it is increasing rather than decreasing risk by hedging if none of its competitors does so. Also, a treasurer may fear criticism from other executives if the company makes a gain from movements in the price of the underlying asset and a loss on the hedge.

An important concept in hedging is basis risk. The basis is the difference between the spot price of an asset and its futures price. Basis risk is created by a hedger's uncertainty as to what the basis will be at maturity of the hedge.

The hedge ratio is the ratio of the size of the position taken in futures contracts to the size of the exposure. It is not always optimal to use a hedge ratio of 1.0. If the hedger wishes to minimize the variance of a position, a hedge ratio different from 1.0 may be appropriate. The optimal hedge ratio is the slope of the best-fit line obtained when changes in the spot price are regressed against changes in the futures price.

Stock index futures can be used to hedge the systematic risk in an equity portfolio. The number of futures contracts required is the beta of the portfolio multiplied by the ratio of the value of the portfolio to the value of the assets underlying one futures contract. Stock index futures can also be used to change the beta of a portfolio without changing the stocks comprising the portfolio.

When there is no liquid futures contract that matures later than the expiration of the hedge, a strategy known as rolling the hedge forward may be appropriate. This involves entering into a sequence of futures contracts. When the first futures contract is near expiration, it is closed out and the hedger enters into a second contract with a later delivery month. When the second contract is close to expiration, it is closed out and the hedger enters into a third contract with a later delivery month; and so on. The result of all this is the creation of a long-dated futures contract by trading a series of short-dated contracts.

FURTHER READING

Allayannis, G. and J. Weston. "The Use of Foreign Currency Derivatives and Firm Market Value," *Review of Financial Studies*, 14, 1 (Spring 2001): 243–276.

Bodnar, G.M., G.S. Hayt, and R.C. Marston. "1998 Wharton Survey of Financial Risk Management by U.S. Non-Financial Firms," *Financial Management* 2, 4 (1998): 70–91.

Brown, G.W. "Managing Foreign Exchange Risk with Derivatives," *Journal of Financial Economics*, 60 (2001): 401–448.

Culp, C. and M. Miller. "Metallgesellschaft and the Economics of Synthetic Storage," *Journal of Applied Corporate Finance* 7, 4 (Winter 1995): 62–76.

Ederington, L.H. "The Hedging Performance of the New Futures Market," *Journal of Finance* 34 (March 1979): 157–170.

Edwards, F.R. and M.S. Canter. "The Collapse of Metallgesellschaft: Unhedgeable Risks, Poor Hedging Strategy, or Just Bad Luck?" *Journal of Applied Corporate Finance*, 8, 1 (Spring 1995): 86–105.

Geczy, C., B.A. Minton, and C. Schrand. "Why Firms Use Currency Derivatives," *Journal of Finance*, 52, 4 (1997): 1323–1354.

Graham, J.R. and C.W. Smith Jr. "Tax Incentives to Hedge," *Journal of Finance*, 54, 6 (1999): 2241–2262.

Haushalter, G. D. "Financing Policy, Basis Risk, and Corporate Hedging: Evidence from Oil and Gas Producers," *Journal of Finance*, 55, 1 (2000): 107–152.

Mello, A. S. and J. E. Parsons. "Hedging and Liquidity," *Review of Financial Studies*, 13 (Spring 2000): 127–153.

Neuberger, A. J. "Hedging Long-Term Exposures with Multiple Short-Term Futures Contracts," *Review of Financial Studies*, 12 (1999): 429–459.

Petersen, M. A. and S. R. Thiagarajan, "Risk Management and Hedging: With and Without Derivatives," *Financial Management*, 29, 4 (Winter 2000): 5–30.

Stulz, R. M. "Optimal Hedging Policies," *Journal of Financial and Quantitative Analysis*, 19 (June 1984): 127–140.

Tufano, P. "Who Manages Risk? An Empirical Examination of Risk Management Practices in the Gold Mining Industry," *Journal of Finance*, 51, 4 (1996): 1097–1138.

Tufano, P. "The Determinants of Stock Price Exposure: Financial Engineering and the Gold Mining Industry," *Journal of Finance*, 53, 3 (1998): 1015–1052.

Quiz (Answers at End of Book)

3.1. Under what circumstances are (a) a short hedge and (b) a long hedge appropriate?

3.2. Explain what is meant by *basis risk* when futures contracts are used for hedging.

3.3. Explain what is meant by a *perfect hedge*. Does a perfect hedge always lead to a better outcome than an imperfect hedge? Explain your answer.

3.4. Under what circumstances does a minimum variance hedge portfolio lead to no hedging at all?

3.5. Give three reasons that the treasurer of a company might not hedge the company's exposure to a particular risk.

3.6. Suppose that the standard deviation of quarterly changes in the prices of a commodity is \$0.65, the standard deviation of quarterly changes in a futures price on the commodity is \$0.81, and the coefficient of correlation between the two changes is 0.8. What is the optimal hedge ratio for a three-month contract? What does it mean?

3.7. A company has a \$20 million portfolio with a beta of 1.2. It would like to use futures contracts on the S&P 500 to hedge its risk. The index is currently standing at 1080, and each contract is for delivery of \$250 times the index. What is the hedge that minimizes risk? What should the company do if it wants to reduce the beta of the portfolio to 0.6?

Questions and Problems (Answers in Solutions Manual/Study Guide)

3.8. In the Chicago Board of Trade's corn futures contract, the following delivery months are available: March, May, July, September, and December. State the contract that should be used for hedging when the expiration of the hedge is in
   a. June
   b. July
   c. January

3.9. Does a perfect hedge always succeed in locking in the current spot price of an asset for a future transaction? Explain your answer.

3.10. Explain why a short hedger's position improves when the basis strengthens unexpectedly and worsens when the basis weakens unexpectedly.

3.11. Imagine you are the treasurer of a Japanese company exporting electronic equipment to the United States. Discuss how you would design a foreign exchange hedging strategy and the arguments you would use to sell the strategy to your fellow executives.

3.12. Suppose that in Trading Note 3.4 the company decides to use a hedge ratio of 0.8. How does the decision affect the way in which the hedge is implemented and the result?

3.13. "If the minimum variance hedge ratio is calculated as 1.0, the hedge must be perfect." Is this statement true? Explain your answer.

3.14. "If there is no basis risk, the minimum variance hedge ratio is always 1.0." Is this statement true? Explain your answer.

3.15. "For an asset where futures prices are usually less than spot prices, long hedges are likely to be particularly attractive." Explain this statement.

3.16. The standard deviation of monthly changes in the spot price of live cattle is (in cents per pound) 1.2. The standard deviation of monthly changes in the futures price of live cattle for the closest contract is 1.4. The correlation between the futures price changes and the spot price changes is 0.7. It is now October 15. A beef producer is committed to purchasing 200,000 pounds of live cattle on November 15. The producer wants to use the December live-cattle futures contracts to hedge its risk. Each contract is for the delivery of 40,000 pounds of cattle. What strategy should the beef producer follow?

3.17. A corn farmer argues: "I do not use futures contracts for hedging. My real risk is not the price of corn. It is that my whole crop gets wiped out by the weather." Discuss this viewpoint. Should the farmer estimate his or her expected production of corn and hedge to try to lock in a price for expected production?

3.18. On July 1, an investor holds 50,000 shares of a certain stock. The market price is \$30 per share. The investor is interested in hedging against movements in the market over the next month and decides to use the September Mini S&P 500 futures contract. The index is currently 1,500 and one contract is for delivery of \$50 times the index. The beta of the stock is 1.3. What strategy should the investor follow?

3.19. Suppose that in Table 3.5 the company decides to use a hedge ratio of 1.5. How does the decision affect the way the hedge is implemented and the result?

3.20. A futures contract is used for hedging. Explain why the marking to market of the contract can give rise to cash flow problems.

Assignment Questions

3.21. It is July 16. A company has a portfolio of stocks worth \$100 million. The beta of the portfolio is 1.2. The company would like to use the CME December futures contract on the S&P 500 to change the beta of the portfolio to 0.5 during the period July 16 to November 16. The index is currently 1,000, and each contract is on \$250 times the index.

a. What position should the company take?

b. Suppose that the company changes its mind and decides to increase the beta of the portfolio from 1.2 to 1.5. What position in futures contracts should it take?

3.22. The following table gives data on monthly changes in the spot price and the futures price for a certain commodity. Use the data to calculate a minimum variance hedge ratio.

Spot price change	+0.50	+0.61	−0.22	−0.35	+0.79
Futures price change	+0.56	+0.63	−0.12	−0.44	+0.60
Spot price change	+0.04	+0.15	+0.70	−0.51	−0.41
Futures price change	−0.06	+0.01	+0.80	−0.56	−0.46

3.23. It is now October 2004. A company anticipates that it will purchase 1 million pounds of copper in each of February 2005, August 2005, February 2006, and August 2006. The company has decided to use the futures contracts traded in the COMEX division of the New York Mercantile Exchange to hedge its risk. One contract is for the delivery of 25,000 pounds of copper. The initial margin is $2,000 per contract and the maintenance margin is $1,500 per contract. The company's policy is to hedge 80% of its exposure. Contracts with maturities up to 13 months into the future are considered to have sufficient liquidity to meet the company's needs. Devise a hedging strategy for the company.

Assume the market prices (in cents per pound) today and at future dates are as follows. What is the impact of the strategy you propose on the price the company pays for copper? What is the initial margin requirement in October 2004? Is the company subject to any margin calls?

Date	*Oct. 2004*	*Feb. 2005*	*Aug. 2005*	*Feb. 2006*	*Aug. 2006*
Spot price	72.00	69.00	65.00	77.00	88.00
Mar. 2005 futures price	72.30	69.10			
Sept. 2005 futures price	72.80	70.20	64.80		
Mar. 2006 futures price		70.70	64.30	76.70	
Sept. 2006 futures price			64.20	76.50	88.20

3.24. A fund manager has a portfolio worth $50 million with a beta of 0.87. The manager is concerned about the performance of the market over the next two months and plans to use three-month futures contracts on the S&P 500 to hedge the risk. The current level of the index is 1,250, one contract is on 250 times the index, the risk-free rate is 6% per annum, and the dividend yield on the index is 3% per annum. The current 3 month futures price is 1,259.

a. What position should the fund manager take to eliminate all exposure to the market over the next two months?

b. Calculate the effect of your strategy on the fund manager's returns if the level of the market in two months is 1,000, 1,100, 1,200, 1,300, and 1,400. Assume that the one-month futures price is 0.25% higher than the index level at this time.

APPENDIX

Proof of the Minimum Variance Hedge Ratio Formula

Suppose we expect to sell N_A units of an asset at time t_2 and choose to hedge at time t_1 by shorting futures contracts on N_F units of a similar asset. The hedge ratio, which we will denote by h, is

$$h = \frac{N_F}{N_A} \tag{3A.1}$$

We will denote the total amount realized for the asset when the profit or loss on the hedge is taken into account by Y, so that

$$Y = S_2 N_A - (F_2 - F_1) N_F$$

or

$$Y = S_1 N_A + (S_2 - S_1) N_A - (F_2 - F_1) N_F \tag{3A.2}$$

where S_1 and S_2 are the asset prices at times t_1 and t_2, and F_1 and F_2 are the futures prices at times t_1 and t_2. From equation (3A.1), the expression for Y in equation (3A.2) can be written

$$Y = S_1 N_A + N_A(\Delta S - h\Delta F) \tag{3A.3}$$

where

$$\Delta S = S_2 - S_1$$

$$\Delta F = F_2 - F_1$$

Because S_1 and N_A are known at time t_1, the variance of Y in equation (3A.3) is minimized when the variance of $\Delta S - h\,\Delta F$ is minimized. The variance of $\Delta S - h\,\Delta F$ equals

$$\sigma_S^2 + h^2\sigma_F^2 - 2h\rho\sigma_S\sigma_F$$

This can be written as

$$(h\sigma_F - \rho\sigma_S)^2 + \sigma_S^2 - \rho^2\sigma_S^2$$

The second and third terms do not involve h. The variance is therefore minimized when $(h\sigma_F - \rho\sigma_S)^2$ is zero, that is, when $h = \rho\sigma_S/\sigma_F$.

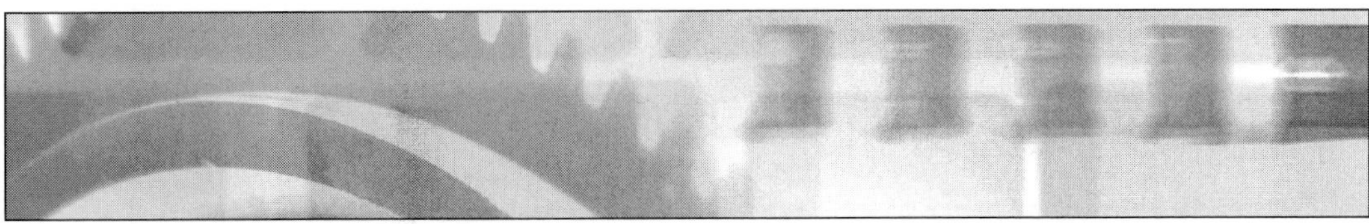

CHAPTER 4

Interest Rates

Interest rates are a factor in the valuation of virtually all derivatives and will feature prominently in much of the material presented in the rest of this book. In this chapter we cover some fundamental issues concerned with the way interest rates are measured and analyzed. We explain the compounding frequency used to define an interest rate and the meaning of continuously compounded interest rates, which are used extensively in the analysis of derivatives. We cover zero rates, par yields, and yield curves. We discuss bond pricing and explain day count conventions. We outline a procedure commonly used by a derivatives trading desk to calculate zero-coupon Treasury interest rates. We also cover forward rates and forward rate agreements, and review different theories of the term structure of interest rates.

4.1 TYPES OF RATES

An interest rate in a particular situation defines the amount of money a borrower promises to pay the lender. For any given currency many different types of interest rates are regularly quoted. These include mortgage rates, deposit rates, prime borrowing rates, and so on. The interest rate applicable in a situation depends on the credit risk. This is the risk that there will be a default by the borrower of funds so that the interest and principal are not paid to the lender as promised. The higher the credit risk, the higher the interest rate that is promised by the borrower.

Treasury Rates

Treasury rates are the rates an investor earns on Treasury bills and Treasury bonds. These are the instruments used by a government to borrow in its own currency. Japanese Treasury rates are the rates at which the Japanese government borrows in yen; U.S. Treasury rates are the rates at which the U.S. government borrows in U.S. dollars; and so on. It is usually assumed that there is no chance that a government will default on an obligation denominated in its own currency.[1] Treasury

[1] The reason for this is that the government can always meet its obligation by printing more money.

rates are therefore totally risk-free rates in the sense that an investor who buys a Treasury bill or Treasury bond is certain that interest and principal payments will be made as promised.

Treasury rates are important because they are used to price Treasury bonds and are sometimes used to define the payoff from a derivative. However, derivatives traders (particularly those active in the over-the-counter market) do not usually use Treasury rates as risk-free rates. Instead they use LIBOR rates.

LIBOR

LIBOR is short for *London Interbank Offer Rate*. A LIBOR quote by a particular bank is the rate of interest at which the bank is prepared to make a large wholesale deposits with other banks. Large banks and other financial institutions quote one-month, three-month, six-month, and twelve-month LIBOR in all major currencies. One-month LIBOR is the rate at which one-month deposits are offered, three-month LIBOR is the rate at which three-month deposits are offered, and so on.

A deposit with a bank can be regarded as a loan to that bank. A bank must therefore satisfy certain creditworthiness criteria in order to be able to accept a LIBOR quote from another bank and receive deposits from that bank at LIBOR. Typically it must have to have a AA credit rating.[2]

AA-rated financial institutions regard LIBOR as their short-term opportunity cost of capital. They can borrow short-term funds at the LIBOR quotes of other financial institutions. Their own LIBOR quotes determine the rate at which surplus funds are lent to other financial institutions. LIBOR rates are not totally free of credit risk. There is a small chance that a AA-rated financial institution will default on a LIBOR loan. However, they are close to risk-free. Derivatives traders regard LIBOR rates as a better indication of the "true" risk-free rate than Treasury rates because a number of tax and regulatory issues cause Treasury rates to be artifically low (see Business Snapshot 4.1). To be consistent with the normal practice in derivatives markets, the term "risk-free rate" in this book should be interpreted as the LIBOR rate.[3]

In addition to quoting LIBOR rates large banks also quote LIBID rates. This is the *London Interbank Bid Rate* and is the rate at which they are prepared to accept deposits from other banks. There is generally a small spread between the LIBID and LIBOR rates quotes by a bank at any time (with LIBOR higher than LIBID). The rates themselves are determined by active trading between banks and are continually changing so that the supply of funds in the interbank market equals the demand for funds in that market. For example, if more banks want to borrow U.S. dollars for three months than lend U.S. dollars for three months, the three-month U.S. LIBID and LIBOR rates quoted by banks will increase. Similarly, if more banks want to lend three-month funds than borrow these funds, the three-month LIBID and LIBOR rate will decrease. LIBOR and LIBID trade in what is known as the *Eurocurrency market*. This market is outside the control of any one government.

---

[2] The best credit rating given to a company by the rating agency S&P is AAA. The second best is AA. The corresponding ratings from the rival rating agency Moody's are Aaa and Aa, respectively.

[3] As we shall see in Chapter 7, it is more accurate to say that the risk-free rate should be interpreted as the rate derived from LIBOR, swap, and Eurodollar futures quotes.

Business Snapshot 4.1 What is the risk-free rate?

It is natural to assume that the rates on Treasury bills and Treasury bonds are the correct benchmark risk-free rates for derivative traders working for financial institutions. In fact these derivative traders usually use LIBOR rates as short-term risk-free rates. This is because they regard LIBOR as their opportunity cost of capital (see Section 4.1). Traders argue that Treasury rates are too low to be used as risk-free rates because:

1. Treasury bills and Treasury bonds must be purchased by financial institutions to fulfill a variety of regulatory requirements. This increases demand for these Treasury instruments driving the price up and the yield down.
2. The amount of capital a bank is required to hold to support an investment in Treasury bills and bonds is substantially smaller than the capital required to support a similar investment in other very low risk instruments.
3. In the United States, Treasury instruments are given a favorable tax treatment compared with most other fixed-income investments because they are not taxed at the state level.

LIBOR is approximately equal to the borrowing rate of a AA-rated company. It is therefore not a perfect proxy for the risk-free rate. There is a small chance that a AA borrower will default within the life of a LIBOR loan. But traders feel it is the best proxy for them to use. LIBOR rates are quoted out to 12 months. As we shall see in Chapter 7, the Eurodollar futures market and the swap market are used to extend the trader's proxy for the risk-free rate beyond 12 months.

Repo Rates

Sometimes trading activities are funded with a *repo* or *repurchase agreement*. This is a contract where an investment dealer who owns securities agrees to sell them to another company now and buy them back later at a slightly higher price. The other company is providing a loan to the investment dealer. The difference between the price at which the securities are sold and the price at which they are repurchased is the interest it earns. The interest rate is referred to as the *repo rate*. If structured carefully, the loan involves very little credit risk. If the borrower does not honor the agreement, the lending company simply keeps the securities. If the lending company does not keep to its side of the agreement, the original owner of the securities keeps the cash.

The most common type of repo is an *overnight repo*, in which the agreement is renegotiated each day. However, longer-term arrangements, known as *term repos*, are sometimes used.

4.2 MEASURING INTEREST RATES

A statement by a bank that the interest rate on one-year deposits is 10% per annum sounds straightforward and unambiguous. In fact, its precise meaning depends on the way the interest rate is measured.

If the interest rate is measured with annual compounding, the bank's statement that the interest rate is 10% means that \$100 grows to

$$\$100 \times 1.1 = \$110$$

at the end of one year. When the interest rate is measured with semiannual compounding, it means that we earn 5% every six months, with the interest being reinvested. In this case \$100 grows to

$$\$100 \times 1.05 \times 1.05 = \$110.25$$

at the end of one year. When the interest rate is measured with quarterly compounding, the bank's statement means that we earn 2.5% every three months, with the interest being reinvested. The \$100 then grows to

$$\$100 \times 1.025^4 = \$110.38$$

at the end of one year. Table 4.1 shows the effect of increasing the compounding frequency further.

The compounding frequency defines the units in which an interest rate is measured. A rate expressed with one compounding frequency can be converted into an equivalent rate with a different compounding frequency. For example, from Table 4.1 we see that 10.25% with annual compounding is equivalent to 10% with semiannual compounding. We can think of the difference between one compounding frequency and another to be analogous to the difference between kilometers and miles. They are two different units of measurement.

To generalize our results, suppose that an amount A is invested for n years at an interest rate of R per annum. If the rate is compounded once per annum, the terminal value of the investment is

$$A(1 + R)^n$$

If the rate is compounded m times per annum, the terminal value of the investment is

$$A\left(1 + \frac{R}{m}\right)^{mn} \tag{4.1}$$

When $m = 1$ the rate is sometimes referred to as the *equivalent annual interest rate*.

Table 4.1 Effect of the compounding frequency on the value of \$100 at the end of one year when the interest rate is 10% per annum

Compounding frequency	*Value of \$100 at end of year (\$)*
Annually ($m = 1$)	110.00
Semiannually ($m = 2$)	110.25
Quarterly ($m = 4$)	110.38
Monthly ($m = 12$)	110.47
Weekly ($m = 52$)	110.51
Daily ($m = 365$)	110.52

Continuous Compounding

The limit as the compounding frequency, m, tends to infinity is known as *continuous compounding*. With continuous compounding, it can be shown (see the Appendix to this chapter) that an amount A invested for n years at rate R grows to

$$Ae^{Rn} \tag{4.2}$$

where $e = 2.71828$. The function e^x is the exponential function and is built into most calculators, so the computation of the expression in equation (4.2) presents no problems. In the example in Table 4.1, $A = 100$, $n = 1$, and $R = 0.1$, so that the value to which A grows with continuous compounding is

$$100e^{0.1} = \$110.52$$

This is (to two decimal places) the same as the value with daily compounding. For most practical purposes, continuous compounding can be thought of as being equivalent to daily compounding. Compounding a sum of money at a continuously compounded rate R for n years involves multiplying it by e^{Rn}. Discounting it at a continuously compounded rate R for n years involves multiplying by e^{-Rn}.

In this book interest rates will be measured with continuous compounding except where otherwise stated. Readers used to working with interest rates that are measured with annual, semiannual, or some other compounding frequency may find this a little strange at first. However, continuously compounded interest rates are used to such a great extent in pricing derivatives that it makes sense to get used to working with them now.

Suppose that R_c is a rate of interest with continuous compounding and R_m is the equivalent rate with compounding m times per annum. From the results in equations (4.1) and (4.2), we must have

$$Ae^{R_c n} = A\left(1 + \frac{R_m}{m}\right)^{mn}$$

or

$$e^{R_c} = \left(1 + \frac{R_m}{m}\right)^{m}$$

This means that

$$R_c = m \ln\left(1 + \frac{R_m}{m}\right) \tag{4.3}$$

and

$$R_m = m(e^{R_c/m} - 1) \tag{4.4}$$

These equations can be used to convert a rate with a compounding frequency of m times per annum to a continuously compounded rate and vice versa. The function $\ln x$ is the natural logarithm function and is built into most calculators. It is defined so that, if $y = \ln x$, then $x = e^y$ (see the Appendix to this chapter).

Examples

1. Consider an interest rate that is quoted as 10% per annum with semiannual compounding. From equation (4.3), with $m = 2$ and $R_m = 0.1$, the equivalent

rate with continuous compounding is

$$2\ln\left(1+\frac{0.1}{2}\right)=0.09758$$

or 9.758% per annum.

2. Suppose that a lender quotes the interest rate on loans as 8% per annum with continuous compounding, and that interest is actually paid quarterly. From equation (4.4), with $m=4$ and $R_c=0.08$, the equivalent rate with quarterly compounding is

$$4(e^{0.08/4}-1)=0.0808$$

or 8.08% per annum. This means that on a \$1,000 loan, interest payments of \$20.20 would be required each quarter.

4.3 ZERO RATES

The n-year zero-coupon interest rate is the rate of interest earned on an investment that starts today and lasts for n years. All the interest and principal is realized at the end of n years. There are no intermediate payments. The n-year zero-coupon interest rate is sometimes also referred to as the n-year *spot rate*, the n-year *zero rate*, or just the n-year *zero*. Suppose a five-year zero rate with continuous compounding is quoted as 5% per annum. This means that \$100, if invested for five years, grows to

$$100\times e^{0.05\times 5}=128.40$$

Many of the interest rates we observe directly in the market are not pure zero rates. Consider a five-year government bond that provides a 6% coupon. The price of this bond does not by itself determine the five-year Treasury zero rate because some of the return on the bond is realized in the form of coupons prior to the end of year five. Later in this chapter we will discuss how we can determine Treasury zero rates from the prices of traded instruments.

4.4 BOND PRICING

Most bonds provide coupons periodically. The bond's principal (which is also known as its par value or face value) is received at the end of its life. The theoretical price of a bond can be calculated as the present value of all the cash flows that will be received by the owner of the bond. Sometimes bond traders use the same discount rate for all the cash flows underlying a bond, but a more accurate approach is to use the appropriate zero rate for each cash flow.

To illustrate this, consider the situation where Treasury zero rates, measured with continuous compounding, are as in Table 4.2. (We explain later how these can be calculated.) Suppose that a two-year Treasury bond with a principal of \$100 provides coupons at the rate of 6% per annum semiannually. To calculate the present value of the first coupon of \$3, we discount it at 5.0% for six months; to calculate the present

Table 4.2 Treasury zero rates

Maturity (years)	*Zero rate (%) (cont. comp.)*
0.5	5.0
1.0	5.8
1.5	6.4
2.0	6.8

value of the second coupon of \$3, we discount it at 5.8% for one year; and so on. The theoretical price of the bond is therefore

$$3e^{-0.05\times0.5} + 3e^{-0.058\times1.0} + 3e^{-0.064\times1.5} + 103e^{-0.068\times2.0} = 98.39$$

or \$98.39.

Bond Yield

The yield on a coupon-bearing bond is the discount rate that equates the cash flows on the bond to its market value. Suppose that the theoretical price of the bond we have been considering, \$98.39, is also its market value (that is, the market's price of the bond is in exact agreement with the data in Table 4.2). If y is the yield on the bond, expressed with continuous compounding, we must have

$$3e^{-y\times0.5} + 3e^{-y\times1.0} + 3e^{-y\times1.5} + 103e^{-y\times2.0} = 98.39$$

This equation can be solved using an iterative ("trial and error") procedure to give $y = 6.76\%$.

Par Yield

The *par yield* for a certain bond maturity is the coupon rate that causes the bond price to equal its par value. (The par value is the same as the principal value). Usually the bond is assumed to provide semiannual coupons. Suppose that the coupon on a two-year bond in our example is c per annum (or $c/2$ per six months). Using the zero rates in Table 4.2, the value of the bond is equal to its par value of 100 when

$$\frac{c}{2}e^{-0.05\times0.5} + \frac{c}{2}e^{-0.058\times1.0} + \frac{c}{2}e^{-0.064\times1.5} + \left(100 + \frac{c}{2}\right)e^{-0.068\times2.0} = 100$$

This equation can be solved in a straightforward way to give $c = 6.87$. The two-year par yield is therefore 6.87% per annum with semiannual compounding (or 6.75% with continuous compounding).

More generally, if d is the present value of \$1 received at the maturity of the bond, A the value of an annuity that pays one dollar on each coupon payment date, and m the number of coupon payments per year, then the par yield c must satisfy

$$100 = A\frac{c}{m} + 100d$$

so that

$$c = \frac{(100 - 100d)m}{A}$$

In our example, $m = 2$, $d = e^{-0.068\times 2} = 0.87284$, and

$$A = e^{-0.05\times 0.5} + e^{-0.058\times 1.0} + e^{-0.064\times 1.5} + e^{-0.068\times 2.0} = 3.70027$$

The formula confirms that the par yield is 6.87% per annum. Note that this is a rate expressed with semiannual compounding. (With continuous compounding it would be 6.75%.)

4.5 DETERMINING TREASURY ZERO RATES

We now discuss how Treasury zero rates can be calculated from the prices of Treasury bonds. The most popular approach is known as the *bootstrap method*. To illustrate the nature of the method, consider the data in Table 4.3 on the prices of five bonds. Because the first three bonds pay no coupons, the zero rates corresponding to the maturities of these bonds can be easily calculated. The three-month bond provides a return of 2.5 in three months on an initial investment of 97.5. With quarterly compounding, the three-month zero rate is $(4 \times 2.5)/97.5 = 10.256\%$ per annum. Equation (4.3) shows that, when the rate is expressed with continuous compounding, it becomes

$$4\ln\left(1 + \frac{0.10256}{4}\right) = 0.10127$$

or 10.127% per annum. The six-month bond provides a return of 5.1 in six months on an initial investment of 94.9. With semiannual compounding the six-month rate is $(2 \times 5.1)/94.9 = 10.748\%$ per annum. Equation (4.3) shows that, when the rate is expressed with continuous compounding, it becomes

$$2\ln\left(1 + \frac{0.10748}{2}\right) = 0.10469$$

Table 4.3 Data for bootstrap method

Bond principal (\$)	*Time to maturity* (*years*)	*Annual coupon** (\$)	*Bond price* (\$)
100	0.25	0	97.5
100	0.50	0	94.9
100	1.00	0	90.0
100	1.50	8	96.0
100	2.00	12	101.6

* Half the stated coupon is assumed to be paid every six months.

Table 4.4 Continuously compounded zero rates determined from data in Table 4.3

Maturity (years)	*Zero rate (%) (cont. comp.)*
0.25	10.127
0.50	10.469
1.00	10.536
1.50	10.681
2.00	10.808

or 10.469% per annum. Similarly, the one-year rate with continuous compounding is

$$\ln\left(1+\frac{10}{90}\right)=0.10536$$

or 10.536% per annum.

The fourth bond lasts 1.5 years. The payments are as follows:

6 months: \$4
1 year: \$4
1.5 years: \$104

From our earlier calculations, we know that the discount rate for the payment at the end of six months is 10.469%, and the discount rate for the payment at the end of one year is 10.536%. We also know that the bond's price, \$96, must equal the present value of all the payments received by the bondholder. Suppose the 1.5-year zero rate is denoted by R. It follows that

$$4e^{-0.10469\times 0.5}+4e^{-0.10536\times 1.0}+104e^{-R\times 1.5}=96$$

This reduces to

$$e^{-1.5R}=0.85196$$

or

$$R=-\frac{\ln(0.85196)}{1.5}=0.10681$$

The 1.5-year zero rate is therefore 10.681%. This is the only zero rate that is consistent with the six-month rate, one-year rate, and the data in Table 4.3.

The two-year zero rate can be calculated similarly from the six-month, one-year, and 1.5-year zero rates, together with the information on the last bond in Table 4.3. If R is the two-year zero rate, then

$$6e^{-0.10469\times 0.5}+6e^{-0.10536\times 1.0}+6e^{-0.10681\times 1.5}+106e^{-R\times 2.0}=101.6$$

This gives $R=0.10808$, or 10.808%.

The rates we have calculated are summarized in Table 4.4. A chart showing the zero rate as a function of maturity is known as the *zero curve*. A common assumption is that the zero curve is linear between the points determined using the bootstrap method.

Figure 4.1 Zero rates given by the bootstrap method

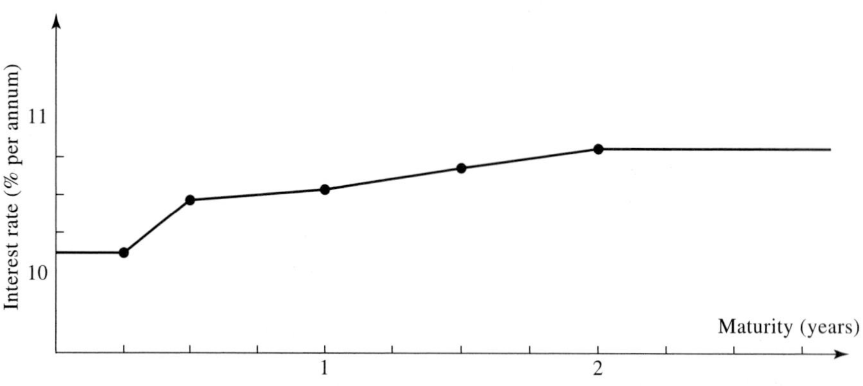

(This means that the 1.25-year zero rate is $0.5 \times 10.536 + 0.5 \times 10.681 = 10.6085\%$ in our example.) It is also usually assumed that the zero curve is horizontal prior to the first point and horizontal beyond the last point. Figure 4.1 shows the zero curve for our data using these assumptions. By using longer maturity bonds, the zero curve would be more accurately determined beyond two years.

In practice, we do not usually have bonds with maturities equal to exactly 1.5 years, 2 years, 2.5 years, and so on. The approach often used by analysts is to interpolate between the bond price data before it is used to calculate the zero curve. For example, if they know that a 2.3-year bond with a coupon of 6% sells for 98 and a 2.7-year bond with a coupon of 6.5% sells for 99, they might assume that a 2.5-year bond with a coupon of 6.25% would sell for 98.5.

4.6 FORWARD RATES

Forward interest rates are the rates of interest implied by current zero rates for periods of time in the future. To illustrate how they are calculated, we suppose that a particular set of zero rates are as shown in the second column of Table 4.5. The rates are assumed

Table 4.5 Calculation of forward rates

Year (n)	*Zero rate for an n-year investment* (*% per annum*)	*Forward rate for nth year* (*% per annum*)
1	3.0	
2	4.0	5.0
3	4.6	5.8
4	5.0	6.2
5	5.3	6.5

to be continuously compounded. Thus, the 3% per annum rate for one year means that, in return for an investment of \$100 today, an investor receives $100e^{0.03\times 1} = \$103.05$ in one year; the 4% per annum rate for two years means that, in return for an investment of \$100 today, the investor receives $100e^{0.04\times 2} = \$108.33$ in two years; and so on.

The forward interest rate in Table 4.5 for year 2 is 5% per annum. This is the rate of interest that is implied by the zero rates for the period of time between the end of the first year and the end of the second year. It can be calculated from the one-year zero interest rate of 3% per annum and the two-year zero interest rate of 4% per annum. It is the rate of interest for year 2 that, when combined with 3% per annum for year 1, gives 4% overall for the two years. To show that the correct answer is 5% per annum, suppose that \$100 is invested. A rate of 3% for the first year and 5% for the second year gives

$$100e^{0.03\times 1}e^{0.05\times 1} = \$108.33$$

at the end of the second year. A rate of 4% per annum for two years gives

$$100e^{0.04\times 2}$$

which is also \$108.33. This example illustrates the general result that when interest rates are continuously compounded and rates in successive time periods are combined, the overall equivalent rate is simply the average rate during the whole period. (This is explained in the Appendix to this chapter.) In our example, 3% for the first year and 5% for the second year average to 4% for the two years. The result is only approximately true when the rates are not continuously compounded.

The forward rate for the year 3 is the rate of interest that is implied by a 4% per annum two-year zero rate and a 4.6% per annum three-year zero rate. It is 5.8% per annum. The reason is that an investment for two years at 4% per annum combined with an investment for one year at 5.8% per annum gives an overall average return for the three years of 4.6% per annum. The other forward rates can be calculated similarly and are shown in the third column of the table. In general, if R_1 and R_2 are the zero rates for maturities T_1 and T_2, respectively, and R_F is the forward interest rate for the period of time between T_1 and T_2:

$$R_F = \frac{R_2T_2 - R_1T_1}{T_2 - T_1} \tag{4.5}$$

To illustrate this formula, consider the calculation of the year 4 forward rate from the data in Table 4.5: $T_1 = 3$, $T_2 = 4$, $R_1 = 0.046$, and $R_2 = 0.05$, and the formula gives $R_F = 0.062$.

Equation (4.5) can be written

$$R_F = R_2 + (R_2 - R_1)\frac{T_1}{T_2 - T_1} \tag{4.6}$$

This shows that, if the zero curve is upward sloping between T_1 and T_2, so that $R_2 > R_1$, then $R_F > R_2$, (i.e., the forward rate is greater than both zero rates). Similarly, if the zero curve is downward sloping with $R_2 < R_1$, then $R_F < R_2$ (i.e., the forward rate is less than both zero rates).

Assuming that the zero rates for borrowing and investing are the same (which is close to the truth for a large financial institution), an investor can lock in the forward rate for a future time period. Suppose, for example, that the zero rates are as in Table 4.5. If an

Business Snapshot 4.2 Orange County's yield curve plays

Suppose an investor can borrow or lend at the rates in Table 4.5 and thinks that one-year interest rates will not change much over the next five years. The investor can borrow one-year funds and invest for five years. The one-year borrowings can be rolled over for further one-year periods at the end of the first, second, third, and fourth years. If interest rates do stay about the same, this strategy will yield a profit of about 2.3% per year because interest will be received at 5.3% and paid at 3%. This type of trading strategy is known as a *yield curve play*. The investor is speculating that rates in the future will be quite different from the forward rates observed in the market today. (In our example forward rates observed in the market today for future one-year periods are 5%, 5.8%, 6.2%, and 6.5%.)

Robert Citron, the Treasurer at Orange County, used yield curve plays similar the one we have just described very successfully in 1992 and 1993. The profit from Mr. Citron's trades became an important contributor Orange County's budget and he was re-elected. (No one listened to his opponent in the election, who said his trading strategy was too risky.)

In 1994 Mr. Citron expanded his yield curve plays. He invested heavily in *inverse floaters*. These pay a rate of interest equal to a fixed rate of interest minus a floating rate. He also leveraged his position by borrowing in the repo market. If short-term interest rates had remained the same or declined he would have continued to do well. As it happened, interest rates rose sharply during 1994. On December 1, 1994, Orange County announced that its investment portfolio had lost $1.5 billion and several days later it filed for bankruptcy protection.

investor borrows $100 at 3% for one year and then invests the money at 4% for two years, the result is a cash outflow of $100e^{0.03\times 1} = \$103.05$ at the end of year 1 and an inflow of $100e^{0.04\times 2} = \$108.33$ at the end of year 2. Because $108.33 = 103.05e^{0.05}$, a return equal to the forward rate (5%) is earned on $103.05 during the second year. Suppose next that the investor borrows $100 for four years at 5% and invests it for three years at 4.6%. The result is a cash inflow of $100e^{0.046\times 3} = \$114.80$ at the end of the third year and a cash outflow of $100e^{0.05\times 4} = \$122.14$ at the end of the fourth year. Because $122.14 = 114.80e^{0.062}$, money is being borrowed for the fourth year at the forward rate of 6.2%.

If an investor thinks that rates in the future will be different from today's forward rates there are many trading strategies that the investor will find attractive (see Business Snapshot 4.2). One of these involves entering into a contract known as a *forward rate agreement*. We will now discuss how this contract works and how it is valued.

4.7 FORWARD RATE AGREEMENTS

A forward rate agreement (FRA) is an over-the-counter agreement that a certain interest rate will apply to either borrowing or lending a certain principal during a specified future period of time. The assumption underlying the contract is that the borrowing or lending would normally be done at LIBOR.

Consider a forward rate agreement where a company X is agreeing to lend money to company Y for the period of time between T_1 and T_2. Define:

R_K: The rate of interest agreed to in the FRA

R_F: The forward LIBOR interest rate for the period between times T_1 and T_2, calculated today[4]

R_M: The actual LIBOR interest rate observed in the market at time T_1 for the period between times T_1 and T_2

L: The principal underlying the contract

We will depart from our usual assumption of continuous compounding and assume that the rates R_K, R_F, and R_M are all measured with a compounding frequency reflecting their maturity. This means that if $T_2 - T_1 = 0.5$, they are expressed with semiannual compounding; if $T_2 - T_1 = 0.25$, they are expressed with quarterly compounding; and so on.

Normally company X would earn R_M from the LIBOR loan. The FRA means that it will earn R_K. The extra interest rate (which may be negative) that it earns as a result of entering into the FRA is $R_K - R_M$. The interest rate is set at time T_1 and paid at time T_2. The extra interest rate therefore leads to a cash flow to company X at time T_2 of

$$L(R_K - R_M)(T_2 - T_1) \tag{4.7}$$

Similarly there is a cash flow to company Y at time T_2 of

$$L(R_M - R_K)(T_2 - T_1) \tag{4.8}$$

From equations (4.7) and (4.8) we see that there is another interpretation of the FRA. It is an agreement where company X will receive interest on the principal between T_1 and T_2 at the fixed rate of R_K and pay interest at the realized market rate of R_M. Company Y will pay interest on the principal between T_1 and T_2 at the fixed rate of R_K and receive interest at R_M.

Usually FRAs are settled at time T_1 rather than T_2. The payoff must then be discounted from time T_2 to T_1. For company X the time T_1 payoff is

$$\frac{L(R_K - R_M)(T_2 - T_1)}{1 + R_M(T_2 - T_1)}$$

and for company Y the time T_1 payoff is

$$\frac{L(R_M - R_K)(T_2 - T_1)}{1 + R_M(T_2 - T_1)}$$

Example

Suppose that a company enters into a FRA that specifies it will receive a fixed rate of 4% on a principal of $1 million for a three-month period starting in three years.

[4] LIBOR forward rates are calculated as described in Section 4.6 from the LIBOR zero curve, which is calculated as described in Section 7.6.

If three-month LIBOR proves to be 4.5% for the three-month period the cash flow to the lender will be

$$1{,}000{,}000 \times (4.0 - 4.5) \times 0.25 = -\$125{,}000$$

at the 3.25 year point. This is equivalent to a cash flow of

$$-\frac{125{,}000}{1 + 0.045 \times 0.25} = -\$123{,}609$$

at the three-year point. The cash flow to the party on the opposite side of the transaction will be +\$125,000 at the 3.25 point or +\$123,609 at the three-year point. (All interest rates in this example are expressed with quarterly compounding.)

Valuation

To value an FRA, we first note that it is always worth zero when $R_K = R_F$.[5] This is because, as noted in the previous section, a large financial institution can at no cost lock in the forward rate for a future time period. For example, it can ensure that it earns the forward rate for the time period between years 2 and 3 by borrowing a certain amount of money for two years and investing it for three years. Similarly, it can ensure that it pays the forward rate for the time period between years 2 and 3 by borrowing a certain amount of money three years and investing it for two years.

Compare two FRAs. The first promises that the LIBOR forward rate R_F will be earned on a principal of L between times T_1 and T_2; the second promises that R_K will be earned on the same principal between the same two dates. The two contracts are the same except for the interest payments received at time T_2. The excess of the value of the second contract over the first is, therefore, the present value of the difference between these interest payment, or

$$L(R_K - R_F)(T_2 - T_1)e^{-R_2 T_2}$$

where R_2 is the continuously compounded riskless zero rate for a maturity T_2.[6] Because the value of the FRA promising R_F is zero, the value of the FRA promising R_K is

$$V_{\text{FRA}} = L(R_K - R_F)(T_2 - T_1)e^{-R_2 T_2} \tag{4.9}$$

Similarly, for the company receiving interest at the floating rate of R_M and paying interest at the fixed rate of R_K, the value of the FRA is given by

$$V_{\text{FRA}} = L(R_F - R_K)(T_2 - T_1)e^{-R_2 T_2} \tag{4.10}$$

Example

Suppose that LIBOR zero and forward rates are as in Table 4.5. Consider an FRA where we will receive a rate of 6%, measured with annual compounding, on a principal of \$1 million between the end of year 1 and the end of year 2. In this

[5] It is usually the case that R_K is set equal to R_F when the FRA is first initiated.

[6] Note that R_K, R, and R_F are expressed with a compounding frequency corresponding to $T_2 - T_1$, whereas R_2 is expressed with continuous compounding.

case, the forward rate is 5% with continuous compounding or 5.127% with annual compounding. From equation (4.9), it follows that the value of the FRA is

$$1{,}000{,}000(0.06 - 0.05127)e^{-0.04\times 2} = \$8{,}058$$

By comparing equations (4.7) and (4.9), we see that an FRA can be valued if we:

1. Calculate the payoff on the assumption that forward rates are realized (that is, on the assumption that $R_M = R_F$
2. Discount this payoff at the risk-free rate

4.8 THEORIES OF THE TERM STRUCTURE OF INTEREST RATES

It is natural to ask what determines the shape of the zero curve. Why is it sometimes downward sloping, sometimes upward sloping, and sometimes partly upward sloping and partly downward sloping? A number of different theories have been proposed. The simplest is *expectations theory*, which conjectures that long-term interest rates should reflect expected future short-term interest rates. More precisely, it argues that a forward interest rate corresponding to a certain future period is equal to the expected future zero interest rate for that period. Another idea, *segmentation theory*, conjectures that there need be no relationship between short-, medium-, and long-term interest rates. Under the theory, a major investor such as a large pension fund invests in bonds of a certain maturity and does not readily switch from one maturity to another. The short-term interest rate is determined by supply and demand in the short-term bond market; the medium-term interest rate is determined by supply and demand in the medium-term bond market; and so on.

The theory that is in some ways most appealing is *liquidity preference theory*, which argues that forward rates should always be higher than expected future zero rates. The basic assumption underlying the theory is that investors prefer to preserve their liquidity and invest funds for short periods of time. Borrowers, on the other hand, usually prefer to borrow at fixed rates for long periods of time. If the interest rates offered by banks and other financial intermediaries corresponded to expectations theory, long-term interest rates would equal the average of expected future short-term interest rates. In the absence of any incentive to do otherwise, investors would tend to deposit their funds for short time periods, and borrowers would tend to choose to borrow for long time periods. Financial intermediaries would then find themselves financing substantial amounts of long-term fixed-rate loans with short-term deposits. Excessive interest rate risk would result. In practice, in order to match depositors with borrowers and avoid interest rate risk, financial intermediaries raise long-term interest rates relative to expected future short-term interest rates. This strategy reduces the demand for long-term fixed-rate borrowing and encourages investors to deposit their funds for long terms.

Liquidity preference theory leads to a situation in which forward rates are greater than expected future zero rates. It is also consistent with the empirical result that yield curves tend to be upward sloping more often than they are downward sloping.

SUMMARY

Two important interest rates for derivatives traders are Treasury rates and LIBOR rates. Treasury rates are the rates paid by a government on borrowings in its own currency. LIBOR rates are short-term lending rates offered by banks in the interbank market.

The compounding frequency used for an interest rate defines the units in which it is measured. The difference between an annually compounded rate and a quarterly compounded rate is analogous to the difference between a distance measured in miles and a distance measured in kilometers. Traders frequently use continuous compounding when analyzing the value of derivatives.

Many different types of interest rate are quoted in financial markets and calculated by analysts. The n-year zero rate or n-year spot rate is the rate applicable to an investment lasting for n years when all of the return is realized at the end. The par yield on a bond of a certain maturity is the coupon rate that causes the bond to sell for its par value. Forward rates are the rates applicable to future periods of time implied by today's zero rates.

The method most commonly used to calculate zero rates is known as the bootstrap method. It involves starting with short-term instruments and moving progressively to longer-term instruments, making sure that the zero rates calculated at each stage are consistent with the prices of the instruments. It is used daily by trading desks to calculate a Treasury zero-rate curve.

A forward rate agreement (FRA) is an over-the-counter agreement that a certain interest rate will apply for either borrowing or lending a certain principal at LIBOR during a specified future period of time. An FRA can be valued by assuming that forward rates are realized and discounting the resulting payoff.

FURTHER READING

Allen, S. L., and A. D. Kleinstein. *Valuing Fixed-Income Investments and Derivative Securities*. New York: New York Institute of Finance, 1991.

Fabozzi, F. J. *Fixed-Income Mathematics: Analytical and Statistical Techniques*. New York: McGraw-Hill, 1996.

Grinblatt, M., and F. A. Longstaff. "Financial Innovation and the Role of Derivatives Securities: An Empirical Analysis of the Treasury Strips Program," *Journal of Finance*, 55, 3 (2000): 1415–36.

Jorion, P. *Big Bets Gone Bad: Derivatives and Bankruptcy in Orange County*. New York: Academic Press, 1995.

Stigum, M., and F. L. Robinson. *Money Markets and Bond Calculations*. Chicago: Irwin, 1996.

Quiz (Answers at End of Book)

4.1. A bank quotes you an interest rate of 14% per annum with quarterly compounding. What is the equivalent rate with (a) continuous compounding and (b) annual compounding?

4.2. What is meant by LIBOR and LIBID. Which is higher?

4.3. The six-month and one-year zero rates are both 10% per annum. For a bond that has a life of 18 months and pays a coupon of 8% per annum (with a coupon payment having just been made), the yield is 10.4% per annum. What is the bond's price? What is the 18-month zero rate? All rates are quoted with semiannual compounding.

4.4. An investor receives $1,100 in one year in return for an investment of $1,000 now. Calculate the percentage return per annum with:
a. Annual compounding
b. Semiannual compounding
c. Monthly compounding
d. Continuous compounding

4.5. Suppose that zero interest rates with continuous compounding are as follows:

Maturity (months)	*Rate (% per annum)*
3	8.0
6	8.2
9	8.4
12	8.5
15	8.6
18	8.7

Calculate forward interest rates for the second, third, fourth, fifth, and sixth quarters.

4.6. Assuming that zero rates are as in Problem 4.5, what is the value of an FRA that enables the holder to earn 9.5% for a three-month period starting in one year on a principal of $1,000,000? The interest rate is expressed with quarterly compounding.

4.7. The term structure of interest rates is upward sloping. Put the following in order of magnitude:
a. The five-year zero rate
b. The yield on a five-year coupon-bearing bond
c. The forward rate corresponding to the period between 5 and 5.25 years in the future
What is the answer to this question when the term structure of interest rates is downward sloping?

Questions and Problems (Answers in Solutions Manual/Study Guide)

4.8. What rate of interest with continuous compounding is equivalent to 15% per annum with monthly compounding?

4.9. A deposit account pays 12% per annum with continuous compounding, but interest is actually paid quarterly. How much interest will be paid each quarter on a $10,000 deposit?

4.10. Suppose that 6-month, 12-month, 18-month, 24-month, and 30-month zero rates continuously compounded are 4%, 4.2%, 4.4%, 4.6%, and 4.8% per annum, respectively. Estimate the cash price of a bond with a face value of 100 that will mature in 30 months pays a coupon of 4% per annum semiannually.

4.11. A three-year bond provides a coupon of 8% semiannually and has a cash price of 104. What is the bond yield?

4.12. Suppose that the 6-month, 12-month, 18-month, and 24-month zero rates are 5%, 6%, 6.5%, and 7%, respectively. What is the two-year par yield?

4.13. Suppose that zero interest rates with continuous compounding are as follows:

Maturity (months)	*Rate (% per annum)*
1	2.0
2	3.0
3	3.7
4	4.2
5	4.5

Calculate forward interest rates for the second, third, fourth, and fifth years.

4.14. Use the rates in Problem 4.13 to value an FRA where you will pay 5% for the third year on $1 million.

4.15. A 10-year 8% coupon bond currently sells for $90. A 10-year 4% coupon bond currently sells for $80. What is the 10-year zero rate? (Hint: Consider taking a long position in two of the 4% coupon bonds and a short position in one of the 8% coupon bonds.)

4.16. Explain carefully why liquidity preference theory is consistent with the observation that the term structure of interest rates tends to be upward sloping more often than it is downward sloping.

4.17. "When the zero curve is upward sloping, the zero rate for a particular maturity is greater than the par yield for that maturity. When the zero curve is downward sloping, the reverse is true." Explain why this is so.

4.18. Why are U.S. Treasury rates significantly lower than other rates that are close to risk-free?

4.19. Why does a loan in the repo market involve very little credit risk?

4.20. Explain why an FRA is equivalent to the exchange of a floating rate of interest for a fixed rate of interest?

Assignment Questions

4.21. An interest rate is quoted as 5% per annum with semiannual compounding. What is the equivalent rate with (a) annual compounding, (b) monthly compounding, and (c) continuous compounding.

4.22. The 6-month, 12-month. 18-month,and 24-month zero rates are 4%, 4.5%, 4.75%, and 5% with semiannual compounding.
   a. What are the rates with continuous compounding?
   b. What is the forward rate for the six-month period beginning in 18 months
   c. What is the value of an FRA that promises to pay you 6% (compounded semiannually) on a principal of $1 million for the six-month period starting in 18 months?

4.23. What is the two-year par yield when the zero rates are as in Problem 4.22? What is the yield on a two-year bond that pays a coupon equal to the par yield?

4.24. The following table gives the prices of bonds:

Bond principal (\$)	*Time to maturity* (*years*)	*Annual coupon** (\$)	*Bond price* (\$)
100	0.50	0.0	98
100	1.00	0.0	95
100	1.50	6.2	101
100	2.00	8.0	104

* Half the stated coupon is assumed to be paid every six months.

a. Calculate zero rates for maturities of 6 months, 12 months, 18 months, and 24 months.
b. What are the forward rates for the periods: 6 months to 12 months, 12 months to 18 months, 18 months to 24 months?
c. What are the 6-month, 12-month, 18-month, and 24-month par yields for bonds that provide semiannual coupon payments?
d. Estimate the price and yield of a two-year bond providing a semiannual coupon of 7% per annum.

APPENDIX

Exponential and Logarithm Functions

The exponential function and the natural logarithm function are widely used in mathematics and in formulas that are encountered in the derivatives business. Here we give a quick review of their properties. The exponential function is closely related to the mathematical constant e. This constant can be defined as an infinite series:

$$e = 1 + \frac{1}{1!} + \frac{1}{2!} + \frac{1}{3!} + \frac{1}{4!} + \cdots$$

where $n! = n \times (n-1) \times (n-2) \times \cdots \times 3 \times 2 \times 1$. It can be calculated to any desired accuracy by evaluating enough terms in the series. Using the first four terms, we get

$$e = 1 + 1 + \frac{1}{2} + \frac{1}{6} = 2.66667$$

Using the first six terms, we get

$$e = 1 + 1 + \frac{1}{2} + \frac{1}{6} + \frac{1}{24} + \frac{1}{120} = 2.71667$$

Using the first ten terms, we get $e = 2.71828$, which is accurate to five decimal places.

The exponential function is e^x. It is sometimes also written as $\exp(x)$. It is calculated as is 2.71828^x. For example, $e^3 = 2.71828^3 = 20.0855$. The exponential function has many interesting properties. One of these is that

$$e^R = \lim_{m \to \infty} \left(1 + \frac{R}{m}\right)^m$$

In other words, as the value of m is increased in the expression on the right-hand side, we get closer and closer to e^R. This property of e leads directly to

$$Ae^{Rn} = \lim_{m \to \infty} \left(1 + \frac{R}{m}\right)^{mn}$$

and shows why we get the result in equation (4.2) from equation (4.1).

An important property of the exponential function is

$$e^x e^y = e^{x+y}$$

(This property arises because exponents add when expressions are multiplied.) Suppose that an investor invests \$100 for five years. The rate of interest is 5% for the first two years and 7% for the last two years, with the rates expressed using continuous compounding. From equation (4.2), by the end of two years the \$100 has grown to $100e^{0.05\times 2} = \$110.52$. During the next two years, this 110.52 grows to $110.52e^{0.07\times 2} = \$127.13$. The value at the end of four years can be written as

$$100e^{0.05\times 2}e^{0.07\times 2} = 100e^{(0.05\times 2)+(0.07\times 2)} = 100e^{0.06\times 4}$$

This shows that continuously compounded rates of 5% for two years and 7% for two years average to 6% for four years. Rates measured with some other compounding frequency do not have this simplifying property.

The natural logarithm function, $\ln(x)$, is the inverse of the exponential function. If $y = e^x$, then $x = \ln(y)$. In our earlier example, we found that $e^3 = 20.0855$. It follows that $\ln 20.0855 = 3$. Important properties of this function are:

$$\ln(XY) = \ln(X) + \ln(Y) \quad \text{and} \quad \ln(X/Y) = \ln(X) - \ln(Y).$$

For example, $\ln(2) = 0.69$, $\ln(3) = 1.10$, and $\ln(6) = 0.69 + 1.10 = 1.79$.

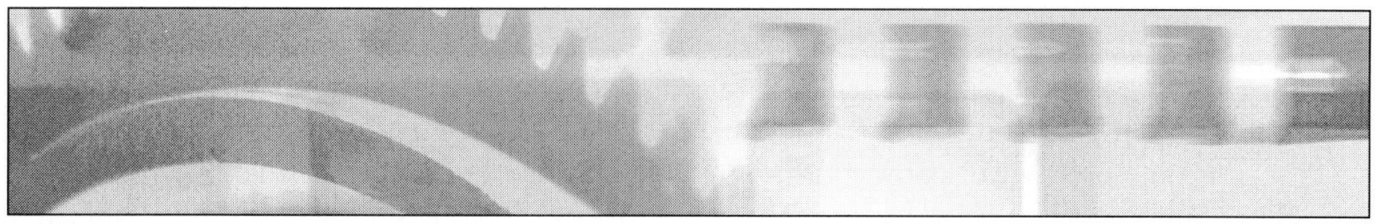

CHAPTER

Determination of Forward and Futures Prices

In this chapter we examine how forward prices and futures prices are related to the spot price of the underlying asset. Forward contracts are easier to analyze than futures contracts because there is no daily settlement—only a single payment at maturity. Luckily it can be shown that the forward price and futures price of an asset are usually very close when the maturities of the two contracts are the same.

In the first part of the chapter we derive some important general results on the relationship between forward prices and spot prices. We then use the results to examine the relationship between futures prices and spot prices for contracts on stock indices, foreign exchange, and commodities. We will consider interest rate futures contracts in the next chapter.

5.1 INVESTMENT ASSETS vs. CONSUMPTION ASSETS

When considering forward and futures contracts, it is important to distinguish between investment assets and consumption assets. An *investment asset* is an asset that is held for investment purposes by significant numbers of investors. Stocks and bonds are clearly investment assets. Gold and silver are also examples of investment assets. Note that investment assets do not have to be held exclusively for investment. Silver, for example, has a number of industrial uses. However, they do have to satisfy the requirement that they are held by significant numbers of investors solely for investment. A *consumption asset* is an asset that is held primarily for consumption and not usually for investment purposes. Examples of consumption assets are commodities such as copper, oil, and pork bellies.

As we will see later in this chapter, we can use arbitrage arguments to determine the forward and futures prices of an investment asset from its spot price and other observable market variables. We cannot do this for consumption assets.

5.2 SHORT SELLING

Some of the arbitrage strategies presented in this chapter involve *short selling*. This trade, usually simply referred to as "shorting," involves selling an asset that is not owned. It is something that is possible for some, but not all, investment assets. We will illustrate how it works by considering a short sale of shares of a stock.

Suppose an investor instructs a broker to short 500 IBM shares. The broker will carry out the instructions by borrowing the shares from another client and selling them in the market in the usual way. The investor can maintain the short position for as long as desired, provided there are always shares for the broker to borrow. At some stage, however, the investor will close out the position by purchasing 500 IBM shares. These are then replaced in the account of the client from which they were borrowed. The investor takes a profit if the stock price has declined and a loss if it has risen. If, at any time while the contract is open, the broker runs out of shares to borrow, the investor is *short-squeezed* and is forced to close out the position immediately, even if not ready to do so.

An investor with a short position must pay to the broker any income, such as dividends or interest, that would normally be received on the securities that have been shorted. The broker will transfer this to the account of the client from whom the securities have been borrowed. Consider the position of an investor who shorts 500 shares in April when the price per share is \$120 and closes out the position by buying them back in July when the price per share is \$100. Suppose that a dividend of \$1 per share is paid in May. The investor receives $500 \times \$120 = \$60{,}000$ in April when the short position is initiated. The dividend leads to a payment by the investor of $500 \times \$1 = \$500$ in May. The investor also pays $500 \times \$100 = \$50{,}000$ for shares when the position is closed out in July. The net gain is, therefore,

$$\$60{,}000 - \$500 - \$50{,}000 = \$9{,}500$$

Table 5.1 illustrates this example and shows that the cash flows from the short sale are the mirror image of the cash flows from purchasing the shares in April and selling them in July.

The investor is required to maintain a *margin account* with the broker. The margin account consists of cash or marketable securities deposited by the investor with the broker to guarantee that the investor will not walk away from the short position if the share price increases. It is similar to the margin account discussed in Chapter 2 for

Table 5.1 Cash flows from short sale and purchase of shares

	Purchase of shares	
April:	Purchase 500 shares for \$120	−\$60,000
May:	Receive dividend	+\$500
July:	Sell 500 shares for \$100 per share	+\$50,000
		Net profit = −\$9,500
	Short sale of shares	
April:	Borrow 500 shares and sell them for \$120	+\$60,000
May:	Pay dividend	−\$500
July:	Buy 500 shares for \$100 per share	−\$50,000
	Replace borrowed shares to close short position	
		Net profit = +\$9,500

futures contracts. An initial margin is required and if there are adverse movements (i.e., increases) in the price of the asset that is being shorted, additional margin may be required. The margin account does not represent a cost to the investor. This is because interest is usually paid on the balance in margin accounts and, if the interest rate offered is unacceptable, marketable securities such as Treasury bills can be used to meet margin requirements. The proceeds of the sale of the asset belong to the investor and normally form part of the initial margin.

Regulators in the United States currently allow a stock to be shorted only on an *uptick*—that is, when the most recent movement in the price of the stock was an increase. An exception is made when traders are shorting a basket of stocks replicating a stock index.

5.3 ASSUMPTIONS AND NOTATION

In this chapter we will assume that the following are all true for some market participants:

1. They are subject to no transactions costs when they trade.
2. They are subject to the same tax rate on all net trading profits.
3. They can borrow money at the same risk-free rate of interest as they can lend money.
4. They take advantage of arbitrage opportunities as they occur.

Note that we do not require these assumptions to be true for all market participants. All that we require is that they be true—or at least approximately true—for a few key market participants such as large investment banks. It is the trading activities of these key market participants and their eagerness to take advantage of arbitrage opportunities as they occur that determine the relationship between forward and spot prices.

The following notation will be used throughout this chapter:

T: Time until delivery date in a forward or futures contract (in years)

S_0: Price of the asset underlying the forward or futures contract today

F_0: Forward or futures price today

r: Zero-coupon risk-free rate of interest per annum, expressed with continuous compounding, for an investment maturing at the delivery date (i.e., in T years)

The risk-free rate, r, is in theory the rate at which money is borrowed or lent when there is no credit risk so that the money is certain to be repaid. As mentioned in Chapter 4, financial institutions and other participants in derivatives markets assume that LIBOR rates rather than Treasury rates are risk-free rates.

5.4 FORWARD PRICE FOR AN INVESTMENT ASSET

The easiest forward contract to value is one written on an investment asset that provides the holder with no income. Non-dividend-paying stocks and zero-coupon bonds are examples of such investment assets.

Illustration

Consider a long forward contract to purchase a non-dividend-paying stock in three months.[1] Assume the current stock price is $40 and the three-month risk-free interest rate is 5% per annum.

Suppose first that the forward price is relatively high at $43. An arbitrageur can borrow $40 at the risk-free interest rate of 5% per annum, buy one share, and short a forward contract to sell one share in three months. At the end of the three months, the arbitrageur delivers the share and receives $43. The sum of money required to pay off the loan is

$$40e^{0.05\times 3/12} = \$40.50$$

By following this strategy, the arbitrageur locks in a profit of $43.00 – $40.50 = $2.50 at the end of the three-month period.

Suppose next that the forward price is relatively low at $39. An arbitrageur can short one share, invest the proceeds of the short sale at 5% per annum for three months, and take a long position in a three-month forward contract. The proceeds of the short sale grow to $40e^{0.05\times 3/12}$, or $40.50, in three months. At the end of the three months, the arbitrageur pays $39, takes delivery of the share under the terms of the forward contract, and uses it to close out the short position. A net gain of

$$\$40.50 - \$39.00 = \$1.50$$

is therefore made at the end of the three months. The two trading strategies we have considered are summarized in Table 5.2.

Under what circumstances do arbitrage opportunities such as those in Table 5.2 not

Table 5.2 Arbitrage opportunities when forward price is out of line with spot price for asset providing no income. (Asset price = $40, interest rate = 5%; maturity of forward contract = 3 months)

Forward Price = $43	*Forward Price = $39*
Action now:	*Action now*:
Borrow $40 at 5% for 3 months	Short 1 unit of asset to realize $40
Buy one unit of asset	Invest $40 at 5% for 3 months
Enter into forward contract to sell asset in 3 months for $43	Enter into a forward contract to buy asset in 3 months for $39
Action in 3 months:	*Action in 3 months*:
Sell asset for $43	Buy asset for $39
Use $40.50 to repay loan with interest	Close short position
	Receive $40.50 from investment
Profit realized = $2.50	Profit realized = $1.50

[1] Forward contracts on individual stocks do not normally arise in practice. However, they form useful examples for developing our ideas. Futures on individual stocks started trading in the United States in November 2002.

exist? The first arbitrage works when the forward price is greater than \$40.50. The second arbitrage works when the forward price is less than \$40.50. We deduce that, for there to be no arbitrage, the forward price must be exactly \$40.50.

A Generalization

To generalize this example, we consider a forward contract on an investment asset with price S_0 that provides no income. Using our notation, T is the time to maturity, r is the risk-free rate, and F_0 is the forward price. The relationship between F_0 and S_0 is

$$F_0 = S_0 e^{rT} \tag{5.1}$$

If $F_0 > S_0 e^{rT}$, arbitrageurs can buy the asset and short forward contracts on the asset. If $F_0 < S_0 e^{rT}$, they can short the asset and enter into long forward contracts on it.[2] In our example, $S_0 = 40$, $r = 0.05$, and $T = 0.25$, so that equation (5.1) gives

$$F_0 = 40e^{0.05 \times 0.25} = \$40.50$$

which is in agreement with our earlier calculations.

A long forward contract and a spot purchase both lead to the asset being owned at time T. The forward price is higher than the spot price because of the cost of financing the spot purchase of the asset during the life of the forward contract. This cost was overlooked by Kidder Peabody (see Business Snapshot 5.1).

Example

Consider a four-month forward contract to buy a zero-coupon bond that will mature one year from today. (This means that the bond will have eight months to go when the forward contract matures.) The current price of the bond is \$930. We assume that the four-month risk-free rate of interest (continuously compounded) is 6% per annum. Because zero-coupon bonds provide no income, we can use equation (5.1), with $T = 4/12$, $r = 0.06$, and $S_0 = 930$. The forward price, F_0, is given by

$$F_0 = 930e^{0.06 \times 4/12} = \$948.79$$

This would be the delivery price in a contract negotiated today.

What If Short Sales Are Not Possible?

Short sales are not possible for all investment assets. As it happens, this does not matter. To derive equation (5.1), we do not need to be able to short the asset. All that we require is that there be a significant number of people who hold the asset purely for investment (and by definition this is always true of an investment asset). If the forward price is too low, they will find it attractive to sell the asset and take a long position in a forward contract.

---

[2] For another way of seeing that equation (5.1) is correct, consider the following strategy: buy one unit of the asset and enter into a short forward contract to sell it for F_0 at time T. This costs S_0 and is certain to lead to a cash inflow of F_0 at time T. So S_0 must equal the present value of F_0; that is, $S_0 = F_0 e^{-rT}$, or equivalently $F_0 = S_0 e^{rT}$.

Business Snapshot 5.1 Kidder Peabody's embarrassing mistake

Investment banks have developed a way of creating a zero-coupon bond, called a *strip*, from a coupon-bearing Treasury bond by selling each of the cash flows underlying the coupon-bearing bond as a separate security. Joseph Jett, a trader working for Kidder Peabody, had a relatively simple trading strategy. He would buy strips and sell them in the forward market. As equation (5.1) shows, the forward price of a security providing no income is always higher than the spot price. Suppose, for example, that the three-month interest rate is 4% per annum and the spot price of a strip is \$70. The three-month forward price of the strip is $70e^{0.04\times3/12} = \$70.70$.

Kidder Peabody's computer system reported a profit on each of Jett's trades equal to the excess of the forward price over the spot price (\$0.70 in our example). In fact this profit was nothing more than the cost of financing the purchase of the strip. But, by rolling his contracts forward, Jett was able to prevent this cost from accruing to him.

The result was that the system reported a profit of \$100 million on Jett's trading (and Jett received a big bonus) when in fact there was a loss in the region of \$350 million. This shows that even large financial institutions can get relatively simple things wrong!

Suppose the underlying asset is gold and assume no storage costs or income. If $F_0 > S_0e^{rT}$ an investor can adopt the following strategy:

1. Borrow S_0 dollars at an interest rate r for T years.
2. Buy one ounce of gold.
3. Short a forward contract on one ounce of gold.

At time T, one ounce of gold is sold for F_0. An amount S_0e^{rT} is required to repay the loan at this time and the investor makes a profit of $F_0 - S_0e^{rT}$.

Suppose next that $F_0 < S_0e^{rT}$. Then an investor who owns one ounce of gold can:

1. Sell the gold for S_0.
2. Invest the proceeds at interest rate r for time T.
3. Take a long position in a forward contract on one ounce of gold.

At time T, the cash invested has grown to S_0e^{rT}. The gold is repurchased for F_0 and the investor makes a profit of $S_0e^{rT} - F_0$ relative to the position the investor would have been in if the gold had been kept.

As in the non-dividend-paying stock example considered earlier, we can expect the forward price to adjust so that neither of the two arbitrage opportunities we have considered exists. This means that the relationship in equation (5.1) must hold.

5.5 KNOWN INCOME

In this section we consider a forward contract on an investment asset that will provide a perfectly predictable cash income to the holder. Examples are stocks paying known dividends and coupon-bearing bonds. We adopt the same approach as in the previous section. We first look at a numerical example and then review the formal arguments.

Illustration

Consider a long forward contract to purchase a coupon-bearing bond whose current price is \$900. We will suppose that the forward contract matures in nine months. We will also suppose that a coupon payment of \$40 is expected after 4 months. We assume the four-month and nine-month risk-free interest rates continuously compounded are 3% and 4% per annum, respectively.

Suppose first that the forward price is relatively high at \$910. An arbitrageur can borrow \$900 to buy the bond and short a forward contract. The first coupon payment has a present value of $40e^{-0.03\times 4/12} = \$39.60$. Of the \$900, \$39.60 is therefore borrowed at 3% per annum for four months so that it can be repaid with the first coupon payment. The remaining \$860.40 is borrowed at 4% per annum for nine months. The amount owing at the end of the year is $860.40e^{0.04\times 0.75} = \$886.60$. A sum of \$910 is received for the bond under the terms of the forward contract. The arbitrageur therefore makes a net profit of

$$910.00 - 886.60 = \$23.40$$

Suppose next that the forward price is relatively low at \$870. An investor can short the bond and enter into a long forward contract. Of the \$900 realized from shorting the bond, \$39.60 is invested for four months at 3% per annum, so that it grows into an amount sufficient to pay the coupon on the bond. The remaining \$860.40 is invested for nine months at 4% per annum and grows to \$886.60. A sum of \$870 is paid under the terms of the forward contract to buy the bond and the short position is closed out. The investor therefore gains

$$886.60 - 870 = \$16.60$$

The two strategies we have considered are summarized in Table 5.3.[3]

The first strategy in Table 5.3 produces a profit when the forward price is greater than \$886.60, whereas the second strategy produces a profit when the forward price is less than \$886.60. It follows that, if there are no arbitrage opportunities, the forward price must be \$886.60.

A Generalization

We can generalize from this example to argue that, when an investment asset provides income with a present value of I during the life of a forward contract, we have

$$F_0 = (S_0 - I)e^{rT} \tag{5.2}$$

In our example, $S_0 = 900.00$, $I = 40e^{-0.03\times 4/12} = 39.60$, $r = 0.04$, and $T = 0.75$, so that

$$F_0 = (900.00 - 39.60)e^{0.04\times 0.75} = \$886.60$$

[3] If shorting the bond is not possible, investors who already own the bond will sell it and buy a forward contract on the bond, thereby increasing the value of their position by \$16.60. This is similar to the strategy we described for gold in Section 5.4.

Table 5.3 Arbitrage opportunities when 9-month forward price is out of line with spot price for asset providing known cash income. (Asset price = \$900; income of \$40 occurs at 4 months; 4-month and 9-month rates are 3% and 4% per annum, respectively)

Forward price = \$910	*Forward price = \$870*
Action now:	*Action now*:
Borrow \$900: \$39.60 for 4 months and \$860.40 for 9 months	Short 1 unit of asset to realize \$900
Buy one unit of asset	Invest \$39.40 for 4 months and \$860.40 for 9 months
Enter into forward contract to sell asset for in 9 months for \$910	Enter into a forward contract to buy asset in 9 months for \$870
Action in 4 months:	*Action in 4 months*:
Receive \$40 of income on asset	Receive \$40 from 4-month investment
Use \$40 to repay first loan with interest	Pay income of \$40 on asset
Action in 9 months:	*Action in 9 months*:
Sell asset for \$910	Receive \$886.60 from 9-month investment
Use \$886.60 to repay second loan with interest	Buy asset for \$870
	Close short position
Profit realized = \$23.40	Profit realized = \$16.60

This is in agreement with our earlier calculation. Equation (5.2) applies to any asset that provides a known cash income.

If $F_0 > (S_0 - I)e^{rT}$, an arbitrageur can lock in a profit by buying the asset and shorting a forward contract on the asset. If $F_0 < (S_0 - I)e^{rT}$ an arbitrageur can lock in a profit by shorting the asset and taking a long position in a forward contract. If short sales are not possible, investors who own the asset will find it profitable to sell the asset and enter into long forward contracts.[4]

Example

Consider a 10-month forward contract on a stock with a price of \$50. We assume that the risk-free rate of interest continuously compounded is 8% per annum for all maturities. We also assume that dividends of \$0.75 per share are expected after three months, six months, and nine months. The present value of the dividends, I, is given by

$$I = 0.75e^{-0.08\times 3/12} + 0.75e^{-0.08\times 6/12} + 0.75e^{-0.08\times 9/12} = 2.162$$

The variable T is 10 months, so that the forward price, F_0, from equation (5.2), is given by

$$F_0 = (50 - 2.162)e^{0.08\times 10/12} = \$51.14$$

[4] For another way of seeing that equation (5.2) is correct, consider the following strategy: buy one unit of the asset and enter into a short forward contract to sell it for F_0 at time T. This costs S_0 and is certain to lead to a cash inflow of F_0 at time T and income with a present value of I. The initial outflow is S_0. The present value of the inflows is $I + F_0e^{-rT}$. Hence $S_0 = I + F_0e^{-rT}$, or equivalently $F_0 = (S_0 - I)e^{rT}$.

If the forward price were less than this, an arbitrageur would short the stock spot and buy forward contracts. If the forward price were greater than this, an arbitrageur would short forward contracts and buy the stock spot.

5.6 KNOWN YIELD

We now consider the situation where the asset underlying a forward contract provides a known yield rather than a known cash income. This means that the income is known when expressed as a percent of the asset's price at the time the income is paid. Suppose that an asset is expected to provide a yield of 5% per annum. This could mean that income is paid once a year and is equal to 5% of the asset price at the time it is paid. (The yield would then be 5% with annual compounding.) It could mean that income is paid twice a year and is equal to 2.5% of the asset price at the time it is paid. (The yield would then be 5% per annum with semiannual compounding.) In Section 4.2 we explained that we will normally measure interest rates with continuous compounding. Similarly we will normally measure yields with continuous compounding. Formulas for translating a yield measured with one compounding frequency to a yield measured with another compounding frequency are the same as those given for interest rates in Section 4.2.

Define q as the average yield per annum on an asset during the life of a forward contract with continuous compounding. It can be shown (see Problem 5.20) that

$$F_0 = S_0 e^{(r-q)T} \tag{5.3}$$

Example

Consider a six-month forward contract on an asset that is expected to provide income equal to 2% of the asset price once during a six-month period. The risk-free rate of interest with continuous compounding is 10% per annum. The asset price is \$25. In this case $S_0 = 25$, $r = 0.10$, and $T = 0.5$. The yield is 4% per annum with semiannual compounding. From equation (5.3), this is 3.96% per annum with continuous compounding. It follows that $q = 0.0396$, so that from equation (5.3) the forward price F_0 is given by

$$F_0 = 25e^{(0.10-0.0396)\times 0.5} = \$25.77$$

5.7 VALUING FORWARD CONTRACTS

The value of a forward contract at the time it is first entered into is zero. At a later stage it may prove to have a positive or negative value. Using the notation introduced earlier, we suppose F_0 is the current forward price for a contract that was negotiated some time ago, the delivery date is T years from today, and r is the T-year risk-free interest rate. We also define:

K: Delivery price in the contract

f: Value of forward contract today

A general result, applicable to all long forward contracts (on both investment assets and consumption assets), is

$$f = (F_0 - K)e^{-rT} \tag{5.4}$$

It is important to understand the difference between F_0, the forward price today and f, the value of the forward contract today. If today happens to be the day when the contract is first negotiated, the delivery price is set equal to the forward price and $f = 0$. As time passes, both the forward price and the value of the forward contract, f, change.

To see why equation (5.4) is correct, we use an argument analogous to the one we used for forward rate agreements in Section 4.7. We compare a long forward contract that has a delivery price of F_0 with an otherwise identical long forward contract that has a delivery price of K. The difference between the two is only in the amount that will be paid for the underlying asset at time T. Under the first contract this amount is F_0; under the second contract it is K. A cash outflow difference of $F_0 - K$ at time T translates to a difference of $(F_0 - K)e^{-rT}$ today. The contract with a delivery price F_0 is therefore less valuable than the contract with delivery price K by an amount $(F_0 - K)e^{-rT}$. The value of the contract that has a delivery price of F_0 is by definition zero. It follows that the value of the contract with a delivery price of K is $(F_0 - K)e^{-rT}$. This proves equation (5.4). Similarly, the value of a short forward contract with delivery price K is

$$(K - F_0)e^{-rT}$$

Example

A long forward contract on a non-dividend-paying stock was entered into some time ago. It currently has six months to maturity. The risk-free rate of interest (with continuous compounding) is 10% per annum, the stock price is \$25, and the delivery price is \$24. In this case $S_0 = 25$, $r = 0.10$, $T = 0.5$, and $K = 24$. From equation (5.1) the six-month forward price, F_0, is given by

$$F_0 = 25e^{0.1\times 0.5} = \$26.28$$

From equation (5.4), the value of the forward contract is

$$f = (26.28 - 24)e^{-0.1\times 0.5} = \$2.17$$

Equation (5.4) shows that we can value a long forward contract on an asset by making the assumption that the price of the asset at the maturity of the forward contract equals the forward price F_0. To see this, note that when we make the assumption, a long forward contract provides a payoff at time T of $F_0 - K$. This has a present value of $(F_0 - K)e^{-rT}$, which is the value of f in equation (5.4). Similarly, we can value a short forward contract on the asset by assuming that the current forward price of the asset is realized. These results are analogous to the result in Section 4.7 that we can value a forward rate agreement on the assumption that forward rates are realized.

Using equation (5.4) in conjunction with (5.1) gives the following expression for the value of a forward contract on an investment asset that provides no income:

$$f = S_0 - Ke^{-rT} \tag{5.5}$$

Similarly, using equation (5.4) in conjunction with (5.2) gives the following expression

Business Snapshot 5.2 A systems error?

A foreign exchange trader working for a bank enters into a long forward contract to buy 1 million pounds sterling at an exchange rate of 1.6000 in three months. At the same time, another trader on the next desk takes a long position in 16 three-month futures contracts on sterling. The futures price is 1.6000 and each contract is on 62,500 pounds. The positions taken by the forward and futures traders are therefore the same. Within minutes of the positions being taken the forward and the futures prices both increase to 1.6040. The bank's systems show that the futures trader has made a profit of $4,000 while the forward trader has made a profit of only $3,900. The forward trader immediately calls the bank's systems department to complain. Does the forward trader have a valid complaint?

The answer is no! The daily settlement of futures contracts ensures that the futures trader realizes an almost immediate profit corresponding to the increase in the futures price. If the forward trader closed out the position by entering into a short contract at 1.6040, the forward trader would have contracted to buy 1 million pounds at 1.6000 in three months and sell 1 million pounds at 1.6040 in three months. This would lead to a $4,000 profit—but not for three months. The forward trader's profit is the present value of $4,000. This is consistent with equation (5.4).

The forward trader can gain some consolation from the fact that gains and losses are treated symmetrically. If the forward/futures prices dropped to 1.5960 instead of rising to 1.6040 the futures trader would take a loss of $4,000, while the forward trader would take a loss of only $3,900.

for the value of a long forward contract on an investment asset that provides a known income with present value I:

$$f = S_0 - I - Ke^{-rT} \tag{5.6}$$

Finally, using equation (5.4) in conjunction with (5.3) gives the following expression for the value of a long forward contract on an investment asset that provides a known yield at rate q:

$$f = S_0e^{-qT} - Ke^{-rT} \tag{5.7}$$

When a futures price changes, the gain or loss on a futures contract is calculated as the change in the futures price multiplied by the size of the position. This gain is realized almost immediately because of the way futures contracts are settled daily. Equation (5.4) shows that, when a forward price changes, the gain or loss is the present value of the change in the forward price multiplied by the size of the position. The difference between the gain/loss on forward and futures contracts often causes confusion on foreign exchange trading desks (see Business Snapshot 5.2).

5.8 ARE FORWARD PRICES AND FUTURES PRICES EQUAL?

The Appendix at the end of this chapter provides an arbitrage argument to show that, when the risk-free interest rate is constant and the same for all maturities, the forward price for a contract with a certain delivery date is the same as the futures price for a contract with that delivery date. The argument in the Appendix can be extended to cover situations where the interest rate is a known function of time.

When interest rates vary unpredictably (as they do in the real world), forward and futures prices are in theory no longer the same. The proof of the relationship between the two is beyond the scope of this book. However, we can get a sense of the nature of the relationship by considering the situation where the price S of the underlying asset is strongly positively correlated with interest rates. When S increases, an investor who holds a long futures position makes an immediate gain because of the daily settlement procedure. The positive correlation indicates that it is likely that interest rates have also increased. The gain will therefore tend to be invested at a higher than average rate of interest. Similarly, when S decreases, the investor will incur an immediate loss. This loss will tend to be financed at a lower than average rate of interest. An investor holding a forward contract rather than a futures contract is not affected in this way by interest rate movements. It follows that a long futures contract will be more attractive than a similar long forward contract. Hence, when S is strongly positively correlated with interest rates, futures prices will tend to be higher than forward prices. When S is strongly negatively correlated with interest rates, a similar argument shows that forward prices will tend to be higher than futures prices.

The theoretical differences between forward and futures prices for contracts that last only a few months are in most circumstances sufficiently small to be ignored. In practice, there are a number of factors not reflected in theoretical models that may cause forward and futures prices to be different. These include taxes, transactions costs, and the treatment of margins. The risk that the counterparty will default is generally less in the case of a futures contract because of the role of the exchange clearinghouse. Also, in some instances, futures contracts are more liquid and easier to trade than forward contracts. Despite all these points, for most purposes it is reasonable to assume that forward and futures prices are the same. This is the assumption we will usually make in this book. We will use the symbol F_0 to represent both the futures price and the forward price of an asset today.

As the life of a futures contract increases, the differences between forward and futures contracts are liable to become significant. It is then dangerous to assume that forward and futures prices are perfect substitutes for each other. This point is particularly relevant to Eurodollar futures contracts because they have maturities as long as ten years. Eurodollar futures contracts are covered in Chapter 6.

5.9 FUTURES PRICES OF STOCK INDICES

We introduced futures on stock indices in Section 3.5 and showed how a stock index futures contract is a useful tool in managing equity portfolios. We are now in a position to consider how index futures prices are determined.

A stock index can usually be regarded as the price of an investment asset that pays dividends.[5] The investment asset is the portfolio of stocks underlying the index, and the dividends paid by the investment asset are the dividends that would be received by the holder of this portfolio. It is usually assumed that the dividends provide a known yield

[5] Occasionally this is not the case: see Business Snapshot 5.3.

> **Business Snapshot 5.3 The CME Nikkei 225 futures contract**
>
> The arguments in this chapter on how index futures prices are determined require that the index be the value of investment asset. This means that it must be the value of a portfolio of assets that can be traded. The asset underlying the Chicago Mercantile Exchange's futures contract on the Nikkei 225 Index does not qualify. The reason is quite subtle. Suppose that S is the value of the Nikkei 225 Index. This is the value of a portfolio of 225 Japanese stocks measured in yen. The variable underlying the CME futures contract on the Nikkei 225 has a *dollar value* of $5S$. In other words, the futures contract takes a variable that is measured in yen and treats it as though it is dollars.
>
> We cannot invest in a portfolio whose value will always be $5S$ dollars. The best we can do is to invest in one that is always worth $5S$ yen or in one that is always worth $5QS$ dollars, where Q is the dollar value of one yen. The variable $5S$ dollars is not therefore the price of an investment asset and equation (5.8) does not apply.
>
> CME's Nikkei 225 futures contract is an example of a *quanto*. A quanto is a derivative where the underlying asset is measured in one currency and the payoff is in another currency.

rather than a known cash income. If q is the dividend yield rate, equation (5.3) gives the futures price, F_0, as

$$F_0 = S_0 e^{(r-q)T} \tag{5.8}$$

Example

Consider a three-month futures contract on the S&P 500. Suppose that the stocks underlying the index provide a dividend yield of 1% per annum, that the current value of the index is 800, and that the continuously compounded risk-free interest rate is 6% per annum. In this case, $r = 0.06$, $S_0 = 800$, $T = 0.25$, and $q = 0.01$. Hence, the futures price, F_0, is given by

$$F_0 = 800e^{(0.06-0.01)\times 0.25} = \$810.06$$

In practice, the dividend yield on the portfolio underlying an index varies week by week throughout the year. For example, a large proportion of the dividends on the NYSE stocks are paid in the first week of February, May, August, and November each year. The chosen value of q should represent the average annualized dividend yield during the life of the contract. The dividends used for estimating q should be those for which the ex-dividend date is during the life of the futures contract. Looking at Table 3.3 of Chapter 3, we see that the settlement prices for futures contracts on the S&P 500 Index appear to be decreasing with the maturity of the futures contract at about 0.4% per annum. This corresponds to the situation where the dividend yield exceeds the risk-free rate by about 0.4% per annum.

Index Arbitrage

If $F_0 > S_0 e^{(r-q)T}$, profits can be made by buying spot (i.e., for immediate delivery) the stocks underlying the index and shorting futures contracts. If $F_0 < S_0 e^{(r-q)T}$, profits can

Business Snapshot 5.4 Index arbitrage in October 1987

To do index arbitrage, a trader must be able to trade both the index futures contract and the portfolio of stocks underlying the index very quickly at the prices quoted in the market. In normal market conditions this is possible using program trading, and the relationship in equation (5.8) holds well. Examples of days when the market was anything but normal are October 19 and 20 of 1987. On what is termed "Black Monday", October 19, 1987, the market fell by more than 20%, and the 604 million shares traded on the New York Stock Exchange easily exceeded all previous records. The exchange's systems were overloaded, and if you placed an order to buy or sell shares on that day there could be a delay of up to two hours before your order was executed.

For most of October 19, 1987, futures prices were at a significant discount to the underlying index. For example, at the close of trading the S&P 500 Index was at 225.06 (down 57.88 on the day), whereas the futures price for December delivery on the S&P 500 was 201.50 (down 80.75 on the day). This was largely because the delays in processing orders made index arbitrage impossible. On the next day, Tuesday, October 20, 1987, the New York Stock Exchange placed temporary restrictions on the way in which program trading could be done. This also made index arbitrage very difficult and the breakdown of the traditional linkage between stock indices and stock index futures continued. At one point the futures price for the December contract was 18% less than the S&P 500 Index. However, after a few days the market returned to normal, and the activities of arbitrageurs ensured that equation (5.8) governed the relationship between futures and spot prices of indices.

be made by doing the reverse—that is, shorting or selling the stocks underlying the index and taking a long position in futures contracts. These strategies are known as *index arbitrage*. When $F_0 < S_0e^{(r-q)T}$, index arbitrage is often done by a pension fund that owns an indexed portfolio of stocks. When $F_0 > S_0e^{(r-q)T}$, it is often done by a corporation holding short-term money market investments. For indices involving many stocks, index arbitrage is sometimes accomplished by trading a relatively small representative sample of stocks whose movements closely mirror those of the index. Often index arbitrage is implemented through *program trading*, whereby a computer system is used to generate the trades.

Most of the time the activities of arbitrageurs ensure that equation (5.8) holds, but occasionally arbitrage is impossible and the futures price does get out of line with the spot price (see Business Snapshot 5.4).

5.10 FORWARD AND FUTURES CONTRACTS ON CURRENCIES

We now move on to consider forward and futures foreign currency contracts from the perspective of a U.S. investor. The underlying asset in such contracts is a certain number of units of the foreign currency. We will therefore define the variable S_0 as the current spot price in dollars of one unit of the foreign currency and F_0 as the

Figure 5.1 Two ways of converting 1,000 units of a foreign currency to dollars at time T. S_0 is spot exchange rate; F_0 is forward exchange rate; r and r_f are dollar and foreign risk-free rates

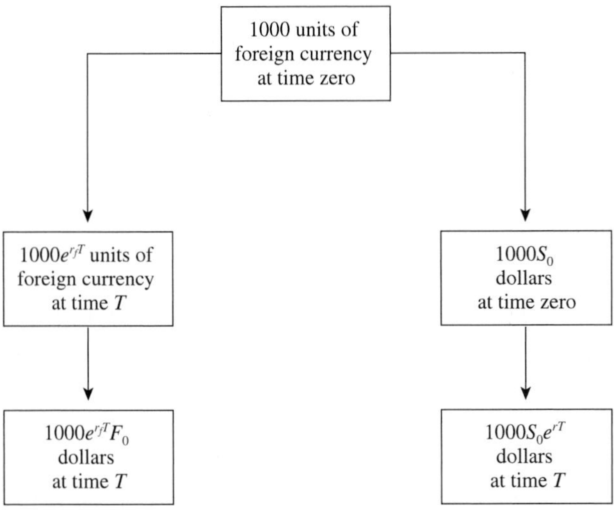

forward or futures price in dollars of one unit of the foreign currency. This is consistent with the way we have defined S_0 and F_0 for other assets underlying forward and futures contracts. However, as mentioned in Section 2.10, it does not necessarily correspond to the way spot and forward exchange rates are quoted. For major exchange rates other than the British pound, euro, Australian dollar, and New Zealand dollar, a spot or forward exchange rate is normally quoted on a foreign currency per dollar basis.

A foreign currency has the property that the holder of the currency can earn interest at the risk-free interest rate prevailing in the foreign country. For example, the holder can invest the currency in a foreign-denominated bond. We define r_f as the value of the foreign risk-free interest rate when money is invested for time T. The variable r is the U.S. dollar risk-free rate when money is invested for this period of time.

The relationship between F_0 and S_0 is

$$F_0 = S_0e^{(r-r_f)T} \tag{5.9}$$

This is the well-known interest rate parity relationship from international finance. The reason it is true is illustrated in Figure 5.1. Suppose that an individual starts with 1,000 units of the foreign currency. There are two ways it can be converted to dollars at time T. One is by investing it for T years at r_f and entering into a forward contract to sell the proceeds for dollars at time T. This generates $1{,}000e^{r_f T}F_0$ dollars. The other is by exchanging the foreign currency for dollars in the spot market and investing the proceeds for T years at rate r. This generates $1{,}000S_0e^{rT}$ dollars. In the absence of arbitrage, the two strategies must give the same result. Hence

$$1{,}000e^{r_f T}F_0 = 1{,}000S_0e^{rT}$$

so that

$$F_0 = S_0 e^{(r-r_f)T}$$

Example

Suppose that the two-year interest rates in Australia and the United States are 5% and 7%, respectively, and the spot exchange rate between the Australian dollar (AUD) and the U.S. dollar (USD) is 0.6200 USD per AUD. From equation (5.9), the two-year forward exchange rate should be

$$0.62e^{(0.07-0.05)\times 2} = 0.6453$$

Suppose first the two-year forward exchange rate is less than this, say 0.6300. An arbitrageur can

1. Borrow 1,000 AUD at 5% per annum for two years, convert to 620 USD and invest the USD at 7%. (Both rates are continuously compounded.)
2. Enter into a forward contract to buy 1,105.17 AUD for $1{,}105.17 \times 0.63 =$ 696.26 USD.

The 620 USD that are invested at 7% grow to $620e^{0.07\times 2} = 713.17$ USD in two years. Of this, 696.26 USD are used to purchase 1,105.17 AUD under the terms of the forward contract. This is exactly enough to repay principal and interest on the 1,000 AUD that are borrowed ($1{,}000e^{0.05\times 2} = 1,105.17$). The strategy therefore gives rise to a riskless profit of $713.17 - 696.26 = 16.91$ USD. (If this does not sound very exciting, consider following a similar strategy where you borrow 100 million AUD!)

Suppose next that the two-year forward rate is 0.6600 (greater than the 0.6453 value given by equation (5.9)). An arbitrageur can:

1. Borrow 1,000 USD at 7% per annum for two years, convert to $1{,}000/0.6200 = 1,612.90$ AUD, and invest the AUD at 5%.
2. Enter into a forward contract to sell 1,782.53 AUD for $1,782.53 \times 0.66 =$ 1,176.47 USD.

The 1,612.90 AUD that are invested at 5% grow to $1{,}612.90e^{0.05\times 2} =$ 1,782.53 AUD in two years. The forward contract has the effect of converting this to 1,176.47 USD. The amount needed to payoff the USD borrowings is $1{,}000e^{0.07\times 2} = 1{,}150.27$ USD. The strategy therefore gives rise to a riskless profit of $1{,}176.47 - 1{,}150.27 = 26.20$ USD.

Table 5.4 shows currency futures quotes on February 4, 2004. In the case of the first eight contracts the quotes are U.S dollars (or cents) per unit of the foreign currency. This is the usual quotation convention for futures contracts. Equation (5.9) applies with r equal to the U.S. risk-free rate and r_f equal to the foreign risk-free rate.

On February 4, 2004, interest rates on the Japanese yen and Swiss franc were lower than the interest rate on the U.S. dollar. This corresponds to the $r > r_f$ situation and explains why futures prices for these currencies increase with maturity in Table 5.4. On the Canadian dollar, the British pound, the Australian dollar, the Mexican peso, and the euro, interest rates were higher than in the United States. This corresponds to the $r_f > r$ situation and explains why the futures prices of these currencies decrease with maturity.

Table 5.4 Foreign exchange futures quotes from the *Wall Street Journal* on February 5, 2004. (Columns show month, open, high, low, settle, change, lifetime high, lifetime low, and open interest, respectively.)

Currency Futures

Month	Open	High	Low	Settle	Change	Lifetime high	Lifetime low	Open interest
Japanese Yen (CME)-¥12,500,000; $ per ¥								
Mar	.9490	.9507	.9476	.9497	.0011	.9515	.8240	161,371
June	.9524	.9529	.9510	.9526	.0011	.9532	.8496	8,070
Est vol 6,229; vol Tue 14,298; open int 169,516, +4,280.								
Canadian Dollar (CME)-CAD 100,000; $ per CAD								
Mar	.7466	.7500	.7431	.7485	.0015	.7863	.6150	57,248
June	.7450	.7480	.7421	.7465	.0015	.7850	.6201	3,453
Sept	.7448	.7460	.7414	.7449	.0015	.7815	.6505	1,635
Dec	.7440	.7445	.7405	.7433	.0015	.7800	.6940	787
Est vol 6,009; vol Tue 12,621; open int 63,329, −2,093.								
British Pound (CME)-£62,500; $ per £								
Mar	1.8335	1.8338	1.8225	1.8277	−.0049	1.8488	1.5654	66,330
June	1.8200	1.8200	1.8060	1.8135	−.0051	1.8373	1.6080	127
Est vol 6,429; vol Tue 14,952; open int 66,822, +2,521.								
Swiss Franc (CME)-CHF 125,000; $ per CHF								
Mar	.8018	.8020	.7970	.8002	−.0008	.8249	.7060	40,580
June	...	...	...	.8019	−.0008	.8248	.7117	216
Est vol 4,223; vol Tue 9,933; open int 40,899, +458.								
Australian Dollar (CME)-AUD 100,000; $ per AUD								
Mar	.7605	.7614	.7545	.7578	−.0034	.7769	.5193	50,309
June	.7490	.7500	.7490	.7494	−.0034	.7686	.5645	843
Est vol 3,108; vol Tue 10,590; open int 51,677, −1,877.								
Mexican Peso (CME)-MXN 500,000; $ per MXN								
Mar	.08990	.09050	.08857	.08920	−00057	.09330	.08600	36,882
June	.08900	.08915	.08780	.08812	−00060	.09125	.08495	594
Est vol 12,680; vol Tue 6,785; open int 38,120, −303.								
Euro/US Dollar (CME)-€125,000; $ per €								
Mar	1.2532	1.2565	1.2478	1.2520	−.0013	1.2875	1.0425	122,318
June	1.2492	1.2520	1.2460	1.2491	−.0013	1.2837	1.0570	1,293
Est vol 20,357; vol Tue 69,168; open int 124,312, +3,721.								
Euro/US Dollar (FINEX)-€200,000; $ per €								
Mar	...	...	...	1.2520	−.0012	1.2841	1.4720	510
Est vol 191; vol Tue 93; open int 512, −12.								
Euro/Japanese Yen (FINEX)-€100,000; ¥ per €								
Mar	131.85	131.85	131.61	131.85	−.28	136.44	130.45	7,752
Est vol 67; vol Tue 287; open int 7,752, +76.								
Euro/British Pound (FINEX)-€100,000; £ per €								
Mar	.6840	.6843	.6832	.6852	.0013	.7094	.6832	9,964
Est vol 198; vol Tue 454; open int 9,964, +360.								

The last two contracts in Table 5.4 involve exchange rates relative to the euro. The quotes are yen per euro and pounds per euro. To use equation (5.9) for the euro/yen contract we can measure S_0 and F_0 as yen per euro, define r as the yen interest rate and r_f as the euro interest rate. Similarly, to use equation (5.9) for the euro/pound contract we can measure S_0 and F_0 as pounds per euro, define r as the sterling interest rate and r_f as the euro interest rate.

Example

The futures price of the Canadian dollar in Table 5.4 appears to be decreasing at a rate of about 1.0% per annum with the maturity of the contract. (The September 2004 settlement price of 0.7449 is about 0.5% below the March 2004 settlement price of 0.7485.) The decrease suggests that short-term interest rates were about 1% per annum higher in the Canada than in the United States on February 4, 2004.

A Foreign Currency as an Asset Providing a Known Yield

Note that equation (5.9) is identical to equation (5.3) with q replaced by r_f. This is not a coincidence. A foreign currency can be regarded as an investment asset paying a known yield. The yield is the risk-free rate of interest in the foreign currency.

To understand this, note that the value of interest paid in a foreign currency depends on the value of the foreign currency. Suppose that the interest rate on British pounds is 5% per annum. To a U.S. investor the British pound provides an income equal to 5% of the value of the British pound per annum. In other words it is an asset that provides a yield of 5% per annum.

5.11 FUTURES ON COMMODITIES

We now move on to consider futures contracts on commodities. First we consider the futures prices of commodities that are investment assets such as gold and silver.[6] We then move on to consider the futures prices of consumption assets.

Income and Storage Costs

As explained in Business Snapshot 3.1, the hedging strategies of gold producers leads to a requirement on the part of investment banks to borrow gold. Gold owners such as central banks charge interest in the form of what is known as the *gold lease rate* when they lend gold. The same is true of silver. Gold and silver can therefore provide income to the holder. Like other commodities they also have storage costs.

Equation (5.1) shows that in the absence of storage costs and income the forward price of a commodity that is an investment asset is given by

$$F_0 = S_0 e^{rT} \tag{5.10}$$

Storage costs can be treated as negative income. If U is the present value of all the storage costs, net of income, during the life of a forward contract, it follows from equation (5.2) that

$$F_0 = (S_0 + U)e^{rT} \tag{5.11}$$

Example

Consider a one-year futures contract on gold. We assume no income and that it costs \$2 per ounce per year to store gold, with the payment being made at the end of the year. Assume that the spot price is \$450 and the risk-free rate is 7% per annum for all maturities. This corresponds to $r = 0.07$, $S_0 = 450$, $T = 1$, and

$$U = 2e^{-0.07\times 1} = 1.865$$

From equation (5.11), the theoretical futures price, F_0, is given by

$$F_0 = (450 + 1.865)e^{0.07\times 1} = \$484.63$$

If the actual gold futures price is greater than 484.63, an arbitrageur can buy gold and short one-year gold futures contracts to lock in a profit. If the actual gold futures price is less than 484.63, an investor who already owns gold can improve the return by selling the gold and buying gold futures contracts. Trading Notes 5.1 and 5.2 illustrate these strategies for the situations where the future price is 500 and 470, respectively.

If the storage costs incurred at any time are proportional to the price of the commodity, they can be treated as negative yield. In this case, from equation (5.3), we have

$$F_0 = S_0 e^{(r+u)T} \tag{5.12}$$

---

[6] Recall that, for an asset to be an investment asset, it need not be held solely for investment purposes. What is required is that some individuals hold it for investment purposes and that these individuals be prepared to sell their holdings and go long forward contracts, if the latter look more attractive. This explains why silver, although it has significant industrial uses, is an investment asset.

where u denotes the storage costs per annum as a proportion of the spot price net of any yield earned on the asset.

Consumption Commodities

Commodities that are consumption assets rather than investment assets usually provide no income, but can be subject to significant storage costs. We now review the arbitrage strategies used to determine futures prices from spot prices carefully.[7] Suppose that, instead of equation (5.11), we have

$$F_0 > (S_0 + U)e^{rT} \tag{5.13}$$

To take advantage of this opportunity, an arbitrageur can implement the following strategy:

1. Borrow an amount $S_0 + U$ at the risk-free rate and use it to purchase one unit of the commodity and to pay storage costs.
2. Short a forward contract on one unit of the commodity.

If we regard the futures contract as a forward contract, this strategy leads to a profit of $F_0 - (S_0 + U)e^{rT}$ at time T. Trading Note 5.1 illustrates the strategy for gold. There is no problem in implementing the strategy for any commodity. However, as arbitrageurs do so, there will be a tendency for S_0 to increase and F_0 to decrease until equation (5.13) is no longer true. We conclude that equation (5.13) cannot hold for any significant length of time.

Suppose next that

$$F_0 < (S_0 + U)e^{rT} \tag{5.14}$$

In the case of investment assets such as gold and silver, we can argue that many investors hold the commodity solely for investment. When they observe the inequality

Trading Note 5.1 Gold futures price too high

The one-year futures price of gold is \$500 per ounce. The spot price is \$450 per ounce and the risk-free interest rate is 7% per annum. The storage costs for gold are \$2 per ounce per year payable in arrears and we assume gold provides no income.

Opportunity

The futures price of gold is too high. An arbitrageur can:

1. Borrow \$45,000 at the risk-free interest rate to buy 100 ounces of gold.
2. Short one gold futures contract for delivery in one year.

At the end of the year \$50,000 is received for the gold under the terms of the futures contract, \$48,263 is used to pay interest and principal on the loan, and \$200 is used to pay storage. The net gain is

$$\$50{,}000 - \$48,263 - \$200 = \$1{,}537$$

[7] For some commodities the spot price depends on the delivery location. We assume that the delivery location for spot and futures are the same.

Trading Note 5.2 Gold futures price too low

The one-year futures price of gold is \$470 per ounce. The spot price is \$450 per ounce and the risk-free interest rate is 7% per annum. The storage costs for gold are \$2 per ounce per year payable in arrears and we assume gold provides no income.

Opportunity
The futures price of gold is too low. An investor who already holds 100 ounces of gold for investment purposes can:

1. Sell the gold for \$45,000.
2. Enter into one long gold futures contract for delivery in one year.

The \$45,000 is invested at the risk-free interest rate for one year and grows to \$48,263. At the end of the year, under the terms of the futures contract, 100 ounces of gold are purchased for \$47,000. The investor therefore ends up with 100 ounces of gold plus

$$\$48{,}263 - \$47{,}000 = \$1{,}263$$

in cash. If the gold is kept throughout the year, the investor ends up with 100 ounces of gold, but has to pay \$200 for storage. The futures contract therefore improves the investor's position by

$$1{,}263 + \$200 = \$1{,}463$$

in equation (5.14), they will find it profitable to:

1. Sell the commodity, save the storage costs, and invest the proceeds at the risk-free interest rate.
2. Take a long position in a forward contract.

This strategy is illustrated for gold in Trading Note 5.2. The result is a riskless profit at maturity of $(S_0 + U)e^{rT} - F_0$ relative to the position the investors would have been in if they had held the commodity. It follows that equation (5.14) cannot hold for long. Because neither equation (5.13) nor (5.14) can hold for long, we must have $F_0 = (S_0 + U)e^{rT}$.

For commodities that are not to any significant extent held for investment, this argument cannot be used. Individuals and companies who keep such a commodity in inventory do so because of its consumption value, not because of its value as an investment. They are reluctant to sell the commodity and buy forward contracts, because forward contracts cannot be consumed. There is therefore nothing to stop equation (5.14) from holding. All we can assert for a consumption commodity is therefore

$$F_0 \leqslant (S_0 + U)e^{rT} \tag{5.15}$$

If storage costs are expressed as a proportion u of the spot price, the equivalent result is

$$F_0 \leqslant S_0 e^{(r+u)T} \tag{5.16}$$

Convenience Yields

We do not necessarily have equality in equations (5.15) and (5.16) because users of a consumption commodity may feel that ownership of the physical commodity provides benefits that are not obtained by holders of futures contracts. For example, an oil refiner is unlikely to regard a futures contract on crude oil in the same way as crude oil held in inventory. The crude oil in inventory can be an input to the refining process whereas a futures contract cannot be used for this purpose. In general, ownership of the physical asset enables a manufacturer to keep a production process running and perhaps profit from temporary local shortages. A futures contract does not do the same. The benefits from holding the physical asset are sometimes referred to as the *convenience yield* provided by the commodity. If the dollar amount of storage costs is known and has a present value, U, the convenience yield, y, is defined so that

$$F_0 e^{yT} = (S_0 + U)e^{rT}$$

If the storage costs per unit are a constant proportion, u, of the spot price, then y is defined so that

$$F_0 e^{yT} = S_0 e^{(r+u)T}$$

or

$$F_0 = S_0 e^{(r+u-y)T} \tag{5.17}$$

The convenience yield simply measures the extent to which the left-hand side is less than the right-hand side in equation (5.15) or (5.16). For investment assets the convenience yield must be zero; otherwise, there are opportunities such as those in Trading Note 5.2. Figure 2.2 of Chapter 2 shows that the futures prices of crude oil tended to decrease as the time to maturity of the contract increased on July 17, 2003. This pattern suggests that the convenience yield, y, is greater than $r + u$ for oil on this date.

The convenience yield reflects the market's expectations concerning the future availability of the commodity. The greater the possibility that shortages will occur, the higher the convenience yield. If users of the commodity have high inventories, there is very little chance of shortages in the near future and the convenience yield tends to be low. On the other hand, low inventories tend to lead to high convenience yields.

5.12 THE COST OF CARRY

The relationship between futures prices and spot prices can be summarized in terms of the *cost of carry*. This measures the storage cost plus the interest that is paid to finance the asset less the income earned on the asset. For a non-dividend-paying stock, the cost of carry is r, because there are no storage costs and no income is earned; for a stock index, it is $r - q$, because income is earned at rate q on the asset. For a currency, it is $r - r_f$; for a commodity that provides income at rate q an requires storage costs at rate u, it is $r - q + u$; and so on.

Define the cost of carry as c. For an investment asset, the futures price is

$$F_0 = S_0 e^{cT} \tag{5.18}$$

For a consumption asset, it is

$$F_0 = S_0 e^{(c-y)T} \tag{5.19}$$

where y is the convenience yield.

5.13 DELIVERY OPTIONS

Whereas a forward contract normally specifies that delivery is to take place on a particular day, a futures contract often allows the party with the short position to choose to deliver at any time during a certain period. (Typically the party has to give a few days' notice of its intention to deliver.) The choice introduces a complication into the determination of futures prices. Should the maturity of the futures contract be assumed to be the beginning, middle, or end of the delivery period? Even though most futures contracts are closed out prior to maturity, it is important to know when delivery would have taken place in order to calculate the theoretical futures price.

If the futures price is an increasing function of the time to maturity, it can be seen from equation (5.19) that $c > y$, so that the benefits from holding the asset (including convenience yield and net of storage costs) are less than the risk-free rate. It is usually optimal in such a case for the party with the short position to deliver as early as possible, because the interest earned on the cash received outweighs the benefits of holding the asset. As a rule, futures prices in these circumstances should be calculated on the basis that delivery will take place at the beginning of the delivery period. If futures prices are decreasing as time to maturity increases ($c < y$), the reverse is true. It is then usually optimal for the party with the short position to deliver as late as possible, and futures prices should, as a rule, be calculated on this assumption.

5.14 FUTURES PRICES AND EXPECTED SPOT PRICES

We refer to the market's average opinion about what the spot price of an asset will be at a certain future time as the *expected spot price* of the asset at that time. Suppose that it is now June and the September futures price of corn is 200 cents. It is interesting to ask what the expected spot price of corn in September is. Is it less that 200 cents, greater than 200 cents, or exactly equal to 200 cents? As illustrated in Figure 2.1, the futures price converges to the spot price at maturity. If the expected spot price is less than 200 cents, the market must be expecting the September futures price to decline so that traders with short positions gain and traders with long positions lose. If the expected spot price is greater than 200 cents the reverse must be true. The market must be expecting the September futures price to increase so that traders with long positions gain while those with short positions lose.

Keynes and Hicks

Economists John Maynard Keynes and John Hicks argued that if hedgers tend to hold short positions and speculators tend to hold long positions, the futures price of an asset will be below the expected spot price.[8] This is because speculators require compensation for the risks they are bearing. They will trade only if they can expect to make money on average. Hedgers will lose money on average, but they are likely to be prepared to accept this because the futures contract reduces their risks. If hedgers tend to hold long

[8] See J.M. Keynes, *A Treatise on Money*. London: Macmillan, 1930; and J.R. Hicks, *Value and Capital*. Oxford: Clarendon Press, 1939.

positions while speculators hold short positions, Keynes and Hicks argued that the futures price will be above the expected spot price for a similar reason.

Risk and Return

The modern approach to explaining the relationship between futures prices and expected spot prices is based on the relationship between risk and expected return in the economy. In general, the higher the risk of an investment, the higher the expected return demanded by an investor. Readers familiar with the capital asset pricing model will know that there are two types of risk in the economy: systematic and nonsystematic. Nonsystematic risk should not be important to an investor. It can be almost completely eliminated by holding a well-diversified portfolio. An investor should not therefore require a higher expected return for bearing nonsystematic risk. Systematic risk, by contrast, cannot be diversified away. It arises from a correlation between returns from the investment and returns from the whole stock market. An investor generally requires a higher expected return than the risk-free interest rate for bearing positive amounts of systematic risk. Also, an investor is prepared to accept a lower expected return than the risk-free interest rate when the systematic risk in an investment is negative.

The Risk in a Futures Position

Let us consider a speculator who takes a long position in a futures contract that lasts for T years in the hope that the spot price of the asset will be above the futures price at the end of the life of the futures contract. We ignore daily settlement and assume that the futures contract can be treated as a forward contract. We suppose that the speculator puts the present value of the futures price into a risk-free investment while simultaneously taking a long futures position. The proceeds of the risk-free investment are used to buy the asset on the delivery date. The asset is then immediately sold for its market price. The cash flows to the speculator are:

Today: $-F_0 e^{-rT}$

End of Futures Contract: $+S_T$

where F_0 is the futures price today, S_T is the price of the asset at time T at the end of the futures contract, and r is the risk-free return on funds invested for time T.

How do we value this investment? The discount rate we use should for the expected cash flow at time T equals an investor's required return on the investment. Suppose that k is an investor's required return for this investment. The present value of this investment is

$$-F_0 e^{-rT} + E(S_T)e^{-kT}$$

where E denotes expected value. We can assume that all investments in securities markets are priced so that they have zero net present value. This means that

$$-F_0 e^{-rT} + E(S_T)e^{-kT} = 0$$

or

$$F_0 = E(S_T)e^{(r-k)T} \tag{5.20}$$

As we have just discussed, the returns investors require on an investment depend on its systematic risk. The investment we have been considering is in essence an investment in the asset underlying the futures contract. If the returns from this asset are uncorrelated with the stock market, the correct discount rate to use is the risk-free rate r, so we should set $k = r$. Equation (2.1) then gives

$$F_0 = E(S_T)$$

This shows that the futures price is an unbiased estimate of the expected future spot price when the return from the underlying asset is uncorrelated with the stock market.

If the return from the asset is positively correlated with the stock market, $k > r$ and equation (2.1) leads to $F_0 < E(S_T)$. This shows that, when the asset underlying the futures contract has positive systematic risk, we should expect the futures price to understate the expected future spot price. An example of an asset that has positive systematic risk is a stock index. The expected return of investors on the stocks underlying an index is generally more than the risk-free rate, r. The dividends provide a return of q. The expected increase in the index must therefore be more than $r - q$. Equation (5.8) is therefore consistent with the prediction that the futures price understates the expected future stock price for a stock index.

If the return from the asset is negatively correlated with the stock market, $k < r$ and equation (5.20) shows that $F_0 > E(S_T)$. This shows that when the asset underlying the futures contract has positive systematic risk we should expect the futures price to overstate the expected future spot price.

Normal Backwardation and Contango

When the futures price is below the expected future spot price, the situation is known as *normal backwardation*; when the futures price is above the expected future spot price, the situation is known as *contango*.

SUMMARY

For most purposes, the futures price of a contract with a certain delivery date can be considered to be the same as the forward price for a contract with the same delivery date. It can be shown that in theory the two should be exactly the same when interest rates are perfectly predictable.

Table 5.5 Summary of results for a contract with time to maturity T on an investment asset with price S_0 when the risk-free interest rate for a T-year period is r

Asset	*Forward/futures price*	*Value of long forward contract with delivery price K*
Provides no income	S_0e^{rT}	$S_0 - Ke^{-rT}$
Provides known income with present value I	$(S_0 - I)e^{rT}$	$S_0 - I - Ke^{-rT}$
Provides known yield, q	$S_0e^{(r-q)T}$	$S_0e^{-qT} - Ke^{-rT}$

For the purposes of understanding futures (or forward) prices, it is convenient to divide futures contracts into two categories: those in which the underlying asset is held for investment by a significant number of investors, and those in which the underlying asset is held primarily for consumption purposes.

In the case of investment assets, we have considered three different situations:

1. The asset provides no income.
2. The asset provides a known dollar income.
3. The asset provides a known yield.

The results are summarized in Table 5.5. They enable futures prices to be obtained for contracts on stock indices, currencies, gold, and silver. Storage costs can be treated as negative income.

In the case of consumption assets, it is not possible to obtain the futures price as a function of the spot price and other observable variables. Here the parameter known as the asset's convenience yield becomes important. It measures the extent to which users of the commodity feel that ownership of the physical asset provides benefits that are not obtained by the holders of the futures contract. These benefits may include the ability to profit from temporary local shortages or the ability to keep a production process running. We can obtain an upper bound for the futures price of consumption assets using arbitrage arguments, but we cannot nail down an equality relationship between futures and spot prices.

The concept of cost of carry is sometimes useful. The cost of carry is the storage cost of the underlying asset plus the cost of financing it minus the income received from it. In the case of investment assets, the futures price is greater than the spot price by an amount reflecting the cost of carry. In the case of consumption assets, the futures price is greater than the spot price by an amount reflecting the cost of carry net of the convenience yield.

FURTHER READING

Cox, J. C., J. E. Ingersoll, and S. A. Ross. "The Relation between Forward Prices and Futures Prices," *Journal of Financial Economics*, 9 (December 1981): 321–46.

Ghon, R. S. and R. P. Chang. "Intra-day Arbitrage in Foreign Exchange and Eurocurrency Markets," *Journal of Finance*, 47, 1 (1992): 363–380.

Jarrow, R. A., and G. S. Oldfield. "Forward Contracts and Futures Contracts," *Journal of Financial Economics*, 9 (December 1981): 373–82.

Kane, E. J. "Market Incompleteness and Divergences between Forward and Futures Interest Rates," *Journal of Finance*, 35 (May 1980): 221–34.

Pindyck R. S. "Inventories and the Short-Run Dynamics of Commodity Prices," *Rand Journal of Economics*, 25, 1 (1994): 141–159.

Richard, S., and M. Sundaresan. "A Continuous-Time Model of Forward and Futures Prices in a Multigood Economy," *Journal of Financial Economics*, 9 (December 1981): 347–72.

Routledge, B. R., D. J. Seppi, and C. S. Spatt. "Equilibrium Forward Curves for Commodities," Journal of Finance, 55, 3 (2000) 1297–1338.

Quiz (Answers at End of Book)

5.1. Explain what happens when an investor shorts a certain share.

5.2. What is the difference between the forward price and the value of a forward contract?

5.3. Suppose that you enter into a six-month forward contract on a non-dividend-paying stock when the stock price is \$30 and the risk-free interest rate (with continuous compounding) is 12% per annum. What is the forward price?

5.4. A stock index currently stands at 350. The risk-free interest rate is 8% per annum (with continuous compounding) and the dividend yield on the index is 4% per annum. What should the futures price for a four-month contract be?

5.5. Explain carefully why the futures price of gold can be calculated from its spot price and other observable variables whereas the futures price of copper cannot.

5.6. Explain carefully the meaning of the terms *convenience yield* and *cost of carry*. What is the relationship between futures price, spot price, convenience yield, and cost of carry?

5.7. Explain why a foreign currency can be treated as an asset providing a known yield.

Questions and Problems (Answers in Solutions Manual/Study Guide)

5.8. Is the futures price of a stock index greater than or less than the expected future value of the index? Explain your answer.

5.9. A one-year long forward contract on a non-dividend-paying stock is entered into when the stock price is \$40 and the risk-free rate of interest is 10% per annum with continuous compounding.
  a. What are the forward price and the initial value of the forward contract?
  b. Six months later, the price of the stock is \$45 and the risk-free interest rate is still 10%. What are the forward price and the value of the forward contract?

5.10. The risk-free rate of interest is 7% per annum with continuous compounding, and the dividend yield on a stock index is 3.2% per annum. The current value of the index is 150. What is the six-month futures price?

5.11. Assume that the risk-free interest rate is 9% per annum with continuous compounding and that the dividend yield on a stock index varies throughout the year. In February, May, August, and November, dividends are paid at a rate of 5% per annum. In other months, dividends are paid at a rate of 2% per annum. Suppose that the value of the index on July 31, 2004, is 300. What is the futures price for a contract deliverable on December 31, 2004?

5.12. Suppose that the risk-free interest rate is 10% per annum with continuous compounding and that the dividend yield on a stock index is 4% per annum. The index is standing at 400, and the futures price for a contract deliverable in four months is 405. What arbitrage opportunities does this create?

5.13. Estimate the difference between short-term interest rates in Mexico and the United States on February 4, 2004, from the information in Table 5.4.

5.14. The two-month interest rates in Switzerland and the United States are 3% and 8% per annum, respectively, with continuous compounding. The spot price of the Swiss franc is \$0.6500. The futures price for a contract deliverable in two months is \$0.6600. What arbitrage opportunities does this create?

5.15. The current price of silver is \$9 per ounce. The storage costs are \$0.24 per ounce per year payable quarterly in advance. Assuming that interest rates are 10% per annum for all maturities, calculate the futures price of silver for delivery in nine months.

5.16. Suppose that F_1 and F_2 are two futures contracts on the same commodity with times to maturity, t_1 and t_2, where $t_2 > t_1$. Prove that

$$F_2 \leqslant F_1 e^{r(t_2 - t_1)}$$

where r is the interest rate (assumed constant) and there are no storage costs. For the purposes of this problem, assume that a futures contract is the same as a forward contract.

5.17. When a known future cash outflow in a foreign currency is hedged by a company using a forward contract, there is no foreign exchange risk. When it is hedged using futures contracts, the marking-to-market process does leave the company exposed to some risk. Explain the nature of this risk. In particular, consider whether the company is better off using a futures contract or a forward contract when:
a. The value of the foreign currency falls rapidly during the life of the contract.
b. The value of the foreign currency rises rapidly during the life of the contract.
c. The value of the foreign currency first rises and then falls back to its initial value.
d. The value of the foreign currency first falls and then rises back to its initial value.
Assume that the forward price equals the futures price.

5.18. It is sometimes argued that a forward exchange rate is an unbiased predictor of future exchange rates. Under what circumstances is this so?

5.19. Show that the growth rate in an index futures price equals the excess return of the index over the risk-free rate. Assume that the risk-free interest rate and the dividend yield are constant.

5.20. Show that equation (5.3) is true by considering an investment in the asset combined with a short position in a futures contract. Assume that all income from the asset is reinvested in the asset. Use an argument similar to that in footnotes 2 and 4 and explain in detail what an arbitrageur would do if equation (5.3) did not hold.

5.21. Explain carefully what is meant by the expected price of a commodity on a particular future date. Suppose that on February 4, 2004, speculators tended to be short crude oil futures and hedgers tended to be long crude oil futures. What does the Keynes and Hicks argument imply about the expected future price of oil? Use Table 2.2.

5.22. The Value Line index is designed to reflect changes in the value of a portfolio of over 1,600 equally weighted stocks. Prior to March 9, 1988, the change in the index from one day to the next was calculated as the *geometric* average of the changes in the prices of the stocks underlying the index. In these circumstances, does equation (5.8) correctly relate the futures price of the index to its cash price? If not, does the equation overstate or understate the futures price?

Assignment Questions

5.23. A stock is expected to pay a dividend of \$1 per share in two months and in five months. The stock price is \$50, and the risk-free rate of interest is 8% per annum with continuous compounding for all maturities. An investor has just taken a short position in a six-month forward contract on the stock.
   a. What are the forward price and the initial value of the forward contract?
   b. Three months later, the price of the stock is \$48 and the risk-free rate of interest is still 8% per annum. What are the forward price and the value of the short position in the forward contract?

5.24. A bank offers a corporate client a choice between borrowing cash at 11% per annum and borrowing gold at 2% per annum. (If gold is borrowed, interest must be repaid in gold. Thus, 100 ounces borrowed today would require 102 ounces to be repaid in one year.) The risk-free interest rate is 9.25% per annum, and storage costs are 0.5% per annum. Discuss whether the rate of interest on the gold loan is too high or too low in relation to the rate of interest on the cash loan. The interest rates on the two loans are expressed with annual compounding. The risk-free interest rate and storage costs are expressed with continuous compounding.

5.25. A company that is uncertain about the exact date when it will pay or receive a foreign currency may try to negotiate with its bank a forward contract that specifies a period during which delivery can be made. The company wants to reserve the right to choose the exact delivery date to fit in with its own cash flows. Put yourself in the position of the bank. How would you price the product that the company wants?

5.26. A trader owns gold as part of a long-term investment portfolio. The trader can buy gold for \$250 per ounce and sell gold for \$249 per ounce. The trader can borrow funds at 6% per year and invest funds at 5.5% per year. (Both interest rates are expressed with annual compounding.) For what range of one-year forward prices of gold does the trader have no arbitrage opportunities? Assume there is no bid–offer spread for forward prices.

5.27. A company enters into a forward contract with a bank to sell a foreign currency for K_1 at time T_1. The exchange rate at time T_1 proves to be S_1 ($> K_1$). The company asks the bank if it can roll the contract forward until time T_2 ($> T_1$) rather than settle at time T_1. The bank agrees to a new delivery price, K_2. Explain how K_2 should be calculated.

APPENDIX

Proof That Forward and Futures Prices Are Equal When Interest Rates Are Constant

This appendix demonstrates that forward and futures prices are equal when interest rates are constant. Suppose that a futures contract lasts for n days and that F_i is the futures price at the end of day i $(0 < i < n)$. Define δ as the risk-free rate per day (assumed constant). Consider the following strategy:[9]

1. Take a long futures position of e^{δ} at the end of day 0 (i.e., at the beginning of the contract).
2. Increase long position to $e^{2\delta}$ at the end of day 1.
3. Increase long position to $e^{3\delta}$ at the end of day 2.

And so on.

This strategy is summarized in Table 5.6. By the beginning of day i, the investor has a long position of $e^{\delta i}$. The profit (possibly negative) from the position on day i is

$$(F_i - F_{i-1})e^{\delta i}$$

Assume that the profit is compounded at the risk-free rate until the end of day n. Its value at the end of day n is

$$(F_i - F_{i-1})e^{\delta i}e^{(n-i)\delta} = (F_i - F_{i-1})e^{n\delta}$$

The value at the end of day n of the entire investment strategy is therefore

$$\sum_{i=1}^{n}(F_i - F_{i-1})e^{n\delta}$$

This is

$$[(F_n - F_{n-1}) + (F_{n-1} - F_{n-2}) + \cdots + (F_1 - F_0)]e^{n\delta} = (F_n - F_0)e^{n\delta}$$

Because F_n is the same as the terminal asset spot price, S_T, the terminal value of the

Table 5.6 The investment strategy to show that futures and forward prices are equal

Day	0	1	2	⋯	$n-1$	n
Futures price	F_0	F_1	F_2	⋯	F_{n-1}	F_n
Futures position	e^{δ}	$e^{2\delta}$	$e^{3\delta}$	⋯	$e^{n\delta}$	0
Gain/loss	0	$(F_1 - F_0)e^{\delta}$	$(F_2 - F_1)e^{2\delta}$	⋯	⋯	$(F_n - F_{n-1})e^{n\delta}$
Gain/loss compounded to day n	0	$(F_1 - F_0)e^{n\delta}$	$(F_2 - F_1)e^{n\delta}$	⋯	⋯	$(F_n - F_{n-1})e^{n\delta}$

[9] This strategy was proposed by J. C. Cox, J. E. Ingersoll, and S. A. Ross, "The Relation between Forward Prices and Futures Prices," *Journal of Financial Economics*, 9 (December 1981): 321–46.

investment strategy can be written

$$(S_T - F_0)e^{n\delta}$$

An investment of F_0 in a risk-free bond combined with the strategy involving futures just given yields

$$F_0 e^{n\delta} + (S_T - F_0)e^{n\delta} = S_T e^{n\delta}$$

at time T. No investment is required for all the long futures positions described. It follows that an amount F_0 can be invested to give an amount $S_T e^{n\delta}$ at time T.

Suppose next that the forward price at the end of day 0 is G_0. Investing G_0 in a riskless bond and taking a long forward position of $e^{n\delta}$ forward contracts also guarantees an amount $S_T e^{n\delta}$ at time T. Thus, there are two investment strategies—one requiring an initial outlay of F_0 and the other requiring an initial outlay of G_0—both of which yield $S_T e^{n\delta}$ at time T. It follows that, in the absence of arbitrage opportunities,

$$F_0 = G_0$$

In other words, the futures price and the forward price are identical. Note that in this proof there is nothing special about the time period of one day. The futures price based on a contract with weekly settlements is also the same as the forward price when corresponding assumptions are made.

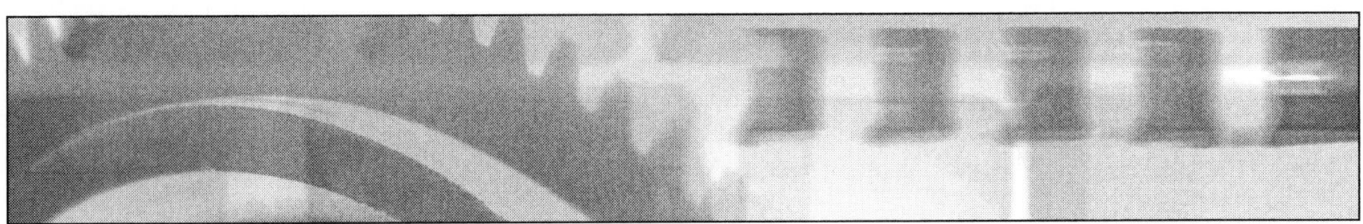

CHAPTER

Interest Rate Futures

So far we have covered futures contracts on commodities, stock indices, and foreign currencies. We have seen how they work, how they are used for hedging, and how futures prices are set. We now move on to consider interest rate futures.

In this chapter we explain the popular Treasury bond futures contracts and Eurodollar futures contracts that trade in the United States. Many of the other interest rate futures contracts throughout the world have been modeled on these contracts. We also discuss the duration measure and show how it can be used to measure the sensitivity of a portfolio to interest rates. We show how interest rate futures contracts, when used in conjunction with the duration measure, can be used to hedge a company's exposure to interest rate movements.

6.1 DAY COUNT CONVENTIONS

As a preliminary to the material in this chapter we consider day count conventions. The day count defines the way in which interest accrues over time. Generally, we know the interest earned over some reference period (e.g., the time between coupon payments), and we are interested in calculating the interest earned over some other period.

The day count convention is usually expressed as X/Y. When we are calculating the interest earned between two dates, X defines the way in which the number of days between the two dates is calculated, and Y defines the way in which the total number of days in the reference period is measured. The interest earned between the two dates is

$$\frac{\text{Number of days between dates}}{\text{Number of days in reference period}} \times \text{Interest earned in reference period}$$

Three day count conventions that are commonly used in the United States are:

1. Actual/actual (in period)
2. 30/360
3. Actual/360

Actual/actual (in period) is used for U.S. Treasury bonds, 30/360 is used for U.S.

Business Snapshot 6.1 Day counts can be deceptive

Between February 28, 2005, and March 1, 2005, you have a choice between owning a U.S. government bond paying a 10% coupon and a U.S. corporate bond paying a 10% coupon. Which would you prefer?

It sounds as though there should not be much difference. In fact, you should have a marked preference for the corporate bond. Under the 30/360 day count convention used for corporate bonds there are three days between February 28, 2005, and March 1, 2005. Under the actual/actual (in period) day count convention used for government bonds, there is only one day. You would earn approximately three times as much interest by holding the corporate bond!

corporate and municipal bonds, and actual/360 is used for U.S. Treasury bills and other money market instruments.

The use of actual/actual (in period) for Treasury bonds indicates that the interest earned between two dates is based on the ratio of the actual days elapsed to the actual number of days in the period between coupon payments. Suppose that the bond principal is \$100, coupon payment dates are March 1 and September 1, the coupon rate is 8%, and we wish to calculate the interest earned between March 1 and July 3. The reference period is from March 1 to September 1. There are 184 (actual) days in this period, and interest of \$4 is earned during the period. There are 124 (actual) days between March 1 and July 3. The interest earned between March 1 and July 3 is therefore

$$\frac{124}{184} \times 4 = 2.6957$$

The use of 30/360 for corporate and municipal bonds indicates that we assume 30 days per month and 360 days per year when carrying out calculations. With 30/360, the total number of days between March 1 and September 1 is 180. The total number of days between March 1 and July 3 is $(4 \times 30) + 2 = 122$. In a corporate bond with the same terms as the Treasury bond just considered, the interest earned between March 1 and July 3 would therefore be

$$\frac{122}{180} \times 4 = 2.7111$$

As shown in Business Snapshot 6.1, sometimes the 30/360 day count convention has surprising consequences.

The use of actual/360 for a money market instrument indicates that the reference period is 360 days. The interest earned during part of a year is calculated by dividing the actual number of elapsed days by 360 and multiplying by the rate. The interest earned in 90 days is therefore exactly one-fourth of the quoted rate. Note that the interest earned in a whole year of 365 days is 365/360 times the quoted rate.

6.2 QUOTATIONS FOR TREASURY BONDS AND BILLS

The price quoted for an interest-bearing instrument is often not the same as the cash price you would have to pay if you purchased it. We illustrate this by considering the way in which prices are quoted for Treasury bonds and Treasury bills in the United States.

Treasury Bonds

Treasury bond prices in the United States are quoted in dollars and thirty-seconds of a dollar. The quoted price is for a bond with a face value of \$100. Thus, a quote of 90-05 indicates that the quoted price for a bond with a face value of \$100,000 is \$90,156.25.

The quoted price, which traders refer to as the *clean price*, is not the same as the cash price, which traders refer to as the *dirty price*. In general, we have

$$\text{Cash price} = \text{Quoted price} + \text{Accrued interest since last coupon date}$$

To illustrate this formula, suppose that it is March 5, 2003, and the bond under consideration is an 11% coupon bond maturing on July 10, 2009, with a quoted price of 95-16 or \$95.50. Because coupons are paid semiannually on government bonds (and the final coupon is at maturity), the most recent coupon date is January 10, 2003, and the next coupon date is July 10, 2003. The number of days between January 10, 2003, and March 5, 2003, is 54, whereas the number of days between January 10, 2003, and July 10, 2003, is 181. On a bond with \$100 face value, the coupon payment is \$5.50 on January 10 and July 10. The accrued interest on March 5, 2003, is the share of the July 10 coupon accruing to the bondholder on March 5, 2003. Because actual/actual in period is used for Treasury bonds (see Section 6.1), this is

$$\frac{54}{181} \times \$5.5 = \$1.64$$

The cash price per \$100 face value for the July 10, 2001, bond is therefore

$$\$95.5 + \$1.64 = \$97.14$$

Thus, the cash price of a \$100,000 bond is \$97,140.

Treasury Bills

As mentioned in Section 6.1, the actual/360 day count convention is used for Treasury bills in the United States. Price quotes are for a Treasury bill with a face value of \$100. There is a difference between the cash price and quoted price for a Treasury bill. If Y is the cash price of a Treasury bill that has a face value of \$100 and n days to maturity, the quoted price is

$$\frac{360}{n}(100 - Y)$$

This is referred to as the *discount rate*. It is the annualized dollar return provided by the Treasury bill expressed as a percentage of the face value. If for a 91-day Treasury bill the cash price, Y, were 98, the quoted price would be $(360/91) \times (100 - 98) = 7.91$.

The discount rate or quoted price is not the same as the rate of return earned on the Treasury bill. The latter is calculated as the dollar return divided by the cost. In the example just given the rate of return would be 2/98, or 2.04% per 91 days. This amounts to

$$\frac{2}{98} \times \frac{365}{91} = 0.08186$$

or 8.186% per annum (actual/365) with compounding every 91 days.

Table 6.1 Interest rate futures quotes from the *Wall Street Journal* on February 5, 2004. (Columns show month, open, high, low, settle, change, lifetime high, lifetime low, and open interest, respectively.)

Interest Rate Futures

Treasury Bonds (CBT)-$100,000; pts 32nds of 100%

Mar	111-25	111-31	109-18	111-17	-3	116-23	101-00	467,134
June	110-09	110-12	109-16	110-03	-3	116-15	104-00	31,215

Est vol 183,502; vol Tue 208,442; open int 499,090, +8,789.

Treasury Notes (CBT)-$100,000; pts 32nds of 100%

Mar	113-29	14-005	113-15	113-22	-4.5	116-10	106-29	1,130,409
June	112-17	112-17	111-29	112-03	-4.5	113-18	107-13	147,892

Est vol 489,439; vol Tue 623,701; open int 1,278,301, -9,178.

5 Yr. Treasury Notes (CBT)-$100,000; pts 32nds of 100%

Mar	12-215	112-24	12-125	112-17	-3.5	19-215	09-145	882,174

Est vol 219,841; vol Tue 268,683; open int 948,759, +6,645.

2 Yr. Treasury Notes (CBT)-$200,000; pts 32nds of 100%

Mar	07-132	07-142	07-102	07-127	-.2	07-205	106-02	164,711

Est vol 15,846; vol Tue 11,507; open int 166,044, +168.

30 Day Federal Funds (CBT)-$5,000,000; 100 - daily avg.

Feb	99.000	99.000	98.995	99.000	...	99.890	98.700	64,359
Mar	99.00	99.00	98.99	98.99	...	99.16	98.74	48,219
Apr	99.00	99.00	98.99	98.99	...	99.17	89.96	71,817
May	98.96	98.96	98.95	98.96	...	99.79	98.40	37,989
June	98.94	98.95	98.94	98.95	...	98.97	98.38	27,460
July	98.87	98.87	98.86	98.87	...	98.93	98.20	26,248
Aug	98.77	98.78	98.77	98.78	.01	98.85	98.24	4,137
Sept	98.70	98.71	98.68	98.71	-.01	98.79	98.22	5,260

Est vol 15,789; vol Tue 16,390; open int 286,642, -49,041.

10 Yr. Interest Rate Swaps (CBT)-$100,000; pts 32nds of 100%

Mar	111-15	111-19	111-03	111-10	-6	113-05	107-20	39,568

Est vol 1,060; vol Tue 968; open int 39,569, +269.

10 Yr. Muni Note Index (CBT)-$1,000 x index

Mar	103-13	103-21	103-08	103-15	1	105-04	99-21	2,249

Est vol 269; vol Tue 194; open int 2,249, +6.
Index: Close 104-15; Yield 4.44.

	OPEN	HIGH	LOW	SETTLE	CHG	YIELD	CHG	OPEN INT
1 Month Libor (CME)-$3,000,000; pts of 100%								
Feb	98.90	98.90	98.89	98.89	...	1.11	...	29,195
Mar	98.89	98.89	98.89	98.89	...	1.11	...	11,060
Apr	98.86	98.86	98.86	98.86	...	1.14	...	8,279
May	98.83	98.83	98.82	98.82	...	1.18	...	2,550
Oct	98.44	98.44	98.43	98.44	...	1.56	...	51,960
Est vol 1,215; vol Tue 2,781; open int 171,119, +1,172.								
Eurodollar (CME)-$1,000,000; pts of 100%								
Feb	98.86	98.86	98.86	98.86	...	1.14	...	32,246
Mar	98.84	98.84	98.83	98.84	...	1.16	...	827,925
Apr	98.80	98.80	98.79	98.80	...	1.20	...	35,531
May	98.75	98.75	98.74	98.74	...	1.26	...	14,543
June	98.69	98.69	98.66	98.68	...	1.32	...	838,794
July	98.58	98.58	98.57	98.58	...	1.42	...	2,150
Sept	98.41	98.43	98.38	98.41	...	1.59	...	794,586
Dec	98.04	98.06	98.00	98.03	...	1.97	...	600,750
Mr05	97.65	97.67	97.58	97.63	...	2.37	...	419,479
June	97.24	97.26	97.19	97.23	...	2.77	...	330,839
Sept	96.88	96.90	96.82	96.86	...	3.14	...	260,971
Dec	96.56	96.59	96.51	96.55	...	3.45	...	191,396
Mr06	96.32	96.33	96.25	96.30	-.01	3.70	.01	172,526
June	96.10	96.11	96.04	96.07	-.01	3.93	.01	128,625
Sept	95.91	95.91	95.83	95.86	-.01	4.14	.01	119,346
Dec	95.69	95.71	95.63	95.66	-.02	4.34	.02	105,045
Mr07	95.47	95.53	95.46	95.49	-.02	4.51	.02	75,659
June	95.34	95.38	95.30	95.33	-.03	4.67	.03	66,675
Sept	95.19	95.23	95.16	95.18	-.03	4.82	.03	73,288
Dec	95.05	95.09	95.02	95.04	-.03	4.96	.03	59,439
Mr08	94.92	94.97	94.90	94.92	-.03	5.08	.03	46,996
June	94.80	94.86	94.79	94.81	-.03	5.19	.03	50,074
Sept	94.71	94.75	94.68	94.71	-.03	5.29	.03	34,029
Dec	94.65	94.65	94.57	94.60	-.03	5.40	.03	26,470
Ju09	94.42	94.47	94.41	94.43	-.03	5.57	.03	9,247
Sept	94.34	94.40	94.34	94.35	-.03	5.65	.03	8,400
Dec	94.26	94.31	94.25	94.27	-.03	5.73	.03	4,633
Mr10	94.19	94.19	94.18	94.19	-.04	5.81	.04	8,192
June	94.12	94.12	94.11	94.12	-.04	5.88	.04	6,761
Sept	94.05	94.05	94.04	94.05	-.04	5.95	.04	4,683
Est vol 780,408; vol Tue 779,833; open int 5,375,781, +11,885.								

	OPEN	HIGH	LOW	SETTLE	CHG	LIFETIME HIGH	LIFETIME LOW	OPEN INT
Euroyen (CME)-¥100,000,000; pts of 100%								
Mar	99.91	99.91	99.91	99.91	...	99.92	99.14	11,530
June	99.91	99.91	99.91	99.91	...	99.92	99.41	9,096
Sept	99.89	99.89	99.89	99.89	...	99.90	99.35	12,320
Mr05	99.82	99.82	99.82	99.82	...	99.84	99.27	4,726
Est vol 431; vol Tue 25; open int 49,808, +775.								
Short Sterling (LIFFE)-£500,000; pts of 100%								
Feb	95.82	95.82	95.82	95.82	...	95.89	95.80	1,913
Mar	95.76	95.77	95.75	95.76	...	96.80	93.01	188,159
June	95.57	95.58	95.54	95.56	...	96.71	93.04	201,882
Sept	95.37	95.40	95.34	95.36	...	96.59	93.35	153,843
Dec	95.21	95.24	95.19	95.20	...	96.48	93.25	139,045
Mr05	95.10	95.13	95.06	95.08	...	96.38	93.29	83,684
June	95.01	95.04	94.98	94.99	...	96.30	93.29	72,583
Sept	94.95	94.97	94.91	94.92	...	96.23	94.06	70,992
Dec	94.88	94.91	94.85	94.86	...	96.15	94.06	35,228
Mr06	94.82	94.84	94.80	94.82	.02	96.10	94.05	27,988
June	94.77	94.81	94.75	94.77	.02	95.97	94.04	28,423
Sept	94.74	94.78	94.72	94.74	.02	95.75	94.32	15,264
Dec	94.74	94.75	94.71	94.72	.02	95.83	94.25	6,356
Mr07	94.69	94.69	94.69	94.71	.02	95.82	94.33	527
June	94.71	94.71	94.71	94.70	.02	95.73	94.66	639
Est vol 142,996; vol Tue 184,402; open int 1,028,552, -284.								
Long Gilt (LIFFE)-£100,000; pts of 100%								
Mar	107.95	108.41	107.95	108.12	.26	109.73	105.39	159,338
Est vol 50,453; vol Tue 36,817; open int 159,339, -153.								
3 Month Euribor (LIFFE)-€1,000,000; pts of 100%								
Feb	97.92	97.93	97.92	97.93	.01	97.96	97.77	13,595
Mar	97.94	97.95	97.93	97.94	.01	98.29	93.83	562,698
June	97.91	97.92	97.89	97.90	.02	98.21	93.79	511,614
Sept	97.77	97.78	97.75	97.76	.03	98.08	93.73	428,741
Dec	97.55	97.57	97.53	97.55	.04	97.91	93.64	436,055
Mr05	97.32	97.34	97.30	97.31	.03	97.77	94.07	301,516
June	97.09	97.10	97.06	97.07	.03	97.60	94.29	197,768
Sept	96.88	96.89	96.84	96.86	.02	97.44	94.29	119,907
Dec	96.68	96.69	96.65	96.66	.02	97.28	94.41	95,512
Mr06	96.51	96.53	96.48	96.50	.02	97.14	94.40	41,992
June	96.35	96.36	96.32	96.33	.02	96.96	94.66	37,197
Sept	96.20	96.21	96.17	96.18	.02	96.81	94.58	22,947
Dec	96.03	96.04	96.01	96.02	.02	96.60	94.62	11,645
Mr07	95.93	95.93	95.93	95.90	.02	96.48	94.57	4,473
June	95.79	95.79	95.79	95.80	.02	96.29	94.57	2,490
Sept	95.69	95.69	95.69	95.70	.02	96.21	95.26	2,204
Est vol 547,848; vol Tue 533,760; open int 2,791,222, +50,205.								
3 Month Euroswiss (LIFFE)-CHF 1,000,000; pts of 100%								
Mar	99.73	99.74	99.72	99.73	...	99.75	96.32	95,989
June	99.61	99.61	99.56	99.57	-.02	99.63	96.98	81,441
Sept	99.37	99.39	99.35	99.36	-.01	99.41	97.60	41,632
Dec	99.14	99.14	99.11	99.12	-.01	99.17	98.00	32,364
Mr05	98.87	98.87	98.86	98.87	-.01	98.93	97.90	7,335
June	98.65	98.65	98.61	98.62	-.01	98.68	97.74	9,694
Sept	98.43	98.44	98.36	98.41	-.02	98.47	97.75	4,732
Dec	98.21	98.22	98.14	98.19	-.01	98.24	97.92	2,745
Est vol 14,180; vol Tue 21,649; open int 275,932, -1,537.								
Canadian Bankers Acceptance (ME)-CAD 1,000,000								
Mar	97.71	97.71	97.67	97.68	-0.02	97.78	93.77	70,087
June	97.78	97.78	97.72	97.75	-0.03	97.88	95.34	97,819
Sept	97.71	97.71	97.65	97.68	-0.03	97.81	94.22	35,605
Dec	97.51	97.51	97.45	97.47	-0.04	97.62	94.10	17,196
Mr05	97.21	97.21	97.16	97.18	-0.04	97.33	94.45	9,163
Sept	96.53	96.53	96.53	96.51	-0.04	96.64	95.21	1,200
Est vol 24,925; vol Tue 21,162; open int 238,828, +585.								
10 Yr. Canadian Govt. Bonds (ME)-CAD 100,000								
Mar	110.58	110.64	110.07	110.39	-0.22	111.61	106.90	90,003
Est vol 6,222; vol Tue 12,898; open int 90,003, +6,036.								

3 Yr. Commonwealth T-Bonds (SFE)-AUD 100,000

Mar	94.38	94.48	94.37	94.47	0.09	94.56	93.96	609,295

Est vol 130,882; vol Tue 72,788; open int 609,295, +83,322.

Euroyen (SGX)-¥100,000,000; pts of 100%

Mar	99.91	99.91	99.91	99.91	...	99.92	98.19	60,509
June	99.91	99.91	99.91	99.92	0.01	99.92	99.45	71,194
Sept	99.89	99.90	99.89	99.90	0.01	99.90	99.34	43,155
Dec	99.87	99.87	99.87	99.87	...	99.87	99.22	45,234
Mr05	99.81	99.82	99.81	99.82	0.01	99.85	99.18	23,103
June	99.78	99.78	99.78	99.78	0.01	99.85	99.10	20,948
Sept	99.70	99.71	99.70	99.71	0.02	99.74	98.95	14,023
Dec	99.61	99.62	99.61	99.61	0.01	99.77	98.80	3,635
Mr06	99.50	99.50	99.50	99.50	0.01	99.76	98.84	3,405
June	99.42	99.42	99.42	99.43	0.02	99.75	98.55	1,380
Dec	99.23	99.23	99.23	99.23	0.02	99.71	98.35	1,851

Est vol 3,160; vol Tue 5,292; open int 295,306, −1,880.

5 Yr. Euro-BOBL (EUREX)-€100,000; pts of 100%

Mar	111.59	111.66	111.47	111.56	...	112.06	108.71	743,330
June	110.79	110.80	110.71	110.75	...	111.16	109.50	7,545

vol Wed 582,579; open int 750,875, +21,654.

10 Yr. Euro-BUND (EUREX)-€100,000; pts of 100%

Mar	114.30	114.45	114.15	114.26	−0.02	117.76	110.73	945,187
June	113.31	113.43	113.26	113.28	−0.01	114.11	110.62	27,345

vol Wed 841,211; open int 972,534, −23,916.

2 Yr. Euro-SCHATZ (EUREX)-€100,000; pts of 100%

Mar	106.18	106.20	106.13	106.17	...	106.35	104.95	683,537
June	105.80	105.84	105.79	105.80	...	105.88	105.21	28,066

vol Wed 437,442; open int 711,603, +22,620.

Source: Reprinted by permission of Dow Jones, Inc., via Copyright Clearance Center, Inc.

6.3 TREASURY BOND FUTURES

Table 6.1 shows interest rate futures quotes as they appeared in the *Wall Street Journal* on February 5, 2004. One of the most popular long-term interest rate futures contracts is the Treasury bond futures contract traded on the Chicago Board of Trade (CBOT). In this contract, any government bond that has more than 15 years to maturity on the first day of the delivery month and is not callable within 15 years from that day can be delivered. As will be explained later in this section, the CBOT has developed a procedure for adjusting the price received by the party with the short position according to the particular bond delivered.

The Treasury note and five-year Treasury note futures contract in the United States are also very popular. In the Treasury note futures, any government bond (or note) with a maturity between $6\frac{1}{2}$ and 10 years can be delivered. In the five-year Treasury note futures contract, any of the four most recently auctioned Treasury notes can be delivered.

The remaining discussion in this section focuses on CBOT Treasury bond futures. The Treasury note futures traded in the United States and many other futures contracts in the rest of the world are designed in a similar way to CBOT Treasury bond futures so that many of the points we will make are applicable to these contracts as well.

Quotes

Treasury bond futures prices are quoted in the same way as the Treasury bond prices themselves (see Section 6.2). Table 6.1 shows that the settlement price on February 4, 2004, for the June 2004 contract was 110-03, or $110\frac{3}{32}$. One contract involves the delivery of $100,000 face value of the bond. Thus, a $1 change in the quoted futures price would lead to a $1,000 change in the value of the futures contract. Delivery can take place at any time during the delivery month.

Conversion Factors

As mentioned, the Treasury bond futures contract allows the party with the short position to choose to deliver any bond that has a maturity of more than 15 years and that is not callable within 15 years. When a particular bond is delivered, a parameter known as its *conversion factor* defines the price received by the party with the short position. The quoted price applicable to the delivery is the product of the conversion factor and the quoted futures price. Taking accrued interest into account, as described in Section 6.2, the cash received for each \$100 face value of bond delivered is

$$(\text{Quoted futures price} \times \text{Conversion factor}) + \text{Accrued interest}$$

Each contract is for the delivery of \$100,000 face value of bonds. Suppose the quoted futures price is 90-00, the conversion factor for the bond delivered is 1.3800, and the accrued interest on this bond at the time of delivery is \$3 per \$100 face value. The cash received by the party with the short position (and paid by the party with the long position) is then

$$(1.3800 \times 90.00) + 3.00 = \$127.20$$

per \$100 face value. A party with the short position in one contract would deliver bonds with face value of \$100,000 and receive \$127,200.

The conversion factor for a bond is equal to the quoted price the bond would have per dollar of principal on the first day of the delivery month on the assumption that the interest rate for all maturities equals 6% per annum (with semiannual compounding). The bond maturity and the times to the coupon payment dates are rounded down to the nearest three months for the purposes of the calculation. The practice enables the CBOT to produce comprehensive tables. If, after rounding, the bond lasts for an exact number of six month periods, the first coupon is assumed to be paid in six months. If, after rounding, the bond does not last for an exact number of six-month periods (i.e., there is an extra three months), the first coupon is assumed to be paid after three months and accrued interest is subtracted.

As a first example of these rules, consider a 10% coupon bond with 20 years and two months to maturity. For the purposes of calculating the conversion factor, the bond is assumed to have exactly 20 years to maturity. The first coupon payment is assumed to be made after six months. Coupon payments are then assumed to be made at six-month intervals until the end of the 20 years when the principal payment is made. Assume that the face value is \$100. When the discount rate is 6% per annum with semiannual compounding (or 3% per six months), the value of the bond is

$$\sum_{i=1}^{40} \frac{5}{1.03^i} + \frac{100}{1.03^{40}} = \$146.23$$

Dividing by the face value gives a credit conversion factor of 1.4623.

As a second example of the rules, consider an 8% coupon bond with 18 years and 4 months to maturity. For the purposes of calculating the conversion factor, the bond is assumed to have exactly 18 years and 3 months to maturity. Discounting all the payments back to a point in time three months from today at 6% per annum (compounded semiannually) gives a value of

$$4 + \sum_{i=1}^{36} \frac{4}{1.03^i} + \frac{100}{1.03^{36}} = \$125.83$$

The interest rate for a three-month period is $\sqrt{1.03} - 1$ or 1.4889%. Hence, discounting back to the present gives the bond's value as $125.83/1.014889 = \$123.99$. Subtracting the accrued interest of 2.0, this becomes \$121.99. The conversion factor is therefore 1.2199.

Cheapest-to-Deliver Bond

At any given time during the delivery month, there are many bonds that can be delivered in the CBOT Treasury bond futures contract. These vary widely as far as coupon and maturity are concerned. The party with the short position can choose which of the available bonds is "cheapest" to deliver. Because the party with the short position receives

$$(\text{Quoted futures price} \times \text{Conversion factor}) + \text{Accrued interest}$$

and the cost of purchasing a bond is

$$\text{Quoted bond price} + \text{Accrued interest}$$

the cheapest-to-deliver bond is the one for which

$$\text{Quoted bond price} - (\text{Quoted futures price} \times \text{Conversion factor})$$

is least. Once the party with the short position has decided to deliver, it can determine the cheapest-to-deliver bond by examining each of the bonds in turn.

Example

The party with the short position has decided to deliver and is trying to choose between the three bonds in Table 6.2. Assume the current quoted futures price is 93-08, or 93.25.

Table 6.2 Deliverable bonds in the Example

Bond	*Quoted bond price ($)*	*Conversion factor*
1	99.50	1.0382
2	143.50	1.5188
3	119.75	1.2615

The cost of delivering each of the bonds is as follows:

Bond 1: $99.50 - (93.25 \times 1.0382) = \$2.69$

Bond 2: $143.50 - (93.25 \times 1.5188) = \$1.87$

Bond 3: $119.75 - (93.25 \times 1.2615) = \$2.12$

The cheapest-to-deliver bond is bond 2.

In addition to the cheapest-to-deliver bond option, the party with a short position has an option known as the wild card play. This is described in Business Snapshot 6.2.

A number of factors determine the cheapest-to-deliver bond. When bond yields are in excess of 6%, the conversion factor system tends to favor the delivery of low-coupon long-maturity bonds. When yields are less than 6%, the system tends to favor the delivery of high-coupon short-maturity bonds. Also, when the yield curve is upward sloping, there is a tendency for bonds with a long time to maturity to be favored, whereas when it is downward sloping, there is a tendency for bonds with a short time to maturity to be delivered.

Business Snapshot 6.2 The wild card play

Trading in the CBOT Treasury bond futures contract ceases at 2:00 p.m. Chicago time. However, Treasury bonds themselves continue trading in the spot market until 4:00 p.m. Furthermore, a trader with a short futures position has until 8:00 p.m. to issue to the clearinghouse a notice of intention to deliver. If the notice is issued, the invoice price is calculated on the basis of the settlement price that day. This is the price at which trading was conducted just before the closing bell at 2:00 p.m.

This practice gives rise to an option known as the *wild card play*. If bond prices decline after 2:00 p.m. on the first day of the delivery month, the party with the short position can issue a notice of intention to deliver at, say, 3:45 p.m. and proceed to buy cheapest-to-deliver bonds for delivery at the 2:00 p.m. futures price. If the bond price does not decline, the party with the short position keeps the position open and waits until the next day when the same strategy can be used.

As with the other options open to the party with the short position, the wild card play is not free. Its value is reflected in the futures price, which is lower than it would be without the option.

Determining the Futures Price

An exact theoretical futures price for the Treasury bond contract is difficult to determine because the short party's options concerned with the timing of delivery and choice of the bond that is delivered cannot easily be valued. However, if we assume that both the cheapest-to-deliver bond and the delivery date are known, the Treasury bond futures contract is a futures contract on a security providing the holder with known income.[1] Equation (5.2) then shows that the futures price, F_0, is related to the spot price, S_0, by

$$F_0 = (S_0 - I)e^{rT} \tag{6.1}$$

where I is the present value of the coupons during the life of the futures contract, T is the time until the futures contract matures, and r is the risk-free interest rate applicable to a time period of length T.

Example

Suppose that, in a Treasury bond futures contract, it is known that the cheapest-to-deliver bond will be a 12% coupon bond with a conversion factor of 1.4000. Suppose also that it is known that delivery will take place in 270 days. Coupons are payable semiannually on the bond. As illustrated in Figure 6.1, the last coupon date was 60 days ago, the next coupon date is in 122 days, and the coupon date thereafter is in 305 days. The term structure is flat, and the rate of interest (with continuous compounding) is 10% per annum. Assume that the current quoted bond price is \$120. The cash price of the bond is obtained by adding to this quoted price the proportion of the next coupon payment that accrues to the

[1] In practice, for the purposes of determining the cheapest-to-deliver in this calculation, analysts usually assume that zero rates at the maturity of the futures contract will equal today's forward rates.

Figure 6.1 Time chart for Example

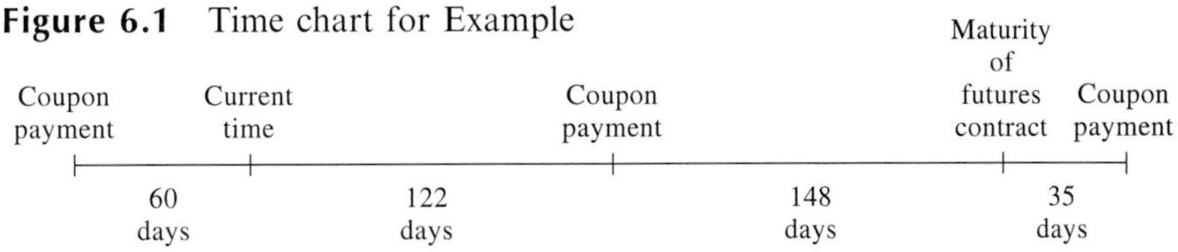

holder. The cash price is therefore

$$120 + \frac{60}{60 + 122} \times 6 = 121.978$$

A coupon of \$6 will be received after 122 days (= 0.3342 year). The present value of this is

$$6e^{-0.1 \times 0.3342} = 5.803$$

The futures contract lasts for 270 days (0.7397 year). The cash futures price if the contract were written on the 12% bond would therefore be

$$(121.978 - 5.803)e^{0.1 \times 0.7397} = 125.094$$

At delivery there are 148 days of accrued interest. The quoted futures price if the contract were written on the 12% bond is calculated by subtracting the accrued interest

$$125.094 - 6 \times \frac{148}{148 + 35} = 120.242$$

From the definition of the conversion factor, 1.4000 standard bonds are considered equivalent to each 12% bond. The quoted futures price should therefore be

$$\frac{120.242}{1.4000} = 85.887$$

6.4 EURODOLLAR FUTURES

The most popular interest rate futures contract in the United States is the three-month Eurodollar futures contract traded on the Chicago Mercantile Exchange (CME). A Eurodollar is a dollar deposited in a U.S. or foreign bank outside the United States. The Eurodollar interest rate is the rate of interest earned on Eurodollars deposited by one bank with another bank. It is essentially the same as the London Interbank Offer Rate (LIBOR) introduced in Chapter 4.

Three-month Eurodollar futures contracts are futures contracts on the three-month Eurodollar interest rate. They allow an investor to lock in an interest rate on \$1 million for a future three-month period. The contracts have maturities in March, June, September, and December for up to 10 years into the future. This means that in 2004 an investor can use Eurodollar futures to lock in an interest rate for three-month periods that are as far into the future as 2014. Short-maturity contracts trade for months other than March, June, September, and December. For example, we see from Table 6.1 that Eurodollar futures with maturities in February, April, May, and July

2004 trade on February 4, 2004. However, these have relatively low open interest. If Q is the quoted price for a Eurodollar futures contract, the exchange defines the value of one contract as

$$10{,}000[100 - 0.25(100 - Q)] \qquad \textbf{(6.2)}$$

Thus, the settlement price of 98.84 for the March 2004 contract in Table 6.1 corresponds to a contract price of

$$10{,}000[100 - 0.25(100 - 98.84)] = \$997{,}100$$

A change of 0.01 (referred to as one basis point) in a Eurodollar futures quote corresponds to a contract price change of \$25. For example, if the March 2004 futures price changed from 98.84 to 98.85, then the contract price would change to

$$10{,}000[100 - 0.25(100 - 98.85)] = \$997{,}125$$

Investors with long positions would gain \$25 and investors with short positions would lose \$25. Similarly, if the futures price changed from 98.84 to 98.83, investors with short positions would gain \$25 and investors with long positions would lose \$25. Note that the contract price moves in the opposite direction to interest rates. If you think interest rates will rise you should take a short Eurodollar futures position; if you think interest rates will fall you should take a long Eurodollar futures position.

When the third Wednesday of the delivery month is reached the contract is settled in cash. The final marking to market sets Q equal to $100 - R$, where R is the actual three-month Eurodollar interest rate on that day, expressed with quarterly compounding and an actual/360 day count convention. Thus, if the three-month Eurodollar interest rate on the third Wednesday of the delivery month is 3%, then the final marking to market is 97 and the final contract price, given by equation (6.2), is

$$10{,}000[100 - 0.25(100 - 97)] = \$992{,}500$$

If Q is a Eurodollar futures quote, $(100 - Q)\%$ is the Eurodollar futures interest rate for a three-month period beginning on the third Wednesday of the delivery month. The settlement price for the March 2004 contract in Table 6.1 is 98.84. This indicates that on February 4, 2004, the futures interest rate for the three-month period beginning Wednesday March 17, 2004, was $100 - 98.84 = 1.16\%$. This is expressed with quarterly compounding and an actual/360 day count convention. We can see that the interest rate term structure in the United States was upward sloping on February 4, 2004. The futures rate for a three-month period beginning March 21, 2007, was 4.51% and for a three-month period beginning March 17, 2010, it was 5.81%.

Other contracts similar to the CME Eurodollar futures contracts trade on interest rates in other countries. As indicated in Table 6.1, the CME trades Euroyen contracts. The London International Financial Futures and Options Exchange trades three-month Euribor contracts (i.e., contracts on the three-month LIBOR rate for the euro) and three-month Euroswiss futures.

Forward vs. Futures Interest Rates

Apart from daily settlement, the Eurodollar futures contract is similar to a forward rate agreement where the three-month forward rate is locked in (see Section 4.7 for a discussion of forward rate agreements). For short maturities (up to one year) the Eurodollar futures interest rate can be assumed to be the same as the corresponding forward interest rate. For longer-dated contracts the differences between futures and forward contracts mentioned in Section 5.8 become important.

Analysts make what is known as a *convexity adjustment* to convert Eurodollar futures rates to forward interest rates. One way of doing this is by using the formula

$$\text{Forward rate} = \text{Futures rate} - \tfrac{1}{2}\sigma^2 t_1 t_2 \qquad \textbf{(6.3)}$$

where t_1 is the time to maturity of the futures contract, t_2 is the time to the maturity of the rate underlying the futures contract, and σ is the standard deviation of the change in the short-term interest rate in one year. Both rates are expressed with continuous compounding.[2] A typical value for σ is 1.2% or 0.012.

Example

Consider the situation where $\sigma = 0.012$ and we wish to calculate the forward rate when the eight-year Eurodollar futures price quote is 94. In this case $t_1 = 8$, $t_2 = 8.25$, and the convexity adjustment is

$$\tfrac{1}{2} \times 0.012^2 \times 8 \times 8.25 = 0.00475$$

or 0.475% (47.5 basis points). The futures rate is 6% per annum on an actual/360 basis with quarterly compounding. This is $6 \times 365/360 = 6.083\%$ per annum on an actual/365 basis with quarterly compounding or 6.038% with continuous compounding. The forward rate is, therefore, $6.038 - 0.475 = 5.563\%$ per annum with continuous compounding. Table 6.3 shows how the size of the adjustment increases with the time to maturity.

Table 6.3 Convexity adjustment for the futures rate in Example

Maturity of futures (years)	*Convexity adjustments (basis points)*
2	3.2
4	12.2
6	27.0
8	47.5
10	73.8

The forward rate is less than the futures rate.[3] As can be seen from Table 6.3, the size of the adjustment is roughly proportional to the square of the time to maturity of the futures contract. Thus, the convexity adjustment for the eight-year contract is approximately 16 times that for a two-year contract.

[2] This formula is based on the Ho–Lee interest rate model. See T. S. Y. Ho and S. B. Lee, "Term Structure Movements and Pricing Interest Rate Contingent Claims," *Journal of Finance*, 41 (December 1986), 1011–29.

[3] The reason for this can be seen from the arguments in Section 5.8. The variable underlying the Eurodollar futures contracts is an interest rate and tends to be highly positively correlated to other interest rates.

6.5 DURATION

The *duration* of a bond, as its name implies, is a measure of how long on average the holder of the bond has to wait before receiving cash payments. A zero-coupon bond that matures in n years has a duration of n years. However, a coupon-bearing bond maturing in n years has a duration of less than n years, because the holder receives some of the cash payments prior to year n.

Suppose that a bond provides the holder with cash flows c_i at time t_i $(1 \leqslant i \leqslant n)$. The price, B, and yield, y (continuously compounded), are related by

$$B = \sum_{i=1}^{n} c_i e^{-yt_i} \tag{6.4}$$

The duration, D, of the bond is defined as

$$D = \frac{\sum_{i=1}^{n} t_i c_i e^{-yt_i}}{B} \tag{6.5}$$

This can be written as

$$D = \sum_{i=1}^{n} t_i \left[\frac{c_i e^{-yt_i}}{B} \right]$$

The term in square brackets is the ratio of the present value of the cash flow at time t_i to the bond price. The bond price is the present value of all payments. The duration is therefore a weighted average of the times when payments are made, with the weight applied to time t_i being equal to the proportion of the bond's total present value provided by the cash flow at time t_i. The sum of the weights is 1.0.

From equation (6.4), it is approximately true that

$$\Delta B = -\Delta y \sum_{i=1}^{n} c_i t_i e^{-yt_i} \tag{6.6}$$

where Δy is a small change in y and ΔB is the corresponding small change in B. (Note that there is a negative relationship between B and y. When bond yields increase, bond prices decrease; and when bond yields decrease, bond prices increase.) From equations (6.5) and (6.6), we can derive the key duration relationship

$$\Delta B = -BD\Delta y \tag{6.7}$$

This can be written

$$\frac{\Delta B}{B} = -D\Delta y \tag{6.8}$$

Equation (6.8) is an approximate relationship between percentage changes in a bond price and changes in its yield. It is easy to use and is the reason why duration, which was suggested by Macaulay in 1938, has become such a popular measure.

Consider a three-year 10% coupon bond with a face value of \$100. Suppose that the yield on the bond is 12% per annum with continuous compounding. This means that $y = 0.12$. Coupon payments of \$5 are made every six months. Table 6.4 shows the calculations necessary to determine the bond's duration. The present values of the bond's cash flows, using the yield as the discount rate, are shown in column 3. (For

Table 6.4 Calculation of duration

Time (years)	*Cash flow ($)*	*Present value*	*Weight*	*Time × Weight*
0.5	5	4.709	0.050	0.025
1.0	5	4.435	0.047	0.047
1.5	5	4.176	0.044	0.066
2.0	5	3.933	0.042	0.083
2.5	5	3.704	0.039	0.098
3.0	105	73.256	0.778	2.333
Total	130	94.213	1.000	2.653

example, the present value of the first cash flow is $5e^{-0.12\times0.5} = 4.709$.) The sum of the numbers in column 3 gives the bond's price as 94.213. The weights are calculated by dividing the numbers in column 3 by 94.213. The sum of the numbers in column 5 gives the duration as 2.653 years.

Small changes in interest rates are often measured in *basis points*. As mentioned earlier, a basis point is 0.01% per annum. The following example investigates the accuracy of the duration relationship in equation (6.7).

Example

For the bond in Table 6.4, the bond price B is 94.213 and the duration D is 2.653, so that equation (6.7) gives

$$\Delta B = -94.213 \times 2.653\Delta y$$

or

$$\Delta B = -249.95\Delta y$$

When the yield on the bond increases by 10 basis points (= 0.1%), $\Delta y = +0.001$. The duration relationship predicts that $\Delta B = -249.95 \times 0.001 = -0.250$, so that the bond price goes down to $94.213 - 0.250 = 93.963$. How accurate is this? When the bond yield increases by 10 basis points to 12.1%, the bond price is

$$5e^{-0.121\times0.5} + 5e^{-0.121\times1.0} + 5e^{-0.121\times1.5} + 5e^{-0.121\times2.0} + 5e^{-0.121\times2.5} + 105e^{-0.121\times3.0} = 93.963$$

which is (to three decimal places) the same as that predicted by the duration relationship.

Modified Duration

The preceding analysis is based on the assumption that y is expressed with continuous compounding. If y is expressed with annual compounding, it can be shown that the approximate relationship in equation (6.7) becomes

$$\Delta B = -\frac{BD\Delta y}{1+y}$$

More generally, if y is expressed with a compounding frequency of m times per year, then

$$\Delta B = -\frac{BD\Delta y}{1 + y/m}$$

A variable D^* defined by

$$D^* = \frac{D}{1 + y/m}$$

is sometimes referred to as the bond's *modified duration*. It allows the duration relationship to be simplified to

$$\Delta B = -BD^*\Delta y \qquad \textbf{(6.9)}$$

when y is expressed with a compounding frequency of m times per year. The following example investigates the accuracy of the modified duration relationship.

Example

The bond in Table 6.4 has a price of 94.213 and a duration of 2.653. The yield, expressed with semiannual compounding, is 12.3673%. The modified duration, D^*, is given by

$$D^* = \frac{2.653}{1 + 0.123673/2} = 2.499$$

From equation (6.9), we have

$$\Delta B = -94.213 \times 2.4985\Delta y$$

or

$$\Delta B = -235.39\Delta y$$

When the yield (semiannually compounded) increases by 10 basis points ($= 0.1\%$), $\Delta y = +0.001$. The duration relationship predicts that we expect ΔB to be $-235.39 \times 0.001 = -0.235$, so that the bond price to goes down to $94.213 - 0.235 = 93.978$. How accurate is this? When the bond yield (semiannually compounded) increases by 10 basis points to 12.4673% (or to 12.0941% with continuous compounding), an exact calculation similar to that in the previous example shows that the bond price becomes 93.978. This shows that the modified duration calculation gives good accuracy.

Bond Portfolios

The duration, D, of a bond portfolio can be defined as a weighted average of the durations of the individual bonds in the portfolio, with the weights being proportional to the bond prices. Equations (6.7) to (6.9) then apply with B being defined as the value of the bond portfolio. They estimate the change in the value of the bond portfolio for a particular change Δy in the yields of all the bonds.

It is important to realize that, when duration is used for bond portfolios, there is an implicit assumption that the yields of all bonds will change by the same amount. When the bonds have widely differing maturities, this happens only when there is a parallel shift in the zero-coupon yield curve. We should therefore interpret equations (6.7) to (6.9) as providing estimates of the impact on the price of a bond portfolio of a parallel shift, Δy, in the zero curve.

Figure 6.2 Two bond portfolios with the same duration

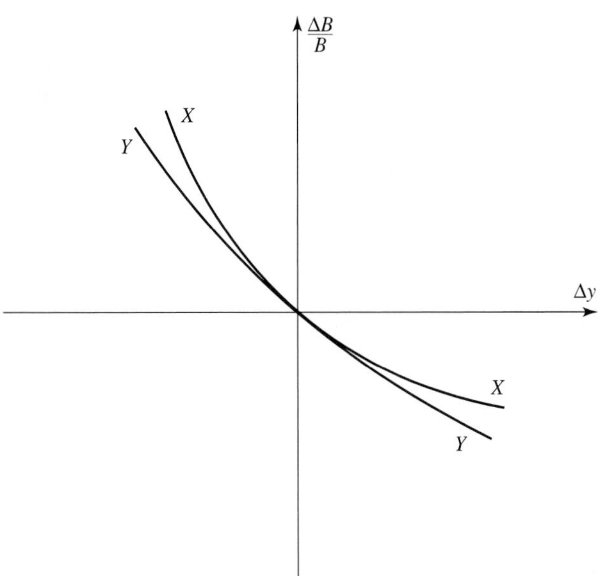

The duration relationship applies only to small changes in yields. This is illustrated in Figure 6.2, which shows the relationship between the percentage change in value and change in yield for two bond portfolios having the same duration. The gradients of the two curves are the same at the origin. This means that both bond portfolios change in value by the same percentage for small yield changes and is consistent with equation (6.8). For large yield changes, the portfolios behave differently. Portfolio X has more curvature in its relationship with yields than portfolio Y. A factor known as *convexity* measures this curvature and can be used to improve the relationship in equation (6.8).

Hedging Portfolios of Assets and Liabilities

Financial institutions frequently attempt to hedge themselves against interest rate risk by ensuring that the average duration of their assets equals the average duration of their liabilities. (The liabilities can be regarded as short positions in bonds.) This strategy is known as *duration matching* or *portfolio immunization*. When implemented it ensures that a small parallel shift in interest rates will have little effect on the value of the portfolio of assets and liabilities. The gain (loss) on the assets should offset the loss (gain) on the liabilities.

Duration matching does not immunize a portfolio against nonparallel shifts in the zero curve. This is a weakness of the approach. In practice, short-term rates are usually more volatile than and are not perfectly correlated with long-term rates. Sometimes it even happens that short- and long-term rates move in opposite directions to each other. Duration matching is therefore only a first step and financial institutions have developed other tools to help them manage their interest rate exposure (see Business Snapshot 6.3).

Business Snapshot 6.3 Asset–liability management by banks

In the 1960s, interest rates were low and not very volatile. Many banks got into the habit of accepting short-term deposits and making long-term loans. In the 1970s, interest rates rose and some of these banks found that they were funding the low-interest long-term loans made in the 1960s with relatively expensive short-term deposits. As a result, there were some spectacular bank failures.

The asset–liability management (ALM) committees of banks now monitor their exposure to interest rates very carefully. Matching the durations of assets and liabilities is a first step, but this does not protect a bank against nonparallel shifts in the yield curve. A popular approach is known as *GAP management*. This involves dividing the zero-coupon yield curve into segments, known as *buckets*. The first bucket might be 0 to 1 month, the second 1 to 3 months, and so on. The ALM committee then investigates the effect on the values of both assets and liabilities of the zero rates corresponding to one bucket changing while those corresponding to all other buckets stay the same.

If there is a mismatch, then corrective action is usually taken. Luckily banks today have many more tools to manage their exposures to interest rates than they had in the 1960s. These tools include swaps, FRAs, bond futures, Eurodollar futures, and other interest rate derivatives.

6.6 DURATION-BASED HEDGING STRATEGIES

Consider the situation where a position in an interest rate dependent asset such as a bond portfolio or a money market security is being hedged using an interest rate futures contract. Define:

F_C: Contract price for the interest rate futures contract

D_F: Duration of the asset underlying the futures contract at the maturity of the futures contract

P: Forward value of the portfolio being hedged at the maturity of the hedge. In practice this is usually assumed to be the same as the portfolio value today.

D_P: Duration of the portfolio at the maturity of the hedge.

If we assume that the change in the yield, Δy, is the same for all maturities, which means that only parallel shifts in the yield curve can occur, it is approximately true that

$$\Delta P = -PD_P\Delta y$$

To a reasonable approximation, it is also true that

$$\Delta F_C = -F_C D_F \Delta y$$

The number of contracts required to hedge against an uncertain Δy is therefore given by

$$N^* = \frac{PD_P}{F_C D_F} \tag{6.10}$$

This is the *duration-based hedge ratio*. It is sometimes also called the *price sensitivity hedge ratio*.[4] Using it has the effect of making the duration of the entire position zero.

When the hedging instrument is a Treasury bond futures contract, the hedger must base D_F on an assumption that one particular bond will be delivered. This means that the hedger must estimate which of the available bonds is likely to be cheapest to deliver at the time the hedge is put in place. If, subsequently, the interest rate environment changes so that it looks as though a different bond will be cheapest to deliver, the hedge has to be adjusted, and its performance may be worse than anticipated.

When hedges are constructed using interest rate futures, it is important to bear in mind that interest rates and futures prices move in opposite directions. When interest rates go up, an interest rate futures price goes down. When interest rates go down, the reverse happens, and the interest rate futures price goes up. Thus, a company in a position to lose money if interest rates drop should hedge by taking a long futures position. Similarly, a company in a position to lose money if interest rates rise should hedge by taking a short futures position.

The hedger tries to choose the futures contract so that the duration of the underlying asset is as close as possible to the duration of the asset being hedged. Eurodollar futures tend to be used for exposures to short-term interest rates, whereas Treasury bond and Treasury note futures contracts are used for exposures to longer-term rates.

Hedging a Bond Portfolio

Suppose it is August 2. A fund manager has \$10 million invested in government bonds and is concerned that interest rates are expected to be highly volatile over the next three months. The fund manager decides to use the December Treasury bond futures contract to hedge the value of the portfolio. The current futures price is 93-02 or 93.0625. Because each contract is for the delivery of \$100,000 face value of bonds, the futures contract price is \$93,062.50.

The duration of the bond portfolio in three months is 6.8 years. The cheapest-to-deliver bond in the Treasury bond contract is expected to be a 20-year 12% per annum coupon bond. The yield on this bond is currently 8.8% per annum, and the duration will be 9.2 years at maturity of the futures contract. This example is summarized in Trading Note 6.1.

The fund manager requires a short position in Treasury bond futures to hedge the bond portfolio. If interest rates go up, a gain will be made on the short futures position, and a loss will be made on the bond portfolio. If interest rates decrease, a loss will be made on the short position, but there will be a gain on the bond portfolio. The number of bond futures contracts that should be shorted can be calculated from equation (6.10) as

$$\frac{10{,}000{,}000 \times 6.80}{93{,}062.50 \times 9.20} = 79.42$$

Rounding to the nearest whole number, the portfolio manager should short 79 contracts.

Suppose that during the period from August 2 to November 2, interest rates decline rapidly and the value of the bond portfolio increases from \$10 million to \$10,450,000. Suppose further that on November 2, the Treasury bond futures price is 98-16. This

[4] For a more detailed discussion of equation (6.10), see R. Rendleman, "Duration-Based Hedging with Treasury Bond Futures," *Journal of Fixed Income*, 9, no. 1 (June 1999): 84–91.

Trading Note 6.1 Hedging a bond portfolio

It is August 2. A fund manager responsible for a \$10 million bond portfolio is concerned that interest rates are expected to be highly volatile over the next three months. The fund manager decides to use Treasury bond futures to hedge the value of the bond portfolio. The quoted price for the December Treasury bond futures contract is 93-02. This means that the contract price is \$93,062.50.

The Strategy

1. Short 79 December Treasury bond futures contracts on August 2.
2. Close out the position on November 2.

The Result

During the period August 2 to November 2, interest rates declined rapidly. The value of the bond portfolio increased from \$10 million to \$10,450,000.

On November 2, the Treasury bond futures price was 98-16. This corresponds to a contract price of \$98,500.00. A loss of 79 × (\$98,500.00 − \$93,062.50) = \$429,562.50 was therefore made on the Treasury bond futures contracts.

Overall, the value of the portfolio manager's position changed by only

\$450,000.00 − \$429,562.50 = \$20,437.50.

corresponds to a contract price of \$98,500. The total loss on the Treasury bond futures contracts is

$$79 \times (\$98{,}500.00 - \$93{,}062.50) = \$429{,}562.50$$

The net change in the value of the portfolio manager's position is therefore only

$$\$450{,}000.00 - \$429{,}562.50 = \$20{,}437.50$$

Because the fund incurs a loss on the futures position, the manager may regret implementing the hedge. On average, we can expect half of our hedges to lead to these sorts of regrets. Unfortunately, we do not know in advance which half of the hedges it will be!

Hedging a Floating-Rate Loan

Interest rate futures can be used to hedge the rate of interest paid by a borrower on a floating-rate loan. Eurodollar futures are ideal for this because the Eurodollar interest rate is closely related to the rate of interest at which corporations borrow. We will consider the use of Eurodollar futures to hedge a three-month loan in which the interest rate is reset every month. This will produce a simple example. The same principles can be used for loans that last far longer than three months.

We suppose that it is April 29, and a company has just borrowed \$15 million for three months. The interest rate for each of the three one-month periods will be the one-month LIBOR rate plus 1%. At the time the loan is negotiated, the one-month LIBOR rate is 8% per annum, so the company must pay 9% per annum for the first month. Because the one-month LIBOR rate is quoted with monthly compounding, the interest for the first month is 0.75% of \$15 million, or \$112,500. This is known for certain at the time the loan is negotiated and does not have to be hedged.

The interest paid at the end of the second month is determined by the one-month LIBOR rate at the beginning of the second month. It can be hedged by taking a position in the June Eurodollar futures contract. Suppose that the quoted price for this contract is 91.88. From Section 6.4, the contract price is

$$10{,}000 \times [100 - 0.25(100 - 91.88)] = \$979{,}700$$

The company will lose money if interest rates rise and gain if interest rates fall. It therefore requires a short position in the futures contracts. The duration of the asset underlying the futures contract at maturity of the contract is three months, or 0.25 years. The duration of the liability being hedged is one month, or 0.08333 years. From equation (6.10), the number of contracts that should be used to hedge the interest payment in the second month is

$$\frac{15{,}000{,}000 \times 0.08333}{979{,}700 \times 0.25} = 5.10$$

Rounding to the nearest whole number, five contracts are required.

For the third month, the September Eurodollar futures contract can be used. Suppose the quoted price for this contract is 91.44, which corresponds to a futures price of \$978,600. The number of futures contracts that should be shorted can be calculated as before:

$$\frac{15{,}000{,}000 \times 0.08333}{978{,}600 \times 0.25} = 5.11$$

Again, we find that, to the nearest whole number, five contracts are required. Thus, five of

---

Trading Note 6.2 Hedging a floating-rate loan

It is April 29. A company has just borrowed \$15 million for three months at an interest rate equal to one-month LIBOR plus 1% and would like to hedge its risk.

Quotes

1. The one-month LIBOR rate is 8%.
2. The June Eurodollar futures price is 91.88.
3. The September Eurodollar futures price is 91.44.

The Strategy

1. Short five June contracts and five September contracts.
2. Close out the June contracts on May 29.
3. Close out the September contracts on June 29.

The Result

On May 29, the one-month LIBOR rate was 8.8%, and the June futures price was 91.12. The company gained 5 × (\$979,700 − \$977,800) = \$9,500 on the five June contracts. This provided compensation for the \$10,000 extra interest payment necessary in the second month because of the increase in LIBOR from 8% to 8.8%.

On June 29, the one-month LIBOR rate was 9.4% and the September futures price was 90.16. The company gained \$16,000 on the five September contracts. This provided compensation for extra interest costs of \$17,500.

---

the June contracts should be shorted to hedge the LIBOR rate applicable to the second month, and five of the September contracts should be shorted to hedge the LIBOR rate applicable to the third month. The June contracts are closed out on May 29, and the September contracts are closed out on June 29.

Suppose that on May 29 the one-month LIBOR rate is 8.8% and the June futures price is 91.12. The latter corresponds to a contract price of \$977,800, so that the company makes a profit of

$$5 \times (\$979{,}700 - \$977{,}800) = \$9{,}500$$

on the June contracts. This provided compensation for the extra \$10,000 interest (one-twelfth of 0.8% of \$15 million) that had to be paid at the end of the second month as a result of the LIBOR increase from 8% to 8.8%.

Suppose further that on June 29 the one-month LIBOR rate is 9.4% and the September futures price is 90.16. A similar calculation to that just given shows that the company gains \$16,000 on the short futures position, but incurs extra interest costs of \$17,500 as a result of the increase in one-month LIBOR from 8% per annum to 9.4% per annum. This example is summarized in Trading Note 6.2.

SUMMARY

Two very popular interest rate contracts are the Treasury bond and Eurodollar futures contracts that trade in the United States. In the Treasury bond futures contracts, the party with the short position has a number of interesting delivery options:

1. Delivery can be made on any day during the delivery month.
2. There are a number of alternative bonds that can be delivered.
3. On any day during the delivery month, the notice of intention to deliver at the 2:00 p.m. settlement price can be made any time up to 8:00 p.m.

These options all tend to reduce the futures price.

The Eurodollar futures contract is a contract on the three-month rate starting on the third Wednesday of the delivery month. Eurodollar futures are frequently used to estimate LIBOR forward rates for the purpose of constructing a LIBOR zero curve. When long-dated contracts are used in this way, it is important to make what is termed a convexity adjustment to allow for the marking to market in the futures contract.

The concept of duration is important in hedging interest rate risk. Duration measures how long on average an investor has to wait before receiving payments. It is a weighted average of the times until payments are received, with the weight for a particular payment time being proportional to the present value of the payment.

A key result underlying the duration-based hedging scheme described in this chapter is

$$\Delta B = -BD\Delta y$$

where B is a bond price, D is its duration, Δy is a small change in its yield (continuously compounded), and ΔB is the resultant small change in B. The equation enables a hedger to assess the sensitivity of a bond price to small changes in its yield. It also enables the hedger to assess the sensitivity of an interest rate futures price to small changes in the yield of the underlying bond. If the hedger is prepared to assume that Δy is the same for all bonds, the result enables the hedger to calculate the number of futures contracts necessary to protect a bond or bond portfolio against small changes in interest rates.

The key assumption underlying the duration-based hedging scheme is that all interest rates change by the same amount. This means that only parallel shifts in the term structure are allowed for. In practice, short-term interest rates are generally more volatile than are long-term interest rates, and hedge performance is liable to be poor if the duration of the bond underlying the futures contract differs markedly from the duration of the asset being hedged.

FURTHER READING

Burghardt, G., and W. Hoskins. "The Convexity Bias in Eurodollar Futures," *Risk*, 8, 3 (1995): 63–70.

Duffie, D. "Debt Management and Interest Rate Risk" in W. Beaver and G. Parker (eds.), *Risk Management: Challenges and Solutions*. New York: McGraw-Hill, 1994.

Fabozzi, F. J. *Duration, Convexity, and Other Bond Risk Measures*, Frank J. Fabozzi Assoc., 1999.

Grinblatt, M., and N. Jegadeesh. "The Relative Price of Eurodollar Futures and Forward Contracts," *Journal of Finance*, 51, 4 (September 1996): 1499–1522.

Quiz (Answers at End of Book)

6.1. A U.S. Treasury bond pays a 7% coupon on January 7 and July 7. How much interest accrues per $100 of principal to the bond holder between July 7, 2004, and August 9, 2004. How would your answer be different if it were a corporate bond?

6.2. It is January 9, 2005. The price of a Treasury bond with a 12% coupon that matures on October 12, 2009, is quoted as 102-07. What is the cash price?

6.3. How is the conversion factor of a bond calculated by the Chicago Board of Trade? How is it used?

6.4. A Eurodollar futures price changes from 96.76 to 96.82. What is the gain or loss to an investor who is long two contracts?

6.5. What is the purpose of the convexity adjustment made to Eurodollar futures rates? Why is the convexity adjustment necessary?

6.6. What does duration tell you about the sensitivity of a bond portfolio to interest rates. What are the limitations of the duration measure?

6.7. It is January 30. You are managing a bond portfolio worth $6 million. The duration of the portfolio in six months will be 8.2 years. The September Treasury bond futures price is currently 108-15, and the cheapest-to-deliver bond will have a duration of 7.6 years in September. How should you hedge against changes in interest rates over the next six months?

Questions and Problems (Answers in Solutions Manual/Study Guide)

6.8. The price of a 90-day Treasury bill is quoted as 10.00. What continuously compounded return (on an actual/365 basis) does an investor earn on the Treasury bill for the 90-day period?

6.9. The cash prices of six-month and one-year Treasury bills are 94.0 and 89.0. A 1.5-year bond that will pay coupons of $4 every six months currently sells for $94.84. A two-year bond that will pay coupons of $5 every six months currently sells for $97.12. Calculate the six-month, one-year, 1.5-year, and two-year zero rates.

6.10. It is May 5, 2003. The quoted price of a government bond with a 12% coupon that matures on July 27, 2011, is 110-17. What is the cash price?

6.11. Suppose that the Treasury bond futures price is 101-12. Which of the following four bonds is cheapest to deliver?

Bond	*Price*	*Conversion factor*
1	125-05	1.2131
2	142-15	1.3792
3	115-31	1.1149
4	144-02	1.4026

6.12. It is July 30, 2005. The cheapest-to-deliver bond in a September 2005 Treasury bond futures contract is a 13% coupon bond, and delivery is expected to be made on September 30, 2005. Coupon payments on the bond are made on February 4 and August 4 each year. The term structure is flat, and the rate of interest with semiannual compounding is 12% per annum. The conversion factor for the bond is 1.5. The current quoted bond price is $110. Calculate the quoted futures price for the contract.

6.13. An investor is looking for arbitrage opportunities in the Treasury bond futures market. What complications are created by the fact that the party with a short position can choose to deliver any bond with a maturity of over 15 years?

6.14. Suppose that the nine-month LIBOR interest rate is 8% per annum and the six-month LIBOR interest rate is 7.5% per annum (both with actual/365 and continuous compounding). Estimate the three-month Eurodollar futures price quote for a contract maturing in six months.

6.15. A five-year bond with a yield of 11% (continuously compounded) pays an 8% coupon at the end of each year.

a. What is the bond's price?
b. What is the bond's duration?
c. Use the duration to calculate the effect on the bond's price of a 0.2% decrease in its yield.
d. Recalculate the bond's price on the basis of a 10.8% per annum yield and verify that the result is in agreement with your answer to (c).

6.16. Suppose that a bond portfolio with a duration of 12 years is hedged using a futures contract in which the underlying asset has a duration of four years. What is likely to be the impact on the hedge of the fact that the 12-year rate is less volatile than the four-year rate?

6.17. Suppose that it is February 20 and a treasurer realizes that on July 17 the company will have to issue $5 million of commercial paper with a maturity of 180 days. If the paper were issued today, the company would realize \$4,820,000. (In other words, the company would receive \$4,820,000 for its paper and have to redeem it at \$5,000,000 in 180 days' time.) The September Eurodollar futures price is quoted as 92.00. How should the treasurer hedge the company's exposure?

6.18. On August 1, a portfolio manager has a bond portfolio worth \$10 million. The duration of the portfolio in October will be 7.1 years. The December Treasury bond futures price is currently 91-12 and the cheapest-to-deliver bond will have a duration of 8.8 years at maturity. How should the portfolio manager immunize the portfolio against changes in interest rates over the next two months?

6.19. How can the portfolio manager change the duration of the portfolio to 3.0 years in Problem 6.18?

6.20. Between October 30, 2006, and November 1, 2006, you have a choice between owning a U.S. government bond paying a 12% coupon and a U.S. corporate bond paying a 12% coupon. Consider carefully the day count conventions discussed in this chapter and decide which of the two bonds you would prefer to own. Ignore the risk of default.

6.21. Suppose that a Eurodollar futures quote is 88 for a contract maturing in 60 days. What is the LIBOR forward rate for the 60- to 150-day period? Ignore the difference between futures and forwards for the purposes of this question.

6.22. The three-month Eurodollar futures price for a contract maturing in six years is quoted as 95.20. The standard deviation of the change in the short-term interest rate in one year is 1.1%. Estimate the forward LIBOR interest rate for the period between 6.00 and 6.25 years in the future.

6.23. Explain why the forward interest rate is less than the corresponding futures interest rate calculated from a Eurodollar futures contract.

Assignment Questions

6.24. Assume that a bank can borrow or lend money at the same interest rate in the LIBOR market. The 91-day rate is 10% per annum, and the 182-day rate is 10.2% per annum, both expressed with continuous compounding. The Eurodollar futures price for a contract maturing in 91 days is quoted as 89.5. What arbitrage opportunities are open to the bank?

6.25. A Canadian company wishes to create a Canadian LIBOR futures contract from a U.S. Eurodollar futures contract and forward contracts on foreign exchange. Using an example, explain how the company should proceed. For the purposes of this problem, assume that a futures contract is the same as a forward contract.

6.26. Portfolio A consists of a one-year zero-coupon bond with a face value of \$2,000 and a 10-year zero-coupon bond with a face value of \$6,000. Portfolio B consists of a 5.95-year zero-coupon bond with a face value of \$5,000. The current yield on all bonds is 10% per annum.
   a. Show that both portfolios have the same duration.
   b. Show that the percentage changes in the values of the two portfolios for a 0.1% per annum increase in yields are the same.
   c. What are the percentage changes in the values of the two portfolios for a 5% per annum increase in yields?

6.27. It is June 25, 2005. The futures price for the June 2005 CBOT bond futures contract is 118-23.

a. Calculate the conversion factor for a bond maturing on January 1, 2021, paying a coupon of 10%.
b. Calculate the conversion factor for a bond maturing on October 1, 2026, paying a coupon of 7%.
c. Suppose that the quoted prices of the bonds in (a) and (b) are 169.00 and 136.00, respectively. Which bond is cheaper to deliver?
d. Assuming that the cheapest to deliver bond is actually delivered, what is the cash price received for the bond?

6.28. A portfolio manager plans to use a Treasury bond futures contract to hedge a bond portfolio over the next three months. The portfolio is worth \$100 million and will have a duration of 4.0 years in three months. The futures price is 122, and each futures contract is on \$100,000 of bonds. The bond that is expected to be cheapest to deliver will have a duration of 9.0 years at the maturity of the futures contract. What position in futures contracts is required?

a. What adjustments to the hedge are necessary if after one month the bond that is expected to be cheapest to deliver changes to one with a duration of seven years?
b. Suppose that all rates increase over the three months, but long-term rates increase less than short-term and medium-term rates. What is the effect of this on the performance of the hedge?

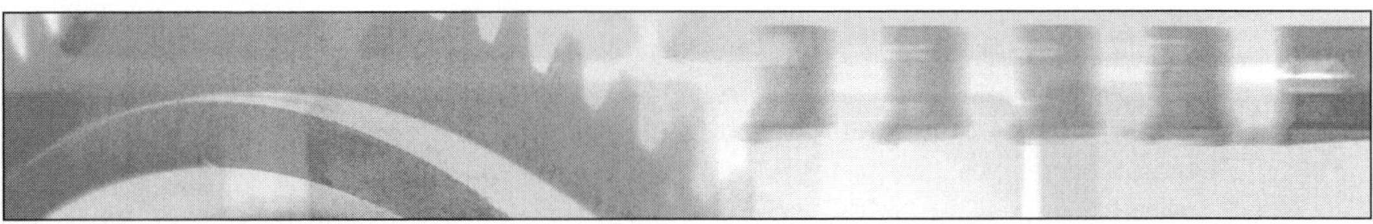

CHAPTER 7 Swaps

The first swap contracts were negotiated in the early 1980s. Since then the market has seen phenomenal growth. Swaps now occupy a position of central importance in the over-the-counter derivatives contract.

A swap is an agreement between two companies to exchange cash flows in the future. The agreement defines the dates when the cash flows are to be paid and the way in which they are to be calculated. Usually the calculation of the cash flows involves the future value of an interest rate, an exchange rate, or other market variable.

A forward contract can be viewed as simple example of a swap. Suppose it is March 1, 2004, and a company enters into a forward contract to buy 100 ounces of gold for \$300 per ounce in one year. The company can sell the gold in one year as soon as it is received. The forward contract is therefore equivalent to a swap where the company agrees that on March 1, 2005, it will pay \$30,000 and receive $100S$, where S is the market price of one ounce of gold on that date.

Whereas a forward contract is equivalent to the exchange of cash flows on just one future date, swaps typically lead to cash flow exchanges taking place on several future dates. In this chapter we examine how swaps are designed and how they are used. Our discussion centers on two popular swaps: plain vanilla interest rate swaps and fixed-for-fixed currency swaps. Other types of swaps are discussed in Chapter 20.

7.1 MECHANICS OF INTEREST RATE SWAPS

The most common type of swap is a "plain vanilla" interest rate swap. In this a company agrees to pay cash flows equal to interest at a predetermined fixed rate on a notional principal for a number of years. In return, it receives interest at a floating rate on the same notional principal for the same period of time.

LIBOR

The floating rate in most interest rate swap agreements is the London Interbank Offer Rate (LIBOR), which we introduced in Chapter 4. It is the rate of interest at which a bank is prepared to deposit money with other banks in the Eurocurrency market.

One-month, three-month, six-month, and 12-month LIBOR are commonly quoted in all major currencies.

Just as prime is often the reference rate of interest for floating-rate loans in the domestic financial market, LIBOR is a reference rate of interest for loans in international financial markets. To understand how it is used, consider a five-year bond with a rate of interest specified as six-month LIBOR plus 0.5% per annum. The life of the bond is divided into 10 periods each six-months in length. For each period, the rate of interest is set at 0.5% per annum above the six-month LIBOR rate at the beginning of the period. Interest is paid at the end of the period.

Illustration

Consider a hypothetical three-year swap initiated on March 5, 2004, between Microsoft and Intel. We suppose Microsoft agrees to pay to Intel an interest rate of 5% per annum on a notional principal of \$100 million, and in return Intel agrees to pay Microsoft the six-month LIBOR rate on the same notional principal. We assume the agreement specifies that payments are to be exchanged every six months, and the 5% interest rate is quoted with semiannual compounding. This swap is represented diagrammatically in Figure 7.1.

The first exchange of payments would take place on September 5, 2004, six months after the initiation of the agreement. Microsoft would pay Intel \$2.5 million. This is the interest on the \$100 million principal for six months at 5%. Intel would pay Microsoft interest on the \$100 million principal at the six-month LIBOR rate prevailing six months prior to September 5, 2004—that is, on March 5, 2004. Suppose that the six-month LIBOR rate on March 5, 2004, is 4.2%. Intel pays Microsoft $0.5 \times 0.042 \times \$100 = \$2.1$ million.[1] Note that there is no uncertainty about this first exchange of payments because it is determined by the LIBOR rate at the time the contract is entered into.

The second exchange of payments would take place on March 5, 2005, one year after the initiation of the agreement. Microsoft would pay \$2.5 million to Intel, and Intel would pay interest on the \$100 million principal to Microsoft at the six-month LIBOR rate prevailing six months prior to March 5, 2005—that is, on September 5, 2004. Suppose that the six-month LIBOR rate on September 5, 2004, is 4.8%. Intel pays $0.5 \times 0.048 \times \$100 = \$2.4$ million to Microsoft.

In total, there are six exchanges of payment on the swap. The fixed payments are always \$2.5 million. The floating-rate payments on a payment date are calculated using the six-month LIBOR rate prevailing six months before the payment date. An

Figure 7.1 Interest rate swap between Microsoft and Intel.

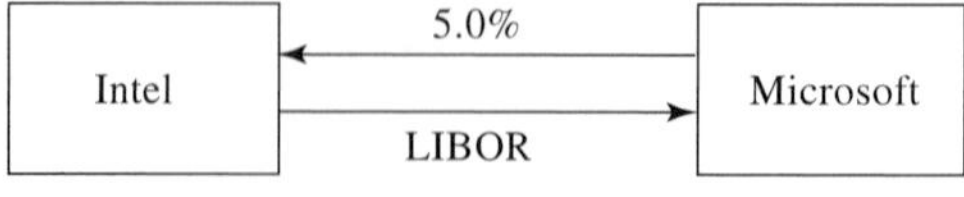

[1] The calculations here are simplified in that they ignore day count conventions. This point is discussed in more detail later in the chapter.

Table 7.1 Cash flows (millions of dollars) to Microsoft in a $100 million three-year interest rate swap when a fixed rate of 5% is paid and LIBOR is received

Date	*Six-month LIBOR rate (%)*	*Floating cash flow received*	*Fixed cash flow paid*	*Net cash flow*
Mar. 5, 2004	4.20			
Sept. 5, 2004	4.80	+2.10	−2.50	−0.40
Mar. 5, 2005	5.30	+2.40	−2.50	−0.10
Sept. 5, 2005	5.50	+2.65	−2.50	+0.15
Mar. 5, 2006	5.60	+2.75	−2.50	+0.25
Sept. 5, 2006	5.90	+2.80	−2.50	+0.30
Mar. 5, 2007	6.40	+2.95	−2.50	+0.45

interest rate swap is generally structured so that one side remits the difference between the two payments to the other side. In our example, Microsoft would pay Intel $0.4 million (= $2.5 million − $2.1 million) on September 5, 2004, and $0.1 million (= $2.5 million − $2.4 million) on March 5, 2005.

Table 7.1 provides a complete example of the payments made under the swap for one particular set of six-month LIBOR rates. The table shows the swap cash flows from the perspective of Microsoft. Note that the $100 million principal is used only for the calculation of interest payments. The principal itself is not exchanged. This is why it is termed the *notional principal.*

If the principal were exchanged at the end of the life of the swap, the nature of the deal would not be changed in any way. The principal is the same for both the fixed and floating payments. Exchanging $100 million for $100 million at the end of the life of the swap is a transaction that would have no financial value to either Microsoft or Intel. Table 7.2 shows the cash flows in Table 7.1 with a final exchange of principal added in. This provides an interesting way of viewing the swap. The cash flows in the third column of this table are the cash flows from a long position in a floating-rate bond. The cash flows in the fourth column of the table are the cash flows from a short position in a

Table 7.2 Cash flows (millions of dollars) from Table 7.1 when there is a final exchange of principal

Date	*Six-month LIBOR rate (%)*	*Floating cash flow received*	*Fixed cash flow paid*	*Net cash flow*
Mar. 5, 2004	4.20			
Sept. 5, 2004	4.80	+2.10	−2.50	−0.40
Mar. 5, 2005	5.30	+2.40	−2.50	−0.10
Sept. 5, 2005	5.50	+2.65	−2.50	+0.15
Mar. 5, 2006	5.60	+2.75	−2.50	+0.25
Sept. 5, 2006	5.90	+2.80	−2.50	+0.30
Mar. 5, 2007	6.40	+102.95	−102.50	+0.45

fixed-rate bond. The table shows that the swap can be regarded as the exchange of a fixed-rate bond for a floating-rate bond. Microsoft, whose position is described by Table 7.2, is long a floating-rate bond and short a fixed-rate bond. Intel is long a fixed-rate bond and short a floating-rate bond.

This characterization of the cash flows in the swap helps to explain why the floating rate in the swap is set six months before it is paid. On a floating-rate bond, interest is generally set at the beginning of the period to which it will apply and is paid at the end of the period. The calculation of the floating-rate payments in a "plain vanilla" interest rate swap such as the one in Table 7.2 reflects this.

Using the Swap to Transform a Liability

For Microsoft, the swap could be used to transform a floating-rate loan into a fixed-rate loan. Suppose that Microsoft has arranged to borrow \$100 million at LIBOR plus 10 basis points. (One basis point is one-hundredth of 1%, so the rate is LIBOR plus 0.1%.) After Microsoft has entered into the swap, it has three sets of cash flows:

1. It pays LIBOR plus 0.1% to its outside lenders.
2. It receives LIBOR under the terms of the swap.
3. It pays 5% under the terms of the swap.

These three sets of cash flows net out to an interest rate payment of 5.1%. Thus, for Microsoft the swap could have the effect of transforming borrowings at a floating rate of LIBOR plus 10 basis points into borrowings at a fixed rate of 5.1%.

For Intel the swap could have the effect of transforming a fixed-rate loan into a floating-rate loan. Suppose that Intel has a three-year \$100 million loan outstanding on which it pays 5.2%. After it has entered into the swap, it has three sets of cash flows:

1. It pays 5.2% to its outside lenders.
2. It pays LIBOR under the terms of the swap.
3. It receives 5% under the terms of the swap.

These three sets of cash flows net out to an interest rate payment of LIBOR plus 0.2% (or LIBOR plus 20 basis points). Thus, for Intel the swap could have the effect of transforming borrowings at a fixed rate of 5.2% into borrowings at a floating rate of LIBOR plus 20 basis points. These potential uses of the swap by Intel and Microsoft are illustrated in Figure 7.2 and summarized in Trading Note 7.1.

Using the Swap to Transform an Asset

Swaps can also be used to transform the nature of an asset. Consider Microsoft in our example. The swap could have the effect of transforming an asset earning a fixed rate of

Figure 7.2 Microsoft and Intel use the swap to transform a liability

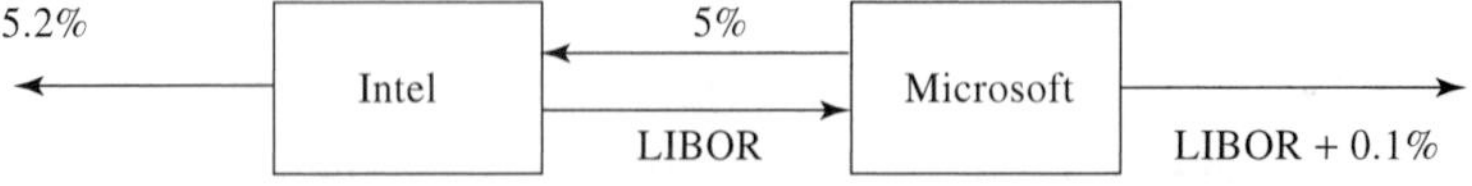

Trading Note 7.1 The versatility of swaps

Swaps have been so successful because they can be used in so many different ways. They are often used to transform the nature of liabilities or assets.

Transforming Liabilities
Using the swap in Figure 7.1, Microsoft switches its borrowings from floating to fixed and Intel does the reverse (see Figure 7.2):

	Microsoft		*Intel*	
Loan payment	LIBOR + 0.1%			5.2%
Add: Paid under swap		5.0%	LIBOR	
Less: Received under swap	−LIBOR			−5.0%
Net payment		5.1%	LIBOR + 0.2%	

Transforming Assets
Using the same swap Microsoft can switch its assets from fixed to floating and Intel can do the reverse (see Figure 7.3):

	Microsoft		*Intel*	
Investment income		4.7%	LIBOR − 0.2%	
Less: Paid under swap		−5.0%	−LIBOR	
Add: Received under swap	LIBOR			5.0%
Net income	LIBOR − 0.3%			4.8%

interest into an asset earning a floating rate of interest. Suppose that Microsoft owns $100 million in bonds that will provide interest at 4.7% per annum over the next three years. After Microsoft has entered into the swap, it has three sets of cash flows:

1. It receives 4.7% on the bonds.
2. It receives LIBOR under the terms of the swap.
3. It pays 5% under the terms of the swap.

These three sets of cash flows net out to an interest rate inflow of LIBOR minus 30 basis points. Thus, one possible use of the swap for Microsoft is to transform an asset earning 4.7% into an asset earning LIBOR minus 30 basis points.

Next, consider Intel. The swap could have the effect of transforming an asset earning a floating rate of interest into an asset earning a fixed rate of interest. Suppose that Intel has an investment of $100 million that yields LIBOR minus 20 basis points. After it has entered into the swap, it has three sets of cash flows:

1. It receives LIBOR minus 20 basis points on its investment.
2. It pays LIBOR under the terms of the swap.
3. It receives 5% under the terms of the swap.

These three sets of cash flows net out to an interest rate inflow of 4.8%. Thus, one possible use of the swap for Intel is to transform an asset earning LIBOR minus 20 basis

Figure 7.3 Microsoft and Intel use the swap to transform an asset

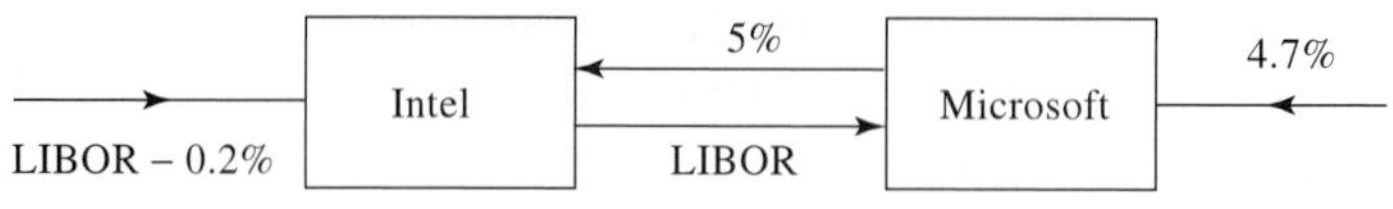

points into an asset earning 4.8%. These potential uses of the swap by Intel and Microsoft are illustrated in Figure 7.3 and summarized in Trading Note 7.1.

Role of Financial Intermediary

Usually two nonfinancial companies such as Intel and Microsoft do not get in touch directly to arrange a swap in the way indicated in Figures 7.2 and 7.3. They each deal with a financial intermediary such as a bank or other financial institution. "Plain vanilla" fixed-for-floating swaps on U.S. interest rates are usually structured so that the financial institution earns about 3 or 4 basis points (0.03% or 0.04%) on a pair of offsetting transactions.

Figure 7.4 shows what the role of the financial institution might be in the situation in Figure 7.2. The financial institution enters into two offsetting swap transactions with Intel and Microsoft. Assuming that both companies honor their obligations, the financial institution is certain to make a profit of 0.03% (3 basis points) per year multiplied by the notional principal of $100 million. (This amounts to $30,000 per year for the three-year period.) Microsoft ends up borrowing at 5.115% (instead of 5.1%, as in Figure 7.2). Intel ends up borrowing at LIBOR plus 21.5 basis points (instead of at LIBOR plus 20 basis points, as in Figure 7.2).

Figure 7.5 illustrates the role of the financial institution in the situation in Figure 7.3. The swap is the same as before and the financial institution is certain to make a profit of three basis points if neither company defaults. Microsoft ends up earning LIBOR minus 31.5 basis points (instead of LIBOR minus 30 basis points, as in Figure 7.3). Intel ends up earning 4.785% (instead of 4.8%, as in Figure 7.3).

Note that in each case the financial institution has two separate contracts: one with Intel and the other with Microsoft. In most instances, Intel will not even know that the financial institution has entered into an offsetting swap with Microsoft, and vice versa. If one of the companies defaults, the financial institution still has to honor its agreement with the other company. The three-basis-point spread earned by the financial institution is partly to compensate it for the risk that one of the two companies will default on the swap payments.

Figure 7.4 Interest rate swap from Figure 7.2 when financial institution is involved

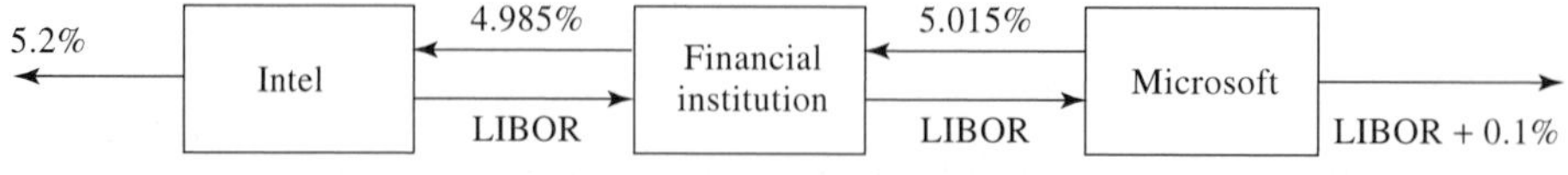

Figure 7.5 Interest rate swap from Figure 7.3 when financial institution is involved

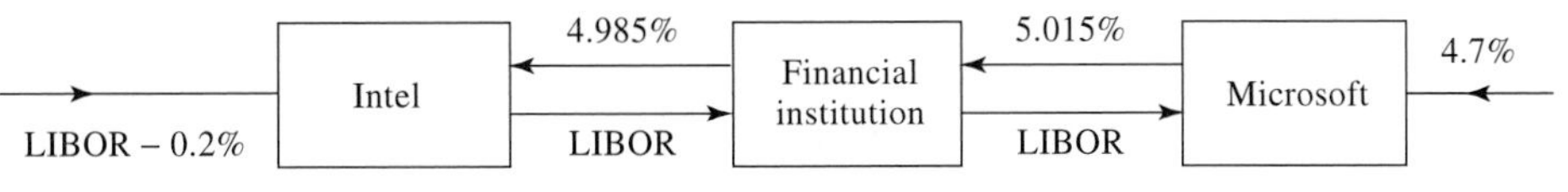

Market Makers

In practice, it is unlikely that two companies will contact a financial institution at the same time and want to take opposite positions in exactly the same swap. For this reason, many large financial institutions act as market makers for swaps. This means that they are prepared to enter into a swap without having an offsetting swap with another counterparty.[2] Market makers must carefully quantify and hedge the risks they are taking. Bonds, forward rate agreements, and interest rate futures are examples of the instruments that can be used for hedging by swap market makers. Table 7.3 shows quotes for plain vanilla U.S. dollar swaps that might be posted by a market maker.[3] Typically, the bid–offer spread is three to four basis points. The average of the bid and offer fixed rates is known as the *swap rate*. This is shown in the final column of Table 7.3.

Consider a new swap where the fixed rate equals the swap rate. It is reasonable to assume that the value of this swap is zero. (Why else would a market maker choose bid–offer quotes centered on the swap rate?) In Table 7.2, we saw that a swap can be characterized as the difference between a fixed-rate and a floating-rate bond. Define:

B_{fix}: Value of fixed-rate bond underlying the swap we are considering

B_{fl}: Value of floating-rate bond underlying the swap we are considering

Because the swap is worth zero, it follows that

$$B_{\text{fix}} = B_{\text{fl}} \tag{7.1}$$

We will use this result later in the chapter when discussing how the LIBOR/swap zero curve is determined.

Table 7.3 Bid and offer fixed rates in the swap market and swap rates (percent per annum); payments exchanged semiannually

Maturity (years)	*Bid*	*Offer*	*Swap rate*
2	6.03	6.06	6.045
3	6.21	6.24	6.225
4	6.35	6.39	6.370
5	6.47	6.51	6.490
7	6.65	6.68	6.665
10	6.83	6.87	6.850

[2] This is sometimes referred to as *warehousing* swaps.

[3] Sometimes the benchmark swap is one where fixed payments made every six months are exchanged for floating LIBOR payments made every three months. As we will see later the fixed rate should in theory be the same regardless of whether floating payments are made every three months or every six months.

7.2 DAY COUNT ISSUES

We discussed day count conventions in Section 6.1. The day count conventions affect payments on a swap, and some of the numbers calculated in the examples we have given do not exactly reflect these day count conventions. Consider, for example, the six-month LIBOR payments in Table 7.1. Because it is a money market rate, six-month LIBOR is quoted on an actual/360 basis. The first floating payment in Table 7.1, based on the LIBOR rate of 4.2%, is shown as \$2.10 million. Because there are 184 days between March 5, 2004, and September 5, 2004, it should be

$$100 \times 0.042 \times \frac{184}{360} = \$2.1467 \text{ million}$$

In general, a LIBOR-based floating-rate cash flow on a swap payment date is calculated as $LRn/360$, where L is the principal, R is the relevant LIBOR rate, and n is the number of days since the last payment date.

The fixed rate that is paid in a swap transaction is similarly quoted with a particular day count basis being specified. As a result, the fixed payments may not be exactly equal on each payment date. The fixed rate is usually quoted as actual/365 or 30/360. It is not therefore directly comparable with LIBOR because it applies to a full year. To make the rates comparable, either the six-month LIBOR rate must be multiplied by 365/360 or the fixed rate must be multiplied by 360/365. For ease of exposition, we will ignore day count issues in the calculations in the rest of this chapter.

7.3 CONFIRMATIONS

A *confirmation* is the legal agreement underlying a swap and is signed by representatives of the two parties. The drafting of confirmations has been facilitated by the work of the International Swaps and Derivatives Association (ISDA) in New York. This organization has produced a number of Master Agreements that consist of clauses defining in some detail the terminology used in swap agreements, what happens in the event of default by either side, and so on. In Business Snapshot 7.1, we show a possible extract from the confirmation for the swap between Microsoft and the financial institution (assumed to be Goldman Sachs) in Figure 7.4. Almost certainly, the full confirmation would state that the provisions of an ISDA Master Agreement apply to the contract.

The confirmation specifies that the following business day convention is to be used and that the U.S. calendar determines which days are business days and which days are holidays. This means that, if a payment date falls on a weekend or a U.S. holiday, the payment is made on the next business day.[4] September 5, 2004, is a Sunday. The first exchange of payments in the swap between Microsoft and Goldman Sachs is therefore on Monday September 6, 2004.

---

[4] Another business day convention that is sometimes specified is the *modified following* business day convention, which is the same as the following business day convention except that, when the next business day falls in a different month from the specified day, the payment is made on the immediately preceding business day. *Preceding* and *modified preceding* business day conventions are defined analogously.

Business Snapshot 7.1 Extract from hypothetical swap confirmation

Trade date:	27-February-2004
Effective date:	5-March-2004
Business day convention (all dates):	Following business day
Holiday calendar:	U.S.
Termination date:	5-March-2007
Fixed amounts	
Fixed-rate payer:	Microsoft
Fixed-rate notional principal:	USD 100 million
Fixed rate:	5.015% per annum
Fixed-rate day count convention:	Actual/365
Fixed-rate payment dates:	Each 5-March and 5-September commencing 5-September, 2004, up to and including 5-March, 2007
Floating amounts	
Floating-rate payer:	Goldman Sachs
Floating-rate notional principal:	USD 100 million
Floating rate:	USD six-month LIBOR
Floating-rate day count convention:	Actual/360
Floating-rate payment dates:	Each 5-March and 5-September commencing 5-September, 2004, up to and including 5-March, 2007

7.4 THE COMPARATIVE-ADVANTAGE ARGUMENT

An explanation commonly put forward to explain the popularity of swaps concerns comparative advantages. Consider the use of an interest rate swap to transform a liability. Some companies, it is argued, have a comparative advantage when borrowing in fixed-rate markets, whereas others have a comparative advantage in floating-rate markets. To obtain a new loan, it makes sense for a company to go to the market where it has a comparative advantage. As a result, the company may borrow fixed when it wants floating, or borrow floating when it wants fixed. The swap is used to transform a fixed-rate loan into a floating-rate loan, and vice versa.

Illustration

Suppose that two companies, AAACorp and BBBCorp, both wish to borrow $10 million for five years and have been offered the rates shown in Table 7.4. AAACorp has a AAA credit rating; BBBCorp has a BBB credit rating.[5] We assume that BBBCorp wants to borrow at a fixed rate of interest, whereas AAACorp wants to borrow at a

[5] The credit ratings assigned to companies by S&P (in order of decreasing creditworthiness) are AAA, AA, A, BBB, BB, B, and CCC. The corresponding ratings assigned by Moody's are Aaa, Aa, A, Baa, Ba, B, and Caa, respectively.

Table 7.4 Borrowing rates that provide a basis for the comparative-advantage argument

	Fixed	*Floating*
AAACorp	10.0%	Six-month LIBOR + 0.3%
BBBCorp	11.2%	Six-month LIBOR + 1.0%

floating rate of interest linked to six-month LIBOR. Because it has a worse credit rating than AAACorp, BBBCorp pays a higher rate of interest than AAACorp in both fixed and floating markets.

A key feature of the rates offered to AAACorp and BBBCorp is that the difference between the two fixed rates is greater than the difference between the two floating rates. BBBCorp pays 1.2% more than AAACorp in fixed-rate markets and only 0.7% more than AAACorp in floating-rate markets. BBBCorp appears to have a comparative advantage in floating-rate markets, whereas AAACorp appears to have a comparative advantage in fixed-rate markets.[6] It is this apparent anomaly that can lead to a swap being negotiated. AAACorp borrows fixed-rate funds at 10% per annum. BBBCorp borrows floating-rate funds at LIBOR plus 1% per annum. They then enter into a swap agreement to ensure that AAACorp ends up with floating-rate funds and BBBCorp ends up with fixed-rate funds.

To understand how the swap might work, we first assume that AAACorp and BBBCorp get in touch with each other directly. The sort of swap they might negotiate is shown in Figure 7.6. This is very similar to our example in Figure 7.2. AAACorp agrees to pay BBBCorp interest at six-month LIBOR on $10 million. In return, BBBCorp agrees to pay AAACorp interest at a fixed rate of 9.95% per annum on $10 million.

AAACorp has three sets of interest rate cash flows:

1. It pays 10% per annum to outside lenders.
2. It receives 9.95% per annum from BBBCorp.
3. It pays LIBOR to BBBCorp.

Figure 7.6 Swap agreement between AAACorp and BBBCorp when the rates in Table 7.4 apply

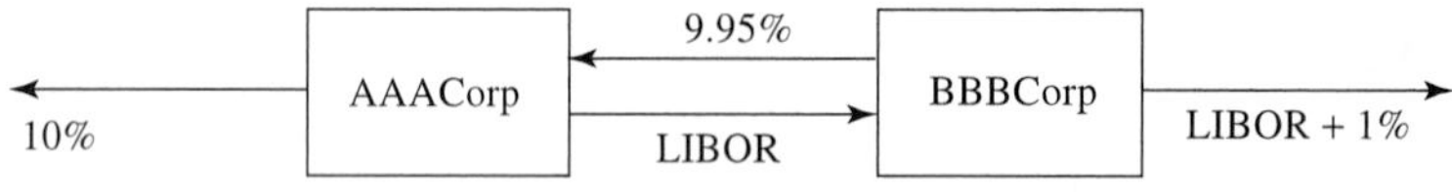

[6] Note that BBBCorp's comparative advantage in floating-rate markets does not imply that BBBCorp pays less than AAACorp in this market. It means that the extra amount that BBBCorp pays over the amount paid by AAACorp is less in this market. One of my students summarized the situation as follows: "AAACorp pays more less in fixed-rate markets; BBBCorp pays less more in floating-rate markets."

Figure 7.7 Swap agreement between AAACorp and BBBCorp when rates in Table 7.4 apply and a financial intermediary is involved

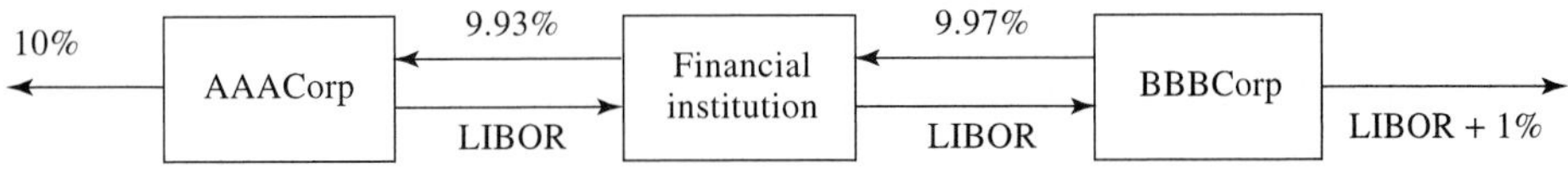

The net effect of the three cash flows is that AAACorp pays LIBOR plus 0.05% per annum. This is 0.25% per annum less than it would pay if it went directly to floating-rate markets. BBBCorp also has three sets of interest rate cash flows:

1. It pays LIBOR + 1% per annum to outside lenders.
2. It receives LIBOR from AAACorp.
3. It pays 9.95% per annum to AAACorp.

The net effect of the three cash flows is that BBBCorp pays 10.95% per annum. This is 0.25% per annum less than it would pay if it went directly to fixed-rate markets.

The swap arrangement appears to improve the position of both AAACorp and BBBCorp by 0.25% per annum. The total gain is therefore 0.5% per annum. It can be shown that the total apparent gain from this type of interest rate swap arrangement is always $a - b$, where a is the difference between the interest rates facing the two companies in fixed-rate markets, and b is the difference between the interest rates facing the two companies in floating-rate markets. In this case, $a = 1.2\%$ and $b = 0.7\%$.

If AAACorp and BBBCorp did not deal directly with each other and used a financial institution, an arrangement such as that shown in Figure 7.7 might result. (This is similar to the example in Figure 7.4.) In this case, AAACorp ends up borrowing at LIBOR + 0.07%, BBBCorp ends up borrowing at 10.97%, and the financial institution earns a spread of four basis points per year. The gain to AAACorp is 0.23%; the gain to BBBCorp is 0.23%; and the gain to the financial institution is 0.04%. The total gain to all three parties is 0.50% as before.

Criticism of the Comparative-Advantage Argument

The comparative-advantage argument we have just outlined for explaining the attractiveness of interest rate swaps is open to question. Why, in Table 7.4, should the spreads between the rates offered to AAACorp and BBBCorp be different in fixed and floating markets? Now that the swap market has been in existence for some time, we might reasonably expect these types of differences to have been arbitraged away.

The reason that spread differentials appear to exist is due to the nature of the contracts available to companies in fixed and floating markets. The 10.0% and 11.2% rates available to AAACorp and BBBCorp in fixed-rate markets are five-year rates (e.g., the rates at which the companies can issue five-year fixed-rate bonds). The LIBOR + 0.3% and LIBOR + 1.0% rates available to AAACorp and BBBCorp in floating-rate markets are six-month rates. In the floating-rate market, the lender usually has the opportunity to review the floating rates every six months. If the creditworthiness of AAACorp or BBBCorp has declined, the lender has the option of increasing the spread over LIBOR that is charged. In extreme circumstances, the lender can refuse to roll over the loan at all. The providers of fixed-rate financing do not have the option to change the terms of the loan in this way.[7]

The spreads between the rates offered to AAACorp and BBBCorp are a reflection of the extent to which BBBCorp is more likely to default than AAACorp. During the next six months, there is very little chance that either AAACorp or BBBCorp will default. As we look further ahead, default statistics show that on average the probability of a default by a company with a relatively low credit rating (such as BBBCorp) increases faster than the probability of a default by a company with a relatively high credit rating (such as AAACorp). This is why the spread between the five-year rates is greater than the spread between the six-month rates.

After negotiating a floating-rate loan at LIBOR + 1.0% and entering into the swap shown in Figure 7.7, BBBCorp appears to obtain a fixed-rate loan at 10.97%. The arguments just presented show that this is not really the case. In practice, the rate paid is 10.97% only if BBBCorp can continue to borrow floating-rate funds at a spread of 1.0% over LIBOR. If, for example, the credit rating of BBBCorp declines so that the floating-rate loan is rolled over at LIBOR + 2.0%, the rate paid by BBBCorp increases to 11.97%. The market expects that BBBCorp's spread over six-month LIBOR will on average rise during the swap's life. BBBCorp's expected average borrowing rate when it enters into the swap is therefore greater than 10.97%.

The swap in Figure 7.7 locks in LIBOR + 0.7% for AAACorp for the whole of the next five years, not just for the next six months. This appears to be a good deal for AAACorp. The downside is that it is bearing the risk of a default by the financial institution. If it borrowed floating-rate funds in the usual way it would not be bearing this risk.

7.5 THE NATURE OF SWAP RATES

At this stage it is appropriate to examine the nature of swap rates and the relationship between swap and LIBOR markets. We explained in Section 4.1 that LIBOR is the rate of interest at which AA-rated banks borrow for periods between 1 and 12 months from other banks. We also explained in Section 7.3 that a swap rate is the average of (a) the fixed rate that a swap market maker is prepared to pay in exchange for receiving LIBOR (its bid rate) and (b) the fixed rate that it prepared to receive in return for paying LIBOR (its offer rate).

Like LIBOR rates, swap rates are not risk-free lending rates. However, they are close to risk-free. A financial institution can earn the five-year swap rate on a certain principal by:

1. Lending the principal for the first six months to a AA borrower and then relending it for successive six-month periods to other AA borrowers, and
2. Entering into a swap to exchange the LIBOR income for the five-year swap rate.

This shows that the five-year swap rate is an interest rate with a credit risk corresponding to the situation where 10 consecutive six-month LIBOR loans to AA companies are made. Similarly the seven-year swap rate is an interest rate with a credit risk

[7] If the floating rate loans are structured so that the spread over LIBOR is guaranteed in advance regardless of changes in credit rating, there is in practice little or no comparative advantage.

corresponding to the situation where 14 consecutive six-month LIBOR loans to AA companies are made. Swap rates of other maturities can be interpreted analogously.

Note that swap rates are less than AA borrowing rates. It is much more attractive to lend money for successive six-month periods to borrowers who are always AA at the beginning of the periods than to lend it to one borrower for the whole five years when all we can be sure of is that the borrower is AA at the beginning of the five years.

7.6 DETERMINING LIBOR/SWAP ZERO RATES

We explained in Section 4.1 that derivatives traders tend to use LIBOR rates as proxies for risk-free rates when valuing derivatives. One problem with LIBOR rates is that direct observations are possible only for maturities out to 12 months. Traders use swap rates for longer term zero rates. In this section we describe how the LIBOR/swap zero curve is determined.

The first point to note is that the value of a newly issued floating-rate bond that pays six-month LIBOR is always equal to its principal value (or par value) when the LIBOR/swap zero curve is used for discounting.[8] The reason is that the bond provides a rate of interest of LIBOR and LIBOR is the discount rate. The interest on the bond exactly matches the discount rate and as a result the bond is fairly priced at par.

In equation (7.1), we showed that for a newly issued swap where the fixed rate equals the swap rate, $B_{\text{fix}} = B_{\text{fl}}$. We have just shown that B_{fl} equals the notional principal. It follows that B_{fix} also equals the swap's notional principal. Swap rates therefore define a set of par yield bonds. For example, from the swap rates in Table 7.3 we can deduce that the two-year LIBOR/swap par yield is 6.045%, the three-year LIBOR/swap par yield is 6.225%,and so on.[9]

The usual method for determining the LIBOR/swap zero curve is the bootstrap method which we used to determine the Treasury zero curve in Section 4.5. LIBOR rates define the zero curve out to one year. Swap rates define par yield bonds that are used to determine longer term rates.

Example

Suppose that the 6-month, 12-month, and 18-month LIBOR/swap zero rates have been determined as 4%, 4.5%, and 4.8% with continuous compounding and that the 2-year swap rate (for a swap where payments are made semiannually) is 5%. This 5% swap rate means that a bond with a principal of \$100 and a semiannual coupon of 5% per annum sells for par. It follows that, if R is the 2-year zero rate, then

$$2.5e^{-0.04\times 0.5} + 2.5e^{-0.045\times 1.0} + 2.5e^{-0.048\times 1.5} + 102.5e^{2R} = 100$$

Solving this, we obtain $R = 4.953\%$. (Note that this calculation is a simplified in that it does not take the swap's day count conventions and holiday calendars into account. See Section 7.2.)

---

[8] The same is true of a newly issued bond that pays 1-month, 3-month, or 12-month LIBOR.

[9] Analysts frequently interpolate between swap rates before calculating the zero curve so that they have swap rates for maturities at six-month intervals. For example, for the data in Table 7.3 the 2.5-year swap rate would be assumed to be 6.135%; the 7.5-year swap rate would be assumed to be 6.696%; and so on.

Using Eurodollar Futures

We discussed Eurodollar futures contracts in Section 6.4. Eurodollar futures contracts maturing in March, June, September, and December are sometimes used to assist in calculating the LIBOR/swap zero curve. Once a convexity adjustment such as that described in Section 6.4 is made, the Eurodollar futures contracts define forward LIBOR rates for future three-month time periods. Suppose that the ith Eurodollar futures contract matures at time T_i $(i = 1, 2, \dots)$. It is usually assumed that the forward interest rate calculated from the ith futures contract applies exactly to the period T_i to T_{i+1}. (In practice, this is close to true.) This enables a bootstrap procedure to be used to determine zero rates. Suppose that F_i is the forward rate calculated from the ith Eurodollar futures contract and R_i is the zero rate for a maturity T_i. From equation (4.5), we have

$$F_i = \frac{R_{i+1}T_{i+1} - R_iT_i}{T_{i+1} - T_i}$$

so that

$$R_{i+1} = \frac{F_i(T_{i+1} - T_i) + R_iT_i}{T_{i+1}} \tag{7.2}$$

Example

The 400-day LIBOR zero rate has been calculated as 4.80% with continuous compounding and, from a Eurodollar futures quote, it has been calculated that the forward rate for a 91-day period beginning in 400 days is 5.30% with continuous compounding. We can use equation (7.2) to obtain the 491-day rate as

$$\frac{0.053 \times 91 + 0.048 \times 400}{491} = 0.04893$$

or 4.893%.

In the United States, spot LIBOR rates are typically used to define the LIBOR zero curve for maturities up to one year. Eurodollar futures are then used for maturities between one and two years—and sometimes for maturities up to five years. Swap rates are used to calculate the zero curve for longer maturities. A similar procedure is followed to determine LIBOR zero rates in other countries. For example, Swiss franc LIBOR zero rates are determined from spot Swiss franc LIBOR rates, three-month Euroswiss futures, and Swiss franc swap rates.

7.7 VALUATION OF INTEREST RATE SWAPS

We now move on to discuss the valuation of interest rate swaps. An interest rate swap is worth zero, or close to zero, when it is first initiated. After it has been in existence for some time, its value may become positive or negative. There are two valuation approaches. The first regards the swap as the difference between two bonds; the second regards it as a portfolio of FRAs.

Valuation in Terms of Bond Prices

Principal payments are not exchanged in an interest rate swap. However, as illustrated in Table 7.2, we can assume that principal payments are both received and paid at the end of the swap without changing its value. By doing this, we find that a swap where fixed cash flows are received and floating cash flows are paid can be regarded as a long position in a fixed-rate bond and a short position in a floating-rate bond, so that

$$V_{\text{swap}} = B_{\text{fix}} - B_{\text{fl}}$$

where V_{swap} is the value of the swap, B_{fl} is the value of the floating rate bond underlying the swap and B_{fix} is the value of the fixed rate payments underlying the swap. Similarly, a swap where floating cash flows are received and fixed cash flows are paid is a long position in a floating-rate bond and a short position in a fixed-rate bond, so that the value of the swap is

$$V_{\text{swap}} = B_{\text{fl}} - B_{\text{fix}}$$

The value of the fixed rate bond, B_{fix} can be determined as described in Section 4.4. To calculate the value of the floating-rate bond, we note that the bond is worth par immediately after an interest payment. This is because at this time the bond is a "fair deal" where the borrower pays LIBOR for each subsequent accrual period.

Suppose that the next exchange of payments is at time t^* and the floating payment that will be made at time t^* (which was determined at the last payment date) is k^*. Immediately after the payment $B_{\text{fl}} = L$ as just explained. It follows that immediately before the payment $B_{\text{fl}} = L + k^*$. The floating-rate bond can therefore be regarded as an instrument providing a single cash flow of $L + k^*$ at time t^*. Discounting this, the value of the floating rate bond today is

$$(L + k^*)e^{-r^*t^*}$$

where r^* is the LIBOR/swap zero rate for a maturity of t^*.

Example

Suppose that a financial institution has agreed to pay six-month LIBOR and receive 8% per annum (with semiannual compounding) on a notional principal of \$100 million. The swap has a remaining life of 1.25 years. The LIBOR rates with continuous compounding for 3-month, 9-month, and 15-month maturities are 10%, 10.5%, and 11%, respectively. The 6-month LIBOR rate at the last payment date was 10.2% (with semiannual compounding).

The calculations for valuing the swap in terms of bonds are summarized in Table 7.5. The fixed rate bond has cash flows of 4, 4, and 104 on the three

Table 7.5 Valuing swap in terms of bonds (\$ millions). B_{fix} is fixed-rate bond underlying swap; B_{fl} is floating-rate bond underlying swap

Time	B_{fix} *cash flow*	B_{fl} *cash flow*	*Discount factor*	*Present value* B_{fix} *cash flow*	*Present value* B_{fl} *cash flow*
0.25	4.0	105.100	0.9753	3.901	102.505
0.75	4.0		0.9243	3.697	
1.25	104.0		0.8715	90.640	
Total				98.238	102.505

payment dates. The discount factors for these cash flows are $e^{-0.1\times 0.25}$, $e^{-0.105\times 0.75}$, and $e^{-0.11\times 1.25}$, respectively, and are shown in the fourth column of Table 7.5. The table shows that the value of the fixed-rate bond (in millions of dollars) is 98.238.

In this example, $k^* = 0.5 \times 0.102 \times 100 = \$5.1$ million and $t^* = 0.25$, so that the floating-rate bond can be valued as though it produces a cash flow of \$105.1 million in three months. The table shows that the value of the floating bond (in millions of dollars) is -102.505.

The value of the swap is the difference between the two bond prices:

$$V_{\text{swap}} = 98.238 - 102.505 = -4.267$$

or -4.267 million dollars.

If the financial institution had been in the opposite position of paying fixed and receiving floating, the value of the swap would be $+\$4.267$ million. Note that our calculations do not take account of day count conventions and holiday calendars.

Valuation in Terms of FRAs

A swap can be characterized as a portfolio of forward rate agreements. Consider the swap between Microsoft and Intel in Figure 7.1. The swap is a three-year deal entered into on March 5, 2004, with semiannual payments. The first exchange of payments is known at the time the swap is negotiated. The other five exchanges can be regarded as FRAs. The exchange on March 5, 2005, is an FRA where interest at 5% is exchanged for interest at the six-month rate observed in the market on September 5, 2004; the exchange on September 5, 2005, is an FRA where interest at 5% is exchanged for interest at the six-month rate observed in the market on March 5, 2005; and so on.

As shown at the end of Section 4.7, an FRA can be valued by assuming that forward interest rates are realized. Because it is nothing more than a portfolio of forward rate agreements, a plain vanilla interest rate swap can also be valued by making the assumption that forward interest rates are realized. The procedure is as follows:

1. Use the LIBOR/swap zero curve to calculate forward rates for each of the LIBOR rates that will determine swap cash flows.
2. Calculate swap cash flows on the assumption that the LIBOR rates will equal the forward rates.
3. Discount these swap cash flows (using the LIBOR/swap zero curve) to obtain the swap value.

Example

Consider again the situation in the previous example. Under the terms of the swap, a financial institution has agreed to pay 6-month LIBOR and receive 8% per annum (with semiannual compounding) on a notional principal of \$100 million. The swap has a remaining life of 1.25 years. The LIBOR rates with continuous compounding for 3-month, 9-month, and 15-month maturities are 10%, 10.5%, and 11%, respectively. The 6-month LIBOR rate at the last payment date was 10.2% (with semiannual compounding).

The calculations are summarized in Table 7.6. The first row of the table shows the cash flows that will be exchanged in three months. These have already been

Table 7.6 Valuing swap in terms of FRAs. Floating cash flows are calculated by assuming that forward rates will be realized

Time	*Fixed cash flow*	*Floating cash flow*	*Net cash flow*	*Discount factor*	*Present value of net cash flow*
0.25	4.0	−5.100	−1.100	0.9753	−1.073
0.75	4.0	−5.522	−1.522	0.9243	−1.407
1.25	4.0	−6.051	−2.051	0.8715	−1.787
Total					−4.267

determined. The fixed rate of 8% will lead to a cash inflow of $10 \times 0.08 \times 0.5 = 4$ million. The floating rate of 10.2% (which was set three months ago) will lead to a cash outflow of $10 \times 0.102 \times 0.5 = 5.1$ million. The second row of the table shows the cash flows that will be exchanged in nine months assuming that forward rates are realized. The cash inflow is 4.0 as before. To calculate the cash outflow, we we must first calculate the forward rate corresponding to the period between three and nine months. From equation (4.5), this is

$$\frac{0.105 \times 0.75 - 0.10 \times 0.25}{0.5} = 0.1075$$

or 10.75% with continuous compounding. From equation (4.4), the forward rate becomes 11.044% with semiannual compounding. The cash outflow is therefore $10 \times 0.11044 \times 0.5 = 5.522$ million. The third row similarly shows the cash flows that will be exchanged in 15 months assuming that forward rates are realized. The discount factors for the three payment dates are $e^{-0.1 \times 0.25}$, $e^{-0.105 \times 0.75}$, and $e^{-0.11 \times 1.25}$, respectively.

The present value of the exchange in three months is −1.073. The values of the FRAs corresponding to the exchanges in nine months and 15 months are −1.4067 and −1.787 respectively. The total value of the swap is −$4.267 million. This is in agreement with the value we calculated earlier by decomposing the swap into a long position in a one bond and a short position in another.

The fixed rate in an interest rate swap is chosen so that the swap is worth zero initially. This means that at the outset of a swap the sum of the values of the FRAs underlying the swap is zero. It does not mean that the value of each individual FRA is zero. In general, some FRAs will have positive values whereas others will have negative values.

Consider the FRAs underlying the swap between the Microsoft and Intel in Figure 7.1:

$$\text{Value of FRA to Microsoft} > 0 \text{ when forward interest rate} > 5.0\%$$
$$\text{Value of FRA to Microsoft} = 0 \text{ when forward interest rate} = 5.0\%$$
$$\text{Value of FRA to Microsoft} < 0 \text{ when forward interest rate} < 5.0\%$$

Suppose that the term structure of interest rates is upward sloping at the time the swap is negotiated. This means that the forward interest rates increase as the maturity of the FRA increases. Because the sum of the values of the FRAs is zero, the forward interest rate must be less than 5.0% for the early payment dates and greater than 5.0% for the

Figure 7.8 Value of forward rate agreements underlying a swap as a function of maturity. In (a) the term structure of interest rates is upward sloping and we receive fixed, or it is downward sloping and we receive floating; in (b) the term structure of interest rates is upward sloping and we receive floating, or it is downward sloping and we receive fixed.

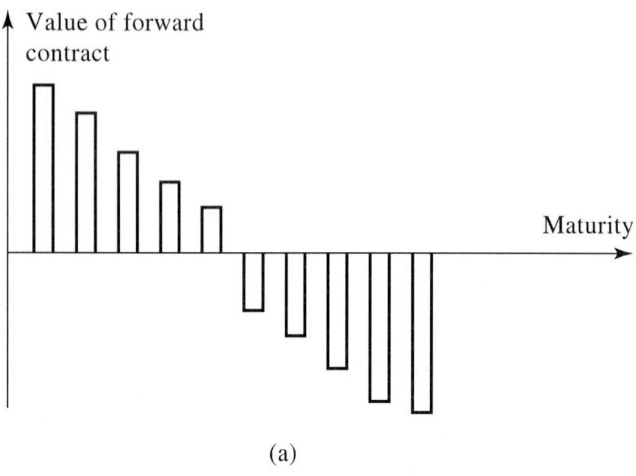

(a)

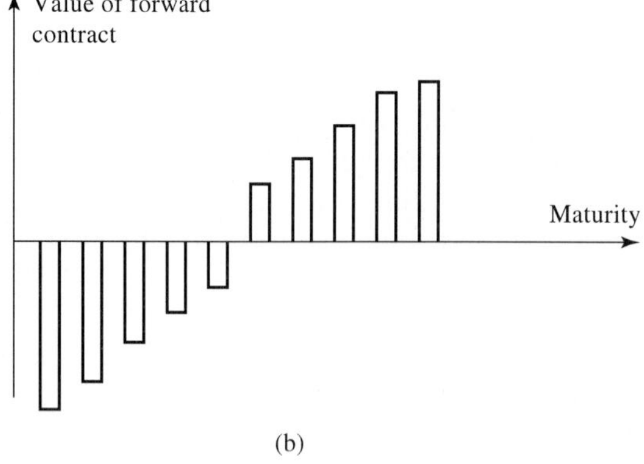

(b)

later payment dates. The value to Microsoft of the FRAs corresponding to early payment dates is therefore negative, whereas the value of the FRAs corresponding to later payment dates is positive. If the term structure of interest rates is downward sloping at the time the swap is negotiated, the reverse is true. The impact of the shape of the term structure of interest rates on the values of the forward contracts underlying a swap is summarized in Figure 7.8.

7.8 CURRENCY SWAPS

Another popular type of swap is known as a *currency swap*. In its simplest form, this involves exchanging principal and interest payments in one currency for principal and interest payments in another currency.

A currency swap agreement requires the principal to be specified in each of the two

Figure 7.9 A currency swap

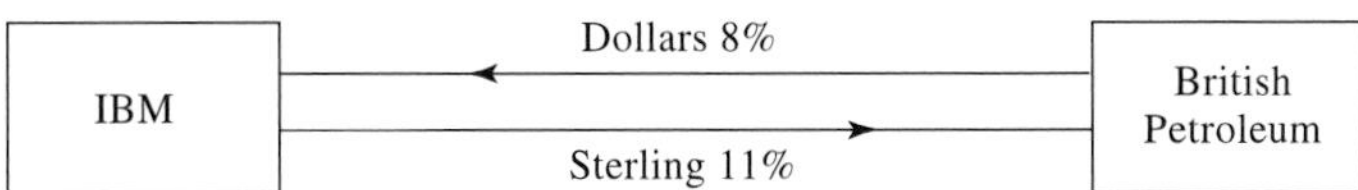

currencies. The principal amounts are usually exchanged at the beginning and at the end of the life of the swap. Usually the principal amounts are chosen to be approximately equivalent using the exchange rate at the swap's initiation.

Illustration

Consider a hypothetical five-year currency swap agreement between IBM and British Petroleum entered into on February 1, 2004. We suppose that IBM pays a fixed rate of interest of 11% in sterling and receives a fixed rate of interest of 8% in dollars from British Petroleum. Interest rate payments are made once a year and the principal amounts are \$15 million and £10 million. This is termed a *fixed-for-fixed* currency swap because the interest rate in both currencies is fixed. The swap is shown in Figure 7.9. Initially, the principal amounts flow in the opposite direction to the arrows in Figure 7.9. The interest payments during the life of the swap and the final principal payment flow in the same direction as the arrows. Thus, at the outset of the swap, IBM pays \$15 million and receives £10 million. Each year during the life of the swap contract, IBM receives \$1.20 million (= 8% of \$15 million) and pays £1.10 million (= 11% of £10 million). At the end of the life of the swap, it pays a principal of £10 million and receives a principal of \$15 million. These cash flows are shown in Table 7.7.

Use of a Currency Swap to Transform Loans and Assets

A swap such as the one just considered can be used to transform borrowings in one currency to borrowings in another currency. Suppose that IBM can issue \$15 million of U.S.-dollar-denominated bonds at 8% interest. The swap has the effect of transforming this transaction into one where IBM has borrowed £10 million at 11% interest. The

Table 7.7 Cash flows to IBM in currency swap

Date	*Dollar cash flow (millions)*	*Sterling cash flow (millions)*
February 1, 2004	−15.00	+10.00
February 1, 2005	+1.20	−1.10
February 1, 2006	+1.20	−1.10
February 1, 2007	+1.20	−1.10
February 1, 2008	+1.20	−1.10
February 1, 2009	+16.20	−11.10

initial exchange of principal converts the proceeds of the bond issue from U.S. dollars to sterling. The subsequent exchanges in the swap have the effect of swapping the interest and principal payments from dollars to sterling.

The swap can also be used to transform the nature of assets. Suppose that IBM can invest £10 million in the U.K. to yield 11% per annum for the next five years, but feels that the U.S. dollar will strengthen against sterling and prefers a U.S.-dollar-denominated investment. The swap has the effect of transforming the U.K. investment into a $15 million investment in the U.S. yielding 8%.

Comparative Advantage

Currency swaps can be motivated by comparative advantage. To illustrate this, we consider another hypothetical example. Suppose the five-year fixed-rate borrowing costs to General Motors and Qantas Airways in U.S. dollars (USD) and Australian dollars (AUD) are as shown in Table 7.8. The data in the table suggest that Australian rates are higher than USD interest rates, and also that General Motors is more creditworthy than Qantas Airways because it is offered a more favorable rate of interest in both currencies. From the viewpoint of a swap trader, the interesting aspect of Table 7.8 is that the spreads between the rates paid by General Motors and Qantas Airways in the two markets are not the same. Qantas Airways pays 2% more than General Motors in the U.S. dollar market and only 0.4% more than General Motors in the AUD market.

This situation is analogous to that in Table 7.4. General Motors has a comparative advantage in the USD market, whereas Qantas Airways has a comparative advantage in the AUD market. In Table 7.4, where a plain vanilla interest rate swap was considered, we argued that comparative advantages were largely illusory. Here we are comparing the rates offered in two different currencies, and it is more likely that the comparative advantages are genuine. One possible source of comparative advantage is tax. General Motors' position might be such that USD borrowings lead to lower taxes on its worldwide income than AUD borrowings. Qantas Airways' position might be the reverse. (Note that we assume that the interest rates in Table 7.8 have been adjusted to reflect these types of tax advantages.)

We suppose that General Motors wants to borrow 20 million AUD and Qantas Airways wants to borrow 12 million USD and that the current exchange rate (USD per AUD) is 0.6000. This creates a perfect situation for a currency swap. General Motors and Qantas Airways each borrow in the market where they have a comparative advantage; that is, General Motors borrows USD and Qantas Airways borrows AUD. They then use a currency swap to transform General Motors' loan into a AUD loan and Qantas Airways' loan into a USD loan.

Table 7.8 Borrowing rates providing basis for currency swap

	*USD**	*AUD**
General Motors	5.0%	12.6%
Qantas Airways	7.0%	13.0%

* Quoted rates have been adjusted to reflect the differential impact of taxes.

Figure 7.10 A currency swap motivated by comparative advantage

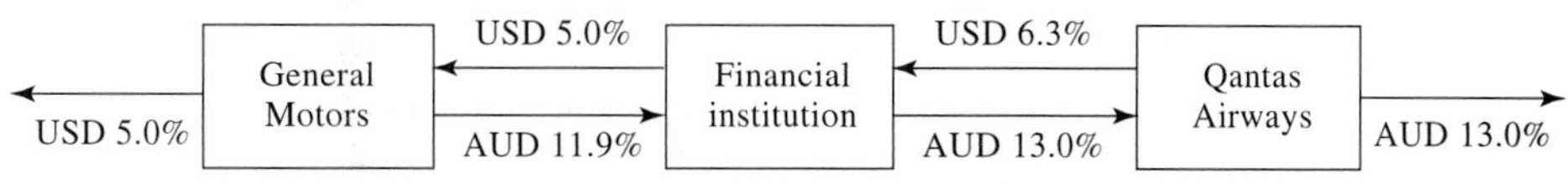

As already mentioned, the difference between the dollar interest rates is 2%, whereas the difference between the AUD interest rates is 0.4%. By analogy with the interest rate swap case, we expect the total gain to all parties to be 2.0 − 0.4 = 1.6% per annum.

There are many ways in which the swap can be arranged. Figure 7.10 shows one way swaps might be entered into with a financial institution. General Motors borrows USD and Qantas Airways borrows AUD. The effect of the swap is to transform the USD interest rate of 5% per annum to an AUD interest rate of 11.9% per annum for General Motors. As a result, General Motors is 0.7% per annum better off than it would be if it went directly to AUD markets. Similarly, Qantas exchanges an AUD loan at 13% per annum for a USD loan at 6.3% per annum and ends up 0.7% per annum better off than it would be if it went directly to USD markets. The financial institution gains 1.3% per annum on its USD cash flows and loses 1.1% per annum on its AUD flows. If we ignore the difference between the two currencies, the financial institution makes a net gain of 0.2% per annum. As predicted, the total gain to all parties is 1.6% per annum.

Each year the financial institution makes a gain of USD 156,000 (= 1.3% of 12 million) and incurs a loss of AUD 220,000 (= 1.1% of 20 million). The financial institution can avoid any foreign exchange risk by buying AUD 220,000 per annum in the forward market for each year of the life of the swap, thus locking in a net gain in USD.

It is possible to redesign the swap so that the financial institution makes a 0.2% spread in USD. Figures 7.11 and 7.12 present two alternatives. These alternatives are unlikely to be used in practice because they do not lead to General Motors and Qantas being free of foreign exchange risk.[10] In Figure 7.11, Qantas bears some foreign exchange risk because it pays 1.1% per annum in AUD and 5.2% per annum in USD. In Figure 7.12, General Motors bears some foreign exchange risk because it receives 1.1% per annum in USD and pays 13% per annum in AUD.

Figure 7.11 Alternative arrangement for currency swap: Qantas Airways bears some foreign exchange risk

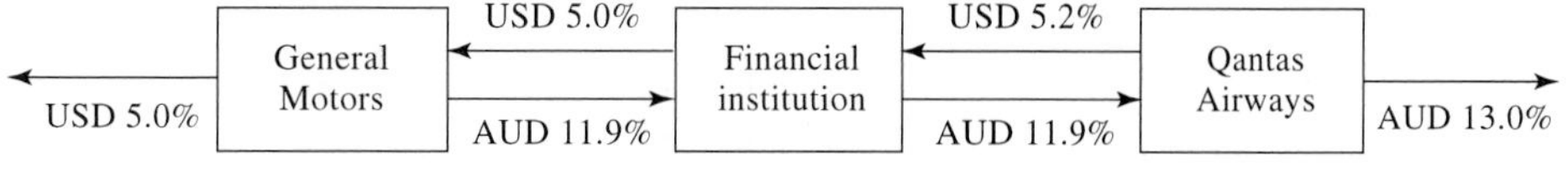

[10] Usually it makes sense for the financial institution to bear the foreign exchange risk, because it is in the best position to hedge the risk.

Figure 7.12 Alternative arrangement for currency swap: General Motors bears some foreign exchange risk

7.9 VALUATION OF CURRENCY SWAPS

Like interest rate swaps, fixed-for-fixed currency swaps can be decomposed into either the difference between two bonds or a portfolio of forward foreign exchange contracts.

Valuation in Terms of Bond Prices

If we define V_{swap} as the value in U.S. dollars of an outstanding swap where dollars are received and a foreign currency is paid

$$V_{\text{swap}} = B_D - S_0 B_F$$

where B_F is the value, measured in the foreign currency, of the bond defined by the foreign cash flows on the swap and B_D is the value of the bond defined by the domestic cash flows on the swap, and S_0 is the spot exchange rate (expressed as number of dollars per unit of foreign currency). The value of a swap can therefore be determined from LIBOR rates in the two currencies, the term structure of interest rates in the domestic currency, and the spot exchange rate.

Similarly, the value of a swap where the foreign currency is received and dollars are paid is

$$V_{\text{swap}} = S_0 B_F - B_D$$

Example

Suppose that the term structure of LIBOR/swap interest rates is flat in both Japan and the United States. The Japanese rate is 4% per annum and the

Table 7.9 Valuation of currency swap in terms of bonds (all amounts in millions)

Time	*Cash flows on dollar bond (\$)*	*Present value (\$)*	*Cash flows forward on yen bond (yen)*	*Present value (yen)*
1	0.8	0.7311	60	57.65
2	0.8	0.6682	60	55.39
3	0.8	0.6107	60	53.22
3	10.0	7.6338	1,200	1,064.30
Total		9.6439		1,230.55

U.S. rate is 9% per annum (both with continuous compounding). A financial institution has entered into a currency swap in which it receives 5% per annum in yen and pays 8% per annum in dollars once a year. The principals in the two currencies are $10 million and 1,200 million yen. The swap will last for another three years, and the current exchange rate is 110 yen = $1.

The calculations are summarized in Table 7.9. In this case the cash flows from the dollar bond underlying the swap are as shown in the second column. The present value of the cash flows using the dollar discount rate of 9% are shown in the third column. The cash flows from the yen bond underlying the swap are shown in the fourth column of the table. The present value of the cash flows using the yen discount rate of 4% are shown in the final column of the table.

The value of the dollar bond, B_D, is 9.5439 million dollars. The value of the yen bond is 1230.55 million yen. The value of the swap in dollars is therefore

$$\frac{1{,}230.55}{110} - 9.5439 = 1.5430 \text{ million}$$

Valuation as Portfolio of Forward Contracts

Each exchange of payments in a fixed-for-fixed currency swap is a forward contract. As shown in Section 5.7, forward foreign exchange contracts can be valued by assuming that forward exchange rates are realized. The forward exchange rates themselves can be calculated from equation (5.9).

Example

Consider again the situation described in the previous example. The LIBOR/swap term structure of interest rates is flat in both Japan and the United States. The Japanese rate is 4% per annum and the U.S. rate is 9% per annum (both with continuous compounding). A financial institution has entered into a currency swap in which it receives 5% per annum in yen and pays 8% per annum in dollars once a year. The principals in the two currencies are $10 million and 1,200 million yen. The swap will last for another three years, and the current exchange rate is 110 yen = $1.

The calculations are summarized in Table 7.10. The financial institution pays $0.08 \times 10 = \$0.8$ million dollars and receives $1{,}200 \times 0.05 = 60$ million yen each year. In addition the dollar principal of $10 million is paid and the yen principal

Table 7.10 Valuation of currency swap as a portfolio of forward contracts (all amounts in millions)

Time	*Dollar cash flow*	*Yen cash flow*	*Forward rate*	*Dollar value of yen cash flow*	*Net cash flow ($)*	*Present value*
1	−0.8	60	0.009557	0.5734	−0.2266	−0.2071
2	−0.8	60	0.010047	0.6028	−0.1972	−0.1647
3	−0.8	60	0.010562	0.6337	−0.1663	−0.1269
3	−10.0	1,200	0.010562	12.6746	+2.6746	2.0417
Total						1.5430

of 1,200 is received at the end of year 3. The current spot rate is 0.009091 dollar per yen. In this case, $r = 4\%$ and $r_f = 9\%$, so that the one-year forward rate is from equation (5.9) $0.009091e^{(0.09-0.04)\times 1} = 0.009557$. The two- and three-year forward rates in Table 7.10 are calculated similarly. The forward contract underlying the swap can be valued by assuming that the forward rates are realized. If the forward rate is realized, the value of yen cash flow in year 1 will be $60 \times 0.009557 = 0.5734$ dollars and the net cash flow at the end of year 1 will be $0.6 - 0.5734 = -0.2266$ dollars. This has a present value of $-0.2266e^{-0.09\times 1} = -0.2071$. This is the value of forward contract corresponding to the exchange of cash flows at the end of year 1. The value of the other forward contracts are calculated similarly. As shown in Table 7.10, the value of the swap is 1.5430. This is in agreement with the value we calculated earlier by decomposing the swap into a long position in one bond and a short position in another.

The value of a currency swap is normally zero when it is first negotiated. If the two principals are worth exactly the same using the exchange rate at the start of the swap, the value of the swap is also zero immediately after the initial exchange of principal. However, as in the case of interest rate swaps, this does not mean that each of the individual forward contracts underlying the swap has zero value. It can be shown that, when interest rates in two currencies are significantly different, the payer of the high-interest-rate currency is in the position where the forward contracts corresponding to the early exchanges of cash flows have negative values, and the forward contract corresponding to final exchange of principals has a positive value. (This is the situation in our example in Table 7.10.) The payer of the low-interest-rate currency is likely to be in the opposite position; that is, the early exchanges of cash flows have positive values and the final exchange has a negative value.

For the payer of the low-interest-rate currency, the swap will tend to have a negative value during most of its life. The forward contracts corresponding to the early exchanges of payments have positive values, and, once these exchanges have taken place, there is a tendency for the remaining forward contracts to have, in total, a negative value. For the payer of the high-interest-rate currency, the reverse is true. The value of the swap will tend to be positive during most of its life. These results are important when the credit risk in the swap is being evaluated.

7.10 CREDIT RISK

Contracts such as swaps that are private arrangements between two companies entail credit risks. Consider a financial institution that has entered into offsetting contracts with two companies (see Figure 7.4, 7.5, or 7.7). If neither party defaults, the financial institution remains fully hedged. A decline in the value of one contract will always be offset by an increase in the value of the other contract. However, there is a chance that one party will get into financial difficulties and default. The financial institution then still has to honor the contract it has with the other party.

Suppose that some time after the initiation of the contracts in Figure 7.4, the contract with Microsoft has a positive value to the financial institution, whereas the contract with Intel has a negative value. If Microsoft defaults, the financial institution is liable to lose the whole of the positive value it has in this contract. To maintain a hedged

Figure 7.13 The credit exposure in a swap

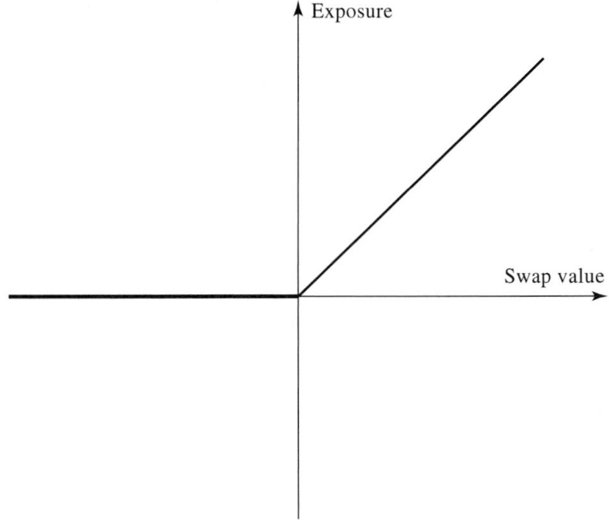

position, it would have to find a third party willing to take Microsoft's position. To induce the third party to take the position, the financial institution would have to pay the third party an amount roughly equal to the value of its contract with Microsoft prior to the default.

A financial institution has credit-risk exposure from a swap only when the value of the swap to the financial institution is positive. What happens when this value is negative and the counterparty gets into financial difficulties? In theory, the financial institution could realize a windfall gain, because a default would lead to it getting rid of a liability. In practice, it is likely that the counterparty would choose to sell the contract to a third party or rearrange its affairs in some way so that its positive value in the contract is not lost. The most realistic assumption for the financial institution is therefore as follows. If the counterparty goes bankrupt, there will be a loss if the value of the swap to the financial institution is positive, and there will be no effect on the financial institution's position if the value of the swap to the financial institution is negative. This situation is summarized in Figure 7.13.

Potential losses from defaults on a swap are much less than the potential losses from defaults on a loan with the same principal. This is because the value of the swap is usually only a small fraction of the value of the loan. Potential losses from defaults on a currency swap are greater than on an interest rate swap. The reason is that, because principal amounts in two different currencies are exchanged at the end of the life of a currency swap, a currency swap is liable to have a greater value at the time of a default than an interest rate swap.

It is important to distinguish between the credit risk and market risk to a financial institution in any contract. As discussed earlier, the credit risk arises from the possibility of a default by the counterparty when the value of the contract to the financial institution is positive. The market risk arises from the possibility that market variables such as interest rates and exchange rates will move in such a way that the value

Business Snapshot 7.2 The Hammersmith and Fulham story

Between 1987 to 1989 the London Borough of Hammersmith and Fulham in Great Britain entered into about 600 interest rate swaps and related instruments with a total notional principal of about 6 billion pounds. The transactions appear to have been entered into for speculative rather than hedging purposes. The two employees of Hammersmith and Fulham that were responsible for the trades had only a sketchy understanding of the risks they were taking and how the products they were trading worked.

By 1989, because of movements in sterling interest rates, Hammersmith and Fulham had lost several hundred million pounds on the swaps. To the banks on the other side of the transactions, the swaps were worth several hundred million pounds. The banks were concerned about credit risk. They had entered into offsetting swaps to hedge their interest rate risks. If Hammersmith and Fulham defaulted they would still have to honor their obligations on the offsetting swaps and would take a huge loss.

What happened was something a little different from a default. Hammersmith and Fulham's auditor asked to have the transactions declared void because Hammersmith and Fulham did not have the authority to enter into the transactions. The British courts agreed. The case was appealed and went all the way to the House of Lords, Britain's highest court. The final decision was that Hammersmith and Fulham did not have the authority to enter into the swaps, but that they ought to have the authority to do so in the future for risk management purposes. Needless to say, banks were furious that their contracts were overturned in this way by the courts.

of a contract to the financial institution becomes negative. Market risks can be hedged by entering into offsetting contracts; credit risks are less easy to hedge.

One of the more bizarre stories in swap markets is outlined in Business Snapshot 7.2. It concerns the British Local Authority, Hammersmith and Fulham, and shows that in addition to bearing credit risk and market risk, banks trading swaps also sometimes bear legal risk.

SUMMARY

The two most common types of swap are interest rate swaps and currency swaps. In an interest rate swap, one party agrees to pay the other party interest at a fixed rate on a notional principal for a number of years. In return, it receives interest at a floating rate on the same notional principal for the same period of time. In a currency swap, one party agrees to pay interest on a principal amount in one currency. In return, it receives interest on a principal amount in another currency.

Principal amounts are not usually exchanged in an interest rate swap. In a currency swap, principal amounts are usually exchanged at both the beginning and the end of the life of the swap. For a party paying interest in the foreign currency, the foreign principal is received, and the domestic principal is paid at the beginning of the life of the swap. At the end of the life of the swap, the foreign principal is paid and the domestic principal is received.

An interest rate swap can be used to transform a floating-rate loan into a fixed-rate loan, or vice versa. It can also be used to transform a floating-rate investment to a fixed-rate investment, or vice versa. A currency swap can be used to transform a loan in one currency into a loan in another currency. It can also be used to transform an investment denominated in one currency into an investment denominated in another currency.

There are two ways of valuing interest rate and currency swaps. In the first, the swap is decomposed into a long position in one bond and a short position in another bond. In the second, it is regarded as a portfolio of forward contracts.

When a financial institution enters into a pair of offsetting swaps with different counterparties, it is exposed to credit risk. If one of the counterparties defaults when the financial institution has positive value in its swap with that counterparty, the financial institution loses money because it still has to honor its swap agreement with the other counterparty.

FURTHER READING

Baz, J., and M. Pascutti. "Alternative Swap Contracts Analysis and Pricing," *Journal of Derivatives*, (Winter 1996): 7–21.

Brown, K.C., and D.J. Smith. *Interest Rate and Currency Swaps: A Tutorial*. Association for Investment Management and Research, 1996.

Cooper, I., and A. Mello. "The Default Risk in Interest Rate Swaps," *Journal of Finance*, 46, 2 (1991): 597–620.

Dattatreya, R.E., and K. Hotta. *Advanced Interest Rate and Currency Swaps: State-of-the Art Products, Strategies, and Risk Management Applications*, Irwin, 1993.

Flavell, R. *Swaps and Other Instruments*. Chichester: Wiley, 2002.

Gupta, A., and M.G. Subrahmanyam. "An Empirical Examination of the Convexity Bias in the Pricing of Interest Rate Swaps," *Journal of Financial Economics*, 55, 2 (2000): 239–79.

Litzenberger, R.H. "Swaps: Plain and Fanciful," *Journal of Finance*, 47, 3 (1992): 831–50.

Minton, B.A. "An Empirical Examination of the Basic Valuation Models for Interest Rate Swaps," *Journal of Financial Economics*, 44, 2 (1997): 251–77.

Sun, T., S. Sundaresan, and C. Wang. "Interest Rate Swaps: An Empirical Investigation," *Journal of Financial Economics*, 34, 1 (1993): 77–99.

Titman, S. "Interest Rate Swaps and Corporate Financing Choices," *Journal of Finance*, 47, 4 (1992): 1503–16.

Quiz (Answers at End of Book)

7.1. Companies A and B have been offered the following rates per annum on a $20 million five-year loan:

	Fixed rate	*Floating rate*
Company A:	12.0%	LIBOR + 0.1%
Company B:	13.4%	LIBOR + 0.6%

Company A requires a floating-rate loan; company B requires a fixed-rate loan. Design a swap that will net a bank, acting as intermediary, 0.1% per annum and that will appear equally attractive to both companies.

7.2. Company X wishes to borrow U.S. dollars at a fixed rate of interest. Company Y wishes to borrow Japanese yen at a fixed rate of interest. The amounts required by the two companies are roughly the same at the current exchange rate. The companies have been quoted the following interest rates, which have been adjusted for the impact of taxes:

	Yen	*Dollars*
Company X:	5.0%	9.6%
Company Y:	6.5%	10.0%

Design a swap that will net a bank, acting as intermediary, 50 basis points per annum. Make the swap equally attractive to the two companies and ensure that all foreign exchange risk is assumed by the bank.

7.3. A \$100 million interest rate swap has a remaining life of 10 months. Under the terms of the swap, six-month LIBOR is exchanged for 12% per annum (compounded semiannually). The average of the bid–offer rate being exchanged for six-month LIBOR in swaps of all maturities is currently 10% per annum with continuous compounding. The six-month LIBOR rate was 9.6% per annum two months ago. What is the current value of the swap to the party paying floating? What is its value to the party paying fixed?

7.4. Explain what a swap rate is. What is the relationship between swap rates and par yields?

7.5. A currency swap has a remaining life of 15 months. It involves exchanging interest at 14% on £20 million for interest at 10% on \$30 million once a year. The term structure of interest rates in both the United Kingdom and the United States is currently flat, and if the swap were negotiated today the interest rates exchanged would be 8% in dollars and 11% in sterling. All interest rates are quoted with annual compounding. The current exchange rate (dollars per pound sterling) is 1.6500. What is the value of the swap to the party paying sterling? What is the value of the swap to the party paying dollars?

7.6. Explain the difference between the credit risk and the market risk in a financial contract.

7.7. A corporate treasurer tells you that he has just negotiated a five-year loan at a competitive fixed rate of interest of 5.2%. The treasurer explains that he achieved the 5.2% rate by borrowing at six-month LIBOR plus 150 basis points and swapping LIBOR for 3.7%. He goes on to say that this was possible because his company has a comparative advantage in the floating-rate market. What has the treasurer overlooked?

Questions and Problems (Answers in Solutions Manual/Study Guide)

7.8. Explain why a bank is subject to credit risk when it enters into two offsetting swap contracts.

7.9. A financial institution has entered into an interest rate swap with company X. Under the terms of the swap, it receives 10% per annum and pays six-month LIBOR on a principal of \$10 million for five years. Payments are made every six months. Suppose that company X defaults on the sixth payment date (end of year 3) when the interest rate (with semiannual compounding) is 8% per annum for all maturities. What is the loss to the financial institution? Assume that six-month LIBOR was 9% per annum halfway through year 3.

7.10. Companies X and Y have been offered the following rates per annum on a $5 million 10-year investment:

	Fixed rate	*Floating rate*
Company X:	8.0%	LIBOR
Company Y:	8.8%	LIBOR

Company X requires a fixed-rate investment; company Y requires a floating-rate investment. Design a swap that will net a bank, acting as intermediary, 0.2% per annum and will appear equally attractive to X and Y.

7.11. A financial institution has entered into a ten-year currency swap with company Y. Under the terms of the swap, the financial institution receives interest at 3% per annum in Swiss francs and pays interest at 8% per annum in U.S. dollars. Interest payments are exchanged once a year. The principal amounts are 7 million dollars and 10 million francs. Suppose that company Y declares bankruptcy at the end of year 6, when the exchange rate is $0.80 per franc. What is the cost to the financial institution? Assume that, at the end of year 6, the interest rate is 3% per annum in Swiss francs and 8% per annum in U.S. dollars for all maturities. All interest rates are quoted with annual compounding.

7.12. Companies A and B face the following interest rates (adjusted for the differential impact of taxes):

	A	B
U.S. dollars (floating rate):	LIBOR + 0.5%	LIBOR + 1.0%
Canadian dollars (fixed rate):	5.0%	6.5%

Assume that A wants to borrow U.S. dollars at a floating rate of interest and B wants to borrow Canadian dollars at a fixed rate of interest. A financial institution is planning to arrange a swap and requires a 50-basis-point spread. If the swap is equally attractive to A and B, what rates of interest will A and B end up paying?

7.13. After it hedges its foreign exchange risk using forward contracts, is the financial institution's average spread in Figure 7.10 likely to be greater than or less than 20 basis points? Explain your answer.

7.14. "Companies with high credit risks are the ones that cannot access fixed-rate markets directly. They are the companies that are most likely to be paying fixed and receiving floating in an interest rate swap." Assume that this statement is true. Do you think it increases or decreases the risk of a financial institution's swap portfolio? Assume that companies are most likely to default when interest rates are high.

7.15. Why is the expected loss from a default on a swap less than the expected loss from the default on a loan with the same principal?

7.16. A bank finds that its assets are not matched with its liabilities. It is taking floating-rate deposits and making fixed-rate loans. How can swaps be used to offset the risk?

7.17. Explain how you would value a swap that is the exchange of a floating rate in one currency for a fixed rate in another currency.

7.18. The LIBOR zero curve is flat at 5% (continuously compounded) out to 1.5 years. Swap rates for 2- and 3-year semiannual pay swaps are 5.4% and 5.6%, respectively. Estimate the LIBOR zero rates for maturities of 2.0, 2.5, and 3.0 years. (Assume that the 2.5-year swap rate is the average of the 2- and 3-year swap rates.)

Assignment Questions

7.19. The one-year LIBOR rate is 10%. A bank trades swaps where a fixed rate of interest is exchanged for 12-month LIBOR with payments being exchanged annually. Two- and three-year swap rates (expressed with annual compounding) are 11% and 12% per annum. Estimate the two- and three-year LIBOR zero rates.

7.20. Company A, a British manufacturer, wishes to borrow U.S. dollars at a fixed rate of interest. Company B, a U.S. multinational, wishes to borrow sterling at a fixed rate of interest. They have been quoted the following rates per annum (adjusted for differential tax effects):

	Sterling	*U.S. dollars*
Company A:	11.0%	7.0%
Company B:	10.6%	6.2%

Design a swap that will net a bank, acting as intermediary, 10 basis points per annum and that will produce a gain of 15 basis points per annum for each of the two companies.

7.21. Under the terms of an interest rate swap, a financial institution has agreed to pay 10% per annum and to receive three-month LIBOR in return on a notional principal of $100 million with payments being exchanged every three months. The swap has a remaining life of 14 months. The average of the bid and offer fixed rates currently being swapped for three-month LIBOR is 12% per annum for all maturities. The three-month LIBOR rate one month ago was 11.8% per annum. All rates are compounded quarterly. What is the value of the swap?

7.22. Suppose that the term structure of interest rates is flat in the United States and Australia. The USD interest rate is 7% per annum and the AUD rate is 9% per annum. The current value of the AUD is 0.62 USD. Under the terms of a swap agreement, a financial institution pays 8% per annum in AUD and receives 4% per annum in USD. The principals in the two currencies are $12 million USD and 20 million AUD. Payments are exchanged every year, with one exchange having just taken place. The swap will last two more years. What is the value of the swap to the financial institution? Assume all interest rates are continuously compounded.

7.23. Company X is based in the United Kingdom and would like to borrow $50 million at a fixed rate of interest for five years in U.S. funds. Because the company is not well known in the United States, this has proved to be impossible. However, the company has been quoted 12% per annum on fixed-rate five-year sterling funds. Company Y is based in the United States and would like to borrow the equivalent of $50 million in sterling funds for five years at a fixed rate of interest. It has been unable to get a quote but has been offered U.S. dollar funds at 10.5% per annum. Five-year government bonds currently yield 9.5% per annum in the United States and 10.5% in the United Kingdom. Suggest an appropriate currency swap that will net the financial intermediary 0.5% per annum.

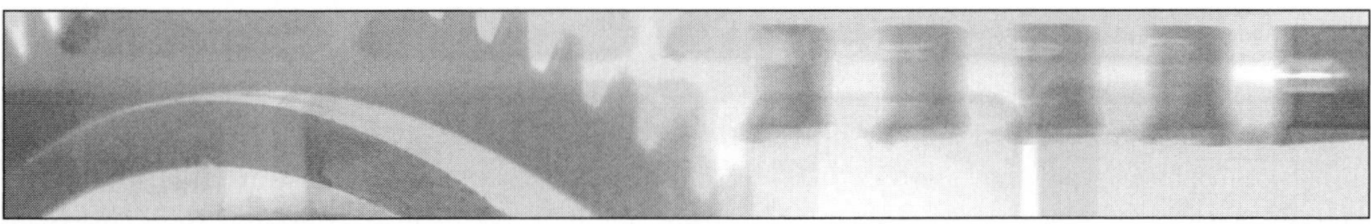

CHAPTER 8

Mechanics of Options Markets

The rest of this book is, for the most part, concerned with options. This chapter explains how options markets are organized, what terminology is used, how the contracts are traded, how margin requirements are set, and so on. Later chapters will examine such topics as trading strategies involving options, the determination of option prices, and the ways in which portfolios of options can be hedged. This chapter is concerned primarily with stock options. Details on the markets for currency options, index options, and futures options are provided in Chapters 13 and 14.

Options are fundamentally different from forward and futures contracts. An option gives the holder of the option the right to do something. The holder does not have to exercise this right. By contrast, in a forward or futures contract, the two parties have committed themselves to some action. It costs a trader nothing (except for the margin requirements) to enter into a forward or futures contract, whereas the purchase of an option requires an up-front payment.

8.1 TYPES OF OPTIONS

As mentioned in Chapter 1, there are two basic types of options. A *call option* gives the holder of the option the right to buy an asset by a certain date for a certain price. A *put option* gives the holder the right to sell an asset by a certain date for a certain price. The date specified in the contract is known as the *expiration date* or the *maturity date*. The price specified in the contract is known as the *exercise price* or the *strike price*.

Options can be either American or European, a distinction that has nothing to do with geographical location. *American options* can be exercised at any time up to the expiration date, whereas *European options* can be exercised only on the expiration date itself. Most of the options that are traded on exchanges are American. However, European options are generally easier to analyze than American options, and some of the properties of an American option are frequently deduced from those of its European counterpart.

Call Options

Consider the situation of an investor who buys a European call option with a strike price of \$100 to purchase 100 eBay shares. Suppose that the current stock price is \$98, the expiration date of the option is in four months, and the price of an option to purchase one share is \$5. The initial investment is \$500. Because the option is European, the investor can exercise only on the expiration date. If the stock price on this date is less than \$100, the investor will clearly choose not to exercise. (There is no point in buying for \$100 a share that has a market value of less than \$100.) In these circumstances, the investor loses the whole of the initial investment of \$500. If the stock price is above \$100 on the expiration date, the option will be exercised. Suppose, for example, that the stock price is \$115. By exercising the option, the investor is able to buy 100 shares for \$100 per share. If the shares are sold immediately, the investor makes a gain of \$15 per share, or \$1,500, ignoring transactions costs. When the initial cost of the option is taken into account, the net profit to the investor is \$1,000.

Trading Note 8.1 summarizes this example. Figure 8.1 shows how the investor's net profit or loss on an option to purchase one share varies with the final stock price in the example. It is important to realize that an investor sometimes exercises an option and makes a loss overall. Suppose that in the example eBay's stock price is \$102 at the expiration of the option. The investor would exercise the option for a gain of $100 \times (\$102 - \$100) = \$200$ and realize a loss overall of \$300 when the initial cost of the option is taken into account. It is tempting to argue that the investor should not exercise the option in these circumstances. However, not exercising would lead to an overall loss of \$500, which is worse than the \$300 loss when the investor exercises. In general, call options should always be exercised at the expiration date if the stock price is above the strike price.

Put Options

Whereas the purchaser of a call option is hoping that the stock price will increase, the purchaser of a put option is hoping that it will decrease. Consider an investor who buys a European put option to sell 100 shares in IBM with a strike price of \$70. Suppose that the current stock price is \$65, the expiration date of the option is in three months, and the price of an option to sell one share is \$7. The initial investment is \$700. Because the option is European, it will be exercised only if the stock price is below \$70 on the expiration date. Suppose that the stock price is \$55 on this date. The investor can buy

---

Trading Note 8.1 Profit from call option

An investor buys a call option to purchase 100 eBay shares.

Strike price = \$100
Current share price = \$98
Price of an option to buy one share = \$5
The initial investment is $100 \times \$5 = \$500$

The Outcome
At the expiration of the option eBay's share price is \$115. At this time, the option is exercised for a gain of

$$(\$115 - \$100) \times 100 = \$1{,}500$$

When the initial cost of the option is taken into account, the net gain is

$$\$1{,}500 - \$500 = \$1{,}000$$

Figure 8.1 Profit from buying a European call option on one eBay share. Option price = \$5; strike price = \$100

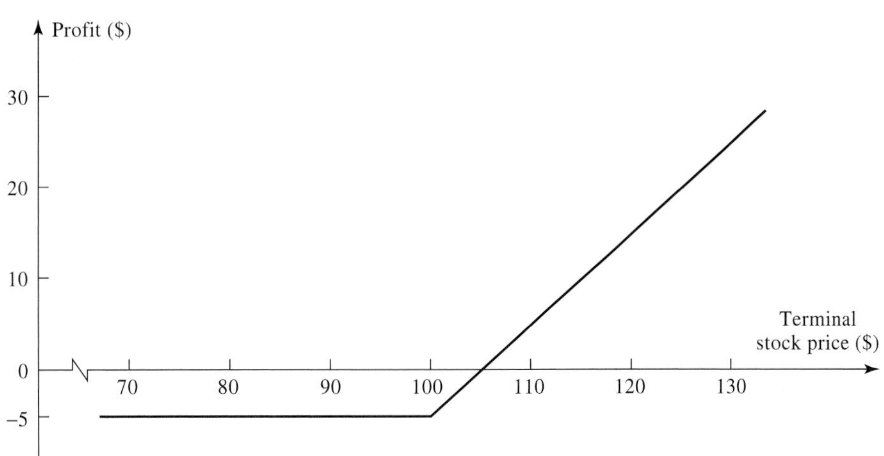

100 shares for \$55 per share and, under the terms of the put option, sell the same shares for \$70 to realize a gain of \$15 per share, or \$1,500 (again, transactions costs are ignored). When the \$700 initial cost of the option is taken into account, the investor's net profit is \$800. There is no guarantee that the investor will make a gain. If the final stock price is above \$70, the put option expires worthless, and the investor loses \$700. Trading Note 8.2 summarizes this example. Figure 8.2 shows the way in which the investor's profit or loss on an option to sell one share varies with the terminal stock price in this example.

Early Exercise

As already mentioned, exchange-traded stock options are generally American rather than European. That is, the investor in the foregoing examples would not have to wait until the

Trading Note 8.2 Profit from put option

An investor buys a put option to sell 100 IBM shares.

Strike price = \$70
Current share price = \$65
Price of put option to sell one share = \$7

The initial investment is 100 × \$7 = \$700.

The Outcome

At the expiration of the option, IBM's share price is \$55. At this time, the investor buys 100 IBM shares and, under the terms of the put option, sells them for \$70 per share to realize a gain of \$15 per share, or \$1,500 in total. When the initial cost of the option is taken into account, the net gain is

\$1,500 − \$700 = \$800

Figure 8.2 Profit from buying a European put option on one IBM share. Option price = \$7; strike price = \$70

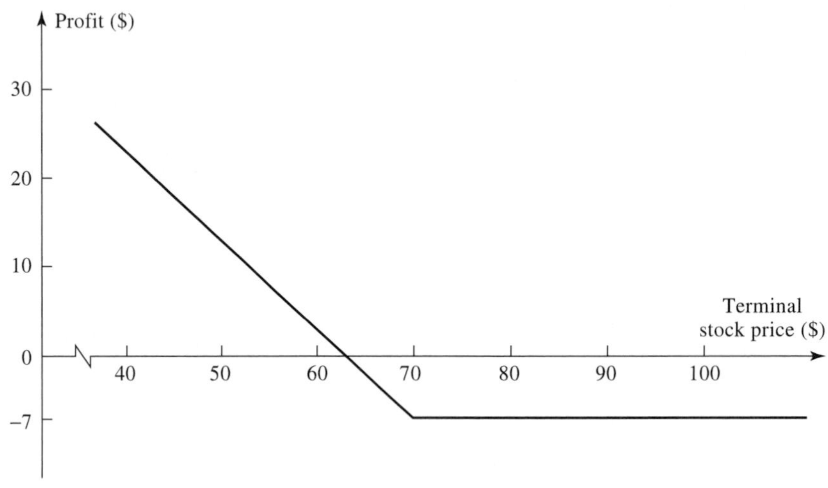

expiration date before exercising the option. We will see later that there are some circumstances under which it is optimal to exercise American options prior to maturity.

8.2 OPTION POSITIONS

There are two sides to every option contract. On one side is the investor who has taken the long position (i.e., has bought the option). On the other side is the investor who has taken a short position (i.e., has sold or *written* the option). The writer of an option receives cash up front, but has potential liabilities later. The writer's profit or loss is the reverse of that for the purchaser of the option. Figures 8.3 and 8.4 show the variation of the profit or loss with the final stock price for writers of the options considered in Figures 8.1 and 8.2.

There are four types of option positions:

1. A long position in a call option
2. A long position in a put option
3. A short position in a call option
4. A short position in a put option

It is often useful to characterize European option positions in terms of the terminal value or payoff to the investor at maturity. The initial cost of the option is not then included in the calculation. If K is the strike price and S_T is the final price of the underlying asset, the payoff from a long position in a European call option is

$$\max(S_T - K, 0)$$

This reflects the fact that the option will be exercised if $S_T > K$ and will not be exercised

Figure 8.3 Profit from writing a European call option on one eBay share. Option price = \$5; strike price = \$100

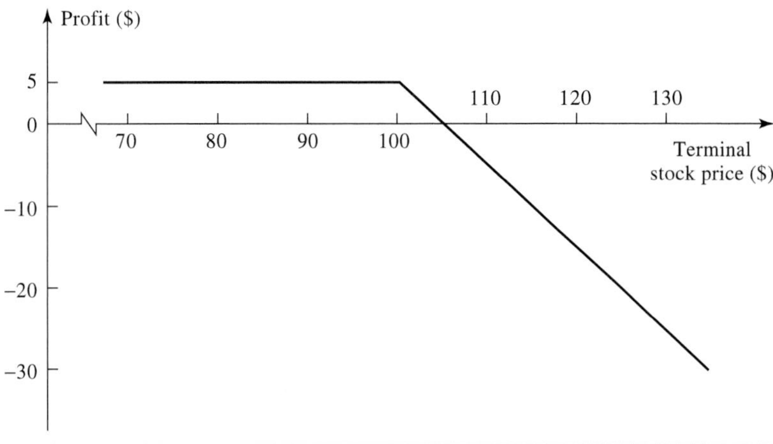

if $S_T \leqslant K$. The payoff to the holder of a short position in the European call option is

$$-\max(S_T - K,\ 0) = \min(K - S_T,\ 0)$$

The payoff to the holder of a long position in a European put option is

$$\max(K - S_T,\ 0)$$

and the payoff from a short position in a European put option is

$$-\max(K - S_T,\ 0) = \min(S_T - K,\ 0)$$

Figure 8.5 illustrates these payoffs.

Figure 8.4 Profit from writing a European put option on one IBM share. Option price = \$7; strike price = \$70

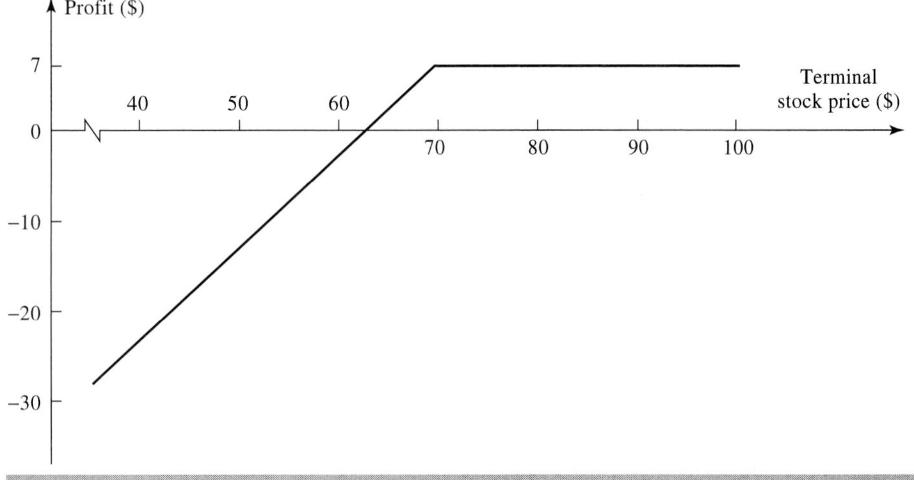

Figure 8.5 Payoffs from positions in European options: (a) long call, (b) short call, (c) long put, (d) short put. Strike price = K; price of asset at maturity = S_T

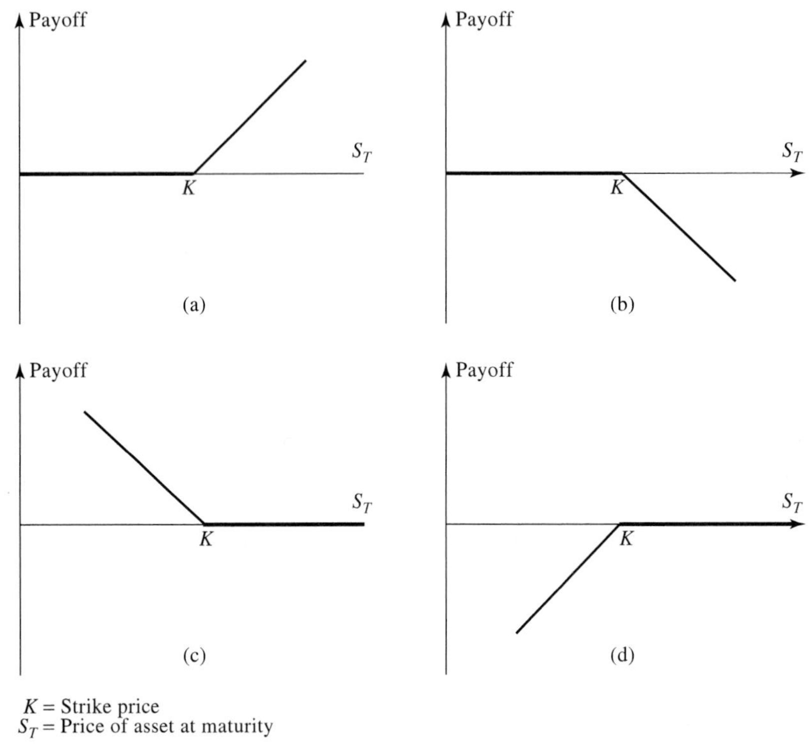

8.3 UNDERLYING ASSETS

In this section we review options on stocks, currencies, stock indices, and futures.

Stock Options

Most trading in stock options is on exchanges. In the United States the exchanges trading stock options are the Chicago Board Options Exchange (www.cboe.com), the Philadelphia Stock Exchange (www.phlx.com), the American Stock Exchange (www.amex.com), the Pacific Exchange (www.pacifex.com), and the International Securities Exchange (www.iseoptions.com). Options trade on more than 1000 different stocks. One contract gives the holder the right to buy or sell 100 shares at the specified strike price. This contract size is convenient because the shares themselves are normally traded in lots of 100.

Foreign Currency Options

Most currency options trading is now in the over-the-counter market, but there is some exchange trading. The major exchange for trading foreign currency options in the

United States is the Philadelphia Stock Exchange. It offers both European and American contracts on a variety of different currencies. The size of one contract depends on the currency. For example, in the case of the British pound, one contract gives the holder the right to buy or sell £31,250; in the case of the Japanese yen, one contract gives the holder the right to buy or sell 6.25 million yen. Foreign currency options contracts are discussed further in Chapter 13.

Index Options

Many different index options currently trade throughout the world in both the over-the-counter market and the exchange-traded market. The most popular exchange-traded contracts in the United States are those on the S&P 500 Index (SPX), the S&P 100 Index (OEX), the Nasdaq 100 Index (NDX), and the Dow Jones Industrial Index (DJX). All of these trade on the Chicago Board Options Exchange. Most of the contracts are European. An exception is the contract on the S&P 100, which is American. One contract is to buy or sell 100 times the index at the specified strike price. Settlement is always in cash, rather than by delivering the portfolio underlying the index. Consider, for example, one call contract on the S&P 100 with a strike price of 980. If it is exercised when the value of the index is 992, the writer of the contract pays the holder $(992 - 980) \times 100 = \$1{,}200$. This cash payment is based on the index value at the end of the day on which exercise instructions are issued. Not surprisingly, investors usually wait until the end of a day before issuing these instructions. Index options are discussed further in Chapter 13.

Futures Options

When an exchange trades a particular futures contract it often also trades options on that contract. A futures option normally matures just before the delivery period in the futures contract. When a call option is exercised, the holder acquires from the writer a long position in the underlying futures contract plus a cash amount equal to the excess of the futures price over the strike price. When a put option is exercised, the holder acquires a short position in the underlying futures contract plus a cash amount equal to the excess of the strike price over the futures price. Futures options contracts are discussed further in Chapter 14.

8.4 SPECIFICATION OF STOCK OPTIONS

In the rest of this chapter, we will focus on stock options. As already mentioned, an exchange-traded stock option in the United States is an American-style option contract to buy or sell 100 shares of the stock. Details of the contract—the expiration date, the strike price, what happens when dividends are declared, how large a position investors can hold, and so on—are specified by the exchange.

Expiration Dates

One of the items used to describe a stock option is the month in which the expiration date occurs. Thus, a January call trading on IBM is a call option on IBM with an expiration date in January. The precise expiration date is the Saturday immediately following the third Friday of the expiration month. The last day on which options trade is the third Friday of the expiration month. An investor with a long position in an option normally has until 4:30 p.m. Central Time on that Friday to instruct a broker to exercise the option. The broker then has until 10:59 p.m. the next day to complete the paperwork notifying the exchange that exercise is to take place.

Stock options are on a January, February, or March cycle. The January cycle consists of the months January, April, July, and October; the February cycle, the months February, May, August, and November; and the March cycle, the months March, June, September, and December. If the expiration date for the current month has not yet been reached, options trade with expiration dates in the current month, the following month, and the next two months in the cycle. If the expiration date of the current month has passed, options trade with expiration dates in the next month, the next-but-one month, and the next two months of the expiration cycle. For example, IBM is on a January cycle. At the beginning of January, options are traded with expiration dates in January, February, April, and July; at the end of January, they are traded with expiration dates in February, March, April, and July; at the beginning of May, they are traded with expiration dates in May, June, July, and October; and so on. When one option reaches expiration, trading in another is started. Longer-term options, known as LEAPS (long-term equity anticipation securities), also trade on about 500 stocks in the United States stocks. These have expiration dates up to three years into the future. The expiration dates for LEAPS on stocks are always in January.

Strike Prices

The exchange normally chooses the strike prices at which options can be written so that they are spaced $2.50, $5, or $10 apart. Typically the spacing is $2.50 when the stock price is between $5 and $25, $5 when the stock price is between $25 and $200, and $10 for stock prices above $200. As will be explained shortly, stock splits and stock dividends can lead to nonstandard strike prices.

When a new expiration date is introduced, the two or three strike prices closest to the current stock price are usually selected by the exchange. If the stock price moves outside the range defined by the highest and lowest strike price, trading is usually introduced in an option with a new strike price. To illustrate these rules, suppose that the stock price is $84 when trading begins in the October options. Call and put options would probably first be offered with strike prices of $80, $85, and $90. If the stock price rose above $90, it is likely that a strike price of $95 would be offered; if it fell below $80, it is likely that a strike price of $75 would be offered; and so on.

Terminology

For any given asset at any given time, many different option contracts may be trading. Consider a stock that has four expiration dates and five strike prices. If call and put options trade with every expiration date and every strike price, there are a total of 40 different contracts. All options of the same type (calls or puts) are referred to as an *option class*. For example, IBM calls are one class, whereas IBM puts are another class. An *option series* consists of all the options of a given class with the same expiration date and strike price. In other words, an option series refers to a particular contract that is traded. The IBM 50 October calls are an option series.

Options are referred to as *in the money*, *at the money*, or *out of the money*. If S is the stock price and K is the strike price, a call option is in the money when $S > K$, at the money when $S = K$, and out of the money when $S < K$. A put option is in the money when $S < K$, at the money when $S = K$, and out of the money when $S > K$. Clearly, an option will be exercised only when it is in the money. In the absence of transactions costs, an in-the-money option will always be exercised on the expiration date if it has not been exercised previously.

The *intrinsic value* of an option is defined as the maximum of zero and the value the option would have if it were exercised immediately. For a call option, the intrinsic value is therefore $\max(S - K, 0)$; for a put option, it is $\max(K - S, 0)$. An in-the-money American option must be worth at least as much as its intrinsic value because the holder can realize a positive intrinsic value by exercising immediately. Often it is optimal for the holder of an in-the-money American option to wait rather than exercise immediately. The option is then said to have *time value*. The total value of an option can be thought of as the sum of its intrinsic value and its time value.

Flex Options

The Chicago Board Options Exchange offers *flex options* on equities and equity indices. These are options where the traders on the floor of the exchange agree to nonstandard terms. These nonstandard terms can involve a strike price or an expiration date that is different from what is usually offered by the exchange. It can also involve the option being European rather than American. Flex options are an attempt by option exchanges to regain business from the over-the-counter markets. The exchange specifies a minimum size (e.g., 100 contracts) for flex option trades.

Dividends and Stock Splits

The early over-the-counter options were dividend protected. If a company declared a cash dividend, the strike price for options on the company's stock was reduced on the ex-dividend day by the amount of the dividend. Exchange-traded options are not usually adjusted for cash dividends. In other words, when a cash dividend occurs, there are no adjustments to the terms of the option contract. An exception is sometimes made for large cash dividends (see the Gucci Group example in Business Snapshot 8.1).

Exchange-traded options are adjusted for stock splits. A stock split occurs when the existing shares are "split" into more shares. For example, in a 3-for-1 stock split, three new shares are issued to replace each existing share. Because a stock split does not change the assets or the earning ability of a company, we should not expect it to have any effect on the wealth of the company's shareholders. All else being equal, the 3-for-1 stock split should cause the stock price to go down to one-third of its previous value. In general, an n-for-m stock split should cause the stock price to go down to m/n of its previous value. The terms of option contracts are adjusted to reflect expected changes in a stock price arising from a stock split. After an n-for-m stock split, the strike price is reduced to m/n of its previous value, and the number of shares covered by one contract is increased to n/m of its previous value. If the stock price declines in the way expected, the positions of both the writer and the purchaser of a contract remain unchanged.

Business Snapshot 8.1 Gucci Group's large dividend

When there is a large cash dividend (typically one more than 10% of the stock price) a committee of the Options Clearing Corporation (OCC) at the Chicago Board Options Exchange can decide to make adjustments to the terms of options traded on the exchange.

On May 28, 2003, Gucci Group N.V. (GUC) declared a cash dividend of 13.50 euros (approximately \$15.88) per common share and this was approved at the GUC annual shareholders meeting on July 16, 2003. The dividend was about 16% of the share price at the time it was declared. In this case the OCC committee decided to adjust the terms of options. As a result, exercise of an option contract required the delivery of 100 shares plus $100 \times 15.88 = \$1{,}588$ of cash. The holder of a call contract paid 100 times the strike price on exercise and received \$1,588 of cash in addition to 100 shares. The holder of a put contract received 100 times the strike price on exercise and delivered \$1,588 of cash in addition to 100 shares.

Adjustments for large dividends are not always made. For example, Deutsche Terminbörse chose not to adjust the terms of options traded on that exchange when Daimler-Benz surprised the marked on March 10, 1998, with a dividend equal to about 12% of its stock price.

Example

> Consider a call option to buy 100 shares of a company for \$30 per share. Suppose that the company makes a 2-for-1 stock split. The terms of the option contract are then changed so that it gives the holder the right to purchase 200 shares for \$15 per share.

Stock options are adjusted for stock dividends. A stock dividend involves a company issuing more shares to its existing shareholders. For example, a 20% stock dividend means that investors receive one new share for each five already owned. A stock dividend, like a stock split, has no effect on either the assets or the earning power of a company. The stock price can be expected to go down as a result of a stock dividend. The 20% stock dividend referred to is essentially the same as a 6-for-5 stock split. All else being equal, it should cause the stock price to decline to 5/6 of its previous value. The terms of an option are adjusted to reflect the expected price decline arising from a stock dividend in the same way as they are for that arising from a stock split.

Example

> Consider a put option to sell 100 shares of a company for \$15 per share. Suppose that the company declares a 25% stock dividend. This is equivalent to a 5-for-4 stock split. The terms of the option contract are changed so that it gives the holder the right to sell 125 shares for \$12.

Adjustments are also made for rights issues. The basic procedure is to calculate the theoretical price of the rights issue and then to reduce the strike price by this amount.

Position Limits and Exercise Limits

The Chicago Board Options Exchange often specifies a *position limit* for option contracts. This defines the maximum number of option contracts that an investor can hold on one side of the market. For this purpose, long calls and short puts are considered to be on the same side of the market. Also, short calls and long puts are considered to be on the same side of the market. The *exercise limit* usually equals the position limit. It defines the maximum number of contracts that can be exercised by any individual (or group of individuals acting together) in any period of five consecutive business days. Options on the largest and most frequently traded stocks have positions limits of 75,000 contracts. Smaller capitalization stocks have position limits of 60,000, 31,500, 22,500, or 13,500 contracts.

Position limits and exercise limits are designed to prevent the market from being unduly influenced by the activities of an individual investor or group of investors. However, whether the limits are really necessary is a controversial issue.

8.5 NEWSPAPER QUOTES

Many newspapers carry options prices. Table 8.1 shows the prices as they appeared in the *Wall Street Journal* of Thursday, February 5, 2004. They refer to last trade on the previous day (Wednesday, February 4, 2004).

The first part of the table shows the 40 most actively traded option contract listed according to their volume of trading. The most active contract was the February 2004 contract on the Nasdaq 100 index. From the table, we see that a call option contract on Cisco expiring in February 2004 with a strike price of $25 traded for $0.40 down $1.60 from the previous day. The closing price of Cisco's stock was $24.08. Similarly, a put option on Peoplesoft expiring in April 2004 with a strike price 20 traded for $0.50 down $0.35 from the previous day. Peoplesoft's stock price closed at $22.70. The second part of the table shows quotes for long-term options (LEAPS). For example, a Cisco call with a strike price of $30 expiring in January 2006 traded for $2.75, while the corresponding put traded for $7.20.

As mentioned earlier, one contract is for the purchase or sale of 100 shares. One contract therefore costs 100 times the price shown. Because most options are priced at less than $10 and some are priced at less than $1, investors do not have to be extremely wealthy to trade options.

The *Wall Street Journal* also shows at the end part of the table the total call volume, put volume, call open interest, and put open interest for each exchange. As in the case of futures contracts, the volume is the total number of contracts traded on a day and the open interest is the number of contracts outstanding.

8.6 TRADING

Traditionally, exchanges have had to provide a large open area for individuals to meet and trade options. This is changing. Eurex, the large European derivatives exchange, is fully electronic, so that traders do not have to physically meet.[1] The International

[1] In September 2003 Eurex announced that it was planning to set up an all-electronic exchange in Chicago.

Table 8.1 Stock option quotes from the *Wall Street Journal* on February 5, 2004

MOST ACTIVE LISTED OPTIONS

Wednesday, February 4, 2004

Composite volume and close for actively traded equity and LEAPS, or long-term options, with results for the corresponding put or call contract. Volume figures are unofficial. Open interest is total outstanding for all exchanges and reflects previous trading day. Close when possible is shown for the underlying stock or primary market. **XC**-Composite. **p**-Put. **o**-Strike price adjusted for split.

OPTION/STRIKE				VOL	EXCH	LAST	NET CHG	CLOSE	OPEN INT
Nasd100Tr	Feb	37		79,072	XC	0.45	-0.30	36.33	179,411
Nasd100Tr	Feb	37	p	77,716	XC	1.10	0.30	36.33	366,260
Cisco	Feb	25	p	65,470	XC	1.30	0.85	24.08	125,149
Nasd100Tr	Mar	37	p	50,099	XC	1.60	0.30	36.33	136,136
Cisco	Feb	25		45,922	XC	0.40	-1.60	24.08	53,363
Nasd100Tr	Feb	38	p	45,379	XC	1.80	0.40	36.33	256,982
Nasd100Tr	Mar	37		40,652	XC	1	-0.30	36.33	85,536
Cisco	Apr	27.50		37,154	XC	0.50	-0.70	24.08	50,310
Nasd100Tr	Feb	36	p	32,848	XC	0.60	0.20	36.33	272,591
Nasd100Tr	Feb	38		32,650	XC	0.20	-0.20	36.33	210,587
Cisco	Feb	27.50		28,459	XC	0.10	-0.55	24.08	159,880
Nasd100Tr	Mar	36	p	23,642	XC	1.15	0.25	36.33	132,833
SemiHTr	Feb	42.50	p	22,758	XC	2.30	0.70	40.58	55,469
JDS Uni	Mar	5		21,315	XC	0.30	-0.15	4.76	47,388
ATT Wrls	Jan 05	10	p	20,942	XC	0.50	-0.05	11.13	9,652
Cisco	Mar	27.50		20,475	XC	0.30	-0.70	24.08	26,565
Nasd100Tr	Jan 06	35		20,087	XC	6.40	-0.30	36.33	105,059
Nasd100Tr	Mar	38		18,915	XC	0.60	-0.25	36.33	65,878
Intel	Feb	30		18,538	XC	0.95	-0.80	30.02	28,975
JohnJn	Feb	55		17,424	XC	0.55	0.25	54.48	18,120

OPTION/STRIKE				VOL	EXCH	LAST	NET CHG	CLOSE	OPEN INT
Cisco	Apr	25		16,786	XC	1.15	-1.40	24.08	35,860
ATT Wrls	Feb	11		16,696	XC	0.35	...	11.13	19,457
FordM	Jan 05	20		16,006	XC	0.35	0.05	13.89	17,243
Nasd100Tr	Feb	35	p	15,424	XC	0.25	...	36.33	80,784
ATT Wrls	Apr	11		14,865	XC	0.70	...	11.13	4,849
Pfizer	Feb	70		14,847	XC	1	0.35	38.27	19,623
Nasd100Tr	Feb	36		14,301	XC	0.95	-0.50	36.33	46,174
Nasd100Tr	Jun	35	p	13,821	XC	1.70	0.25	36.33	70,112
Peoplesoft	Apr	20	p	12,605	XC	0.50	-0.35	22.70	7,767
Peoplesoft	Mar	22.50	p	12,542	XC	1.05	-0.50	22.70	289
SemiHTr	Feb	40	p	12,235	XC	0.95	0.45	40.58	34,513
Pfizer	Mar	40		12,164	XC	0.40	0.15	38.27	9,707
Cisco	Mar	25		11,453	XC	0.85	-1.45	24.08	7,877
ATT Wrls	Jul	12.50		11,056	XC	0.30	-0.05	11.13	65,795
Conseco	Jun	15	p	11,006	XC	0.45	0.30	21.86	547
Nasd100Tr	Feb	39	p	10,906	XC	2.70	0.55	36.33	52,208
Pfizer	Mar	70		10,676	XC	1.45	0.40	38.27	42,155
WalMart	Feb	55		10,613	XC	1.10	0.15	55.39	47,678
Dellinc	Feb	32.50	p	10,542	XC	0.95	0.50	32.39	27,928
Cisco	Feb	27.50	p	10,526	XC	3.40	1.75	24.08	40,102

Volume & Open Interest Summaries

AMERICAN			
Call Vol:	507,923	Open Int:	45,122,029
Put Vol:	435,069	Open Int:	34,155,216
CHICAGO BOARD			
Call Vol:	803,225	Open Int:	59,856,094
Put Vol:	647,213	Open Int:	49,257,435
INTL SECURITIES			
Call Vol:	1,006,254	Open Int:	51,961,968
Put Vol:	704,231	Open Int:	41,896,347
PHILADELPHIA			
Call Vol:	424,568	Open Int:	43,397,779
Put Vol:	263,640	Open Int:	33,690,351
PACIFIC			
Call Vol:	234,706	Open Int:	54,541,910
Put Vol:	159,733	Open Int:	43,234,469
TOTAL			
Call Vol:	2,976,676		
Put Vol:	2,209,886		

LEAPS-LONG TERM OPTIONS

OPTION/STRIKE		EXP	-CALL- VOL	-CALL- LAST	-PUT- VOL	-PUT- LAST
AT&T	15	Jan 05	...	...	4450	0.80
19.14	17.50	Jan 05	315	2.80	3615	1.70
19.14	20	Jan 05	898	1.65	1414	3.20
ATT Wrls	10	Jan 05	430	1.70	20942	0.50
AMD	7.50	Jan 06	...	...	7520	0.95
14.13	17.50	Jan 05	3109	2.05	...	...
Amgen	70	Jan 05	1431	4.90	...	...
ApldMat	15	Jan 05	35	7.40	3040	0.85
21.38	17.50	Jan 05	10	5.40	6290	1.45
Broadcom	40	Jan 05	2255	6.30	120	7.30
Cisco	22.50	Jan 05	804	4.30	2899	2.40
24.08	25	Jan 05	4397	3.10	633	3.60
24.08	25	Jan 06	3272	4.60	228	4.60
24.08	30	Jan 05	5208	1.45	214	6.90
24.08	30	Jan 06	3147	2.75	40	7.20
24.08	40	Jan 06	1988	0.95	...	...
CompAsc	25	Jan 05	1800	4.70	300	3.10
ContlAir	10	Jan 06	...	...	1500	2.20
Corning	12.50	Jan 05	2622	1.90	160	2.20
11.99	12.50	Jan 06	3942	3.30	34	3.10
DJIA Diam	116	Jan 05	1500	1.85	...	...
Dell Inc	35	Jan 06	87	4.50	1623	5.90
DukeEgy	22.50	Jan 06	3457	2.05	...	...
ElPasoCp	5	Jan 05	...	...	3500	0.50
8.16	7.50	Jan 05	5302	1.85	1207	1.25
FordM	12.50	Jan 05	2079	2.60	2	1.30
13.89	12.50	Jan 06	2009	3.10	4011	1.90
13.89	15	Jan 06	3527	2.10	20	3.20
13.89	20	Jan 05	16006	0.35	...	...
FredMac	60	Jan 05	192	7.50	2550	5.30
GenMotrs	10	Jan 06	...	...	9100	0.20

OPTION/STRIKE		EXP	-CALL- VOL	-CALL- LAST	-PUT- VOL	-PUT- LAST
47.97	15	Jan 06	...	...	3500	0.45
47.97	20	Jan 06	...	...	3690	0.75
47.97	40	Jan 06	2040	9.70	105	4.40
47.97	55	Jan 06	2245	3.40	...	...
Gillette	45	Jan 05	1450	0.40	...	...
HomeDp	30	Jan 05	...	...	1500	1.45
Intel	30	Jan 05	1127	4.10	2389	3.60
JohnJns	55	Jan 05	107	3.60	1457	4.20
LillyEli	65	Jan 05	52	10.50	1575	5.80
70.50	70	Jan 05	1862	8	1515	8
70.50	75	Jan 05	2445	5.80	...	...
Lucent	2.50	Jan 05	1885	1.90	20	0.20
4.20	5	Jan 05	3845	0.70	703	1.45
LucentT	5	Jan 06	2023	1.10	260	1.75
Lyondell	12.50	Jan 05	...	...	5016	1.10
Maxim	45	Jan 05	10	9.90	5000	5
48.69	55	Jan 05	5075	5	60	10.30
MicronT	22.50	Jan 06	...	...	5000	7.90
Microsft	22.50	Jan 05	22	5.80	1480	0.90
Microsoft	30	Jan 06	1912	2.85	...	...
Nasd100Tr	34	Jan 06	21	6.90	2510	3.40
36.33	35	Jan 05	1713	4.50	233	2.85
36.33	35	Jan 06	20087	6.40	37	4
36.33	38	Jan 06	1731	4.70	1956	5.30
36.33	47	Jan 05	1510	0.55	...	...
36.33	49	Jan 06	2500	1.35	...	...
NortelNw	7.50	Jan 05	1995	1.70	504	1.55
7.50	10	Jan 05	1822	0.95	66	3.40
Pfizer	40	Jan 05	1766	2.15	24	4.10
RylCarb	15	Jan 06	...	...	2250	0.45
SBC Com	20	Jan 06	47	6.20	1531	1.50

OPTION/STRIKE		EXP	-CALL- VOL	-CALL- LAST	-PUT- VOL	-PUT- LAST
SwstAirl	15	Jan 06	5561	2.90	5151	2.90
SprntFON	20	Jan 06	...	...	2620	4.40
SunMicro	5	Jan 06	1784	1.45	241	1.20
TenetHlt	7.50	Jan 06	...	...	2010	1.15
TimeWarn	15	Jan 05	185	3.30	3205	0.90
17.19	15	Jan 06	24	4.10	5000	1.35
17.19	17.50	Jan 06	8	2.75	3649	2.40
17.19	20	Jan 06	2581	1.70	...	...
UltraPet	25	Jan 05	...	...	2000	4.10
Verizon	30	Jan 06	...	...	2714	2.55
WalMart	55	Jan 06	2033	6.80	2478	5.30
WinnDix	2.50	Jan 05	...	...	3080	0.40
XM Sat	5	Jan 06	...	...	2930	0.40

Volume & Open Interest Summaries

CHICAGO BOARD			
Call Vol:	31,142	Open Int:	5,520,851
Put Vol:	27,750	Open Int:	6,222,730
INTL SECURITIES			
Call Vol:	108,287	Open Int:	21,850,815
Put Vol:	75,548	Open Int:	20,174,219
PACIFIC			
Call Vol:	41,886	Open Int:	21,859,348
Put Vol:	43,151	Open Int:	20,109,861
TOTAL			
Call Vol:	181,315		
Put Vol:	146,449		

Source: Reprinted by permission of Dow Jones, Inc., via Copyright Clearance Center, Inc.

Securities Exchange (www.iseoptions.com) launched the first all-electronic options market for equities in the United States in May 2000. The Chicago Board Options Exchange has CBOEdirect and the CME has GLOBEX. Both are electronic systems that run side by side with their floor-based open-outcry markets.

Market Makers

Most options exchanges use market makers to facilitate trading. A market maker for a certain option is an individual who, when asked to do so, will quote both a bid and an offer price on the option. The bid is the price at which the market maker is prepared to buy, and the offer is the price at which the market maker is prepared to sell. At the time the bid and the offer are quoted, the market maker does not know whether the trader who asked for the quotes wants to buy or sell the option. The offer is always higher than the bid, and the amount by which the offer exceeds the bid is referred to as the bid–offer spread. The exchange sets upper limits for the bid–offer spread. For example, it might specify that the spread be no more than \$0.25 for options priced at less than \$0.50, \$0.50 for options priced between \$0.50 and \$10, \$0.75 for options priced between \$10 and \$20, and \$1 for options priced over \$20.

The existence of the market maker ensures that buy and sell orders can always be executed at some price without any delays. Market makers therefore add liquidity to the market. The market makers themselves make their profits from the bid–offer spread. They use some of the schemes discussed later in this book to hedge their risks.

Offsetting Orders

An investor who has purchased an option can close out the position by issuing an offsetting order to sell the same option. Similarly, an investor who has written an option can close out the position by issuing an offsetting order to buy the same option. If, when an options contract is traded, neither investor is offsetting an existing position, the open interest increases by one contract. If one investor is offsetting an existing position and the other is not, the open interest stays the same. If both investors are offsetting existing positions, the open interest goes down by one contract.

8.7 COMMISSIONS

The types of orders that can be placed with a broker for options trading are similar to those for futures trading (see Section 2.7). A market order is to be executed immediately; a limit order specifies the least favorable price at which the order can be executed; and so on.

For a retail investor, commissions vary significantly from broker to broker. Discount brokers generally charge lower commissions than full-service brokers. The actual amount charged is often calculated as a fixed cost plus a proportion of the dollar amount of the trade. Table 8.2 shows the sort of schedule that might be offered by a discount broker. Thus, the purchase of eight contracts when the option price is \$3 would cost $\$20 + (0.02 \times \$2{,}400) = \$68$ in commissions.

If an option position is closed out by entering into an offsetting trade, the commission must be paid again. If the option is exercised, the commission is the same as it

Table 8.2 A typical commission schedule for a discount broker

Dollar amount of trade	*Commission**
< \$2,500	\$20 + 0.02 of dollar amount
\$2,500 to \$10,000	\$45 + 0.01 of dollar amount
> \$10,000	\$120 + 0.0025 of dollar amount

* Maximum commission is \$30 per contract for the first five contracts plus \$20 per contract for each additional contract. Minimum commission is \$30 per contract for the first contract plus \$2 per contract for each additional contract.

would be if the investor placed an order to buy or sell the underlying stock. Typically, this is 1% to 2% of the stock's value.

Consider an investor who buys one call contract with a strike price of \$50 when the stock price is \$49. We suppose the option price is \$4.50, so that the cost of the contract is \$450. Under the schedule in Table 8.2, the purchase or sale of one contract always costs \$30 (both the maximum and minimum commission is \$30 for the first contract). Suppose that the stock price rises and the option is exercised when the stock reaches \$60. Assuming that the investor pays 1.5% commission on stock trades, the commission payable when the option is exercised is

$$0.015 \times \$60 \times 100 = \$90$$

The total commission paid is therefore \$120, and the net profit to the investor is

$$\$1{,}000 - \$450 - \$120 = \$430$$

Note that selling the option for \$10 instead of exercising it would save the investor \$60 in commissions. (The commission payable when an option is sold is only \$30 in our example.) In general, the commission system tends to push retail investors in the direction of selling options rather than exercising them.

A hidden cost in option trading (and in stock trading) is the market maker's bid–offer spread. Suppose that, in the example just considered, the bid price was \$4.00 and the offer price was \$4.50 at the time the option was purchased. We can reasonably assume that a "fair" price for the option is halfway between the bid and the offer price, or \$4.25. The cost to the buyer and to the seller of the market maker system is the difference between the fair price and the price paid. This is \$0.25 per option, or \$25 per contract.

8.8 MARGINS

In the United States, when shares are purchased, an investor can either pay cash or borrow using a margin account (this is known as *buying on margin*). The initial margin is usually 50% of the value of the shares, and the maintenance margin is usually 25% of the value of the shares. The margin account operates similarly to that for a futures contract (see Chapter 2).

When call or put options are purchased, the option price must be paid in full. Investors are not allowed to buy options on margin because options already contain substantial leverage. Buying on margin would raise this leverage to an unacceptable level. An investor who writes options is required to maintain funds in a margin account. Both the investor's broker and the exchange want to be satisfied that the investor will not default if the option is exercised. The size of the margin required depends on the circumstances.

Writing Naked Options

A *naked option* is an option that is not combined with an offsetting position in the underlying stock. The initial margin for a written naked call option is the greater of the following two calculations:

1. A total of 100% of the proceeds of the sale plus 20% of the underlying share price less the amount if any by which the option is out of the money
2. A total of 100% of the option proceeds plus 10% of the underlying share price

For a written naked put option, it is the greater of

1. A total of 100% of the proceeds of the sale plus 20% of the underlying share price less the amount if any by which the option is out of the money
2. A total of 100% of the option proceeds plus 10% of the exercise price

The 20% in the preceding calculations is replaced by 15% for options on a broadly based stock index because a stock index is usually less volatile than the price of an individual stock.

Example

An investor writes four naked call option contracts on a stock. The option price is \$5, the strike price is \$40, and the stock price is \$38. Because the option is \$2 out of the money, the first calculation gives

$$400(5 + 0.2 \times 38 - 2) = \$4{,}240$$

The second calculation gives

$$400(5 + 0.1 \times 38) = \$3{,}520$$

The initial margin requirement is therefore \$4,240. Note that if the option had been a put, it would be \$2 in the money and the margin requirement would be

$$400(5 + 0.2 \times 38) = \$5{,}040$$

In both cases the proceeds of the sale, \$2,000, can be used to form part of the margin account.

A calculation similar to the initial margin calculation (but with the current market price replacing the proceeds of sale) is repeated every day. Funds can be withdrawn from the margin account when the calculation indicates that the margin required is less than the current balance in the margin account. When the calculation indicates that a significantly greater margin is required, a margin call will be made.

Writing Covered Calls

Writing covered calls involves writing call options when the shares that might have to be delivered are already owned. Covered calls are far less risky than naked calls, because the worst that can happen is that the investor is required to sell shares already owned at below their market value. If covered call options are out of the money, no margin is required. The shares owned can be purchased using a margin account, as described previously, and the price received for the option can be used to partially fulfill this margin requirement. If the options are in the money, no margin is required for the options. However, for the purposes of calculating the investor's equity position, the share price is reduced by the extent, if any, to which the option is in the money. This may limit the amount that the investor can withdraw from the margin account if the share price increases.

Example

An investor in the United States decides to buy 200 shares of a certain stock on margin and to write two call option contracts on the stock. The stock price is \$63, the strike price is \$60, and the price of the option is \$7. The margin account allows the investor to borrow 50% of the price of the shares, or \$6,300. The investor is also able to use the price received for the options, $\$7 \times 200 = \$1{,}400$, to finance the purchase of the shares. The shares cost $\$63 \times 200 = \$12{,}600$. The minimum cash initially required from the investor for the trades is therefore

$$\$12{,}600 - \$6{,}300 - \$1{,}400 = \$4{,}900$$

In Chapter 10, we will examine more complicated option trading strategies such as spreads, combinations, straddles, and strangles. There are special rules for determining the margin requirements when these trading strategies are used.

8.9 THE OPTIONS CLEARING CORPORATION

The Options Clearing Corporation (OCC) performs much the same function for options markets as the clearinghouse does for futures markets (see Chapter 2). It guarantees that options writers will fulfill their obligations under the terms of options contracts and keeps a record of all long and short positions. The OCC has a number of members, and all options trades must be cleared through a member. If a brokerage house is not itself a member of an exchange's OCC, it must arrange to clear its trades with a member. Members are required to have a certain minimum amount of capital and to contribute to a special fund that can be used if any member defaults on an option obligation.

When purchasing an option, the buyer must pay for it in full by the morning of the next business day. The funds are deposited with the OCC. The writer of the option maintains a margin account with a broker, as described earlier. The broker maintains a margin account with the OCC member that clears its trades. The OCC member in turn maintains a margin account with the OCC. The margin requirements described in the previous section are the margin requirements imposed by the OCC on its members. A brokerage house may require higher margins from its clients. However, it cannot require lower margins.

Exercising an Option

When an investor notifies a broker to exercise an option, the broker in turn notifies the OCC member that clears its trades. This member then places an exercise order with the OCC. The OCC randomly selects a member with an outstanding short position in the same option. The member, using a procedure established in advance, selects a particular investor who has written the option. If the option is a call, this investor is required to sell stock at the strike price. If it is a put, the investor is required to buy stock at the strike price. The investor is said to be *assigned*. When an option is exercised, the open interest goes down by one.

At the expiration of the option, all in-the-money options should be exercised unless the transactions costs are so high as to wipe out the payoff from the option. Some brokerage firms will automatically exercise options for their clients at expiration when it is in a client's interest to do so. Many exchanges also have rules for exercising options that are in the money at expiration.

8.10 REGULATION

Options markets are regulated in a number of different ways. Both the exchange and its Options Clearing Corporation have rules governing the behavior of traders. In addition, there are both federal and state regulatory authorities. In general, options markets have demonstrated a willingness to regulate themselves. There have been no major scandals or defaults by OCC members. Investors can have a high level of confidence in the way the market is run.

The Securities and Exchange Commission is responsible for regulating options markets in stocks, stock indices, currencies, and bonds at the federal level. The Commodity Futures Trading Commission is responsible for regulating markets for options on futures. The major options markets are in the states of Illinois and New York. These states actively enforce their own laws on unacceptable trading practices.

8.11 TAXATION

Determining the tax implications of options strategies can be tricky, and an investor who is in doubt about this should consult a tax specialist. In the United States, the general rule is that (unless the taxpayer is a professional trader) gains and losses from the trading of stock options are taxed as capital gains or losses. The way that capital gains and losses are taxed in the United States was discussed in Section 2.9. For both the holder and the writer of a stock option, a gain or loss is recognized when (a) the option expires unexercised, or (b) the option position is closed out. If the option is exercised, the gain or loss from the option is rolled into the position taken in the stock and recognized when the stock position is closed out. For example, when a call option is exercised, the party with a long position is deemed to have purchased the stock at the strike price plus the call price. This is then used as a basis for calculating this party's gain or loss when the stock is eventually sold. Similarly, the party with the short call position is deemed to have sold the stock at the strike price plus the call price. When a put option is exercised, the seller of the option is deemed to have bought stock for the strike price less the original put price and the purchaser of the option is deemed to have sold the stock for the strike price less the original put price.

Wash Sale Rule

One tax consideration in option trading in the United States is the wash sale rule. To understand this rule, imagine an investor who buys a stock when the price is $60 and plans to keep it for the long term. If the stock price drops to $40, the investor might be tempted to sell the stock and then immediately repurchase it so that the $20 loss is realized for tax purposes. To prevent this sort of thing, the tax authorities have ruled that when the repurchase is within 30 days of the sale (i.e., between 30 days before the sale and 30 days after the sale), any loss on the sale is not deductible. The disallowance also applies where, within the 61-day period, the taxpayer enters into an option or similar contract to acquire the stock. Thus, selling a stock at a loss and buying a call option within a 30-day period will lead to the loss being disallowed. The wash sale rule does not apply if the taxpayer is a dealer in stocks or securities and the loss is sustained in the ordinary course of business.

Constructive Sales

Prior to 1997, if a United States taxpayer shorted a security while holding a long position in a substantially identical security, no gain or loss was recognized until the short position was closed out. This means that short positions could be used to defer recognition of a gain for tax purposes. The situation was changed by the Tax Relief Act of 1997. An appreciated property is now treated as "constructively sold" when the owner does one of the following:

1. Enters into a short sale of the same or substantially identical property
2. Enters into a futures or forward contract to deliver the same or substantially identical property
3. Enters into one or more positions that eliminate substantially all of the loss and opportunity for gain

It should be noted that transactions reducing only the risk of loss or only the opportunity for gain should not result in constructive sales. Therefore, an investor holding a long position in a stock can buy in-the-money put options on the stock without triggering a constructive sale.

Tax practitioners sometimes use options to minimize tax costs or maximize tax benefits (see example in Business Snapshot 8.2). Tax authorities in many jurisdictions have proposed legislation designed to combat the use of derivatives for tax purposes. Before entering into any tax-motivated transaction, a corporate treasurer or private individual should explore in detail how the structure could be unwound in the event of legislative change and how costly this process could be.

8.12 WARRANTS, EXECUTIVE STOCK OPTIONS, AND CONVERTIBLES

Usually, when a call option on a stock is exercised, the party with the short position acquires shares that have already been issued and sells them to the party with the long

Business Snapshot 8.2 Tax planning using options

As a simple example of a possible tax planning strategy using options, suppose that Country A has a tax regime where the tax is low on interest and dividends and a high on capital gains, while Country B has a tax regime where tax is high on interest and dividends and low on capital gains. It is advantageous for a company to receive the income from a security in Country A and the capital gain, if there is one, in Country B. The company would like to keep capital losses in Country A where they can be used to offset capital gains on other items. All of this can be accomplished by arranging for a subsidiary company in Country A to have legal ownership of the security and for a subsidiary company in Country B to buy a call option on the security from the company in country A with the strike price of the option equal to the current value of the security. During the life of the option income from the security is earned in Country A. If the security price rises sharply the option will be exercised and the capital gain will be realized in Country B. If it falls sharply, the option will not be exercised and the capital loss will be realized in Country A.

position for the strike price. The company whose stock underlies the option is not involved in any way. Warrants and executive stock options are call options that work slightly differently. They are written by a company on its own stock. When they are exercised, the company issues more of its own stock and sells them to the option holder for the strike price. The exercise of a warrant or executive stock option therefore leads to an increase in the number of shares of the company's stock that are outstanding.

Warrants are call options that often come into existence as a result of a bond issue. They are added to the bond issue to make it more attractive to investors. Typically, a warrant lasts for a number of years. Once they have been created, they sometimes trade separately from the bonds to which they were originally attached.

Executive stock options are call options issued to executives to motivate them to act in the best interests of the company's shareholders (see the discussion in Business Snapshot 8.3). Recently there has been a great deal of controversy about whether executive stock options should be expensed by companies on their income statements. Some companies and their accountants argue that there is no reliable way of doing this. Options experts contend that executive stock options can be valued at least as precisely as other items in financial statements.

A *convertible bond* is a bond issued by a company that can be converted into equity at certain times using a predetermined exchange ratio. It is therefore a bond with an embedded call option on the company's stock. Convertibles are like warrants and executive stock options in that their exercise leads to more shares being issued by the company.

8.13 OVER-THE-COUNTER MARKETS

Most of this chapter has focused on exchange-traded options markets. The over-the-counter market for options has become increasingly important since the early 1980s and is now larger than the exchange-traded market. As explained in Chapter 1, in the over-the-counter market, financial institutions, corporate treasurers, and fund managers

Business Snapshot 8.3 Executive stock options

Stock options became an increasingly popular type of compensation for executives and other employees in the 1990s and early 2000s. In a typical arrangement, an executive is granted a certain number of call options on the stock of the company for which he or she works. The options are at the money on the grant date. They often last for ten years or even longer and there is a vesting period of up to five years. The options cannot be exercised during the vesting period, but can be exercised any time after the vesting period ends. If the executive leaves the company during the vesting period the options are forfeited. If the executive leaves the company after the end of the vesting period, in-the-money options are exercised immediately while out-of-the-money options are forfeited. Options cannot be sold to another party by the executive.

One reason why executive stock options have been so attractive has been their accounting treatment. The compensation cost charged to the income statement for an employee stock option in the United States and other countries has traditionally been its intrinsic value. Because most executive stock options are at the money when they are issued this compensation cost is zero. In 1995 accounting standard FAS 123 was issued. This encouraged, but did not require, companies to expense the "fair value" of the options on their income statement. (If the fair value was not expensed on the income statement it had to be reported in a footnote to the company's accounts.) Very few companies chose to expense options in the 1990s, but in the aftermath of Enron, WorldCom, and other extreme examples of managerial behavior an increasing number of companies are doing so.

Accounting standards throughout the world are now changing to require the expensing of stock options at their fair value on the income statement. In February 2004, the International Accounting Standards Board issued IASB 2 requiring companies to start expensing stock options in 2005. In March 2004, the Financial Accounting Standards Board in the United States issued an exposure draft that is expected to lead to an accounting standard requiring the expensing of options.

Executive stock options tend to be exercised earlier than similar exchange-traded or over-the-counter options because the executive is not allowed to sell the options. If an executive wants to realize cash from the options, he or she has to exercise the options and sell the stock. For this reason, valuing executive stock options is not as easy as valuing regular options. It requires a model of the executives' early-exercise behavior.

trade over the phone. There is a wide range of assets underlying the options. Over-the-counter options on foreign exchange and interest rates are particularly popular. The chief potential disadvantage of the over-the-counter market is that option writer may default. This means that the purchaser is subject to some credit risk. In an attempt to overcome this disadvantage, market participants are adopting a number of measures such as requiring counterparties to post collateral. This was discussed in Section 2.4.

The instruments traded in the over-the-counter market are often structured by financial institutions to meet the precise needs of their clients. Sometimes this involves choosing exercise dates, strike prices, and contract sizes that are different from those traded by the exchange. In other cases the structure of the option is different from standard calls and puts. The option is then referred to as an *exotic option*. Chapter 20 describes a number of different types of exotic options.

SUMMARY

There are two types of options: calls and puts. A call option gives the holder the right to buy the underlying asset for a certain price by a certain date. A put option gives the holder the right to sell the underlying asset by a certain date for a certain price. There are four possible positions in options markets: a long position in a call, a short position in a call, a long position in a put, and a short position in a put. Taking a short position in an option is known as writing it. Options are currently traded on stocks, stock indices, foreign currencies, futures contracts, and other assets.

An exchange must specify the terms of the option contracts it trades. In particular, it must specify the size of the contract, the precise expiration time, and the strike price. In the United States one stock option contract gives the holder the right to buy or sell 100 shares. The expiration of a stock option contract is 10:59 p.m. Central Time on the Saturday immediately following the third Friday of the expiration month. Options with several different expiration months trade at any given time. Strike prices are at $\$2\frac{1}{2}$, \$5, or \$10 intervals, depending on the stock price. The strike price is generally fairly close to the stock price when trading in an option begins.

The terms of a stock option are not normally adjusted for cash dividends. However, they are adjusted for stock dividends, stock splits, and rights issues. The aim of the adjustment is to keep the positions of both the writer and the buyer of a contract unchanged.

Most options exchanges use market makers. These are individuals who are prepared to quote both a bid price (at which they are prepared to buy) and an offer price (at which they are prepared to sell). Market makers improve the liquidity of the market and ensure that there is never any delay in executing market orders. They themselves make a profit from the difference between their bid and offer prices (known as their bid–offer spread). The exchange has rules specifying upper limits for the bid–offer spread.

Writers of options have potential liabilities and are required to maintain margins with their brokers. If it is not a member of the Options Clearing Corporation, the broker will maintain a margin account with a firm that is a member. This firm will in turn maintain a margin account with the Options Clearing Corporation. The Options Clearing Corporation is responsible for keeping a record of all outstanding contracts, handling exercise orders, and so on.

Not all options are traded on exchanges. Many options are traded by phone in the over-the-counter market. An advantage of over-the-counter options is that they can be tailored by a financial institution to meet the particular needs of a corporate treasurer or fund manager.

FURTHER READING

Arzac, E. R. "PERCs, DECs, and Other Manadatory Convertibles." *Journal of Applied Corporate Finance*, 10, 1 (1997): 54–63.

Core, J. E., and W. R. Guay. "Stock Option Plans for non-Executive Employees." *Journal of Financial Economics*, 61, 2 (2001): 253–87.

Cox, J. C., and M. Rubinstein. *Options Markets.* Upper Saddle River, NJ: Prentice Hall, 1985.

Hull, J. C., and A. White. "How to Value Employee Stock Options," *Financial Analysts Journal*, 60, 1 (January/February 2004): 114–19.

Rubinstein, M. "On the Accounting Valuation of Employee Stock Options," *Journal of Derivatives*, 3, 1 (Fall 1995): 8–24.

Quiz (Answers at End of Book)

8.1. An investor buys a European put on a share for $3. The stock price is $42 and the strike price is $40. Under what circumstances does the investor make a profit? Under what circumstances will the option be exercised? Draw a diagram showing the variation of the investor's profit with the stock price at the maturity of the option.

8.2. An investor sells a European call on a share for $4. The stock price is $47 and the strike price is $50. Under what circumstances does the investor make a profit? Under what circumstances will the option be exercised? Draw a diagram showing the variation of the investor's profit with the stock price at the maturity of the option.

8.3. An investor sells a European call option with strike price of K and maturity T and writes a put with the same strike price and maturity. Describe the investor's position.

8.4. Explain why brokers require margins when clients write options but not when they buy options.

8.5. A stock option is on a February, May, August, and November cycle. What options trade on (a) April 1, and (b) May 30?

8.6. A company declares a 2-for-1 stock split. Explain how the terms change for a call option with a strike price of $60.

8.7. How is an executive stock option different from a regular exchange-traded or over-the-counter American-style stock option?

Questions and Problems (Answers in Solutions Manual/Study Guide)

8.8. A corporate treasurer is designing a hedging program involving foreign currency options. What are the pros and cons of using (a) the Philadelphia Stock Exchange and (b) the over-the-counter market for trading?

8.9. Suppose that a European call option to buy a share for $100.00 costs $5.00 and is held until maturity. Under what circumstances will the holder of the option make a profit? Under what circumstances will the option be exercised? Draw a diagram illustrating how the profit from a long position in the option depends on the stock price at maturity of the option.

8.10. Suppose that a European put option to sell a share for $60 costs $8 and is held until maturity. Under what circumstances will the seller of the option (the party with the short position) make a profit? Under what circumstances will the option be exercised? Draw a diagram illustrating how the profit from a short position in the option depends on the stock price at maturity of the option.

8.11. Describe the terminal value of the following portfolio: a newly entered-into long forward contract on an asset and a long position in a European put option on the asset with the same maturity as the forward contract and a strike price that is equal to the forward price of the asset at the time the portfolio is set up. Show that the European put option has the same value as a European call option with the same strike price and maturity.

8.12. A trader buys a call option with a strike price of \$45 and a put option with a strike price of \$40. Both options have the same maturity. The call costs \$3 and the put costs \$4. Draw a diagram showing the variation of the trader's profit with the asset price.

8.13. Explain why an American option is always worth at least as much as a European option on the same asset with the same strike price and exercise date.

8.14. Explain why an American option is always worth at least as much as its intrinsic value.

8.15. Explain carefully the difference between writing a put option and buying a call option.

8.16. The treasurer of a corporation is trying to choose between options and forward contracts to hedge the corporation's foreign exchange risk. Discuss the advantages and disadvantages of each.

8.17. Suppose that sterling–U.S. dollar spot and forward exchange rates are as follows:

Spot:	1.8470
90-day forward:	1.8381
180-day forward:	1.8291

What opportunities are open to an investor in the following situations:
a. A 180-day European call option to buy £1 for \$1.80 costs \$0.0250?
b. A 90-day European put option to sell £1 for \$1.86 costs \$0.0200?

8.18. Consider an exchange-traded call option contract to buy 500 shares with a strike price of \$40 and maturity in four months. Explain how the terms of the option contract change when there is
a. A 10% stock dividend
b. A 10% cash dividend
c. A 4-for-1 stock split

8.19. "If most of the call options on a stock are in the money, it is likely that the stock price has risen rapidly in the last few months." Discuss this statement.

8.20. What is the effect of an unexpected cash dividend on (a) a call option price and (b) a put option price?

8.21. Options on General Motors stock are on a March, June, September, and December cycle. What options trade on (a) March 1, (b) June 30, and (c) August 5?

8.22. Explain why the market maker's bid–offer spread represents a real cost to options investors.

8.23. A United States investor writes five naked call option contracts. The option price is \$3.50, the strike price is \$60.00, and the stock price is \$57.00. What is the initial margin requirement?

Assignment Questions

8.24. A United States investor buys 500 shares of a stock and sells five call option contracts on the stock. The strike price is \$30. The price of the option is \$3. What is the investor's minimum cash investment (a) if the stock price is \$28, and (b) if it is \$32?

8.25. The price of a stock is \$40. The price of a one-year European put option on the stock with a strike price of \$30 is quoted as \$7 and the price of a one-year European call option on the stock with a strike price of \$50 is quoted as \$5. Suppose that an investor buys 100 shares, shorts 100 call options, and buys 100 put options. Draw a diagram illustrating how the investor's profit or loss varies with the stock price over the next year. How does your answer change if the investor buys 100 shares, shorts 200 call options, and buys 200 put options?

8.26. "If a company does not do better than its competitors but the stock market goes up, executives do very well from their stock options. This makes no sense." Discuss this viewpoint. Can you think of alternatives to the usual executive stock option plan that take the viewpoint into account.

8.27. Use DerivaGem to calculate the value of an American put option on a non-dividend-paying stock when the stock price is \$30, the strike price is \$32, the risk-free rate is 5%, the volatility is 30%, and the time to maturity is 1.5 years. (Choose binomial American for the "option type" and 50 time steps.)

a. What is the option's intrinsic value?

b. What is the option's time value?

c. What would a time value of zero indicate? What is the value of an option with zero time value?

d. Using a trial and error approach calculate how low the stock price would have to be for the time value of the option to be zero.

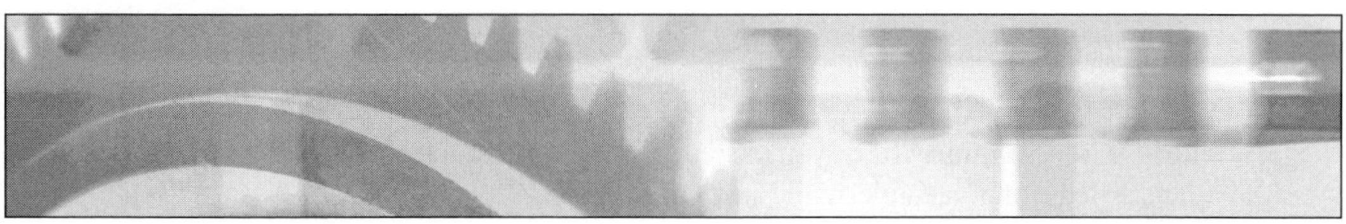

CHAPTER 9

Properties of Stock Options

In this chapter we look at the factors affecting stock option prices. We use a number of different arbitrage arguments to explore the relationships between European option prices, American option prices, and the underlying stock price. The most important of these relationships is put–call parity, which is a relationship between European call option prices and European put option prices.

The chapter examines whether American options should be exercised early. It shows that it is never optimal to exercise an American call option on a non-dividend-paying stock prior to the option's expiration, but that under some circumstances the early exercise of an American put option on such a stock is optimal.

9.1 FACTORS AFFECTING OPTION PRICES

There are six factors affecting the price of a stock option:

1. The current stock price, S_0
2. The strike price, K
3. The time to expiration, T
4. The volatility of the stock price, σ
5. The risk-free interest rate, r
6. The dividends expected during the life of the option

In this section we consider what happens to option prices when one of these factors changes with all the others remaining fixed. The results are summarized in Table 9.1.

Figures 9.1 and 9.2 show how the price of a European call and put depends on the first five factors in the situation where $S_0 = 50$, $K = 50$, $r = 5\%$ per annum, $\sigma = 30\%$ per annum, $T = 1$ year, and there are no dividends. In this case the call price is 7.116 and the put price is 4.677.

Stock Price and Strike Price

If a call option is exercised at some future time, the payoff will be the amount by which the stock price exceeds the strike price. Call options therefore become more valuable as

Table 9.1 Summary of the effect on the price of a stock option of increasing one variable while keeping all others fixed*

Variable	*European call*	*European put*	*American call*	*American put*
Current stock price	+	−	+	−
Strike price	−	+	−	+
Time to expiration	?	?	+	+
Volatility	+	+	+	+
Risk-free rate	+	−	+	−
Dividends	−	+	−	+

* + indicates that an increase in the variable causes the option price to increase; − indicates that an increase in the variable causes the option price to decrease; ? indicates that the relationship is uncertain.

the stock price increases and less valuable as the strike price increases. For a put option, the payoff on exercise is the amount by which the strike price exceeds the stock price. Put options, therefore, behave in the opposite way from call options. They become less valuable as the stock price increases and more valuable as the strike price increases. Figures 9.1a, b, c, d illustrate the way in which put and call prices depend on the stock price and strike price.

Time to Expiration

Consider next the effect of the expiration date. Both put and call American options become more valuable as the time to expiration increases. Consider two options that differ only as far as the expiration date is concerned. The owner of the long-life option has all the exercise opportunities open to the owner of the short-life option—and more. The long-life option must therefore always be worth at least as much as the short-life option.

Although European put and call options usually become more valuable as the time to expiration increases (see, e.g., Figures 9.1e, f), this is not always the case. Consider two European call options on a stock: one with an expiration date in one month, the other with an expiration date in two months. Suppose that a very large dividend is expected in six weeks. The dividend will cause the stock price to decline, so that the short-life option could be worth more than the long-life option.

Volatility

The precise way in which volatility is defined is discussed in Chapter 12. Roughly speaking, the *volatility* of a stock price is a measure of how uncertain we are about future stock price movements. As volatility increases, the chance that the stock will do very well or very poorly increases. For the owner of a stock, these two outcomes tend to offset each other. However, this is not so for the owner of a call or put. The owner of a call benefits from price increases but has limited downside risk in the event of price decreases because the most the owner can lose is the price of the option. Similarly, the owner of a put benefits from price decreases, but has limited downside risk in the event of price increases. The values of both calls and puts therefore increase as volatility increases (see Figures 9.2a, b).

Risk-Free Interest Rate

The risk-free interest rate affects the price of an option in a less clear-cut way. As interest rates in the economy increase, the expected return required by investors from

Figure 9.1 Effect of changes in stock price, strike price, and expiration date on option prices when $S_0 = 50$, $K = 50$, $r = 5\%$, $\sigma = 30\%$, and $T = 1$

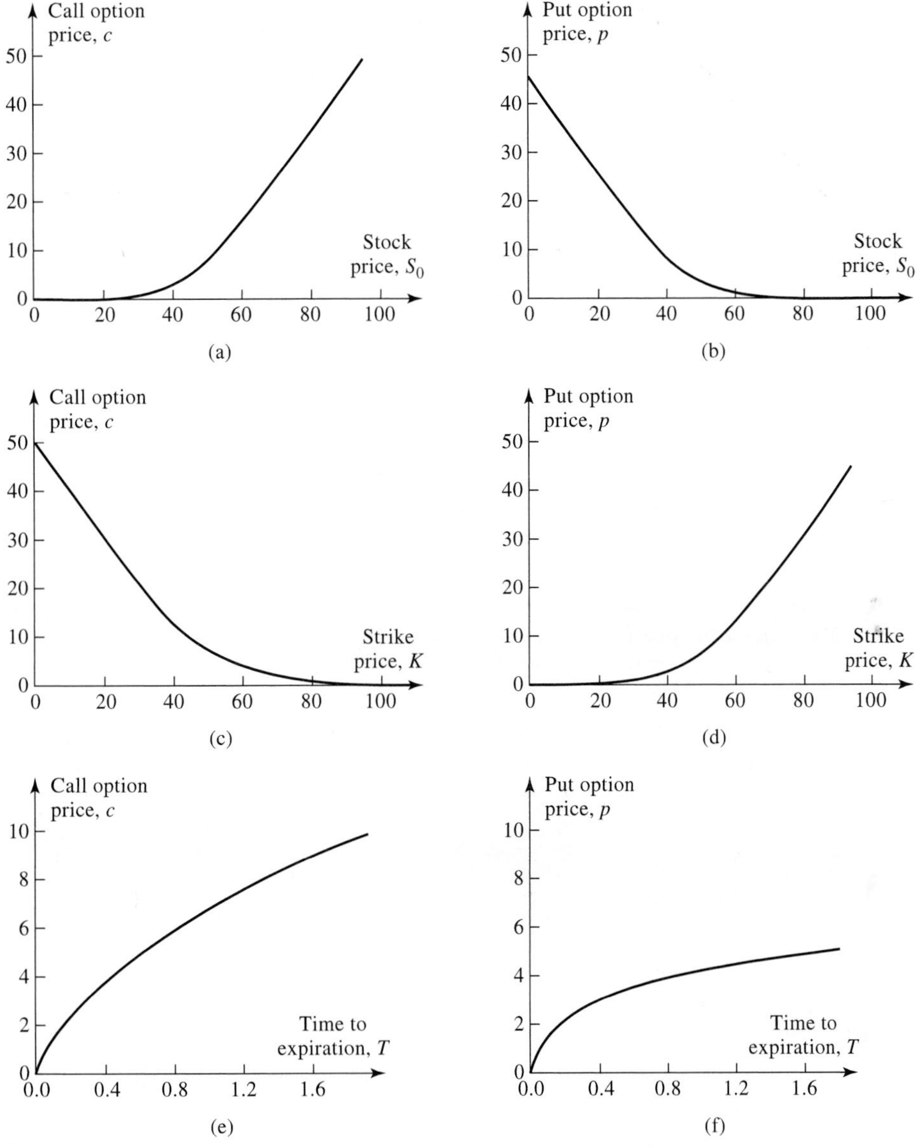

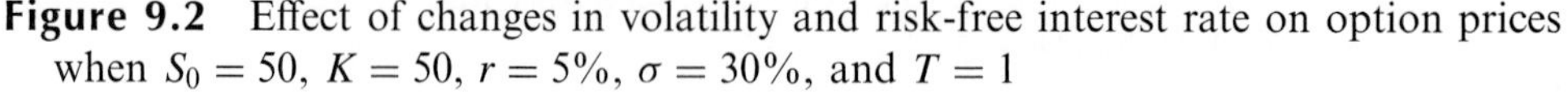

Figure 9.2 Effect of changes in volatility and risk-free interest rate on option prices when $S_0 = 50$, $K = 50$, $r = 5\%$, $\sigma = 30\%$, and $T = 1$

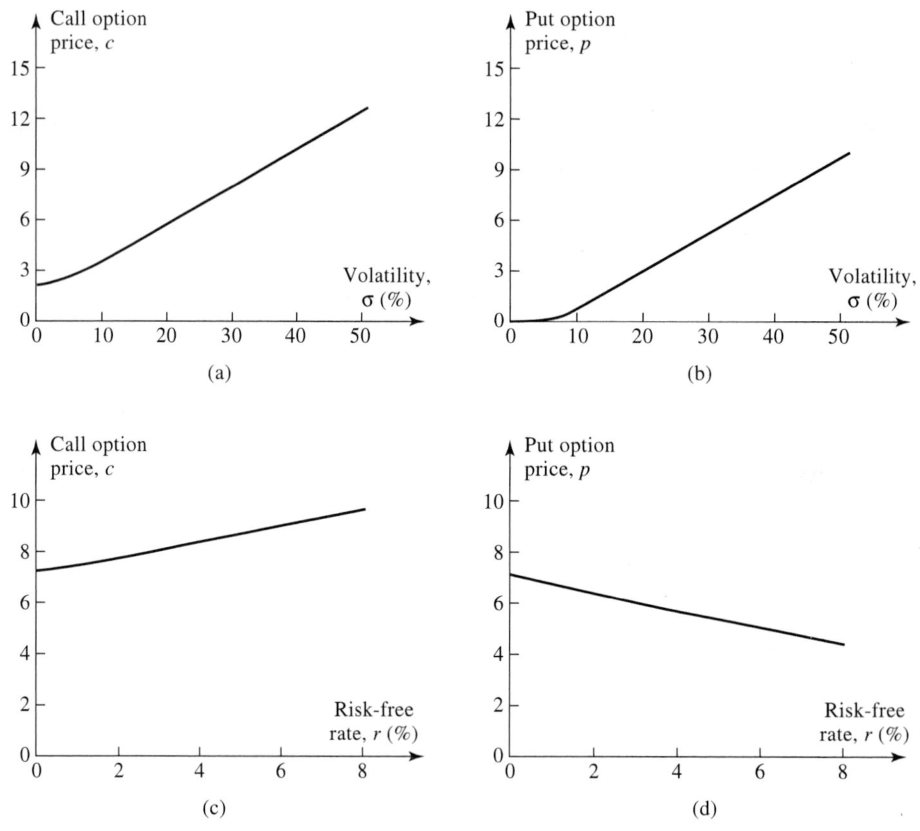

the stock tends to increase. In addition, the present value of any future cash flow received by the holder of the option decreases. The combined impact of these two effects is to decrease the value of call options and increase the value of put options (see Figures 9.2c, d).

It is important to emphasize that we are assuming that interest rates change while all other variables stay the same. In particular we are assuming that interest rates change while the stock price remains the same. In practice, when interest rates rise (fall), stock prices tend to fall (rise). The net effect of an interest rate increase and the accompanying stock price decrease can be to decrease the value of a call option and increase the value of a put option. Similarly, the net effect of an interest rate decrease and the accompanying stock price increase can be to increase the value of a call option and decrease the value of a put option.

Dividends

Dividends have the effect of reducing the stock price on the ex-dividend date. This is bad news for the value of call options and good news for the value of put options. The value of a call option is therefore negatively related to the size of any anticipated dividends, and the value of a put option is positively related to the size of any anticipated dividends.

9.2 ASSUMPTIONS AND NOTATION

In this chapter we will make assumptions similar to those made for deriving forward and futures prices in Chapter 5. We assume that there are some market participants, such as large investment banks, for which the following statements are true:

1. There are no transactions costs.
2. All trading profits (net of trading losses) are subject to the same tax rate.
3. Borrowing and lending are possible at the risk-free interest rate.

We assume that these market participants are prepared to take advantage of arbitrage opportunities as they arise. As discussed in Chapters 1 and 5, this means that any available arbitrage opportunities disappear very quickly. For the purposes of our analyses, it is therefore reasonable to assume that there are no arbitrage opportunities.

We will use the following notation:

S_0: Current stock price
K: Strike price of option
T: Time to expiration of option
S_T: Stock price at maturity
r: Continuously compounded risk-free rate of interest for an investment maturing in time T
C: Value of American call option to buy one share
P: Value of American put option to sell one share
c: Value of European call option to buy one share
p: Value of European put option to sell one share

It should be noted that r is the nominal rate of interest, not the real rate of interest. We can assume that $r > 0$. Otherwise, a risk-free investment would provide no advantages over cash. (Indeed, if $r < 0$, cash would be preferable to a risk-free investment.)

9.3 UPPER AND LOWER BOUNDS FOR OPTION PRICES

In this section we derive upper and lower bounds for option prices. These bounds do not depend on any particular assumptions about the factors mentioned in Section 9.1 (except $r > 0$). If an option price is above the upper bound or below the lower bound, there are profitable opportunities for arbitrageurs.

Upper Bounds

An American or European call option gives the holder the right to buy one share of a stock for a certain price. No matter what happens, the option can never be worth more than the stock. Hence, the stock price is an upper bound to the option price:

$$c \leqslant S_0 \quad \text{and} \quad C \leqslant S_0$$

If these relationships were not true, an arbitrageur could easily make a riskless profit by buying the stock and selling the call option.

An American or European put option gives the holder the right to sell one share of a stock for K. No matter how low the stock price becomes, the option can never be worth more than K. Hence,

$$p \leqslant K \quad \text{and} \quad P \leqslant K$$

For European options, we know that at maturity the option cannot be worth more than K. It follows that it cannot be worth more than the present value of K today:

$$p \leqslant Ke^{-rT}$$

If this were not true, an arbitrageur could make a riskless profit by writing the option and investing the proceeds of the sale at the risk-free interest rate.

Lower Bound for Calls on Non-Dividend-Paying Stocks

A lower bound for the price of a European call option on a non-dividend-paying stock is

$$S_0 - Ke^{-rT}$$

We first look at a numerical example and then consider a more formal argument.

Suppose that $S_0 = \$20$, $K = \$18$, $r = 10\%$ per annum, and $T = 1$ year. In this case,

$$S_0 - Ke^{-rT} = 20 - 18e^{-0.1} = 3.71$$

or \$3.71. Consider the situation where the European call price is \$3.00, which is less than the theoretical minimum of \$3.71. An arbitrageur can short the stock and buy the call to provide a cash inflow of \$20.00 – \$3.00 = \$17.00. If invested for one year at 10% per annum, the \$17.00 grows to $17e^{0.1} = \$18.79$. At the end of the year, the option expires. If the stock price is greater than \$18.00, the arbitrageur exercises the option for \$18.00, closes out the short position, and makes a profit of

$$\$18.79 - \$18.00 = \$0.79$$

If the stock price is less than \$18.00, the stock is bought in market and the short position is closed out. The arbitrageur then makes an even greater profit. For example, if the stock price is \$17.00, the arbitrageur's profit is

$$\$18.79 - \$17.00 = \$1.79$$

This example is illustrated in Trading Note 9.1.

For a more formal argument, we consider the following two portfolios:

Portfolio A: one European call option plus an amount of cash equal to Ke^{-rT}

Portfolio B: one share

In portfolio A, the cash, if it is invested at the risk-free interest rate, will grow to K in time T. If $S_T > K$, the call option is exercised at maturity and portfolio A is worth S_T.

Trading Note 9.1 Call option price too low

A European call option on a non-dividend-paying stock with a strike price of \$18 and an expiration date in one year costs \$3. The stock price is \$20 and the risk-free interest rate is 10% per annum.

Action Now

Buy the option for \$3
Short the stock to realize \$20
Invest \$17 for 1 year

Action in One Year

If $S_T > 18$:	If $S_T < 18$:
Exercise the option to buy stock for \$18	Buy stock for S_T
Use stock to close out short position	Use stock to close out short position
Receive \$18.79 from investment	Receive \$18.79 from investment
Net gain = \$0.79	Net gain = $18.79 - S_T$ (> \$0.79)

If $S_T < K$, the call option expires worthless and the portfolio is worth K. Hence, at time T, portfolio A is worth

$$\max(S_T, K)$$

Portfolio B is worth S_T at time T. Hence, portfolio A is always worth as much as, and can be worth more than, portfolio B at the option's maturity. It follows that in the absence of arbitrage opportunities this must also be true today. Hence,

$$c + Ke^{-rT} \geqslant S_0$$

or

$$c \geqslant S_0 - Ke^{-rT}$$

Because the worst that can happen to a call option is that it expires worthless, its value cannot be negative. This means that $c \geqslant 0$ and therefore

$$c \geqslant \max(S_0 - Ke^{-rT}, 0) \tag{9.1}$$

Example

Consider a European call option on a non-dividend-paying stock when the stock price is \$51, the strike price is \$50, the time to maturity is six months, and the risk-free rate of interest is 12% per annum. In this case, $S_0 = 51$, $K = 50$, $T = 0.5$, and $r = 0.12$. From equation (9.1), a lower bound for the option price is $S_0 - Ke^{-rT}$, or

$$51 - 50e^{-0.12\times0.5} = \$3.91$$

Lower Bound for Puts on Non-Dividend-Paying Stocks

For a European put option on a non-dividend-paying stock, a lower bound for the price is

$$Ke^{-rT} - S_0$$

Trading Note 9.2 Put option price too low

A European put option on a non-dividend-paying stock with a strike price of \$40 and an expiration date in six months costs \$1. The stock price is \$37 and the risk-free interest rate is 5% per annum.

Action Now

Borrow \$38 for six months
Buy the option for \$1
Buy the stock for \$37

Action in Six Months

If $S_T < 40$:	If $S_T > 40$:
Exercise the option to sell stock for \$40	Sell the stock for $+S_T$
Use \$38.96 to repay borrowings	Use \$38.96 to repay borrowings
Net gain = \$1.04	Net gain = $S_T - 38.96 > \$1.04$

Again, we first consider a numerical example and then look at a more formal argument. Suppose that $S_0 = \$37$, $K = \$40$, $r = 5\%$ per annum, and $T = 0.5$ years. In this case,

$$Ke^{-rT} - S_0 = 40e^{-0.05\times 0.5} - 37 = \$2.01$$

Consider the situation where the European put price is \$1.00, which is less than the theoretical minimum of \$2.01. An arbitrageur can borrow \$38.00 for six months to buy both the put and the stock. At the end of the six months, the arbitrageur will be required to repay $38e^{0.05\times 0.5} = \$38.96$. If the stock price is below \$40.00, the arbitrageur exercises the option to sell the stock for \$40.00, repays the loan, and makes a profit of

$$\$40.00 - \$38.96 = \$1.04$$

If the stock price is greater than \$40.00, the arbitrageur discards the option, sells the stock, and repays the loan for an even greater profit. For example, if the stock price is \$42.00, the arbitrageur's profit is

$$\$42.00 - \$38.96 = \$3.04$$

This example is illustrated in Trading Note 9.2.

For a more formal argument, we consider the following two portfolios:

Portfolio C: one European put option plus one share
Portfolio D: an amount of cash equal to Ke^{-rT}

If $S_T < K$, the option in portfolio C is exercised at option maturity and the portfolio becomes worth K. If $S_T > K$, the put option expires worthless and the portfolio is worth S_T at this time. Hence, portfolio C is worth

$$\max(S_T, K)$$

in time T. Assuming the cash is invested at the risk-free interest rate, portfolio D is worth K in time T. Hence, portfolio C is always worth as much as, and can sometimes be worth more than, portfolio D in time T. It follows that in the absence of arbitrage opportunities portfolio C must be worth at least as much as portfolio D today. Hence,

$$p + S_0 \geqslant Ke^{-rT}$$

or

$$p \geqslant Ke^{-rT} - S_0$$

Because the worst that can happen to a put option is that it expires worthless, its value cannot be negative. This means that

$$p \geqslant \max(Ke^{-rT} - S_0,\ 0) \tag{9.2}$$

Example

Consider a European put option on a non-dividend-paying stock when the stock price is \$38, the exercise price is \$40, the time to maturity is three months, and the risk-free rate of interest is 10% per annum. In this case, $S_0 = 38$, $K = 40$, $T = 0.25$, and $r = 0.10$. From equation (9.2), a lower bound for the option price is $Ke^{-rT} - S_0$, or

$$40e^{-0.1\times 0.25} - 38 = \$1.01$$

9.4 PUT–CALL PARITY

We now derive an important relationship between p and c. Consider the following two portfolios that were used in the previous section:

Portfolio A: one European call option plus an amount of cash equal to Ke^{-rT}

Portfolio C: one European put option plus one share

Both are worth

$$\max(S_T,\ K)$$

at expiration of the options. Because the options are European, they cannot be exercised prior to the expiration date. The portfolios must therefore have identical values today. This means that

$$c + Ke^{-rT} = p + S_0 \tag{9.3}$$

This relationship is known as *put–call parity*. It shows that the value of a European call with a certain exercise price and exercise date can be deduced from the value of a European put with the same exercise price and exercise date, and vice versa.

If equation (9.3) does not hold, there are arbitrage opportunities. Suppose that the stock price is \$31, the exercise price is \$30, the risk-free interest rate is 10% per annum, the price of a three-month European call option is \$3, and the price of a three-month European put option is \$2.25. In this case,

$$c + Ke^{-rT} = 3 + 30e^{-0.1\times 3/12} = \$32.26$$

$$p + S_0 = 2.25 + 31 = \$33.25$$

Portfolio C is overpriced relative to portfolio A. The correct arbitrage strategy is to buy the securities in portfolio A and short the securities in portfolio C. The strategy involves buying the call and shorting both the put and the stock, generating a positive cash flow of

$$-3 + 2.25 + 31 = \$30.25$$

up front. When invested at the risk-free interest rate, this amount grows to $30.25e^{0.1\times0.25} = \$31.02$ in three months.

If the stock price at expiration of the option is greater than \$30, the call will be exercised. If it is less than \$30, the put will be exercised. In either case, the investor ends up buying one share for \$30. This share can be used to close out the short position. The net profit is therefore

$$\$31.02 - \$30.00 = \$1.02$$

For an alternative situation, suppose that the call price is \$3 and the put price is \$1. In this case,

$$c + Ke^{-rT} = 3 + 30e^{-0.1\times3/12} = \$32.26$$

$$p + S_0 = 1 + 31 = \$32.00$$

Portfolio A is overpriced relative to portfolio C. An arbitrageur can short the securities in portfolio A and buy the securities in portfolio C to lock in a profit. The strategy involves shorting the call and buying both the put and the stock with an initial investment of

$$\$31 + \$1 - \$3 = \$29$$

When the investment is financed at the risk-free interest rate, a repayment of $29e^{0.1\times0.25} = \$29.73$ is required at the end of the three months. As in the previous case, either the call or the put will be exercised. The short call and long put option position

Table 9.2 Arbitrage opportunities when put–call parity does not hold. Stock price = \$31; interest rate = 10%; call price = \$3. Both put and call have strike price of \$30 and three months to maturity

Three-month put price = \$2.25	***Three-month put price = \$1***
Action now:	*Action now*:
Buy call for \$3	Borrow \$29 for 3 months
Short put to realize \$2.25	Short call to realize \$3
Short the stock to realize \$31	Buy put for \$1
Invest \$30.25 for 3 months	Buy the stock for \$31
Action in 3 months if $S_T > 30$:	*Action in 3 months if* $S_T > 30$:
Receive \$31.02 from investment	Call exercised: sell stock for \$30
Exercise call to buy stock for \$30	Use \$29.73 to repay loan
Net profit = \$1.02	Net profit = \$0.27
Action in 3 months if $S_T < 30$:	*Action in 3 months if* $S_T < 30$:
Receive \$31.02 from investment	Exercise put to sell stock for \$30
Put exercised: buy stock for \$30	Use \$29.73 to repay loan
Net profit = \$1.02	Net profit = \$0.27

Business Snapshot 9.1 Put–call parity and capital structure

The pioneers of option pricing were Fischer Black, Myron Scholes, and Robert Merton. In the early 1970s they showed that options can be used to characterize the capital structure of a company. Today this model is widely used by financial institutions to assess a company's credit risk.

To illustrate the model, consider a company that has assets that are financed with zero-coupon bonds and equity. Suppose that the bonds mature in five years at which time a principal payment of K is required. The company pays no dividends. If the assets are worth more than K in five years, the equity holders choose to repay the bond holders. If the assets are worth less than K, the equity holders choose to declare bankruptcy and the bond holders end up owning the company.

The value of the equity in five years is therefore $\max(A_T - K, 0)$, where A_T is the value of the company's assets at that time. This shows that the equity holders have a five-year European call option on the assets of the company with a strike price of K. What about the bondholders? They get $\min(A_T, K)$ in five years. This is the same as $K - \max(K - A_T, 0)$. The bondholders have given the equity holders the right to sell the company's assets to them for K in five years. The bonds are therefore worth the present value of K minus the value of a five-year European put option on the assets with a strike price of K.

To summarize, if c and p are the values of the call and put options, respectively, then

$$\text{Value of equity} = c$$

$$\text{Value of debt} = PV(K) - p$$

Denote the value of the assets of the company today by A_0. The value of the assets must equal the total value of the instruments used to finance the assets. This means that it must equal the sum of the value of the equity and the value of the debt, so that

$$A_0 = c + [PV(K) - p]$$

Rearranging this equation, we have

$$c + PV(K) = p + A_0$$

This is the put–call parity result in equation (9.3) for call and put options on the assets of the company.

therefore leads to the stock being sold for \$30.00. The net profit is therefore

$$\$30.00 - \$29.73 = \$0.27$$

These examples are illustrated in Table 9.2. Business Snapshot 9.1 shows how options and put–call parity can help us understand the positions of the debt holders and equity holders in a company.

American Options

Put–call parity holds only for European options. However, it is possible to derive some results for American option prices. It can be shown (see Problem 9.18) that, when there are no dividends,

$$S_0 - K \leqslant C - P \leqslant S_0 - Ke^{-rT} \tag{9.4}$$

Example

An American call option on a non-dividend-paying stock with exercise price \$20.00 and maturity in five months is worth \$1.50. Suppose that the current stock price is \$19.00 and the risk-free interest rate is 10% per annum. From equation (9.4), we have

$$19 - 20 \leqslant C - P \leqslant 19 - 20e^{-0.1 \times 5/12}$$

or

$$1 \geqslant P - C \geqslant 0.18$$

showing that $P - C$ lies between \$1.00 and \$0.18. With C at \$1.50, P must lie between \$1.68 and \$2.50. In other words, upper and lower bounds for the price of an American put with the same strike price and expiration date as the American call are \$2.50 and \$1.68.

9.5 EARLY EXERCISE: CALLS ON A NON-DIVIDEND-PAYING STOCK

This section demonstrates that it is never optimal to exercise an American call option on a non-dividend-paying stock before the expiration date.

To illustrate the general nature of the argument, consider an American call option on a non-dividend-paying stock with one month to expiration when the stock price is \$50 and the strike price is \$40. The option is deep in the money, and the investor who owns the option might well be tempted to exercise it immediately. However, if the investor plans to hold the stock obtained by exercising the option for more than one month, this is not the best strategy. A better course of action is to keep the option and exercise it at the end of the month. The \$40 strike price is then paid out one month later than it would be if the option were exercised immediately, so that interest is earned on the \$40 for one month. Because the stock pays no dividends, no income from the stock is sacrificed. A further advantage of waiting rather than exercising immediately is that there is some chance (however remote) that the stock price will fall below \$40 in one month. In this case the investor will not exercise in one month and will be glad that the decision to exercise early was not taken!

This argument shows that there are no advantages to exercising early if the investor plans to keep the stock for the remaining life of the option (one month, in this case). What if the investor thinks the stock is currently overpriced and is wondering whether to exercise the option and sell the stock? In this case, the investor is better off selling the option than exercising it.[1] The option will be bought by another investor who does want to hold the stock. Such investors must exist. Otherwise the current stock price would not be \$50. The price obtained for the option will be greater than its intrinsic value of \$10, for the reasons mentioned earlier.

[1] As an alternative strategy, the investor can keep the option and short the stock to lock in a better profit than \$10.

Figure 9.3 Variation of price of an American or European call option on a non-dividend-paying stock with the stock price S_0

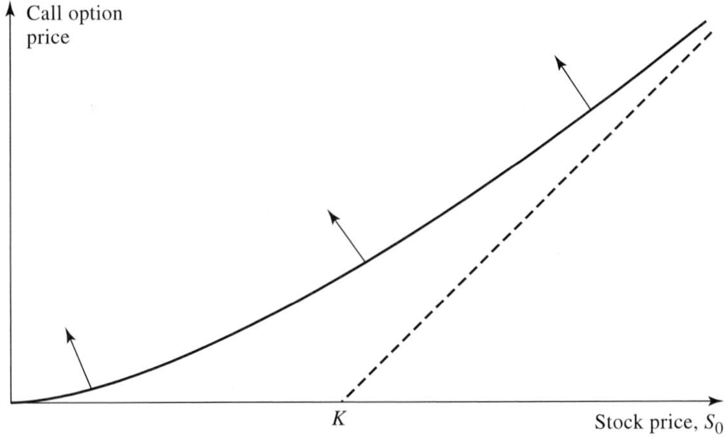

For a more formal argument, we can use equation (9.1):

$$c \geqslant S_0 - Ke^{-rT}$$

Because the owner of an American call has all the exercise opportunities open to the owner of the corresponding European call, we must have

$$C \geqslant c$$

Hence,

$$C \geqslant S_0 - Ke^{-rT}$$

Given $r > 0$, it follows that $C > S_0 - K$. If it were optimal to exercise early, then C would equal $S_0 - K$. We deduce that it can never be optimal to exercise early.

Figure 9.3 shows the general way in which the call price varies with S_0 and K. It indicates that the call price is always above its intrinsic value of $\max(S_0 - K, 0)$. As r or T or the volatility increases, the line relating the call price to the stock price moves in the direction indicated by the arrows (i.e., farther away from the intrinsic value).

To summarize, there are two reasons an American call on a non-dividend-paying stock should not be exercised early. One relates to the insurance that it provides. A call option, when held instead of the stock itself, in effect insures the holder against the stock price falling below the strike price. Once the option has been exercised and the strike price has been exchanged for the stock price, this insurance vanishes. The other reason concerns the time value of money. From the perspective of the option holder, the later the strike price is paid out the better.

9.6 EARLY EXERCISE: PUTS ON A NON-DIVIDEND-PAYING STOCK

It can be optimal to exercise an American put option on a non-dividend-paying stock early. Indeed, at any given time during its life, a put option should always be exercised early if it is sufficiently deep in the money.

To illustrate, consider an extreme situation. Suppose that the strike price is \$10 and the stock price is virtually zero. By exercising immediately, an investor makes an immediate gain of \$10. If the investor waits, the gain from exercise might be less than \$10, but it cannot be more than \$10, because negative stock prices are impossible. Furthermore, receiving \$10 now is preferable to receiving \$10 in the future. It follows that the option should be exercised immediately.

Like a call option, a put option can be viewed as providing insurance. A put option, when held in conjunction with the stock, insures the holder against the stock price falling below a certain level. However, a put option is different from a call option in that it may be optimal for an investor to forgo this insurance and exercise early in order to realize the strike price immediately. In general, the early exercise of a put option becomes more attractive as S_0 decreases, as r increases, and as the volatility decreases.

It will be recalled from equation (9.2) that

$$p \geqslant Ke^{-rT} - S_0$$

For an American put with price P, the stronger condition

$$P \geqslant K - S_0$$

must always hold because immediate exercise is always possible.

Figure 9.4 shows the general way in which the price of an American put varies with S_0. Provided that $r > 0$, it is always optimal to exercise an American put immediately when the stock price is sufficiently low. When early exercise is optimal, the value of the option is $K - S_0$. The curve representing the value of the put therefore merges into the put's intrinsic value, $K - S_0$, for a sufficiently small value of S_0. In Figure 9.4, this value of S_0 is shown as point A. The line relating the put price to the stock price moves in the direction indicated by the arrows when r decreases, when the volatility increases, and when T increases.

Because there are some circumstances when it is desirable to exercise an American put option early, it follows that an American put option is always worth more than the

Figure 9.4 Variation of price of an American put option with stock price S_0

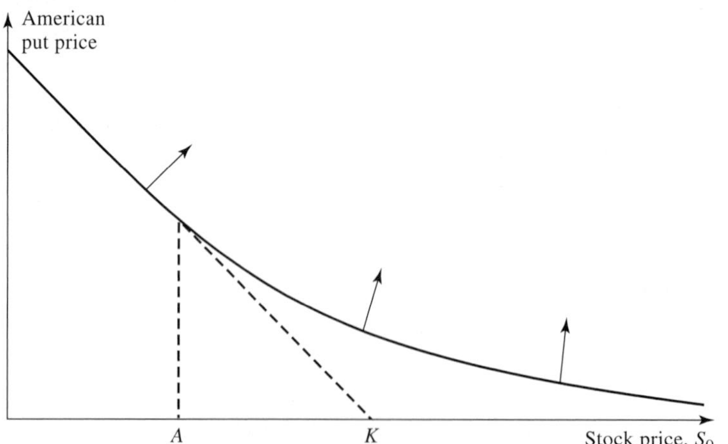

Figure 9.5 Variation of price of a European put option with the stock price S_0

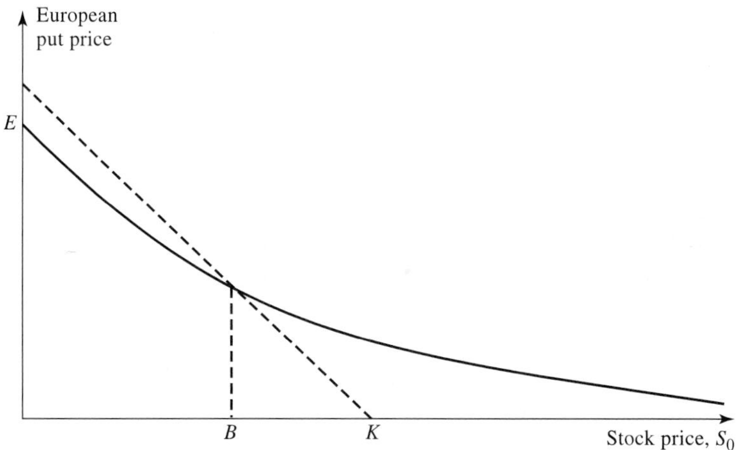

corresponding European put option. Furthermore, because an American put is sometimes worth its intrinsic value (see Figure 9.4), it follows that a European put option must sometimes be worth less than its intrinsic value. Figure 9.5 shows the variation of the European put price with the stock price. Note that point B in Figure 9.5, at which the price of the option is equal to its intrinsic value, must represent a higher value of the stock price than point A in Figure 9.4. Point E in Figure 9.5 is where $S_0 = 0$ and the European put price is Ke^{-rT}.

9.7 EFFECT OF DIVIDENDS

The results produced so far in this chapter have assumed that we are dealing with options on a non-dividend-paying stock. In this section we examine the impact of dividends. In the United States most exchange-traded stock options have a life of less than one year and dividends payable during the life of the option can usually be predicted with reasonable accuracy. We will use D to denote the present value of the dividends during the life of the option. In the calculation of D, a dividend is assumed to occur at the time of its ex-dividend date.

Lower Bound for Calls and Puts

We can redefine portfolios A and B as follows:

Portfolio A: one European call option plus an amount of cash equal to $D + Ke^{-rT}$

Portfolio B: one share

A similar argument to the one used to derive equation (9.1) shows that

$$c \geqslant S_0 - D - Ke^{-rT} \tag{9.5}$$

We can also redefine portfolios C and D as follows:

Portfolio C: one European put option plus one share

Portfolio D: an amount of cash equal to $D + Ke^{-rT}$

A similar argument to the one used to derive equation (9.2) shows that

$$p \geqslant D + Ke^{-rT} - S_0 \tag{9.6}$$

Early Exercise

When dividends are expected, we can no longer assert than an American call option will not be exercised early. Sometimes it is optimal to exercise an American call immediately prior to an ex-dividend date. It is never optimal to exercise a call at other times. This point is discussed further in the Appendix to Chapter 12.

Put–Call Parity

Comparing the value at option maturity of the redefined portfolios A and C shows that, with dividends, the put–call parity result in equation (9.3) becomes

$$c + D + Ke^{-rT} = p + S_0 \tag{9.7}$$

Dividends cause equation (9.4) to be modified (see Problem 9.19) to

$$S_0 - D - K \leqslant C - P \leqslant S_0 - Ke^{-rT} \tag{9.8}$$

SUMMARY

There are six factors affecting the value of a stock option: the current stock price, the strike price, the expiration date, the stock price volatility, the risk-free interest rate, and the dividends expected during the life of the option. The value of a call generally increases as the current stock price, the time to expiration, the volatility, and the risk-free interest rate increase. The value of a call decreases as the strike price and expected dividends increase. The value of a put generally increases as the strike price, the time to expiration, the volatility, and the expected dividends increase. The value of a put decreases as the current stock price and the risk-free interest rate increase.

It is possible to reach some conclusions about the value of stock options without making any assumptions about the volatility of stock prices. For example, the price of a call option on a stock must always be worth less than the price of the stock itself. Similarly, the price of a put option on a stock must always be worth less than the option's strike price.

A European call option on a non-dividend-paying stock must be worth more than

$$\max(S_0 - Ke^{-rT}, 0)$$

where S_0 is the stock price, K is the exercise price, r is the risk-free interest rate, and T is the time to expiration. A European put option on a non-dividend-paying stock must be worth more than

$$\max(Ke^{-rT} - S_0, 0)$$

When dividends with present value D will be paid, the lower bound for a European call option becomes

$$\max(S_0 - D - Ke^{-rT},\ 0)$$

and the lower bound for a European put option becomes

$$\max(Ke^{-rT} + D - S_0,\ 0)$$

Put–call parity is a relationship between the price, c, of a European call option on a stock and the price, p, of a European put option on a stock. For a non-dividend-paying stock, it is

$$c + Ke^{-rT} = p + S_0$$

For a dividend-paying stock, the put–call parity relationship is

$$c + D + Ke^{-rT} = p + S_0$$

Put–call parity does not hold for American options. However, it is possible to use arbitrage arguments to obtain upper and lower bounds for the difference between the price of an American call and the price of an American put.

In Chapter 12 we will carry the analyses in this chapter further by making specific assumptions about the probabilistic behavior of stock prices. This will enable us to derive exact pricing formulas for European stock options. In Chapters 11 and 16, we will see how numerical procedures can be used to price American options.

FURTHER READING

Black, F., and M. Scholes. "The Pricing of Options and Corporate Liabilities," *Journal of Political Economy*, 81 (May–June 1973): 637–59.

Broadie, M., and J. Detemple. "American Option Valuation: New Bounds, Approximations, and a Comparison of Existing Methods," *Review of Financial Studies*, 9, 4 (1996): 1211–50.

Merton, R. C. "On the Pricing of Corporate Debt: The Risk Structure of Interest Rates," *Journal of Finance*, 29, 2 (1974): 449–70.

Merton, R. C. "Theory of Rational Option Pricing," *Bell Journal of Economics and Management Science*, 4 (Spring 1973): 141–83.

Merton, R. C. "The Relationship between Put and Call Prices: Comment," *Journal of Finance*, 28 (March 1973): 183–84.

Stoll, H. R. "The Relationship between Put and Call Option Prices," *Journal of Finance*, 31 (May 1969): 319–32.

Quiz (Answers at End of Book)

9.1. List the six factors affecting stock option prices.

9.2. What is a lower bound for the price of a four-month call option on a non-dividend-paying stock when the stock price is \$28, the strike price is \$25, and the risk-free interest rate is 8% per annum?

9.3. What is a lower bound for the price of a one-month European put option on a non-dividend-paying stock when the stock price is \$12, the strike price is \$15, and the risk-free interest rate is 6% per annum?

9.4. Give two reasons that the early exercise of an American call option on a non-dividend-paying stock is not optimal. The first reason should involve the time value of money. The second reason should apply even if interest rates are zero.

9.5. "The early exercise of an American put is a trade-off between the time value of money and the insurance value of a put." Explain this statement.

9.6. Explain why an American call option on a dividend-paying stock is always worth at least as much as its intrinsic value. Is the same true of a European call option? Explain your answer.

9.7. The price of a non-dividend paying stock is \$19 and the price of a three-month European call option on the stock with a strike price of \$20 is \$1. The risk-free rate is 4% per annum. What is the price of a three-month European put option with a strike price of \$20?

Questions and Problems (Answers in Solutions Manual/Study Guide)

9.8. Explain why the arguments leading to put–call parity for European options cannot be used to give a similar result for American options.

9.9. What is a lower bound for the price of a six-month call option on a non-dividend-paying stock when the stock price is \$80, the strike price is \$75, and the risk-free interest rate is 10% per annum?

9.10. What is a lower bound for the price of a two-month European put option on a non-dividend-paying stock when the stock price is \$58, the strike price is \$65, and the risk-free interest rate is 5% per annum?

9.11. A four-month European call option on a dividend-paying stock is currently selling for \$5. The stock price is \$64, the strike price is \$60, and a dividend of \$0.80 is expected in one month. The risk-free interest rate is 12% per annum for all maturities. What opportunities are there for an arbitrageur?

9.12. A one-month European put option on a non-dividend-paying stock is currently selling for \$2.50. The stock price is \$47, the strike price is \$50, and the risk-free interest rate is 6% per annum. What opportunities are there for an arbitrageur?

9.13. Give an intuitive explanation of why the early exercise of an American put becomes more attractive as the risk-free rate increases and volatility decreases.

9.14. The price of a European call that expires in six months and has a strike price of \$30 is \$2. The underlying stock price is \$29, and a dividend of \$0.50 is expected in two months and again in five months. The term structure is flat, with all risk-free interest rates being 10%. What is the price of a European put option that expires in six months and has a strike price of \$30?

9.15. Explain carefully the arbitrage opportunities in Problem 9.14 if the European put price is \$3.

9.16. The price of an American call on a non-dividend-paying stock is \$4. The stock price is \$31, the strike price is \$30, and the expiration date is in three months. The risk-free interest rate is 8%. Derive upper and lower bounds for the price of an American put on the same stock with the same strike price and expiration date.

9.17. Explain carefully the arbitrage opportunities in Problem 9.16 if the American put price is greater than the calculated upper bound.

9.18. Prove the result in equation (9.4). (*Hint*: For the first part of the relationship, consider (a) a portfolio consisting of a European call plus an amount of cash equal to K, and (b) a portfolio consisting of an American put option plus one share.)

9.19. Prove the result in equation (9.8). (*Hint*: For the first part of the relationship consider (a) a portfolio consisting of a European call plus an amount of cash equal to $D + K$, and (b) a portfolio consisting of an American put option plus one share.)

9.20. Regular call options on non-dividend-paying stocks should not be exercised early, but there is a tendency for executive stock options to be exercised early even when the company pays no dividends (see Business Snapshot 8.3 for a discussion of executive stock options). Give a possible reason for this.

9.21. Use the software DerivaGem to verify that Figures 9.1 and 9.2 are correct.

Assignment Questions

9.22. A European call option and put option on a stock both have a strike price of \$20 and an expiration date in three months. Both sell for \$3. The risk-free interest rate is 10% per annum, the current stock price is \$19, and a \$1 dividend is expected in one month. Identify the arbitrage opportunity open to a trader.

9.23. Suppose that c_1, c_2, and c_3 are the prices of European call options with strike prices K_1, K_2, and K_3, respectively, where $K_3 > K_2 > K_1$ and $K_3 - K_2 = K_2 - K_1$. All options have the same maturity. Show that

$$c_2 \leqslant 0.5(c_1 + c_3)$$

(*Hint*: Consider a portfolio that is long one option with strike price K_1, long one option with strike price K_3, and short two options with strike price K_2.)

9.24. What is the result corresponding to that in Problem 9.23 for European put options?

9.25. Suppose that you are the manager and sole owner of a highly leveraged company. All the debt will mature in one year. If at that time the value of the company is greater than the face value of the debt, you will pay off the debt. If the value of the company is less than the face value of the debt, you will declare bankruptcy and the debt holders will own the company.

a. Express your position as an option on the value of the company.

b. Express the position of the debt holders in terms of options on the value of the company.

c. What can you do to increase the value of your position?

9.26. Consider an option on a stock when the stock price is \$41, the strike price is \$40, the risk-free rate is 6%, the volatility is 35%, and the time to maturity is one year. Assume that a dividend of \$0.50 is expected after six months.

a. Use DerivaGem to value the option assuming it is a European call.

b. Use DerivaGem to value the option assuming it is a European put.

c. Verify that put–call parity holds.

d. Explore using DerivaGem what happens to the price of the options as the time to maturity becomes very large. For this purpose, assume there are no dividends. Explain the results you get.

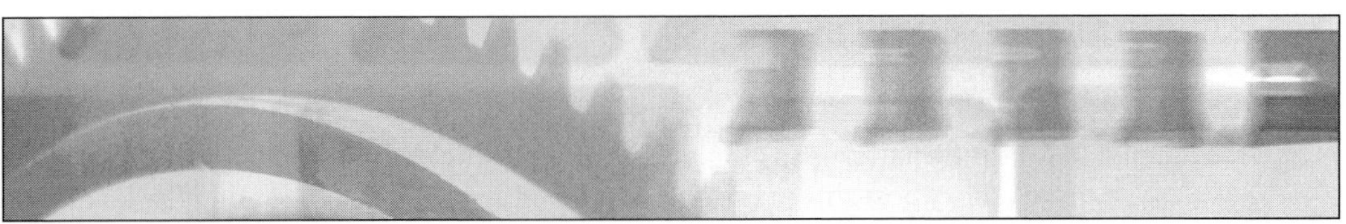

CHAPTER 10 Trading Strategies Involving Options

We discussed the profit pattern from an investment in a single stock option in Chapter 8. In this chapter we cover more fully the range of profit patterns obtainable using options. We assume that the underlying asset is a stock. Similar results can be obtained for other underlying assets, such as foreign currencies, stock indices, and futures contracts. The options used in the strategies we discuss are European. American options may lead to slightly different outcomes because of the possibility of early exercise.

In the first section we consider what happens when a position in a stock option is combined with a position in the stock itself. We then move on to examine the profit patterns obtained when an investment is made in two or more different options on the same stock. One of the attractions of options is that they can be used to create a wide range of different payoff functions. (A payoff function is the payoff as a function of the stock price.) If European options were available with every single possible strike price, then any payoff function could in theory be created.

For ease of exposition, the figures and tables showing the profit from a trading strategy will ignore the time value of money. The profit will be shown as the final payoff minus the initial cost. (In theory, it should be calculated as the present value of the final payoff minus the initial cost.)

10.1 STRATEGIES INVOLVING A SINGLE OPTION AND A STOCK

There are a number of different trading strategies involving a single option on a stock and the stock itself. The profits from these are illustrated in Figure 10.1. In this figure and in other figures throughout this chapter, the dashed line shows the relationship between profit and the stock price for the individual securities constituting the portfolio, whereas the solid line shows the relationship between profit and the stock price for the whole portfolio.

In Figure 10.1a, the portfolio consists of a long position in a stock plus a short position in a call option. This is known as *writing a covered call*. The long stock position "covers" or protects the investor from the payoff on the short call that becomes

Figure 10.1 Profit patterns (a) long position in a stock combined with short position in a call; (b) short position in a stock combined with long position in a call; (c) long position in a put combined with long position in a stock; (d) short position in a put combined with short position in a stock

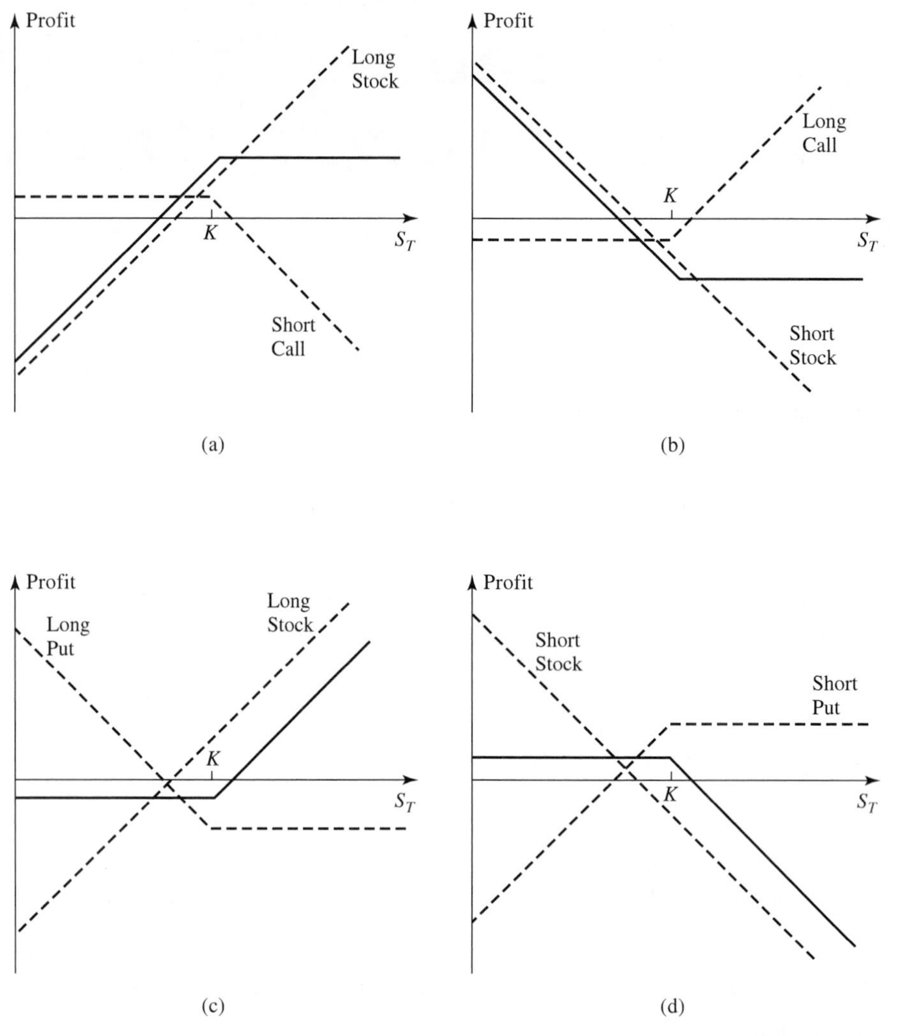

necessary if there is a sharp rise in the stock price. In Figure 10.1b, a short position in a stock is combined with a long position in a call option. This is the reverse of writing a covered call. In Figure 10.1c, the investment strategy involves buying a put option on a stock and the stock itself. The approach is sometimes referred to as a *protective put* strategy. In Figure 10.1d, a short position in a put option is combined with a short position in the stock. This is the reverse of a protective put.

The profit patterns in Figures 10.1a, b, c, d have the same general shape as the profit patterns discussed in Chapter 8 for short put, long put, long call, and short call, respectively. Put–call parity provides a way of understanding why this is so. From

Chapter 9, the put–call parity relationship is

$$p + S_0 = c + Ke^{-rT} + D \tag{10.1}$$

where p is the price of a European put, S_0 is the stock price, c is the price of a European call, K is the strike price of both call and put, r is the risk-free interest rate, T is the time to maturity of both call and put, and D is the present value of the dividends anticipated during the life of the options.

Equation (10.1) shows that a long position in a put combined with a long position in the stock is equivalent to a long call position plus a certain amount ($= Ke^{-rT} + D$) of cash. This explains why the profit pattern in Figure 10.1c is similar to the profit pattern from a long call position. The position in Figure 10.1d is the reverse of that in Figure 10.1c and therefore leads to a profit pattern similar to that from a short call position.

Equation (10.1) can be rearranged to become

$$S_0 - c = Ke^{-rT} + D - p$$

In other words, a long position in a stock combined with a short position in a call is equivalent to a short put position plus a certain amount ($= Ke^{-rT} + D$) of cash. This equality explains why the profit pattern in Figure 10.1a is similar to the profit pattern from a short put position. The position in Figure 10.1b is the reverse of that in Figure 10.1a and therefore leads to a profit pattern similar to that from a long put position.

10.2 SPREADS

A spread trading strategy involves taking a position in two or more options of the same type (i.e., two or more calls or two or more puts).

Bull Spreads

One of the most popular types of spreads is a *bull spread*. This can be created by buying a call option on a stock with a certain strike price and selling a call option on the same

Figure 10.2 Profit from bull spread created using call options

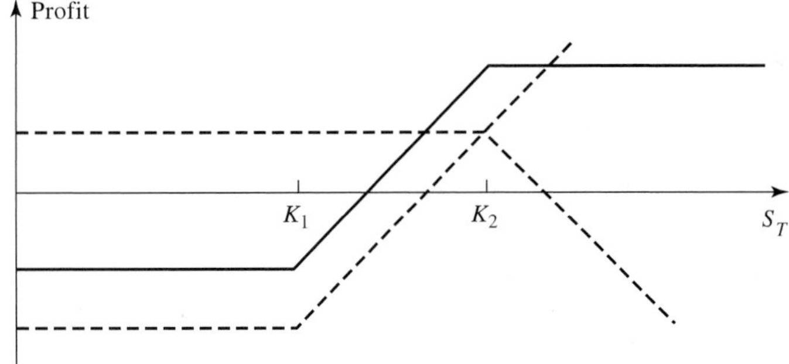

Table 10.1 Payoff from a bull spread created using calls

Stock price range	*Payoff from long call option*	*Payoff from short call option*	*Total payoff*
$S_T \geqslant K_2$	$S_T - K_1$	$K_2 - S_T$	$K_2 - K_1$
$K_1 < S_T < K_2$	$S_T - K_1$	0	$S_T - K_1$
$S_T \leqslant K_1$	0	0	0

stock with a higher strike price. Both options have the same expiration date. The strategy is illustrated in Figure 10.2. The profits from the two option positions taken separately are shown by the dashed lines. The profit from the whole strategy is the sum of the profits given by the dashed lines and is indicated by the solid line. Because a call price always decreases as the strike price increases, the value of the option sold is always less than the value of the option bought. A bull spread, when created from calls, therefore requires an initial investment.

Suppose that K_1 is the strike price of the call option bought, K_2 is the strike price of the call option sold, and S_T is the stock price on the expiration date of the options. Table 10.1 shows the total payoff that will be realized from a bull spread in different circumstances. If the stock price does well and is greater than the higher strike price, the payoff is the difference between the two strike prices, or $K_2 - K_1$. If the stock price on the expiration date lies between the two strike prices, the payoff is $S_T - K_1$. If the stock price on the expiration date is below the lower strike price, the payoff is zero. The profit in Figure 10.2 is calculated by subtracting the initial investment from the payoff.

A bull spread strategy limits the investor's upside as well as downside risk. The strategy can be described by saying that the investor has a call option with a strike price equal to K_1 and has chosen to give up some upside potential by selling a call option with strike price K_2 ($K_2 > K_1$). In return for giving up the upside potential, the investor gets the

Figure 10.3 Profit from bull spread created using put options

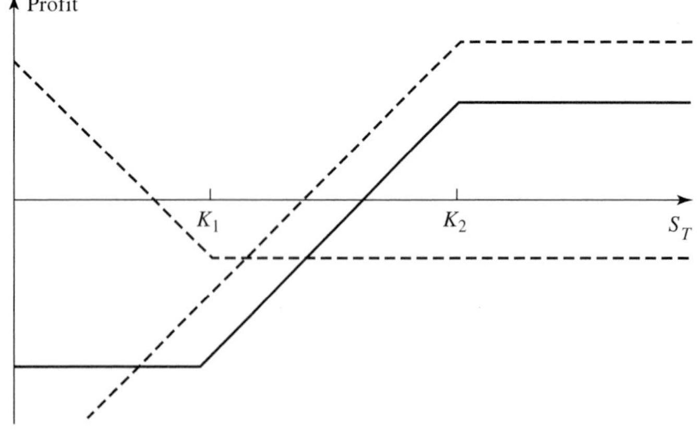

price of the option with strike price K_2. Three types of bull spread can be distinguished:

1. Both calls are initially out of the money.
2. One call is initially in the money; the other call is initially out of the money.
3. Both calls are initially in the money.

The most aggressive bull spreads are those of type 1. They cost very little to set up and have a small probability of giving a relatively high payoff ($= K_2 - K_1$). As we move from type 1 to type 2 and from type 2 to type 3, the spreads become more conservative.

Example

An investor buys for \$3 a call with a strike price of \$30 and sells for \$1 a call with a strike price of \$35. The payoff from this bull spread strategy is \$5 if the stock price is above \$35 and zero if it is below \$30. If the stock price is between \$30 and \$35, the payoff is the amount by which the stock price exceeds \$30. The cost of the strategy is \$3 − \$1 = \$2. The profit is therefore as follows:

Stock price range	*Profit*
$S_T \leqslant 30$	-2
$30 < S_T < 35$	$S_T - 32$
$S_T \geqslant 35$	$+3$

Bull spreads can also be created by buying a put with a low strike price and selling a put with a high strike price, as illustrated in Figure 10.3. Unlike the bull spread created from calls, bull spreads created from puts involve a positive cash flow to the investor up front (ignoring margin requirements) and a payoff that is either negative or zero.

Bear Spreads

An investor who enters into a bull spread is hoping that the stock price will increase. By contrast, an investor who enters into a *bear spread* is hoping that the stock price will decline. Bear spreads can be created by buying a put with one strike price and selling a put with another strike price. The strike price of the option purchased is greater than the strike price of the option sold. (This is in contrast to a bull spread where the strike price of

Figure 10.4 Profit from bear spread created using put options

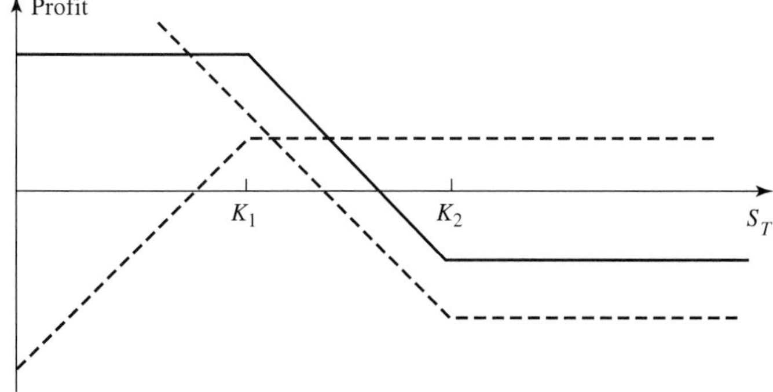

Table 10.2 Payoff from a bear spread created with put options

Stock price range	*Payoff from long put option*	*Payoff from short put option*	*Total payoff*
$S_T \geqslant K_2$	0	0	0
$K_1 < S_T < K_2$	$K_2 - S_T$	0	$K_2 - S_T$
$S_T \leqslant K_1$	$K_2 - S_T$	$K_1 - S_T$	$K_2 - K_1$

the option purchased is always less than the strike price of the option sold.) In Figure 10.4, the profit from the spread is shown by the solid line. A bear spread created from puts involves an initial cash outflow because the price of the put sold is less than the price of the put purchased. In essence, the investor has bought a put with a certain strike price and chosen to give up some of the profit potential by selling a put with a lower strike price. In return for the profit given up, the investor gets the price of the option sold.

Assume that the strike prices are K_1 and K_2, with $K_1 < K_2$. Table 10.2 shows the payoff that will be realized from a bear spread in different circumstances. If the stock price is greater than K_2, the payoff is zero. If the stock price is less than K_1, the payoff is $K_2 - K_1$. If the stock price is between K_1 and K_2, the payoff is $K_2 - S_T$. The profit is calculated by subtracting the initial cost from the payoff.

Example

An investor buys for \$3 a put with a strike price of \$35 and sells for \$1 a put with a strike price of \$30. The payoff from this bear spread strategy is zero if the stock price is above \$35 and \$5 if it is below \$30. If the stock price is between \$30 and \$35, the payoff is $35 - S_T$. The options cost \$3 – \$1 = \$2 up front. The profit is therefore as follows:

Stock price range	*Profit*
$S_T \leqslant 30$	+3
$30 < S_T < 35$	$33 - S_T$
$S_T \geqslant 35$	−2

Figure 10.5 Profit from bear spread created using call options

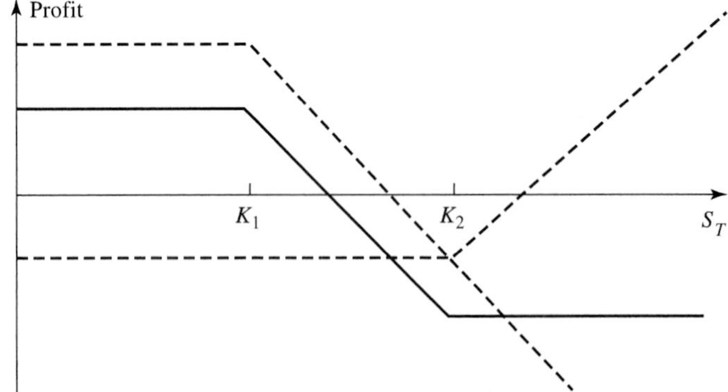

Table 10.3 Payoff from a box spread

Stock price range	*Payoff from bull call spread*	*Payoff from bear put spread*	*Total payoff*
$S_T \geqslant K_2$	$K_2 - K_1$	0	$K_2 - K_1$
$K_1 < S_T < K_2$	$S_T - K_1$	$K_2 - S_T$	$K_2 - K_1$
$S_T \leqslant K_1$	0	$K_2 - K_1$	$K_2 - K_1$

Like bull spreads, bear spreads limit both the upside profit potential and the downside risk. Bear spreads can be created using calls instead of puts. The investor buys a call with a high strike price and sells a call with a low strike price, as illustrated in Figure 10.5. Bear spreads created with calls involve an initial cash inflow (ignoring margin requirements).

Box Spreads

A box spread is a combination of a bull call spread with strike prices K_1 and K_2 and a bear put spread with the same two strike prices. As shown in Table 10.3, the payoff from a box spread is always $K_2 - K_1$. The value of a box spread is therefore always the present value of this payoff or $(K_2 - K_1)e^{-rT}$. If it has a different value, there is an arbitrage opportunity. If the market price of the box spread is too low, it is profitable to buy the box. This involves buying a call with strike price K_1, buying a put with strike price K_2, selling a call with strike price K_2, and selling a put with strike price K_1. If the market price of the box spread is too high, it is profitable to sell the box. This involves buying a call with strike price K_2, buying a put with strike price K_1, selling a call with strike price K_1, and selling a put with strike price K_2.

It is important to realize that a box spread arbitrage only works with European options. Most of the options that trade on exchanges are American. As shown in Business Snapshot 10.1, inexperienced traders who treat American options as European are liable to lose money.

Butterfly Spreads

A *butterfly spread* involves positions in options with three different strike prices. It can be created by buying a call option with a relatively low strike price, K_1; buying a call

Table 10.4 Values of two-month and American options on non-dividend-paying stock. Stock price = \$50; interest rate = 8% per annum; volatility = 30% per annum

Option type	*Strike price*	*European option price*	*American option price*
Call	60	0.26	0.26
Call	55	0.76	0.76
Put	60	9.46	10.00
Put	55	5.23	5.44

Business Snapshot 10.1 Losing money with box spreads

Suppose that a stock has a price of \$50 and a volatility of 30%. No dividends are expected and the risk-free rate is 8%. A trader offers you the chance to sell on the CBOE a two-month box spread where the strike prices are \$55 and \$60 for \$5.10. Should you do the trade?

The trade certainly sounds attractive. In this case, $K_1 = 55$, $K_2 = 60$, and the payoff is certain to be \$5 in two months. By selling the box spread for \$5.10 and investing the funds for two months, you would have more than enough funds to meet the \$5 payoff in two months. The theoretical value of the box spread today is $5 \times e^{0.08\times2/12} = \$4.93$.

Unfortunately there is a snag. CBOE stock options are American and the \$5 payoff from the box spread is calculated on the assumption that the options comprising the box are European. Option prices for this example (calculated using DerivaGem) are shown in Table 10.4. A bull call spread where the strike prices are \$55 and \$60 costs $0.96 - 0.26 = \$0.70$. (This is the same for both European and American options because, as we saw in Chapter 9, the price of a European call is the same as the price of an American call when there are no dividends.) A bear put spread with the same strike prices costs $9.46 - 5.23 = \$4.23$ if the options are European and $10.00 - 5.44 = \$4.56$ if they are American. The combined value of both spreads if they are created with European options is $0.70 + 4.23 = \$4.93$. This is the theoretical box spread price calculated above. The combined value of buying both spreads if they are American is $0.70 + 4.56 = \$5.26$. Selling a box spread created with American options for \$5.10 would not be a good trade. You would realize this almost immediately as the trade involves selling a \$60 strike put and this would be exercised against you almost as soon as you sold it!

option with a relatively high strike price, K_3; and selling two call options with a strike price, K_2, halfway between K_1 and K_3. Generally K_2 is close to the current stock price. The pattern of profits from the strategy is shown in Figure 10.6. A butterfly spread leads to a profit if the stock price stays close to K_2, but gives rise to a small loss if there is a significant stock price move in either direction. It is therefore an appropriate strategy for

Figure 10.6 Profit from butterfly spread using call options

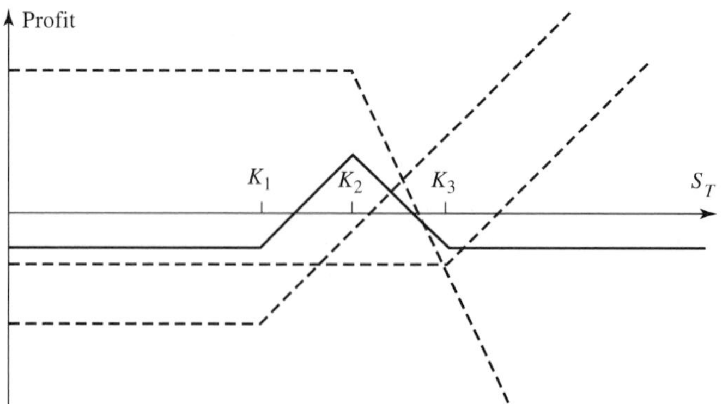

Table 10.5 Payoff from a butterfly spread

Stock price range	*Payoff from first long call*	*Payoff from second long call*	*Payoff from short calls*	*Total payoff**
$S_T < K_1$	0	0	0	0
$K_1 < S_T < K_2$	$S_T - K_1$	0	0	$S_T - K_1$
$K_2 < S_T < K_3$	$S_T - K_1$	0	$-2(S_T - K_2)$	$K_3 - S_T$
$S_T > K_3$	$S_T - K_1$	$S_T - K_3$	$-2(S_T - K_2)$	0

* These payoffs are calculated using the relationship $K_2 = 0.5(K_1 + K_3)$.

an investor who feels that large stock price moves are unlikely. The strategy requires a small investment initially. The payoff from a butterfly spread is shown in Table 10.5.

Suppose that a certain stock is currently worth \$61. Consider an investor who feels that a significant price move in the next six months is unlikely. Suppose that the market prices of six-month calls are as follows:

Strike price (\$)	*Call price* (\$)
55	10
60	7
65	5

The investor could create a butterfly spread by buying one call with a \$55 strike price, buying one call with a \$65 strike price, and selling two calls with a \$60 strike price. It costs $\$10 + \$5 - (2 \times \$7) = \$1$ to create the spread. If the stock price in six months is greater than \$65 or less than \$55, the total payoff is zero and the investor incurs a net loss of \$1. If the stock price is between \$56 and \$64, a profit is made. The maximum profit, \$4, occurs when the stock price in six months is \$60.

Butterfly spreads can be created using put options. The investor buys a put with a low strike price, buys a put with a high strike price, and sells two puts with an intermediate strike price, as illustrated in Figure 10.7. The butterfly spread in the example just

Figure 10.7 Profit from butterfly spread using put options

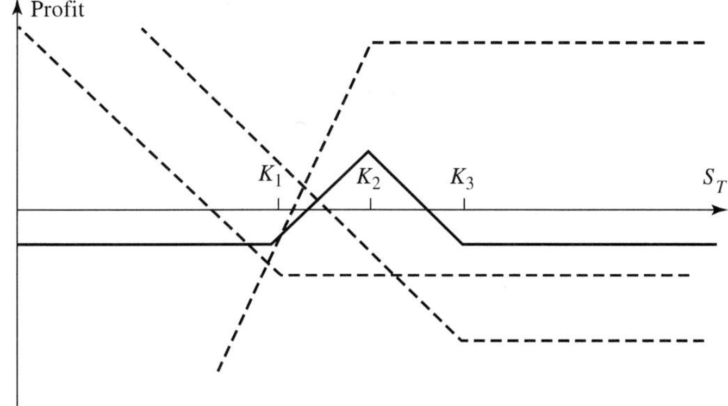

considered would be created by buying a put with a strike price of \$55, buying a put with a strike price of \$65, and selling two puts with a strike price of \$60. If all options are European, the use of put options results in exactly the same spread as the use of call options. Put–call parity can be used to show that the initial investment is the same in both cases.

A butterfly spread can be sold or shorted by following the reverse strategy. Options are sold with strike prices of K_1 and K_3, and two options with the middle strike price K_2 are purchased. This strategy produces a modest profit if there is a significant movement in the stock price.

Calendar Spreads

Up to now we have assumed that the options used to create a spread all expire at the same time. We now move on to *calendar spreads* in which the options have the same strike price and different expiration dates.

A calendar spread can be created by selling a call option with a certain strike price and buying a longer-maturity call option with the same strike price. The longer the maturity of an option, the more expensive it usually is. A calendar spread therefore usually requires an initial investment. Profit diagrams for calendar spreads are usually produced so that they show the profit when the short-maturity option expires on the assumption that the long-maturity option is sold at that time. The profit pattern for a calendar spread produced from call options is shown in Figure 10.8. The pattern is similar to the profit from the butterfly spread in Figure 10.6. The investor makes a profit if the stock price at the expiration of the short-maturity option is close to the strike price of the short-maturity option. However, a loss is incurred when the stock price is significantly above or significantly below this strike price.

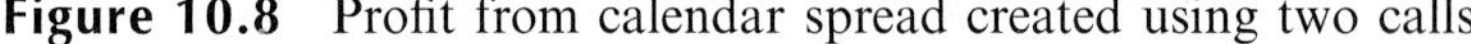

Figure 10.8 Profit from calendar spread created using two calls

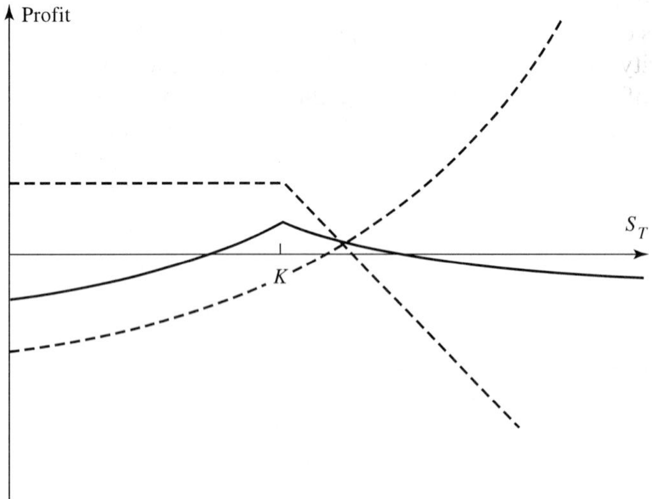

Figure 10.9 Profit from calendar spread created using two puts

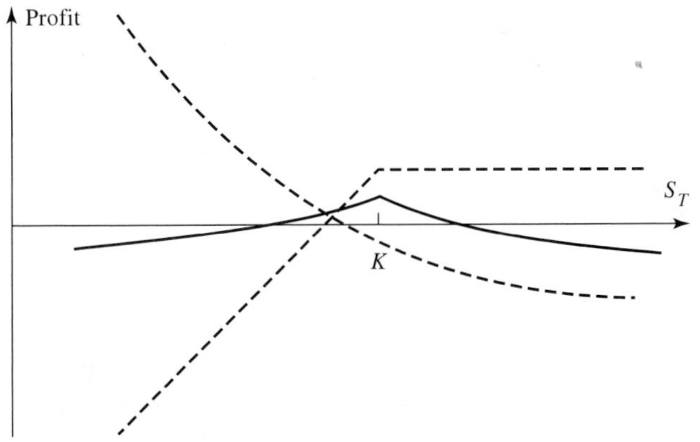

To understand the profit pattern from a calendar spread, first consider what happens if the stock price is very low when the short-maturity option expires. The short-maturity option is worthless and the value of the long-maturity option is close to zero. The investor therefore incurs a loss that is close to the cost of setting up the spread initially. Consider next what happens if the stock price, S_T, is very high when the short-maturity option expires. The short-maturity option costs the investor $S_T - K$, and the long-maturity option (assuming early exercise is not optimal) is worth a little more than $S_T - K$, where K is the strike price of the options. Again, the investor makes a net loss that is close to the cost of setting up the spread initially. If S_T is close to K, the short-maturity option costs the investor either a small amount or nothing at all. However, the long-maturity option is still quite valuable. In this case a significant net profit is made.

In a *neutral calendar spread*, a strike price close to the current stock price is chosen. A *bullish calendar spread* involves a higher strike price, whereas a *bearish calendar spread* involves a lower strike price.

Calendar spreads can be created with put options as well as call options. The investor buys a long-maturity put option and sells a short-maturity put option. As shown in Figure 10.9, the profit pattern is similar to that obtained from using calls.

A *reverse calendar spread* is the opposite to that in Figures 10.8 and 10.9. The investor buys a short-maturity option and sells a long-maturity option. A small profit arises if the stock price at the expiration of the short-maturity option is well above or well below the strike price of the short-maturity option. However, a significant loss results if it is close to the strike price.

Table 10.6 Payoff from a straddle

Range of stock price	*Payoff from call*	*Payoff from put*	*Total payoff*
$S_T \leqslant K$	0	$K - S_T$	$K - S_T$
$S_T > K$	$S_T - K$	0	$S_T - K$

Diagonal Spreads

Bull, bear, and calendar spreads can all be created from a long position in one call and a short position in another call. In the case of bull and bear spreads, the calls have different strike prices and the same expiration date. In the case of calendar spreads, the calls have the same strike price and different expiration dates. In a *diagonal spread* both the expiration date and the strike price of the calls are different. This increases the range of profit patterns that are possible.

10.3 COMBINATIONS

A *combination* is an option trading strategy that involves taking a position in both calls and puts on the same stock. We will consider straddles, strips, straps, and strangles.

Straddle

One popular combination is a *straddle*, which involves buying a call and put with the same strike price and expiration date. The profit pattern is shown in Figure 10.10. The strike price is denoted by K. If the stock price is close to this strike price at expiration of the options, the straddle leads to a loss. However, if there is a sufficiently large move in either direction, a significant profit will result. The payoff from a straddle is calculated in Table 10.6.

A straddle is appropriate when an investor is expecting a large move in a stock price but does not know in which direction the move will be. Consider an investor who feels that the price of a certain stock, currently valued at \$69 by the market, will move significantly in the next three months. The investor could create a straddle by buying both a put and a call with a strike price of \$70 and an expiration date in three months. Suppose that the call costs \$4 and the put costs \$3. If the stock price stays at \$69, it is easy to see that the strategy costs the investor \$6 (an up-front investment of \$7 is required, the call expires worthless, and the put expires worth \$1). If the stock price moves to \$70, a loss of \$7 is experienced (this is the worst that can happen). However, if the stock price jumps up to \$90, a profit of \$13 is made; if the stock moves down to \$55, a profit of \$8 is made; and so on. As indicated in Business Snapshot 10.2 an investor

Figure 10.10 Profit from a straddle

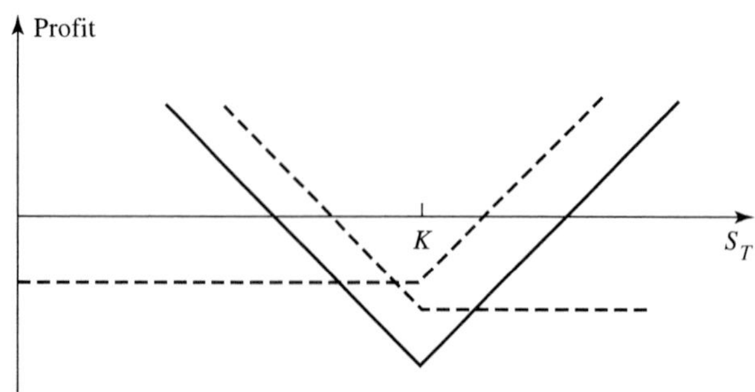

Business Snapshot 10.2 How to make money from trading straddles

Suppose that a big move is expected in a company's stock price because there is a takeover bid for the company or the outcome of a major lawsuit involving the company is about to be announced. Should you trade a straddle?

A straddle seems a natural trading strategy in this case. However, if your view of the company's situation is much the same as that of other market participants, this view will be reflected in the prices of options. Options on the stock will be significantly more expensive than options on a similar stock for which no jump is expected. The V-shaped profit pattern from the straddle in Figure 10.10 will have moved downward, so that a bigger move in the stock price is necessary for you to make a profit.

For a straddle to be an effective strategy, you must believe that there are likely to be big movements in the stock price and these beliefs must be different from those of most other investors. Market prices incorporate the beliefs of market participants. To make money from any investment strategy, you must take a view that is different from most of the rest of the market—and you must be right!

should carefully consider whether the jump that he or she anticipates is already reflected in option prices before putting on a straddle trade.

The straddle in Figure 10.10 is sometimes referred to as a *bottom straddle* or straddle purchase. A *top straddle* or *straddle write* is the reverse position. It is created by selling a call and a put with the same exercise price and expiration date. It is a highly risky strategy. If the stock price on the expiration date is close to the strike price, a significant profit results. However, the loss arising from a large move in either direction is unlimited.

Strips and Straps

A *strip* consists of a long position in one call and two puts with the same strike price and expiration date. A *strap* consists of a long position in two calls and one put with the

Figure 10.11 Profit from a strip and a strap

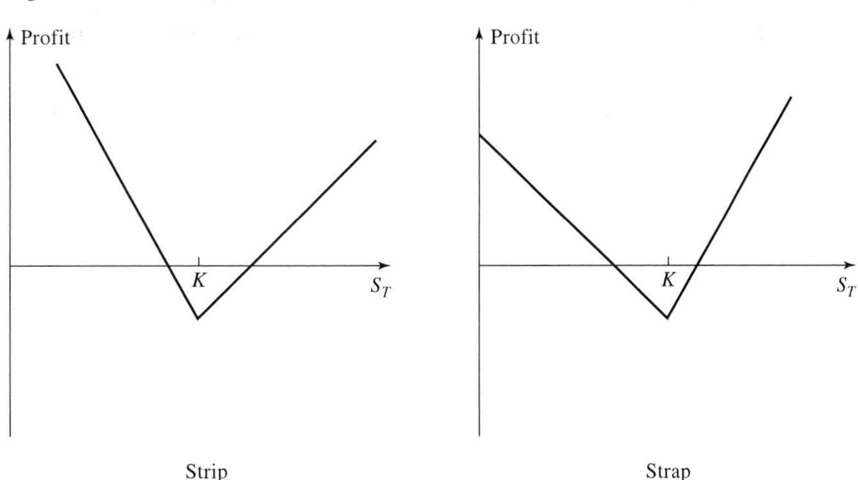

Figure 10.12 Profit from a strangle

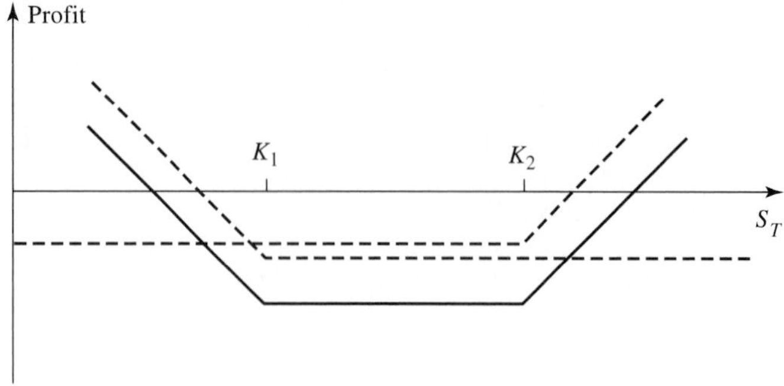

same strike price and expiration date. The profit patterns from strips and straps are shown in Figure 10.11. In a strip the investor is betting that there will be a big stock price move and considers a decrease in the stock price to be more likely than an increase. In a strap the investor is also betting that there will be a big stock price move. However, in this case, an increase in the stock price is considered to be more likely than a decrease.

Strangles

In a *strangle*, sometimes called a *bottom vertical combination*, an investor buys a put and a call with the same expiration date and different strike prices. The profit pattern that is obtained is shown in Figure 10.12. The call strike price, K_2, is higher than the put strike price, K_1. The payoff function for a strangle is calculated in Table 10.7.

A strangle is a similar strategy to a straddle. The investor is betting that there will be a large price move, but is uncertain whether it will be an increase or a decrease. Comparing Figures 10.12 and 10.10, we see that the stock price has to move farther in a strangle than in a straddle for the investor to make a profit. However, the downside risk if the stock price ends up at a central value is less with a strangle.

The profit pattern obtained with a strangle depends on how close together the strike prices are. The farther they are apart, the less the downside risk and the farther the stock price has to move for a profit to be realized.

The sale of a strangle is sometimes referred to as a *top vertical combination*. It can be appropriate for an investor who feels that large stock price moves are unlikely. However, as with sale of a straddle, it is a risky strategy involving unlimited potential loss to the investor.

Table 10.7 Payoff from a strangle

Range of stock price	*Payoff from call*	*Payoff from put*	*Total payoff*
$S_T \leqslant K_1$	0	$K_1 - S_T$	$K_1 - S_T$
$K_1 < S_T < K_2$	0	0	0
$S_T \geqslant K_2$	$S_T - K_2$	0	$S_T - K_2$

Figure 10.13 Payoff from a butterfly spread

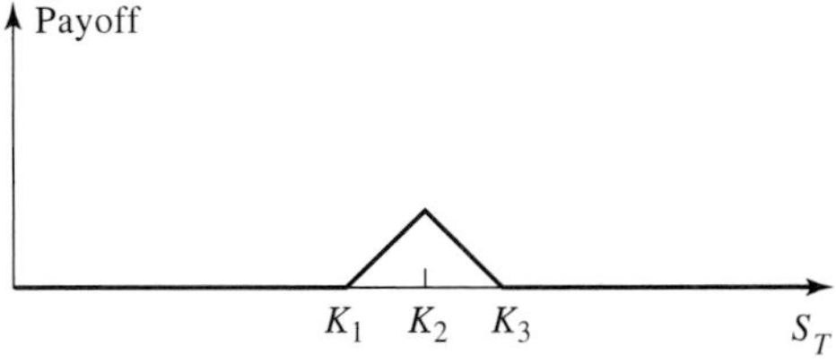

10.4 OTHER PAYOFFS

This chapter has demonstrated just a few of the ways in which options can be used to produce an interesting relationship between profit and stock price. If European options expiring at time T were available with every single possible strike price, any payoff function at time T could in theory be obtained. The easiest illustration of this involves a series of butterfly spreads. Recall that a butterfly spread is created by buying options with strike prices K_1 and K_3 and selling two options with strike price K_2 where $K_1 < K_2 < K_3$ and $K_3 - K_2 = K_2 - K_1$. Figure 10.13 shows the payoff from a butterfly spread. The pattern could be described as a spike. As K_1 and K_3 move closer together, the spike becomes smaller. Through the judicious combination of a large number of very small spikes, any payoff function can be approximated.

SUMMARY

A number of common trading strategies involve a single option and the underlying stock. For example, writing a covered call involves buying the stock and selling a call option on the stock; a protective put involves buying a put option and buying the stock. The former is similar to selling a put option; the latter is similar to buying a call option.

Spreads involve either taking a position in two or more calls or taking a position in two or more puts. A bull spread can be created by buying a call (put) with a low strike price and selling a put (call) with a high strike price. A bear spread can be created by buying a put (call) with a high strike price and selling a put (call) with a low strike price. A butterfly spread involves buying calls (puts) with a low and high strike price and selling two calls (puts) with some intermediate strike price. A calendar spread involves selling a call (put) with a short time to expiration and buying a call (put) with a longer time to expiration. A diagonal spread involves a long position in one option and a short position in another option such that both the strike price and the expiration date are different.

Combinations involve taking a position in both calls and puts on the same stock. A straddle combination involves taking a long position in a call and a long position in a put with the same strike price and expiration date. A strip consists of a long position in one call and two puts with the same strike price and expiration date. A strap consists of a long position in two calls and one put with the same strike price and expiration date. A strangle consists of a long position in a call and a put with different strike prices and the same expiration date. There are many other ways in which options can be used to produce interesting payoffs. It is not surprising that option trading has steadily increased in popularity and continues to fascinate investors.

FURTHER READING

Bharadwaj, A., and J. B. Wiggins. "Box Spread and Put–Call Parity Tests for the S&P Index LEAPS Markets," *Journal of Derivatives*, 8, 4 (Summer 2001): 62–71.

Chaput, J. S., and L. H. Ederington, "Option Spread and Combination Trading," *Journal of Derivatives*, 10, 4 (Summer 2003): 70–88.

McMillan, L. G. *Options as a Strategic Investment*, 4th edn. Upper Saddle River: Prentice Hall, 2001.

Rendleman, R. J. "Covered Call Writing from an Expected Utility Perspective," *Journal of Derivatives*, 8, 3 (Spring 2001): 63–75.

Ronn, A. G., and E. I. Ronn. "The Box-Spread Arbitrage Conditions," *Review of Financial Studies*, 2, 1 (1989): 91–108.

Quiz (Answers at End of Book)

10.1. What is meant by a protective put? What position in call options is equivalent to a protective put?

10.2. Explain two ways in which a bear spread can be created.

10.3. When is it appropriate for an investor to purchase a butterfly spread?

10.4. Call options on a stock are available with strike prices of \$15, \$17$\frac{1}{2}$, and \$20 and expiration dates in three months. Their prices are \$4, \$2, and \$$\frac{1}{2}$, respectively. Explain how the options can be used to create a butterfly spread. Construct a table showing how profit varies with stock price for the butterfly spread.

10.5. What trading strategy creates a reverse calendar spread?

10.6. What is the difference between a strangle and a straddle?

10.7. A call option with a strike price of \$50 costs \$2. A put option with a strike price of \$45 costs \$3. Explain how a strangle can be created from these two options. What is the pattern of profits from the strangle?

Questions and Problems (Answers in Solutions Manual/Study Guide)

10.8. Use put–call parity to relate the initial investment for a bull spread created using calls to the initial investment for a bull spread created using puts.

10.9. Explain how an aggressive bear spread can be created using put options.

10.10. Suppose that put options on a stock with strike prices \$30 and \$35 cost \$4 and \$7, respectively. How can the options be used to create (a) a bull spread and (b) a bear spread? Construct a table that shows the profit and payoff for both spreads.

10.11. Use put–call parity to show that the cost of a butterfly spread created from European puts is identical to the cost of a butterfly spread created from European calls.

10.12. A call with a strike price of \$60 costs \$6. A put with the same strike price and expiration date costs \$4. Construct a table that shows the profit from a straddle. For what range of stock prices would the straddle lead to a loss?

10.13. Construct a table showing the payoff from a bull spread when puts with strike prices K_1 and K_2 are used ($K_2 > K_1$).

10.14. An investor believes that there will be a big jump in a stock price, but is uncertain as to the direction. Identify six different strategies the investor can follow and explain the differences among them.

10.15. How can a forward contract on a stock with a particular delivery price and delivery date be created from options?

10.16. "A box spread comprises four options. Two can be combined to create a long forward position and two can be combined to create a short forward position." Explain this statement.

10.17. What is the result if the strike price of the put is higher than the strike price of the call in a strangle?

10.18. One Australian dollar is currently worth \$0.64. A one-year butterfly spread is set up using European call options with strike prices of \$0.60, \$0.65, and \$0.70. The risk-free interest rates in the United States and Australia are 5% and 4%, respectively, and the volatility of the exchange rate is 15%. Use the DerivaGem software to calculate the cost of setting up the butterfly spread position. Show that the cost is the same if European put options are used instead of European call options.

Assignment Questions

10.19. Three put options on a stock have the same expiration date and strike prices of \$55, \$60, and \$65. The market prices are \$3, \$5, and \$8, respectively. Explain how a butterfly spread can be created. Construct a table showing the profit from the strategy. For what range of stock prices would the butterfly spread lead to a loss?

10.20. A diagonal spread is created by buying a call with strike price K_2 and exercise date T_2 and selling a call with strike price K_1 and exercise date T_1 ($T_2 > T_1$). Draw a diagram showing the profit when (a) $K_2 > K_1$ and (b) $K_2 < K_1$.

10.21. Draw a diagram showing the variation of an investor's profit and loss with the terminal stock price for a portfolio consisting of:

a. One share and a short position in one call option
b. Two shares and a short position in one call option
c. One share and a short position in two call options
d. One share and a short position in four call options

In each case, assume the call option has an exercise price equal to the current stock price.

10.22. Suppose that the price of a non-dividend-paying stock is \$32, its volatility is 30%, and the risk-free rate for all maturities is 5% per annum. Use DerivaGem to calculate the cost of setting up the following positions. In each case provide a table showing the relationship between profit and final stock price. Ignore the impact of discounting.

a. A bull spread using European call options with strike prices of \$25 and \$30 and a maturity of six months

b. A bear spread using European put options with strike prices of \$25 and \$30 and a maturity of six months
c. A butterfly spread using European call options with strike prices of \$25, \$30, and \$35 and a maturity of one year
d. A butterfly spread using European put options with strike prices of \$25, \$30, and \$35 and a maturity of one year
e. A straddle using options with a strike price of \$30 and a six-month maturity
f. A strangle using options with strike prices of \$25 and \$35 and a six-month maturity

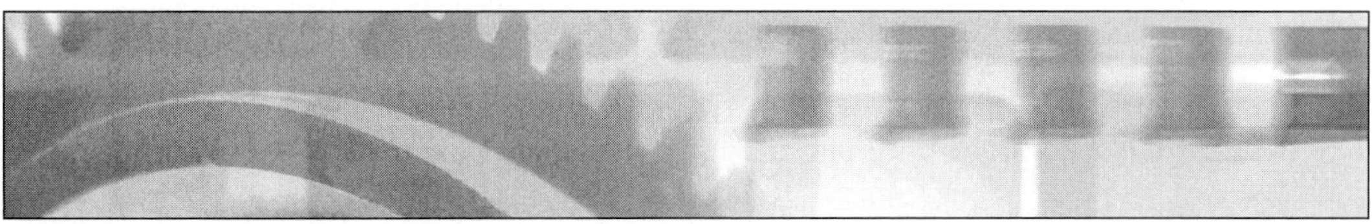

CHAPTER 11

Introduction to Binomial Trees

A useful and very popular technique for pricing an option involves constructing a *binomial tree*. This is a diagram that represents different possible paths that might be followed by the stock price over the life of the option. In this chapter we will take a first look at binomial trees and their relationship to an important principle known as risk-neutral valuation. The general approach adopted here is similar to that in an important paper published by Cox, Ross, and Rubinstein in 1979.

The material in this chapter is intended to be introductory. Numerical procedures involving binomial trees are discussed in more detail in Chapter 16.

11.1 A ONE-STEP BINOMIAL MODEL

We start by considering a very simple situation. A stock price is currently \$20, and it is known that at the end of three months it will be either \$22 or \$18. We are interested in valuing a European call option to buy the stock for \$21 in three months. This option will have one of two values at the end of the three months. If the stock price turns out to be \$22, the value of the option will be \$1; if the stock price turns out to be \$18, the value of the option will be zero. The situation is illustrated in Figure 11.1.

It turns out that a relatively simple argument can be used to price the option in this example. The only assumption needed is that no arbitrage opportunities exist. We set up a portfolio of the stock and the option in such a way that there is no uncertainty about the value of the portfolio at the end of the three months. We then argue that, because the portfolio has no risk, the return it earns must equal the risk-free interest rate. This enables us to work out the cost of setting up the portfolio and therefore the option's price. Because there are two securities (the stock and the stock option) and only two possible outcomes, it is always possible to set up the riskless portfolio.

Consider a portfolio consisting of a long position in Δ shares of the stock and a short position in one call option. We calculate the value of Δ that makes the portfolio riskless. If the stock price moves up from \$20 to \$22, the value of the shares is 22Δ and the value of the option is 1, so that the total value of the portfolio is $22\Delta - 1$. If the stock price moves down from \$20 to \$18, the value of the shares is 18Δ and the value of the option is zero, so that the total value of the portfolio is 18Δ. The portfolio is

Figure 11.1 Stock price movements in numerical example

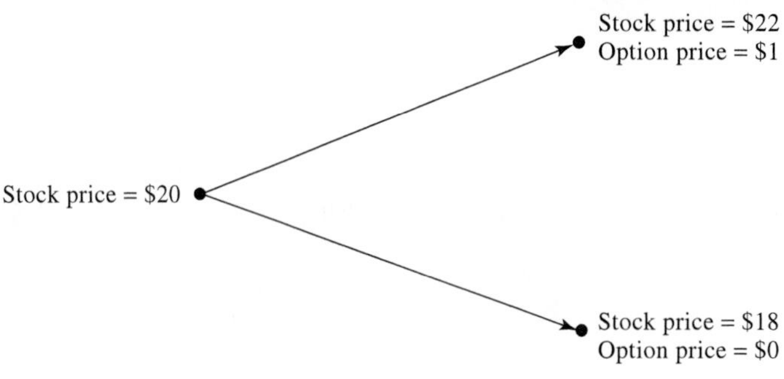

riskless if the value of Δ is chosen so that the final value of the portfolio is the same for both alternatives. This means

$$22\Delta - 1 = 18\Delta$$

or

$$\Delta = 0.25$$

A riskless portfolio is therefore

Long: 0.25 shares
Short: 1 option

If the stock price moves up to $22, the value of the portfolio is

$$22 \times 0.25 - 1 = 4.5$$

If the stock price moves down to $18, the value of the portfolio is

$$18 \times 0.25 = 4.5$$

Regardless of whether the stock price moves up or down, the value of the portfolio is always 4.5 at the end of the life of the option.

Riskless portfolios must, in the absence of arbitrage opportunities, earn the risk-free rate of interest. Suppose that in this case the risk-free rate is 12% per annum. It follows that the value of the portfolio today must be the present value of 4.5, or

$$4.5e^{-0.12\times 3/12} = 4.367$$

The value of the stock price today is known to be $20. Suppose the option price is denoted by f. The value of the portfolio today is

$$20 \times 0.25 - f = 5 - f$$

It follows that

$$5 - f = 4.367$$

or

$$f = 0.633$$

This shows that, in the absence of arbitrage opportunities, the current value of the option must be 0.633. If the value of the option were more than 0.633, the portfolio would cost less than 4.367 to set up and would earn more than the risk-free rate. If the value of the option were less than 0.633, shorting the portfolio would provide a way of borrowing money at less than the risk-free rate.

A Generalization

We can generalize the argument just presented by considering a stock whose price is S_0 and an option on the stock whose current price is f. We suppose that the option lasts for time T and that during the life of the option the stock price can either move up from S_0 to a new level, S_0u, or down from S_0 to a new level, S_0d ($u > 1$; $d < 1$). The proportional increase in the stock price when there is an up movement is $u - 1$; the proportional decrease when there is a down movement is $1 - d$. If the stock price moves up to S_0u, we suppose that the payoff from the option is f_u; if the stock price moves down to S_0d, we suppose the payoff from the option is f_d. The situation is illustrated in Figure 11.2.

As before, we imagine a portfolio consisting of a long position in Δ shares and a short position in one option. We calculate the value of Δ that makes the portfolio riskless. If there is an up movement in the stock price, the value of the portfolio at the end of the life of the option is

$$S_0u\Delta - f_u$$

If there is a down movement in the stock price, the value becomes

$$S_0d\Delta - f_d$$

The two are equal when

$$S_0u\Delta - f_u = S_0d\Delta - f_d$$

or

$$\Delta = \frac{f_u - f_d}{S_0u - S_0d} \tag{11.1}$$

In this case, the portfolio is riskless and must earn the risk-free interest rate. Equation (11.1) shows that Δ is the ratio of the change in the option price to the change in the stock price as we move between the nodes.

If we denote the risk-free interest rate by r, the present value of the portfolio is

$$(S_0u\Delta - f_u)e^{-rT}$$

Figure 11.2 Stock and option prices in a general one-step tree

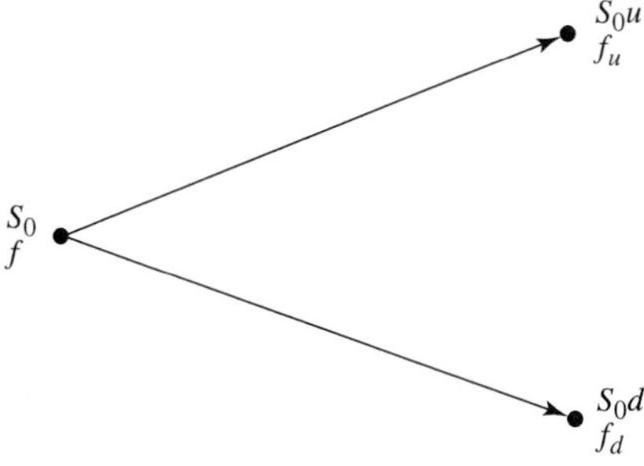

The cost of setting up the portfolio is

$$S_0\Delta - f$$

It follows that

$$S_0\Delta - f = (S_0 u\Delta - f_u)e^{-rT}$$

or

$$f = S_0\Delta(1 - ue^{-rT}) + f_u e^{-rT}$$

Substituting from equation (11.1) for Δ and simplifying, we can reduce this equation to

$$f = e^{-rT}[pf_u + (1-p)f_d] \tag{11.2}$$

where

$$p = \frac{e^{rT} - d}{u - d} \tag{11.3}$$

Equations (11.2) and (11.3) enable an option to be priced using a one-step binomial model.

In the numerical example considered previously (see Figure 11.1), $u = 1.1$, $d = 0.9$, $r = 0.12$, $T = 0.25$, $f_u = 1$, and $f_d = 0$. From equation (11.3),

$$p = \frac{e^{0.12\times 3/12} - 0.9}{1.1 - 0.9} = 0.6523$$

and, from equation (11.2),

$$f = e^{-0.12\times 0.25}(0.6523 \times 1 + 0.3477 \times 0) = 0.633$$

The result agrees with the answer obtained earlier in this section.

Irrelevance of the Stock's Expected Return

The option pricing formula in equation (11.2) does not involve the probabilities of the stock price moving up or down. For example, we get the same option price when the probability of an upward movement is 0.5 as we do when it is 0.9. This is surprising and seems counterintuitive. It is natural to assume that as the probability of an upward movement in the stock price increases, the value of a call option on the stock increases and the value of a put option on the stock decreases. This is not the case.

The key reason is that we are not valuing the option in absolute terms. We are calculating its value in terms of the price of the underlying stock. The probabilities of future up or down movements are already incorporated into the price of the stock. It turns out that we do not need to take them into account again when valuing the option in terms of the stock price.

11.2 RISK-NEUTRAL VALUATION

Although we do not need to make any assumptions about the probabilities of up and down movements in order to derive equation (11.2), it is natural to interpret the variable p in equation (11.2) as the probability of an up movement in the stock price. The variable $1 - p$ is then the probability of a down movement, and the expression

$$pf_u + (1-p)f_d$$

is the expected payoff from the option. With this interpretation of p, equation (11.2) then states that the value of the option today is its expected future payoff discounted at the risk-free rate. We now investigate the expected return from the stock when the probability of an up movement is assumed to be p. The expected stock price at time T, $E(S_T)$, is given by

$$E(S_T) = pS_0u + (1 - p)S_0d$$

or

$$E(S_T) = pS_0(u - d) + S_0d$$

Substituting from equation (11.3) for p, we obtain

$$E(S_T) = S_0e^{rT} \tag{11.4}$$

showing that the stock price grows on average at the risk-free rate. Setting the probability of the up movement equal to p is therefore equivalent to assuming that the return on the stock equals the risk-free rate.

In a *risk-neutral world* all individuals are indifferent to risk. In such a world investors require no compensation for risk, and the expected return on all securities is the risk-free interest rate. Equation (11.4) shows that we are assuming a risk-neutral world when we set the probability of an up movement to p. Equation (11.2) shows that the value of the option is its expected payoff in a risk-neutral world discounted at the risk-free rate.

This result is an example of an important general principle in option pricing known as *risk-neutral valuation*. The principle states that we can with complete impunity assume the world is risk neutral when pricing options. The resulting prices are correct not just in a risk-neutral world, but in other worlds as well.

The One-Step Binomial Example Revisited

We now return to the example in Figure 11.1 and show that risk-neutral valuation gives the same answer as no-arbitrage arguments. In Figure 11.1, the stock price is currently \$20 and will move either up to \$22 or down to \$18 at the end of three months. The option considered is a European call option with a strike price of \$21 and an expiration date in three months. The risk-free interest rate is 12% per annum.

We define p as the probability of an upward movement in the stock price in a risk-neutral world. We can calculate p from equation (11.3). Alternatively, we can argue that the expected return on the stock in a risk-neutral world must be the risk-free rate of 12%. This means that p must satisfy

$$22p + 18(1 - p) = 20e^{0.12\times3/12}$$

or

$$4p = 20e^{0.12\times3/12} - 18$$

That is, p must be 0.6523.

At the end of the three months, the call option has a 0.6523 probability of being worth 1 and a 0.3477 probability of being worth zero. Its expected value is therefore

$$0.6523 \times 1 + 0.3477 \times 0 = 0.6523$$

In a risk-neutral world this should be discounted at the risk-free rate. The value of the option today is therefore

$$0.6523e^{-0.12\times3/12}$$

or $0.633. This is the same as the value obtained earlier, demonstrating that no-arbitrage arguments and risk-neutral valuation give the same answer.

Real World vs. Risk-Neutral World

It should be emphasized that p is the probability of a up movement in a risk-neutral world. In general this is not the same as the probability of an up movement in the real world. In our example $p = 0.6523$. When the probability of an up movement is 0.6523, the expected return on both the stock and the option is the risk-free rate of 12%. Suppose that in the real world the expected return on the stock is 16%, and q is the probability of an up movement in the real world. It follows that

$$22q + 18(1 - q) = 20e^{0.16\times 3/12}$$

so that $q = 0.7041$.

The expected payoff from the option in the real world is then

$$q \times 1 + (1 - q) \times 0$$

This is 0.7041. Unfortunately it is not easy to know the correct discount rate to apply to the expected payoff in the real world. A position in a call option is riskier than a position in the stock. As a result the discount rate to be applied to the payoff from a call option is greater than 16%. Without knowing the option's value, we do not know how much greater than 16% it should be.[1] Using risk-neutral valuation is convenient because we know that in a risk-neutral world the expected return on all assets (and therefore the discount rate to use for all expected payoffs) is the risk-free rate.

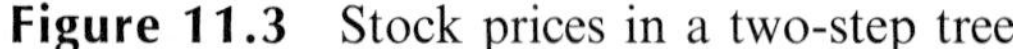

Figure 11.3 Stock prices in a two-step tree

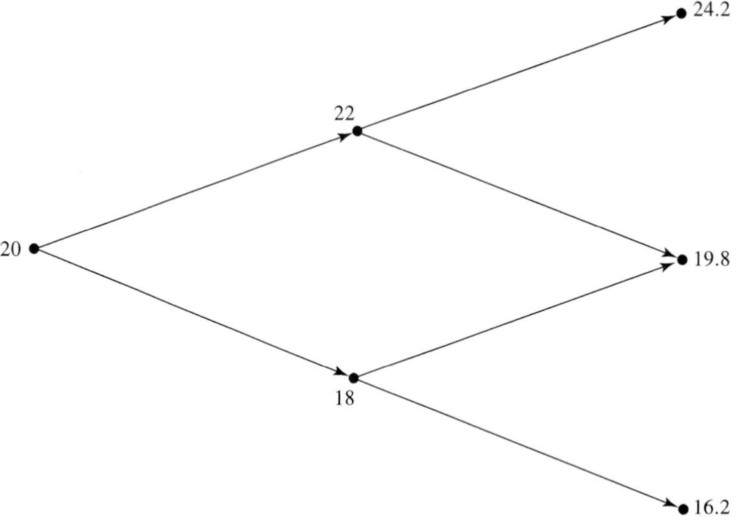

[1] Because the correct value of the option is 0.633, we can deduce that the correct discount rate is 42.58%. This is because $0.633 = 0.7041e^{-0.4258\times 3/12}$.

11.3 TWO-STEP BINOMIAL TREES

We can extend the analysis to a two-step binomial tree such as that shown in Figure 11.3. Here the stock price starts at \$20 and in each of two time steps may go up by 10% or down by 10%. We suppose that each time step is three months long and the risk-free interest rate is 12% per annum. As before, we consider an option with a strike price of \$21.

The objective of the analysis is to calculate the option price at the initial node of the tree. This can be done by repeatedly applying the principles established earlier in the chapter. Figure 11.4 shows the same tree as Figure 11.3, but with both the stock price and the option price at each node. (The stock price is the upper number and the option price the lower.) The option prices at the final nodes of the tree are easily calculated. They are the payoffs from the option. At node D the stock price is 24.2 and the option price is $24.2 - 21 = 3.2$; at nodes E and F the option is out of the money and its value is zero.

At node C the option price is zero, because node C leads to either node E or node F and at both nodes the option price is zero. We calculate the option price at node B by focusing our attention on the part of the tree shown in Figure 11.5. Using the notation introduced earlier in the chapter, $u = 1.1$, $d = 0.9$, $r = 0.12$, and $T = 0.25$, so that $p = 0.6523$ and equation (11.2) gives the value of the option at node B as

$$e^{-0.12\times 3/12}(0.6523 \times 3.2 + 0.3477 \times 0) = 2.0257$$

It remains for us to calculate to option price at the initial node A. We do so by focusing on the first step of the tree. We know that the value of the option at node B is 2.0257

Figure 11.4 Stock and option prices in a two-step tree. The upper number at each node is the stock price; the lower number is the option price

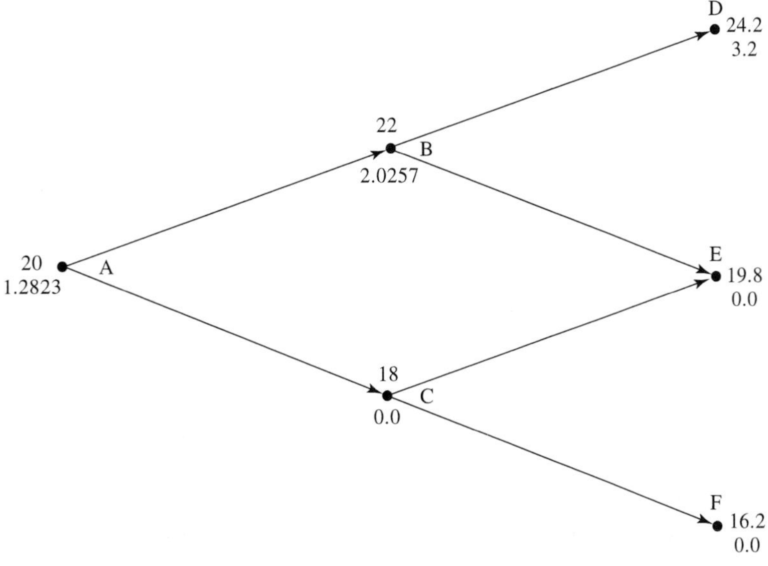

Figure 11.5 Evaluation of option price at node B

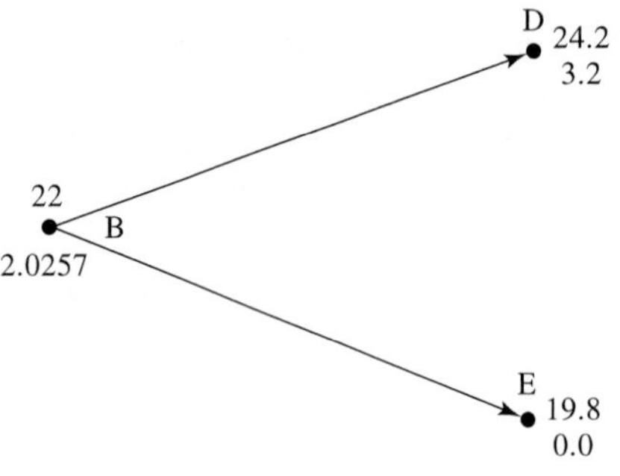

and that at node C it is zero. Equation (11.2) therefore gives the value at node A as

$$e^{-0.12\times 3/12}(0.6523 \times 2.0257 + 0.3477 \times 0) = 1.2823$$

The value of the option is \$1.2823.

Note that this example was constructed so that u and d (the proportional up and down movements) were the same at each node of the tree and so that the time steps were of the same length. As a result, the risk-neutral probability, p, as calculated by equation (11.3) is the same at each node.

A Generalization

We can generalize the case of two time steps by considering the situation in Figure 11.6. The stock price is initially S_0. During each time step, it either moves up to u times its

Figure 11.6 Stock and option prices in general two-step tree

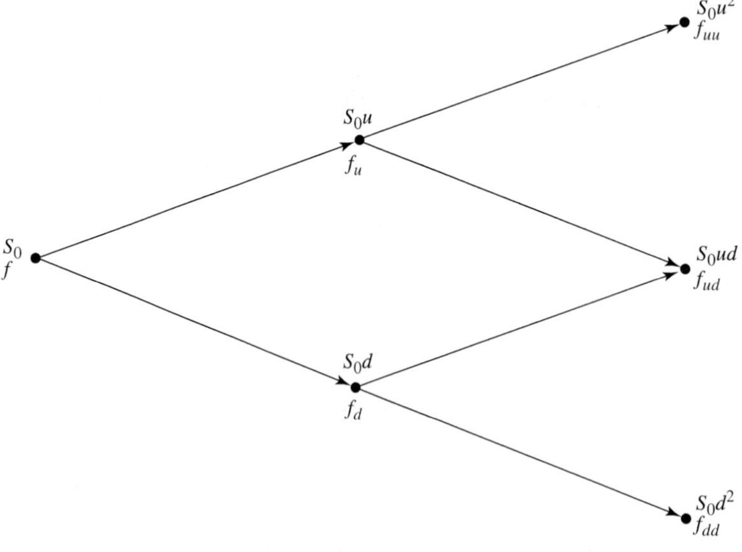

initial value or moves down to d times its initial value. The notation for the value of the option is shown on the tree. (For example, after two up movements the value of the option is f_{uu}.) We suppose that the risk-free interest rate is r and the length of the time step is Δt years.

Because the length of a time step is now Δt rather than T, equations (11.2) and (11.3) become

$$f = e^{-r\Delta t}[pf_u + (1-p)f_d] \tag{11.5}$$

$$p = \frac{e^{r\Delta t} - d}{u - d} \tag{11.6}$$

Repeated application of equation (11.5) gives

$$f_u = e^{-r\Delta t}[pf_{uu} + (1-p)f_{ud}] \tag{11.7}$$

$$f_d = e^{-r\Delta t}[pf_{ud} + (1-p)f_{dd}] \tag{11.8}$$

$$f = e^{-r\Delta t}[pf_u + (1-p)f_d] \tag{11.9}$$

Substituting from equations (11.7) and (11.8) into (11.9), we get

$$f = e^{-2r\Delta t}[p^2 f_{uu} + 2p(1-p)f_{ud} + (1-p)^2 f_{dd}] \tag{11.10}$$

This is consistent with the principle of risk-neutral valuation mentioned earlier. The variables p^2, $2p(1-p)$, and $(1-p)^2$ are the probabilities that the upper, middle, and lower final nodes will be reached. The option price is equal to its expected payoff in a risk-neutral world discounted at the risk-free interest rate.

As we add more steps to the binomial tree, the risk-neutral valuation principle continues to hold. The option price is always equal to its expected payoff in a risk-neutral world, discounted at the risk-free interest rate.

11.4 A PUT EXAMPLE

The procedures described in this chapter can be used to price puts as well as calls. Consider a two-year European put with a strike price of \$52 on a stock whose current price is \$50. We suppose that there are two time steps of one year, and in each time step the stock price either moves up by a proportional amount of 20% or moves down by a proportional amount of 20%. We also suppose that the risk-free interest rate is 5%.

The tree is shown in Figure 11.7. In this case, $u = 1.2$, $d = 0.8$, $\Delta t = 1$, and $r = 0.05$. From equation (11.6), the value of the risk-neutral probability, p, is given by

$$p = \frac{e^{0.05\times 1} - 0.8}{1.2 - 0.8} = 0.6282$$

The possible final stock prices are: \$72, \$48, and \$32. In this case, $f_{uu} = 0$, $f_{ud} = 4$, and $f_{dd} = 20$. From equation (11.8),

$$f = e^{-2\times 0.05\times 1}(0.6282^2 \times 0 + 2 \times 0.6282 \times 0.3718 \times 4 + 0.3718^2 \times 20) = 4.1923$$

The value of the put is \$4.1923. This result can also be obtained using equation (11.5)

Figure 11.7 Use of two-step tree to value European put option. At each node the upper number is the stock price; the lower number is the option price

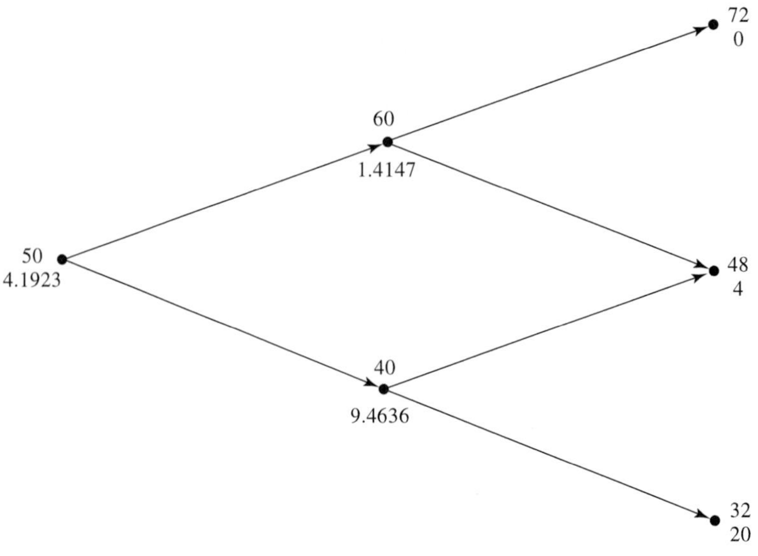

and working back through the tree one step at a time. Figure 11.7 shows the intermediate option prices that are calculated.

11.5 AMERICAN OPTIONS

Up to now all the options we have considered have been European. We now move on to consider how American options can be valued using binomial trees such as those in Figures 11.4 and 11.7. The procedure is to work back through the tree from the end to the beginning, testing at each node to see whether early exercise is optimal. The value of the option at the final nodes is the same as for the European option. At earlier nodes the value of the option is the greater of:

1. The value given by equation (11.5)
2. The payoff from early exercise

Figure 11.8 shows how Figure 11.7 is affected if the option under consideration is American rather than European. The stock prices and their probabilities are unchanged. The values for the option at the final nodes are also unchanged. At node B, equation (11.2) gives the value of the option as 1.4147, whereas the payoff from early exercise is negative ($= -8$). Clearly early exercise is not optimal at node B, and the value of the option at this node is 1.4147. At node C, equation (11.5) gives the value of the option as 9.4636, whereas the payoff from early exercise is 12. In this case, early exercise is optimal and the value of the option at the node is 12. At the initial node A, the value given by equation (11.5) is

$$e^{-0.05\times 1}(0.6282 \times 1.4147 + 0.3718 \times 12.0) = 5.0894$$

Figure 11.8 Use of two-step tree to value American put option. At each node the upper number is the stock price; the lower number is the option price

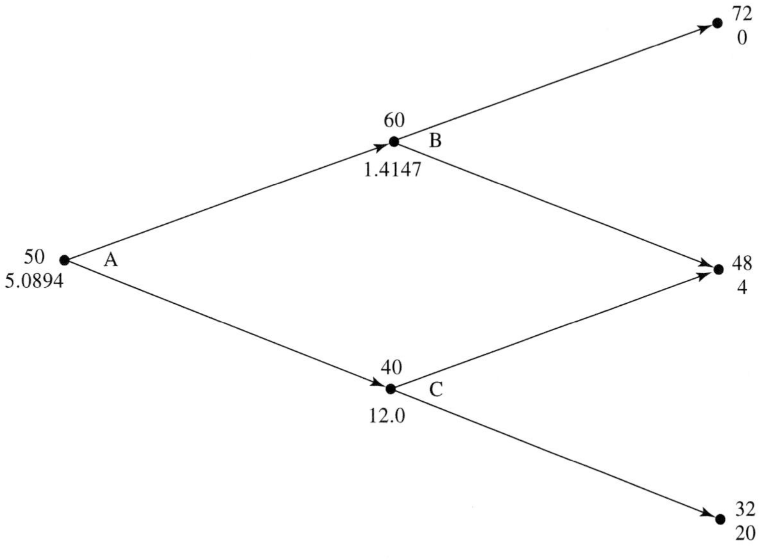

and the payoff from early exercise is 2. In this case early exercise is not optimal. The value of the option is therefore \$5.0894.

11.6 DELTA

At this stage it is appropriate to introduce *delta*, an important parameter in the pricing and hedging of options.

The delta of a stock option is the ratio of the change in the price of the stock option to the change in the price of the underlying stock. It is the number of units of the stock we should hold for each option shorted in order to create a riskless hedge. It is the same as the Δ introduced earlier in this chapter. The construction of a riskless hedge is sometimes referred to as *delta hedging*. The delta of a call option is positive, whereas the delta of a put option is negative.

From Figure 11.1, we can calculate the value of the delta of the call option being considered as

$$\frac{1-0}{22-18} = 0.25$$

This is because when the stock price changes from \$18 to \$22, the option price changes from \$0 to \$1.

In Figure 11.4, the delta corresponding to stock price movements over the first time step is

$$\frac{2.0257-0}{22-18} = 0.5064$$

The delta for stock price movements over the second time step is

$$\frac{3.2 - 0}{24.2 - 19.8} = 0.7273$$

if there is an upward movement over the first time step, and

$$\frac{0 - 0}{19.8 - 16.2} = 0$$

if there is a downward movement over the first time step.

From Figure 11.7, delta is

$$\frac{1.4147 - 9.4636}{60 - 40} = -0.4024$$

at the end of the first time step and either

$$\frac{0 - 4}{72 - 48} = -0.1667$$

or

$$\frac{4 - 20}{48 - 32} = -1.0000$$

at the end of the second time step.

The two-step examples show that delta changes over time. (In Figure 11.4, delta changes from 0.5064 to either 0.7273 or 0; in Figure 11.7, it changes from −0.4024 to either −0.1667 or −1.0000.) Thus, in order to maintain a riskless hedge using an option and the underlying stock, we need to adjust our holdings in the stock periodically. This is a feature of options that we will return to in Chapters 12 and 15.

11.7 DETERMINING u AND d

Up to now we have assumed values for u and d. For example, in Figure 11.8, we assumed that $u = 1.2$ and $d = 0.8$. In practice, u and d are determined from the stock price volatility, σ. The formulas are

$$u = e^{\sigma\sqrt{\Delta t}} \tag{11.11}$$

$$d = \frac{1}{u} \tag{11.12}$$

where Δt is the length of one time step on the tree. These formulas will be explained further in Chapter 16. The complete set of equations defining the tree are equation (11.11) and equation (11.12), together with equation (11.6), which can be written

$$p = \frac{a - d}{u - d} \tag{11.13}$$

where

$$a = e^{r\,\Delta t} \tag{11.14}$$

Consider again the situation in Figures 11.7 and 11.8, where the stock price is \$50, the

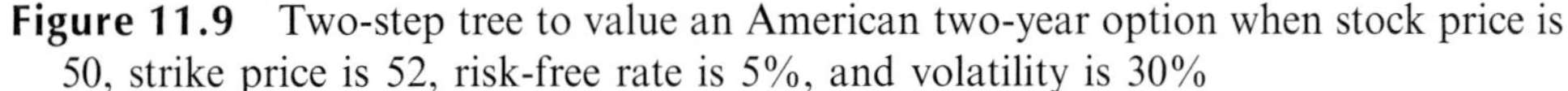

Figure 11.9 Two-step tree to value an American two-year option when stock price is 50, strike price is 52, risk-free rate is 5%, and volatility is 30%

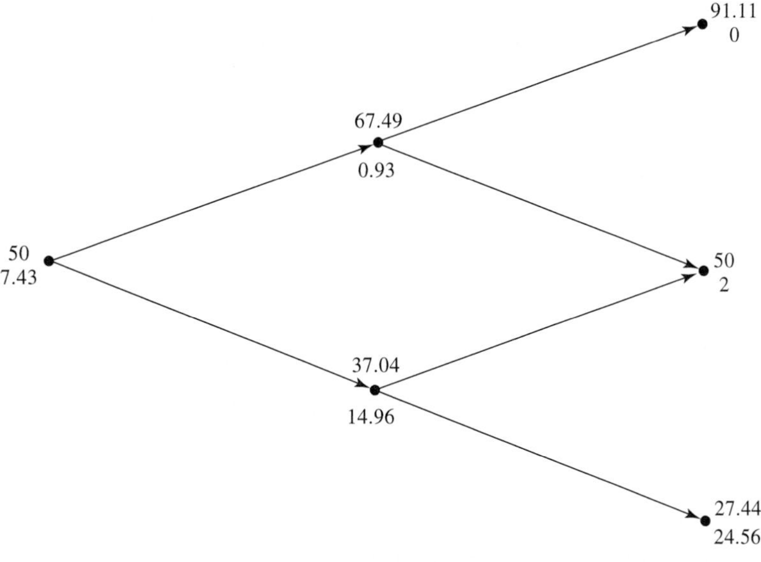

strike price is \$52, the risk-free rate is 5%, the life of the option is two years, and there are two time steps. In this case, $\Delta t = 1$. Suppose that the volatility σ is 30%. Then, from equations (11.11) to (11.14), we have

$$u = e^{0.3\times 1} = 1.3499$$

$$d = \frac{1}{1.3499} = 0.7408$$

$$a = e^{0.05\times 1} = 1.0513$$

and

$$p = \frac{1.053 - 0.7408}{1.3499 - 0.7408} = 0.5097$$

The tree is shown in Figure 11.9. The value of the option is 7.428. This is different from the value obtained in Figure 11.8 by assuming $u = 1.2$ and $d = 0.8$.

11.8 INCREASING THE NUMBER OF STEPS

The binomial models presented so far have been unrealistically simple. Clearly an analyst can expect to obtain only a very rough approximation to an option price by assuming that stock price movements during the life of the option consist of one or two binomial steps.

When binomial trees are used in practice, the life of the option is typically divided into 30 or more time steps. In each time step there is a binomial stock price movement.

With 30 time steps, there are 31 terminal stock prices and 2^{30}, or about 1 billion, possible stock price paths are considered.

The equations defining the tree are equations (11.11) to (11.14), regardless of the number of time steps. Suppose, for example, that there are five steps instead of two steps in the example we considered in Figure 11.9. The parameters would be $\Delta t = 2/5 = 0.4$, $r = 0.05$, and $\sigma = 0.3$. These give $u = e^{0.3\times\sqrt{0.4}} = 1.2089$, $d = 1/1.2089 = 0.8272$, $a = e^{0.05\times 0.4} = 1.0202$, and $p = (1.0202 - 0.8272)/(1.2089 - 0.8272) = 0.5056$.

Use of DerivaGem

The software accompanying this book, DerivaGem, is a useful tool for becoming comfortable with binomial trees. After loading the software in the way described at the end of this book, go to the Equity_Index_FX_Futures_Options worksheet. Choose Equity as the Underlying Type and select Binomial American as the Option Type. Enter the stock price, volatility, risk-free rate, time to expiration, exercise price, and tree steps as 50, 30%, 5%, 2, 52, and 2, respectively. Click on the *Put* button and then on *Calculate*. The price of the option is shown as 7.428 in the box labeled Price. Now click on *Display Tree* and you will see the equivalent of Figure 11.9. (The red numbers indicate the nodes where the option is exercised.)

Return to the Equity_Index_FX_Futures_Options worksheet and change the number of time steps to 5. Hit *Enter* and click on *Calculate*. You will find that the value of the option changes to 7.671. By clicking on *Display Tree* the five-step tree is displayed together with the values of u, d, a, and p we have just calculated.

DerivaGem can display trees that have up to 10 steps, but the calculations can be done for up to 500 steps. In our example, 500 steps gives the option price (to two decimal places) as 7.47. This is an accurate answer. By changing the Option Type to Binomial European, we can use the tree to value a European option. Using 500 time steps, the value of a European option with the same parameters as the American option is 6.76. (By changing the option type to Analytic European, we can display the value the option using the Black–Scholes formula that will be presented in the next chapter. This is also 6.76.)

By changing the Underlying Type, we can consider options on assets other than stocks. We will now discuss these types of option.

11.9 OPTIONS ON OTHER ASSETS

We introduced options on indices, currencies, and futures contracts in Chapter 8 and will cover them in more detail in Chapters 13 and 14. It turns out that we can construct and use binomial trees for these options in exactly the same way as for options on stocks except that in equations (11.9) to (11.12):

(a) For options on an index, we set $a = e^{(r-q)\Delta t}$, where q is the average dividend yield on the index during the life of the option.

(b) For options on a currency, we set $a = e^{(r-r_f)\Delta t}$, where r_f is the risk-free interest rate in the currency.

(c) For options on a futures contract, we set $a = 1$.

As in the case of options on stocks, equation (11.2) applies, so that the value at a node (before the possibility of early exercise is considered) is p times the value if there is an up movement plus $1 - p$ times the value if there is a down movement, discounted at the risk-free rate.

Examples

1. A stock index is currently 810 and has a volatility of 20% and a dividend yield of 2%. The risk-free rate is 5%. Figure 11.10 shows the output from DerivaGem for valuing a European six-month call option with a strike price of 800 using a two-step tree. In this case,

$$\Delta t = 0.25, \quad u = e^{0.20\times\sqrt{0.25}} = 1.1052, \quad d = 1/u = 0.9048,$$

$$a = e^{(0.05-0.02)\times 0.25} = 1.0075, \quad p = \frac{1.0075 - 0.9048}{1.1052 - 0.9048} = 0.5126$$

The value of the option is 53.39.

Figure 11.10 Two-step tree to value an European six-month call option on an index when index level is 810, strike price is 800, risk-free rate is 5%, volatility is 20%, and dividend yield is 2%

At each node:
Upper value = Underlying Asset Price
Lower value = Option Price
Shading indicates where option is exercised

Strike price = 800
Discount factor per step = 0.9876
Time step, dt = 0.2500 years, 91.25 days
Growth factor per step, a = 1.0075
Probability of up move, p = 0.5126
Up step size, u = 1.1052
Down step size, d = 0.9048

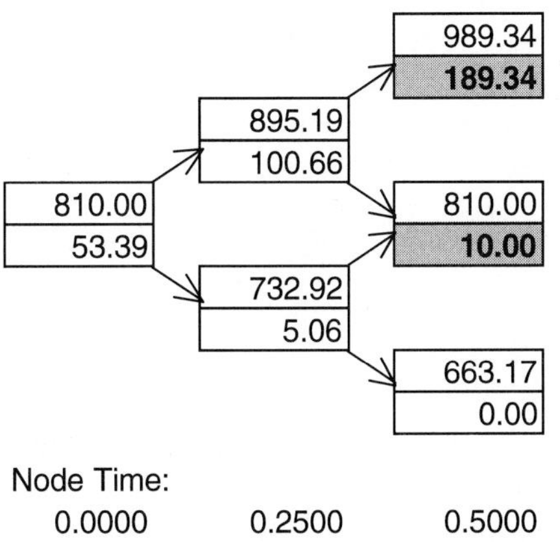

Figure 11.11 Three-step tree to value an American three-month call option on a currency when value of currency is 0.6100, strike price is 0.6000, risk-free rate is 5%, volatility is 12%, and foreign risk-free rate is 7%

At each node:
Upper value = Underlying Asset Price
Lower value = Option Price
Shading indicates where option is exercised

Strike price = 0.6
Discount factor per step = 0.9958
Time step, dt = 0.0833 years, 30.42 days
Growth factor per step, a = 0.9983
Probability of up move, p = 0.4673
Up step size, u = 1.0352
Down step size, d = 0.9660

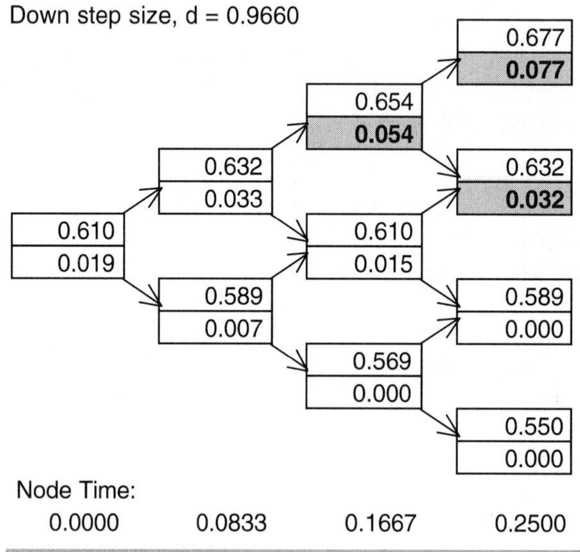

2. The Australian dollar is currently worth 0.6100 U.S. dollars and this exchange rate has a volatility of 12%. The Australian risk-free rate is 7% and the U.S. risk-free rate is 5%. Figure 11.11 shows the output from DerivaGem for valuing a three-month American call option with a strike price of 0.6000 using a three-step tree. In this case,

$$\Delta t = 0.08333, \quad u = e^{0.12\times\sqrt{0.08333}} = 1.0352, \quad d = 1/u = 0.9660,$$

$$a = e^{(0.05-0.07)\times 0.08333} = 0.9983, \quad p = \frac{0.9983 - 0.9660}{1.0352 - 0.9660} = 0.4673$$

The value of the option is 0.019.

3. A futures price is currently 31 and it has a volatility of 30%. The risk-free rate is 5%. Figure 11.12 shows the output from DerivaGem for valuing a nine-month American put option with a strike price of 30 using a three-step

Figure 11.12 Three-step tree to value an American nine-month put option on a futures contract when futures price is 31, strike price is 30, risk-free rate is 5%, and volatility is 30%

At each node:
Upper value = Underlying Asset Price
Lower value = Option Price
Shading indicates where option is exercised

Strike price = 30
Discount factor per step = 0.9876
Time step, dt = 0.2500 years, 91.25 days
Growth factor per step, a = 1.000
Probability of up move, p = 0.4626
Up step size, u = 1.1618
Down step size, d = 0.8607

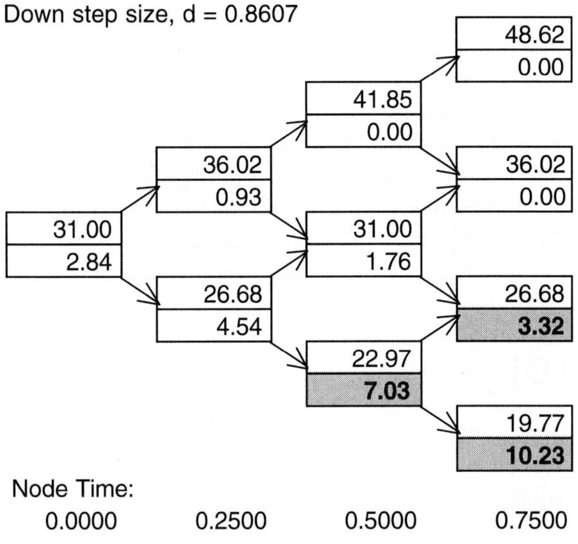

tree. In this case,

$$\Delta t = 0.25, \quad u = e^{0.3\sqrt{0.25}} = 1.1618, \quad d = 1/u = 1/1.1618 = 0.8607,$$

$$a = 1, \quad p = \frac{1 - 0.8607}{1.1618 - 0.8607} = 0.4626$$

The value of the option is 2.84.

SUMMARY

This chapter has provided a first look at the valuation of options on stocks and other assets. In the simple situation where movements in the price of a stock during the life of an option are governed by a one-step binomial tree, it is possible to set up a portfolio consisting of a stock option and the stock that is riskless. In a world with no arbitrage opportunities, riskless portfolios must earn the risk-free interest. This enables the stock option to be priced in terms of the stock. It is interesting to note that no assumptions are required about the probabilities of up and down movements in the stock price at each node of the tree.

When stock price movements are governed by a multistep binomial tree, we can treat each binomial step separately and work back from the end of the life of the option to the beginning to obtain the current value of the option. Again only no-arbitrage arguments are used, and no assumptions are required about the probabilities of up and down movements in the stock price at each node.

Another approach to valuing stock options involves risk-neutral valuation. This very important principle states that it is permissible to assume the world is risk neutral when valuing an option in terms of the underlying stock. This chapter has shown, through both numerical examples and algebra, that no-arbitrage arguments and risk-neutral valuation are equivalent and lead to the same option prices.

The delta of a stock option, Δ, considers the effect of a small change in the underlying stock price on the change in the option price. It is the ratio of the change in the option price to the change in the stock price. For a riskless position an investor should buy Δ shares for each option sold. An inspection of a typical binomial tree shows that delta changes during the life of an option. This means that to hedge a particular option position, we must change our holding in the underlying stock periodically.

Constructing binomial trees for valuing options on stock indices, currencies, futures contracts is very similar to doing so for valuing options on stocks. In Chapter 16, we will return to binomial trees and give a further details on how they can be used in practice.

FURTHER READING

Coval, J. E., and T. Shumway. "Expected Option Returns," *Journal of Finance*, 56, 3 (2001), 983–1009.

Cox, J., S. Ross, and M. Rubinstein. "Option Pricing: A Simplified Approach." *Journal of Financial Economics*, 7 (October 1979): 229–64.

Rendleman, R., and B. Bartter. "Two State Option Pricing." *Journal of Finance*, 34 (1979): 1092–1110.

Quiz (Answers at End of Book)

11.1. A stock price is currently \$40. It is known that at the end of one month it will be either \$42 or \$38. The risk-free interest rate is 8% per annum with continuous compounding. What is the value of a one-month European call option with a strike price of \$39?

11.2. Explain the no-arbitrage and risk-neutral valuation approaches to valuing a European option using a one-step binomial tree.

11.3. What is meant by the delta of a stock option?

11.4. A stock price is currently \$50. It is known that at the end of six months it will be either \$45 or \$55. The risk-free interest rate is 10% per annum with continuous compounding. What is the the value of a six-month European put option with a strike price of \$50?

11.5. A stock price is currently \$100. Over each of the next two six-month periods it is expected to go up by 10% or down by 10%. The risk-free interest rate is 8% per annum with continuous compounding. What is the value of a one-year European call option with a strike price of \$100?

11.6. For the situation considered in Quiz 11.5, what is the value of a one-year European put option with a strike price of \$100? Verify that the European call and European put prices satisfy put–call parity.

11.7. What are the formulas for u and d in terms of the volatility of an asset price?

Questions and Problems (Answers in Solutions Manual/Study Guide)

11.8. Consider the situation in which stock price movements during the life of a European option are governed by a two-step binomial tree. Explain why it is not possible to set up a position in the stock and the option that remains riskless for the whole of the life of the option.

11.9. A stock price is currently \$50. It is known that at the end of two months it will be either \$53 or \$48. The risk-free interest rate is 10% per annum with continuous compounding. What is the value of a two-month European call option with a strike price of \$49? Use no-arbitrage arguments.

11.10. A stock price is currently \$80. It is known that at the end of four months it will be either \$75 or \$85. The risk-free interest rate is 5% per annum with continuous compounding. What is the value of a four-month European put option with a strike price of \$80? Use no-arbitrage arguments.

11.11. A stock price is currently \$40. It is known that at the end of three months it will be either \$45 or \$35. The risk-free rate of interest with quarterly compounding is 8% per annum. Calculate the value of a three-month European put option on the stock with an exercise price of \$40. Verify that no-arbitrage arguments and risk-neutral valuation arguments give the same answers.

11.12. A stock price is currently \$50. Over each of the next two three-month periods it is expected to go up by 6% or down by 5%. The risk-free interest rate is 5% per annum with continuous compounding. What is the value of a six-month European call option with a strike price of \$51?

11.13. For the situation considered in Problem 11.12, what is the value of a six-month European put option with a strike price of \$51? Verify that the European call and European put prices satisfy put–call parity. If the put option were American, would it ever be optimal to exercise it early at any of the nodes on the tree?

11.14. A stock price is currently \$25. It is known that at the end of two months it will be either \$23 or \$27. The risk-free interest rate is 10% per annum with continuous compounding. Suppose S_T is the stock price at the end of two months. What is the value of a derivative that pays off S_T^2 at this time?

11.15. Calculate u, d, and p when a binomial tree is constructed to value an option on a foreign currency. The tree step size is one month, the domestic interest rate is 5% per annum, the foreign interest rate is 8% per annum, and the volatility is 12% per annum.

Assignment Questions

11.16. A stock price is currently $50. It is known that at the end of six months it will be either $60 or $42. The risk-free rate of interest with continuous compounding is 12% per annum. Calculate the value of a six-month European call option on the stock with an exercise price of $48. Verify that no-arbitrage arguments and risk-neutral valuation arguments give the same answers.

11.17. A stock price is currently $40. Over each of the next two three-month periods it is expected to go up by 10% or down by 10%. The risk-free interest rate is 12% per annum with continuous compounding.

a. What is the value of a six-month European put option with a strike price of $42?

b. What is the value of a six-month American put option with a strike price of $42?

11.18. Using a "trial-and-error" approach, estimate how high the strike price has to be in Problem 11.17 for it to be optimal to exercise the put option immediately.

11.19. A stock price is currently $30. During each two-month period for the next four months it is expected to increase by 8% or reduce by 10%. The risk-free interest rate is 5%. Use a two-step tree to calculate the value of a derivative that pays off $[\max(30 - S_T, 0)]^2$ where S_T is the stock price in two months? If the derivative is American-style, should it be exercised early?

11.20. Consider a European call option on a non-dividend-paying stock where the stock price is $40, the strike price is $40, the risk-free rate is 4% per annum, the volatility is 30% per annum, and the time to maturity is six months.

a. Calculate u, d, and p for a two step tree.

b. Value the option using a two step tree.

c. Verify that DerivaGem gives the same answer.

d. Use DerivaGem to value the option with 5, 50, 100, and 500 time steps.

11.21. Repeat Problem 11.20 for an American put option on a futures contract. The strike price and the futures price are $50, the risk-free rate is 10%, the time to maturity is six months, and the volatility is 40% per annum.

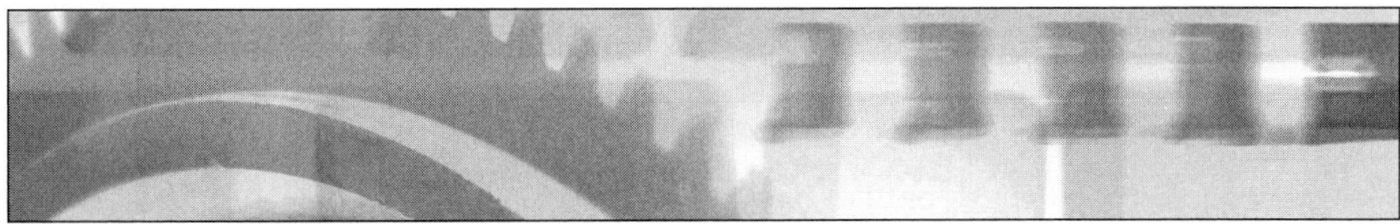

CHAPTER 12

Valuing Stock Options: The Black–Scholes Model

In the early 1970s, Fischer Black, Myron Scholes, and Robert Merton made a major breakthrough in the pricing of stock options.[1] This involved the development of what has become known as the Black–Scholes model. This model has had a huge influence on the way in which traders price and hedge options. It has also been pivotal to the growth and success of financial engineering in the last 20 years. An acknowledgment of the importance of the model came in 1997 when Myron Scholes and Robert Merton were awarded the Nobel prize for economics. Sadly, Fischer Black died in 1995. Otherwise he would undoubtedly also have been one of the recipients of this prize.

In this chapter we present the Black–Scholes model for valuing European call and put options on a non-dividend-paying stock and discuss the assumptions on which it is based. We also consider more fully than in previous chapters the meaning of volatility and show how volatility can be either estimated from historical data or implied from option prices. Toward the end of the chapter we explain how the Black–Scholes results can be extended to deal with European call and put options on dividend-paying stocks.

12.1 ASSUMPTIONS ABOUT HOW STOCK PRICES EVOLVE

A stock option pricing model must make some assumptions about how stock prices evolve over time. If a stock price is \$100 today, what is the probability distribution for the price in one day or in one week or in one year?

The assumption underlying the Black–Scholes model is that (in the absence of dividends) percentage changes in the stock price in a short period of time are approximately normally distributed. The changes in successive short periods of time are independent. The percentage change in the stock price is the return provided by the stock, and a variable with independent random changes in successive time periods is said to follow a *random walk*. The assumption is therefore that stock price returns follow a

[1] See F. Black and M. Scholes, "The Pricing of Options and Corporate Liabilities," *Journal of Political Economy*, 81 (May/June 1973): 637–59; and R. C. Merton, "Theory of Rational Option Pricing," *Bell Journal of Economics and Management Science* 4 (Spring 1973): 141–83.

random walk. Define:

μ: Expected return on the stock per year

σ: Volatility of the stock price per year

The mean of the percentage change in time Δt is $\mu\,\Delta t$. The standard deviation of the percentage change is $\sigma\sqrt{\Delta t}$. The assumption underlying Black–Scholes is therefore

$$\frac{\Delta S}{S} \sim \phi(\mu\,\Delta t, \sigma\sqrt{\Delta t}) \tag{12.1}$$

where ΔS is the change in the stock price S in time Δt, and $\phi(m, s)$ denotes a normal distribution with mean m and standard deviation s.

The Lognormal Distribution

The assumption in equation (12.1) implies that the stock price at any future time has a *lognormal* distribution. The general shape of a lognormal distribution is shown in Figure 12.1. It can be contrasted with the more familiar normal distribution in Figure 12.2. Whereas a variable with a normal distribution can take any positive or negative value, a lognormally distributed variable is restricted to being positive. A normal distribution is symmetrical; a lognormal distribution is skewed with the mean, median, and mode all different.

A variable with a lognormal distribution has the property that its natural logarithm is normally distributed. The Black–Scholes assumption for stock prices therefore implies that $\ln S_T$ is normal, where S_T is the stock price at a future time T. The mean and standard deviation of $\ln S_T$ can be shown to be

$$\ln S_0 + \left(\mu - \frac{\sigma^2}{2}\right)T \quad \text{and} \quad \sigma\sqrt{T}$$

where S_0 is the current stock price. We can write this result as

$$\ln S_T \sim \phi\left[\ln S_0 + \left(\mu - \frac{\sigma^2}{2}\right)T, \ \sigma\sqrt{T}\right] \tag{12.2}$$

Figure 12.1 A lognormal distribution

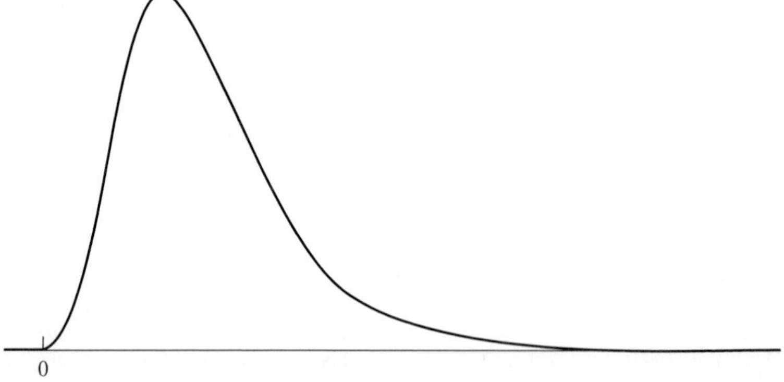

Figure 12.2 A normal distribution

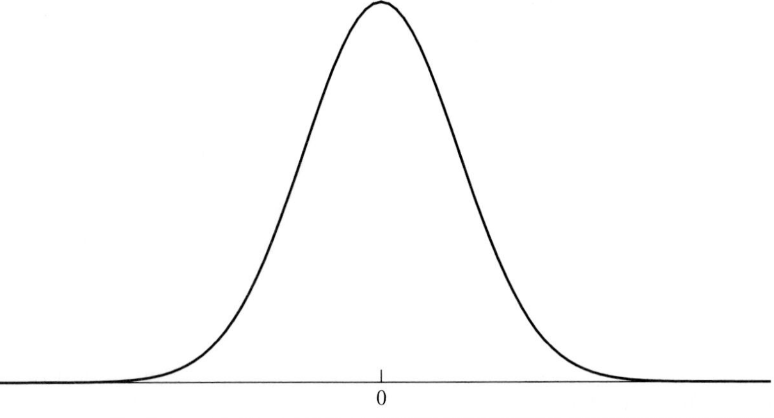

The expected value or mean value, $E(S_T)$, of S_T is given by

$$E(S_T) = S_0 e^{\mu T} \tag{12.3}$$

The variance, $\text{var}(S_T)$, of S_T can be shown to be given by

$$\text{var}(S_T) = S_0^2 e^{2\mu T}(e^{\sigma^2 T} - 1)$$

Example

Consider a stock with an initial price of \$40, an expected return of 16% per annum, and a volatility of 20% per annum. From equation (12.2), the probability distribution of the stock price, S_T, in six months is given by

$$\ln S_T \sim \phi\left[\ln 40 + \left(0.16 - \frac{0.2^2}{2}\right)0.5,\ 0.2\sqrt{0.5}\right]$$

or

$$\ln S_T \sim \phi(3.759, 0.141)$$

There is a 95% probability that a normally distributed variable has a value within 1.96 standard deviations of its mean. Hence, with 95% confidence,

$$3.759 - 1.96 \times 0.141 < \ln S_T < 3.759 + 1.96 \times 0.141$$

This implies

$$e^{3.759-1.96\times0.141} < S_T < e^{3.759+1.96\times0.141}$$

or

$$32.55 < S_T < 56.56$$

Thus, there is a 95% probability that the stock price in six months will lie between 32.55 and 56.56. The mean and variance of S_T are

$$40e^{0.16\times0.5} = 43.33$$

and

$$40^2 e^{2\times0.16\times0.5}(e^{0.2\times0.2\times0.5} - 1) = 37.93$$

From equation (12.2) and the properties of the normal distribution, we have

$$\ln S_T - \ln S_0 \sim \phi\left[\left(\mu - \frac{\sigma^2}{2}\right)T,\ \sigma\sqrt{T}\right]$$

or

$$\ln\frac{S_T}{S_0} \sim \phi\left[\left(\mu - \frac{\sigma^2}{2}\right)T,\ \sigma\sqrt{T}\right] \quad \textbf{(12.4)}$$

When $T = 1$, the expression $\ln(S_T/S_0)$ is the continuously compounded return provided by the stock in one year.[2] The mean and standard deviation of the continuously compounded return in one year are therefore $\mu - \sigma^2/2$ and σ, respectively.

Example

Consider a stock with an expected return of 17% per annum and a volatility of 20% per annum. The probability distribution for the rate of return (continuously compounded) realized over one year is normal, with mean

$$0.17 - \frac{0.2^2}{2} = 0.15$$

or 15% and standard deviation 20%. Because there is a 95% chance that a normally distributed variable will lie within 1.96 standard deviations of its mean, we can be 95% confident that the return realized over one year will be between −24.2% and +54.2%.

We now consider in more detail the nature of the expected return and volatility parameter in the lognormal stock price model.

12.2 EXPECTED RETURN

The expected return, μ, required by investors from a stock depends on the riskiness of the stock. The higher the risk, the higher the expected return. It also depends on the level of interest rates in the economy. The higher the level of interest rates, the higher the expected return required on any given stock. Fortunately, we do not have to concern ourselves with the determinants of μ in any detail. It turns out that the value of a stock option, when expressed in terms of the value of the underlying stock, does not depend on μ at all. Nevertheless, there is one aspect of the expected return from a stock that frequently causes confusion and is worth explaining.

Equation (12.1) shows that $\mu\,\Delta t$ is the expected percentage change in the stock price in a very short period of time, Δt. It is natural to assume from this that μ is the expected continuously compounded return on the stock. However, this is not the case. Denote by R the continuously compounded return actually realized over a period of time of length T years. This satisfies

$$S_T = S_0 e^{RT}$$

---

[2] As discussed in Chapter 4, it is important to distinguish between the continuously compounded return and the return with annual compounding. The former is $\ln(S_T/S_0)$; the latter is $(S_T - S_0)/S_0$.

so that

$$R = \frac{1}{T}\ln\frac{S_T}{S_0}$$

Equation (12.4) shows that the expected value, $E(R)$, of R is $\mu - \sigma^2/2$.

The reason why the expected continuously compounded return is different from μ is subtle, but important. Suppose we consider a very large number of very short periods of time of length Δt. Define S_i as the stock price at the end of the ith interval and ΔS_i as $S_{i+1} - S_i$. Under the assumptions we are making for stock price behavior, the average of the returns on the stock in each interval is close to μ. In other words, $\mu\,\Delta t$ is close to the arithmetic mean of the $\Delta S_i/S_i$. However, the expected return over the whole period covered by the data, expressed with a compounding period of Δt, is close to $\mu - \sigma^2/2$, not μ.[3] Business Snapshot 12.1 provides a numerical example related to the mutual fund industry that illustrates the point being made here.

For a mathematical explanation of what is going on, we start with equation (12.3):

$$E(S_T) = S_0 e^{\mu T}$$

Taking logarithms, we get

$$\ln[E(S_T)] = \ln(S_0) + \mu T$$

It is now tempting to set $\ln[E(S_T)] = E[\ln(S_T)]$, so that $E[\ln(S_T)] - \ln(S_0) = \mu T$, or $E[\ln(S_T/S_0)] = \mu T$, which leads to $E(R) = \mu$. However, we cannot do this because ln is a nonlinear function. In fact, $\ln[E(S_T)] > E[\ln(S_T)]$, so that $E[\ln(S_T/S_0)] < \mu T$, which leads to $E(R) < \mu$. (As pointed out above, $E(R) = \mu - \sigma^2/2$.)

12.3 VOLATILITY

The volatility of a stock, σ, is a measure of our uncertainty about the returns provided by the stock. Stocks typically have volatilities between 15% and 50%.

From equation (12.4), the volatility of a stock price can be defined as the standard deviation of the return provided by the stock in one year when the return is expressed using continuous compounding.

When T is small, equation (12.1) shows that $\sigma\sqrt{T}$ is approximately equal to the standard deviation of the percentage change in the stock price in time T. Suppose that $\sigma = 0.3$, or 30% per annum, and the current stock price is \$50. The standard deviation of the percentage change in the stock price in one week is approximately

$$30 \times \sqrt{\frac{1}{52}} = 4.16\%$$

A one-standard-deviation move in the stock price in one week is therefore 50×0.0416, or \$2.08.

Equation (12.1) shows that our uncertainty about a future stock price, as measured by its standard deviation, increases—at least approximately—with the square root of how far ahead we are looking. For example, the standard deviation of the stock price in four weeks is approximately twice the standard deviation in one week.

[3] The arguments in this section show that the term "expected return" is ambiguous. It can refer either to μ or to $\mu - \sigma^2/2$. Unless otherwise stated, it will be used to refer to μ throughout this book.

Business Snapshot 12.1 Mutual fund returns can be misleading

The difference between μ and $\mu - \sigma^2/2$ is closely related to an issue in the reporting of mutual fund returns. Suppose that the following is a sequence of returns per annum reported by a mutual fund manager over the last five years (measured using annual compounding):

$$15\%,\quad 20\%,\quad 30\%,\quad -20\%,\quad 25\%$$

The arithmetic mean of the returns, calculated by taking the sum of the returns and dividing by 5, is 14%. However, an investor would actually earn less than 14% per annum by leaving the money invested in the fund for five years. The dollar value of \$100 at the end of the five years would be

$$100 \times 1.15 \times 1.20 \times 1.30 \times 0.80 \times 1.25 = \$179.40$$

By contrast, a 14% return with annual compounding would give

$$100 \times 1.14^5 = \$192.54$$

The return that gives \$179.40 at the end of five years is 12.4%. This is because

$$100 \times (1.0124)^5 = 179.40$$

What average return should the fund manager report? It is tempting for the manager to make a statement such as: "The average of the returns per year that we have realized in the last five years is 14%." Although true, this is misleading. It is much less misleading to say "The average return realized by someone who invested with us for the last five years is 12.4% per year." In some jurisdictions regulatory standards require fund managers to report returns the second way.

This phenomenon is an example of a result that is well known by mathematicians. The geometric mean of a set of numbers (not all the same) is always less than the arithmetic mean. In our example, the return multipliers each year are 1.15, 1.20, 1.30, 0.80, and 1.25. The arithmetic mean of these numbers is 1.140, but the geometric mean is only 1.124.

12.4 ESTIMATING VOLATILITY FROM HISTORICAL DATA

A record of stock price movements can be used to estimate volatility. The stock price is usually observed at fixed intervals of time (e.g., every day, every week, or every month). We define:

$n+1$: Number of observations

S_i: Stock price at end of ith interval, where $i = 0, 1, \dots, n$

τ: Length of time interval in years

and let

$$u_i = \ln\left(\frac{S_i}{S_{i-1}}\right)$$

An estimate, s, of the standard deviation of the u_i is given by

$$s = \sqrt{\frac{1}{n-1}\sum_{i=1}^{n}(u_i - \bar{u})^2}$$

or

$$s = \sqrt{\frac{1}{n-1}\sum_{i=1}^{n} u_i^2 - \frac{1}{n(n-1)}\left(\sum_{i=1}^{n} u_i\right)^2}$$

where $\bar{u}$ is the mean of the u_i.

From equation (12.4), the standard deviation of the u_i is $\sigma\sqrt{\tau}$. The variable s is therefore an estimate of $\sigma\sqrt{\tau}$. It follows that σ itself can be estimated as $\hat{\sigma}$, where

$$\hat{\sigma} = \frac{s}{\sqrt{\tau}}$$

The standard error of this estimate can be shown to be approximately $\hat{\sigma}/\sqrt{2n}$.

Choosing an appropriate value for n is not easy. More data generally lead to more accuracy, but σ does change over time and data that are too old may not be relevant for predicting the future volatility. A compromise that seems to work reasonably well is to use closing prices from daily data over the most recent 90 to 180 days. An often-used rule of thumb is to set n equal to the number of days to which the volatility is to be applied. Thus, if the volatility estimate is to be used to value a two-year option, it is calculated from daily data over the last two years.

Example

Table 12.1 shows a possible sequence of stock prices during 21 consecutive trading days. In this case,

$$\sum u_i = 0.09531 \quad \text{and} \quad \sum u_i^2 = 0.00326$$

and the estimate of the standard deviation of the daily return is

$$\sqrt{\frac{0.00326}{19} - \frac{0.09531^2}{380}} = 0.01216$$

or 1.216%. Assuming that there are 252 trading days per year, $\tau = 1/252$ and the data give an estimate for the volatility per annum of $0.01216\sqrt{252} = 0.193$ or 19.3%. The standard error of this estimate is

$$\frac{0.193}{\sqrt{2 \times 20}} = 0.031$$

or 3.1% per annum.

The foregoing analysis assumes that the stock pays no dividends. It can be adapted to accommodate dividend-paying stocks. The return, u_i, during a time interval that includes an ex-dividend day is given by

$$u_i = \ln\frac{S_i + D}{S_{i-1}}$$

Table 12.1 Computation of volatility

Day	*Closing stock price* (\$)	*Price relative* S_i/S_{i-1}	*Daily return* $u_i = \ln(S_i/S_{i-1})$
0	20.00		
1	20.10	1.00500	0.00499
2	19.90	0.99005	−0.01000
3	20.00	1.00503	0.00501
4	20.50	1.02500	0.02469
5	20.25	0.98780	−0.01227
6	20.90	1.03210	0.03159
7	20.90	1.00000	0.00000
8	20.90	1.00000	0.00000
9	20.75	0.99282	−0.00720
10	20.75	1.00000	0.00000
11	21.00	1.01205	0.01198
12	21.10	1.00476	0.00475
13	20.90	0.99052	−0.00952
14	20.90	1.00000	0.00000
15	21.25	1.01675	0.01661
16	21.40	1.00706	0.00703
17	21.40	1.00000	0.00000
18	21.25	0.99299	−0.00703
19	21.75	1.02353	0.02326
20	22.00	1.01149	0.01143

where D is the amount of the dividend. The return in other time intervals is still

$$u_i = \ln\frac{S_i}{S_{i-1}}$$

However, because tax factors play a part in determining returns around an ex-dividend date, it is probably best to discard altogether data for intervals that include an ex-dividend date when daily or weekly data is used.

Trading Days vs. Calendar Days

There is an important issue concerned with whether time should be measured in calendar days or trading days when volatility parameters are being estimated and used. As shown in Business Snapshot 12.2, research shows that volatility is much higher when the exchange is open for trading than when it is closed. As a result, practitioners tend to ignore days when the exchange is closed when estimating volatility from historical data and when calculating the life of an option. The volatility per annum is calculated from the volatility per trading day using the formula

$$\text{Volatility per annum} = \text{Volatility per trading day} \times \sqrt{\begin{matrix}\text{Number of trading}\\ \text{days per annum}\end{matrix}}$$

Business Snapshot 12.2 What causes volatility?

It is natural to assume that the volatility of a stock is caused by new information reaching the market. This new information causes people to revise their opinions about the value of the stock. The price of the stock changes and volatility results. This view of what causes volatility is not supported by research.

With several years of daily stock price data researchers can calculate:

1. The variance of stock price returns between the close of trading on one day and the close of trading on the next day when there are no intervening nontrading days.
2. The variance of the stock price returns between the close of trading on Friday and the close of trading on Monday.

The second variance is the variance of returns over a three-day period. The first is a variance over a one-day period. We might reasonably expect the second variance to be three times as great as the first variance. Fama (1965), French (1980), and French and Roll (1986) show that this is not the case. These three research studies estimate the second variance to be, respectively, 22%, 19%, and 10.7% higher than the first variance.

At this stage you might be tempted to argue that these results are explained by more news reaching the market when the market is open for trading. But research by Roll (1984) does not support this explanation. Roll looked at the prices of orange juice futures. By far the most important news for orange juice futures prices is news about the weather and news about the weather is equally likely to arrive on any day. When Roll did a similar analysis to that just described for stocks he found that the second (Friday-to-Monday) variance is only 1.54 times the first variance.

The only reasonable conclusion from all this is that volatility is to a large extent caused by trading itself. (Traders usually have no difficulty accepting this conclusion!)

This is what we did when calculating volatility from the data in Table 12.1. The number of trading days in a year is usually assumed to be 252 for stocks.

The life of an option is also usually measured using trading days rather than calendar days. It is calculated as T years, where

$$T = \frac{\text{Number of trading days until option maturity}}{252}$$

12.5 ASSUMPTIONS UNDERLYING BLACK–SCHOLES

The assumptions made by Black and Scholes when they derived their option pricing formula were as follows:

1. Stock price behavior corresponds to the lognormal model (developed earlier in this chapter) with μ and σ constant.
2. There are no transactions costs or taxes. All securities are perfectly divisible.
3. There are no dividends on the stock during the life of the option.

4. There are no riskless arbitrage opportunities.
5. Security trading is continuous.
6. Investors can borrow or lend at the same risk-free rate of interest.
7. The short-term risk-free rate of interest, r, is constant.

Some of these assumptions have been relaxed by other researchers. For example, variations on the Black–Scholes formula can be used when r and σ are functions of time, and as we will see later in this chapter the formula can be adjusted to take dividends into account.

12.6 THE BLACK–SCHOLES/MERTON ANALYSIS

The Black–Scholes/Merton arguments are analogous to the no-arbitrage arguments used in Chapter 11 to value options when stock price changes are binomial. A riskless portfolio consisting of a position in the option and a position in the underlying stock is set up. In the absence of arbitrage opportunities, the return from the portfolio must be the risk-free interest rate, r. This results in a differential equation that must be satisfied by the option.

The reason a riskless portfolio can be set up is that the stock price and the option price are both affected by the same underlying source of uncertainty: stock price movements. In any short period of time, the price of a call option is perfectly positively correlated with the price of the underlying stock; the price of a put option is perfectly negatively correlated with the price of the underlying stock. In both cases, when an appropriate portfolio of the stock and the option is set up, the gain or loss from the stock position always offsets the gain or loss from the option position so that the overall value of the portfolio at the end of the short period of time is known with certainty.

Suppose, for example, that at a particular point in time the relationship between a small change in the stock price, ΔS, and the resultant small change in the price of a European call option, Δc, is given by

$$\Delta c = 0.4\Delta S$$

This means that the slope of the line representing the relationship between Δc and ΔS is 0.4, as indicated in Figure 12.3. A riskless portfolio would consist of:

1. A long position in 40 shares
2. A short position in 100 call options

Suppose for example that the stock price increases by 10 cents. The option price will increase by 4 cents and the $40 \times 0.10 = \$4$ gain on the shares is equal to the $100 \times 0.04 = \$40$ loss on the short option position.

There is one important difference between the Black–Scholes/Merton analysis and the analysis using a binomial model in Chapter 11. In Black–Scholes/Merton, the position that is set up is riskless for only a very short period of time. (Theoretically, it remains riskless only for an instantaneously short period of time.) To remain riskless, it must be frequently adjusted or *rebalanced*.[4] For example, the relationship between Δc

[4] We will examine the rebalancing of portfolios in more detail in Chapter 15.

Figure 12.3 Relationship between call price and stock price. Current stock price is S_0

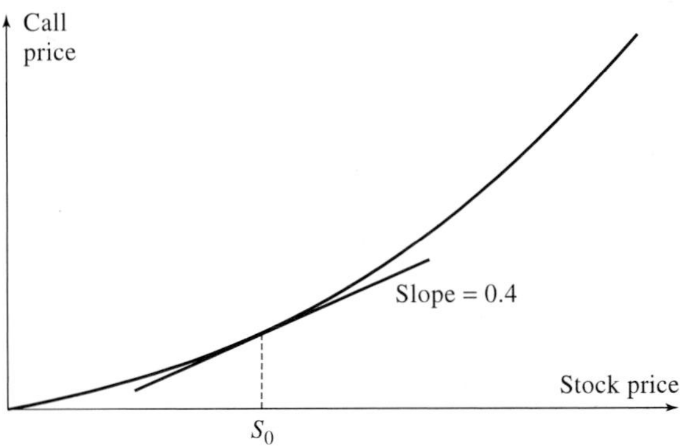

and ΔS might change from $\Delta c = 0.4\,\Delta S$ today to $\Delta c = 0.5\,\Delta S$ in two weeks. (If so, an extra 0.1 shares must be purchased for each call option sold to maintain a riskless portfolio.) It is nevertheless true that the return from the riskless portfolio in any short period of time must be the risk-free interest rate. This is the key element in the Black–Scholes/Merton arguments and leads to their pricing formulas.

The Pricing Formulas

The Black–Scholes formulas for the prices of European calls and puts on non-dividend-paying stocks are[5]

$$c = S_0 N(d_1) - Ke^{-rT} N(d_2) \tag{12.5}$$

$$p = Ke^{-rT} N(-d_2) - S_0 N(-d_1) \tag{12.6}$$

where

$$d_1 = \frac{\ln(S_0/K) + (r + \sigma^2/2)T}{\sigma\sqrt{T}}$$

$$d_2 = \frac{\ln(S_0/K) + (r - \sigma^2/2)T}{\sigma\sqrt{T}} = d_1 - \sigma\sqrt{T}$$

The function $N(x)$ is the cumulative probability function for a standardized normal variable. In other words, it is the probability that a variable with a standard normal distribution, $\phi(0, 1)$, will be less than x. It is illustrated in Figure 12.4. The remaining notation in equations (12.5) and (12.6) should be familiar. The variables c and p are the European call and put prices, S_0 is the stock price, K is the strike price, r is the risk-free interest rate (expressed with continuous compounding), T is the time to expiration, and σ is the volatility of the stock price. Because the American call price, C, equals the European call price, c, for a non-dividend-paying stock, equation (12.5) also gives the price of an American call. There is no exact analytic formula to value an American put, but binomial trees such as those introduced in Chapter 11 can be used.

In theory, the Black–Scholes formula is correct only if the short-term interest rate, r,

[5] The software that accompanies this book can be used to carry out Black–Scholes calculations for options on stocks, currencies, indices, and futures contracts.

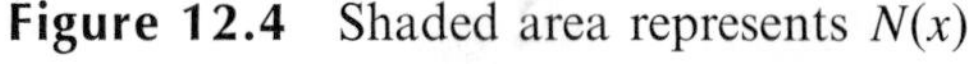

Figure 12.4 Shaded area represents $N(x)$

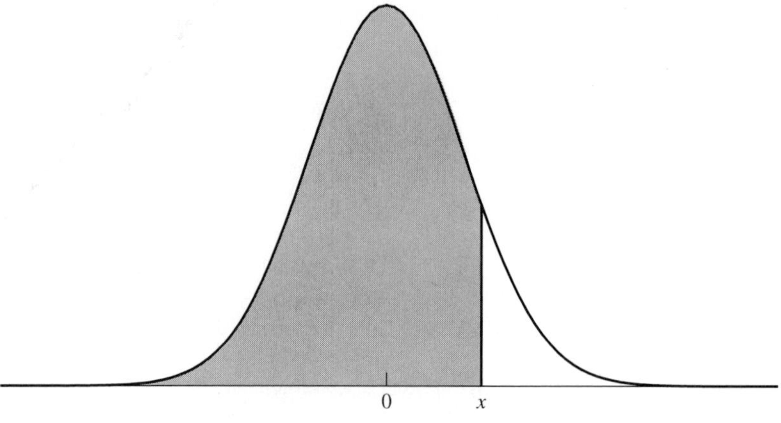

is constant. In practice, the formula is usually used with the interest rate, r, being set equal to the risk-free interest rate on an investment that lasts for time T.

Properties of the Black–Scholes Formulas

A full proof of the Black–Scholes formulas is beyond the scope of this book. At this stage we show that the formulas have the right general properties by considering what happens when some of the parameters take extreme values.

When the stock price, S_0, becomes very large, a call option is almost certain to be exercised. It then becomes very similar to a forward contract with delivery price K. From equation (5.5) we therefore expect the call price to be

$$S_0 - Ke^{-rT}$$

This is, in fact, the call price given by equation (12.5) because, when S_0 becomes very large, both d_1 and d_2 become very large, and $N(d_1)$ and $N(d_2)$ are both close to 1.0.

When the stock price becomes very large, the price of a European put option, p, approaches zero. This result is consistent with equation (12.6) because $N(-d_1)$ and $N(-d_2)$ are both close to zero when S_0 is large.

When the stock price becomes very small, both d_1 and d_2 become very large and negative. This means that $N(d_1)$ and $N(d_2)$ are then both very close to zero, and equation (12.5) gives a price close to zero for the call option. This is as expected. Also, $N(-d_1)$ and $N(-d_2)$ become close to 1, so that the price of the put option given by equation (12.6) is close to $Ke^{-rT} - S_0$. This is also as expected.

The only problem in applying equations (12.5) and (12.6) is the computation of the cumulative normal distribution function, N. Tables for N are provided at the end of this book. The function can also be evaluated using the NORMSDIST function in Excel. A polynomial approximation that gives accuracy to six decimal places is

$$N(x) = \begin{cases} 1 - N'(x)(a_1k + a_2k^2 + a_3k^3 + a_4k^4 + a_5k^5) & \text{if } x \geqslant 0 \\ 1 - N(-x) & \text{if } x < 0 \end{cases}$$

where

$$k = \frac{1}{1+\gamma x}, \qquad \gamma = 0.2316419$$

$$a_1 = 0.319381530, \quad a_2 = -0.356563782$$

$$a_3 = 1.781477937, \quad a_4 = -1.821255978 \quad a_5 = 1.330274429$$

and

$$N'(x) = \frac{1}{\sqrt{2\pi}} e^{-x^2/2}$$

Example

The stock price six months from the expiration of an option is \$42, the exercise price of the option is \$40, the risk-free interest rate is 10% per annum, and the volatility is 20% per annum. This means that $S_0 = 42$, $K = 40$, $r = 0.1$, $\sigma = 0.2$, $T = 0.5$,

$$d_1 = \frac{\ln(42/40) + (0.1 + 0.2^2/2) \times 0.5}{0.2\sqrt{0.5}} = 0.7693$$

$$d_2 = \frac{\ln(42/40) + (0.1 - 0.2^2/2) \times 0.5}{0.2\sqrt{0.5}} = 0.6278$$

and

$$Ke^{-rT} = 40e^{-0.1\times 0.5} = 38.049$$

Hence, if the option is a European call, its value, c, is given by

$$c = 42N(0.7693) - 38.049N(0.6278)$$

If the option is a European put, its value, p, is given by

$$p = 38.049N(-0.6278) - 42N(-0.7693)$$

Using the polynomial approximation just given or the tables at the end of the book, we get

$$N(0.7693) = 0.7791, \quad N(-0.7693) = 0.2209$$

$$N(0.6278) = 0.7349, \quad N(-0.6278) = 0.2651$$

so that

$$c = 4.76 \quad \text{and} \quad p = 0.81$$

Ignoring the time value of money, the stock price has to rise by \$2.76 for the purchaser of the call to break even. Similarly, the stock price has to fall by \$2.81 for the purchaser of the put to break even.

12.7 RISK-NEUTRAL VALUATION

A very important result in the pricing of derivatives is known as risk-neutral valuation. The principle was introduced in Chapter 11 and can be stated as follows:

> Any security dependent on other traded securities can be valued on the assumption that investors are risk neutral.

Note that risk-neutral valuation does not state that investors are risk neutral. What it does state is that derivatives such as options can be valued on the assumption that investors are risk neutral. It means that investors' risk preferences have no effect on the value of a stock option when it is expressed as a function of the price of the underlying stock. It explains why equations (12.5) and (12.6) do not involve the stock's expected return, μ. Risk-neutral valuation is a very powerful tool because in a risk-neutral world two particularly simple results hold:

1. The expected return from all investment assets is the risk-free interest rate.
2. The risk-free interest rate is the appropriate discount rate to apply to any expected future cash flow.

Options and other derivatives can be valued using risk-neutral valuation. The procedure is as follows:

1. Assume that the expected return from the underlying asset is the risk-free interest rate r (i.e., assume $\mu = r$).
2. Calculate the expected payoff.
3. Discount the expected payoff at the risk-free interest rate.

Application to Forward Contracts

This procedure can be used to derive the Black–Scholes formulas, but the mathematics is fairly complicated and will not be presented here. Instead, as an illustration, we will show how the procedure can be used to value a forward contract on a non-dividend-paying stock. (This contract has already been valued in Chapter 5 using a different approach.) We will make the assumption that interest rates are constant and equal to r.

Consider a long forward contract that matures at time T with delivery price K. The value of the contract at maturity is

$$S_T - K$$

The expected value of S_T was shown earlier in this chapter to be $S_0 e^{\mu T}$. In a risk-neutral world, it becomes $S_0 e^{rT}$. The expected payoff from the contract at maturity in a risk-neutral world is therefore

$$S_0 e^{rT} - K$$

Discounting at the risk-free rate r for time T gives the value, f, of the forward contract today as

$$f = e^{-rT}(S_0 e^{rT} - K) = S_0 - K e^{-rT}$$

This is in agreement with the result in equation (5.5).

12.8 IMPLIED VOLATILITIES

The one parameter in the Black–Scholes pricing formulas that cannot be observed directly is the volatility of the stock price. Earlier in this chapter we saw how volatility can be estimated from a history of the stock price. We now show how to calculate what is known as an *implied volatility*. This is the volatility implied by an option price observed in the market.[6]

[6] Implied volatilities for European and American options on stocks, stock indices, foreign currencies, and futures can be calculated using the DerivaGem software supplied with this book.

To illustrate the basic idea, suppose that the value of a European call option on a non-dividend-paying stock is 1.90 when $S_0 = 21$, $K = 20$, $r = 0.1$, and $T = 0.25$. The implied volatility is the value of σ that, when substituted into equation (12.5), gives $c = 1.90$. It is not possible to invert equation (12.5) so that σ is expressed as a function of S_0, K, r, T, and c, but an iterative search procedure can be used to find the implied σ. We could start by trying $\sigma = 0.20$. This gives a value of c equal to 1.76, which is too low. Because c is an increasing function of σ, a higher value of σ is required. We could next try a value of 0.30 for σ. This gives a value of c equal to 2.10, which is too high, and means that σ must lie between 0.20 and 0.30. Next, we try a value of 0.25 for σ. This also proves to be too high, showing that σ lies between 0.20 and 0.25. Proceeding in this way, we can halve the range for σ at each iteration and thereby calculate the correct value of σ to any required accuracy.[7] In this example, the implied volatility is 0.242, or 24.2% per annum.

Implied volatilities can be used to monitor the market's opinion about the volatility of a particular stock. Analysts often calculate implied volatilities from actively traded options on a certain stock and use them to calculate the price of a less actively traded option on the same stock. The way they do this is described in Chapter 17.

The prices of at-the-money options are quite sensitive to volatility and implied volatilities calculated from these option are reliable indicators of the market's view of volatility. The prices of deep-in-the-money and deep-out-of-the-money options are relatively insensitive to volatility. Implied volatilities calculated from these options may therefore be less reliable.

12.9 DIVIDENDS

Up to now we have assumed that the stock on which the option is written pays no dividends. In practice, this is not always the case. We now extend our results by assuming that the dividends paid on the stock during the life of an option can be predicted with certainty. When options last for relatively short periods of time (less than one year), the assumption is not unreasonable.

The date on which the dividend is paid should be assumed to be the ex-dividend date. On this date the stock price declines by the amount of the dividend.[8] The effect is to reduce the value of calls and increase the value of puts.

European Options

European options can be analyzed by assuming that the stock price is the sum of two components: a riskless component that will be used to pay the known dividends during the life of the option and a risky component. The riskless component at any given time is the present value of all the dividends during the life of the option discounted from the ex-dividend dates to the present at the risk-free rate. The Black–Scholes formula is then

[7] This method is presented for illustration. Other, more powerful, procedures are usually used in practice.

[8] For tax reasons the stock price may go down by somewhat less than the cash amount of the dividend. To take account of this phenomenon, we need to interpret the word *dividend* in the context of option pricing as the reduction in the stock price on the ex-dividend date caused by the dividend. Thus, if a dividend of $1 per share is anticipated and the share price normally goes down by 80% of the dividend on the ex-dividend date, the dividend should be assumed to be $0.80 for the purposes of the analysis.

correct if S_0 is set equal to the risky component. Operationally this means that the Black–Scholes formula can be used provided the stock price is reduced by the present value of all the dividends during the life of the option, the discounting being done from the ex-dividend dates at the risk-free rate. A dividend is included in the calculations only if its ex-dividend date occurs during the life of the option.

Example

Consider a European call option on a stock with ex-dividend dates in two months and five months. The dividend on each ex-dividend date is expected to be \$0.50. The current share price is \$40, the exercise price is \$40, the stock price volatility is 30% per annum, the risk-free rate of interest is 9% per annum, and the time to maturity is six months. The present value of the dividends is

$$0.5e^{-0.09\times 2/12} + 0.5e^{-0.09\times 5/12} = 0.9741$$

The option price can therefore be calculated from the Black–Scholes formula with $S_0 = 40 - 0.9741 = 39.0259$, $K = 40$, $r = 0.09$, $\sigma = 0.3$, and $T = 0.5$:

$$d_1 = \frac{\ln(39.0259/40) + (0.09 + 0.3^2/2)\times 0.5}{0.3\sqrt{0.5}} = 0.2017$$

$$d_2 = \frac{\ln(39.0259/40) + (0.09 - 0.3^2/2)\times 0.5}{0.3\sqrt{0.5}} = -0.0104$$

Using the polynomial approximation gives

$$N(d_1) = 0.5800 \quad \text{and} \quad N(d_2) = 0.4959$$

and from equation (12.5) the call price is

$$39.0259 \times 0.5800 - 40e^{-0.09\times 0.5} \times 0.4959 = 3.67$$

or \$3.67.

With this procedure, σ in the Black–Scholes formula should be the volatility of the risky component of the stock price—not the volatility of the stock price itself. In practice, the two are often assumed to be the same. In theory, the volatility of the risky component is approximately $S_0/(S_0 - D)$ times the volatility of the stock price, where D is the present value of the remaining dividends and S_0 is the stock price.

American Call Options

In Chapter 9, we saw that American call options should never be exercised early when the underlying stock pays no dividends. When dividends are paid, it is sometimes optimal to exercise at a time immediately before the stock goes ex-dividend. The reason is easy to understand. The dividend will make both the stock and the call option less valuable. If the dividend is sufficiently large and the call option is sufficiently in the money, it may be worth forgoing the remaining time value of the option in order to avoid the adverse effects of the dividend on the stock price.

In practice, call options are most likely to be exercised early immediately before the final ex-dividend date. The analysis in the Appendix at the end of this chapter indicates why this is so and derives the conditions under which early exercise can be optimal.

Here we will describe an approximate procedure suggested by Fischer Black for valuing American calls on dividend-paying stocks.

Black's Approximation

Black's approximation involves calculating the prices of two European options:

1. A European option that matures at the same time as the American option
2. A European option maturing just before the latest ex-dividend date that occurs during the life of the option

The strike price, initial stock price, risk-free interest rate, and volatility are the same as for the option under consideration. The American option price is set equal to the higher of these two European option prices.

Example

Return to the previous example but suppose that the option is American rather than European. The present value of the first dividend is given by

$$0.5e^{-0.09\times 2/12} = 0.4926$$

The value of the option on the assumption that it expires just before the final ex-dividend date can be calculated using the Black–Scholes formula, with $S_0 = 40 - 0.4926 = 39.5074$, $K = 40$, $r = 0.09$, $\sigma = 0.30$, and $T = 0.4167$. It is \$3.52. Black's approximation involves taking the greater of this value and the value of the option when it can be exercised only at the end of six months. From the previous example, we know that the latter is \$3.67. Black's approximation therefore gives the value of the American call as \$3.67.

SUMMARY

The usual assumption in stock option pricing is that the price of a stock at some future time given its price today is lognormal. This in turn implies that the continuously compounded return from the stock in a period of time is normally distributed. Our uncertainty about future stock prices increases as we look further ahead. As a rough approximation, we can say that the standard deviation of the stock price is proportional to the square root of how far ahead we are looking.

To estimate the volatility, σ, of a stock price empirically, we need to observe the stock price at fixed intervals of time (e.g., every day, every week, or every month). For each time period, the natural logarithm of the ratio of the stock price at the end of the time period to the stock price at the beginning of the time period is calculated. The volatility is estimated as the standard deviation of these numbers divided by the square root of the length of the time period in years. Usually days when the exchanges are closed are ignored in measuring time for the purposes of volatility calculations.

Stock option valuation involves setting up a riskless position in the option and the stock. Because the stock price and the option price both depend on the same underlying source of uncertainty, such a position can always be achieved. The position remains riskless for only a very short period of time. However, the return on a riskless position must always be the risk-free interest rate if there are to be no arbitrage opportunities. It is this fact that enables the option price to be valued in terms of the stock price. The original Black–Scholes equation gives the value of a European call or put option on a non-dividend-paying stock in terms of five variables: the stock price, the strike price, the risk-free interest rate, the volatility, and the time to expiration.

Surprisingly the expected return on the stock does not enter into the Black–Scholes equation. There is a general principle known as risk-neutral valuation, which states that any security dependent on other traded securities can be valued on the assumption that the world is risk neutral. The result proves to be very useful in practice. In a risk-neutral world the expected return from all securities is the risk-free interest rate, and the correct discount rate for expected cash flows is also the risk-free interest rate.

An implied volatility is the volatility that, when substituted into the Black–Scholes equation or its extensions, gives the market price of the option. Traders monitor implied volatilities and sometimes use the implied volatility from one stock option price to calculate the price of another option on the same stock. Empirical results show that the volatility of a stock is much higher when the exchange is open than when it is closed. This suggests that to some extent trading itself causes stock price volatility.

The Black–Scholes results can be extended to cover European call and put options on dividend-paying stocks. One procedure is to use the Black–Scholes formula with the stock price reduced by the present value of the dividends anticipated during the life of the option and the volatility equal to the volatility of the stock price net of the present value of these dividends. Fischer Black has suggested an approximate way of valuing American call options on a dividend-paying stock. His approach involves setting the price equal to the greater of two European option prices. The first European option expires at the same time as the American option; the second expires immediately prior to the final ex-dividend date.

FURTHER READING

On the Black–Scholes formula and its extensions

Black, F. "Fact and Fantasy in the Use of Options and Corporate Liabilities," *Financial Analysts Journal*, 31 (July/August 1975): 36–41, 61–72.

Black, F. "How We Came Up with the Option Pricing Formula," *Journal of Portfolio Management*, 15, 2 (1989): 4–8.

Black, F., and M. Scholes. "The Pricing of Options and Corporate Liabilities," *Journal of Political Economy*, 81 (May–June 1973): 637–59.

Hull, J. *Options, Futures, and Other Derivatives*. 5th edn. Upper Saddle River, NJ: Prentice Hall, 2003.

Merton, R. C. "Theory of Rational Option Pricing," *Bell Journal of Economics and Management Science*, 4 (Spring 1973): 141–83.

On the causes of volatility

Fama, E. E. "The Behavior of Stock Market Prices," *Journal of Business*, 38 (January 1965): 34–105.

French, K. R. "Stock Returns and the Weekend Effect," Journal of Financial Economics, 8 (March 1980): 55–69.

French, K. R., and R. Roll. "Stock Return Variances: The Arrival of Information and the Reaction of Traders," *Journal of Financial Economics*, 17 (September 1986): 5–26.

Roll, R. "Orange Juice and Weather," *American Economic Review*, 74, 5 (December 1984): 861–80.

Quiz (Answers at End of Book)

12.1. What does the Black–Scholes stock option pricing model assume about the probability distribution of the stock price in one year? What does it assume about the continuously compounded rate of return on the stock during the year?

12.2. The volatility of a stock price is 30% per annum. What is the standard deviation of the percentage price change in one trading day?

12.3. Explain how risk-neutral valuation could be used to derive the Black–Scholes formulas.

12.4. Calculate the price of a three-month European put option on a non-dividend-paying stock with a strike price of \$50 when the current stock price is \$50, the risk-free interest rate is 10% per annum, and the volatility is 30% per annum.

12.5. What difference does it make to your calculations in the previous question if a dividend of \$1.50 is expected in two months?

12.6. What is meant by implied volatility? How would you calculate the volatility implied by a European put option price?

12.7. What is Black's approximation for valuing an American call option on a dividend-paying stock?

Questions and Problems (Answers in Solutions Manual/Study Guide)

12.8. A stock price is currently \$40. Assume that the expected return from the stock is 15% and its volatility is 25%. What is the probability distribution for the rate of return (with continuous compounding) earned over a one-year period?

12.9. A stock price has an expected return of 16% and a volatility of 35%. The current price is \$38.

a. What is the probability that a European call option on the stock with an exercise price of \$40 and a maturity date in six months will be exercised?

b. What is the probability that a European put option on the stock with the same exercise price and maturity will be exercised?

12.10. Prove that, with the notation in the chapter, a 95% confidence interval for S_T is between

$$S_0 e^{(\mu-\sigma^2/2)T-1.96\sigma\sqrt{T}} \quad \text{and} \quad S_0 e^{(\mu-\sigma^2/2)T+1.96\sigma\sqrt{T}}$$

12.11. A portfolio manager announces that the average of the returns realized in each of the last 10 years is 20% per annum. In what respect is this statement misleading?

12.12. Assume that a non-dividend-paying stock has an expected return of μ and a volatility of σ. An innovative financial institution has just announced that it will trade a derivative that pays off a dollar amount equal to

$$\frac{1}{T}\ln\left(\frac{S_T}{S_0}\right)$$

at time T. The variables S_0 and S_T denote the values of the stock price at time zero and time T.

a. Describe the payoff from this derivative.

b. Use risk-neutral valuation to calculate the price of the derivative at time zero.

12.13. What is the price of a European call option on a non-dividend-paying stock when the stock price is \$52, the strike price is \$50, the risk-free interest rate is 12% per annum, the volatility is 30% per annum, and the time to maturity is three months?

12.14. What is the price of a European put option on a non-dividend-paying stock when the stock price is \$69, the strike price is \$70, the risk-free interest rate is 5% per annum, the volatility is 35% per annum, and the time to maturity is six months?

12.15. A call option on a non-dividend-paying stock has a market price of \$2.50. The stock price is \$15, the exercise price is \$13, the time to maturity is three months, and the risk-free interest rate is 5% per annum. What is the implied volatility?

12.16. Show that the Black–Scholes formula for a call option gives a price that tends to $\max(S_0 - K, 0)$ as $T \to 0$.

12.17. Explain carefully why Black's approach to evaluating an American call option on a dividend-paying stock may give an approximate answer even when only one dividend is anticipated. Does the answer given by Black's approach understate or overstate the true option value? Explain your answer.

12.18. Consider an American call option on a stock. The stock price is \$70, the time to maturity is eight months, the risk-free rate of interest is 10% per annum, the exercise price is \$65, and the volatility is 32%. A dividend of \$1 is expected after three months and again after six months. Use the results in the appendix to show that it can never be optimal to exercise the option on either of the two dividend dates. Use DerivaGem to calculate the price of the option.

12.19. A stock price is currently \$50 and the risk-free interest rate is 5%. Use the DerivaGem software to translate the following table of European call options on the stock into a table of implied volatilities, assuming no dividends. Are the option prices consistent with the assumptions underlying Black–Scholes?

	Maturity (months)		
Strike price (\$)	*3*	*6*	*12*
45	7.00	8.30	10.50
50	3.50	5.20	7.50
55	1.60	2.90	5.10

12.20. Show that the Black–Scholes formulas for call and put options satisfy put–call parity.

12.21. Show that the probability that a European call option will be exercised in a risk-neutral world is, with the notation introduced in this chapter, $N(d_2)$. What is an expression for the value of a derivative that pays off \$100 if the price of a stock at time T is greater than K?

Assignment Questions

12.22. A stock price is currently \$50. Assume that the expected return from the stock is 18% per annum and its volatility is 30% per annum. What is the probability distribution for the stock price in two years? Calculate the mean and standard deviation of the distribution. Determine the 95% confidence interval.

12.23. Suppose that observations on a stock price (in dollars) at the end of each of 15 consecutive weeks are as follows:

30.2, 32.0, 31.1, 30.1, 30.2, 30.3, 30.6, 33.0, 32.9, 33.0, 33.5, 33.5, 33.7, 33.5, 33.2

Estimate the stock price volatility. What is the standard error of your estimate?

12.24. A financial institution plans to offer a derivative that pays off a dollar amount equal to S_T^2 at time T, where S_T is the stock price at time T. Assume no dividends. Defining other variables as necessary use risk-neutral valuation to calculate the price of the derivative at time zero. (*Hint*: The expected value of S_T^2 can be calculated from the mean and variance of S_T given in Section 12.1.)

12.25. Consider an option on a non-dividend-paying stock when the stock price is \$30, the exercise price is \$29, the risk-free interest rate is 5% per annum, the volatility is 25% per annum, and the time to maturity is four months.
a. What is the price of the option if it is a European call?
b. What is the price of the option if it is an American call?
c. What is the price of the option if it is a European put?
d. Verify that put–call parity holds.

12.26. Assume that the stock in Problem 12.25 is due to go ex-dividend in 1.5 months. The expected dividend is 50 cents.
a. What is the price of the option if it is a European call?
b. What is the price of the option if it is a European put?
c. Use the results in the Appendix to this chapter to determine whether there are any circumstances under which the option is exercised early.

12.27. Consider an American call option when the stock price is \$18, the exercise price is \$20, the time to maturity is six months, the volatility is 30% per annum, and the risk-free interest rate is 10% per annum. Two equal dividends of 40 cents are expected during the life of the option, with ex-dividend dates at the end of two months and five months. Use Black's approximation and the DerivaGem software to value the option. Suppose now that the dividend is D on each ex-dividend date. Use the results in the Appendix to determine how high D can be without the American option being exercised early.

APPENDIX

The Early Exercise of American Call Options on Dividend-Paying Stocks

In Chapter 9, we saw that it is never optimal to exercise an American call option on a non-dividend-paying stock before the expiration date. A similar argument shows that the only times when a call option on a dividend-paying stock should be exercised are immediately before an ex-dividend date and on the expiration date. We assume that n ex-dividend dates are anticipated and that they are at times $t_1, t_2, \ldots, t_n$, with $t_1 < t_2 < \cdots < t_n$. The dividends will be denoted by $D_1, D_2, \ldots, D_n$, respectively.

We start by considering the possibility of early exercise immediately prior to the final ex-dividend date (i.e., at time t_n). If the option is exercised at time t_n, the investor receives

$$S(t_n) - K$$

where $S(t)$ denotes the stock price at time t.

If the option is not exercised, the stock price drops to $S(t_n) - D_n$. As shown in Chapter 9, a lower bound for the price of the option is then

$$S(t_n) - D_n - Ke^{-r(T-t_n)}$$

It follows that if

$$S(t_n) - D_n - Ke^{-r(T-t_n)} \geqslant S(t_n) - K$$

that is,

$$D_n \leqslant K(1 - e^{-r(T-t_n)}) \qquad \textbf{(12A.1)}$$

it cannot be optimal to exercise at time t_n. On the other hand, if

$$D_n > K(1 - e^{-r(T-t_n)}) \qquad \textbf{(12A.2)}$$

it can be shown that it is always optimal to exercise at time t_n for a sufficiently high value of $S(t_n)$. The inequality in equation (12A.2) is most likely to be satisfied when the final ex-dividend date is fairly close to the maturity of the option (i.e., when $T - t_n$ is small) and the dividend is large.

Consider next time t_{n-1}, the penultimate ex-dividend date. If the option is exercised immediately prior to time t_{n-1}, the investor receives

$$S(t_{n-1}) - K$$

If the option is not exercised at time t_{n-1}, the stock price drops to $S(t_{n-1}) - D_{n-1}$ and the earliest subsequent time at which exercise could take place is t_n. A lower bound to the option price if it is not exercised at time t_{n-1} is

$$S(t_{n-1}) - D_{n-1} - Ke^{-r(t_n-t_{n-1})}$$

It follows that if

$$S(t_{n-1}) - D_{n-1} - Ke^{-r(t_n-t_{n-1})} \geqslant S(t_{n-1}) - K$$

or

$$D_{n-1} \leqslant K(1 - e^{-r(t_n-t_{n-1})})$$

it is not optimal to exercise at time t_{n-1}. Similarly, for any $i < n$, if

$$D_i \leqslant K(1 - e^{-r(t_{i+1}-t_i)}) \tag{12A.3}$$

it is not optimal to exercise immediately prior to time t_i.

The inequality in equation (12A.3) is approximately equivalent to

$$D_i \leqslant Kr(t_{i+1} - t_i)$$

Assuming that K is fairly close to the current stock price, the dividend yield on the stock has to be either close to or above the risk-free rate of interest for the inequality not to be satisfied.

We can conclude from this analysis that, in many circumstances, the most likely time for the early exercise of an American call is the final ex-dividend date, t_n. Furthermore, if the inequality in equation (12A.3) holds for $i = 1, 2, \dots, n - 1$ and the inequality in equation (12A.1) also holds, then we can be certain that early exercise is never optimal.

Example

Consider the example that was used in this chapter to value European options on dividend-paying stocks: $S_0 = 40$, $K = 40$, $r = 0.09$, $\sigma = 0.30$, $t_1 = 0.1667$, $t_2 = 0.4167$, $T = 0.5$, $D_1 = D_2 = 0.5$. We suppose that the option is American rather than European. In this case,

$$K(1 - e^{-r(t_2-t_1)}) = 40(1 - e^{-0.09\times 0.25}) = 0.89$$

Because this is greater than 0.5, it follows from equation (12A.3) that the option should never be exercised on the first ex-dividend date. Also,

$$K(1 - e^{-r(T-t_2)}) = 40(1 - e^{-0.09\times 0.08333}) = 0.30$$

Because this is less than 0.5, it follows from equation (12A.1) that when the option is sufficiently deep in the money it should be exercised on the second ex-dividend date.

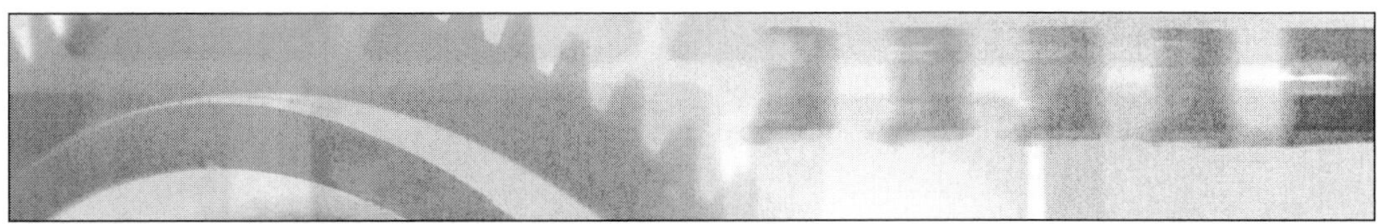

CHAPTER 13

Options on Stock Indices and Currencies

In this chapter we tackle the problem of valuing options on stock indices and currencies. As a first step, some of the results in Chapters 9, 11, and 12 are extended to cover European options on a stock paying a known dividend yield. It is then argued that both stock indices and currencies are analogous to stocks paying dividend yields. This enables the results for options on a stock paying a dividend yield to be applied to these types of options as well.

13.1 A SIMPLE RULE

In this section we produce a simple rule that enables results produced for European options on a non-dividend-paying stock to be extended so that they apply to European options on a stock paying a known dividend yield.

Dividends cause stock prices to reduce on the ex-dividend date by the amount of the dividend payment. The payment of a dividend yield at rate q therefore causes the growth rate in the stock price to be less than it would otherwise be by an amount q. If, with a dividend yield of q, the stock price grows from S_0 today to S_T at time T, then in the absence of dividends it would grow from S_0 today to $S_T e^{qT}$ at time T. Alternatively, in the absence of dividends it would grow from $S_0 e^{-qT}$ today to S_T at time T.

This argument shows that we get the same probability distribution for the stock price at time T in each of the following two cases:

1. The stock starts at price S_0 and provides a dividend yield at rate q.
2. The stock starts at price $S_0 e^{-qT}$ and pays no dividends.

This leads to a simple rule. When valuing a European option lasting for time T on a stock paying a known dividend yield at rate q, we reduce the current stock price from S_0 to $S_0 e^{-qT}$ and then value the option as though the stock pays no dividends.

Lower Bounds for Option Prices

As a first application of this rule, consider the problem of determining bounds for the price of a European option on a stock paying a dividend yield at rate q. Substituting

S_0e^{-qT} for S_0 in equation (9.1), we see that a lower bound for the European call option price, c, is given by

$$c \geqslant S_0e^{-qT} - Ke^{-rT} \tag{13.1}$$

We can also prove this directly by considering the following two portfolios:

Portfolio A: one European call option plus an amount of cash equal to Ke^{-rT}

Portfolio B: e^{-qT} shares with dividends being reinvested in additional shares

In portfolio A, the cash, if it is invested at the risk-free interest rate, will grow to K in time T. If $S_T > K$, the call option is exercised at time T and portfolio A is worth S_T. If $S_T < K$, the call option expires worthless, and the portfolio is worth K. Hence, at time T, portfolio A is worth

$$\max(S_T,\ K)$$

Because of the reinvestment of dividends, portfolio B becomes one share at time T. It is therefore worth S_T at this time. It follows that portfolio A is always worth as much as, and is sometimes worth more than, portfolio B at time T. In the absence of arbitrage opportunities, this must also be true today. Hence,

$$c + Ke^{-rT} \geqslant S_0e^{-qT}$$

or

$$c \geqslant S_0e^{-qT} - Ke^{-rT}$$

To obtain a lower bound for a European put option, we can similarly replace S_0 by S_0e^{-qT} in equation (9.2) to get

$$p \geqslant Ke^{-rT} - S_0e^{-qT} \tag{13.2}$$

This result can also be proved directly by considering the following portfolios:

Portfolio C: one European put option plus e^{-qT} shares with dividends on the shares being reinvested in additional shares

Portfolio D: an amount of cash equal to Ke^{-rT}

Put–Call Parity

Replacing S_0 by S_0e^{-qT} in equation (9.3) we obtain put–call parity for an option on a stock paying a dividend yield at rate q:

$$c + Ke^{-rT} = p + S_0e^{-qT} \tag{13.3}$$

This result can also be proved directly by considering the following two portfolios:

Portfolio A: one European call option plus an amount of cash equal to Ke^{-rT}

Portfolio C: one European put option plus e^{-qT} shares with dividends on the shares being reinvested in additional shares

Both portfolios are both worth $\max(S_T,\ K)$ at time T. They must therefore be worth the same today, and the put–call parity result in equation (13.3) follows. For American options, the put–call parity relationship is (see Problem 13.12)

$$S_0e^{-qT} - K \leqslant C - P \leqslant S_0 - Ke^{-rT}$$

13.2 PRICING FORMULAS

By replacing S_0 by S_0e^{-qT} in the Black–Scholes formulas, equations (12.5) and (12.6), we obtain the price, c, of a European call and the price, p, of a European put on a stock paying a dividend yield at rate q as

$$c = S_0e^{-qT}N(d_1) - Ke^{-rT}N(d_2) \tag{13.4}$$

$$p = Ke^{-rT}N(-d_2) - S_0e^{-qT}N(-d_1) \tag{13.5}$$

Since

$$\ln\frac{S_0e^{-qT}}{K} = \ln\frac{S_0}{K} - qT$$

it follows that d_1 and d_2 are given by

$$d_1 = \frac{\ln(S_0/K) + (r - q + \sigma^2/2)T}{\sigma\sqrt{T}}$$

$$d_2 = \frac{\ln(S_0/K) + (r - q - \sigma^2/2)T}{\sigma\sqrt{T}} = d_1 - \sigma\sqrt{T}$$

These results were first derived by Merton.[1] As discussed in Chapter 12, the word *dividend* should, for the purposes of option valuation, be defined as the reduction in the stock price on the ex-dividend date arising from any dividends declared. If the dividend yield rate is known but not constant during the life of the option, equations (13.4) and (13.5) are still true, with q equal to the average annualized dividend yield during the option's life.

13.3 BINOMIAL TREES

We now move on to examine, more formally than in Chapter 11, the effect of a dividend yield equal to q on binomial trees.

Consider the situation shown in Figure 13.1, in which a stock price starts at S_0 and moves either up to S_0u or down to S_0d. As in Chapter 11, we define p as the probability of an up movement in a risk-neutral world. The total return provided by the stock in a risk-neutral world must be the risk-free interest rate, r. The dividends provide a return equal to q. The return in the form of capital gains must therefore be $r - q$. This means that p must satisfy

$$pS_0u + (1 - p)S_0d = S_0e^{(r-q)T} \tag{13.6}$$

or

$$p = \frac{e^{(r-q)T} - d}{u - d} \tag{13.7}$$

This is consistent with the result in Section 11.8.

---

[1] See R.C. Merton, "Theory of Rational Option Pricing," *Bell Journal of Economics and Management Science*, 4 (Spring 1973): 141–83.

Figure 13.1 Stock price and option price in one-step binomial tree when stock pays a dividend at rate q

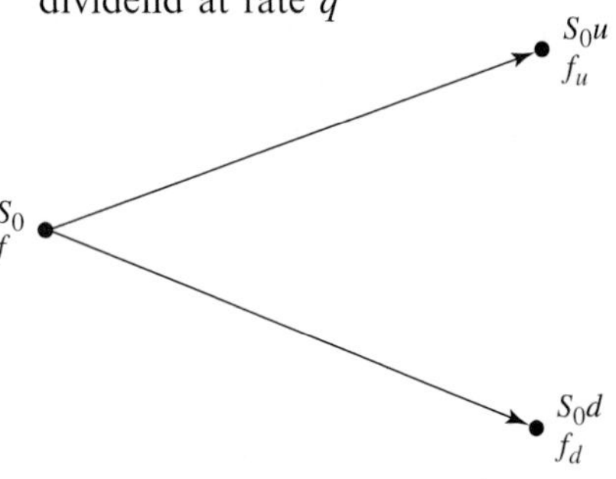

As explained in Chapter 11, the value of the derivative at time zero is the expected payoff in a risk-neutral world discounted at the risk-free rate:

$$f = e^{-rT}[pf_u + (1-p)f_d] \tag{13.8}$$

Example

Suppose that the initial stock price is \$30 and the stock price will either move up to \$36 or down to \$24 during a six-month period. The six-month risk-free interest rate is 5% and the stock is expected to provide a dividend yield of 3% during the six-month period. In this case, $u = 1.2$, $d = 0.8$, and

$$p = \frac{e^{(0.05-0.03)\times 6/12} - 0.8}{1.2 - 0.8} = 0.5251$$

Consider a six-month put option on the stock with a strike price of \$28. If the stock price moves up, the payoff is zero; if it moves down, the payoff is 4. The value of the option is therefore

$$e^{-0.05\times 0.5}[0.5251 \times 0 + 0.4749 \times 4] = 1.85$$

13.4 OPTIONS ON STOCK INDICES

As discussed in Chapter 8, several exchanges trade options on stock indices. Some of the indices track the movement of the market as a whole. Others are based on the performance of a particular sector (e.g., computer technology, oil and gas, transportation, or telecoms).

Quotes

Table 13.1 shows quotes for options on the Dow Jones Industrial Average (DJX) and S&P 500 (SPX) as they appeared in the Money and Investing section of the *Wall Street Journal* on Thursday February 5, 2004. The *Wall Street Journal* also shows quotes for options on a number of other indices including the Nasdaq 100 (NDX), Russell 2000 (RUT), and S&P 100 (OEX). All the options trade on the Chicago

Table 13.1 Quotes for stock index options from the *Wall Street Journal*, February 5, 2004

Wednesday, Feb. 4, 2004
Volume, last, net change and open interest for all contracts. Volume figures are unofficial. Open interest reflects previous trading day. p-Put c-Call. The totals for call and put volume are midday figures

CHICAGO

	STRIKE	VOL	LAST	NET CHG	OPEN INT
DJ INDUS AVG(DJX)					
Mar	90 p	5	0.15	−0.05	5,844
Mar	92 p	105	0.20	0.05	14,161
Apr	92 p	1	0.55	0.05	40
Mar	96 p	310	0.40	...	11,814
Feb	98 p	40	0.10	−0.05	7,602
Mar	98 p	775	0.60	0.05	4,211
Feb	99 c	10	5.90	0.10	328
Feb	99 p	200	0.15	...	2,190
Apr	99 p	3	1.35	0.05	606
Feb	100 p	179	0.20	...	6,935
Mar	100 p	3	0.90	0.05	21,574
Apr	100 p	3	1.35	−0.05	2,248
Mar	101 c	10	4.80	−0.70	3,075
Mar	101 p	3	1	−0.10	4,772
Feb	102 p	151	0.40	−0.10	2,925
Apr	102 p	2,133	2	0.15	2,206
Feb	104 c	40	1.75	−0.05	5,265
Feb	104 p	422	1.05	0.15	7,282
Mar	104 c	378	2.50	−0.30	11,255
Mar	104 p	458	2.10	0.20	12,458
Apr	104 p	5	2.85	0.10	1,799
Feb	105 c	2,068	1.05	−0.15	13,467
Feb	105 p	2,335	1.50	0.20	15,555
Mar	105 c	646	1.90	−0.15	39,444
Mar	105 p	122	2.35	0.05	21,489
Apr	105 c	200	2.75	0.05	1,914
Apr	105 p	102	3	...	895
Feb	106 c	1,071	0.65	−0.10	4,647
Feb	106 p	65	2.10	0.15	3,485
Mar	106 p	30	3	0.25	5,426
Apr	106 p	5	3.80	0.20	1,547
Feb	107 c	118	0.35	−0.10	4,414
Mar	107 p	2	3.50	...	125
Apr	107 c	10	1.50	−0.75	617
Apr	107 p	5	4.30	0.20	742
Feb	108 c	6	0.20	−0.10	3,305
Feb	108 p	2	3.90	0.40	2,585
Mar	108 c	182	0.85	...	11,472
Mar	108 p	41	4	...	614
Apr	108 p	40	5	0.20	88
Feb	112 p	23	7.30	0.10	435
Call Vol.		8,251	Open Int.		313,904
Put Vol.		14,484	Open Int.		370,073
S & P 500(SPX)					
Feb	850 p	10	0.05	...	1,434
Mar	850 p	430	0.40	0.10	29,388
Apr	850 p	10	1.05	...	311
Feb	875 p	5	0.05	...	613
Apr	875 p	5	1.65	0.20	16
Mar	900 p	5	0.80	...	37,089
Apr	900 p	85	1.90	−0.15	2
Feb	925 c	140	199.50	2.50	690
Feb	925 p	4	0.10	−0.05	3,579
Mar	925 p	96	1.05	0.05	14,592
Feb	950 p	200	0.40	0.30	17,129
Feb	975 p	2,090	0.25	0.10	18,301
Mar	975 c	10	155	6.50	9,718
Mar	975 p	360	2.05	0.05	40,001
Apr	975 p	26	5.20	1.20	2,027
Feb	995 p	23	0.30	...	13,445
Mar	995 p	2,004	2.70	0.10	27,317
Apr	995 p	4	5.70	...	2,658
Feb	1005 p	256	0.35	0.05	36,093
Mar	1005 c	11	125	−12.50	2,370
Mar	1005 p	1,173	2.90	−0.10	25,947
Feb	1025 c	10	100.50	−9.50	5,757
Feb	1025 p	6,227	0.60	0.05	45,995
Mar	1025 p	515	4.60	0.50	55,930
Apr	1025 p	225	9	1.00	5,171
Feb	1035 p	306	0.70	...	2,864
Feb	1040 p	10	1	0.25	4,270
Feb	1050 c	1,789	76.30	−15.20	9,986
Feb	1050 p	1,929	1.10	...	42,107
Mar	1050 c	10	84	−5.80	19,676
Mar	1050 p	36	6.90	0.90	48,190
Feb	1055 p	130	1.40	0.10	3,134
Mar	1060 c	1	73	−6.50	3,391
Mar	1060 p	2,305	8.10	1.30	7,272
Mar	1070 p	600	9	0.90	7,919
Feb	1075 c	27	57.80	−3.70	11,711
Feb	1075 p	11,023	2.70	0.60	28,638
Mar	1075 c	16	64.50	−3.50	33,222
Mar	1075 p	519	10.40	1.80	38,840
Apr	1075 p	185	16.40	1.30	1,138
Feb	1085 c	4	48.80	−0.20	204
Feb	1085 p	583	3.70	1.00	6,492
Mar	1085 p	305	12	2.50	5,608
Feb	1090 c	30	43.60	−5.40	319
Feb	1090 p	85	4	0.70	5,371
Feb	1100 c	447	31.30	−8.10	21,191
Feb	1100 p	2,617	6.40	2.10	32,392
Mar	1100 c	33	40.50	−6.50	40,878
Mar	1100 p	4,203	15.80	1.80	44,776
Apr	1100 c	32	50	−4.50	462
Apr	1100 p	8,895	24	4.00	9,380
Feb	1105 p	124	7.20	1.70	1,734
Feb	1110 c	6	26.50	−5.50	13
Feb	1110 p	3,828	8.50	2.20	6,048
Mar	1110 c	11	34.40	−9.80	20,786
Mar	1110 p	688	18.10	2.10	18,829
Feb	1115 c	4	20.60	−5.20	973
Feb	1115 p	115	10.30	3.10	9,530
Feb	1120 c	93	18	−6.00	152
Feb	1120 p	255	12.10	3.50	6,774
Feb	1125 c	1,803	14	−7.00	19,486
Feb	1125 p	1,570	14.50	4.50	32,185
Mar	1125 c	4,980	24.70	−4.90	80,288
Mar	1125 p	4,764	25	4.00	78,162
Apr	1125 c	36	32.90	−4.80	2,641
Apr	1125 p	327	32	3.20	2,931
Feb	1130 c	1,156	11.30	−5.20	4,741
Feb	1130 p	2,693	16.60	4.20	11,001
Mar	1130 c	2,829	21.50	−5.00	12,667
Mar	1130 p	2,864	27	3.80	13,475
Feb	1135 c	322	9	−4.50	1,262
Feb	1135 p	396	19.90	5.60	2,600
Mar	1135 c	413	19.90	−4.10	9,978
Mar	1135 p	851	30	5.00	9,651
Feb	1140 c	1,779	7	−5.00	6,401
Feb	1140 p	948	22	5.50	8,040
Mar	1140 c	1,401	18	−3.00	3,698
Mar	1140 p	1	30	2.00	2,151
Feb	1145 c	52	6.60	−2.90	944
Feb	1145 p	47	26	5.00	1,584
Feb	1150 c	3,479	4.20	−3.30	26,943
Feb	1150 p	943	28.70	6.20	6,483
Mar	1150 c	520	13	−3.70	35,491
Mar	1150 p	52	38	5.00	23,226
Apr	1150 c	23	20.60	−3.40	2,122
Feb	1155 c	179	3.80	−2.00	1,557
Feb	1160 c	1,351	2.55	−1.85	6,062
Feb	1160 p	126	37	7.80	1,159
Mar	1160 c	402	10	−2.90	2,098
Maf	1160 p	1	45	1.00	14
Feb	1170 c	3,054	1.50	−0.90	6,733
Feb	1170 p	13	42.80	3.80	261
Feb	1175 c	1,617	1.15	−0.85	28,065
Feb	1175 p	55	49	6.00	2,196
Mar	1175 c	614	6	−2.00	26,761
Mar	1175 p	3	57.10	8.10	2,304
Apr	1175 c	558	12.20	−1.50	2,095
Feb	1180 c	420	0.80	−0.55	1,543
Feb	1185 c	7	0.85	−0.25	731
Feb	1190 c	86	0.50	−0.35	2,597
Mar	1190 c	104	4.70	...	...
Feb	1200 c	1,259	0.35	−0.20	22,677
Feb	1200 p	16	70.70	5.70	315
Mar	1200 c	1,965	3	−0.50	23,307
Mar	1200 p	1	73.40	4.90	463
Apr	1200 c	25	7	−0.60	3,481
Feb	1210 c	10	0.25	−0.10	1,424
Feb	1215 c	13	0.25	−0.15	963
Feb	1225 c	72	0.10	−0.10	5,124
Mar	1225 c	1	1.20	−0.30	3,018
Mar	1225 p	2	96.90	−4.60	11
Apr	1225 c	20	3.20	−0.50	2,845
Feb	1250 c	55	0.05	−0.10	8,403
Mar	1250 c	14	0.55	−0.05	11,441
Mar	1250 p	30	120	0.50	515
Apr	1250 c	3	1.50	−0.40	410
Call Vol.		37,739	Open Int.		1,200,003
Put Vol.		85,508	Open Int.		1,976,864
LEAPS-LONG TERM					
DJ INDUS AVG - CB					
Dec 05	76 p	10	2	...	...
Dec 05	104 c	1	9.20	0.40	11,701
Dec 05	108 c	500	6.90	0.40	82
Dec 05	108 p	500	10	1.00	20
Call Vol.		501	Open Int.		13,617
Put Vol.		510	Open Int.		12,357
S & P 500 - CB					
Dec 04	80 c	60	33.10	...	7,895
Dec 05	80 p	10	1.75	0.05	12,238
Dec 04	90 p	132	1.60	0.20	38,870
Dec 05	90 c	61	26	...	24,696
Dec 05	90 p	3	3.50	0.50	18,418
Dec 04	95 p	10	2.20	0.05	5,595
Dec 04	100 p	87	3.10	0.15	25,728
Dec 05	100 p	10	5	0.30	28,972
Dec 04	105 p	8	4.30	0.10	2,324
Dec 04	110 p	12	5.60	0.60	25,390
Dec 06	110 c	11	14.70	−1.00	4,328
Dec 06	110 p	10	9.10	0.70	33,811
Dec 04	120 c	4	3.40	−0.20	9,911
Call Vol.		136	Open Int.		480,710
Put Vol.		282	Open.Int.		435,054

Source: Reprinted by permission of Dow Jones, Inc., via Copyright Clearance Center, Inc.

Board Options Exchange and all are European, except the contract on the S&P 100, which is American. The quotes refer to the price at which the last trade was made on Wednesday, February 4, 2004. The closing prices of the DJX and SPX on February 4, 2004, were 104.71 and 1,126.52, respectively.

One index option contract is on 100 times the index. (Note that the Dow Jones index used for index options is 0.01 times the usually quoted Dow Jones index.) Index options are settled in cash. This means that, on exercise of the option, the holder of a call option contract receives $(S - K) \times 100$ in cash and the writer of the option pays this amount in cash, where S is the value of the index at the close of trading on the day of the exercise and K is the strike price. Similarly, the holder of a put option contract receives $(K - S) \times 100$ in cash and the writer of the option pays this amount in cash.

Table 13.1 shows that, in addition to relatively short-dated options, the exchanges trade longer-maturity contracts known as LEAPS. The acronym LEAPS stands for Long-term Equity AnticiPation Securities and was originated by the CBOE. LEAPS are exchange-traded options that last up to three years. The index is divided by five for the purposes of quoting the strike price and the option price. One contract is an option on 100 times one-fifth of the index (or 20 times the index). LEAPS on indices have expiration dates in December. As mentioned in Chapter 8, the CBOE and several other exchanges also trade LEAPS on many individual stocks. These have expirations in January.

The CBOE also trades *flex options* on indices. As mentioned in Chapter 8, these are options where the trader can choose the expiration date, the strike price, and whether the option is American or European.

Valuation

In valuing index futures in Chapter 5, we assumed that the index could be treated as a security paying a known dividend yield. In valuing index options, we make similar assumptions. This means that equations (13.1) and (13.2) provide a lower bound for European index options; equation (13.3) is the put–call parity result for European index options; and equations (13.4) and (13.5) can be used to value European options on an index. In all cases, S_0 is equal to the value of the index, σ is equal to the volatility of the index, and q is equal to the average annualized dividend yield on the index during the life of the option. The calculation of q should include only dividends whose ex-dividend date occurs during the life of the option.

In the United States ex-dividend dates tend to occur during the first week of February, May, August, and November. At any given time the correct value of q is therefore likely to depend on the life of the option. This is even more true for some foreign indices. In Japan, for example, all companies tend to use the same ex-dividend dates.

Example

Consider a European call option on the S&P 500 that is two months from maturity. The current value of the index is 930, the exercise price is 900, the risk-free interest rate is 8% per annum, and the volatility of the index is 20% per annum. Dividend yields of 0.2% and 0.3% are expected in the first month and the second month, respectively. In this case $S_0 = 930$, $K = 900$, $r = 0.08$, $\sigma = 0.2$, and $T = 2/12$. The total dividend yield during the option's life is $0.2 + 0.3 = 0.5\%$. This is 3% per annum. Hence, $q = 0.03$ and

$$d_1 = \frac{\ln(930/900) + (0.08 - 0.03 + 0.2^2/2) \times 2/12}{0.2\sqrt{2/12}} = 0.5444$$

$$d_2 = \frac{\ln(930/900) + (0.08 - 0.03 - 0.2^2/2) \times 2/12}{0.2\sqrt{2/12}} = 0.4628$$

$$N(d_1) = 0.7069, \qquad N(d_2) = 0.6782$$

so that the call price, c, is given by equation (13.4) as

$$c = 930 \times 0.7069e^{-0.03\times 2/12} - 900 \times 0.6782e^{-0.08\times 2/12} = 51.83$$

One contract would cost \$5,183.

If the absolute amount of the dividend that will be paid on the stocks underlying the index (rather than the dividend yield) is assumed to be known, the basic Black–Scholes formula can be used with the initial stock price being reduced by the present value of the dividends. This is the approach recommended in Chapter 12 for a stock paying known dividends. However, it may be difficult to implement for a broadly based stock index because it requires a knowledge of the dividends expected on every stock underlying the index.

In some circumstances it is optimal to exercise American put and call options on an index prior to the expiration date. The binomial tree methodology can be used to value American-style index options. This will be discussed further in Chapter 16.

Portfolio Insurance

Portfolio managers can use index options to limit their downside risk. Suppose that the value of an index today is S_0. Consider a manager in charge of a well-diversified portfolio whose beta is 1.0. A beta of 1.0 implies that the returns from the portfolio mirror those from the index. Assuming the dividend yield from the portfolio is the same as the dividend yield from the index, the percentage changes in the value of the portfolio can be expected to be approximately the same as the percentage changes in the value of the index. Each contract on the S&P 500 is on 100 times the index. It follows that the value of the portfolio is protected against the possibility of the index falling below K if, for each $100S_0$ dollars in the portfolio, the manager buys one put option contract with strike price K. Suppose that the manager's portfolio is worth \$500,000 and the value of the index is 1,000. The portfolio is worth 500 times the index. The manager can obtain insurance against the value of the portfolio dropping below \$450,000 in the next three months by buying five put option contracts with a strike price of 900. Suppose that the risk-free rate is 12%, the dividend yield on the index is 4%, and the volatility of the index is 22%. The parameters of the option are as follows:

$$S = 1000, \quad K = 900, \quad r = 0.12, \quad \sigma = 0.22, \quad T = 0.25, \quad q = 0.04$$

From equation (13.5), the value of the option is \$6.48. The cost of the insurance is therefore $5 \times 100 \times 6.48 = \$3{,}240$.

To illustrate how the insurance works, consider the situation where the index drops to 880 in three months. The portfolio will be worth about \$440,000. The payoff from the options will be $5 \times (900 - 880) \times 100 = \$10{,}000$, bringing the total value of the portfolio up to the insured value of \$450,000 (or \$446,760 when the cost of the options are taken into account). This example is summarized in Trading Note 13.1.

It is sometimes argued that the return from stocks is certain to beat the return from bonds in the long run. If this were true, long-dated portfolio insurance would not cost very much. However, Business Snapshot 13.1 shows that it can be quite expensive.

When the Portfolio's Beta Is Not 1.0

If the portfolio's returns are not expected to equal those of an index, the capital asset pricing model can be used. This model asserts that the expected excess return of a portfolio over the risk-free interest rate equals beta times the excess return of a market index over the risk-free interest rate. Suppose that the \$500,000 portfolio just considered has a beta of 2.0 instead of 1.0. As before, we assume that the S&P 500 index is

Trading Note 13.1 Protecting the value of a portfolio that mirrors the S&P 500

A manager in charge of a portfolio worth \$500,000 is concerned that the market might decline rapidly during the next three months and would like to use index options as a hedge against the portfolio declining below \$450,000. The portfolio is expected to mirror closely the S&P 500, which is currently standing at 1,000.

The Strategy
The manager buys five put option contracts with a strike price of 900 on the S&P 500 for a total cost of \$3,240.

The Result
The index dropped to 880.
The value of the portfolio dropped to \$440,000.
There was a payoff of \$10,000 from the five put option contracts.

currently 1,000, the risk-free rate is 12% and the dividend yield on the index is 4%. Table 13.2 shows the expected relationship between the level of the index and the value of the portfolio in three months. To illustrate the sequence of calculations necessary to derive Table 13.2, Table 13.3 shows the calculations for the case when the value of the index in three months proves to be 1,040.

Suppose that S_0 is the value of the index. It can be shown that, for each $100S_0$ dollars in the portfolio, a total of beta put contracts should be purchased. The strike price should be the value that the index is expected to have when the value of the portfolio reaches the insured value. Assume that the required insured value is \$450,000, as in the beta = 1.0 case. Table 13.2 shows that the appropriate strike price for the put options purchased is 960. The option parameters are

$$S = 1000, \quad K = 960, \quad r = 0.12, \quad \sigma = 0.22, \quad T = 0.25, \quad q = 0.04$$

and equation (13.5) gives the value of the option as \$19.21. In this case $100S_0 = \$100,000$ and beta = 2.0, so that two put contracts are required for each \$100,000 in the portfolio. Because the portfolio is worth \$500,000, a total of 10 contracts should be purchased. The total cost of the insurance is therefore $10 \times 100 \times 19.21 = \$19,210$.

Table 13.2 Relationship between value of index and value of portfolio for Beta = 2.0

Value of index in three months	*Value of portfolio in three months (\$)*
1,080	570,000
1,040	530,000
1,000	490,000
960	450,000
920	410,000
880	370,000

Business Snapshot 13.1 Can we guarantee that stocks will beat bonds in the long run?

It is often said that if you are a long-term investor you should buy stocks rather than bonds. Consider a U.S. fund manager who is trying to persuade investors to buy, as a long-term investment, an equity fund that is expected to mirror the S&P 500. The manager might be tempted to offer purchasers of the fund a guarantee that their return will be at least as good as the return on risk-free bonds over the next 10 years. Historically stocks have outperformed bonds in the United States over almost any 10-year period. It appears that the fund manager would not be giving much away.

In fact, this type of guarantee is surprisingly expensive. Suppose that an equity index is 1,000 today, the dividend yield on the index is 1% per annum, the volatility of the index is 15% per annum, and the 10-year risk-free rate is 5% per annum. To outperform bonds, the stocks underlying the index must earn more than 5% per annum. The dividend yield will provide 1% per annum. The capital gains on the stocks must therefore provide 4% per annum. This means that we require the index level to be at least $1{,}000e^{0.04\times 10} = 1{,}492$ in 10 years.

A guarantee that the return on $1,000 invested in the S&P 500 will be greater than the return on $1,000 invested in bonds over the over the next 10 years is therefore equivalent to the right to sell the index for 1,492 in 10 years. This is a European put option on the index and can be valued from equation (13.5) with $S_0 = 1{,}000$, $K = 1{,}492$, $r = 5\%$, $\sigma = 15\%$, $T = 10$, and $q = 1\%$. The value of the put option is 169.7. This shows that the guarantee contemplated by the fund manager is worth about 17% of the fund—hardly something that should be given away!

Table 13.3 Calculations for Table 13.2 when the value of the index is 1,040 in three months

Value of index in three months:	1,040
Return from change in index:	40/1,000, or 4% per three months
Dividends from index:	$0.25 \times 4 = 1\%$ per three months
Total return from index:	$4 + 1 = 5\%$ per three months
Risk-free interest rate:	$0.25 \times 12 = 3\%$ per three months
Excess return from index over risk-free interest rate:	$5 - 3 = 2\%$ per three months
Excess return from portfolio over risk-free interest rate:	$2 \times 2 = 4\%$ per three months
Return from portfolio:	$3 + 4 = 7\%$ per three months
Dividends from portfolio:	$0.25 \times 4 = 1\%$ per three months
Increase in value of portfolio:	$7 - 1 = 6\%$ per three months
Value of portfolio:	$\$500{,}000 \times 1.06 = \$530{,}000$

Trading Note 13.2 Protecting the value of a portfolio that has a beta of 2.0

A manager in charge of a portfolio worth \$500,000 is concerned that the market might decline rapidly during the next three months and would like to use index options as a hedge against the value of the portfolio declining below \$450,000. The portfolio has a beta of 2.0 and the S&P 500 is standing at 1000.

The Strategy
The manager buys 10 put option contracts with a strike price of 960 for a total cost of \$19,210.

The Outcome
The index dropped to 880.
The value of the portfolio dropped to \$370,000.
There was a payoff of \$80,000 from the five put option contracts

To illustrate that the required result is obtained, consider what happens if the value of the index falls to 880. As shown in Table 13.2, the value of the portfolio is then about \$370,000. The put options pay off $(960 - 880) \times 10 \times 100 =$ \$80,000, and this is exactly what is necessary to move the total value of the portfolio manager's position up from \$370,000 to the required level of \$450,000. (After the cost of the options are taken into account, the value of the portfolio is \$430,790.) This example is summarized in Trading Note 13.2.

Comparing Trading Notes 13.1 and 13.2, we see that there are two reasons why the cost of hedging increases as the beta of a portfolio increases. More put options are required and they have a higher strike price.

13.5 CURRENCY OPTIONS

Currency options are primarily traded in the over-the-counter market. The advantage of this market is that large trades are possible, with strike prices, expiration dates, and other features tailored to meet the needs of corporate treasurers. Although European and American currency options do trade on the Philadelphia Stock Exchange in the United States, the exchange-traded market for these options is much smaller than the over-the-counter market.

For a corporation wishing to hedge a foreign exchange exposure, foreign currency options are an interesting alternative to forward contracts. A company due to receive sterling at a known time in the future can hedge its risk by buying put options on sterling that mature at that time. The strategy guarantees that the value of the sterling will not be less than the strike price, while allowing the company to benefit from any favorable exchange-rate movements. Similarly, a company due to pay sterling at a known time in the future can hedge by buying calls on sterling that mature at that time. The approach guarantees that the cost of the sterling will not be greater than a certain amount while allowing the company to benefit from favorable exchange-rate movements. Whereas a forward contract locks in the exchange rate for a future transaction, an option provides a type of insurance. This insurance is not free. It costs nothing to enter into a forward transaction, whereas options require a premium to be paid up front.

Valuation

To value currency options, we define S_0 as the spot exchange rate. To be precise, S_0 is the value of one unit of the foreign currency in U.S. dollars. As explained in Chapter 5, a foreign currency is analogous to a stock paying a known dividend yield. The owner of foreign currency receives a yield equal to the risk-free interest rate, r_f, in the foreign currency. Equations (13.1) and (13.2), with q replaced by r_f, provide bounds for the European call price, c, and the European put price, p:

$$c \geqslant S_0 e^{-r_f T} - K e^{-rT}$$

$$p \geqslant K e^{-rT} - S_0 e^{-r_f T}$$

Equation (13.3), with q replaced by r_f, provides the put–call parity result for currency options:

$$c + K e^{-rT} = p + S_0 e^{-r_f T}$$

Finally, equations (13.4) and (13.5) provide the pricing formulas for currency options when q is replaced by r_f:

$$c = S_0 e^{-r_f T} N(d_1) - K e^{-rT} N(d_2) \tag{13.9}$$

$$p = K e^{-rT} N(-d_2) - S_0 e^{-r_f T} N(-d_1) \tag{13.10}$$

where

$$d_1 = \frac{\ln(S_0/K) + (r - r_f + \sigma^2/2)T}{\sigma\sqrt{T}}$$

$$d_2 = \frac{\ln(S_0/K) + (r - r_f - \sigma^2/2)T}{\sigma\sqrt{T}} = d_1 - \sigma\sqrt{T}$$

Both the domestic interest rate, r, and the foreign interest rate, r_f, are the rates for a maturity T. Put and call options on a currency are symmetrical in that a put option to sell currency A for currency B at an exercise price K is the same as a call option to buy B with A at $1/K$.

Example

Consider a four-month European call option on the British pound. Suppose that the current exchange rate is 1.6000, the exercise price is 1.6000, the risk-free interest rate in the United States is 8% per annum, the risk-free interest rate in Britain is 11% per annum, and the option price is 4.3 cents. In this case, $S_0 = 1.6$, $K = 1.6$, $r = 0.08$, $r_f = 0.11$, $T = 0.3333$, and $c = 0.043$. The implied volatility can be calculated by trial and error. A volatility of 20% gives an option price of 0.0639; a volatility of 10% gives an option price of 0.0285; and so on. The implied volatility is 14.1%.

From equation (5.9), the forward rate, F_0, for a maturity T is given by

$$F_0 = S_0 e^{(r - r_f)T}$$

This relationship allows equations (13.9) and (13.10) to be simplified to

$$c = e^{-rT}[F_0N(d_1) - KN(d_2)] \tag{13.11}$$

$$p = e^{-rT}[KN(-d_2) - F_0N(-d_1)] \tag{13.12}$$

where

$$d_1 = \frac{\ln(F_0/K) + \sigma^2T/2}{\sigma\sqrt{T}}$$

$$d_2 = \frac{\ln(F_0/K) - \sigma^2T/2}{\sigma\sqrt{T}} = d_1 - \sigma\sqrt{T}$$

Note that, for equations (13.11) and (13.12) to be the correct equations for valuing a European option on the spot foreign exchange rate, the maturities of the forward contract and the option must be the same.

In some circumstances it is optimal to exercise American currency options prior to maturity. Thus, American currency options are worth more than their European counterparts. In general, call options on high-interest currencies and put options on low-interest currencies are the most likely to be exercised prior to maturity. The reason is that a high-interest currency is expected to depreciate and a low-interest currency is expected to appreciate.

SUMMARY

The Black–Scholes formula for valuing European options on a non-dividend-paying stock can be extended to cover European options on a stock paying a known dividend yield. This is useful because a number of other assets on which options are written can be considered to be analogous to a stock paying a dividend yield. This chapter has used the following results:

1. A stock index is analogous to a stock paying a dividend yield. The dividend yield is the dividend yield on the stocks that make up the index.
2. A foreign currency is analogous to a stock paying a dividend yield. The foreign risk-free interest rate plays the role of the dividend yield.

The extension to Black–Scholes can therefore be used to value European options on stock indices and foreign currencies.

Index options are settled in cash. On exercise of an index call option, the holder receives 100 times the amount by which the index exceeds the strike price. Similarly, on exercise of an index put option contract, the holder receives 100 times the amount by which the strike price exceeds the index. Index options can be used for portfolio insurance. If the value of the portfolio mirrors the index, it is appropriate to buy one put option contract for each $100S_0$ dollars in the portfolio, where S_0 is the value of the index. If the portfolio does not mirror the index, β put option contracts should be purchased for each $100S_0$ dollars in the portfolio, where β is the beta of the portfolio calculated using the capital asset pricing model. The strike price of the put options purchased should reflect the level of insurance required.

Currency options are traded both on organized exchanges and over the counter. They can be used by corporate treasurers to hedge foreign exchange exposure. For example, a U.S. corporate treasurer who knows that the company will be receiving sterling at a certain time in the future can hedge by buying put options that mature at that time. Similarly, a U.S. corporate treasurer who knows that the company will be paying sterling at a certain time in the future can hedge by buying call options that mature at that time.

FURTHER READING

Amin, K., and R. A. Jarrow. "Pricing Foreign Currency Options under Stochastic Interest Rates," *Journal of International Money and Finance*, 10 (1991): 310–29.

Biger, N., and J. C. Hull. "The Valuation of Currency Options," *Financial Management*, 12 (Spring 1983): 24–28.

Bodie, Z. "On the Risk of Stocks in the Long Run," *Financial Analysts Journal*, 51, 3 (1995): 18–22.

Garman, M. B., and S. W. Kohlhagen. "Foreign Currency Option Values," *Journal of International Money and Finance*, 2 (December 1983): 231–37.

Giddy, I. H., and G. Dufey. "Uses and Abuses of Currency Options," *Journal of Applied Corporate Finance*, 8, 3 (1995): 49–57.

Grabbe, J. O. "The Pricing of Call and Put Options on Foreign Exchange," *Journal of International Money and Finance*, 2 (December 1983): 239–53.

Jorion, P. "Predicting Volatility in the Foreign Exchange Market," *Journal of Finance* 50, 2(1995): 507–28.

Merton, R. C. "Theory of Rational Option Pricing," *Bell Journal of Economics and Management Science*, 4 (Spring 1973): 141–83.

Quiz (Answers at End of Book)

13.1. A portfolio is currently worth $10 million and has a beta of 1.0. The S&P 100 is currently standing at 800. Explain how a put option on the S&P 100 with a strike price of 700 can be used to provide portfolio insurance.

13.2. "Once we know how to value options on a stock paying a dividend yield, we know how to value options on stock indices and currencies." Explain this statement.

13.3. A stock index is currently 300, the dividend yield on the index is 3% per annum, and the risk-free interest rate is 8% per annum. What is a lower bound for the price of a six-month European call option on the index when the strike price is 290?

13.4. A currency is currently worth $0.80. Over each of the next two months it is expected to increase or decrease in value by 2%. The domestic and foreign risk-free interest rates are 6% and 8%, respectively. What is the value of a two-month European call option with a strike price of $0.80?

13.5. Explain how corporations can use currency options to hedge their foreign exchange risk.

13.6. Calculate the value of a three-month at-the-money European call option on a stock index when the index is at 250, the risk-free interest rate is 10% per annum, the volatility of the index is 18% per annum, and the dividend yield on the index is 3% per annum.

13.7. Calculate the value of an eight-month European put option on a currency with a strike price of 0.50. The current exchange rate is 0.52, the volatility of the exchange rate is 12%, the domestic risk-free interest rate is 4% per annum, and the foreign risk-free interest rate is 8% per annum.

Questions and Problems (Answers in Solutions Manual/Study Guide)

13.8. Suppose that an exchange constructs a stock index that tracks the return, including dividends, on a certain portfolio. Explain how you would value (a) futures contracts and (b) European options on the index.

13.9. A foreign currency is currently worth \$1.50. The domestic and foreign risk-free interest rates are 5% and 9%, respectively. Calculate a lower bound for the value of a six-month call option on the currency with a strike price of \$1.40 if it is (a) European and (b) American.

13.10. Consider a stock index currently standing at 250. The dividend yield on the index is 4% per annum, and the risk-free rate is 6% per annum. A three-month European call option on the index with a strike price of 245 is currently worth \$10. What is the value of a three-month put option on the index with a strike price of 245?

13.11. An index currently stands at 696 and has a volatility of 30% per annum. The risk-free rate of interest is 7% per annum and the index provides a dividend yield of 4% per annum. Calculate the value of a three-month European put with an exercise price of 700.

13.12. Show that, if C is the price of an American call with exercise price K and maturity T on a stock paying a dividend yield of q, and P is the price of an American put on the same stock with the same strike price and exercise date, then

$$S_0e^{-qT} - K < C - P < S_0 - Ke^{-rT},$$

where S_0 is the stock price, r is the risk-free rate, and $r > 0$. (*Hint*: To obtain the first half of the inequality, consider possible values of:

Portfolio A: a European call option plus an amount K invested at the risk-free rate
Portfolio B: an American put option plus e^{-qT} of stock with dividends being reinvested in the stock

To obtain the second half of the inequality, consider possible values of:

Portfolio C: an American call option plus an amount Ke^{-rT} invested at the risk-free rate
Portfolio D: a European put option plus one stock with dividends being reinvested in the stock.)

13.13. Show that a call option on a currency has the same price as the corresponding put option on the currency when the forward price equals the strike price.

13.14. Would you expect the volatility of a stock index to be greater or less than the volatility of a typical stock? Explain your answer.

13.15. Does the cost of portfolio insurance increase or decrease as the beta of a portfolio increases? Explain your answer.

13.16. Suppose that a portfolio is worth \$60 million and the S&P 500 is at 1200. If the value of the portfolio mirrors the value of the index, what options should be purchased to provide protection against the value of the portfolio falling below \$54 million in one year's time?

13.17. Consider again the situation in Problem 13.16. Suppose that the portfolio has a beta of 2.0, the risk-free interest rate is 5% per annum, and the dividend yield on both the portfolio and the index is 3% per annum. What options should be purchased to provide protection against the value of the portfolio falling below $54 million in one year's time?

Assignment Questions

13.18. Use the DerivaGem software to calculate implied volatilities for the March 104 call and the March 104 put on the Dow Jones Industrial Average (DJX) in Table 13.1. The value of the DJX on February 4, 2004, was 104.71. Assume that the risk-free interest rate was 1.2% and the dividend yield was 3.5%. The options expire on March 20, 2004. Are the quotes for the two options consistent with put–call parity?

13.19. A stock index currently stands at 300. It is expected to increase or decrease by 10% over each of the next two time periods of three months. The risk-free interest rate is 8% and the dividend yield on the index is 3%. What is the value of a six-month put option on the index with a strike price of 300 if it is (a) European and (b) American?

13.20. Suppose that the spot price of the Canadian dollar is U.S. $0.75 and that the Canadian dollar/U.S. dollar exchange rate has a volatility of 4% per annum. The risk-free rates of interest in Canada and the United States are 9% and 7% per annum, respectively. Calculate the value of a European call option to buy one Canadian dollar for U.S. $0.75 in nine months. Use put–call parity to calculate the price of a European put option to sell one Canadian dollar for U.S. $0.75 in nine months. What is the price of a call option to buy U.S. $0.75 with one Canadian dollar in nine months?

13.21. A mutual fund announces that the salaries of its fund managers will depend on the performance of the fund. If the fund loses money, the salaries will be zero. If the fund makes a profit, the salaries will be proportional to the profit. Describe the salary of a fund manager as an option. How is a fund manager motivated to behave with this type of remuneration package?

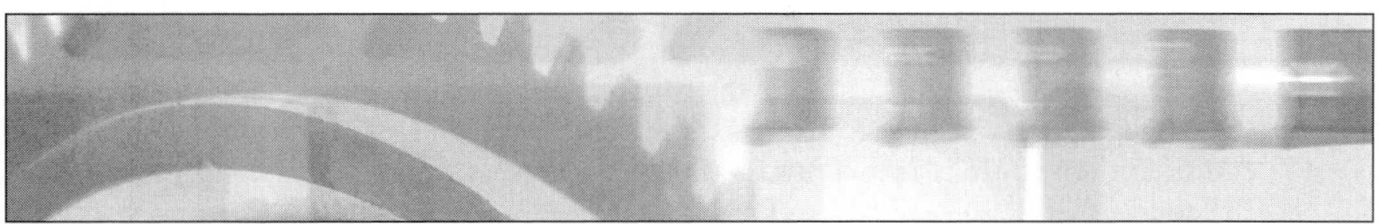

CHAPTER 14 Futures Options

The options we have considered so far provide the holder with the right to buy or sell a certain asset by a certain date. They are sometimes termed *options on spot* or *spot options* because, when the options are exercised, the sale or purchase of the asset at the agreed-on price takes place immediately. In this chapter we move on to consider *options on futures*, also known as *futures options*. In these contracts, exercise of the option gives the holder a position in a futures contract.

The Commodity Futures Trading Commission authorized the trading of options on futures on an experimental basis in 1982. Permanent trading was approved in 1987, and since then the popularity of the contract with investors has grown very fast.

In this chapter we consider how futures options work and the differences between these options and spot options. We examine how futures options can be priced using either binomial trees or formulas similar to those produced by Black, Scholes, and Merton for stock options. We also explore the relative pricing of futures options and spot options.

14.1 NATURE OF FUTURES OPTIONS

A futures option is the right, but not the obligation, to enter into a futures contract at a certain futures price by a certain date. Specifically, a call futures option is the right to enter into a long futures contract at a certain price; a put futures option is the right to enter into a short futures contract at a certain price. Most futures options are American; that is, they can be exercised any time during the life of the contract.

To illustrate the operation of futures options contracts, consider the position of an investor who has bought a July call futures option on gold with a strike price of \$300 per ounce. The asset underlying one contract is 100 ounces of gold. As with other exchange-traded option contracts, the investor is required to pay for the option at the time the contract is entered into. If the call futures option is exercised, the investor obtains a long futures contract, and there is a cash settlement to reflect the investor entering into the futures contract at the strike price. Suppose that the July futures price at the time the option is exercised is 340 and the most recent settlement price for the July futures contract is 338. The investor receives a cash amount equal to the excess of the most recent settlement price over the strike price. This amount, $(338 - 300) \times 100 =$ \$3,800 in our example, is added to the investor's margin account.

If the investor closes out the July futures contract immediately, the gain on the futures contract is $(340 - 338) \times 100$, or \$200. The total payoff from exercising the futures option contract is therefore \$4,000. This corresponds to the July futures price at the time of exercise less the strike price. If the investor keeps the futures contract, additional margin may be required. The example is summarized in Trading Note 14.1.

The investor who sells (or writes) a call futures option receives the option premium, but takes the risk that the contract will be exercised. When the contract is exercised, this investor assumes a short futures position. An amount equal to $F - K$ is deducted from the investor's margin account, where F is the most recent settlement price. The exchange clearinghouse arranges for this sum to be transferred to the investor on the other side of the transaction who chose to exercise the option.

Put futures options work analogously to call options. Consider an investor who buys a September put futures option on corn with a strike price of 200 cents per bushel. Each contract is on 5,000 bushels of corn. If the put futures option is exercised, the investor obtains a short futures contract plus a cash settlement. Suppose the contract is exercised when the September futures price is 180 cents and the most recent settlement price is 179 cents. The investor receives a cash amount equal to the excess of the strike price over the most recent settlement price. The cash amount received, i.e. $(2.00 - 1.79) \times 5{,}000 =$ \$1,050 in our example, is added to the investor's margin account. If the investor closes out the futures contract immediately, the loss on the short futures contract is $(1.80 - 1.79) \times 5{,}000 = \$50$. The total payoff from exercising the futures option contract is therefore \$1,000. This corresponds to the strike price minus the futures price at the time of exercise. As in the case of call futures, additional margin may be required if the investor decides to keep the futures position. The example is summarized in Trading Note 14.2.

The investor on the other side of the transaction (i.e., the investor who sold the put futures option) obtains a long futures position when the option is exercised, and the excess of the strike price over the most recent settlement price is deducted from the investor's margin account.

14.2 QUOTES

Futures options are referred to by the month in which the underlying futures contract matures—not by the expiration month of the option. As mentioned earlier, most futures

Trading Note 14.1 Call futures options

An investor buys a July call futures option contract on gold. The contract size is 100 ounces. The strike price is 300.

The Exercise Decision

The investor exercises when the July gold futures price is 340 and the most recent settlement price is 338.

The Outcome

1. The investor receives a cash amount equal to $(338 - 300) \times 100 = \$3{,}800$.
2. The investor receives a long futures contract.
3. The investor closes out the long futures contract immediately for a gain of $(340 - 338) \times 100 = \$200$.
4. Total payoff $= \$4{,}000$.

Trading Note 14.2 Put futures options

An investor buys a September put futures option contract on corn. The contract size is 5,000 bushels. The strike price is 200 cents.

The Exercise Decision
The investor exercises when the September corn futures price is 180 and the most recent settlement price is 179.

The Outcome
1. The investor receives a cash amount of $(2.00 - 1.79) \times 5{,}000 = \$1{,}050$.
2. The investor receives a short futures contract.
3. The investor decides to close out the short futures position immediately for a loss of $(1.80 - 1.79) \times 5{,}000 = \$50$.
4. Total payoff = $1,000.

options are American. The expiration date of a futures option contract is usually on, or a few days before, the earliest delivery date of the underlying futures contract. (For example, the CBOT Treasury bond futures option expires on the first Friday preceding by at least five business days the end of the month, just prior to the futures contract expiration month.) An exception is the CME mid-curve Eurodollar contract where the futures contract expires either one or two years after the options contract.

Table 14.1 shows quotes for futures options as they appeared in the *Wall Street Journal* on February 5, 2004. The most popular contracts (as measured by open interest) are those on corn, soybeans, cotton, sugar-world, crude oil, natural gas, gold, Treasury bonds, Treasury notes, five-year Treasury notes, 30-day federal funds, Eurodollars, one-year and two-year mid-curve Eurodollars, Euribor, Eurobunds, and the S&P 500.

14.3 REASONS FOR THE POPULARITY OF FUTURES OPTIONS

It is natural to ask why people choose to trade options on futures rather than options on the underlying asset. The main reason appears to be that a futures contract is, in many circumstances, more liquid and easier to trade than the underlying asset. Furthermore, a futures price is known immediately from trading on the futures exchange, whereas the spot price of the underlying asset may not be so readily available.

Consider Treasury bonds. The market for Treasury bond futures is much more active than the market for any particular Treasury bond. Also, a Treasury bond futures price is known immediately from trading on the Chicago Board of Trade. By contrast, the current market price of a bond can be obtained only by contacting one or more dealers. It is not surprising that investors would rather take delivery of a Treasury bond futures contract than Treasury bonds.

Futures on commodities are also often easier to trade than the commodities themselves. For example, it is much easier and more convenient to make or take delivery of a live-cattle futures contract than it is to make or take delivery of the cattle themselves.

An important point about a futures option is that exercising it does not usually lead to delivery of the underlying asset, as in most circumstances the underlying futures

Table 14.1 Closing prices of futures options on February 4, 2004

Wednesday, February 4, 2004

Final or settlement prices of selected contracts. Volume and open interest are totals in all contract months.

Grain and Oilseed

Corn (CBT)

5,000 bu.; cents per bu.

STRIKE	CALLS-SETTLE			PUTS-SETTLE		
Price	Mar	May	Jly	Mar	May	Jly
260	11.875	20.250	26.750	1.625	5.250	8.500
270	5.500	14.750	21.250	5.250	9.500	13.500
280	2.250	10.500	17.250	12.000	15.500	19.000
290	.750	7.375	14.000	20.500	22.000	25.625
300	.250	5.125	11.375	30.000	29.625	32.625
310	.125	3.500	9.250	...	...	...

Est vol 14,610 Tu 8,885 calls 6,364 puts
Op int Tues 323,990 calls 227,010 puts

Soybeans (CBT)

5,000 bu.; cents per bu.

Price	Mar	May	Jly	Mar	May	Jly
760	47.500	58.500	60.000	1.875	13.000	28.500
780	31.250	46.500	50.250	5.500	20.750	38.500
800	18.875	36.250	42.000	13.125	30.750	50.000
820	10.250	28.500	35.000	24.500	42.250	62.750
840	5.125	22.000	29.500	39.375	56.000	77.000
860	2.500	17.000	24.750	56.625	70.750	92.000

Est vol 17,482 Tu 16,204 calls 6,863 puts
Op int Tues 153,237 calls 125,007 puts

Soybean Meal (CBT)

100 tons; $ per ton

Price	Mar	May	Jly	Mar	May	Jly
235	...	...	...	...	...	...
240	9.00	13.50	14.50	2.00	7.25	11.75
245	...	...	...	...	...	...
250	3.75	9.30	10.90	6.75	12.60	18.25
255	...	...	...	...	...	...
260	1.35	6.50	8.50	14.40	19.75	25.70

Est vol 2,445 Tu 2,767 calls 2,418 puts
Op int Tues 39,831 calls 36,748 puts

Soybean Oil (CBT)

60,000 lbs.; cents per lb.

Price	Mar	May	Jly	Mar	May	Jly
290	1.080	1.770	2.070	.250	1.000	1.620
295	.750	1.545	1.870	.400	1.280	...
300	.550	1.325	1.700	.700	1.570	2.240
305	...	...	...	...	...	...
310	.250	1.000	1.410	...	...	...
315	...	...	...	...	...	...

Est vol 6,036 Tu 2,484 calls 2,045 puts
Op int Tues 55,851 calls 44,819 puts

Wheat (CBT)

5,000 bu.; cents per bu.

Price	Mar	May	Jly	Mar	May	Jly
360	19.250	32.375	34.500	3.250	10.000	17.250
370	12.750	26.500	29.750	6.750	14.000	22.500
380	8.000	21.500	25.250	12.000	19.000	28.000
390	4.500	17.500	21.500	18.500	25.000	34.250
400	2.500	14.125	18.250	26.375	31.500	41.000
410	1.375	11.250	15.500	35.250	38.625	48.000

Est vol 4,768 Tu 2,369 calls 1,615 puts
Op int Tues 76,609 calls 56,869 puts

Wheat (KC)

5,000 bu.; cents per bu.

Price	Mar	May	Jly	Mar	May	Jly
360	22.500	30.625	36.375	2.000	10.250	16.000
370	15.000	24.875	31.250	4.500	14.500	20.750
380	9.125	20.000	26.625	8.625	19.500	26.125
390	5.250	16.125	22.750	14.750	25.625	32.125
400	2.875	14.000	19.375	22.375	32.500	38.750
410	2.000	10.500	16.500	31.000	...	...

Est vol 2,045 Tu 437 calls 315 puts
Op int Tues 21,347 calls 19,365 puts

Food and Fiber

Cotton (NYCE)

50,000 lbs.; cents per lb.

STRIKE	CALLS-SETTLE			PUTS-SETTLE		
Price	Mar	May	Jly	Mar	May	Jly
67	2.44	5.85	7.13	.19	1.60	1.87
68	1.64	5.21	6.47	.39	1.95	2.20
69	.90	4.60	5.86	.65	2.34	2.58
70	.46	4.04	5.28	1.21	2.78	3.00
71	.28	3.54	4.75	2.03	3.27	3.46
72	.15	3.07	4.25	2.90	3.80	3.95

Est vol 9,021 Tu 8,443 calls 5,904 puts
Op int Tues 217,446 calls 113,615 puts

Orange Juice (NYCE)

15,000 lbs.; cents per lb.

Price	Mar	May	Jly	Mar	May	Jly
50	11.65	14.45	17.10	.05	.15	.25
55	6.75	9.75	12.60	.10	.40	.75
60	2.40	5.75	8.25	.75	1.35	1.40
65	.45	3.05	5.05	3.50	3.50	3.00
70	.15	1.55	2.95	8.35	7.05	5.90
75	.10	.80	1.70	13.35	11.40	9.55

Est vol 412 Tu 1,547 calls 843 puts
Op int Tues 42,351 calls 14,369 puts

Coffee (CSCE)

37,500 lbs.; cents per lb.

Price	Mar	Apr	May	Mar	Apr	May
67.5	5.40	8.17	9.06	0.30	0.98	1.94
70	3.35	6.38	7.53	0.75	1.85	2.90
72.5	1.85	4.94	6.24	1.75	2.79	4.10
75	1.00	3.82	5.18	3.30	4.17	5.52
77.5	0.49	2.98	4.30	5.39	5.82	7.14
80	0.23	2.34	3.58	7.63	7.68	8.91

Est vol 9,420 Tu 2,864 calls 2,718 puts
Op int Tues 78,119 calls 38,500 puts

Sugar-World (CSCE)

112,000 lbs.; cents per lb.

Price	Mar	Apr	May	Mar	Apr	May
450	1.19	1.39	1.40	0.01	0.01	0.02
500	0.69	0.89	0.93	0.01	0.02	0.06
550	0.25	0.47	0.55	0.07	0.09	0.17
600	0.02	0.18	0.27	0.34	0.30	0.39
650	0.01	0.05	0.12	0.83	0.67	0.74
700	0.01	0.01	0.06	1.33	1.13	1.17

Est vol 2,533 Tu 1,814 calls 1,889 puts
Op int Tues 154,632 calls 112,414 puts

Cocoa (CSCE)

10 metric tons; $ per ton

Price	Mar	Apr	May	Mar	Apr	May
1500	84	108	133	3	39	64
1550	42	78	105	11	59	86
1600	14	54	81	33	85	112
1650	4	36	61	73	117	142
1700	1	24	45	120	155	176
1750	1	15	34	170	196	214

Est vol 1,663 Tu 439 calls 341 puts
Op int Tues 18,472 calls 15,125 puts

Petroleum

Crude Oil (NYM)

1,000 bbls.; $ per bbl.

Price	Mar	Apr	May	Mar	Apr	May
3200	1.53	1.36	1.39	0.43	1.37	2.07
3250	1.20	1.12	1.18	0.60	1.63	2.36
3300	0.91	0.93	1.00	0.81	1.94	2.67
3350	0.66	0.75	0.84	1.06	2.26	3.01
3400	0.49	0.61	0.70	1.39	2.62	3.37
3450	0.33	0.50	0.00	1.73	3.00	...

Est vol 43,517 Tu 13,264 calls 17,244 puts
Op int Tues 341,383 calls 486,295 puts

Heating Oil No.2 (NYM)

42,000 gal.; $ per gal.

STRIKE	CALLS-SETTLE			PUTS-SETTLE		
Price	Mar	Apr	May	Mar	Apr	May
87	.0437	.0426	.0335	.0240	.0540	...
88	.0381	.0386	.0303	.0284	.0600	.0850
89	.0330	.0348	.0275	.0333	.0661	...
90	.0290	.0314	.0248	.0393	.0727	...
91	.0245	.0282	.0224	.0448	.0795	...
92	.0210	.0254	...	.0513	.0866	...

Est vol 815 Tu 800 calls 300 puts
Op int Tues 27,374 calls 19,492 puts

Gasoline-Unlead (NYM)

42,000 gal.; $ per gal.

Price	Mar	Apr	May	Mar	Apr	May
97	.0462	...	.0932	.0305	.0301	.0484
98	.0409	.0842	.0877	.0352	.0338	.0528
99	.0361	...	.0823	.0404	.0378	.0574
100	.0318	.0725	.0773	.0461	.0421	.0623
101	.0279	.0671	.0724	.0522	.0466	.0674
102	.0243	.0619	.0680	.0586	.0514	...

Est vol 2,854 Tu 1,831 calls 1,008 puts
Op int Tues 21,736 calls 17,368 puts

Natural Gas (NYM)

10,000 MMBtu.; $ per MMBtu.

Price	Mar	Apr	May	Mar	Apr	May
555	.382	.276	...	.278	.486	...
560	.358	.260	.238	.304	.519	...
565	.334	.244	...	.330	.553	...
570	.313	.230	.210	.359	.589	...
575	.293	.216	.197	.389	.625	...
580	.275	.203	.185	.421	.662	...

Est vol 37,627 Tu 17,111 calls 19,795 puts
Op int Tues 316,788 calls 386,608 puts

Brent Crude (IPE)

1,000 net bbls.; $ per bbl.

Price	Mar	Apr	May	Mar	Apr	May
	Data not available from source.				...	...
...	...	...				...
	...	...	...	...	...	...
	...	...	...	...	...	...
	...	...	...	...	...	...
	...	...	...	...	...	...
	...	...	...	...	...	...

Est vol Tu calls puts
Op int Tues calls puts

Livestock

Cattle-Feeder (CME)

50,000 lbs.; cents per lb.

Price	Mar	Apr	May	Mar	Apr	May
8000	4.00	5.50	6.28	3.00	2.80	3.10
8100	...	...	...	...	...	...
8200	2.50	4.00	...	3.50	3.30	3.90
8300	2.10	...	...	4.10	...	...
8400	1.60	3.10	4.00	4.60	4.40	4.80
8500	1.20	...	...	5.20	...	...

Est vol 534 Tu 183 calls 261 puts
Op int Tues 3,298 calls 5,427 puts

Cattle-Live (CME)

40,000 lbs.; cents per lb.

Price	Feb	Mar	Apr	Feb	Mar	Apr
73	1.50	...	2.00	0.50	...	4.05
74	0.80	...	1.70	0.80	...	4.75
75	0.35	...	1.50	1.35	...	5.55
76	0.18	...	1.25	2.18	...	6.28
77	0.08	...	1.05	3.08	...	7.08
78	0.03	...	0.85	4.03	...	7.88

Est vol 1,903 Tu 690 calls 855 puts
Op int Tues 40,381 calls 42,076 puts

Hogs-Lean (CME)

40,000 lbs.; cents per lb.

Price	Feb	Apr	May	Feb	Apr	May
57	2.63	3.80	...	0.20	1.93	...
58	1.78	3.18	4.80	0.35	2.30	2.18
59	1.08	2.65	...	0.65	2.78	...
60	0.53	2.15	3.63	1.10	3.28	2.98
61	0.28	1.73	...	...	...	...
62	0.15	1.35	2.68	2.73	...	...

Est vol 243 Tu 207 calls 358 puts
Op int Tues 5,619 calls 6,176 puts

STRIKE CALLS-SETTLE PUTS-SETTLE

Metals

Copper (CMX)

25,000 lbs.; cents per lb.

Price	Mar	Apr	May	Mar	Apr	May
114	5.00	6.00	7.15	1.55	2.90	4.65
116	3.70	4.90	6.15	2.25	3.80	5.60
118	2.55	3.95	5.20	3.10	4.85	6.65
120	1.75	3.10	4.40	4.30	6.00	7.85
122	1.15	1.80	3.70	5.70	9.65	9.10
124	0.70	1.00	3.05	7.25	13.90	10.50

Est vol 1,650 Tu 247 calls 23 puts
Op int Tues 12,848 calls 3,638 puts

Gold (CMX)

100 troy ounces; $ per troy ounce

Price	Mar	Apr	Jun	Mar	Apr	Jun
390	13.50	16.80	21.80	1.90	5.10	9.20
395	10.00	13.70	19.00	3.30	7.00	11.40
400	7.00	11.00	17.50	5.30	9.30	14.90
405	4.80	8.80	14.30	8.10	12.10	16.60
410	3.20	6.60	12.50	11.50	14.90	19.70
415	2.10	5.50	10.80	15.40	18.80	23.00

Est vol 18,000 Tu 4,487 calls 5,463 puts
Op int Tues 306,159 calls 227,854 puts

Silver (CMX)

5,000 troy ounces; cts per troy ounce

Price	Mar	Apr	May	Mar	Apr	May
610	20.30	30.50	38.40	15.50	24.40	32.20
620	15.90	26.30	34.30	21.10	30.10	38.10
625	14.00	24.40	32.40	24.20	33.20	41.20
630	12.40	22.70	30.70	27.60	36.40	44.40
640	9.70	19.50	27.50	34.90	43.20	51.20
650	7.60	16.80	24.70	42.70	50.50	58.40

Est vol 1,800 Tu 1,474 calls 1,954 puts
Op int Tues 66,669 calls 26,556 puts

Interest Rate

T-Bonds (CBT)

$100,000; points and 64ths of 100%

Price	Mar	Apr	May	Mar	Apr	May
110	2-06	2-03	2-35	0-36	1-61	2-29
111	1-28	1-36	...	0-58	2-30	...
112	0-58	1-11	1-42	1-24	3-04	...
113	0-34	0-54	...	2-00	3-48	...
114	0-19	0-39	...	2-49	4-32	...
115	0-10	0-27	0-49	3-40	5-20	...

Est vol 23,701;
Tu vol 14,191 calls 17,000 puts
Op int Tues 412,644 calls 444,891 puts

T-Notes (CBT)

$100,000; points and 64ths of 100%

Price	Mar	Apr	May	Mar	Apr	May
112	2-00	1-30	1-52	0-20	1-25	1-46
113	1-17	1-00	...	0-37	1-58	...
114	0-44	0-41	0-59	1-00	...	...
115	0-20	0-24	0-40	1-40	...	...
116	0-08	0-14	0-26	2-28	...	...
117	0-03	0-08	0-16	...	...	...

Est vol 150,806 Tu 61,052 calls 65,301 puts
Op int Tues 1,045,055 calls 1,083,950 puts

5 Yr Treas Notes (CBT)

$100,000; points and 64ths of 100%

Price	Mar	Apr	May	Mar	Apr	May
11150	1-16	0-49	0-62	0-15	1-08	1-21
11200	0-56	0-36	...	0-22	1-27	...
11250	0-36	0-25	...	0-34	...	...
11300	0-22	0-17	...	0-52	...	...
11350	0-12	0-11	...	1-10	...	...
11400	0-06	...	...	1-36	...	...

Est vol 17,994 Tu 4,736 calls 25,086 puts
Op int Tues 125,023 calls 426,615 puts

30 Day Federal Funds (CBT)

$5,000,000; 100 minus daily average

Price	Feb	Mar	Apr	Feb	Mar	Apr
988750	.127	.117	.120	.002	.002	.005
989375	.065	.062	.060	.002	.007	.007
990000	.007	.007	.007	.007	.017	.017
990625	...	.002	.002	...	...	...
991250	.002	.002	...	...	...	...
991875	...	...	...	...	...	...

Est vol 330 Tu 1,199 calls 1,303 puts
Op int Tues 128,420 calls 162,873 puts

Eurodollar (CME)

$ million; pts. of 100%

Price	Feb	Mar	Apr	Feb	Mar	Apr
9825	...	5.90	...	0.00	0.00	0.12
9850	...	3.42	2.22	0.00	0.02	0.37
9875	0.95	1.02	0.45	0.05	0.12	1.10
9900	...	0.05	0.02	...	1.65	...
9925	...	0.00	...	...	4.10	...
9950	...	0.00	...	...	6.60	...

Est vol 288,753;
Tu vol 83,303 calls 142,595 puts
Op int Tues 4,268,863 calls 4,408,535 puts

1 Yr. Mid-Curve Eurodlr (CME)

$1,000,000 contract units; pts. of 100%

Price	Feb	Mar	Apr	Feb	Mar	Apr
9725	4.02	4.65	2.75	0.17	0.80	2.95
9750	2.05	2.87	1.60	0.70	1.52	...
9775	0.70	1.55	0.82	1.85	2.70	...
9800	0.15	0.65	0.35	3.80	4.30	...
9825	0.02	0.20	0.15	...	6.35	...
9850	0.00	0.05	...	...	...	...

Est vol 210,600 Tu 61,545 calls 129,840 puts
Op int Tues 934,544 calls 932,093 puts

2 Yr. Mid-Curve Eurodlr (CME)

$1,000,000 contract units; pts. of 100%

Price	Mar	Jun	Sep	Mar	Jun	Sep
9575	6.00	5.70	...	0.50	2.45	...
9600	4.00	4.10	4.05	1.00	3.35	5.40
9625	2.45	2.82	2.90	1.95	4.57	...
9650	1.27	1.85	...	3.27	6.07	...
9675	0.60	1.12	...	5.10	...	...
9700	0.17	0.50	...	7.17	...	...

Est vol 800 Tu 8,400 calls 0 puts
Op int Tues 158,035 calls 33,178 puts

Euribor (LIFFE)

Euro 1,000,000

Price	Feb	Mar	Apr	Feb	Mar	Apr
97750	0.18	0.19	0.17	...	0.00	0.02
97875	0.06	0.07	0.08	0.00	0.01	0.06
98000	0.01	0.03	0.03	0.07	0.09	0.13
98125	...	0.01	0.01	0.19	0.20	0.24
98250	...	0.00	0.00	0.31	0.32	0.35
98375	...	...	0.00	0.44	0.44	0.48

Vol Wd 327,805 calls 29,183 puts
Op int Tues 5,655,304 calls 1,807,541 puts

Euro-BUND (EUREX)

100,000; pts. In 100%

Price	Mar	Apr	May	Mar	Apr	May
11350	1.01	0.78	1.02	0.25	1.00	1.24
11400	0.68	0.56	0.78	0.42	1.28	1.50
11450	0.42	0.39	0.61	0.66	1.61	1.83
11500	0.22	0.26	0.46	0.96	1.98	2.18
11550	0.11	0.17	0.34	1.35	2.39	2.56
11600	0.06	0.10	...	1.80	2.82	...

Vol Wd 35,857 calls 42,186 puts
Op int Tues 366,384 calls 479,188 puts

Currency

Japanese Yen (CME)

12,500,000 yen; cents per 100 yen

Price	Feb	Mar	Apr	Feb	Mar	Apr
9400	1.03	1.72	2.30	0.06	0.75	1.04
9450	0.60	1.44	2.03	0.13	0.97	1.27
9500	0.30	1.19	1.78	0.33	1.22	1.52
9550	0.13	0.98	1.56	0.66	...	...
9600	0.06	0.81	1.36	1.09	1.84	...
9650	0.04	0.67	...	...	...	...

Est vol 1,352 Tu 1,271 calls 531 puts
Op int Tues 23,459 calls 20,676 puts

Canadian Dollar (CME)

100,000 Can.$, cents per Can.$

Price	Feb	Mar	Apr	Feb	Mar	Apr
7400	...	1.35	...	0.07	0.50	...
7450	0.51	1.04	...	0.16	0.69	...
7500	0.23	0.77	1.03	0.38	0.92	1.38
7550	0.10	0.57	...	0.75	1.22	...
7600	0.05	0.42	...	1.19	1.57	...
7650	0.02	0.31	...	1.67	1.96	...

Est vol 419 Tu 219 calls 163 puts
Op int Tues 12,761 calls 9,409 puts

British Pound (CME)

62,500 pounds; cents per pound

Price	Feb	Mar	Apr	Feb	Mar	Apr
1810	2.01	3.13	...	0.24	1.36	...
1820	1.13	2.53	...	0.36	1.76	...
1830	0.68	2.04	...	0.91	2.27	...
1840	0.34	1.60	...	1.57	2.83	...
1850	0.16	1.24	1.66	...	...	...
1860	0.08	0.96	1.42	3.31	...	...

Est vol 755 Tu 242 calls 625 puts
Op int Tues 6,257 calls 5,097 puts

Swiss Franc (CME)

125,000 francs; cents per franc

Price	Feb	Mar	Apr	Feb	Mar	Apr
7900	1.10	1.70	...	0.08	0.68	...
7950	0.69	1.39	...	0.17	0.87	...
8000	0.37	1.11	...	0.35	1.09	...
8050	0.18	0.89	...	0.66	1.37	...
8100	0.10	0.71	...	1.08	1.69	...
8150	0.05	0.55	...	1.53	2.03	...

Est vol 189 Tu 44 calls 384 puts
Op int Tues 1,690 calls 2,356 puts

Euro Fx (CME)

125,000 euros; cents per euro

Price	Feb	Mar	Apr	Feb	Mar	Apr
12400	1.35	2.36	2.82	0.15	1.16	1.91
12450	0.98	2.07	2.55	0.28	1.37	2.14
12500	0.66	1.81	2.31	0.46	1.61	2.40
12550	0.42	1.56	2.08	0.72	1.86	2.67
12600	0.26	1.34	1.87	1.06	2.14	2.96
12650	0.15	1.14	1.68	1.45	2.44	3.27

Est vol 3,767 Tu 3,252 calls 2,088 puts
Op int Tues 39,137 calls 43,286 puts

Index

DJ Industrial Avg (CBOT)

$100 times premium

Price	Feb	Mar	Apr	Feb	Mar	Apr
102	28.50	37.00	42.40	4.50	13.25	20.50
103	21.00	30.00	35.50	7.00	16.25	...
104	14.50	24.00	29.75	10.50	20.00	...
105	9.00	18.50	24.25	15.00	24.50	...
106	5.50	14.00	19.50	21.50	30.00	...
107	3.00	10.00	...	29.00	...	...

Est vol 124 Tu 111 calls 72 puts
Op int Tues 5,861 calls 5,480 puts

S&P 500 Stock Index (CME)

$250 times premium

Price	Feb	Mar	Apr	Feb	Mar	Apr
1115	19.70	29.90	37.80	10.80	21.00	29.90
1120	16.60	26.90	34.90	12.70	23.00	32.00
1125	13.80	24.00	32.00	14.90	25.10	34.10
1130	11.30	21.40	29.30	17.40	27.50	36.40
1135	9.10	19.00	26.80	20.20	30.10	...
1140	7.20	16.70	24.30	23.30	32.80	41.30

Est vol 14,455 Tu 4,759 calls 10,464 puts
Op int Tues 88,723 calls 228,763 puts

Other Options

Nasdaq 100 (CME)

$100 times NASDAQ 100 Index

Price	Feb	Mar	Apr	Feb	Mar	Apr
1460	...	...	...	...	...	...

Est vol 41 Tu 3 calls 2 puts
Op int Tues 2,185 calls 958 puts

NYSE Composite (NYFE)

$50 times premium

Price	Feb	Mar	Apr	Feb	Mar	Apr
6500	7450	12100	16400	6500	11150	16450

Est vol 0 Tu 3 calls 20 puts
Op int Tues 1 calls 9,514 puts

contract is closed out prior to delivery. Futures options are therefore normally eventually settled in cash. This is appealing to many investors, particularly those with limited capital who may find it difficult to come up with the funds to buy the underlying asset when an option is exercised. Another advantage sometimes cited for futures options is that futures and futures options are traded in pits side by side in the same exchange. This facilitates hedging, arbitrage, and speculation. It also tends to make the markets more efficient. A final point is that futures options tend to entail lower transactions costs than spot options in many situations.

14.4 PUT–CALL PARITY

In Chapter 9 we derived a put–call parity relationship for European stock options. We now consider a similar argument to derive a put–call parity relationship for European futures options. Consider European call and put futures options, both with strike price K and time to expiration T. We can form two portfolios:

Portfolio A: a European call futures option plus an amount of cash equal to Ke^{-rT}

Portfolio B: a European put futures option plus a long futures contract plus an amount of cash equal to F_0e^{-rT}, where F_0 is the futures price

In portfolio A, the cash can be invested at the risk-free rate, r, and grows to K at time T. Let F_T be the futures price at maturity of the option. If $F_T > K$, the call option in portfolio A is exercised and portfolio A is worth F_T. If $F_T \leqslant K$, the call is not exercised and portfolio A is worth K. The value of portfolio A at time T is therefore

$$\max(F_T, K)$$

In portfolio B, the cash can be invested at the risk-free rate to grow to F_0 at time T. The put option provides a payoff of $\max(K - F_T, 0)$. The futures contract provides a payoff of $F_T - F_0$.[1] The value of portfolio B at time T is therefore

$$F_0 + (F_T - F_0) + \max(K - F_T, 0) = \max(F_T, K)$$

Because the two portfolios have the same value at time T and European options cannot be exercised early, it follows that they are worth the same today. The value of portfolio A today is

$$c + Ke^{-rT}$$

where c is the price of the call futures option. The marking-to-market process ensures that the futures contract in portfolio B is worth zero today. Portfolio B is therefore worth

$$p + F_0e^{-rT}$$

where p is the price of the put futures option. Hence

$$c + Ke^{-rT} = p + F_0e^{-rT} \tag{14.1}$$

The difference between this put–call parity relationship and the one for a non-dividend-

[1] This analysis assumes that a futures contract is like a forward contract and settled at the end of its life rather than on a day-to-day basis.

paying stock in equation (9.3) is that the stock price, S_0, is replaced by the discounted futures price, F_0e^{-rT}.

For American futures, the put–call parity relationship is (see Problem 14.19)

$$F_0e^{-rT} - K < C - P < F_0 - Ke^{-rT} \tag{14.2}$$

Example

Suppose that the price of a European call option on silver futures for delivery in six months is \$0.56 per ounce when the exercise price is \$8.50. Assume that the silver futures price for delivery in six months is currently \$8.00, and the risk-free interest rate for an investment that matures in six months is 10% per annum. From a rearrangement of equation (14.1), the price of a European put option on silver futures with the same maturity and exercise date as the call option is

$$0.56 + 8.50e^{-0.1\times6/12} - 8.00e^{-0.1\times6/12} = 1.04$$

14.5 BOUNDS FOR FUTURES OPTIONS

The put–call parity relationship in equation (14.1) provides bounds for European call and put options. Because the price of a put, p, cannot be negative, it follows from equation (14.1) that

$$c + Ke^{-rT} \geqslant F_0e^{-rT}$$

or

$$c \geqslant (F_0 - K)e^{-rT} \tag{14.3}$$

Similarly, because the price of a call option cannot be negative, it follows from equation (14.1) that

$$Ke^{-rT} \leqslant F_0e^{-rT} + p$$

or

$$p \geqslant (K - F_0)e^{-rT} \tag{14.4}$$

These bounds are similar to the ones derived for European stock options in Chapter 9. The prices of European call and put options are very close to their lower bounds when the options are deep in the money. To see why this is so, we return to the put–call parity relationship in equation (14.1). When a call option is deep in the money, the corresponding put option is deep out of the money. This means that p is very close to zero. The difference between c and its lower bound equals p, so that the price of the call option must be very close to its lower bound. A similar argument applies to put options.

Because American futures options can be exercised at any time, we must have

$$C \geqslant F_0 - K$$

and

$$P \geqslant K - F_0$$

Thus, if interest rates are positive, the lower bound for an American option price is always higher than the lower bound for a European option. This is because there is always some chance that an American futures option will be exercised early.

14.6 VALUATION OF FUTURES OPTIONS USING BINOMIAL TREES

This section examines, more formally than in Chapter 11, how binomial trees can be used to price futures options. A key difference between futures options and stock options is that there are no up-front costs when a futures contract is entered into.

Suppose that the current futures price is 30 and that it will move either up to 33 or down to 28 over the next month. We consider a one-month call option on the futures with a strike price of 29 and ignore daily settlement. The situation is as indicated in Figure 14.1. If the futures price proves to be 33, the payoff from the option is 4 and the value of the futures contract is 3. If the futures price proves to be 28, the payoff from the option is zero and the value of the futures contract is −2.

To set up a riskless hedge, we consider a portfolio consisting of a short position in one options contract and a long position in Δ futures contracts. If the futures price moves up to 33, the value of the portfolio is $3\Delta - 4$; if it moves down to 28, the value of the portfolio is -2Δ. The portfolio is riskless when these are the same, that is, when

$$3\Delta - 4 = -2\Delta$$

or $\Delta = 0.8$.

For this value of Δ, we know the portfolio will be worth $3 \times 0.8 - 4 = -1.6$ in one month. Assume a risk-free interest rate of 6%. The value of the portfolio today must be

$$-1.6e^{-0.06\times 1/12} = -1.592$$

The portfolio consists of one short option and Δ futures contracts. Because the value of the futures contract today is zero, the value of the option today must be 1.592.

A Generalization

We can generalize this analysis by considering a futures price that starts at F_0 and is anticipated to rise to F_0u or move down to F_0d over the time period T. We consider an option maturing at time T and suppose that its payoff is f_u if the futures price moves up and f_d if it moves down. The situation is summarized in Figure 14.2.

The riskless portfolio in this case consists of a short position in one option combined

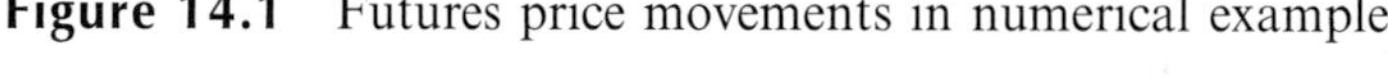

Figure 14.1 Futures price movements in numerical example

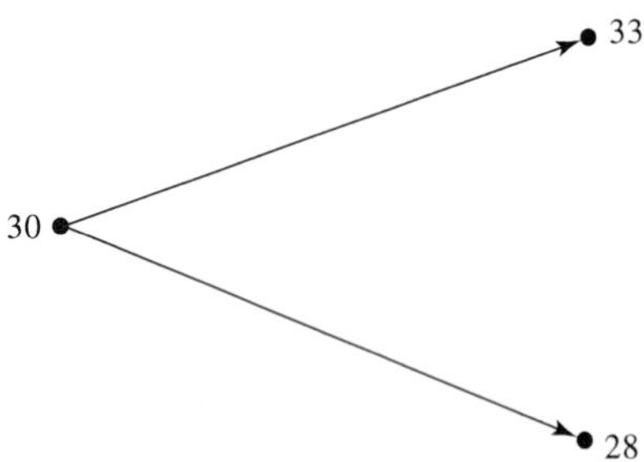

Figure 14.2 Futures price and option price in general situation

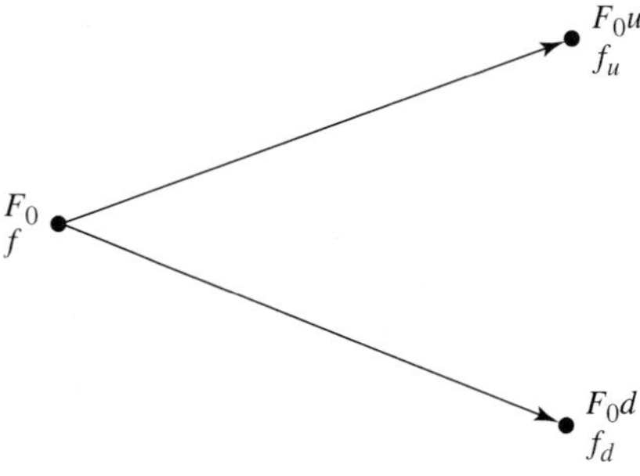

with a long position in Δ futures contracts, where

$$\Delta = \frac{f_u - f_d}{F_0u - F_0d}$$

The value of the portfolio at time T is then always

$$(F_0u - F_0)\Delta - f_u$$

Denoting the risk-free interest rate by r, we obtain the value of the portfolio today as

$$[(F_0u - F_0)\Delta - f_u]e^{-rT}$$

Another expression for the present value of the portfolio is $-f$, where f is the value of the option today. It follows that

$$-f = [(F_0u - F_0)\Delta - f_u]e^{-rT}$$

Substituting for Δ and simplifying reduces this equation to

$$f = e^{-rT}[pf_u + (1-p)f_d] \tag{14.5}$$

where

$$p = \frac{1-d}{u-d} \tag{14.6}$$

This agrees with the result in Section 11.9.

In the numerical example considered previously (see Figure 14.1), $u = 1.1$, $d = 0.9333$, $r = 0.06$, $T = 1/12$, $f_u = 4$, and $f_d = 0$. From equation (14.6),

$$p = \frac{1 - 0.9333}{1.1 - 0.9333} = 0.4$$

and, from equation (14.5),

$$f = e^{-0.06\times 1/12}[0.4 \times 4 + 0.6 \times 0] = 1.592$$

This result agrees with the answer obtained for this example earlier.

14.7 A FUTURES PRICE AS AN ASSET PROVIDING A YIELD

There is a general result that makes the analysis of futures options analogous to the analysis of options on a stock paying a dividend yield. This result is that futures prices behave in the same way as a stock paying a dividend yield at the domestic risk-free rate r.

One clue that this might be so is given by comparing equations (14.5) and (14.6) with equations (13.7) and (13.8). The two sets of equations are identical when we set $q = r$. Another clue is that the lower bounds for futures options prices and the put–call parity relationship for futures options prices are the same as those for options on a stock paying a dividend yield at rate q when the stock price is replaced by the futures price and $q = r$.

We can understand the general result by noting that a futures contract requires zero investment. In a risk-neutral world the expected profit from holding a position in an investment that costs zero to set up must be zero. The expected payoff from a futures contract in a risk-neutral world must therefore be zero. It follows that the expected growth rate of the futures price in a risk-neutral world must be zero. As pointed out in Chapter 13, a stock paying a dividend at rate q grows at an expected rate of $r - q$ in a risk-neutral world. If we set $q = r$, the expected growth rate of the stock price is zero, making it analogous to a futures price.

14.8 BLACK'S MODEL FOR VALUING FUTURES OPTIONS

European futures options can be valued using equations (13.4) and (13.5) with $q = r$. Fischer Black was the first to show this in a paper published in 1976. The underlying assumption is that futures prices have the same lognormal property that we assumed for stock prices in Chapter 12. The European call price, c, and the European put price, p, for a futures option are given by equations (13.4) and (13.5) with S_0 replaced by F_0 and $q = r$:

$$c = e^{-rT}[F_0 N(d_1) - KN(d_2)] \tag{14.7}$$

$$p = e^{-rT}[KN(-d_2) - F_0 N(-d_1)] \tag{14.8}$$

where

$$d_1 = \frac{\ln(F_0/K) + \sigma^2 T/2}{\sigma\sqrt{T}}$$

$$d_2 = \frac{\ln(F_0/K) - \sigma^2 T/2}{\sigma\sqrt{T}} = d_1 - \sigma\sqrt{T}$$

and σ is the volatility of the futures price.[2] Note that Black's formula for valuing futures options does not require the option contract and the futures contract to mature at the same time.

Example

Consider a European put futures option on crude oil. The time to the option's maturity is four months, the current futures price is \$20, the exercise price is \$20, the risk-free interest rate is 9% per annum, and the volatility of the futures price

[2] When the cost of carry and the convenience yield are functions only of time, it can be shown that the volatility of the futures price is the same as the volatility of the underlying asset.

is 25% per annum. In this case, $F_0 = 20$, $K = 20$, $r = 0.09$, $T = 4/12$, $\sigma = 0.25$, and $\ln(F_0/K) = 0$, so that

$$d_1 = \frac{\sigma\sqrt{T}}{2} = 0.07216$$

$$d_2 = -\frac{\sigma\sqrt{T}}{2} = -0.07216$$

$$N(-d_1) = 0.4712, \qquad N(-d_2) = 0.5288$$

and the put price p is given by

$$p = e^{-0.09\times 4/12}(20 \times 0.5288 - 20 \times 0.4712) = 1.12$$

or \$1.12.

14.9 FUTURES OPTIONS vs. SPOT OPTIONS

The payoff from a European spot call option with strike price K is

$$\max(S_T - K,\ 0)$$

where S_T is the spot price at the option's maturity. The payoff from a European futures call option with the same strike price is

$$\max(F_T - K,\ 0)$$

where F_T is the futures price at the option's maturity. If the European futures option matures at the same time as the futures contract, $F_T = S_T$ and the two options are in theory equivalent. If the European call futures option matures before the futures contract, it is worth more than the corresponding spot option in a normal market (where futures prices are higher than spot prices) and less than the corresponding spot option in an inverted market (where futures prices are lower than spot prices).[3]

Similarly, a European futures put option is worth the same as its spot option counterpart when the futures option matures at the same time as the futures contract. If the European put futures option matures before the futures contract, it is worth less than the corresponding spot option in a normal market and more than the corresponding spot option in an inverted market.

Results for American Options

Traded futures options are in practice usually American. Assuming that the risk-free rate of interest, r, is positive, there is always some chance that it will be optimal to exercise an American futures option early. American futures options are therefore worth more than their European counterparts.

It is not generally true that an American futures option is worth the same as the corresponding American spot option when the futures and options contracts have the same maturity. Suppose, for example, that there is a normal market with futures prices consistently higher than spot prices prior to maturity. This is the case with most stock

[3] The spot option "corresponding" to a futures option is defined here as one with the same strike price and the same expiration date.

indices, gold, silver, low-interest currencies, and some commodities. An American call futures option must be worth more than the corresponding American spot call option. The reason is that in some situations the futures option will be exercised early, in which case it will provide a greater profit to the holder. Similarly, an American put futures option must be worth less than the corresponding American spot put option. If there is an inverted market with futures prices consistently lower than spot prices, as is the case with high-interest currencies and some commodities, the reverse must be true. American call futures options are worth less than the corresponding American spot call option, whereas American put futures options are worth more than the corresponding American spot put option.

The differences just described between American futures options and American spot options hold true when the futures contract expires later than the options contract as well as when the two expire at the same time. In fact, the later the futures contract expires the greater the differences tend to be.

SUMMARY

Futures options require delivery of the underlying futures contract on exercise. When a call is exercised, the holder acquires a long futures position plus a cash amount equal to the excess of the futures price over the strike price. Similarly, when a put is exercised the holder acquires a short position plus a cash amount equal to the excess of the strike price over the futures price. The futures contract that is delivered usually expires slightly later than the option.

A futures price behaves in the same way as a stock that provides a dividend yield equal to the risk-free rate, r. This means that the results produced in Chapter 13 for options on stock paying a dividend yield apply to futures options if we replace the stock price by the futures price and set the dividend yield equal to the risk-free interest rate. Pricing formulas for European futures options were first produced by Fischer Black in 1976. They assume that the futures price is lognormally distributed at the expiration of the option.

If we assume that the two expiration dates are the same, a European futures option is worth exactly the same as the corresponding European spot option. This is not true of American options. If the futures market is normal, an American call futures is worth more than the corresponding American spot call option, while an American put futures is worth less than the corresponding American spot put option. If the futures market is inverted, the reverse is true.

FURTHER READING

Black, F. "The Pricing of Commodity Contracts," *Journal of Financial Economics*, 3 (1976): 167–79.

Hilliard, J. E., and J. Reis. "Valuation of Commodity Futures and Options under Stochastic Convenience Yields, Interest Rates, and Jump Diffusions in the Spot," *Journal of Financial and Quantitative Analysis*, 33, 1 (March 1998): 61–86.

Miltersen, K. R., and E. S. Schwartz. "Pricing of Options on Commodity Futures with Stochastic Term Structures of Convenience Yields and Interest Rates," *Journal of Financial and Quantitative Analysis*, 33, 1 (March 1998): 33–59.

Quiz (Answers at End of Book)

14.1. Explain the difference between a call option on yen and a call option on yen futures.

14.2. Why are options on bond futures more actively traded than options on bonds?

14.3. "A futures price is like a stock paying a dividend yield." What is the dividend yield?

14.4. A futures price is currently 50. At the end of six months it will be either 56 or 46. The risk-free interest rate is 6% per annum. What is the value of a six-month European call option with a strike price of 50?

14.5. How does the put–call parity formula for a futures option differ from put–call parity for an option on a non-dividend-paying stock?

14.6. Consider an American futures call option where the futures contract and the option contract expire at the same time. Under what circumstances is the futures option worth more than the corresponding American option on the underlying asset?

14.7. Calculate the value of a five-month European put futures option when the futures price is \$19, the strike price is \$20, the risk-free interest rate is 12% per annum, and the volatility of the futures price is 20% per annum.

Questions and Problems (Answers in Solutions Manual/Study Guide)

14.8. Suppose you buy a put option contract on October gold futures with a strike price of \$400 per ounce. Each contract is for the delivery of 100 ounces. What happens if you exercise when the October futures price is \$380?

14.9. Suppose you sell a call option contract on April live cattle futures with a strike price of 70 cents per pound. Each contract is for the delivery of 40,000 pounds. What happens if the contract is exercised when the futures price is 75 cents?

14.10. Consider a two-month call futures option with a strike price of 40 when the risk-free interest rate is 10% per annum. The current futures price is 47. What is a lower bound for the value of the futures option if it is (a) European and (b) American?

14.11. Consider a four-month put futures option with a strike price of 50 when the risk-free interest rate is 10% per annum. The current futures price is 47. What is a lower bound for the value of the futures option if it is (a) European and (b) American?

14.12. A futures price is currently 60. It is known that over each of the next two three-month periods it will either rise by 10% or fall by 10%. The risk-free interest rate is 8% per annum. What is the value of a six-month European call option on the futures with a strike price of 60? If the call were American, would it ever be worth exercising it early?

14.13. In Problem 14.12, what is the value of a six-month European put option on futures with a strike price of 60? If the put were American, would it ever be worth exercising it early? Verify that the call prices calculated in Problem 14.12 and the put prices calculated here satisfy put–call parity relationships.

14.14. A futures price is currently 25, its volatility is 30% per annum, and the risk-free interest rate is 10% per annum. What is the value of a nine-month European call on the futures with a strike price of 26?

14.15. A futures price is currently 70, its volatility is 20% per annum, and the risk-free interest rate is 6% per annum. What is the value of a five-month European put on the futures with a strike price of 65?

14.16. Suppose that a one-year futures price is currently 35. A one-year European call option and a one-year European put option on the futures with a strike price of 34 are both priced at 2 in the market. The risk-free interest rate is 10% per annum. Identify an arbitrage opportunity.

14.17. "The price of an at-the-money European call futures option always equals the price of a similar at-the-money European put futures option." Explain why this statement is true.

14.18. Suppose that a futures price is currently 30. The risk-free interest rate is 5% per annum. A three-month American call futures option with a strike price of 28 is worth 4. Calculate bounds for the price of a three-month American put futures option with a strike price of 28.

14.19. Show that, if C is the price of an American call option on a futures contract when the strike price is K and the maturity is T, and P is the price of an American put on the same futures contract with the same strike price and exercise date, then

$$F_0 e^{-rT} - K < C - P < F_0 - K e^{-rT}$$

where F_0 is the futures price and r is the risk-free rate. Assume that $r > 0$ and that there is no difference between forward and futures contracts. (*Hint*: Use an analogous approach to that indicated for Problem 13.12.)

Assignment Questions

14.20. A futures price is currently 40. It is known that at the end of three months the price will be either 35 or 45. What is the value of a three-month European call option on the futures with a strike price of 42 if the risk-free interest rate is 7% per annum?

14.21. Calculate the implied volatility of soybean futures prices from the following information concerning a European put on soybean futures:

Current futures price	525
Exercise price	525
Risk-free rate	6% per annum
Time to maturity	5 months
Put price	20

14.22. Use the DerivaGem software to calculate implied volatilities for the July options on corn futures in Table 14.1. Assume the futures prices in Table 2.2 apply and that the risk-free rate is 1.1% per annum. Treat the options as American and use 100 time steps. The options mature on June 19, 2004. Can you draw any conclusions from the pattern of implied volatilities you obtain?

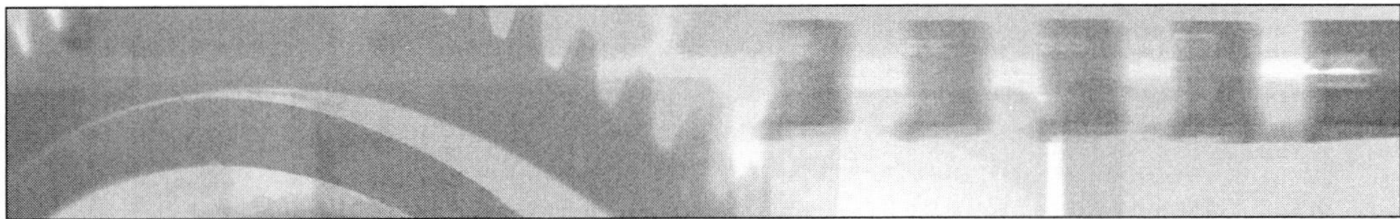

CHAPTER 15

The Greek Letters

A financial institution that sells an option to a client in the over-the-counter market is faced with the problem of managing its risk. If the option happens to be the same as one that is traded on an exchange, the financial institution can neutralize its exposure by buying on the exchange the same option as it has sold. But when the option has been tailored to the needs of a client and does not correspond to the standardized products traded by exchanges, hedging the exposure is more difficult.

In this chapter we discuss some of the alternative approaches to this problem. We cover what are commonly referred to as the "Greek letters," or simply the "Greeks." Each Greek letter measures a different dimension to the risk in an option position and the aim of a trader is to manage the Greeks so that all risks are acceptable. The analysis presented in this chapter is applicable to market makers in options on an exchange as well as to over-the-counter traders working for financial institutions.

Toward the end of the chapter, we will consider the creation of options synthetically. This turns out to be very closely related to the hedging of options. Creating an option position synthetically is essentially the same task as hedging the opposite option position. For example, creating a long call option synthetically is the same as hedging a short position in the call option.

15.1 ILLUSTRATION

In the next few sections, we use as an example the position of a financial institution that has sold for \$300,000 a European call option on 100,000 shares of a non-dividend-paying stock. We assume that the stock price is \$49, the strike price is \$50, the risk-free interest rate is 5% per annum, the stock price volatility is 20% per annum, the time to maturity is 20 weeks (0.3846 years), and the expected return from the stock is 13% per annum.[1] With our usual notation, this means that

$$S_0 = 49, \quad K = 50, \quad r = 0.05, \quad \sigma = 0.20, \quad T = 0.3846, \quad \mu = 0.13$$

The Black–Scholes price of the option is about \$240,000. The financial institution has

[1] As shown in Chapters 11 and 12, the expected return is irrelevant to the pricing of an option. It is given here because it can have some bearing on the effectiveness of a hedging scheme.

therefore sold the option for $60,000 more than its theoretical value. But it is faced with the problem of hedging the risks.[2]

15.2 NAKED AND COVERED POSITIONS

One strategy open to the financial institution is to do nothing. This is sometimes referred to as adopting a *naked position*. It is a strategy that works well if the stock price is below $50 at the end of the 20 weeks. The option then costs the financial institution nothing and it makes a profit of $300,000. A naked position works less well if the call is exercised because the financial institution then has to buy 100,000 shares at the market price prevailing in 20 weeks to cover the call. The cost to the financial institution is 100,000 times the amount by which the stock price exceeds the strike price. For example, if after 20 weeks the stock price is $60, the option costs the financial institution $1,000,000. This is considerably greater than the $300,000 charged for the option.

As an alternative to a naked position, the financial institution can adopt a *covered position*. This involves buying 100,000 shares as soon as the option has been sold. If the option is exercised, this strategy works well, but in other circumstances it could lead to a significant loss. For example, if the stock price drops to $40, the financial institution loses $900,000 on its stock position. This is considerably greater than the $300,000 charged for the option.[3]

Neither a naked position nor a covered position provides a good hedge. If the assumptions underlying the Black–Scholes formula hold, the cost to the financial institution should always be $240,000 on average for both approaches.[4] But on any one occasion the cost is liable to range from zero to over $1,000,000. A good hedge would ensure that the cost is always close to $240,000.

15.3 A STOP-LOSS STRATEGY

One interesting hedging scheme that is sometimes proposed involves a *stop-loss strategy*. To illustrate the basic idea, consider an institution that has written a call option with strike price K to buy one unit of a stock. The hedging scheme involves buying one unit of the stock as soon as its price rises above K and selling it as soon as its price falls below K. The objective is to hold a naked position whenever the stock price is less than K and a covered position whenever the stock price is greater than K. The scheme is designed to ensure that at time T the institution owns the stock if the option closes in the money and does not own it if the option closes out of the money. The strategy appears to produce payoffs that are the same as the payoffs on the option. In the situation illustrated in Figure 15.1, it involves buying the stock at time t_1, selling it at

[2] A call option on a non-dividend-paying stock is a convenient example with which to develop our ideas. The points that will be made apply to other types of options and to other derivatives.

[3] Put–call parity shows that the exposure from writing a covered call is the same as the exposure from writing a naked put.

[4] More precisely, the present value of the expected cost is $240,000 for both approaches assuming that appropriate risk-adjusted discount rates are used.

time t_2, buying it at time t_3, selling it at time t_4, buying it at time t_5, and delivering it at time T.

As usual, we denote the initial stock price by S_0. The cost of setting up the hedge initially is S_0 if $S_0 > K$ and zero otherwise. It seems as though the total cost, Q, of writing and hedging the option is equal to the intrinsic value of the option:

$$Q = \max(S_0 - K,\ 0) \qquad \textbf{(15.1)}$$

This is because all purchases and sales subsequent to time zero are made at price K. If this were in fact correct, the hedging scheme would work perfectly in the absence of transactions costs. Furthermore, the cost of hedging the option would always be less than its Black–Scholes price. Thus, an investor could earn riskless profits by writing options and hedging them.

There are two basic reasons why equation (15.1) is incorrect. The first is that the cash flows to the hedger occur at different times and must be discounted. The second is that purchases and sales cannot be made at exactly the same price K. This second point is critical. If we assume a risk-neutral world with zero interest rates, we can justify ignoring the time value of money. But we cannot legitimately assume that both purchases and sales are made at the same price. If markets are efficient, the hedger cannot know whether, when the stock price equals K, it will continue above or below K.

As a practical matter, purchases must be made at a price $K + \epsilon$ and sales must be made at a price $K - \epsilon$, for some small positive number, ϵ. Thus, every purchase and subsequent sale involves a cost (apart from transaction costs) of 2ϵ. A natural response on the part of the hedger is to monitor price movements more closely so that ϵ is reduced. Assuming that stock prices change continuously, ϵ can be made arbitrarily small by monitoring the stock prices closely. But as ϵ is made smaller, trades tend to occur more frequently. Thus,

Figure 15.1 A stop-loss strategy

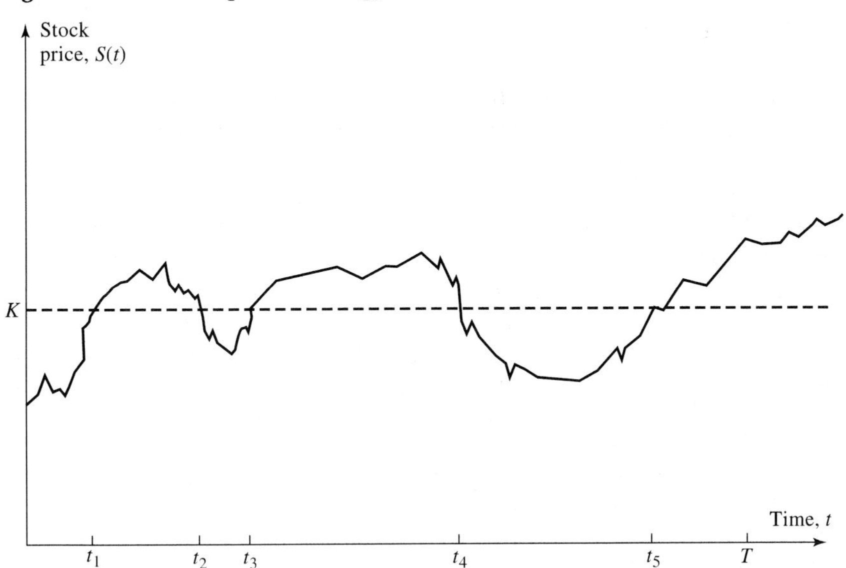

Table 15.1 Performance of stop-loss strategy. (The performance measure is the ratio of the standard deviation of the cost of writing the option and hedging it to the theoretical price of the option.)

Δt (weeks):	5	4	2	1	0.5	0.25
Hedge performance:	1.02	0.93	0.82	0.77	0.76	0.76

the lower cost per trade is offset by the increasing frequency of trading. As $\epsilon \to 0$, the expected number of trades tends to infinity.

A stop-loss strategy, although superficially attractive, does not work particularly well as a hedging scheme. Consider its use for an out-of-the-money option. If the stock price never reaches the strike price of K, the hedging scheme costs nothing. If the path of the stock price crosses the strike price level many times, the scheme is quite expensive. Monte Carlo simulation can be used to assess the overall performance of stop-loss hedging. This involves randomly sampling paths for the stock price and observing the results of using the scheme. Table 15.1 shows the results for the option considered in Section 15.1. It assumes that the stock price is observed at the end of time intervals of length Δt.[5] The hedge performance measure is the ratio of the standard deviation of the cost of hedging the option to the Black–Scholes price of the option. Each result is based on 1,000 sample paths for the stock price and has a standard error of about 2%. It appears to be impossible to produce a value for the hedge performance measure below 0.70 regardless of how small Δt is made.

15.4 DELTA HEDGING

Most traders use more sophisticated hedging schemes than those mentioned so far. These involve calculating measures such as delta, gamma, and vega. In this section we consider the role played by delta.

The *delta* of an option, Δ, was introduced in Chapter 11. It is defined as the rate of change of the option price with respect to the price of the underlying asset. It is the slope of the curve that relates the option price to the underlying asset price. Suppose that the delta of a call option on a stock is 0.6. This means that when the stock price changes by a small amount, the option price changes by about 60% of that amount. Figure 15.2 shows the relationship between a call price and the underlying stock price. When the stock price corresponds to point A, the option price corresponds to point B, and Δ is the slope of the line indicated. In general, the delta of a call equals $\Delta c/\Delta S$, where ΔS is a small change in the stock price and Δc the resulting change in the call price.

Suppose that, in Figure 15.2, the stock price is \$100 and the option price is \$10. Consider a trader working for a financial institution who sells 20 call option contracts on a stock—that is, options to buy 2,000 shares. The trader's position could be hedged

[5] The precise hedging rule used was as follows. If the stock price moves from below K to above K in a time interval of length Δt, it is bought at the end of the interval. If it moves from above K to below K in the time interval, it is sold at the end of the interval. Otherwise, no action is taken.

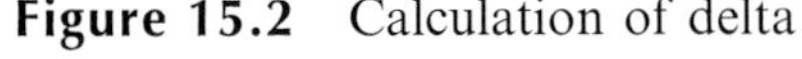

Figure 15.2 Calculation of delta

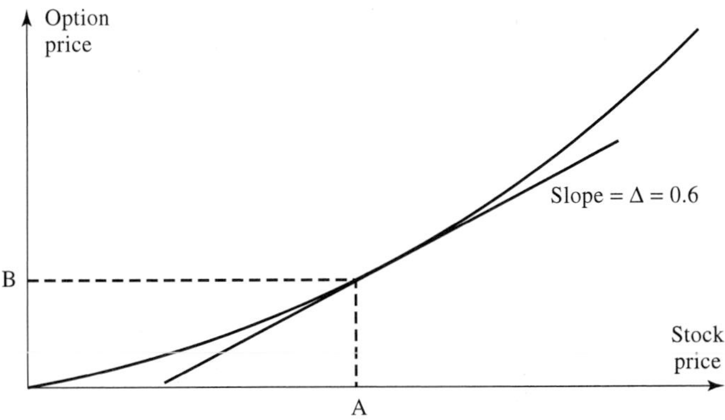

by buying $0.6 \times 2{,}000 = 1{,}200$ shares. The gain (loss) on the option position would then tend to be offset by the loss (gain) on the stock position. For example, if the stock price goes up by \$1 (producing a gain of \$1,200 on the shares purchased), the option price will tend to go up by $0.6 \times \$1 = \$0.60$ (producing a loss of \$1,200 on the options written); if the stock price goes down by \$1 (producing a loss of \$1,200 on the shares purchased), the option price will tend to go down by \$0.60 (producing a gain of \$1,200 on the options written).

In this example, the delta of the trader's option position is $0.6 \times (-2{,}000) = -1{,}200$. In other words, the trader loses $1{,}200\Delta S$ on the short option position when the stock price increases by ΔS. The delta of the stock is 1.0, so that the long position in 1,200 shares has a delta of +1,200. The delta of the investor's overall position is, therefore, zero. The delta of the stock position offsets the delta of the option position. A position with a delta of zero is referred to as being *delta neutral.*

It is important to realize that, because delta changes, the investor's position remains delta hedged (or delta neutral) for only a relatively short period of time. The hedge has to be adjusted periodically. This is known as *rebalancing*. In our example, at the end of one day the stock price might increase to \$110. As indicated by Figure 15.2, an increase in the stock price leads to an increase in delta. Suppose that delta rises from 0.60 to 0.65. An extra $0.05 \times 2{,}000 = 100$ shares would then have to be purchased to maintain the hedge. The example is summarized in Trading Note 15.1.

The delta-hedging scheme just described is an example of a *dynamic-hedging scheme*. It can be contrasted with *static-hedging schemes*, where the hedge is set up initially and never adjusted. Static-hedging schemes are sometimes also referred to as *hedge-and-forget schemes*. Delta is closely related to the Black–Scholes analysis. As explained in Chapter 12, Black and Scholes showed that it is possible to set up a riskless portfolio consisting of a position in an option on a stock and a position in the stock. Expressed in terms of Δ, the Black and Scholes portfolio is

$$\begin{cases} -1: & \text{option} \\ +\Delta: & \text{shares of the stock} \end{cases}$$

Using our new terminology, we can say that Black and Scholes valued options by

Trading Note 15.1 Use of delta hedging

A trader working for a financial institution sells 20 call option contracts (2,000 options) on a certain stock. The option price is \$10, the stock price is \$100, and the option's delta is 0.6.

First Hedge
The trader buys $0.6 \times 2{,}000 = 1{,}200$ shares.

Price Change
During the next day the stock price increases to \$110 and the delta changes to 0.65

Hedge Rebalancing
The trader buys a further $0.05 \times 2{,}000 = 100$ shares.

setting up a delta-neutral position and arguing that the return on the position should be the risk-free interest rate.

Delta of European Stock Options

For a European call option on a non-dividend-paying stock, it can be shown that

$$\Delta = N(d_1)$$

where d_1 is defined as in equation (12.5). Using delta hedging for a short position in a European call option therefore involves keeping a long position of $N(d_1)$ shares at any given time. Similarly, using delta hedging for a long position in a European call option involves maintaining a short position of $N(d_1)$ shares at any given time.

For a European put option on a non-dividend-paying stock, delta is given by

$$\Delta = N(d_1) - 1$$

Delta is negative, which means that a long position in a put option should be hedged

Figure 15.3 Variation of delta with stock price for (a) call option and (b) put option on a non-dividend-paying stock

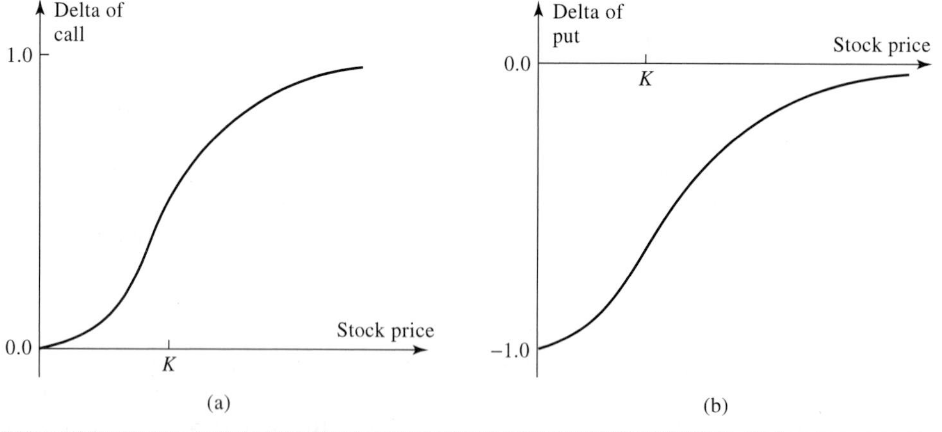

Figure 15.4 Typical patterns for variation of delta with time to maturity for a call option

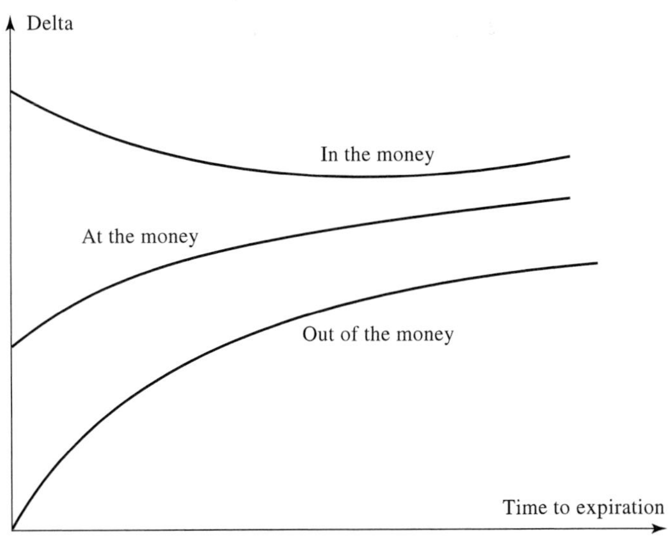

with a long position in the underlying stock, and a short position in a put option should be hedged with a short position in the underlying stock. Figure 15.3 shows the variation of the delta of a call option and a put option with the stock price. Figure 15.4 shows the variation of delta with the time to maturity for in-the-money, at-the-money, and out-of-the-money call options.

Delta of Other European Options

For European call options on an asset paying a dividend yield q,

$$\Delta = e^{-qT}N(d_1)$$

where d_1 is defined by equation (13.4). For European put options on the asset,

$$\Delta = e^{-qT}[N(d_1) - 1]$$

When the asset is a stock index, these formulas are correct with q equal to the dividend yield on the index. When the asset is a currency, they are correct with q equal to the foreign risk-free rate, r_f. When the asset is a futures contract, they are correct with q equal to the domestic risk-free rate, r, and $S_0 = F_0$ in the definition of d_1. (In the latter case, delta gives the rate of change of the option price with respect to the futures price.)

Example

A U.S. bank has sold six-month put options on £1 million with a strike price of 1.6000 and wishes to make its portfolio delta neutral. Suppose that the current exchange rate is 1.6200, the risk-free interest rate in the United Kingdom is 13% per annum, the risk-free interest rate in the United States is 10% per annum, and the volatility of sterling is 15%. In this case, $S_0 = 1.6200$, $K = 1.6000$, $r = 0.10$, $r_f = 0.13$, $\sigma = 0.15$, and $T = 0.5$. The delta of a put option on a currency is

$$[N(d_1) - 1]e^{-r_f T}$$

where d_1 is given by equation (13.9). It can be shown that

$$d_1 = 0.0287 \quad \text{and} \quad N(d_1) = 0.5115$$

so that the delta of the put option is –0.458. This is the delta of a long position in one put option. (It means that when the exchange rate increases by ΔS, the price of the put goes down by 45.8% of ΔS.) The delta of the bank's total short option position is +458,000. To make the position delta neutral, we must therefore add a short sterling position of £458,000 to the option position. This short sterling position has a delta of –458,000 and neutralizes the delta of the option position.

Delta of Forward Contracts

The concept of delta can be applied to financial instruments other than options. Consider a forward contract on a non-dividend-paying stock. Equation (5.5) shows that the value of a forward contract is $S_0 - Ke^{-rT}$ where K is the delivery price and T is the forward contract's time to maturity. When the price of the stock changes by ΔS, with all else remaining the same, the value of a forward contract on the stock also changes by ΔS. The delta of a forward contract on one share of the stock is therefore always 1.0. This means that a short forward contract on one share can be hedged by purchasing one share; a long forward contract on one share can be hedged by shorting one share.[6]

For an asset providing a dividend yield at rate q, equation (5.7) shows that the forward contract's delta is e^{-qT}. In the case of a stock index, q is set equal to the dividend yield on the index. For a currency, it is set equal to the foreign risk-free rate, r_f.

Delta of a Futures Contract

From equation (5.1), the futures price for a contract on a non-dividend-paying stock is $S_0 e^{rT}$, where T is the time to maturity of the futures contract. This shows that when the price of the stock changes by ΔS, with all else remaining the same, the futures price changes by $\Delta S\, e^{rT}$. Because futures contracts are marked to market daily, the holder of a long futures contract makes an almost immediate gain of this amount. The delta of a futures contract is therefore e^{rT}. For a futures contract on an asset providing a dividend yield at rate q, equation (5.3) shows similarly that delta is $e^{(r-q)T}$. It is interesting that the impact of marking to market is to make the deltas of futures and forward contracts slightly different. This is true even when interest rates are constant and the forward price equals the futures price.

Sometimes a futures contract is used to achieve a delta-neutral position. Define:

T: Maturity of futures contract

H_A: Required position in asset for delta hedging

H_F: Alternative required position in futures contracts for delta hedging

---

[6] These are hedge-and-forget schemes. Because delta is always 1.0, no changes need to be made to the position in the stock during the life of the contract.

If the underlying asset is a non-dividend-paying stock, the analysis we have just given shows that

$$H_F = e^{-rT} H_A \tag{15.2}$$

When the underlying asset pays a dividend yield q,

$$H_F = e^{-(r-q)T} H_A \tag{15.3}$$

For a stock index, we set q equal to the dividend yield on the index; for a currency, we set it equal to the foreign risk-free rate, r_f, so that

$$H_F = e^{-(r-r_f)T} H_A \tag{15.4}$$

Example

Consider the option in the previous example where hedging using the currency requires a short position of 458,000 pounds sterling. From equation (15.4), hedging using nine-month currency futures requires a short futures position

$$e^{-(0.10-0.13)\times 9/12} \times 458{,}000$$

or £468,442. Because each futures contract is for the purchase or sale of £62,500, seven contracts should be shorted. (Seven is the nearest whole number to 468,442/62,500.)

Dynamic Aspects of Delta Hedging

Tables 15.2 and 15.3 provide two examples of the operation of delta hedging for the example in Section 15.1. The hedge is assumed to be adjusted or rebalanced weekly. The initial value of delta can be calculated from the data in Section 15.1 as 0.522. This means that as soon as the option is written, \$2,557,800 must be borrowed to buy 52,200 shares at a price of \$49. The rate of interest is 5%. As a result, an interest cost of approximately \$2,500 is incurred in the first week.

In Table 15.2, the stock price falls by the end of the first week to \$48.12. The delta declines to 0.458, and 6,400 of shares are sold to maintain the hedge. The strategy realizes \$308,000 in cash, and the cumulative borrowings at the end of Week 1 are reduced to \$2,252,300. During the second week, the stock price reduces to \$47.37, delta declines again, and so on. Toward the end of the life of the option, it becomes apparent that the option will be exercised and delta approaches 1.0. By Week 20, therefore, the hedger has a fully covered position. The hedger receives \$5 million for the stock held, so that the total cost of writing the option and hedging it is \$263,300.

Table 15.3 illustrates an alternative sequence of events such that the option closes out of the money. As it becomes clear that the option will not be exercised, delta approaches zero. By Week 20, the hedger has a naked position and has incurred costs totaling \$256,600.

In Tables 15.2 and 15.3, the costs of hedging the option, when discounted to the beginning of the period, are close to, but not exactly the same as, the Black–Scholes price of \$240,000. If the hedging scheme worked perfectly, the cost of hedging would, after discounting, be exactly equal to the Black–Scholes price for every simulated stock price path. The reason for the variation in the cost of delta hedging is that the hedge is rebalanced only once a week. As rebalancing takes place more frequently, the variation in the cost of hedging is reduced. Of course, the examples in Tables 15.2 and 15.3 are idealized in that they assume that the volatility is constant and there are no transaction costs.

Table 15.4 shows statistics on the performance of delta hedging obtained from 1,000 random stock price paths in our example. As in Table 15.1, the performance measure is the ratio of the standard deviation of the cost of hedging the option to the Black–Scholes price of the option. It is clear that delta hedging is a great improvement over a stop-loss strategy. Unlike a stop-loss strategy, the performance of delta-hedging strategy gets steadily better as the hedge is monitored more frequently.

Delta hedging aims to keep the value of the financial institution's position as close to unchanged as possible. Initially, the value of the written option is \$240,000. In the situation depicted in Table 15.2, the value of the option can be calculated as \$414,500 in Week 9. Thus, the financial institution has lost \$174,500 on its option position. Its cash position, as measured by the cumulative cost, is \$1,442,900 worse in Week 9 than in Week 0. The value of the shares held has increased from \$2,557,800 to \$4,171,100. The net effect of all this is that the value of the financial institution's position has changed by only \$4,100 during the nine-week period.

Table 15.2 Simulation of delta hedging. Option closes in the money and cost of hedging is \$263,300

Week	*Stock price*	*Delta*	*Shares purchased*	*Cost of shares purchased (\$000)*	*Cumulative cost including interest (\$000)*	*Interest cost (\$000)*
0	49.00	0.522	52,200	2,557.8	2,557.8	2.5
1	48.12	0.458	(6,400)	(308.0)	2,252.3	2.2
2	47.37	0.400	(5,800)	(274.7	1,979.8	1.9
3	50.25	0.596	19,600	984.9	2,966.6	2.9
4	51.75	0.693	9,700	502.0	3,471.5	3.3
5	53.12	0.774	8,100	430.3	3,905.1	3.8
6	53.00	0.771	(300)	(15.9)	3,893.0	3.7
7	51.87	0.706	(6,500)	(337.2)	3,559.5	3.4
8	51.38	0.674	(3,200)	(164.4)	3,398.5	3.3
9	53.00	0.787	11,300	598.9	4,000.7	3.8
10	49.88	0.550	(23,700)	(1,182.2)	2,822.3	2.7
11	48.50	0.413	(13,700)	(664.4)	2,160.6	2.1
12	49.88	0.542	12,900	643.5	2,806.2	2.7
13	50.37	0.591	4,900	246.8	3,055.7	2.9
14	52.13	0.768	17,700	922.7	3,981.3	3.8
15	51.88	0.759	(900)	(46.7)	3,938.4	3.8
16	52.87	0.865	10,600	560.4	4,502.6	4.3
17	54.87	0.978	11,300	620.0	5,126.9	4.9
18	54.62	0.990	1,200	65.5	5,197.3	5.0
19	55.87	1.000	1,000	55.9	5,258.2	5.1
20	57.25	1.000	0	0.0	5,263.3	

Table 15.3 Simulation of delta hedging. Option closes out of the money and cost of hedging = $256,600

Week	*Stock price*	*Delta*	*Shares purchased*	*Cost of shares purchased ($000)*	*Cumulative cost including interest ($000)*	*Interest cost ($000)*
0	49.00	0.522	52,200	2,557.8	2,557.8	2.5
1	49.75	0.568	4,600	228.9	2,789.2	2.7
2	52.00	0.705	13,700	712.4	3,504.3	3.4
3	50.00	0.579	(12,600)	(630.0)	2,877.7	2.8
4	48.38	0.459	(12,000)	(580.6)	2,299.9	2.2
5	48.25	0.443	(1,600)	(77.2)	2,224.9	2.1
6	48.75	0.475	3,200	156.0	2,383.0	2.3
7	49.63	0.540	6,500	322.6	2,707.9	2.6
8	48.25	0.420	(12,000)	(579.0)	2,131.5	2.1
9	48.25	0.410	(1,000)	(48.2)	2,085.4	2.0
10	51.12	0.658	24,800	1,267.8	3,355.2	3.2
11	51.50	0.692	3,400	175.1	3,533.5	3.4
12	49.88	0.542	(15,000)	(748.2)	2,788.7	2.7
13	49.88	0.538	(400)	(20.0)	2,771.4	2.7
14	48.75	0.400	(13,800)	(672.7)	2,101.4	2.0
15	47.50	0.236	(16,400)	(779.0)	1,324.4	1.3
16	48.00	0.261	2,500	120.0	1,445.7	1.4
17	46.25	0.062	(19,900)	(920.4)	526.7	0.5
18	48.13	0.183	12,100	582.4	1,109.6	1.1
19	46.63	0.007	(17,600)	(820.7)	290.0	0.3
20	48.12	0.000	(700)	(33.7)	256.6	

Where the Cost Comes From

The delta-hedging scheme in Tables 15.2 and 15.3 in effect creates a long position in the option synthetically. This neutralizes the short position arising from the option that has been written. The scheme generally involves selling stock just after the price has gone down and buying stock just after the price has gone up. It might be termed a buy-high, sell-low scheme! The cost of $240,000 comes from the average difference between the price paid for the stock and the price realized for it.

Table 15.4 Performance of delta hedging. The performance measure is the ratio of the standard deviation of the cost of writing the option and hedging it to the theoretical price of the option.

Time between hedge rebalancing (weeks):	5	4	2	1	0.5	0.25
Performance measure:	0.43	0.39	0.26	0.19	0.14	0.09

Delta of a Portfolio

The delta of a portfolio of options or other derivatives dependent on a single asset whose price is S is given by

$$\frac{\Delta\Pi}{\Delta S}$$

where ΔS is a small change in the price of the asset and $\Delta\Pi$ is the resultant change in the value of the portfolio.

The delta of the portfolio can be calculated from the deltas of the individual options in the portfolio. If a portfolio consists of a quantity w_i of option i ($1 \leqslant i \leqslant n$), the delta of the portfolio is given by

$$\Delta = \sum_{i=1}^{n} w_i \Delta_i$$

where Δ_i is the delta of ith option. The formula can be used to calculate the position in the underlying asset or in a futures contract on the underlying asset necessary to make the delta of the portfolio zero. When this position has been taken, the portfolio is referred to as being *delta neutral.*

Suppose a financial institution in the United States has the following three positions in options on the Australian dollar:

1. A long position in 100,000 call options with strike price 0.55 and an expiration date in three months. The delta of each option is 0.533.
2. A short position in 200,000 call options with strike price 0.56 and an expiration date in five months. The delta of each option is 0.468.
3. A short position in 50,000 put options with strike price 0.56 and an expiration date in two months. The delta of each option is −0.508.

The delta of the whole portfolio is

$$100{,}000 \times 0.533 - 200{,}000 \times 0.468 - 50{,}000 \times (-0.508) = -14{,}900$$

This means that the portfolio can be made delta neutral with a long position of 14,900 Australian dollars.

A six-month forward contract could also be used to achieve delta neutrality in this example. Suppose that the risk-free rate of interest is 8% per annum in Australia and 5% in the United States ($r = 0.05$ and $r_f = 0.08$). The delta of a forward contract maturing at time T on one Australian dollar is $e^{-r_f T}$ or $e^{-0.08\times 0.5} = 0.9608$. The long position in Australian dollar forward contracts for delta neutrality is therefore $14{,}900/0.9608 = 15{,}508$.

Another alternative is to use a six-month futures contract. From equation (15.4), the long position in Australian dollar futures for delta neutrality is

$$14{,}900e^{-(0.05-0.08)\times 0.5} = 15{,}125$$

Transaction Costs

Maintaining a delta-neutral position in a single option and the underlying asset, in the way that has just been described, is liable to be prohibitively expensive because of the transaction costs incurred on trades. For a large portfolio of options, delta neutrality is more feasible. Only one trade in the underlying asset is necessary to zero out delta for the whole portfolio. The hedging transactions costs are absorbed by the profits on many different trades.

15.5 THETA

The *theta* of a portfolio of options, Θ, is the rate of change of the value of the portfolio with respect to the passage of time with all else remaining the same. Specifically,

$$\Theta = \frac{\Delta \Pi}{\Delta t}$$

where $\Delta \Pi$ is change in the value of the portfolio when an amount of time Δt passes with all else remaining the same. Theta is sometimes referred to as the *time decay* of the portfolio. For a European call option on a non-dividend-paying stock, it can be shown from the Black–Scholes formula that

$$\Theta = -\frac{S_0 N'(d_1)\sigma}{2\sqrt{T}} - rKe^{-rT}N(d_2)$$

where d_1 and d_2 are defined as in equation (12.5) and

$$N'(x) = \frac{1}{\sqrt{2\pi}} e^{-x^2/2} \tag{15.5}$$

For a European put option on the stock,

$$\Theta = -\frac{S_0 N'(d_1)\sigma}{2\sqrt{T}} + rKe^{-rT}N(-d_2)$$

For a European call option on an asset paying a dividend at rate q,

$$\Theta = -\frac{S_0 N'(d_1)\sigma e^{-qT}}{2\sqrt{T}} + qS_0 N(d_1)e^{-qT} - rKe^{-rT}N(d_2)$$

where d_1 and d_2 are defined as in equation (13.4), and for a European put option on the asset

$$\Theta = -\frac{S_0 N'(d_1)\sigma e^{-qT}}{2\sqrt{T}} - qS_0 N(-d_1)e^{-qT} + rKe^{-rT}N(-d_2)$$

When the asset is a stock index, these last two equations are true with q equal to the dividend yield on the index. When it is a currency, they are true with q equal to the foreign risk-free rate, r_f. When it is a futures contract, they are true with $S_0 = F_0$ and $q = r$.

In these formulas, time is measured in years. Usually, when theta is quoted, time is measured in days, so that theta is the change in the portfolio value when one day passes with all else remaining the same. We can either measure theta "per calendar day" or "per trading day." To obtain the theta per calendar day, the formula for theta must be divided by 365; to obtain theta per trading day, it must be divided by 252. (DerivaGem measures theta per calendar day.)

Figure 15.5 Variation of theta of a European call option with stock price

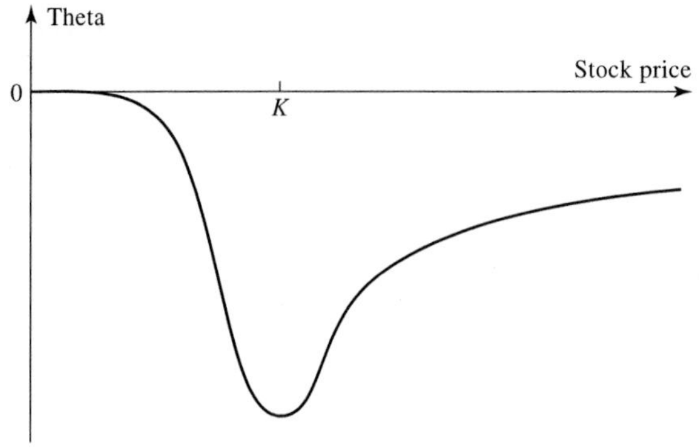

Theta

Stock price

0

K

Example

Consider a four-month put option on a stock index. The current value of the index is 305, the strike price is 300, the dividend yield is 3% per annum, the risk-free interest rate is 8% per annum, and the volatility of the index is 25% per annum. In this case, $S_0 = 305$, $K = 300$, $q = 0.03$, $r = 0.08$, $\sigma = 0.25$, and $T = 0.3333$. The option's theta is

$$-\frac{S_0 N'(d_1)\sigma e^{-qT}}{2\sqrt{T}} - qS_0 N(-d_1)e^{-qT} + rKe^{-rT}N(-d_2) = -18.15$$

The theta is $-18.15/365 = -0.0497$ per calendar day or $-18.15/252 = -0.0720$ per trading day.

Figure 15.6 Typical patterns for variation of theta of a European call option with time to maturity

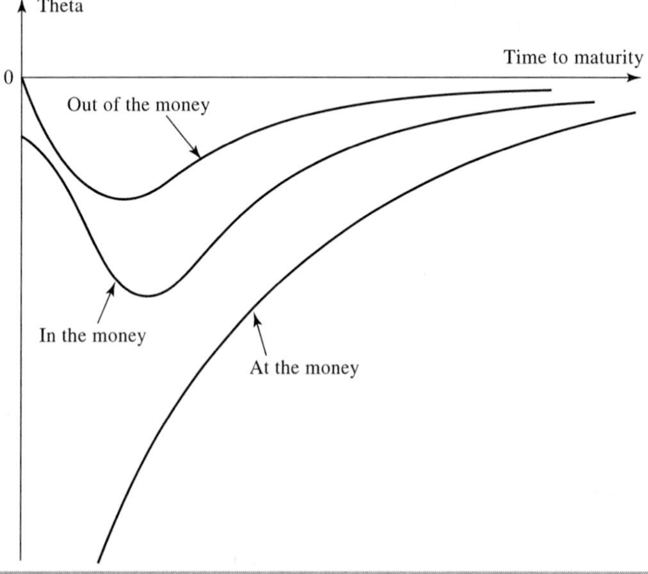

Theta is usually negative for an option.[7] This is because as the time to maturity decreases with all else remaining the same, the option tends to become less valuable. The variation of Θ with stock price for a call option on a stock is shown in Figure 15.5. When the stock price is very low, theta is close to zero. For an at-the-money call option, theta is large and negative. As the stock price becomes larger, theta tends to $-rKe^{-rT}$. Figure 15.6 shows typical patterns for the variation of Θ with the time to maturity for in-the-money, at-the-money, and out-of-the-money call options.

Theta is not the same type of hedge parameter as delta. There is uncertainty about the future stock price, but there is no uncertainty about the passage of time. It makes sense to hedge against changes in the price of the underlying asset, but it does not make any sense to hedge against the effect of the passage of time on an option portfolio. In spite of this, many traders regard theta as a useful descriptive statistic for a portfolio. This is because, as we will see later, in a delta-neutral portfolio theta is a proxy for gamma.

15.6 GAMMA

The *gamma*, Γ, of a portfolio of options on an underlying asset is the rate of change of the portfolio's delta with respect to the price of the underlying asset. If gamma is small, delta changes slowly, and adjustments to keep a portfolio delta neutral need to be made only relatively infrequently. However, if gamma is large in absolute terms, delta is highly sensitive to the price of the underlying asset. It is then quite risky to leave a delta-neutral portfolio unchanged for any length of time. Figure 15.7 illustrates this point. When the stock price moves from S to S', delta hedging assumes that the option price moves from C to C', when in fact it moves from C to C''. The difference between C' and C'' leads to a hedging error. This error depends on the curvature of the relationship between the option price and the stock price. Gamma measures this curvature.[8]

Suppose that ΔS is the change in the price of an underlying asset in a small interval of time, Δt, and $\Delta\Pi$ is the corresponding change in the price of the portfolio. For a

Figure 15.7 Hedging error introduced by nonlinearity

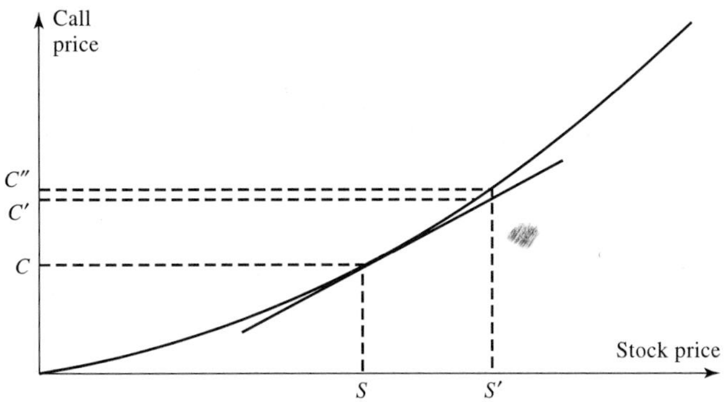

[7] An exception to this could be an in-the-money European put option on a non-dividend-paying stock or an in-the-money European call option on a currency with a very high interest rate.

[8] Indeed, the gamma of an option is sometimes referred to as its *curvature* by practitioners.

delta-neutral portfolio, it is approximately true that

$$\Delta\Pi = \Theta\,\Delta t + \frac{\Gamma\,\Delta S^2}{2} \tag{15.6}$$

where Θ is the theta of the portfolio.

Example

Suppose that the gamma of a delta-neutral portfolio of options on an asset is $-10{,}000$. Equation (15.6) shows that if a change of $+2$ or -2 in the price of the asset occurs over a short period of time, there is an unexpected decrease in the value of the portfolio of approximately $0.5 \times 10{,}000 \times 2^2 = \$20{,}000$.

Figure 15.8 shows the nature of this relationship between $\Delta\Pi$ and ΔS for a delta-neutral portfolio. It shows that when gamma is positive, the portfolio declines in value if there is no change in S but increases in value if there is a large positive or negative change in S. When gamma is negative, the reverse is true: the portfolio increases in value if there is no change in S but decreases in value if there is a large positive or negative change in S. As the absolute value of gamma increases, the sensitivity of the value of the portfolio to ΔS increases.

Figure 15.8 Alternative relationships between $\Delta\Pi$ and ΔS for a delta-neutral portfolio: (a) slightly positive gamma, (b) large positive gamma, (c) slightly negative gamma, and (d) large negative gamma

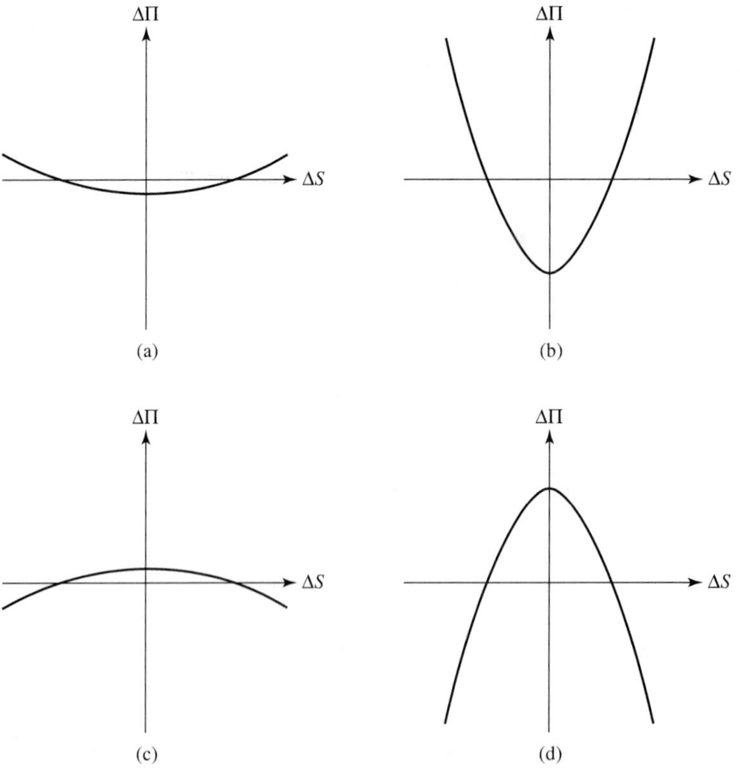

Making a Portfolio Gamma Neutral

A position in the underlying asset itself or a forward contract on the underlying asset both have zero gamma and cannot be used to change the gamma of a portfolio. What is required is a position in an instrument such as an option that is not linearly dependent on the underlying asset.

Suppose that a delta-neutral portfolio has a gamma equal to Γ, and a traded option has a gamma equal to Γ_T. If the number of traded options added to the portfolio is w_T, then the gamma of the portfolio is

$$w_T \Gamma_T + \Gamma$$

Hence, the position in the traded option necessary to make the portfolio gamma neutral is $-\Gamma/\Gamma_T$. Including the traded option is likely to change the delta of the portfolio, so the position in the underlying asset then has to be changed to maintain delta neutrality. Note that the portfolio is gamma neutral only for a short period of time. As time passes, gamma neutrality can be maintained only if the position in the traded option is adjusted so that it is always equal to $-\Gamma/\Gamma_T$.

Making a delta-neutral portfolio gamma neutral can be regarded as a first correction for the fact that the position in the underlying asset cannot be changed continuously when delta hedging is used. Delta neutrality provides protection against relatively small stock price moves between rebalancing. Gamma neutrality provides protection against larger movements in this stock price between hedge rebalancing. Suppose that a portfolio is delta neutral and has a gamma of −3,000. The delta and gamma of a particular traded call option are 0.62 and 1.50, respectively. The portfolio can be made gamma neutral by including in the portfolio a long position of

$$\frac{3{,}000}{1.5} = 2{,}000$$

in the call option. However, the delta of the portfolio will then change from zero to $2{,}000 \times 0.62 = 1{,}240$. A quantity, 1,240, of the underlying asset must therefore be sold from the portfolio to keep it delta neutral. This example is summarized in Trading Note 15.2.

Calculation of Gamma

For a European call or put option on a non-dividend-paying stock, the gamma is given by

$$\Gamma = \frac{N'(d_1)}{S_0 \sigma \sqrt{T}}$$

where d_1 is defined as in equation (12.5) and $N'(x)$ is as given by equation (15.5). The

---

Trading Note 15.2 Making a portfolio gamma and delta neutral

A trader's portfolio is delta neutral and has a gamma of −3,000. The delta and gamma of a particular traded call option are 0.62 and 1.50, respectively. The trader would like to make the portfolio gamma neutral as well as delta neutral.

The Strategy

1. Make portfolio gamma neutral buying 2,000 options (20 contracts).

2. Sell quantity, 1,240, of the underlying asset to maintain delta neutrality.

---

gamma of a long option position is always positive and varies with S_0 in the way indicated in Figure 15.9. The variation of gamma with time to maturity for out-of-the-money, at-the-money, and in-the-money options is shown in Figure 15.10. For an at-the-money option, gamma increases as the time to maturity decreases. Short-life at-the-money options have very high gammas, which means that the value of the option holder's position is highly sensitive to jumps in the stock price.

For a European call or put option on an asset paying a continuous dividend at rate q,

$$\Gamma = \frac{N'(d_1)e^{-qT}}{S_0\sigma\sqrt{T}}$$

where d_1 is defined as in equation (13.4). When the asset is a stock index, q is set equal to the dividend yield on the index. When it is a currency, q is set equal to the foreign risk-free rate, r_f. When it is a futures contract, $S_0 = F_0$ and $q = r$.

Example

Consider a four-month put option on a stock index. The current value of the index is 305, the strike price is 300, the dividend yield is 3% per annum, the risk-free interest rate is 8% per annum, and volatility of the index is 25% per annum. In this case, $S_0 = 305$, $K = 300$, $q = 0.03$, $r = 0.08$, $\sigma = 0.25$, and $T = 4/12$. The gamma of the index option is given by

$$\frac{N'(d_1)e^{-qT}}{S_0\sigma\sqrt{T}} = 0.00857$$

Thus, an increase of 1 in the index (from 305 to 306) increases the delta of the option by approximately 0.00857.

15.7 RELATIONSHIP BETWEEN DELTA, THETA, AND GAMMA

The Black–Scholes analysis shows that the Greek letters for a portfolio of calls, puts, and other financial instruments dependent on an asset paying a dividend yield of q

Figure 15.9 Variation of gamma with stock price for an option

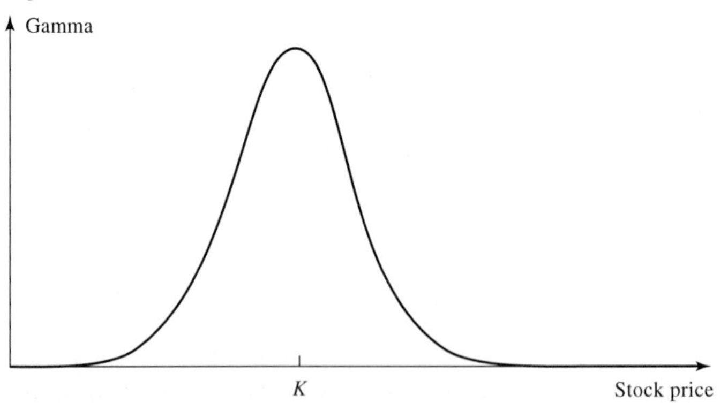

Figure 15.10 Variation of gamma with time to maturity for a stock option

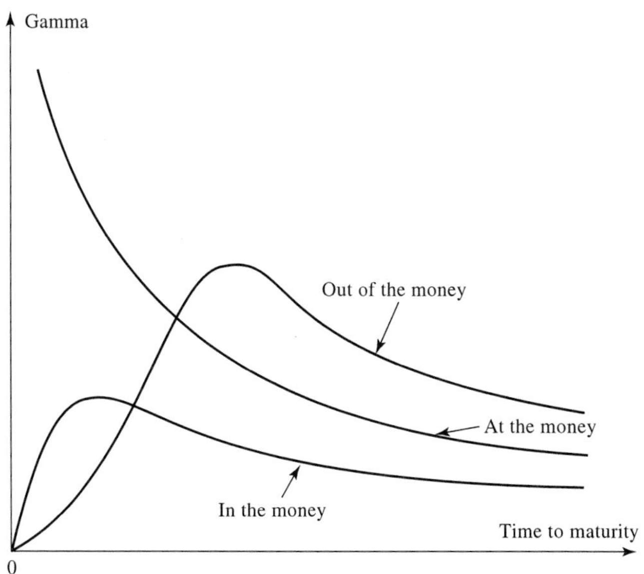

must satisfy

$$\Theta + (r - q)S_0\Delta + \tfrac{1}{2}\sigma^2 S_0^2\Gamma = r\Pi \quad \textbf{(15.7)}$$

where S_0 is the asset price and Π is the value of the portfolio.

For a delta-neutral portfolio, $\Delta = 0$, so that

$$\Theta + \tfrac{1}{2}\sigma^2 S_0^2\Gamma = r\Pi$$

This shows that when Θ is large and positive, gamma of a portfolio tends to be large and negative, and vice versa. This is consistent with the way Figure 15.8 has been drawn and explains why theta is sometimes regarded as a proxy for gamma in a delta-neutral portfolio.

15.8 VEGA

Up to now we have implicitly assumed that the volatility of the asset underlying a derivative is constant. In practice, volatilities change over time. This means that the value of a derivative is liable to change because of movements in volatility as well as because of changes in the asset price and the passage of time.

The *vega* of a portfolio of derivatives, $\mathcal{V}$, is the rate of change of the value of the portfolio with respect to the volatility of the underlying asset.[9] If vega is high in absolute terms, the portfolio's value is very sensitive to small changes in volatility. If vega is low in absolute terms, volatility changes have relatively little impact on the value of the portfolio.

[9] Vega is the name given to one of the "Greek letters" in option pricing, but it is not one of the letters in the Greek alphabet.

A position in the underlying asset has zero vega. However, the vega of a portfolio can be changed by adding a position in a traded option. If $\mathcal{V}$ is the vega of the portfolio and $\mathcal{V}_T$ is the vega of a traded option, a position of $-\mathcal{V}/\mathcal{V}_T$ in the traded option makes the portfolio instantaneously vega neutral. Unfortunately, a portfolio that is gamma neutral will not in general be vega neutral, and vice versa. If a hedger requires a portfolio to be both gamma and vega neutral, at least two traded derivatives dependent on the underlying asset must usually be used.

Example

Consider a portfolio that is delta neutral, with a gamma of −5,000 and a vega of −8,000. A traded option has a gamma of 0.5, a vega of 2.0, and a delta of 0.6. The portfolio can be made vega neutral by including a long position in 4,000 traded options. This would increase delta to 2,400 and require that 2,400 units of the asset be sold to maintain delta neutrality. The gamma of the portfolio would change from −5,000 to −3,000.

To make the portfolio gamma and vega neutral, we suppose that there is a second traded option with a gamma of 0.8, a vega of 1.2, and a delta of 0.5. If w_1 and w_2 are the quantities of the two traded options included in the portfolio, we require

$$-5{,}000 + 0.5w_1 + 0.8w_2 = 0$$

$$-8{,}000 + 2.0w_1 + 1.2w_2 = 0$$

The solution to these equations is $w_1 = 400$, $w_2 = 6{,}000$. The portfolio can therefore be made gamma and vega neutral by including 400 of the first traded option and 6,000 of the second traded option. The delta of the portfolio after the addition of the positions in the two traded options is $400 \times 0.6 + 6{,}000 \times 0.5 = 3{,}240$. Hence, 3,240 units of the asset would have to be sold to maintain delta neutrality.

For a European call or put option on a non-dividend-paying stock, vega is given by

$$\mathcal{V} = S_0\sqrt{T}\,N'(d_1)$$

where d_1 is defined as in equation (12.5). The formula for $N'(x)$ is given in equation (15.5). For a European call or put option on an asset providing a dividend

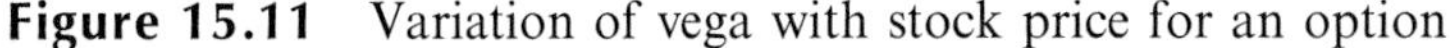

Figure 15.11 Variation of vega with stock price for an option

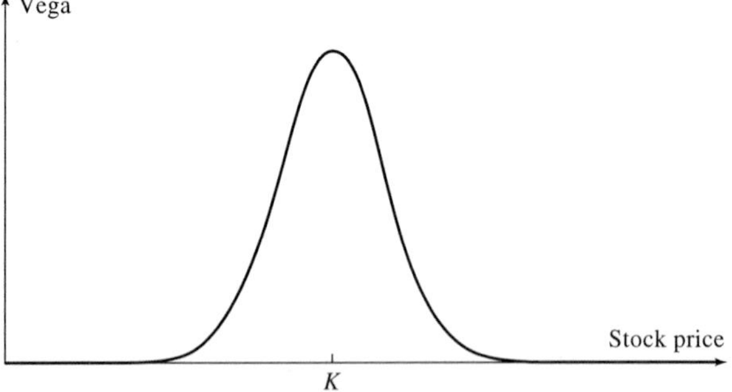

yield at rate q,

$$\mathcal{V} = S_0\sqrt{T}\,N'(d_1)e^{-qT}$$

where d_1 is defined as in equation (13.4). When the asset is a stock index, q is set equal to the dividend yield on the index. When it is a currency, q is set equal to the foreign risk-free rate, r_f. When it is a futures contract, $S_0 = F_0$ and $q = r$.

The vega of a long position in a regular European or American option is always positive. The general way in which vega varies with S_0 is shown in Figure 15.11.

Example

Consider a four-month put option on a stock index. The current value of the index is 305, the strike price is 300, the dividend yield is 3% per annum, the risk-free interest rate is 8% per annum, and the volatility of the index is 25% per annum. In this case $S_0 = 305$, $K = 300$, $q = 0.03$, $r = 0.08$, $\sigma = 0.25$, and $T = 4/12$. The option's vega is given by

$$S_0\sqrt{T}\,N'(d_1)e^{-qT} = 66.44$$

Thus a 1% (0.01) increase in volatility (from 25% to 26%) increases the value of the option by approximately 0.6644 (= 0.01 × 66.44).

Calculating vega from the Black–Scholes model and its extensions may seem strange because one of the assumptions underlying Black–Scholes is that volatility is constant. It would be theoretically more correct to calculate vega from a model in which volatility is assumed to be stochastic. However, it turns out that the vega calculated from a stochastic volatility model is very similar to the Black–Scholes vega so the practice of calculating vega from a model in which volatility is constant works reasonably well.[10]

Gamma neutrality protects against large changes in the price of the underlying asset between hedge rebalancing. Vega neutrality protects for a variable σ. As might be expected, whether it is best to use an available traded option for vega or gamma hedging depends on the time between hedge rebalancing and the volatility of the volatility.[11]

15.9 RHO

The *rho* of a portfolio of options is the rate of change of the value of the portfolio with respect to the interest rate. It measures the sensitivity of the value of a portfolio to interest rates. For a European call option on a non-dividend-paying stock,

$$\text{rho} = KTe^{-rT}N(d_2)$$

---

[10] See J. C. Hull and A. White, "The Pricing of Options on Assets with Stochastic Volatilities," *Journal of Finance*, 42 (June 1987): 281–300; J. C. Hull and A. White, "An Analysis of the Bias in Option Pricing Caused by a Stochastic Volatility," *Advances in Futures and Options Research*, 3 (1988): 27–61.

[11] For a discussion of this issue, see J. C. Hull and A. White. "Hedging the Risks from Writing Foreign Currency Options," *Journal of International Money and Finance*, 6 (June 1987): 131–52.

where d_2 is defined as in equation (12.5). For a European put option,

$$\text{rho} = -KTe^{-rT}N(-d_2)$$

These same formulas apply to European call and put options on stocks and stock indices paying known dividend yields when d_2 is as in equation (13.4).

Example

Consider a four-month put option on a stock index. The current value of the index is 305, the strike price is 300, the dividend yield is 3% per annum, the risk-free interest rate is 8% per annum, and the volatility of the index is 25% per annum. In this case $S_0 = 305$, $K = 300$, $q = 0.03$, $r = 0.08$, $\sigma = 0.25$, and $T = 4/12$. The option's rho is

$$-KTe^{-rT}N(-d_2) = -42.6$$

This means that for a 1% (0.01) change in the risk-free interest rate (from 8% to 9%) the value of the option decreases by 0.426 ($= 0.01 \times 42.6$).

In the case of currency options, there are two rhos corresponding to the two interest rates. The rho corresponding to the domestic interest rate is given by the formulas already presented with d_2 as in equation (13.9). The rho corresponding to the foreign interest rate for a European call on a currency is

$$\text{rho} = -Te^{-r_f T}S_0N(d_1)$$

For a European put, it is

$$\text{rho} = Te^{-r_f T}S_0N(-d_1)$$

where d_1 is given by equation (13.9).

For a European call futures option rho is $-cT$, and for a European put futures option it is $-pT$, where c and p are the European call and put option prices, respectively.

15.10 THE REALITIES OF HEDGING

In an ideal world, traders working for financial institutions would be able to rebalance their portfolios very frequently in order to maintain a zero delta, a zero gamma, a zero vega, and so on. In practice, this is not possible. When managing a large portfolio dependent on a single underlying asset, traders usually make delta zero, or close to zero, at least once a day by trading the underlying asset. Unfortunately, a zero gamma and a zero vega are less easy to achieve, because it is difficult to find options or other nonlinear derivatives that can be traded in the volume required at competitive prices (see discussion of dynamic hedging in Business Snapshot 15.1).

There are big economies of scale in being an options trader. As noted earlier, maintaining delta neutrality for an individual option on, say, the S&P 500 by trading daily would be prohibitively expensive. But it is realistic to do this for a portfolio of several hundred options on the S&P 500. This is because the cost of daily rebalancing (either by trading the stocks underlying the index or by trading index futures) is covered by the profit on many different trades.

Business Snapshot 15.1 Dynamic hedging in practice

In a typical arrangement at a financial institution, the responsibility for a portfolio of derivatives dependent on a particular underlying asset is assigned to one trader or to a group of traders working together. For example, one trader at Goldman Sachs might be assigned responsibility for all derivatives dependent on the value of the Australian dollar. A computer system calculates the value of the portfolio and Greek letters for the portfolio. Limits are defined for each Greek letter and special permission is required if a trader wants to exceed a limit at the end of a trading day.

The delta limit is often expressed as the equivalent maximum position in the underlying asset. For example, the delta limit of Goldman Sachs on Microsoft might be \$10 million. If the Microsoft stock price is \$50, this means that the absolute value of delta as we have calculated it can be no more that 200,000. The vega limit is usually expressed as a maximum dollar exposure per 1% change in the volatility.

As a matter of course, options traders make themselves delta neutral—or close to delta neutral—at the end of each day. Gamma and vega are monitored, but are not usually managed on a daily basis. Financial institutions often find that their business with clients involves writing options and that as a result they accumulate negative gamma and vega. They are then always looking out for opportunities to manage their gamma and vega risks by buying options at competitive prices.

There is one aspect of an options portfolio that mitigates problems of managing gamma and vega somewhat. Options are often close to the money when they are first sold so that they have relatively high gammas and vegas. But after some time has elapsed, the underlying asset price has often changed enough for them to become deep out of the money or deep in the money. Their gammas and vegas are then very small and of little consequence. The nightmare scenario for an options trader is where written options remain very close to the money as the maturity date is approached.

15.11 SCENARIO ANALYSIS

In addition to monitoring risks such as delta, gamma, and vega, option traders often also carry out a scenario analysis. The analysis involves calculating the gain or loss on their portfolio over a specified period under a variety of different scenarios. The time period chosen is likely to depend on the liquidity of the instruments. The scenarios can be either chosen by management or generated by a model.

Consider a bank with a portfolio of options on a foreign currency. There are two main variables on which the value of the portfolio depends. These are the exchange rate and the exchange rate volatility. Suppose that the exchange rate is currently 1.0000 and its volatility is 10% per annum. The bank could calculate a table such as Table 15.5 showing the profit or loss experienced during a two-week period under different scenarios. This table considers seven different exchange rates and three different volatilities. Because a one-standard-deviation move in the exchange rate during a two-week period is about 0.02, the exchange rate moves considered are approximately one, two, and three standard deviations.

Table 15.5 Profit or loss realized in two weeks under different scenarios (millions of dollars)

Volatility	*Exchange rate*						
	0.94	*0.96*	*0.98*	*1.00*	*1.02*	*1.04*	*1.06*
8%	+102	+55	+25	+6	−10	−34	−80
10%	+80	+40	+17	+2	−14	−38	−85
12%	+60	+25	+9	−2	−18	−42	−90

In Table 15.5 the greatest loss is in the lower right corner of the table. The loss corresponds to the volatility increasing to 12% and the exchange rate moving up to 1.06. Usually the greatest loss in such a table occurs at one of the corners, but this is not always so. Consider, for example, the situation where a bank's portfolio consists of a reverse butterfly spread (see Section 10.2). The greatest loss will be experienced if the exchange rate stays where it is.

15.12 CREATING OPTIONS SYNTHETICALLY FOR PORTFOLIO INSURANCE

A portfolio manager is often interested in acquiring a put option on his or her portfolio. This provides protection against market declines while preserving the potential for a gain if the market does well. One approach (discussed in Chapter 13) is to buy put options on a market index such as the S&P 500. An alternative is to create the options synthetically.

Creating an option synthetically involves maintaining a position in the underlying asset (or futures on the underlying asset) so that the delta of the position is equal to the delta of the required option. The position necessary to create an option synthetically is the reverse of that necessary to hedge it. This is because the procedure for hedging an option involves the creation of an equal and opposite option synthetically.

There are two reasons why it may be more attractive for the portfolio manager to create the required put option synthetically than to buy it in the market. The first is that options markets do not always have the liquidity to absorb the trades that managers of large funds would like to carry out. The second is that fund managers often require strike prices and exercise dates that are different from those available in exchange-traded options markets.

The synthetic option can be created from trading the portfolio or from trading in index futures contracts. We first examine the creation of a put option by trading the portfolio. Recall that the delta of a European put on the portfolio is

$$\Delta = e^{-qT}[N(d_1) - 1] \tag{15.8}$$

where, with our usual notation,

$$d_1 = \frac{\ln(S_0/K) + (r - q + \sigma^2/2)T}{\sigma\sqrt{T}}$$

with S_0 the value of the portfolio, K the strike price, r the risk-free rate, q the dividend yield on the portfolio, σ the volatility of the portfolio, and T the life of the option.

To create the put option synthetically, the fund manager should ensure that at any given time a proportion

$$e^{-qT}[1 - N(d_1)]$$

of the stocks in the original portfolio has been sold and the proceeds invested in riskless assets. As the value of the original portfolio declines, the delta of the put given by equation (15.8) becomes more negative and the proportion of the original portfolio sold must be increased. As the value of the original portfolio increases, the delta of the put becomes less negative and the proportion of the original portfolio sold must be decreased (i.e., some of the original portfolio must be repurchased).

Using this strategy to create portfolio insurance means that at any given time funds are divided between the stock portfolio on which insurance is required and riskless assets. As the value of the stock portfolio increases, riskless assets are sold and the position in the stock portfolio is increased. As the value of the stock portfolio declines, the position in the stock portfolio is decreased and riskless assets are purchased. The cost of the insurance arises from the fact that the portfolio manager is always selling after a decline in the market and buying after a rise in the market.

Example

A portfolio is worth \$90 million. To protect against market downturns the managers of the portfolio require a six-month European put option on the portfolio with a strike price of \$87 million. The risk-free rate is 9% per annum, the dividend yield is 3% per annum, and the volatility of the portfolio is 25% per annum. The S&P 500 index stands at 900. As the portfolio is considered to mimic the S&P 500 fairly closely, one alternative is to buy 1,000 put option contracts on the S&P 500 with a strike price of 870. Another alternative is to create the required option synthetically. In this case, $S_0 = 90$ million, $K = 87$ million, $r = 0.09$, $q = 0.03$, $\sigma = 0.25$, and $T = 0.5$, so that

$$d_1 = \frac{\ln(90/87) + (0.09 - 0.03 + 0.25^2/2)0.5}{0.25\sqrt{0.5}} = 0.4499$$

and the delta of the required option is initially

$$e^{-qT}[N(d_1) - 1] = -0.3215$$

This shows that 32.15% of the portfolio should be sold initially to match the delta of the required option. The amount of the portfolio sold must be monitored frequently. For example, if the value of the portfolio reduces to \$88 million after one day, the delta of the required option changes to −0.3679 and a further 4.64% of the original portfolio should be sold. If the value of the portfolio increases to \$92 million, the delta of the required option changes to −0.2787 and 4.28% of the original portfolio should be repurchased.

Use of Index Futures

Using index futures to create options synthetically can be preferable to using the underlying stocks because the transaction costs associated with trades in index futures are generally lower than those associated with the corresponding trades in the underlying stocks. The dollar amount of the futures contracts shorted as a proportion of the value of the portfolio should from equations (15.3) and (15.8) be

$$e^{-qT}e^{-(r-q)T^*}[1 - N(d_1)] = e^{q(T^*-T)}e^{-rT^*}[1 - N(d_1)]$$

where T^* is the maturity time of the futures contract. If the portfolio is worth A_1 times the index and each index futures contract is on A_2 times the index, the number of futures contracts shorted at any given time should be

$$e^{q(T^*-T)}e^{-rT^*}[1 - N(d_1)]\frac{A_1}{A_2}$$

Example

Suppose that in the previous example futures contracts on the S&P 500 maturing in nine months are used to create the option synthetically. In this case initially $T = 0.5$, $T^* = 0.75$, $A_1 = 100{,}000$, $A_2 = 250$, and $d_1 = 0.4499$, so that the number of futures contracts shorted should be

$$e^{q(T^*-T)}e^{-rT^*}[1 - N(d_1)]\frac{A_1}{A_2} = 122.95$$

or 123 rounding to the nearest whole number. As time passes and index changes, the position in futures contracts must be adjusted.

Up to now we have assumed that the portfolio mirrors the index. As discussed in Section 13.4, the hedging scheme can be adjusted to deal with other situations. The strike price for the options used should be the expected level of the market index when the portfolio's value reaches its insured value. The number of index options used should be β times the number of options that would be required if the portfolio had a beta of 1.0. The volatility of portfolio can be assumed to be its beta times the volatility of an appropriate well-diversified index.

15.13 STOCK MARKET VOLATILITY

We discussed in Chapter 12 the issue of whether volatility is caused solely by the arrival of new information or whether trading itself generates volatility. Portfolio insurance schemes such as those just described have the potential to increase volatility. When the market declines, they cause portfolio managers either to sell stock or to sell index futures contracts. Either action may accentuate the decline (see Business Snapshot 15.2). The sale of stock is liable to drive down the market index further in a direct way. The sale of index futures contracts is liable to drive down futures prices. This creates selling pressure on stocks via the mechanism of index arbitrage (see Chapter 5), so that the market index is liable to be driven down in this case as well. Similarly, when the market rises, the portfolio insurance schemes cause portfolio managers either to buy stock or to buy futures contracts. This may accentuate the rise.

In addition to formal portfolio insurance schemes, we can speculate that many investors consciously or subconsciously follow portfolio insurance schemes of their own. For example, an investor may be inclined to enter the market when it is rising but will sell when it is falling to limit the downside risk.

Business Snapshot 15.2 Was portfolio insurance to blame for the crash of 1987?

On Monday, October 19, 1987, the Dow Jones Industrial Average dropped by more than 20%. Many people feel that portfolio insurance played a major role in this crash.

In October 1987 between $60 billion and $90 billion of equity assets were subject to portfolio insurance schemes where put options were created synthetically in the way discussed in Section 15.12. During the period Wednesday, October 14, 1987, to Friday, October 16, 1987, the market declined by about 10% with much of this decline taking place on Friday afternoon. The portfolio insurance schemes should have generated at least $12 billion of equity or index futures sales as a result of this decline. In fact, portfolio insurers had time to sell only $4 billion and they approached the following week with huge amounts of selling already dictated by their models. It is estimated that on Monday, October 19, sell programs by three portfolio insurers accounted for almost 10% of the sales on the New York Stock Exchange, and that portfolio insurance sales amounted to 21.3% of all sales in index futures markets. It is likely that the decline in equity prices was exacerbated by investors other than portfolio insurers selling heavily because they anticipated the actions of portfolio insurers.

Because the market declined so fast and the stock exchange systems were overloaded, many portfolio insurers were unable to execute the trades generated by their models and failed to obtain the protection they required. Needless to say, the popularity of portfolio insurance schemes has declined significantly since 1987. One of the morals of this story is that it is dangerous to follow a particular trading strategy—even a hedging strategy—when many other market participants are doing the same thing.

Whether portfolio insurance schemes (formal or informal) affect volatility depends on how easily the market can absorb the trades that are generated by portfolio insurance. If portfolio insurance trades are a very small fraction of all trades, there is likely to be no effect. As portfolio insurance becomes more popular, it is liable to have a destabilizing effect on the market.

SUMMARY

Financial institutions offer a variety of option products to their clients. Often the options do not correspond to the standardized products traded by exchanges. The financial institutions are then faced with the problem of hedging their exposure. Naked and covered positions leave them subject to an unacceptable level of risk. One course of action that is sometimes proposed is a stop-loss strategy. This involves holding a naked position when an option is out of the money and converting it to a covered position as soon as the option moves into the money. Although superficially attractive, the strategy does not provide a good hedge.

The delta, Δ, of an option is the rate of change of its price with respect to the price of the underlying asset. Delta hedging involves creating a position with zero delta (sometimes referred to as a delta-neutral position). Because the delta of the underlying asset is 1.0, one way of hedging is to take a position of $-\Delta$ in the underlying asset for each long option being hedged. The delta of an option changes over time. This means that the position in the underlying asset has to be frequently adjusted.

Once an option position has been made delta neutral, the next stage is often to look at its gamma. The gamma of an option is the rate of change of its delta with respect to the price of the underlying asset. It is a measure of the curvature of the relationship between the option price and the asset price. The impact of this curvature on the performance of delta hedging can be reduced by making an option position gamma neutral. If Γ is the gamma of the position being hedged, this reduction is usually achieved by taking a position in a traded option that has a gamma of $-\Gamma$.

Delta and gamma hedging are both based on the assumption that the volatility of the underlying asset is constant. In practice, volatilities do change over time. The vega of an option or an option portfolio measures the rate of change of its value with respect to volatility. A trader who wishes to hedge an option position against volatility changes can make the position vega neutral. As with the procedure for creating gamma neutrality, this usually involves taking an offsetting position in a traded option. If the trader wishes to achieve both gamma and vega neutrality, two traded options are usually required.

Two other measures of the risk of an option position are theta and rho. Theta measures the rate of change of the value of the position with respect to the passage of time, with all else remaining constant. Rho measures the rate of change of the value of the position with respect to the interest rate, with all else remaining constant.

In practice, option traders usually rebalance their portfolios at least once a day to maintain delta neutrality. It is usually not feasible to maintain gamma and vega neutrality on a regular basis. Typically a trader monitors these measures. If they get too large, either corrective action is taken or trading is curtailed.

Portfolio managers are sometimes interested in creating put options synthetically for the purposes of insuring an equity portfolio. They can do so either by trading the portfolio or by trading index futures on the portfolio. Trading the portfolio involves splitting the portfolio between equities and risk-free securities. As the market declines, more is invested in risk-free securities; as the market increases, more is invested in equities. Trading index futures involves keeping the equity portfolio intact and selling index futures. As the market declines, more index futures are sold; as it rises, fewer are sold. This type of portfolio insurance works well under normal conditions. On Monday, October 19, 1987, when the Dow Jones Industrial Average dropped very sharply, it worked badly. Portfolio insurers were unable to sell either stocks or index futures fast enough to protect their positions.

FURTHER READING

Taleeb, N. N. *Dynamic Hedging: Managing Vanilla and Exotic Options*. New York: Wiley, 1996.

Quiz (Answers at End of Book)

15.1. Explain how a stop-loss hedging scheme can be implemented for the writer of an out-of-the-money call option. Why does it provide a relatively poor hedge?

15.2. What does it mean to assert that the delta of a call option is 0.7? How can a short position in 1,000 call options be made delta neutral when the delta of each option is 0.7?

15.3. Calculate the delta of an at-the-money six-month European call option on a non-dividend-paying stock when the risk-free interest rate is 10% per annum and the stock price volatility is 25% per annum.

15.4. Can the vega of a derivatives portfolio be changed by taking a position in the underlying asset? Explain your answer.

15.5. What is meant by the gamma of an option position? What are the risks in the situation where the gamma of a position is large and negative and the delta is zero?

15.6. "The procedure for creating an option position synthetically is the reverse of the procedure for hedging the option position." Explain this statement.

15.7. Explain why portfolio insurance may have played a part in the stock market crash of October 19, 1987.

Questions and Problems (Answers in Solutions Manual/Study Guide)

15.8. What does it mean to assert that the theta of an option position is −0.1 when time is measured in years? If a trader feels that neither a stock price nor its implied volatility will change, what type of option position is appropriate?

15.9. The Black–Scholes price of an out-of-the-money call option with an exercise price of $40 is $4. A trader who has written the option plans to use a stop-loss strategy. The trader's plan is to buy at $40.10 and to sell at $39.90. Estimate the expected number of times the stock will be bought or sold.

15.10. Suppose that a stock price is currently $20 and that a call option with an exercise price of $25 is created synthetically using a continually changing position in the stock. Consider the following two scenarios:
a. Stock price increases steadily from $20 to $35 during the life of the option.
b. Stock price oscillates wildly, ending up at $35.

Which scenario would make the synthetically created option more expensive? Explain your answer.

15.11. What is the delta of a short position in 1,000 European call options on silver futures? The options mature in eight months, and the futures contract underlying the option matures in nine months. The current nine-month futures price is $8 per ounce, the exercise price of the options is $8, the risk-free interest rate is 12% per annum, and the volatility of silver is 18% per annum.

15.12. In Problem 15.11, what initial position in nine-month silver futures is necessary for delta hedging? If silver itself is used, what is the initial position? If one-year silver futures are used, what is the initial position? Assume no storage costs for silver.

15.13. A company uses delta hedging to hedge a portfolio of long positions in put and call options on a currency. Which of the following would give the most favorable result?
a. A virtually constant spot rate
b. Wild movements in the spot rate
Explain your answer.

15.14. Repeat Problem 15.13 for a financial institution with a portfolio of short positions in put and call options on a currency.

15.15. A financial institution has just sold 1,000 seven-month European call options on the Japanese yen. Suppose that the spot exchange rate is 0.80 cent per yen, the exercise price is 0.81 cent per yen, the risk-free interest rate in the United States is 8% per annum, the risk-free interest rate in Japan is 5% per annum, and the volatility of the yen is 15% per annum. Calculate the delta, gamma, vega, theta, and rho of the financial institution's position. Interpret each number.

15.16. Under what circumstances is it possible to make a European option on a stock index both gamma neutral and vega neutral by adding a position in one other European option?

15.17. A fund manager has a well-diversified portfolio that mirrors the performance of the S&P 500 and is worth $360 million. The value of the S&P 500 is 1,200, and the portfolio manager would like to buy insurance against a reduction of more than 5% in the value of the portfolio over the next six months. The risk-free interest rate is 6% per annum. The dividend yield on both the portfolio and the S&P 500 is 3%, and the volatility of the index is 30% per annum.

a. If the fund manager buys traded European put options, how much would the insurance cost?

b. Explain carefully alternative strategies open to the fund manager involving traded European call options, and show that they lead to the same result.

c. If the fund manager decides to provide insurance by keeping part of the portfolio in risk-free securities, what should the initial position be?

d. If the fund manager decides to provide insurance by using nine-month index futures, what should the initial position be?

15.18. Repeat Problem 15.17 on the assumption that the portfolio has a beta of 1.5. Assume that the dividend yield on the portfolio is 4% per annum.

15.19. Show by substituting for the various terms in equation (15.7) that the equation is true for:

a. A single European call option on a non-dividend-paying stock

b. A single European put option on a non-dividend-paying stock

c. Any portfolio of European put and call options on a non-dividend-paying stock

15.20. Suppose that $70 billion of equity assets are the subject of portfolio insurance schemes. Assume that the schemes are designed to provide insurance against the value of the assets declining by more than 5% within one year. Making whatever estimates you find necessary, use the DerivaGem software to calculate the value of the stock or futures contracts that the administrators of the portfolio insurance schemes will attempt to sell if the market falls by 23% in a single day.

15.21. Does a forward contract on a stock index have the same delta as the corresponding futures contract? Explain your answer.

15.22. A bank's position in options on the dollar–euro exchange rate has a delta of 30,000 and a gamma of −80,000. Explain how these numbers can be interpreted. The exchange rate (dollars per euro) is 0.90. What position would you take to make the position delta neutral? After a short period of time, the exchange rate moves to 0.93. Estimate the new delta. What additional trade is necessary to keep the position delta neutral? Assuming the bank did set up a delta-neutral position originally, has it gained or lost money from the exchange-rate movement?

Assignment Questions

15.23. Consider a one-year European call option on a stock when the stock price is \$30, the strike price is \$30, the risk-free rate is 5%, and the volatility is 25% per annum. Use the DerivaGem software to calculate the price, delta, gamma, vega, theta, and rho of the option. Verify that delta is correct by changing the stock price to \$30.1 and recomputing the option price. Verify that gamma is correct by recomputing the delta for the situation where the stock price is \$30.1. Carry out similar calculations to verify that vega, theta, and rho are correct. Use the DerivaGem software to plot the option price, delta, gamma, vega, theta, and rho against the stock price for the stock option.

15.24. A financial institution has the following portfolio of over-the-counter options on sterling:

Type	*Position*	*Delta of option*	*Gamma of option*	*Vega of option*
Call	−1,000	0.50	2.2	1.8
Call	−500	0.80	0.6	0.2
Put	−2,000	−0.40	1.3	0.7
Call	−500	0.70	1.8	1.4

A traded option is available with a delta of 0.6, a gamma of 1.5, and a vega of 0.8.

a. What position in the traded option and in sterling would make the portfolio both gamma neutral and delta neutral?
b. What position in the traded option and in sterling would make the portfolio both vega neutral and delta neutral?

15.25. Consider again the situation in Problem 15.24. Suppose that a second traded option with a delta of 0.1, a gamma of 0.5, and a vega of 0.6 is available. How could the portfolio be made delta, gamma, and vega neutral?

15.26. A deposit instrument offered by a bank guarantees that investors will receive a return during a six-month period that is the greater of (a) zero and (b) 40% of the return provided by a market index. An investor is planning to put \$100,000 in the instrument. Describe the payoff as an option on the index. Assuming that the risk-free rate of interest is 8% per annum, the dividend yield on the index is 3% per annum, and the volatility of the index is 25% per annum, is the product a good deal for the investor?

15.27. Use DerivaGem to check that equation (15.7) is satisfied for the option considered in Section 15.1. (*Note*: DerivaGem produces a value of theta "per calendar day." The theta in equation (15.7) is "per year.")

15.28. Use the DerivaGem Application Builder functions to reproduce Table 15.2. (Note that in Table 15.2 the stock position is rounded to the nearest 100 shares.) Calculate the gamma and theta of the position each week. Calculate the change in the value of the portfolio each week and check whether equation (15.6) is approximately satisfied. (*Note*: DerivaGem produces a value of theta "per calendar day." The theta in equation (15.6) is "per year.")

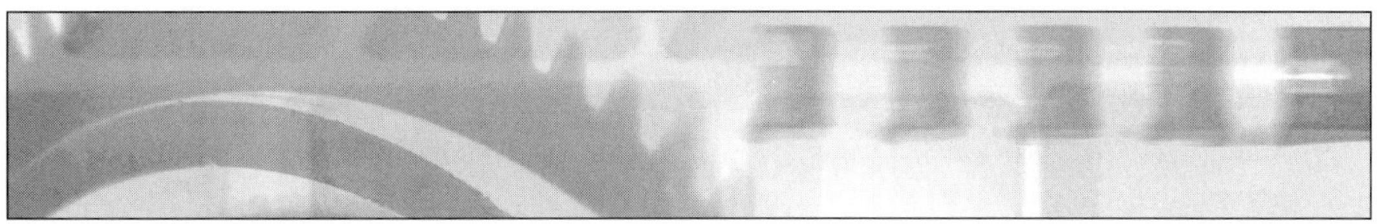

CHAPTER 16 Binomial Trees in Practice

As we have seen in Chapters 12, 13, and 14, the Black–Scholes model and its extensions can be used to value European call and put options on stocks, stock indices, currencies, and futures contracts. For American options we rely on binomial trees. In this chapter we cover, more completely than in Chapter 11, how binomial trees are used in practice. In particular, we explain how the binomial tree methodology can be used to value American options on a range of different underlying assets including dividend-paying stocks and how it can be used to calculate the Greek letters that were introduced in Chapter 15. As explained in Section 11.8, the DerivaGem software that accompanies this book can be used to carry out the calculations described in the chapter and view the trees that are produced.

16.1 THE BINOMIAL MODEL FOR A NON-DIVIDEND-PAYING STOCK

The binomial tree methodology for handling American-style options was first proposed by Cox, Ross, and Rubinstein.[1] Consider the evaluation of an option on a non-dividend-paying stock. We start by dividing the life of the option into a large number of small time intervals of length Δt. We assume that in each time interval the stock price moves from its initial value of S_0 to one of two new values, S_0u and S_0d. This model is illustrated in Figure 16.1. In general, $u > 1$ and $d < 1$. The movement from S_0 to S_0u is, therefore, an "up" movement and the movement from S_0 to S_0d is a "down" movement. The probability of an up movement will be denoted by p. The probability of a down movement is $1 - p$.

Risk-Neutral Valuation

The risk-neutral valuation principle, discussed in Chapters 11 and 12, states that any security dependent on a stock price can be valued on the assumption that the world is

[1] See J.C. Cox, S.A. Ross, and M. Rubinstein, "Option Pricing: A Simplified Approach," *Journal of Financial Economics*, 7 (October 1979), 229–64.

Figure 16.1 Stock price movements in time Δt under the binomial model

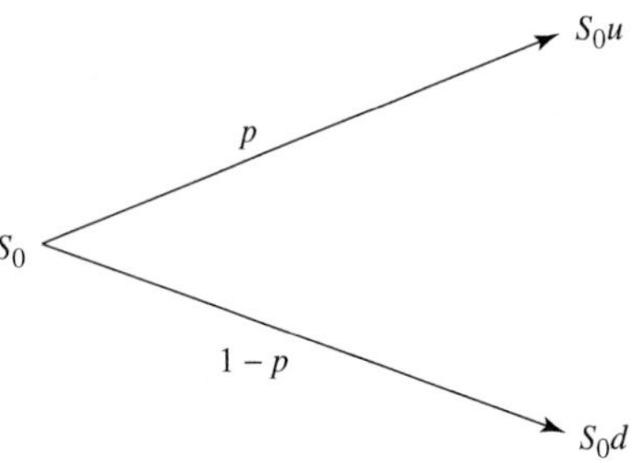

risk neutral. This means that, for the purposes of valuing an option (or any other derivative), we can assume the following:

1. The expected return from all traded securities is the risk-free interest rate.
2. Future cash flows can be valued by discounting their expected values at the risk-free interest rate.

We will make use of this result when using a binomial tree.

Determination of p, u, and d

We design the tree to represent the behavior of a stock price in a risk-neutral world. The parameters p, u, and d must give correct values for the mean and variance of the stock price during a time interval Δt in this world. The expected return from a stock is the risk-free interest rate, r. Hence, the expected value of the stock price at the end of a time interval Δt is $Se^{r\Delta t}$, where S is the stock price at the beginning of the time interval. It follows that

$$Se^{r\Delta t} = pSu + (1-p)Sd \tag{16.1}$$

or

$$e^{r\Delta t} = pu + (1-p)d \tag{16.2}$$

As explained in Chapter 12, the standard deviation of the percentage change in the stock price in a small time interval Δt is $\sigma\sqrt{\Delta t}$. The variance of this percentage change is $\sigma^2\Delta t$. The variance of a variable Q is defined as $E(Q^2) - E(Q)^2$, where E denotes expected value. There is a probability p that the percentage change is u and a probability $1-p$ that it is d. It follows that

$$\sigma^2\Delta t = pu^2 + (1-p)d^2 - [pu + (1-p)d]^2 \tag{16.3}$$

Equations (16.2) and (16.3) impose two conditions on p, u, and d. A third condition used by Cox, Ross, and Rubinstein is

$$u = \frac{1}{d}$$

It can be shown that provided Δt is small, the three conditions imply that

$$p = \frac{a - d}{u - d} \tag{16.4}$$

$$u = e^{\sigma\sqrt{\Delta t}} \tag{16.5}$$

$$d = e^{-\sigma\sqrt{\Delta t}} \tag{16.6}$$

where

$$a = e^{r\Delta t} \tag{16.7}$$

The variable a is sometimes referred to as the *growth factor*. Note that equations (16.4) to (16.7) are the same as equations (11.9) to (11.12) in Chapter 11.

The Tree of Stock Prices

Figure 16.2 illustrates the complete tree of stock prices that is considered when the binomial model is used. At time zero, the stock price, S_0, is known. At time Δt, there are two possible stock prices, S_0u and S_0d; at time $2\Delta t$, there are three possible stock prices, S_0u^2, S_0, and S_0d^2; and so on. In general, at time $i\Delta t$, we consider $i + 1$ stock prices. These are

$$S_0u^jd^{i-j} \quad (j = 0, 1, \dots, i)$$

Note that the relationship $u = 1/d$ is used in computing the stock price at each node of the tree in Figure 16.2. For example, $S_0u^2d = S_0u$. Note also that the tree recombines in

Figure 16.2 Tree used to value a stock option

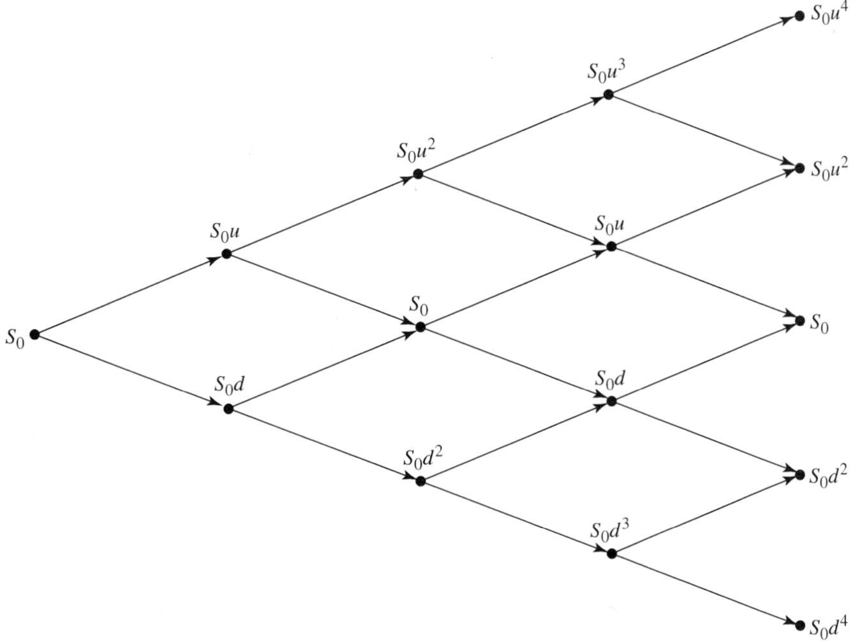

the sense that an up movement followed by a down movement leads to the same stock price as a down movement followed by an up movement.

Working Backward through the Tree

Options are evaluated by starting at the end of the tree (time T) and working backward, a procedure known as *backwards induction*. The value of the option is known at time T. For example, a put option is worth $\max(K - S_T, 0)$ and a call option is worth $\max(S_T - K, 0)$, where S_T is the stock price at time T and K is the strike price. Because a risk-neutral world is assumed, the value at each node at time $T - \Delta t$ can be calculated as the expected value at time T discounted at rate r for a time period Δt. Similarly, the value at each node at time $T - 2\Delta t$ can be calculated as the expected value at time $T - \Delta t$ discounted for a time period Δt at rate r, and so on. If the option is American, it is necessary to check at each node to see whether early exercise is preferable to holding the option for a further time period Δt. Eventually, by working back through all the nodes, we obtain the value of the option at time zero.

Illustration

An example will make the procedure clear. Consider a five-month American put option on a non-dividend-paying stock when the stock price is \$50, the strike price is \$50, the risk-free interest rate is 10% per annum, and the volatility is 40% per annum. With our usual notation, this means that $S_0 = 50$, $K = 50$, $r = 0.10$, $\sigma = 0.40$, and $T = 0.4167$. Suppose that we divide the life of the option into five intervals of length one month for the purposes of constructing a binomial tree. Then $\Delta t = 1/12$ and, using equations (16.4) to (16.7),

$$u = e^{\sigma\sqrt{\Delta t}} = 1.1224, \qquad d = e^{-\sigma\sqrt{\Delta t}} = 0.8909, \qquad a = e^{r\Delta t} = 1.0084$$

$$p = \frac{a-d}{u-d} = 0.5073, \qquad 1 - p = 0.4927$$

Figure 16.3 shows the binomial tree produced by DerivaGem. At each node there are two numbers. The top one shows the stock price at the node; the lower one shows the value of the option at the node. The probability of an up movement is always 0.5073; the probability of a down movement is always 0.4927.

The stock price at the jth $(j = 0, 1, \dots, i)$ node at time $i\Delta t$ $(i = 0, 1, \dots, 5)$ is calculated as $S_0 u^j d^{i-j}$. For example, the stock price at node A $(i = 4, j = 1)$ (i.e., the second node up at the end of the fourth time step) is $50 \times 1.1224 \times 0.8909^3 = \$39.69$.

The option prices at the final nodes are calculated as $\max(K - S_T, 0)$. For example, the option price at node G is $50.00 - 35.36 = 14.64$. The option prices at the penultimate nodes are calculated from the option prices at the final nodes. First, we assume no exercise of the option at the nodes. This means that the option price is calculated as the present value of the expected option price one time step later. For example, at node E, the option price is calculated as

$$(0.5073 \times 0 + 0.4927 \times 5.45)e^{-0.10\times 1/12} = 2.66$$

whereas at node A it is calculated as

$$(0.5073 \times 5.45 + 0.4927 \times 14.64)e^{-0.10\times 1/12} = 9.90$$

Figure 16.3 Binomial tree from DerivaGem for American put on non-dividend-paying stock

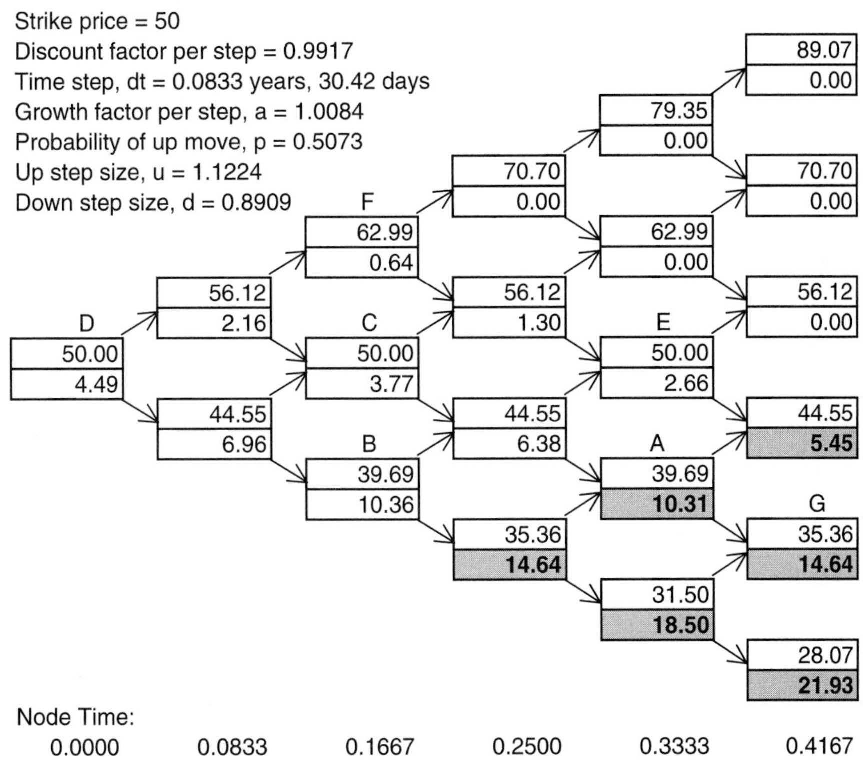

We then check to see if early exercise is preferable to waiting. At node E, early exercise would give a value for the option of zero because both the stock price and strike price are \$50. Clearly, it is best to wait. The correct value for the option at node E is, therefore, \$2.66. At node A, it is a different story. If the option is exercised, it is worth \$50.00 – \$39.69, or \$10.31. This is more than \$9.90. If node A is reached, the option should, therefore, be exercised and the correct value for the option at node A is \$10.31.

Option prices at earlier nodes are calculated in a similar way. Note that it is not always best to exercise an option early when it is in the money. Consider node B. If the option is exercised, it is worth \$50.00 – \$39.69, or \$10.31. However, if it is held, it is worth

$$(0.5073 \times 6.38 + 0.4927 \times 14.64)e^{-0.10\times 1/12} = 10.36$$

The option should, therefore, not be exercised at this node, and the correct option value at the node is \$10.36.

Working back through the tree, we find the value of the option at the initial node to be \$4.49. This is our numerical estimate for the option's current value. In practice, a smaller value of Δt, and many more nodes, would be used. DerivaGem shows that with 30, 50, and 100 time steps we get values for the option of 4.263, 4.272, and 4.278, respectively.

Expressing the Approach Algebraically

Suppose that the life of an American put option on a non-dividend-paying stock is divided into N subintervals of length Δt. We will refer to the jth node at time $i\Delta t$ as the (i, j) node, where $0 \leqslant i \leqslant N$ and $0 \leqslant j \leqslant i$. Define $f_{i,j}$ as the value of the option at the (i, j) node. The stock price at the (i, j) node is $S_0 u^j d^{i-j}$. Because the value of an American put at its expiration date is $\max(K - S_T, 0)$, we know that

$$f_{N,j} = \max(K - S_0 u^j d^{N-j}, 0) \quad (j = 0, 1, \dots, N)$$

There is a probability, p, of moving from the (i, j) node at time $i\Delta t$ to the $(i+1, j+1)$ node at time $(i+1)\Delta t$, and a probability $1 - p$ of moving from the (i, j) node at time $i\Delta t$ to the $(i+1, j)$ node at time $(i+1)\Delta t$. Assuming no early exercise, risk-neutral valuation gives

$$f_{i,j} = e^{-r\Delta t}[p f_{i+1,j+1} + (1-p) f_{i+1,j}]$$

for $0 \leqslant i \leqslant N-1$ and $0 \leqslant j \leqslant i$. When early exercise is taken into account, this value for $f_{i,j}$ must be compared with the option's intrinsic value, and we obtain

$$f_{i,j} = \max\{K - S_0 u^j d^{i-j},\ e^{-r\Delta t}[p f_{i+1,j+1} + (1-p) f_{i+1,j}]\}$$

Note that, because the calculations start at time T and work backward, the value at time $i\Delta t$ captures not only the effect of early exercise possibilities at time $i\Delta t$, but also the effect of early exercise at subsequent times.

In the limit as Δt tends to zero, an exact value for the American put is obtained. In

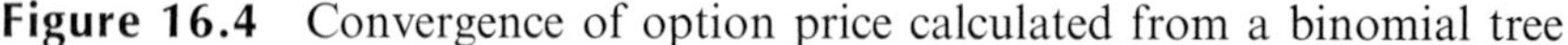

Figure 16.4 Convergence of option price calculated from a binomial tree

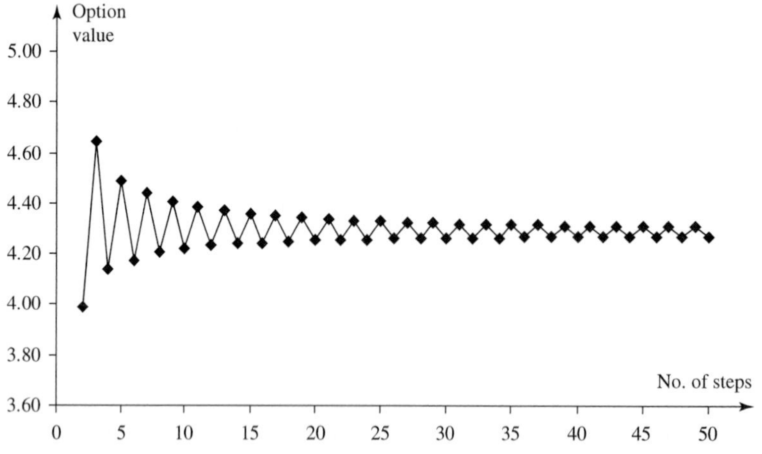

practice, $N = 30$ usually gives reasonable results. Figure 16.4 shows the convergence of the option price in the example we have been considering. This figure was calculated using the Application Builder functions provided with the DerivaGem software (see Sample Application A).

Estimating Delta and Other Greek Letters

It will be recalled that the delta, Δ, of an option is the rate of change of its price with respect to the underlying stock price. It can be calculated as

$$\frac{\Delta f}{\Delta S}$$

where ΔS is a small change in the stock price and Δf is the corresponding small change in the option price. At time Δt, we have an estimate f_{11} for the option price when the stock price is S_0u and an estimate f_{10} for the option price when the stock price is S_0d. In other words, when $\Delta S = S_0u - S_0d$, we have $\Delta f = f_{11} - f_{10}$. An estimate of Δ at time Δt is therefore

$$\Delta = \frac{f_{11} - f_{10}}{S_0u - S_0d} \tag{16.8}$$

To determine gamma, Γ, we note that there are two estimates of Δ at time $2\Delta t$. When the stock price is $(S_0u^2 + S_0)/2$ (halfway between the second and third node at time $2\Delta t$), delta is $(f_{22} - f_{21})/(S_0u^2 - S_0)$; when the stock price is $(S_0 + S_0d^2)/2$ (halfway between the first and second node at time $2\Delta t$), delta is $(f_{21} - f_{20})/(S_0 - S_0d^2)$. The difference between the two stock prices is h, where

$$h = 0.5(S_0u^2 - S_0d^2)$$

Gamma is the change in delta divided by h, or

$$\Gamma = \frac{[(f_{22} - f_{21})/(S_0u^2 - S_0)] - [(f_{21} - f_{20})/(S_0 - S_0d^2)]}{h} \tag{16.9}$$

These procedures provide estimates of delta at time Δt and of gamma at time $2\Delta t$. In practice, they are usually used as estimates of delta and gamma at time zero as well.[2]

A further hedge parameter that can be obtained directly from the tree is theta, Θ. This is the rate of change of the option price with time when all else is kept constant. An estimate of theta is therefore

$$\Theta = \frac{f_{21} - f_{00}}{2\Delta t} \tag{16.10}$$

Vega can be calculated by making a small change, $\Delta\sigma$, in the volatility and constructing a new tree to obtain a new value of the option (Δt should be kept the same). The estimate of vega is

$$\mathcal{V} = \frac{f^* - f}{\Delta\sigma}$$

---

[2] If slightly more accuracy is required for delta and gamma, we can start the binomial tree at time $-2\Delta t$ and assume that the stock price is S_0 at this time. This leads to the option price being calculated for three different stock prices at time zero.

where f and f^* are the estimates of the option price from the original and the new tree, respectively. Rho can be calculated similarly.

As an illustration, consider the tree in Figure 16.3. In this case, $f_{1,0} = 6.96$ and $f_{1,1} = 2.16$. Equation (16.8) gives an estimate of delta of

$$\frac{2.16 - 6.96}{56.12 - 44.55} = -0.41$$

From equation (16.9), an estimate of the gamma of the option can be obtained from the values at nodes B, C, and F as

$$\frac{[(0.64 - 3.77)/(62.99 - 50.00)] - [(3.77 - 10.36)/(50.00 - 39.69)]}{11.65} = 0.03$$

From equation (16.10), an estimate of the theta of the option can be obtained from the values at nodes D and C as

$$\frac{3.77 - 4.49}{0.1667} = -4.3 \text{ per year}$$

or -0.012 per calendar day. These are, of course, only rough estimates. They become progressively better as the number of time steps on the tree is increased. Using 50 time steps, DerivaGem provides estimates of -0.414, 0.033, and -0.0117 for delta, gamma, and theta, respectively.

16.2 USING THE BINOMIAL TREE FOR OPTIONS ON INDICES, CURRENCIES, AND FUTURES CONTRACTS

As shown in Section 13.3, the binomial tree approach to valuing options on non-dividend-paying stocks can easily be adapted to valuing American calls and puts on a stock paying a continuous dividend yield at rate q.

Because the dividends provide a return of q, the stock price itself must, on average, in a risk-neutral world provide a return of $r - q$. Hence, equation (16.1) becomes

$$Se^{(r-q)\Delta t} = pSu + (1 - p)Sd$$

so that

$$e^{(r-q)\Delta t} = pu + (1 - p)d$$

The parameters p, u, and d must satisfy this equation and equation (16.3). It turns out that equations (16.4), (16.5), and (16.6) are still correct but with

$$a = e^{(r-q)\Delta t} \tag{16.11}$$

The binomial tree numerical procedure can therefore be used exactly as before with this new value of a.

We showed in Chapters 13 and 14 that stock indices, currencies, and futures contracts can for the purposes of option evaluation be considered as stocks paying continuous dividend yields. In the case of a stock index, the relevant dividend yield is the dividend yield on the stock portfolio underlying the index; in the case of a currency, it is the foreign risk-free interest rate; in the case of a futures contract, it is the domestic risk-free interest rate. We are, therefore, now in a position to use binomial trees to value options on indices, currencies, and futures contracts.

Example 1

Consider a four-month American call option on index futures. The current futures price is 300, the exercise price is 300, the risk-free interest rate is 8% per annum, and the volatility of the index is 30% per annum. We divide the life of the option into four one-month intervals for the purposes of constructing the tree. In this case, $F_0 = 300$, $K = 300$, $r = 0.08$, $\sigma = 0.3$, $T = 4/12$, and $\Delta t = 1/12$. Because a futures contract is analogous to a stock paying dividends at a continuous rate r, q should be set equal to r in equation (16.11). This gives $a = 1$. The other parameters necessary to construct the tree are

$$u = e^{\sigma\sqrt{\Delta t}} = 1.0905, \quad d = \frac{1}{u} = 0.9170, \quad p = \frac{a-d}{u-d} = 0.4784, \quad 1 - p = 0.5216$$

The tree is shown in Figure 16.5 (the upper number is the futures price; the lower number is the option price). The estimated value of the option is 19.16. More accuracy is obtained with more steps. With 50 time steps DerivaGem gives a value of 20.18; with 100 time steps it gives a value of 20.22.

Figure 16.5 Binomial tree produced by DerivaGem for American call option on an index futures contract (Example 1)

At each node:
Upper value = Underlying Asset Price
Lower value = Option Price
Shading indicates where option is exercised

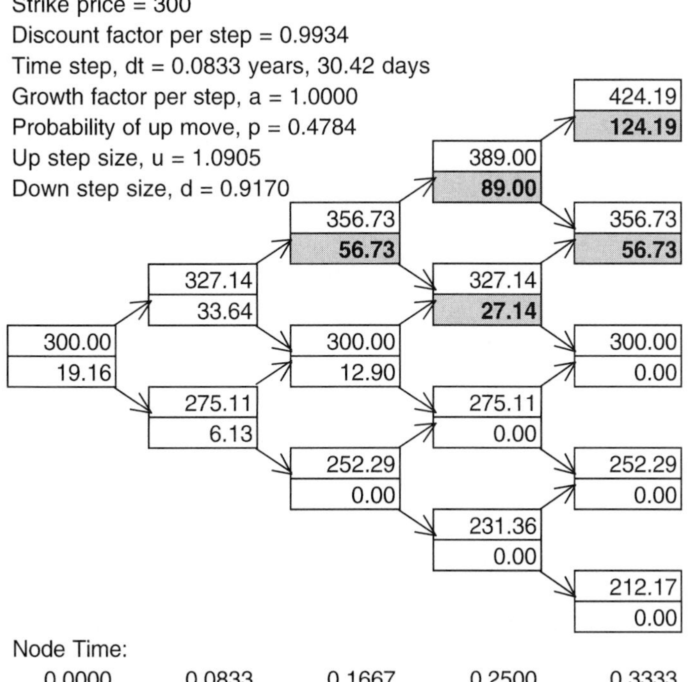

Example 2

Consider a one-year American put option on the British pound. The current exchange rate is 1.6100, the strike price is 1.6000, the U.S. risk-free interest rate is 8% per annum, the sterling risk-free interest rate is 9% per annum, and the volatility of the sterling exchange rate is 12% per annum. In this case, $S_0 = 1.61$, $K = 1.60$, $r = 0.08$, $r_f = 0.09$, $\sigma = 0.12$, and $T = 1.0$. We divide the life of the option into four three-month periods for the purposes of constructing the tree so that $\Delta t = 0.25$. In this case, $q = r_f$ and equation (16.11) gives

$$a = e^{(0.08-0.09)\times 0.25} = 0.9975$$

The other parameters necessary to construct the tree are:

$$u = e^{\sigma\sqrt{\Delta t}} = 1.0618, \quad d = \frac{1}{u} = 0.9418, \quad p = \frac{a-d}{u-d} = 0.4642, \quad 1 - p = 0.5358$$

The tree is shown in Figure 16.6 (the upper number is the exchange rate; the lower number is the option price). The estimated value of the option is \$0.0710. Using

Figure 16.6 Binomial tree produced by DerivaGem for American put option on a currency (Example 2)

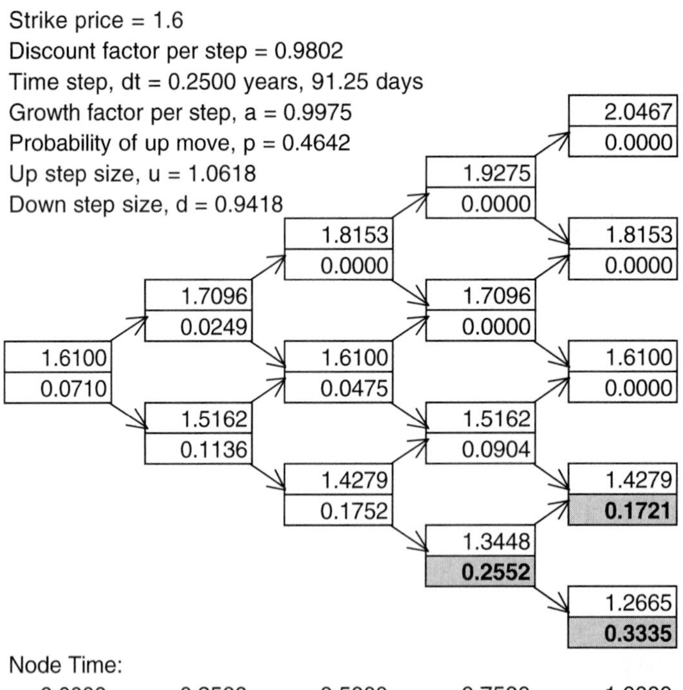

50 time steps, DerivaGem gives the value of the option as 0.0738; with 100 time steps, it also gives the value 0.0738.

16.3 THE BINOMIAL MODEL FOR A DIVIDEND-PAYING STOCK

We now move on to the more tricky issue of how the binomial model can be used for a stock paying discrete dividends. As in Chapter 12, the word *dividend* will for the purposes of our discussion be used to refer to the reduction in the stock price on the ex-dividend date as a result of the dividend.

Known Dividend Yield

If it is assumed that a single dividend will be paid at a certain time and that it will be a proportion, δ, of the stock price at that time, the tree takes the form shown in Figure 16.7 and can be analyzed in a way that is analogous to that just described. If the time $i\Delta t$ is prior to the stock going ex-dividend, the nodes on the tree correspond to stock prices

$$S_0 u^j d^{i-j} \quad (j = 0, 1, \ldots, i)$$

where u and d are defined as in equations (16.5) and (16.6). If the time $i\Delta t$ is after the

Figure 16.7 Tree when stock pays a known dividend yield at one particular time

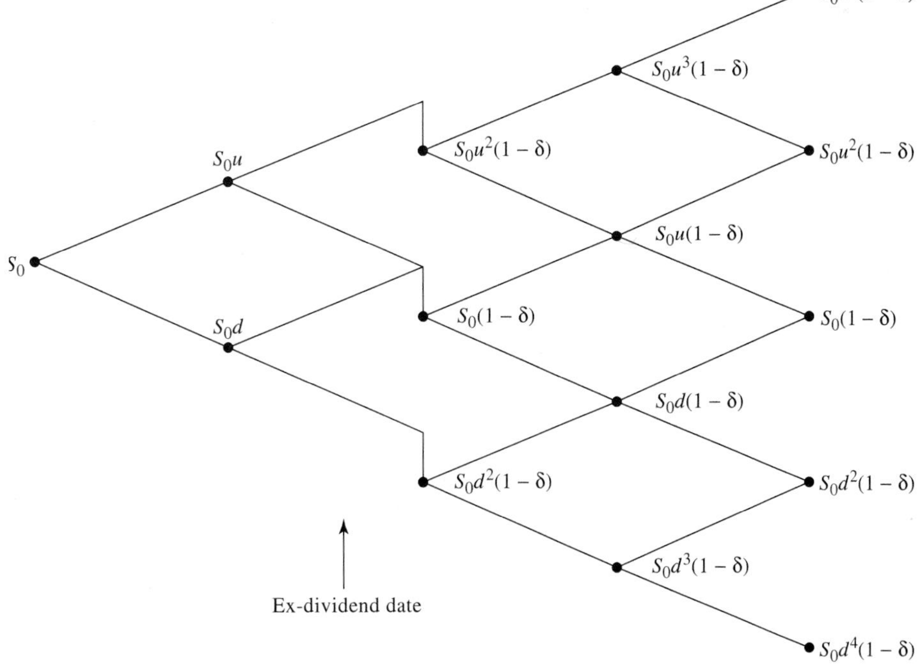

stock goes ex-dividend, the nodes correspond to stock prices

$$S_0(1-\delta)u^j d^{i-j} \quad (j=0,1,\ldots,i)$$

Several known dividends during the life of an option can be dealt with similarly. If δ_i is the total dividend yield associated with all ex-dividend dates between time zero and time $i\Delta t$, the nodes at time $i\Delta t$ correspond to stock prices

$$S_0(1-\delta_i)u^j d^{i-j}$$

Known Dollar Dividend

In some situations, it is more realistic to assume that the dollar amount of the dividend rather than the dividend yield is known in advance. If the volatility of the stock, σ, is assumed constant, the tree takes the form shown in Figure 16.8. It does not recombine, which means that the number of nodes that have to be evaluated, particularly if there are several dividends, is liable to become very large. Suppose that there is only one dividend, that the ex-dividend date, τ, is between $k\Delta t$ and $(k+1)\Delta t$, and that the dollar amount of the dividend is D. When $i \leqslant k$, the nodes on the tree at time $i\Delta t$ correspond to stock prices

$$S_0 u^j d^{i-j} \quad (j=0,1,2,\ldots,i)$$

as before. When $i = k+1$, the nodes on the tree correspond to stock prices

$$S_0 u^j d^{i-j} - D \quad (j=0,1,2,\ldots,i)$$

Figure 16.8 Tree when dollar amount of dividend is assumed known and volatility is assumed constant

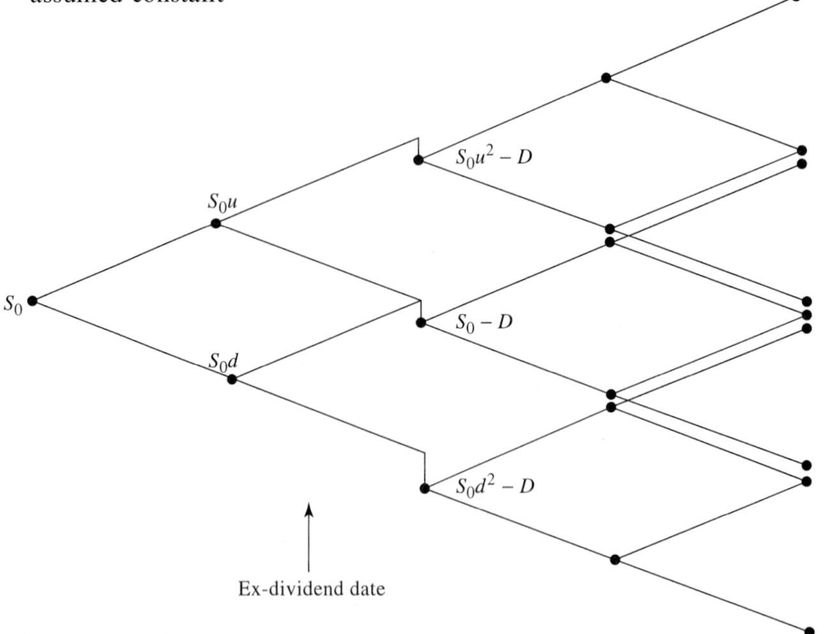

When $i = k + 2$, the nodes on the tree correspond to stock prices

$$(S_0 u^j d^{i-1-j} - D)u \quad \text{and} \quad (S_0 u^j d^{i-1-j} - D)d$$

for $j = 0, 1, 2, \dots, i - 1$, so that there are $2i$ rather than $i + 1$ nodes. At time $(k + m)\Delta t$, there are $m(k + 2)$ rather than $k + m + 1$ nodes.

The problem can be simplified by assuming, as in the analysis of European options in Chapter 12, that the stock price has two components: a part that is uncertain and a part that is the present value of all future dividends during the life of the option. Suppose, as before, that there is only one ex-dividend date, τ, during the life of the option and that $k\Delta t \leqslant \tau \leqslant (k + 1)\Delta t$. The value of the uncertain component, S^*, at time $i\Delta t$ is given by

$$S^* = S \quad \text{when } i\Delta t > \tau$$

and

$$S^* = S - De^{-r(\tau - i\Delta t)} \quad \text{when } i\Delta t \leqslant \tau$$

where D is the dividend. Define σ^* as the volatility of S^* and assume that σ^* is constant.[3] The parameters p, u, and d can be calculated from equations (16.4), (16.5), (16.6), and (16.7) with σ replaced by σ^*, and a tree can be constructed in the usual way to model S^*. By adding to the stock price at each node the present value of future dividends (if any), the tree can be converted into another tree that models S. Suppose that is the value of S^* at time zero. At time $i\Delta t$, the nodes on this tree correspond to the stock prices

$$S_0^* u^j d^{i-j} + De^{-r(\tau - i\Delta t)} \quad (j = 0, 1, \dots, i)$$

when $i\Delta t < \tau$ and

$$S_0^* u^j d^{i-j} \quad (j = 0, 1, \dots, i)$$

when $i\Delta t > \tau$. This approach, which has the advantage of being consistent with the approach for European options in Section 12.9, succeeds in achieving a situation where the tree recombines so that there are $i + 1$ nodes at time $i\Delta t$. It can be generalized in a straightforward way to deal with the situation where there are several dividends.

Illustration

To provide an example of how the approach works in a particular case, consider a five-month American put option on a stock that is expected to pay a single dividend of \$2.06 during the life of the option. The initial stock price is \$52, the strike price is \$50, the risk-free interest rate is 10% per annum, the volatility is 40% per annum, and the ex-dividend date is in 3.5 months.

We first construct a tree to model S^*, the stock price less the present value of future dividends during the life of the option. Initially, the present value of the dividend is

$$2.06e^{-0.1 \times 3.5/12} = 2.00$$

The initial value of S^* is therefore 50. Assuming that the 40% per annum volatility refers to S^*, Figure 16.3 provides a binomial tree for S^*. (S^* has the same initial value and volatility as the stock price on which Figure 16.3 was based.) Adding the present

[3] In theory σ^* is slightly greater than σ, the volatility of S. In practice no distinction is usually made between the two.

Figure 16.9 Tree produced by DerivaGem for put option on a stock paying a single dividend

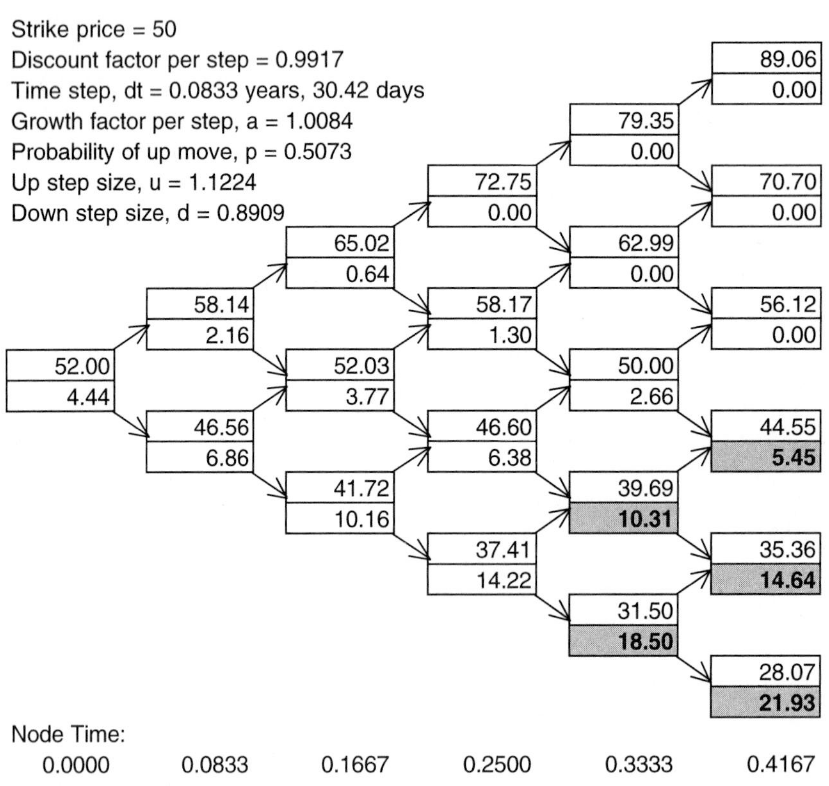

value of the dividend at each node leads to Figure 16.9, which is a binomial model for S. The probabilities at each node are, as in Figure 16.3, 0.5073 for an up movement and 0.4927 for a down movement. Working back through the tree in the usual way gives the option price as \$4.44.

16.4 EXTENSIONS OF THE BASIC TREE APPROACH

We now explain two ways in which the binomial tree approach can be extended.

Time-Dependent Interest Rates

Up to now we have been assuming that interest rates are constant. When the term structure is steeply upward or downward sloping and American options are being valued, this may not be a satisfactory assumption. It is more appropriate to assume that the interest rate for a period of length Δt in the future equals the current forward interest rate for that period. We can accommodate this assumption by setting

$$a = e^{f(t)\Delta t} \tag{16.12}$$

for nodes at time t where $f(t)$ is the forward rate between times t and $t + \Delta t$. This does not change the geometry of the tree because u and d do not depend on a. The probabilities on the branches emanating from nodes at time t are as before:[4]

$$p = \frac{a - d}{u - d} \quad \text{and} \quad 1 - p = \frac{u - a}{u - d}$$

The rest of the way in which we use the tree is the same as before, except that when discounting from time $t + \Delta t$ to time t we use $f(t)$. A similar modification of the basic tree can be used to value index options, foreign exchange options, and futures options. In these applications the dividend yield on an index or a foreign risk-free rate can be made a function of time by following a similar approach to that just described.

The Control Variate Technique

A technique known as the *control variate technique* can be used for the evaluation of an American option.[5] This involves using the same tree to calculate both the value of the American option, f_A, and the value of the corresponding European option, f_E. We also calculate the Black–Scholes price of the European option, f_{BS}. The error given by the tree in the pricing of the European option is assumed equal to that given by the tree in the pricing of the American option. This gives the estimate of the price of the American option to be

$$f_A + f_{BS} - f_E$$

To illustrate this approach, Figure 16.10 values the option in Figure 16.3 on the assumption that it is European. The price obtained is \$4.32. From the Black–Scholes formula, the true European price of the option is \$4.08. The estimate of the American price in Figure 16.3 is \$4.49. The control variate estimate of the American price is therefore

$$4.49 + 4.08 - 4.32 = 4.25$$

A good estimate of the American price, calculated using 100 steps, is 4.278. The control variate approach does, therefore, produce a considerable improvement over the basic tree estimate of 4.49 in this case. In effect, it uses the tree to calculate the difference between the European and the American price rather than the American price itself.

16.5 ALTERNATIVE PROCEDURE FOR CONSTRUCTING TREES

The Cox, Ross, and Rubinstein approach is not the only way of building a binomial tree. Instead of imposing the assumption $u = 1/d$ on equations (16.2) and (16.3), we

---

[4] For a sufficiently large number of time steps, these probabilities are always positive.

[5] See J. C. Hull and A. White, "The Use of the Control Variate Technique in Option Pricing," *Journal of Financial and Quantitative Analysis* 23 (September 1988): 237–51.

Figure 16.10 Tree produced by DerivaGem for European version of option in Figure 16.3. At each node, the upper number is the stock price and the lower number is the option price

At each node:
Upper value = Underlying Asset Price
Lower value = Option Price
Shading indicates where option is exercised

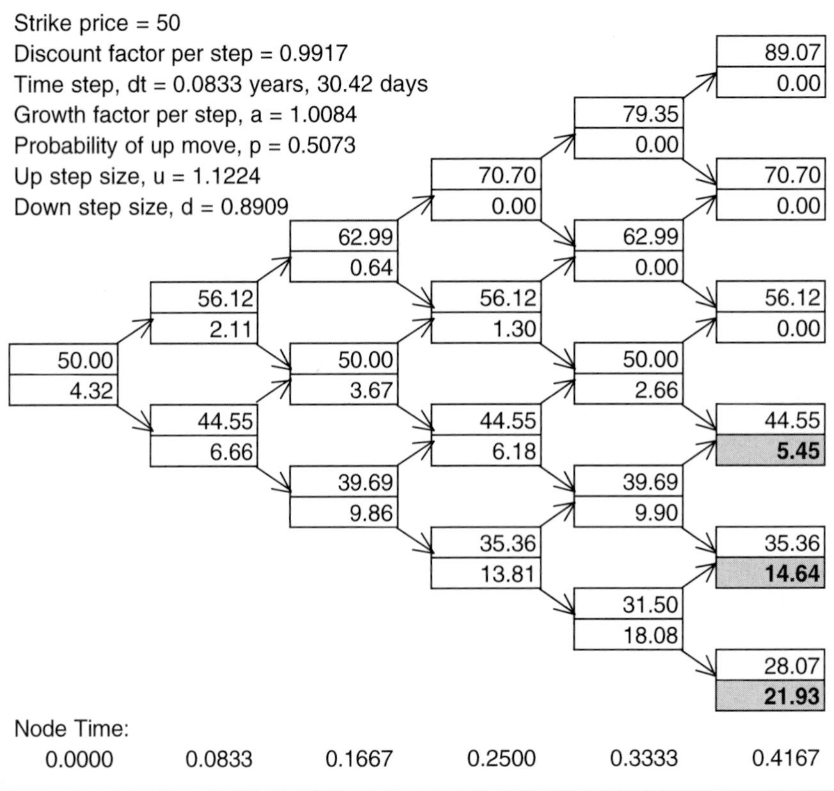

can set $p = 0.5$. A solution to the equations for small Δt is

$$u = e^{(r-\sigma^2/2)\Delta t+\sigma\sqrt{\Delta t}}, \quad d = e^{(r-\sigma^2/2)\Delta t-\sigma\sqrt{\Delta t}}$$

When the stock provides a continuous dividend yield at rate q, the variable r becomes $r - q$ in these formulas. This allows trees with $p = 0.5$ to be built for options on indices, foreign exchange, and futures.

This alternative tree-building procedure has the advantage over the Cox, Ross, and Rubinstein approach that the probabilities are always 0.5 regardless of the value of σ or the number of time steps.[6] Its disadvantage is that the calculation of delta, gamma, and

[6] In the unusual situation that time steps are so large that $\sigma < |(r-q)\sqrt{\Delta t}|$, the Cox, Ross, and Rubinstein tree gives negative probabilities. The alternative procedure described here does not have that drawback.

theta from the tree is not as accurate because the values of the underlying asset at times Δt and $2\Delta t$ are no longer centered at S_0.

Example

A nine-month American call option on the Canadian dollar has a strike price of 0.7950. The current exchange rate is 0.7900, the U.S. risk-free interest rate is 6% per annum, the Canadian risk-free interest rate is 10% per annum, and the volatility of the exchange rate is 4% per annum. In this case, $S_0 = 0.79$, $K = 0.795$, $r = 0.06$, $r_f = 0.10$, $\sigma = 0.04$, and $T = 0.75$. We divide the life of the option into three-month periods for the purposes of constructing the tree so that $\Delta t = 0.25$. We set the probabilities on each branch to 0.5 and

$$u = e^{(0.06-0.10-0.0016/2)0.25+0.04\sqrt{0.25}} = 1.0098$$

$$d = e^{(0.06-0.10-0.0016/2)0.25-0.04\sqrt{0.25}} = 0.9703$$

The tree for the exchange rate is shown in Figure 16.11. The tree gives the value of the option as 0.0026.

Figure 16.11 Binomial tree for American call option on the Canadian dollar. At each node, the uppermost number is the spot exchange rate, all probabilities are 0.5, and the lower number is option price

At each node:
Upper value = Underlying Asset Price
Lower value = Option Price
Shading indicates where option is exercised

Strike price = 0.795
Discount factor per step = 0.9851
Time step, dt = 0.2500 years, 91.25 days

Probability of up move, p = 0.5000

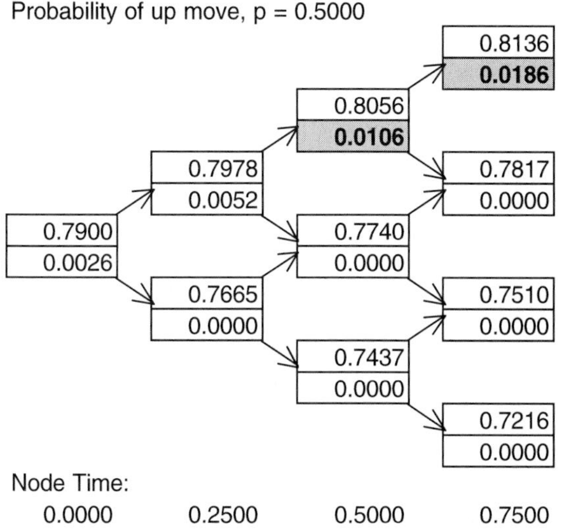

16.6 MONTE CARLO SIMULATION

Binomial trees can be used in conjunction with Monte Carlo simulation for valuing derivatives. Once the tree has been constructed, we randomly sample paths through it. Instead of working backward from the end of the tree to the beginning, we work forward through the tree. The basic procedure is as follows. At the first node we sample a random number between 0 and 1. If the number lies between 0 and p, we take the upper branch; if it lies between p and 1, we take the lower branch. We repeat this procedure at the node that is then reached and at all subsequent nodes that are reached until we get to the end of the tree. We then calculate the payoff on the option for the particular path sampled. This completes the first trial. We carry out many more trials by repeating the whole procedure. Our estimate of the value of the option is the arithmetic average of the payoffs from all the trials discounted at the risk-free interest rate.

Monte Carlo simulation, as just described, cannot easily be used for American options, because we have no way of knowing whether early exercise is optimal when a certain node is reached. It can be used to value European options so that a check is provided on the pricing formulas for these options. It can also be used to price some of the exotic options we will discuss in Chapter 20 (e.g. Asian options and lookback options).

Example

Suppose that the tree in Figure 16.3 is used to value an option that pays off $\max(S_{ave} - 50, 0)$ where S_{ave} is the average stock price during the five months (with the first and last stock price being included in the average). This is known

Table 16.1 Monte Carlo simulation to value an Asian option from the tree in Figure 16.3. The payoff is amount by which the average stock price exceeds $50. U = up movement; D = down movement

Trial	*Path*	*Average stock price*	*Option payoff*
1	UUUUD	64.98	14.98
2	UUUDD	59.82	9.82
3	DDDUU	42.31	0.00
4	UUUUU	68.04	18.04
5	UUDDU	55.22	5.22
6	UDUUD	55.22	5.22
7	DDUDD	42.31	0.00
8	UUDDU	55.22	5.22
9	UUUDU	62.25	12.25
10	DDUUD	45.56	0.00
Average			7.08

as an Asian option. When ten simulation trials are used one possible result is shown in Table 16.1. The value of the option is calculated as the average payoff discounted at the risk-free rate. In this case, the average payoff is \$7.08 and the risk-free rate is 10%, and so the calculated value is $7.08e^{-0.1\times 5/12} = 6.79$. (This illustrates the method. In practice we would have to use more time steps on the tree and many more simulation trials to get an accurate answer.)

SUMMARY

This chapter has described how options can be valued using the binomial tree approach. This approach involves dividing the life of the option into a number of small intervals of length Δt and assuming that an asset price at the beginning of an interval can lead to only one of two alternative asset prices at the end of the interval. One of these alternative asset prices involves an up movement; the other involves a down movement.

The sizes of the up movements and down movements, and their associated probabilities, are chosen so that the change in the asset price has the correct mean and standard deviation for a risk-neutral world. Option prices are calculated by starting at the end of the tree and working backward. At the end of the tree, the price of an option is its intrinsic value. At earlier nodes on the tree, the value of an option, if it is American, must be calculated as the greater of

1. The value it has if exercised immediately
2. The value it has if held for a further period of time of length Δt

If it is exercised at a node, the value of the option is its intrinsic value. If it is held for a further period of length Δt, the value of the option is its expected value at the end of the time period Δt discounted at the risk-free rate.

Delta, gamma, and theta can be estimated directly from the values of the option at the various nodes of the tree. Vega can be estimated by making a small change to the volatility and recomputing the value of the option using a similar tree. Rho can similarly be estimated by making a small change to the interest rate and recomputing the tree.

The binomial tree approach can handle options on stocks paying continuous dividend yields. Because stock indices, currencies, and most futures contracts can be regarded as analogous to stocks paying continuous yields, binomial trees can handle options on these assets as well.

When the binomial tree approach is used to value options on a stock paying known dollar dividends, it is convenient to use the tree to model the stock price less the present value of all future dividends during the life of the option. This keeps the number of nodes on the tree from becoming unmanageable and is consistent with the way European options on dividend-paying stocks are valued.

The computational efficiency of the binomial model can be improved by using the control variate technique. This involves valuing both the American option that is of interest and the corresponding European option using the same tree. The error in the price of the European option is used as an estimate of the error in the price of the American option.

FURTHER READING

Boyle, P. P. "Options: A Monte Carlo Approach," *Journal of Financial Economics*, 4 (1977): 323–28.

Boyle, P. P., M. Broadie, and P. Glasserman. "Monte Carlo Methods for Security Pricing," *Journal of Economic Dynamics and Control*, 21 (1997): 1267–1322.

Cox, J. C., S. A. Ross, and M. Rubinstein. "Option Pricing: A Simplified Approach," *Journal of Financial Economics*, 7 (October 1979): 229–64.

Figlewski, S., and B. Gao. "The Adaptive Mesh Model: A New Approach to Efficient Option Pricing," *Journal of Financial Economics*, 53 (1999), 313–51.

Hull, J. C., and A. White. "The Use of the Control Variate Technique in Option Pricing," *Journal of Financial and Quantitative Analysis*, 23 (September 1988): 237–51.

Longstaff, F. A. and E. S. Schwartz. "Valuing American Options by Simulation: A Least Squares Approach," *Review of Financial Studies*, 14, 1 (2001): 113–47.

Rendleman, R., and B. Bartter. "Two State Option Pricing," *Journal of Finance*, 34 (1979): 1092–1110.

Quiz (Answers at End of Book)

16.1. Which of the following can be estimated for an American option by constructing a single binomial tree: delta, gamma, vega, theta, rho?

16.2. The probability for an up-movement on a binomial tree is $(a - d)/(u - d)$. Explain how the growth factor a is calculated for (a) a non-dividend-paying stock, (b) a stock index, (c) a foreign currency, and (d) a futures contract.

16.3. Calculate the price of a three-month American put option on a non-dividend-paying stock when the stock price is \$60, the strike price is \$60, the risk-free interest rate is 10% per annum, and the volatility is 45% per annum. Use a binomial tree with a time step of one month.

16.4. Explain how the control variate technique is implemented.

16.5. Calculate the price of a nine-month American call option on corn futures when the current futures price is 198 cents, the strike price is 200 cents, the risk-free interest rate is 8% per annum, and the volatility is 30% per annum. Use a binomial tree with a time step of three months.

16.6. "For a dividend-paying stock the tree for the stock price does not recombine, but the tree for the stock price less the present value of future dividends does recombine." Explain this statement.

16.7. Explain the problem in using Monte Carlo simulation to value an American option.

Questions and Problems (Answers in Solutions Manual/Study Guide)

16.8. Consider an option that pays off the amount by which the final stock price exceeds the average stock price achieved during the life of the option. Can this be valued from a binomial tree using backwards induction?

16.9. A nine-month American put option on a non-dividend-paying stock has a strike price of \$49. The stock price is \$50, the risk-free rate is 5% per annum, and the volatility is 30% per annum. Use a three-step binomial tree to calculate the option price.

16.10. Use a three-time-step tree to value a nine-month American call option on wheat futures. The current futures price is 400 cents, the strike price is 420 cents, the risk-free rate is 6%, and the volatility is 35% per annum. Estimate the delta of the option from your tree.

16.11. A three-month American call option on a stock has a strike price of \$20. The stock price is \$20, the risk-free rate is 3% per annum, and the volatility is 25% per annum. A dividend of \$2 is expected in 1.5 months. Use a three-step binomial tree to calculate the option price.

16.12. A one-year American put option on a non-dividend-paying stock has an exercise price of \$18. The current stock price is \$20, the risk-free interest rate is 15% per annum, and the volatility of the stock is 40% per annum. Use the DerivaGem software with four three-month time steps to estimate the value of the option. Display the tree and verify that the option prices at the final and penultimate nodes are correct. Use DerivaGem to value the European version of the option. Use the control variate technique to improve your estimate of the price of the American option.

16.13. A two-month American put option on a stock index has an exercise price of 480. The current level of the index is 484, the risk-free interest rate is 10% per annum, the dividend yield on the index is 3% per annum, and the volatility of the index is 25% per annum. Divide the life of the option into four half-month periods and use the binomial tree approach to estimate the value of the option.

16.14. How would you use the control variate approach to improve the estimate of the delta of an American option when the binomial tree approach is used?

16.15. How would you use the binomial tree approach to value an American option on a stock index when the dividend yield on the index is a function of time?

Assignment Questions

16.16. An American put option to sell a Swiss franc for dollars has a strike price of \$0.80 and a time to maturity of one year. The volatility of the Swiss franc is 10%, the dollar interest rate is 6%, the Swiss franc interest rate is 3%, and the current exchange rate is 0.81. Use a tree with three time steps to value the option. Estimate the delta of the option from your tree.

16.17. A one-year American call option on silver futures has an exercise price of \$9.00. The current futures price is \$8.50, the risk-free rate of interest is 12% per annum, and the volatility of the futures price is 25% per annum. Use the DerivaGem software with four three-month time steps to estimate the value of the option. Display the tree and verify that the option prices at the final and penultimate nodes are correct. Use DerivaGem to value the European version of the option. Use the control variate technique to improve your estimate of the price of the American option.

16.18. A six-month American call option on a stock is expected to pay dividends of \$1 per share at the end of the second month and the fifth month. The current stock price is \$30, the exercise price is \$34, the risk-free interest rate is 10% per annum, and the volatility of the part of the stock price that will not be used to pay the dividends is 30% per annum.

Use the DerivaGem software with the life of the option divided into 100 time steps to estimate the value of the option. Compare your answer with that given by Black's approximation (see Section 12.9).

16.19. The DerivaGem Application Builder functions enable you to investigate how the prices of options calculated from a binomial tree converge to the correct value as the number of time steps increases (see Figure 16.4 and Sample Application A in DerivaGem). Consider a put option on a stock index where the index level is 900, the strike price is 900, the risk-free rate is 5%, the dividend yield is 2%, and the time to maturity is 2 years:

a. Produce results similar to Sample Application A on convergence for the situation where the option is European and the volatility of the index is 20%.
b. Produce results similar to Sample Application A on convergence for the situation where the option is American and the volatility of the index is 20%.
c. Produce a chart showing the pricing of the American option when the volatility is 20% as a function of the number of time steps when the control variate technique is used.
d. Suppose that the price of the American option in the market is 85.0. Produce a chart showing the implied volatility estimate as a function of the number of time steps.

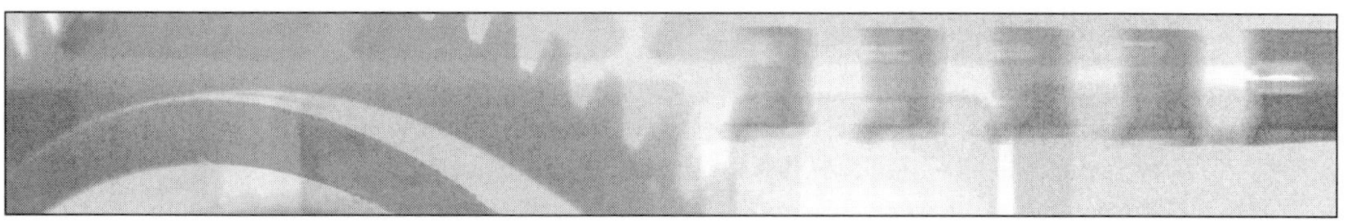

CHAPTER 17 Volatility Smiles

How close are the market prices of options to those predicted by Black–Scholes? Do traders really use Black–Scholes when determining a price for an option? Are the probability distributions of asset prices really lognormal? What research has been carried out to test the validity of the Black–Scholes formulas? In this chapter we answer these questions. We explain that traders do use the Black–Scholes model—but not in exactly the way that Black and Scholes originally intended. This is because they allow the volatility used to price an option to depend on its strike price and time to maturity.

A plot of the implied volatility of an option as a function of its strike price is known as a *volatility smile*. In this chapter we describe the volatility smiles that traders use in equity and foreign currency markets. We explain the relationship between a volatility smile and the probability distribution being assumed for the future asset price. We also discuss how option traders vary volatility with option maturity and how they use volatility surfaces as pricing tools.

17.1 PUT–CALL PARITY REVISITED

Put–call parity, which we explained in Chapters 9 and 13, provides a good starting point for understanding volatility smiles. It is an important relationship between the price, c, of a European call and the price, p, of a European put:

$$p + S_0e^{-qT} = c + Ke^{-rT} \tag{17.1}$$

The call and the put have the same strike price, K, and time to maturity, T. The variable S_0 is the price of the underlying asset today, r is the risk-free interest rate for maturity T, and q is the yield on the asset.

A key feature of the put–call parity relationship is that it is based on a relatively simple arbitrage argument. It does not require any assumption about the future probability distribution of the asset price. It is true both when the asset price distribution is lognormal and when it is not lognormal.

Suppose that, for a particular value of the volatility, p_{bs} and c_{bs} are the values of European put and call options calculated using the Black–Scholes model. Suppose further that p_{mkt} and c_{mkt} are the market values of these options. Because put–call parity holds for the Black–Scholes model, we must have

$$p_{\mathrm{bs}} + S_0 e^{-qT} = c_{\mathrm{bs}} + Ke^{-rT}$$

Because it holds for the market prices too, we also have

$$p_{\mathrm{mkt}} + S_0 e^{-qT} = c_{\mathrm{mkt}} + Ke^{-rT}$$

Subtracting the second of these two equations from the first, we obtain

$$p_{\mathrm{bs}} - p_{\mathrm{mkt}} = c_{\mathrm{bs}} - c_{\mathrm{mkt}} \tag{17.2}$$

This shows that the dollar pricing error when the Black–Scholes model is used to price a European put option should be exactly the same as the dollar pricing error when it is used to price a European call option with the same strike price and time to maturity.

Suppose that the implied volatility of the put option is 22%. This means that $p_{\mathrm{bs}} = p_{\mathrm{mkt}}$ when a volatility of 22% is used in the Black–Scholes model. From equation (17.2), it follows that $c_{\mathrm{bs}} = c_{\mathrm{mkt}}$ when this volatility is used. The implied volatility of the call, therefore, is also 22%. This argument shows that the implied volatility of a European call option is always the same as the implied volatility of a European put option when the two have the same strike price and maturity date. To put this another way, for a given strike price and maturity, the correct volatility to use in conjunction with the Black–Scholes model to price a European call should always be the same as that used to price a European put. This is also approximately true for American options. It follows that when traders refer to the relationship between implied volatility and strike price, or to the relationship between implied volatility and maturity, they do not need to state whether they are talking about calls or puts. The relationship is the same for both.

Example

The value of the Australian dollar is \$0.60. The risk-free interest rate is 5% per annum in the United States and 10% per annum in Australia. The market price of a European call option on the Australian dollar with a maturity of one year and a strike price of \$0.59 is 0.0236. DerivaGem shows that the implied volatility of the call is 14.5%. For there to be no arbitrage, the put–call parity relationship in equation (17.1) must apply with q equal to the foreign risk-free rate. The price, p, of a European put option with a strike price of \$0.59 and maturity of one year therefore satisfies

$$p + 0.60e^{-0.10\times 1} = 0.0236 + 0.59e^{-0.05\times 1}$$

so that $p = 0.0419$. DerivaGem shows that, when the put has this price, its implied volatility is also 14.5%. This is what we expect from the analysis just given.

17.2 FOREIGN CURRENCY OPTIONS

The volatility smile used by traders to price foreign currency options has the general form shown in Figure 17.1. The volatility is relatively low for at-the- money options, but becomes progressively higher as an option moves either into the money or out of the money.

Figure 17.1 Volatility smile for foreign currency options

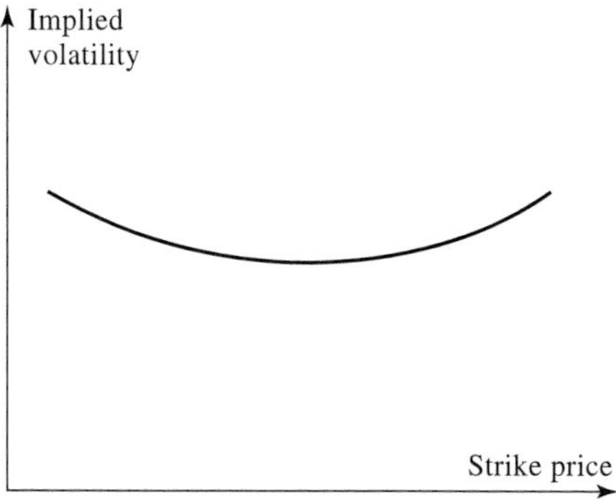

The volatility smile in Figure 17.1 corresponds to the probability distribution shown by the solid line in Figure 17.2. We will refer to this as the *implied distribution*. A lognormal distribution with the same mean and standard deviation as the implied distribution is shown by the dashed line in Figure 17.2. It can be seen that the implied distribution has heavier tails than the lognormal distribution.[1]

To see that Figures 17.1 and 17.2 are consistent with each other, consider first a deep-out-of-the-money call option with a high strike price of K_2. This option pays off only if the exchange rate proves to be above K_2. Figure 17.2 shows that the probability

Figure 17.2 Implied distribution and lognormal distribution for foreign currency options

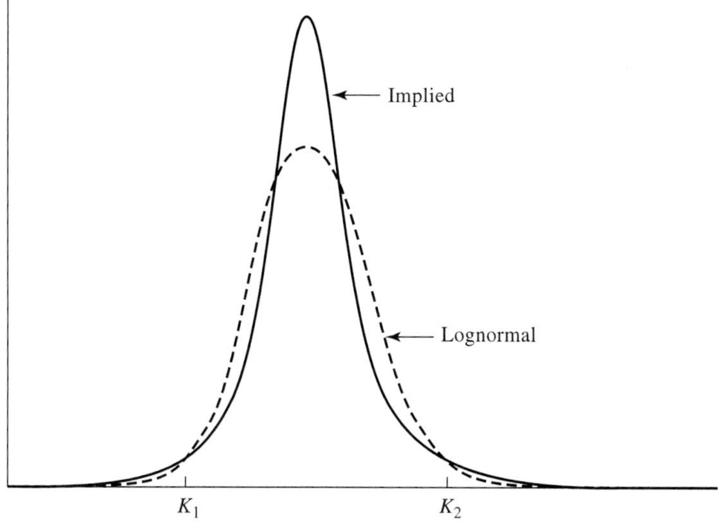

[1] This is known as kurtosis. Note that, in addition to having a heavier tail, the implied distribution is more "peaked." Both small and large movements in the exchange rate are more likely than with the lognormal distribution. Intermediate movements are less likely.

of this is higher for the implied probability distribution than for the lognormal distribution. We therefore expect the implied distribution to give a relatively high price for the option. A relatively high price leads to a relatively high implied volatility—and this is exactly what we observe in Figure 17.1 for the option. The two figures are therefore consistent with each other for high strike prices. Consider next a deep-out-of-the-money put option with a low strike price of K_1. This option pays off only if the exchange rate proves to be below K_1. Figure 17.2 shows that the probability of this is also higher for implied probability distribution than for the lognormal distribution. We therefore expect the implied distribution to give a relatively high price, and a relatively high implied volatility, for this option as well. Again, this is exactly what we observe in Figure 17.1.

Empirical Results

We have just shown that the smile used by traders for foreign currency options implies that they consider that the lognormal distribution understates the probability of extreme movements in exchange rates. To test whether they are right, Table 17.1 examines the daily movements in 12 different exchange rates over a 10-year period. The first step in the production of the table is to calculate the standard deviation of daily percentage change in each exchange rate. The next stage is to note how often the actual percentage change exceeded one standard deviation, two standard deviations, and so on. The final stage is to calculate how often this would have happened if the percentage changes had been normally distributed. (The lognormal model implies that percentage changes are almost exactly normally distributed over a one-day time period.) The results are shown in Table 17.1.[2]

Daily changes exceed three standard deviations on 1.34% of days. The lognormal model predicts that this should happen on only 0.27% of days. Daily changes exceed four, five, and six standard deviations on 0.29%, 0.08%, and 0.03% of days, respectively. The lognormal model predicts that we should hardly ever observe this happening. The table therefore provides evidence to support the existence of heavy

Table 17.1 Percent of days when daily exchange rate moves are greater than one, two,..., six standard deviations (S.D. = standard deviation of daily change)

	Real world	*Lognormal model*
> 1 S.D.	25.04	31.73
> 2 S.D.	5.27	4.55
> 3 S.D.	1.34	0.27
> 4 S.D.	0.29	0.01
> 5 S.D.	0.08	0.00
> 6 S.D.	0.03	0.00

[2] This table is taken from J. C. Hull and A. White, "Value at Risk When Daily Changes in Market Variables Are Not Normally Distributed," *Journal of Derivatives*, 5, no. 3 (Spring 1998): 9–19.

Business Snapshot 17.1 Making money from foreign currency options

Suppose that most market participants think that exchange rates are lognormally distributed. They will be comfortable using the same volatility to value all options on a particular exchange rate. You have just done the analysis in Table 17.1 and know that the lognormal assumption is not a good one for exchange rates. What should you do?

The answer is that you should buy deep-out-the-money call and put options on a variety of different currencies—and wait. These options will be relatively inexpensive and more of them will close in the money than the lognormal model predicts. The present value of your payoffs will on average be much greater than the cost of the options.

In the mid-1980s, a few traders knew about the heavy tails of foreign exchange probability distributions. Everyone else thought that the lognormal assumption of Black–Scholes was reasonable. The few traders who were well informed followed the strategy we have described—and made lots of money. By the late 1980s everyone realized that foreign currency options should be priced with a volatility smile and the trading opportunity disappeared.

tails and the volatility smile used by traders. Business Snapshot 17.1 shows how you could have made money if you had done the analysis in Table 17.1 ahead of the rest of the market.

Reasons for the Smile in Foreign Currency Options

Why are exchange rates not lognormally distributed? Two of the conditions for an asset price to have a lognormal distribution are:

1. The volatility of the asset is constant.
2. The price of the asset changes smoothly with no jumps.

In practice, neither of these conditions is satisfied for an exchange rate. The volatility of an exchange rate is far from constant, and exchange rates frequently exhibit jumps.[3] It turns out that the effect of both a nonconstant volatility and jumps is that extreme outcomes become more likely.

The impact of jumps and nonconstant volatility depends on the option maturity. The percentage impact of a nonconstant volatility on prices becomes more pronounced as the maturity of the option is increased, but the volatility smile created by the nonconstant volatility usually becomes less pronounced. The percentage impact of jumps on both prices and the volatility smile becomes less pronounced as the maturity of the option is increased. When we look at sufficiently long-dated options, jumps tend to get "averaged out," so that the stock price distribution when there are jumps is almost indistinguishable from that obtained when the stock price changes smoothly.

[3] Often the jumps are in response to the actions of central banks.

17.3 EQUITY OPTIONS

The volatility smile for equity options has been studied by Rubinstein (1985), Rubinstein (1994), and Jackwerth and Rubinstein (1996). Prior to 1987, there was no marked volatility smile. Since 1987 the volatility smile used by traders to price equity options (both those on individual stocks and those on stock indices) has the general form shown in Figure 17.3. This is sometimes referred to as a *volatility skew*. The volatility decreases as the strike price increases. The volatility used to price an option with a low strike price (i.e., a deep-out-of-the-money put or a deep-in-the-money call) is significantly higher than that used to price an option with a high strike price (i.e., a deep-in-the-money put or a deep-out-of-the-money call).

The volatility smile for equity options corresponds to the implied probability distribution given by the solid line in Figure 17.4. A lognormal distribution with the same mean and standard deviation as the implied distribution is represented by the dotted line. It can be seen that the implied distribution has a heavier left tail and less heavy right tail than the lognormal distribution.

To see that Figures 17.3 and 17.4 are consistent with each other, we proceed as for Figures 17.1 and 17.2 and consider options that are deep out of the money. From Figure 17.4, a deep-out-of-the-money call with a strike price of K_2 has a lower price when the implied distribution is used than when the lognormal distribution is used. This is because the option pays off only if the stock price proves to be above K_2, and the probability of this is lower for the implied probability distribution than for the lognormal distribution. We therefore expect the implied distribution to give a relatively low price for the option. A relatively low price leads to a relatively low implied volatility—and this is exactly what we observe in Figure 17.3 for the option. Consider

Figure 17.3 Volatility smile for equities

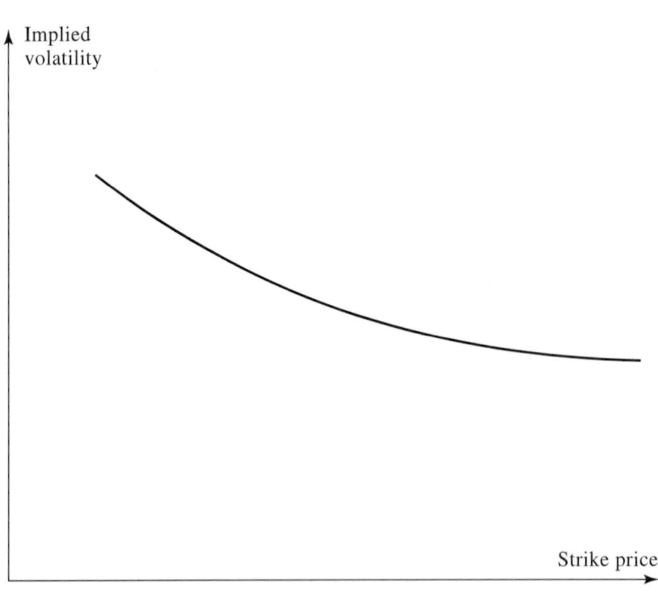

Figure 17.4 Implied distribution and lognormal distribution for equity options

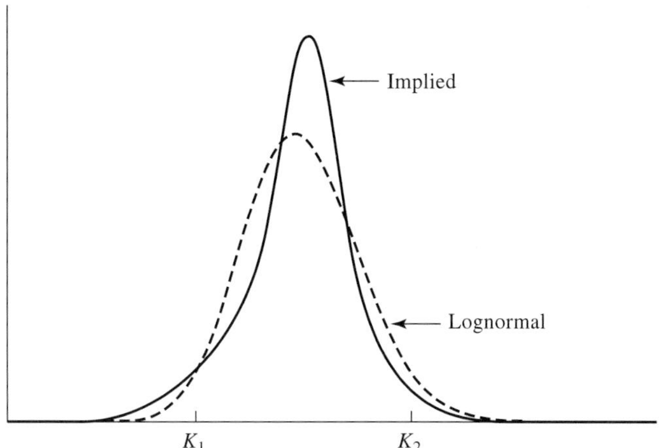

next a deep-out-of-the-money put option with a strike price of K_1. This option pays off only if the stock price proves to be below K_1. Figure 17.4 shows that the probability of this is higher for implied probability distribution than for the lognormal distribution. We therefore expect the implied distribution to give a relatively high price, and a relatively high implied volatility, for this option. Again, this is exactly what we observe in Figure 17.3.

The Reason for the Smile in Equity Options

One possible explanation for the smile in equity options concerns leverage. As a company's equity declines in value, the company's leverage increases. This means that the equity becomes more risky and its volatility increases. As a company's equity increases in value, leverage decreases. The equity then becomes less risky and its volatility decreases. This argument shows that we can expect the volatility of equity to be a decreasing function of price and is consistent with Figures 17.3 and 17.4. Another explanation is crashophobia (see Business Snapshot 17.2).

17.4 THE VOLATILITY TERM STRUCTURE AND VOLATILITY SURFACES

In addition to a volatility smile, traders use a volatility term structure when pricing options. This means that the volatility used to price an at-the-money option depends on the maturity of the option. Volatility tends to be an increasing function of maturity when short-dated volatilities are historically low. This is because there is then an expectation that volatilities will increase. Similarly, volatility tends to be an decreasing function of maturity when short-dated volatilities are historically high. This is because there is then an expectation that volatilities will decrease.

Volatility surfaces combine volatility smiles with the volatility term structure to

Business Snapshot 17.2 Crashophobia

It is interesting that the pattern for equities in Figure 17.3 has existed only since the stock market crash of October 1987. Prior to October 1987, implied volatilities were much less dependent on strike price. This has led Mark Rubinstein to suggest that one reason for the equity volatility smile may be "crashophobia." Traders are concerned about the possibility of another crash similar to October 1987, and they price options accordingly.

There is some empirical support for this explanation. Declines in the S&P 500 tend to be accompanied by a steepening of the skew. When the S&P 500 increases, the skew tends to become less steep.

tabulate the volatilities appropriate for pricing an option with any strike price and any maturity. An example of a volatility surface that might be used for foreign currency options is shown in Table 17.2.

One dimension of a volatility surface is strike price; the other is time to maturity. The main body of the volatility surface shows implied volatilities calculated from the Black–Scholes model. At any given time, some of the entries in the volatility surface are likely to correspond to options for which reliable market data are available. The implied volatilities for these options are calculated directly from their market prices and entered into the table. The rest of the volatility surface is determined using linear interpolation.

When a new option has to be valued, financial engineers look up the appropriate volatility in the table. For example, when valuing a nine-month option with a strike price of 1.05, a financial engineer would interpolate between 13.4 and 14.0 to obtain a volatility of 13.7%. This is the volatility that would be used in the Black–Scholes formula or in a binomial tree.

The shape of the volatility smile depends on the option maturity. As illustrated in Table 17.2, the smile tends to become less pronounced as the option maturity increases. Define T as the time to maturity and F_0 as the forward price of the asset. Some financial engineers choose to define the volatility smile as the relationship between implied volatility and

$$\frac{1}{\sqrt{T}}\ln\frac{K}{F_0}$$

Table 17.2 Volatility surface

Option maturity	*Strike price*				
	0.90	*0.95*	*1.00*	*1.05*	*1.10*
1 month	14.2	13.0	12.0	13.1	14.5
3 months	14.0	13.0	12.0	13.1	14.2
6 months	14.1	13.3	12.5	13.4	14.3
1 year	14.7	14.0	13.5	14.0	14.8
2 years	15.0	14.4	14.0	14.5	15.1
5 years	14.8	14.6	14.4	14.7	15.0

rather than as the relationship between the implied volatility and K. The smile is then usually much less dependent on the time to maturity.[4]

The Role of the Model

How important is the pricing model if traders are prepared to use a different volatility for every deal? It can be argued that the Black–Scholes model is no more than a sophisticated interpolation tool used by traders for ensuring that an option is priced consistently with the market prices of other actively traded options. If traders stopped using Black–Scholes and switched to another plausible model, the volatility surface would change and the shape of the smile would change. But arguably, the dollar prices quoted in the market would not change appreciably.

17.5 WHEN A SINGLE LARGE JUMP IS ANTICIPATED

We now consider an example of how an unusual volatility smile could arise in equity markets. Suppose that a stock price is currently \$50 and an important news announcement in a few days is expected to either increase the stock price by \$8 or reduce it by \$8. (This announcement might concern the outcome of a takeover attempt or the verdict in an important lawsuit.)

The probability distribution of the stock price in, say, one month might then consist of a mixture of two lognormal distributions, the first corresponding to favorable news, and the second to unfavorable news. The situation is illustrated in Figure 17.5. The solid line shows the mixed-lognormal distribution for the stock price in one month; the dashed line shows a lognormal distribution with the same mean and standard deviation as this distribution.

Figure 17.5 Effect of a single large jump. The solid line is the true distribution; the dashed line is the lognormal distribution

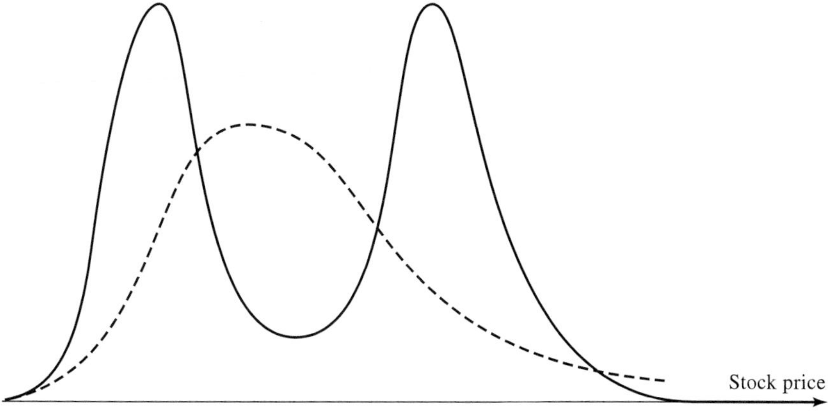

[4] For a discussion of this approach, see S. Natenberg, *Option Pricing and Volatility: Advanced Trading Strategies and Techniques*, 2nd edn. McGraw-Hill, 1994; R. Tompkins, *Options Analysis: A State of the Art Guide to Options Pricing*, Burr Ridge, IL: Irwin, 1994.

Figure 17.6 Change in stock price in one month

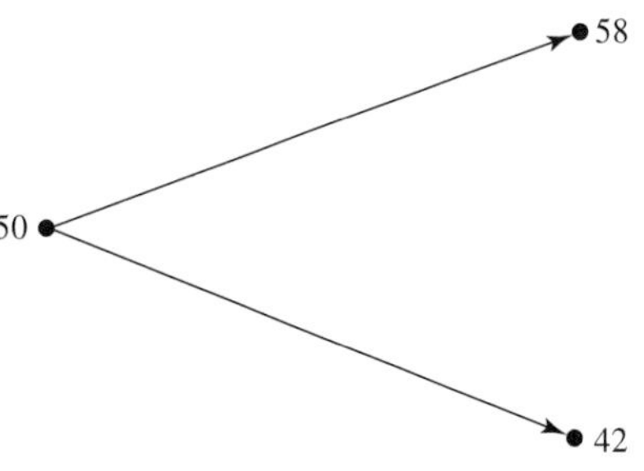

The true probability distribution is bimodal (certainly not lognormal). On easy way to investigate the general effect of a bimodal stock price distribution is to consider the extreme case where the distribution is binomial. This is what we will now do. Suppose that the stock price is currently \$50 and that it is known that in one month it will be either \$42 or \$58. Suppose further that the risk-free rate is 12% per annum. The situation is illustrated in Figure 17.6. Options can be valued using the binomial model from Chapters 11 and 16. In this case, $u = 1.16$, $d = 0.84$, $a = 1.0101$, and $p = 0.5314$. The results from valuing a range of different options are shown in Table 17.3. The first column shows alternative strike prices; the second shows prices of one-month European call options; the third shows the prices of one-month European put option prices; and the fourth shows implied volatilities. (As demonstrated in Section 17.1, the implied volatility of a European put option is the same as that of a European call option when they have the same strike price and maturity.) Figure 17.7 shows that volatility smile. It is actually a "frown" (the opposite of that observed for currencies) with volatilities declining as we move out of or into the money. The volatility implied from an option with a strike price of 50 will overprice an option with a strike price of 44 or 56.

Table 17.3 Implied volatilities in situation where true distribution is binomial

Strike price (\$)	*Call price (\$)*	*Put price (\$)*	*Implied volatility (%)*
42	8.42	0.00	0.0
44	7.37	0.93	58.8
46	6.31	1.86	66.6
48	5.26	2.78	69.5
50	4.21	3.71	69.2
52	3.16	4.64	66.1
54	2.10	5.57	60.0
56	1.05	6.50	49.0
58	0.00	7.42	0.0

Figure 17.7 Volatility smile for situation in Table 17.3

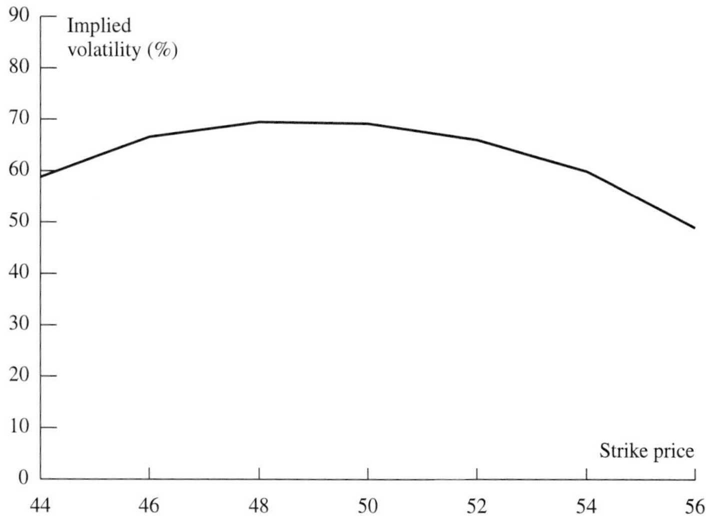

SUMMARY

The Black–Scholes model and its extensions assume that the probability distribution of the underlying asset at any given future time is lognormal. This assumption is not the one made by traders. They assume the probability distribution of an equity price has a heavier left tail and less heavy right tail than the lognormal distribution. They also assume that the probability of an exchange rate has a heavier right tail and a heavier left tail than the lognormal distribution.

Traders use volatility smiles to allow for nonlognormality. The volatility smile defines the relationship between the implied volatility of an option and its strike price. For equity options, the volatility smile tends to be downward sloping. This means that out-of-the-money puts and in-the-money calls tend to have high implied volatilities whereas out-of-the-money calls and in-the-money puts tend to have low implied volatilities. For foreign currency options, the volatility smile is U-shaped. Both out-of-the-money and in-the-money options have higher implied volatilities than at-the-money options.

Often traders also use a volatility term structure. The implied volatility of an option then depends on its life. When volatility smiles and volatility term structures are combined, they produce a volatility surface. This defines implied volatility as a function of both the strike price and the time to maturity.

FURTHER READING

Bakshi, G., C. Cao, and Z. Chen. "Empirical Performance of Alternative Option Pricing Models," *Journal of Finance*, 52, no. 5 (December 1997): 2004–49.

Bates, D. S. "Post-'87 Crash Fears in the S&P Futures Market," *Journal of Econometrics*, 94 (Jan./Feb. 2000): 181–238.

Derman, E. "Regimes of Volatility," *Risk*, April 1999: 55–59.

Ederington, L., and W. Guan. "Why Are Those Options Smiling," *Journal of Derivatives*, 10, 2 (2002): 9–34.

Jackwerth, J. C., and M. Rubinstein. "Recovering Probability Distributions from Option Prices," *Journal of Finance*, 51 (December 1996): 1611–31.

Lauterbach, B., and P. Schultz. "Pricing Warrants: An Empirical Study of the Black–Scholes Model and Its Alternatives," *Journal of Finance*, 4, no. 4 (September 1990): 1181–1210.

Melick, W. R., and C. P. Thomas. "Recovering an Asset's Implied Probability Density Function from Option Prices: An Application to Crude Oil during the Gulf Crisis," *Journal of Financial and Quantitative Analysis*, 32, no. 1 (March 1997): 91–115.

Rubinstein, M. "Nonparametric Tests of Alternative Option Pricing Models Using All Reported Trades and Quotes on the 30 Most Active CBOE Option Classes from August 23, 1976, through August 31, 1978," *Journal of Finance*, 40 (June 1985): 455–80.

Rubinstein, M. "Implied Binomial Trees," *Journal of Finance*, 49, no. 3 (July 1994): 771–818.

Xu, X., and S. J. Taylor. "The Term Structure of Volatility Implied by Foreign Exchange Options," *Journal of Financial and Quantitative Analysis*, 29 (1994): 57–74.

Quiz (Answers at End of Book)

17.1. What volatility smile is likely to be observed when:
   a. Both tails of the stock price distribution are less heavy than those of the lognormal distribution?
   b. The right tail is heavier, and the left tail is less heavy, than that of a lognormal distribution?

17.2. What volatility smile is observed for equities?

17.3. What volatility smile is likely to be caused by jumps in the underlying asset price? Is the pattern likely to be more pronounced for a two-year rather than a three-month option?

17.4. A European call and put option have the same strike price and time to maturity. The call has an implied volatility of 30% and the put has an implied volatility of 25%. What trades would you do?

17.5. Explain carefully why a distribution with a heavier left tail and less heavy right tail than the lognormal distribution gives rise to a downward sloping volatility smile.

17.6. The market price of a European call is $3.00 and its price given by Black–Scholes model with a volatility of 30% is $3.50. The price given by this Black–Scholes model for a European put option with the same strike price and time to maturity is $1.00. What should the market price of the put option be? Explain the reasons for your answer.

17.7. Explain what is meant by crashophobia.

Questions and Problems (Answers in Solutions Manual/Study Guide)

17.8. A stock price is currently $20. Tomorrow, news is expected to be announced that will either increase the price by $5 or decrease the price by $5. What are the problems in using Black–Scholes to value one-month options on the stock?

17.9. What volatility smile is likely to be observed for six-month options when the volatility is uncertain and positively correlated to the stock price?

17.10. What problems do you think would be encountered in testing a stock option pricing model empirically?

17.11. Suppose that a central bank's policy is to allow an exchange rate to fluctuate between 0.97 and 1.03. What pattern of implied volatilities for options on the exchange rate would you expect to see?

17.12. Option traders sometimes refer to deep-out-of-the-money options as being options on volatility. Why do you think they do this?

17.13. A European call option on a certain stock has a strike price of \$30, a time to maturity of one year, and an implied volatility of 30%. A European put option on the same stock has a strike price of \$30, a time to maturity of one year, and an implied volatility of 33%. What is the arbitrage opportunity open to a trader? Does the arbitrage work only when the lognormal assumption underlying Black–Scholes holds? Explain the reasons for your answer carefully.

17.14. Suppose that the result of a major lawsuit affecting Microsoft is due to be announced tomorrow. Microsoft's stock price is currently \$60. If the ruling is favorable to Microsoft, the stock price is expected to jump to \$75. If it is unfavorable, the stock is expected to jump to \$50. What is the risk-neutral probability of a favorable ruling? Assume that the volatility of Microsoft's stock will be 25% for six months after the ruling if the ruling is favorable and 40% if it is unfavorable. Use DerivaGem to calculate the relationship between implied volatility and strike price for six-month European options on Microsoft today. Microsoft does not pay dividends. Assume that the six-month risk-free rate is 6%. Consider call options with strike prices of 30, 40, 50, 60, 70, and 80.

17.15. An exchange rate is currently 0.8000. The volatility of the exchange rate is quoted as 12% and interest rates in the two countries are the same. Using the lognormal assumption, estimate the probability that the exchange rate in three months will be (a) less than 0.7000, (b) between 0.7000 and 0.7500, (c) between 0.7500 and 0.8000, (d) between 0.8000 and 0.8500, (e) between 0.8500 and 0.9000, and (f) greater than 0.9000. Based on the volatility smile usually observed in the market for exchange rates, which of these estimates would you expect to be too low and which would you expect to be too high?

17.16. The price of a stock is \$40. A six-month European call option on the stock with a strike price of \$30 has an implied volatility of 35%. A six-month European call option on the stock with a strike price of \$50 has an implied volatility of 28%. The six-month risk-free rate is 5% and no dividends are expected. Explain why the two implied volatilities are different. Use DerivaGem to calculate the prices of the two options. Use put–call parity to calculate the prices of six-month European put options with strike prices of \$30 and \$50. Use DerivaGem to calculate the implied volatilities of these two put options.

17.17. "The Black–Scholes model is used by traders as an interpolation tool." Discuss this view.

Assignment Questions

17.18. A company's stock is selling for \$4. The company has no outstanding debt. Analysts consider the liquidation value of the company to be at least \$300,000 and there are 100,000 shares outstanding. What volatility smile would you expect to see?

17.19. A company is currently awaiting the outcome of a major lawsuit. This is expected to be known within one month. The stock price is currently \$20. If the outcome is positive, the stock price is expected to be \$24 at the end of one month. If the outcome is negative, it is expected to be \$18 at this time. The one-month risk-free interest rate is 8% per annum.

a. What is the risk-neutral probability of a positive outcome?
b. What are the values of one-month call options with strike prices of \$19, \$20, \$21, \$22, and \$23?
c. Use DerivaGem to calculate a volatility smile for one-month call options.
d. Verify that the same volatility smile is obtained for one-month put options.

17.20. A futures price is currently \$40. The risk-free interest rate is 5%. Some news is expected tomorrow that will cause the volatility over the next three months to be either 10% or 30%. There is a 60% chance of the first outcome and a 40% chance of the second outcome. Use DerivaGem to calculate a volatility smile for three-month options.

17.21. Data for a number of foreign currencies are provided on the author's website:

`http://www.rotman.utoronto.ca/~hull/data`

Choose a currency and use the data to produce a table similar to Table 17.1.

17.22. Data for a number of stock indices are provided on the author's website:

`http://www.rotman.utoronto.ca/~hull/data`

Choose an index and test whether a three standard deviation down movement happens more often than a three standard deviation up movement.

17.23. Consider a European call and a European put with the same strike price and time to maturity. Show that they change in value by the same amount when the volatility increases from a level, σ_1, to a new level, σ_2 within a short period of time. (*Hint*: Use put–call parity.)

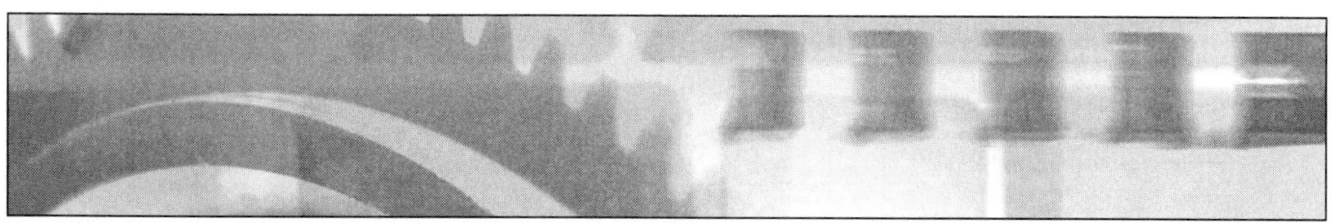

CHAPTER 18 Value at Risk

In Chapter 15 we examined measures such as delta, gamma, and vega for describing different aspects of the risk in a portfolio consisting of options and other financial assets. A financial institution usually calculates each of these measures each day for every market variable to which it is exposed. Often there are hundreds, or even thousands, of these market variables. A delta–gamma–vega analysis, therefore, leads to a huge number of different risk measures being produced each day. These risk measures provide valuable information for a trader who is responsible for managing the part of the financial institution's portfolio that is dependent on the particular market variable, but they are of limited use to senior management.

Value at risk (VaR) is an attempt to provide a single number summarizing the total risk in a portfolio of financial assets for senior management. It has become widely used by corporate treasurers and fund managers as well as by financial institutions. Central bank regulators also use VaR in determining the capital a bank is required to keep to reflect the market risks it is bearing.

In this chapter we explain the VaR measure and describe the two main approaches for calculating it. These are known as the *historical simulation* approach and the *model-building* approach.

18.1 THE VaR MEASURE

When using the value-at-risk (VaR) measure, we are interested in making a statement of the following form:

> We are X percent certain that we will not lose more than V dollars in the next N days.

Here, V is the VaR of the portfolio. It is a function of two parameters: the time horizon, N days, and the confidence level, X percent. It is the loss level over N days that we are X percent certain will not be exceeded. Bank regulators require banks to calculate VaR with $N = 10$ and $X = 99$ (see the discussion in Business Snapshot 18.1).

In general, when N days is the time horizon and X percent is the confidence level, VaR is the loss corresponding to the $(100 - X)$th percentile of the distribution of the change in the value of the portfolio over the next N days. For example, when $N = 5$ and $X = 97$, VaR is the third percentile of the distribution of changes in the value of

Business Snapshot 18.1 How bank regulators use VaR

The Basle Committee on Bank Supervision is a committee of the world's bank regulators that meets regularly in Basle, Switzerland. In 1988 it published what has become known as *The 1988 BIS Accord* or just *The Accord*. This is an agreement between the regulators on how the capital a bank is required to hold for credit risk should be calculated. Several years later the Basle Committee published *The 1996 Amendment* which was implemented in 1998 and required banks to hold capital for market risk as well as credit risk. The Amendment distinguishes between a bank's trading book and its banking book. The banking book consists primarily of loans and is not usually revalued on a regular basis for managerial and accounting purposes. The trading book consists of the myriad of different instruments that are traded by the bank (stocks, bonds, swaps, forward contracts, options, etc.) and is normally revalued daily.

The 1996 BIS Amendment calculates capital for the trading book using the VaR measure with $N = 10$ and $X = 99$. This means that it focuses on the revaluation loss over a 10-day period that is expected to be exceeded only 1% of the time. The capital it requires the bank to hold is k times this VaR measure (with an adjustment for what are termed specific risks). The multiplier k is chosen on a bank-by-bank basis by the regulators and must be at least 3.0. For a bank with excellent well-tested VaR estimation procedures, it is likely that k will be set equal to the minimum value of 3.0. For other banks it may be higher.

the portfolio over the next five days. VaR is illustrated for the situation where the change in the value of the portfolio is approximately normally distributed in Figure 18.1.

VaR is an attractive measure because it is easy to understand. In essence, it asks the simple question "How bad can things get?" This is the question all senior managers want answered. They are very comfortable with the idea of compressing all the Greek letters for all the market variables underlying a portfolio into a single number.

If we accept that it is useful to have a single number to describe the risk of a portfolio, an interesting question is whether VaR is the best alternative. Some

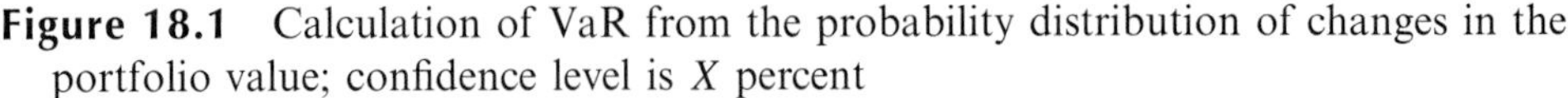

Figure 18.1 Calculation of VaR from the probability distribution of changes in the portfolio value; confidence level is X percent

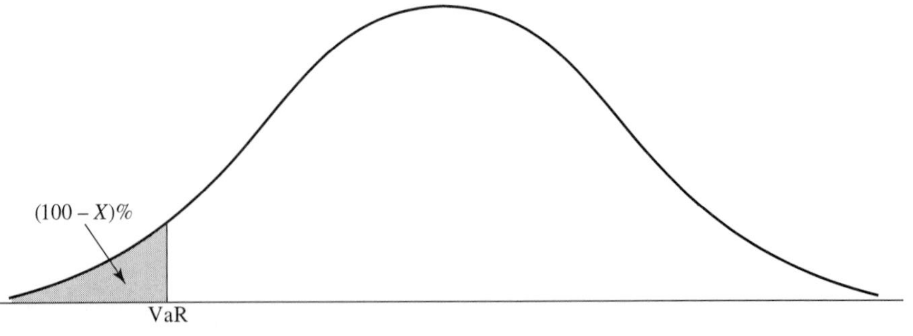

Figure 18.2 Alternative situation to Figure 18.1; VaR is the same, but the potential loss is larger

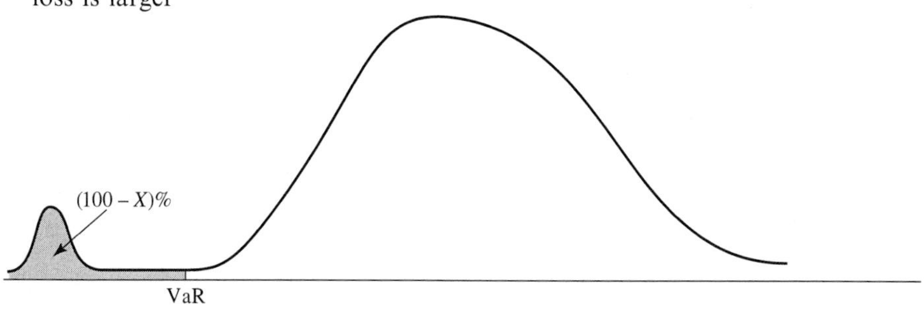

researchers have argued that VaR may tempt traders to choose a portfolio with a return distribution similar to that in Figure 18.2. The portfolios in Figures 18.1 and 18.2 have the same VaR, but the portfolio in Figure 18.2 is much riskier because potential losses are much larger.

A measure that deals with the problem we have just mentioned is *conditional VaR* (C-VaR).[1] Whereas VaR asks the question "How bad can things get?", C-VaR asks: "If things do get bad, how much can we expect to lose?" C-VaR is the expected loss during an N-day period conditional that we are in the $(100 - X)$ percent left tail of the distribution. For example, with $X = 99$ and $N = 10$, C-VaR is the average amount we lose over a 10-day period assuming that a 1% worst-case event occurs.

In spite of its weaknesses, VaR (not C-VaR) is the most popular measure of risk among both regulators and senior management. We will therefore devote most of the rest of this chapter to the ways in which it can be measured.

The Time Horizon

In theory, VaR has two parameters. These are the time horizon, N, measured in days, and the confidence interval, X. In practice, analysts almost invariably set $N = 1$ in the first instance. This is because there is not enough data to estimate directly the behavior of market variables over periods of time longer than one day. The usual assumption is

$$N\text{-day VaR} = 1\text{-day VaR} \times \sqrt{N}$$

This formula is exactly true when the changes in the value of the portfolio on successive days have independent identical normal distributions with mean zero. In other cases, it is an approximation.

We mentioned in Business Snapshot 18.1 that regulators require a bank's capital to be at least three times the 10-day 99% VaR. Given the way a 10-day VaR is calculated, this capital level is, to all intents and purposes, $3 \times \sqrt{10} = 9.49$ times the 1-day 99% VaR.

[1] This measure, which is also known as *expected shortfall* or *tail loss*, was suggested by P. Artzner, F. Delbaen, J. M. Eber, and D. Heath, "Coherent Measures of Risk," *Mathematical Finance*, 9 (1999): 203–28. These authors define certain properties that a good risk measure should have and show that the standard VaR measure does not have all of them.

18.2 HISTORICAL SIMULATION

Historical simulation is one popular way of estimating VaR. It involves using past data in a very direct way as a guide to what might happen in the future. Suppose that we wish to calculate VaR for a portfolio using a one-day time horizon, a 99% confidence level, and 500 days of data. The first step is to identify the market variables affecting the portfolio. These will typically be exchange rates, equity prices, interest rates, and so on. We then collect data on the movements in these market variables over the most recent 500 days. This provides us with 500 alternative scenarios for what can happen between today and tomorrow. Scenario 1 is where the percentage changes in the values of all variables are the same as they were on the first day for which we have collected data; scenario 2 is where they are the same as on the second day for which we have data; and so on. For each scenario we calculate the dollar change in the value of the portfolio between today and tomorrow. This defines a probability distribution for daily changes in the value of our portfolio. The fifth-worst daily change is the first percentile of the distribution. The estimate of VaR is the loss when we are at this first percentile point. Assuming that the last 500 days are a good guide to what could happen during the next day, we are 99% certain that we will not take a loss greater than our VaR estimate.

The historical simulation methodology is illustrated in Tables 18.1 and 18.2. Table 18.1 shows observations on market variables over the last 500 days. The observations are taken at some particular point in time during the day (usually the close of trading). We denote the first day for which we have data as Day 0; the second as Day 1; and so on. Today is Day 500; tomorrow is Day 501.

Table 18.2 shows the values of the market variables tomorrow if their percentage changes between today and tomorrow are the same as they were between Day $i-1$ and Day i for $1 \leqslant i \leqslant 500$. The first row in Table 18.2 shows the values of market variables tomorrow assuming their percentage changes between today and tomorrow are the same as they were between Day 0 and Day 1; the second row shows the values of market variables tomorrow assuming their percentage changes between Day 1 and Day 2 occur; and so on. The 500 rows in Table 18.2 are the 500 scenarios considered.

Table 18.1 Data for VaR historical simulation calculation

Day	*Market variable 1*	*Market variable 2*	...	*Market variable N*
0	20.33	0.1132	...	65.37
1	20.78	0.1159	...	64.91
2	21.44	0.1162	...	65.02
3	20.97	0.1184	...	64.90
⋮	⋮	⋮	⋮	⋮
498	25.72	0.1312	...	62.22
499	25.75	0.1323	...	61.99
500	25.85	0.1343	...	62.10

Table 18.2 Scenarios generated for tomorrow (Day 501) using data in Table 18.1

Scenario number	*Market variable 1*	*Market variable 2*	...	*Market variable N*	*Portfolio value* ($ millions)
1	26.42	0.1375	...	61.66	23.71
2	26.67	0.1346	...	62.21	23.12
3	25.28	0.1368	...	61.99	22.94
⋮	⋮	⋮	⋮	⋮	⋮
499	25.88	0.1354	...	61.87	23.63
500	25.95	0.1363	...	62.21	22.87

Define v_i as the value of a market variable on Day i and suppose that today is Day m. The ith scenario assumes that the value of the market variable tomorrow will be

$$v_m \frac{v_i}{v_{i-1}}$$

In our example, $m = 500$. For the first variable, the value today, v_{500}, is 25.85. We also have $v_0 = 20.33$ and $v_1 = 20.78$. It follows that the value of the first market variable in the first scenario is

$$25.85 \times \frac{20.78}{20.33} = 26.42$$

The final column of Table 18.2 shows the value of the portfolio tomorrow for each of the 500 scenarios. The value of the portfolio today is known. Suppose this is \$23.50 million. We can calculate the change in the value of the portfolio between today and tomorrow for all the different scenarios. For Scenario 1, it is +\$210,000; for Scenario 2, it is −\$380,000; and so on. These changes in value are then ranked. The fifth-worst loss is the one-day 99% VaR. As mentioned in the previous section, the N-day VaR for a 99% confidence level is calculated as $\sqrt{N}$ times the one-day VaR.

The VaR estimate in our example would be updated each day using the most recent 500 days of data. Consider, for example, what happens on Day 501. We find out new values for all the market variables and are able to calculate a new value for our portfolio.[2] We then go through the procedure we have outlined to calculate a new VaR. We use data on the market variables from Day 1 to Day 501. (This gives us the required 500 observations on the percentage changes in market variables; the Day-0 values of the market variables are no longer used.) Similarly, on Day 502 we use data from Day 2 to Day 502 to determine VaR; and so on.

18.3 MODEL-BUILDING APPROACH

The main alternative to historical simulation is the model-building approach (sometimes also called the variance–covariance approach). Before getting into the details of

[2] Note that the portfolio's composition may have changed between Day 500 and Day 501.

the approach, it is appropriate to mention one issue concerned with the units for measuring volatility.

Daily Volatilities

In option pricing we usually measure time in years, and the volatility of an asset is usually quoted as a "volatility per year." When using the model-building approach to calculate VaR, we usually measure time in days and the volatility of an asset is usually quoted as a "volatility per day."

What is the relationship between the volatility per year used in option pricing and the volatility per day used in VaR calculations? Let us define σ_{year} as the volatility per year of a certain asset and σ_{day} as the equivalent volatility per day of the asset. Assuming 252 trading days in a year, we can use equation (12.4) to write the standard deviation of the continuously compounded return on the asset in one year as either σ_{year} or $\sigma_{\text{day}}\sqrt{252}$. It follows that

$$\sigma_{\text{year}} = \sigma_{\text{day}}\sqrt{252}$$

or

$$\sigma_{\text{day}} = \frac{\sigma_{\text{year}}}{\sqrt{252}}$$

so that daily volatility is about 6% of annual volatility.

As pointed out in Section 12.3, σ_{day} is approximately equal to the standard deviation of the percentage change in the asset price in one day. For the purposes of calculating VaR, we assume exact equality. We define the daily volatility of an asset price (or any other variable) as equal to the standard deviation of the percentage change in one day.

Our discussion in the next few sections assumes we have estimates of daily volatilities and correlations. Later in the chapter, we discuss how the estimates can be produced.

Single-Asset Case

We now consider how VaR is calculated using the model-building approach in a very simple situation where the portfolio consists of a position in a single stock. The portfolio we consider is one consisting of $10 million in shares of Microsoft. We suppose that $N = 10$ and $X = 99$, so that we are interested in the loss level over 10 days that we are 99% confident will not be exceeded. Initially, we consider a one-day time horizon.

We assume that the volatility of Microsoft is 2% per day (corresponding to about 32% per year). Because the size of the position is $10 million, the standard deviation of daily changes in the value of the position is 2% of $10 million, or $200,000.

It is customary in the model-building approach to assume that the expected change in a market variable over the time period considered is zero. This is not exactly true, but it is a reasonable assumption. The expected change in the price of a market variable over a short time period is generally small when compared with the standard deviation of the change. Suppose, for example, that Microsoft has an expected return of 20% per annum. Over a one-day period, the expected return is 0.20/252, or about 0.08%, whereas the standard deviation of the return is 2%. Over a 10-day period, the expected return is 0.08×10, or about 0.8%, whereas the standard deviation of the return is $2\sqrt{10}$, or about 6.3%.

So far, we have established that the change in the value of the portfolio of Microsoft shares over a one-day period has a standard deviation of $200,000 and (at least approximately) a mean of zero. We assume that the change is normally distributed.[3] From the tables at the end of this book, we find that $N(-2.33) = 0.01$. This means that there is a 1% probability that a normally distributed variable will decrease in value by more than 2.33 standard deviations. Equivalently, it means that we are 99% certain that a normally distributed variable will not decrease in value by more than 2.33 standard deviations. Therefore the one-day 99% VaR for our portfolio consisting of a \$10 million position in Microsoft is

$$2.33 \times 200{,}000 = \$466{,}000$$

As discussed earlier, the N-day VaR is calculated as $\sqrt{N}$ times the one-day VaR. The 10-day 99% VaR for Microsoft is therefore

$$466{,}000 \times \sqrt{10} = \$1{,}473{,}621$$

Consider next a portfolio consisting of a \$5 million position in AT&T, and suppose the daily volatility of AT&T is 1% (approximately 16% per year). A similar calculation to that for Microsoft shows that the standard deviation of the change in the value of the portfolio in one day is

$$5{,}000{,}000 \times 0.01 = 50{,}000$$

Assuming the change is normally distributed, the one-day 99% VaR is

$$50{,}000 \times 2.33 = \$116{,}500$$

and the 10-day 99% VaR is

$$116{,}500 \times \sqrt{10} = \$368{,}405$$

Two-Asset Case

Now consider a portfolio consisting of both \$10 million of Microsoft shares and \$5 million of AT&T shares. We suppose that the returns on the two shares have a bivariate normal distribution with a correlation of 0.3. A standard result in statistics tells us that, if two variables X and Y have standard deviations equal to σ_X and σ_Y, with the coefficient of correlation between them being equal to ρ, then the standard deviation of $X + Y$ is given by

$$\sigma_{X+Y} = \sqrt{\sigma_X^2 + \sigma_Y^2 + 2\rho\sigma_X\sigma_Y}$$

To apply this result, we set X equal to the change in the value of the position in Microsoft over a one-day period and Y equal to the change in the value of the position in AT&T over a one-day period, so that

$$\sigma_X = 200{,}000, \qquad \sigma_Y = 50{,}000$$

Therefore the standard deviation of the change in the value of the portfolio consisting of both stocks over a one-day period is

$$\sqrt{200{,}000^2 + 50{,}000^2 + 2 \times 0.3 \times 200{,}000 \times 50{,}000} = 220{,}227$$

[3] To be consistent with the option pricing assumption in Chapter 12, we could assume that the price of Microsoft is lognormal tomorrow. Because one day is such a short period of time, this is almost indistinguishable from the assumption we do make—that the change in the stock price between today and tomorrow is normal.

Trading Note 18.1 Calculation of VaR in a simple situation

A company has a portfolio consisting of \$10 million invested in Microsoft and \$5 million invested in AT&T. The daily volatility of Microsoft is 2%, the daily volatility of AT&T is 1%, and the coefficient of correlation between the returns from Microsoft and AT&T is 0.3.

Calculation of VaR

1. The standard deviation of the change in value of the Microsoft position per day is $10{,}000{,}000 \times 0.02 = \$200{,}000$.
2. The standard deviation of the change in value of the AT&T position per day is $5{,}000{,}000 \times 0.01 = \$50{,}000$.
3. The standard deviation of the change in the portfolio value per day is therefore:

$$\sqrt{200{,}000^2 + 50{,}000^2 + 2 \times 0.3 \times 200{,}000 \times 50{,}000} = 220{,}227$$

4. The one-day 99% VaR is therefore:

$$220{,}227 \times 2.33 = \$513{,}129$$

5. The 10-day 99% VaR is $\sqrt{10} \times 513{,}129$, or \$1,622,657.

The change is normally distributed and the mean change is assumed to be zero. So the one-day 99% VaR is

$$220{,}227 \times 2.33 = \$513{,}129$$

The 10-day 99% VaR is $\sqrt{10}$ times this or \$1,622,657. This example is summarized in Trading Note 18.1.

The Benefits of Diversification

In the example we have just considered:

1. The 10-day 99% VaR for the portfolio of Microsoft shares is \$1,473,621.
2. The 10-day 99% VaR for the portfolio of AT&T shares is \$368,405.
3. The 10-day 99% VaR for the portfolio of both Microsoft and AT&T shares is \$1,622,657.

The amount

$$(1{,}473{,}621 + 368{,}405) - 1{,}622{,}657 = \$219{,}369$$

represents the benefits of diversification. If Microsoft and AT&T were perfectly correlated, the VaR for the portfolio of both Microsoft and AT&T would equal the VaR for the Microsoft portfolio plus the VaR for the AT&T portfolio. Less than perfect correlation leads to some of the risk being "diversified away."[4]

---

[4] Harry Markowitz was one of the first researchers to study the benefits of diversification to a portfolio manager. He was awarded a Nobel prize for this research in 1990. See H. Markowitz, "Portfolio Selection," *Journal of Finance* 7, no. 1 (March 1952): 77–91.

18.4 LINEAR MODEL

The examples we have just considered are simple illustrations of the use of the linear model for calculating VaR. Suppose that we have a portfolio worth P consisting of n assets with an amount w_i being invested in asset i $(1 \leqslant i \leqslant n)$. We define Δx_i as the return on asset i in one day. It follows that the dollar change in the value of our investment in asset i in one day is $w_i\,\Delta x_i$ and

$$\Delta P = \sum_{i=1}^{n} w_i\,\Delta x_i \tag{18.1}$$

where ΔP is the dollar change in the value of the whole portfolio in one day.

In the example considered in the previous section, \$10 million was invested in the first asset (Microsoft) and \$5 million was invested in the second asset (AT&T), so that (in millions of dollars) $w_1 = 10$, $w_2 = 5$, and

$$\Delta P = 10\Delta x_1 + 5\Delta x_2$$

If we assume that the Δx_i in equation (18.1) are multivariate normal, ΔP is normally distributed. To calculate VaR, we therefore need to calculate only the mean and standard deviation of ΔP. We assume, as discussed in the previous section, that the expected value of each Δx_i is zero. This implies that the mean of ΔP is zero.

To calculate the standard deviation of ΔP, we define σ_i as the daily volatility of the ith asset and ρ_{ij} as the coefficient of correlation between returns on asset i and asset j. This means that σ_i is the standard deviation of Δx_i, and ρ_{ij} is the coefficient of correlation between Δx_i and Δx_j. The variance of ΔP, which we will denote by σ_P^2, is given by

$$\sigma_P^2 = \sum_{i=1}^{n}\sum_{j=1}^{n} \rho_{ij} w_i w_j \sigma_i \sigma_j$$

This equation can also be written as

$$\sigma_P^2 = \sum_{i=1}^{n} w_i^2 \sigma_i^2 + 2\sum_{i=1}^{n}\sum_{j<i} \rho_{ij} w_i w_j \sigma_i \sigma_j \tag{18.2}$$

The standard deviation of the change over N days is $\sigma_P\sqrt{N}$, and the 99% VaR for an N-day time horizon is $2.33\sigma_P\sqrt{N}$.

In the example considered in the previous section, $\sigma_1 = 0.02$, $\sigma_2 = 0.01$, and $\rho_{12} = 0.3$. As already noted, $w_1 = 10$ and $w_2 = 5$, so that

$$\sigma_P^2 = 10^2 \times 0.02^2 + 5^2 \times 0.01^2 + 2 \times 10 \times 5 \times 0.3 \times 0.02 \times 0.01 = 0.0485$$

and $\sigma_P = 0.220$. This is the standard deviation of the change in the portfolio value per day (in millions of dollars). The 10-day 99% VaR is $2.33 \times 0.220 \times \sqrt{10} =$ \$1.623 million. This agrees with the calculation in the previous section.

Handling Interest Rates

It is out of the question to define a separate market variable for every single bond price or interest rate to which a company is exposed. Some simplifications are necessary. The usual approach is to choose as market variables the prices of zero-coupon bonds with standard maturities: 1 month, 3 months, 6 months, 1 year, 2 years, 5 years, 7 years, 10 years, and 30 years. For the purposes of calculating VaR, the cash flows from instruments in the portfolio are mapped into cash flows occurring on the standard maturity dates. Consider a \$1 million position in a Treasury bond lasting 1.2 years that pays a coupon of 6% semiannually. Coupons are paid in 0.2, 0.7, and 1.2 years, and the principal is paid in 1.2 years. This bond is therefore, in the first instance, regarded as a \$30,000 position in 0.2-year zero-coupon bond plus a \$30,000 position in a 0.7-year zero-coupon bond plus a \$1.03 million position in a 1.2-year zero-coupon bond. The position in the 0.2-year bond is then replaced by an equivalent position in 1-month and 3-month zero-coupon bonds; the position in the 0.7-year bond is replaced by an equivalent position in 6-month and 1-year zero-coupon bonds; and the position in the 1.2-year bond is replaced by an equivalent position in 1-year and 2-year zero-coupon bonds. The result is that the position in the 1.2-year coupon-bearing bond is, for VaR purposes, regarded as a position in zero-coupon bonds having maturities of 1 month, 3 months, 6 months, 1 year, and 2 years.

This procedure is known as *cash-flow mapping*. One way of doing it is explained in the Appendix to this chapter.

Applications of the Linear Model

The simplest application of the linear model is to a portfolio with no derivatives consisting of positions in stocks, bonds, foreign exchange, and commodities. In this case the change in the value of the portfolio is linearly dependent on the percentage changes in the prices of the assets comprising the portfolio. Note that, for the purposes of VaR calculations, all asset prices are measured in the domestic currency. The market variables considered by a large bank in the United States are therefore likely to include the value of the Nikkei 225 index in dollars, the price of a 10-year sterling zero-coupon bond measured in dollars, and so on.

An example of a derivative that can be handled by the linear model is a forward contract to buy a foreign currency. Suppose the contract matures at time T. It can be regarded as the exchange of a foreign zero-coupon bond maturing at time T for a domestic zero-coupon bond maturing at time T. For the purposes of calculating VaR, the forward contract is therefore treated as a long position in the foreign bond combined with a short position in the domestic bond. Each bond can be handled using the cash-flow mapping procedure outlined above.

Consider next an interest rate swap. As explained in Chapter 7, this can be regarded as the exchange of a floating-rate bond for a fixed-rate bond. The fixed-rate bond is a regular coupon-bearing bond. The floating-rate bond is worth par just after the next payment date. It can be regarded as a zero-coupon bond with a maturity date equal to the next payment date. Therefore, the interest rate swap reduces to a portfolio of long and short positions in bonds and can be handled using the cash-flow mapping procedure outlined above.

The Linear Model and Options

We now consider how the linear model can be used when there are options. Consider first a portfolio consisting of options on a single stock whose current price is S. Suppose that the delta of the position (calculated in the way described in Chapter 15) is δ.[5] Because δ is the rate of change of the value of the portfolio with S, it is approximately true that

$$\delta = \frac{\Delta P}{\Delta S}$$

so that

$$\Delta P = \delta \, \Delta S \tag{18.3}$$

where ΔS is the dollar change in the stock price in one day and ΔP is, as usual, the dollar change in the portfolio in one day. We define Δx as the percentage change in the stock price in one day:

$$\Delta x = \frac{\Delta S}{S}$$

It follows that an approximate relationship between ΔP and Δx is

$$\Delta P = S\delta \, \Delta x$$

When we have a position in several underlying market variables that includes options, we can derive an approximate linear relationship between ΔP and the Δx_i similarly. This relationship is

$$\Delta P = \sum_{i=1}^{n} S_i \delta_i \, \Delta x_i \tag{18.4}$$

where S_i is the value of the ith market variable and δ_i is the delta of the portfolio with respect to the ith market variable. This corresponds to equation (18.1):

$$\Delta P = \sum_{i=1}^{n} w_i \, \Delta x_i$$

with $w_i = S_i \delta_i$. Equation (18.2) can therefore be used to calculate the standard deviation of ΔP.

Example

A portfolio consists of options on Microsoft and AT&T. The options on Microsoft have a delta of 1,000, and the options on AT&T have a delta of 20,000. The Microsoft share price is \$120, and the AT&T share price is \$30. From equation (18.4), it is approximately true that

$$\Delta P = 120 \times 1{,}000 \times \Delta x_1 + 30 \times 20{,}000 \times \Delta x_2$$

or

$$\Delta P = 120{,}000 \Delta x_1 + 600{,}000 \Delta x_2$$

where Δx_1 and Δx_2 are the returns from Microsoft and AT&T in one day and ΔP is the resultant change in the value of the portfolio. (The portfolio is assumed to be equivalent to an investment of \$120,000 in Microsoft and \$600,000 in AT&T.) Assuming that the daily volatility of Microsoft is 2% and the daily volatility of

[5] Normally we denote the delta and gamma of a portfolio by Δ and Γ. In this section and the next one, we use the lower case Greek letters δ and γ to avoid overworking Δ.

AT&T is 1%, and the correlation between the daily changes is 0.3, the standard deviation of ΔP (in thousands of dollars) is

$$\sqrt{(120 \times 0.02)^2 + (600 \times 0.01)^2 + 2 \times 120 \times 0.02 \times 600 \times 0.01 \times 0.3} = 7.099$$

Because $N(-1.65) = 0.05$, the 5-day 95% value at risk is

$$1.65 \times \sqrt{5} \times 7{,}099 = \$26{,}193$$

18.5 QUADRATIC MODEL

When a portfolio includes options, the linear model is an approximation. It does not take account of the gamma of the portfolio. As discussed in Chapter 15, delta is defined as the rate of change of the portfolio value with respect to an underlying market variable and gamma is defined as the rate of change of the delta with respect to the market variable. Gamma measures the curvature of the relationship between the portfolio value and an underlying market variable.

Figure 18.3 shows the impact of a nonzero gamma on the probability distribution of the value of the portfolio. When gamma is positive, the probability distribution of ΔP tends to be positively skewed; when gamma is negative, it tends to be negatively skewed. Figures 18.4 and 18.5 illustrate the reason for this result. Figure 18.4 shows the relationship between the value of a long call option and the price of the underlying asset. A long call is an example of an option position with positive gamma. The figure shows that, when the probability distribution for the price of the underlying asset at the end of one day is normal, the probability distribution for the option price is positively skewed.[6] Figure 18.5 shows the relationship between the value of a short call position and the price of the underlying asset. A short call position has negative gamma. In this case we see that a normal distribution for the price of the underlying asset at the end of one day gets mapped into a negatively skewed distribution for the value of the option position.

Figure 18.3 Probability distribution for value of portfolio: (a) positive gamma, (b) negative gamma

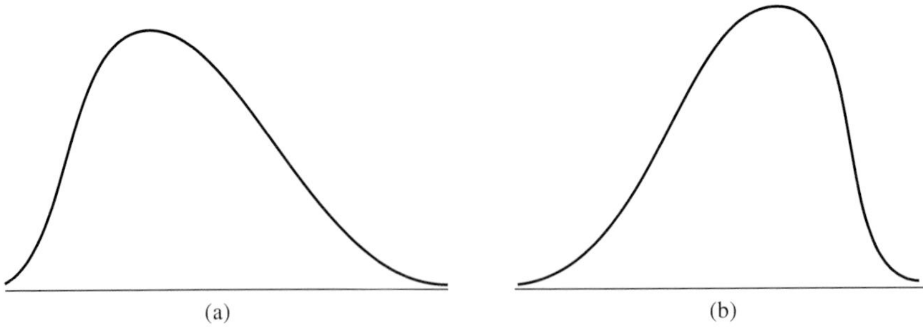

[6] As mentioned in footnote 3, we can use the normal distribution as an approximation to the lognormal distribution in VaR calculations.

Figure 18.4 Translation of normal probability distribution for asset into probability distribution for value of a long call on asset

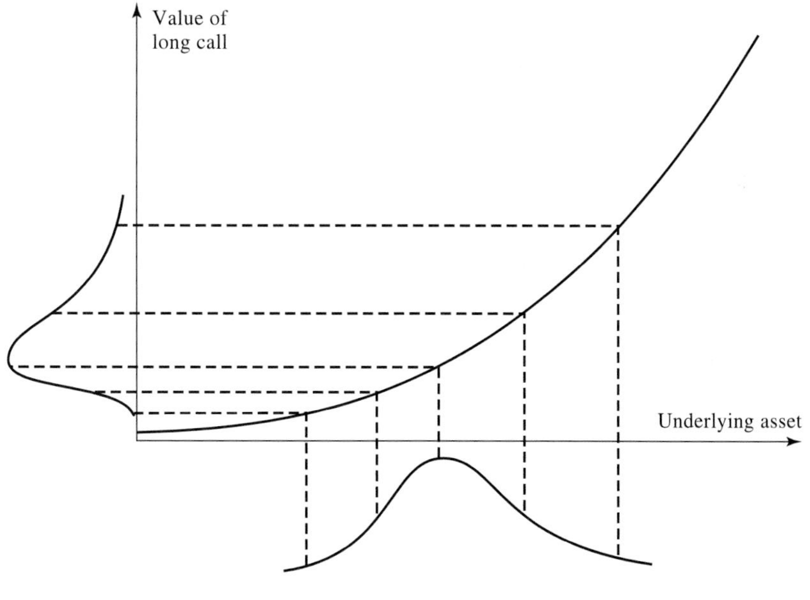

Figure 18.5 Translation of normal probability distribution for asset into probability distribution for value of a short call on asset

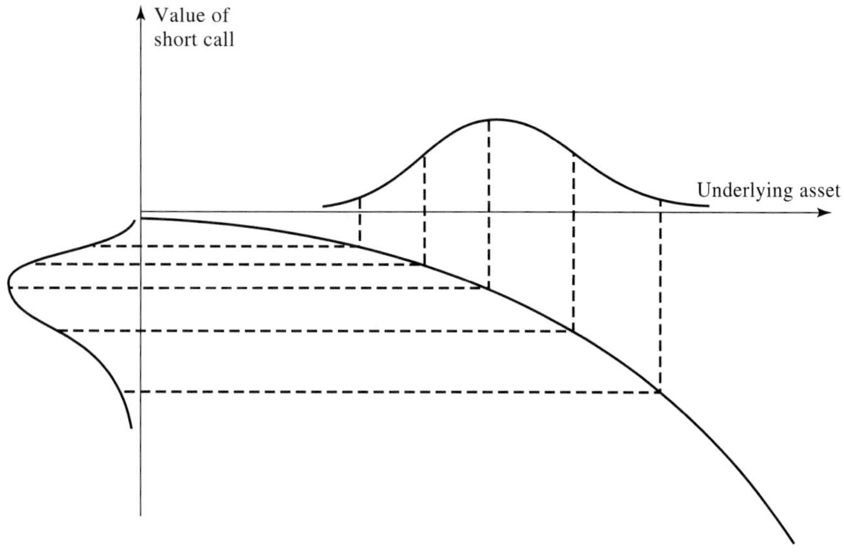

The VaR for a portfolio is critically dependent on the left tail of the probability distribution of ΔP. For example, when the confidence level used is 99%, the VaR is calculated as the value in the left tail below which there is only 1% of the distribution. As indicated in Figures 18.3a and 18.4, a positive gamma portfolio tends to have a less heavy left tail than the normal distribution. If we assume the distribution is normal, we will tend to calculate a VaR that is too high. Similarly, as indicated in Figures 18.3b and 18.5, a negative gamma portfolio tends to have a heavier left tail than the normal distribution. If we assume the distribution is normal, we will tend to calculate a VaR that is too low.

For a more accurate estimate of VaR than that given by the linear model, we can use both delta and gamma measures to relate ΔP to the Δx_i. Consider a portfolio dependent on a single asset whose price is S. Suppose that the delta of a portfolio is δ and its gamma is γ. An improvement over the approximation in equation (18.3) is

$$\Delta P = \delta\,\Delta S + \tfrac{1}{2}\gamma(\Delta S)^2$$

Setting

$$\Delta x = \frac{\Delta S}{S}$$

reduces this to

$$\Delta P = S\delta\,\Delta x + \tfrac{1}{2}S^2\gamma(\Delta x)^2 \qquad \textbf{(18.5)}$$

A similar quadratic equation relating ΔP to the Δx_i applies when there is more than one market variable. One approach to calculating VaR is to use the quadratic equation in conjunction with Monte Carlo simulation. This methodology is similar to historical simulation methodology described in Section 18.2 except that alternative movements in market variables are sampled from an assumed multivariate distribution rather than being calculated from historical data. In addition, the change in the portfolio value is calculated from the quadratic equation.

18.6 ESTIMATING VOLATILITIES AND CORRELATIONS

The model-building approach requires daily volatilities for all market variables and correlations between each pair of market variables. We now consider how these can be obtained.

In this section we define σ_n as the volatility per day of a market variable on day n, as estimated at the end of day $n-1$. (This is a change of notation. Earlier in this chapter, σ_n was used to denote the volatility of the nth variable.) The square of the volatility, σ_n^2, on day n is the *variance rate*. The standard approach to estimating σ_n from historical data was described in Section 12.4. Suppose that the value of the market variable at the end of day i is S_i. The variable u_i is defined as the continuously compounded return during day i (between the end of day $i-1$ and the end of day i):

$$u_i = \ln\frac{S_i}{S_{i-1}}$$

An unbiased estimate σ_n^2 of the variance rate per day, using the most recent m observations on the u_i, is given by

$$\sigma_n^2 = \frac{1}{m-1}\sum_{i=1}^{m}(u_{n-i} - \bar{u})^2 \tag{18.6}$$

where $\bar{u}$ is the mean of the u_i:

$$\bar{u} = \frac{1}{m}\sum_{i=1}^{m} u_{n-i}$$

For the purposes of calculating VaR, the formula in equation (18.6) is usually changed in a number of ways:

1. u_i is defined as the percentage change in the market variable between the end of day $i-1$ and the end of day i, so that[7]

$$u_i = \frac{S_i - S_{i-1}}{S_{i-1}} \tag{18.7}$$

2. $\bar{u}$ is assumed to be zero.[8]
3. $m-1$ is replaced by m.

These three changes make very little difference to the variance estimates that are calculated. They result in equation (18.6) being replaced by

$$\sigma_n^2 = \frac{1}{m}\sum_{i=1}^{m} u_{n-i}^2 \tag{18.8}$$

where u_i is given by equation (18.7).

Weighting Schemes

Equation (18.8) gives equal weight to $u_{n-1}^2, u_{n-2}^2, \dots, u_{n-m}^2$. Given that the objective is to monitor the current level of volatility, it is appropriate to give more weight to recent data. A model that does this is

$$\sigma_n^2 = \sum_{i=1}^{m} \alpha_i u_{n-i}^2 \tag{18.9}$$

The variable α_i is the amount of weight given to the observation i days ago. The α's are positive. Because we wish to give less weight to older observations, $\alpha_i < \alpha_j$ when $i > j$. The weights must sum to unity, so that

$$\sum_{i=1}^{m} \alpha_i = 1$$

The exponentially weighted moving average (EWMA) model is a particular case of the

[7] This is consistent with the point made in Section 18.3 about the way that volatility is defined for the purposes of VaR calculations.

[8] As explained in Section 18.3, this assumption usually has very little effect on estimates of the variance because the expected change in a variable in one day is very small when compared with the standard deviation of changes. As an alternative to the assumption, we can define u_i as the realized return minus the expected return on day i.

model in equation (18.9) where the weights, α_i, decrease exponentially as we move back through time. Specifically, $\alpha_{i+1} = \lambda\alpha_i$, where λ is a constant between zero and one.

It turns out that this weighting scheme leads to a particularly simple formula for updating volatility estimates. The formula is

$$\sigma_n^2 = \lambda\sigma_{n-1}^2 + (1-\lambda)u_{n-1}^2 \quad \textbf{(18.10)}$$

The estimate σ_n of the volatility for day n (made at the end of day $n-1$) is calculated from σ_{n-1} (the estimate that was made at the end of day $n-2$) and u_{n-1} (the most recent daily percent change in the market variable).

Example

The EWMA parameter λ is 0.90, the volatility estimated for day $n-1$ is 1% per day, and the change in the market variable during day $n-1$ is 2%. In this case, $\sigma_{n-1}^2 = 0.01^2 = 0.0001$ and $u_{n-1}^2 = 0.02^2 = 0.0004$. Equation (18.10) gives

$$\sigma_n^2 = 0.9 \times 0.0001 + 0.1 \times 0.0004 = 0.00013$$

The estimate σ_n of the volatility for day n, therefore, is $\sqrt{0.00013}$, or 1.14% per day. Note that the expected value of u_{n-1}^2 is σ_{n-1}^2 or 0.0001. In this example, the realized value of u_{n-1}^2 is greater than the expected value, and as a result the volatility estimate increases. If the realized value of u_{n-1}^2 had been less than its expected value, the estimate of the volatility would have decreased.

To understand why equation (18.10) corresponds to weights that decrease exponentially, we substitute for σ_{n-1}^2, to get

$$\sigma_n^2 = \lambda[\lambda\sigma_{n-2}^2 + (1-\lambda)u_{n-2}^2] + (1-\lambda)u_{n-1}^2$$

or

$$\sigma_n^2 = (1-\lambda)(u_{n-1}^2 + \lambda u_{n-2}^2) + \lambda^2\sigma_{n-2}^2$$

Substituting in a similar way for σ_{n-2}^2 gives

$$\sigma_n^2 = (1-\lambda)(u_{n-1}^2 + \lambda u_{n-2}^2 + \lambda^2 u_{n-3}^2) + \lambda^3\sigma_{n-3}^2$$

Continuing in this way, we see that

$$\sigma_n^2 = (1-\lambda)\sum_{i=1}^{m}\lambda^{i-1}u_{n-i}^2 + \lambda^m\sigma_{n-m}^2$$

For large m, the term $\lambda^m\sigma_{n-m}^2$ is sufficiently small to be ignored, so that equation (18.10) is the same as equation (18.9) with $\alpha_i = (1-\lambda)\lambda^{i-1}$. The weights for the u_i decline at rate λ as we move back through time. Each weight is λ times the previous weight.

The EWMA approach has the attractive feature that relatively little data need to be stored. At any given time, we need to remember only the current estimate of the variance rate and the most recent observation on the value of the market variable. When we get a new observation on the value of the market variable, we calculate a new u^2 and use equation (18.10) to update our estimate of the variance rate. The old estimate of the variance rate and the old value of the market variable can then be discarded.

The EWMA approach is designed to track changes in the volatility. Suppose there is a big move in the market variable on day $n-1$, so that u_{n-1}^2 is large. From equation (18.10), this causes σ_n, our estimate of the daily volatility for day n, to move upward. The value of λ governs how responsive the estimate of the daily volatility is to the most recent observations on the daily changes. A low value of λ leads to a great deal of weight being given to the u_{n-1}^2 when σ_n is calculated. In this case, the estimates produced for the volatility on successive days are themselves highly volatile. A high value of λ (i.e., a value close to 1.0) produces estimates of the daily volatility that respond relatively slowly to new information provided by the daily changes.

Correlations

The correlation between two variables X and Y can be defined as

$$\frac{\text{cov}(X, Y)}{\sigma_X \sigma_Y}$$

where σ_X and σ_Y are the standard deviation of X and Y and $\text{cov}(X, Y)$ is the covariance between X and Y. The covariance between X and Y is defined as

$$E[(X - \mu_X)(Y - \mu_Y)]$$

where μ_X and μ_Y are the means of X and Y, and E denotes expected value. Although it is easier to develop intuition about the meaning of a correlation than of a covariance, it is covariances that are the fundamental variables of our analysis.

Consider two different market variables, U and V. We define u_i and v_i as the percentage changes in U and V between the end of day $i - 1$ and the end of day i:

$$u_i = \frac{U_i - U_{i-1}}{U_{i-1}}, \qquad v_i = \frac{V_i - V_{i-1}}{V_{i-1}}$$

where U_i and V_i are the values of U and V at the end of day i. We also define:

$\sigma_{u,n}$: Daily volatility of variable U, estimated for day n

$\sigma_{v,n}$: Daily volatility of variable V, estimated for day n

cov_n: Estimate of covariance between daily changes in U and V, calculated on day n

Our estimate of the correlation between U and V on day n is

$$\frac{\text{cov}_n}{\sigma_{u,n}\sigma_{v,n}}$$

Using an equal-weighting scheme and assuming that the means of u_i and v_i are zero, equation (18.8) shows that we can estimate the variance rates of U and V from the most recent m observations as

$$\sigma_{u,n}^2 = \frac{1}{m}\sum_{i=1}^{m} u_{n-i}^2 \quad \text{and} \quad \sigma_{v,n}^2 = \frac{1}{m}\sum_{i=1}^{m} v_{n-i}^2$$

A similar estimate for the covariance between U and V is

$$\text{cov}_n = \frac{1}{m}\sum_{i=1}^{m} u_{n-i}v_{n-i} \qquad \textbf{(18.11)}$$

One alternative is an EWMA model similar to equation (18.10). The formula for updating the covariance estimate is then

$$\text{cov}_n = \lambda\,\text{cov}_{n-1} + (1-\lambda)u_{n-1}v_{n-1} \qquad \textbf{(18.12)}$$

A similar analysis to that presented for the EWMA volatility model shows that the weights given to observations on the $u_i v_i$ decline as we move back through time. The lower the value of λ, the greater the weight that is given to recent observations.

Example

The EWMA parameter λ is 0.95 and the estimate of the correlation between two variables U and V on day $n-1$ is 0.6. The estimate of the volatilities of U and V on day $n-1$ are 1% and 2%, respectively. The actual changes in U and V on day $n-1$ are 0.5% and 2.5%, respectively. In this case, from the relationship between correlation and covariance, the estimate of the covariance between the U and V on day $n-1$ is

$$0.6 \times 0.01 \times 0.02 = 0.00012$$

The variance and covariance for day n are calculated as follows:

$$\sigma_{u,n}^2 = 0.95 \times 0.01^2 + 0.05 \times 0.005^2 = 0.00009625$$

$$\sigma_{v,n}^2 = 0.95 \times 0.02^2 + 0.05 \times 0.025^2 = 0.00041125$$

$$\text{cov}_n = 0.95 \times 0.00012 + 0.05 \times 0.005 \times 0.025 = 0.00012025$$

The new volatility of U is $\sqrt{0.00009625} = 0.981\%$ and the new volatility of V is $\sqrt{0.00041125} = 2.028\%$. The new coefficient of correlation between U and V is

$$\frac{0.00012025}{0.00981 \times 0.02028} = 0.6044$$

RiskMetrics

Many companies rely on the data and models that are provided by RiskMetrics (www.riskmetrics.com) to calculate VaR. RiskMetrics uses the EWMA method to update variances and covariances for a large number of different market variables daily. It uses a value of λ equal to 0.94. The company found that, across a range of different market variables, this value of λ gives forecasts of the variance rate that come closest to the realized variance rate over the subsequent 25 days.

18.7 COMPARISON OF APPROACHES

We have discussed two methods for estimating VaR: the historical simulation approach and the model-building approach. The advantages of the model-building approach are that results can be produced very quickly and it can be used in conjunction with volatility updating schemes such as EWMA. The main disadvantage of the model-building approach is that it assumes that the market variables have a multivariate normal distribution. In practice, daily changes in market variables often have distributions that are quite different from normal (see, for example, Table 17.1). It is also the case that the model-building approach tends to give poor results for low-delta portfolios.

The historical simulation approach has the advantage that historical data determine the joint probability distribution of the market variables. It also avoids the need for cash-flow mapping. The main disadvantages of historical simulation are that it is computationally slow and does not easily allow volatility updating schemes to be used.

18.8 STRESS TESTING AND BACK TESTING

In addition to calculating a VaR, many companies carry out what is known as a *stress test* of their portfolio. Stress testing involves estimating how the portfolio would have performed under some of the most extreme market moves seen in the last 10 to 20 years.

For example, to test the impact of an extreme movement in U.S. equity prices, a company might set the percentage changes in all market variables equal to those on October 19, 1987, when the S&P 500 moved by 22.3 standard deviations. If this is considered to be too extreme, the company might choose January 8, 1988, when the S&P 500 moved by 6.8 standard deviations. To test the effect of extreme movements in U.K. interest rates, the company might set the percentage changes in all market variables equal to those on April 10, 1992, when 10-year bond yields moved by 7.7 standard deviations.

Stress testing can be considered as a way of taking into account extreme events that do occur from time to time but that are virtually impossible according to the probability distributions assumed for market variables. A 5-standard-deviation daily move in a market variable is one such extreme event. Under the assumption of a normal distribution, it happens about once every 7,000 years, but, in practice, it is not uncommon to see a 5-standard-deviation daily move once or twice every 10 years.

Whatever the method used for calculating VaR, an important reality check is *back testing*. It involves testing how well the VaR estimates would have performed in the past. Suppose that we are calculating a one-day 99% VaR. Back testing would involve looking at how often the loss in a day exceeded the one-day 99% VaR calculated for that day. If this happened on about 1% of the days, we can feel reasonably comfortable with the methodology for calculating VaR. If it happened on, say, 7% of days, the methodology is suspect.

SUMMARY

A value at risk (VaR) calculation is aimed at making a statement of the form: "We are X percent certain that we will not lose more than V dollars in the next N days." The variable V is the VaR, X percent is the confidence level, and N days is the time horizon.

One approach to calculating VaR is historical simulation. This involves creating a database consisting of the daily movements in all market variables over a period of time. The first simulation trial assumes that the percentage changes in each market variable are the same as those on the first day covered by the database; the second simulation trial assumes that the percentage changes are the same as those on the second day; and so on. The change ΔP in the portfolio value is calculated for each simulation trial, and the VaR is calculated as the appropriate percentile of the probability distribution of ΔP.

An alternative is the model-building approach. This is relatively straightforward if two assumptions can be made:

1. The change in the value of the portfolio (ΔP) is linearly dependent on percentage changes in the market variables.
2. The percentage changes in the market variables are multivariate normally distributed.

The probability distribution of ΔP is then normal, and there are analytic formulas for relating the standard deviation of ΔP to the volatilities and correlations of the underlying market variables. The VaR can be calculated from well-known properties of the normal distribution.

When a portfolio includes options, ΔP is not linearly related to the percentage changes in the market variables and is not normally distributed. The calculation of VaR using the model building approach is then more difficult and may involve Monte Carlo simulation.

When the model-building approach is used, volatilities and correlations are usually updated daily. A popular approach is the exponentially weighted moving average method. In this the weights given to observations decline as they become older. The weight given to data from i days ago is λ times the weight given to data from $i - 1$ days ago for some parameter λ between zero and one.

FURTHER READING

Artzner P., F. Delbaen, J. M. Eber, and D. Heath. "Coherent Measures of Risk," *Mathematical Finance*, 9 (1999): 203–28.

Basak, S., and A. Shapiro. "Value-at-Risk-Based Risk Management: Optimal Policies and Asset Prices," *Review of Financial Studies*, 14, 2 (2001): 371–405.

Beder, T. "VaR: Seductive But Dangerous," *Financial Analysts Journal*, 51, 5 (1995): 12–24.

Boudoukh, J., M. Richardson, and R. Whitelaw. "The Best of Both Worlds," *Risk*, May 1998: 64–67.

Dowd, K. *Beyond Value at Risk: The New Science of Risk Management*. New York: Wiley, 1998.

Duffie, D., and J. Pan. "An Overview of Value at Risk," *Journal of Derivatives*, 4, 3 (Spring 1997): 7–49.

Embrechts, P., C. Kluppelberg, and T. Mikosch. *Modeling Extremal Events for Insurance and Finance*. New York: Springer, 1997.

Frye, J. "Principals of Risk: Finding VAR through Factor-Based Interest Rate Scenarios," in *VAR: Understanding and Applying Value at Risk*, pp. 275–88. London: Risk Publications, 1997.

Hendricks, D. "Evaluation of Value-at-Risk Models Using Historical Data," *Economic Policy Review*, Federal Reserve Bank of New York, 2 (April 1996): 39–69.

Hopper, G. "Value at Risk: A New Methodology for Measuring Portfolio Risk," *Business Review*, Federal Reserve Bank of Philadelphia, July/Aug. 1996: 19–29.

Hua, P., and P. Wilmott, "Crash Courses," *Risk*, June 1997: 64–67.

Hull, J. C., and A. White. "Value at Risk When Daily Changes in Market Variables Are Not Normally Distributed," *Journal of Derivatives*, 5 (Spring 1998): 9–19.

Hull, J. C., and A. White. 'Incorporating Volatility Updating into the Historical Simulation Method for Value at Risk," *Journal of Risk*, 1, 1 (1998): 5–19.

Jackson, P., D.J. Maude, and W. Perraudin. "Bank Capital and Value at Risk," *Journal of Derivatives*, 4, 3 (Spring 1997): 73–90.

Jamshidian, F., and Y. Zhu. "Scenario Simulation Model: Theory and Methodology," *Finance and Stochastics*, 1 (1997): 43–67.

Jorion, P. *Value at Risk*. 2nd edn. McGraw-Hill, 2001.

Longin, F.M. "Beyond the VaR," *Journal of Derivatives*, 8, 4 (Summer 2001): 36–48.

Marshall, C., and M. Siegel. "Value at Risk: Implementing a Risk Measurement Standard," *Journal of Derivatives*, 4, 3 (Spring 1997): 91–111.

Neftci, S.N. "Value at Risk Calculations, Extreme Events and Tail Estimation," *Journal of Derivatives*, 7, 3 (Spring 2000): 23–38.

Rich, D. "Second Generation VaR and Risk-Adjusted Return on Capital," *Journal of Derivatives*, 10, 4 (Summer 2003): 51–61.

Quiz (Answers at End of Book)

18.1. Explain the historical simulation method for calculating VaR.

18.2. Explain the exponentially weighted moving average (EWMA) model for estimating volatility from historical data.

18.3. The most recent estimate of the daily volatility of an asset is 1.5%, and the price of the asset at the close of trading yesterday was $30.00. The parameter λ in the EWMA model is 0.94. Suppose that the price of the asset at the close of trading today is $30.50. How will this cause the volatility to be updated by the EWMA model?

18.4. Consider a position consisting of a $300,000 investment in asset A and a $500,000 investment in asset B. Assume that the daily volatilities of the assets are 1.8% and 1.2%, respectively, and that the coefficient of correlation between their returns is 0.3. What is the five-day 95% value at risk for the portfolio?

18.5. A financial institution owns a portfolio of options on the U.S. dollar/sterling exchange rate. The delta of the portfolio is 56.0. The current exchange rate is 1.5000. Derive an approximate linear relationship between the change in the portfolio value and the percentage change in the exchange rate. If the daily volatility of the exchange rate is 0.7%, estimate the 10-day 99% VaR.

18.6. Suppose you know that the gamma of the portfolio in the previous quiz question is 16.2. How does this change your estimate of the relationship between the change in the portfolio value and the percentage change in the exchange rate?

18.7. Suppose a company has a portfolio consisting of positions in stocks, bonds, foreign exchange, and commodities. Assume there are no derivatives. Explain the assumptions underlying (a) the historical simulation and (b) the model-building approach for calculating VaR.

Questions and Problems (Answers in Solutions Manual/Study Guide)

18.8. A company uses an EWMA model for forecasting volatility. It decides to change the parameter λ from 0.95 to 0.85. Explain the likely impact on the forecasts.

18.9. Explain the difference between value at risk and conditional value at risk.

18.10. Consider a position consisting of a \$100,000 investment in asset A and a \$100,000 investment in asset B. Assume that the daily volatilities of both assets are 1% and that the coefficient of correlation between their returns is 0.3. What is the five-day 99% value at risk for the portfolio?

18.11. The volatility of a certain market variable is 30% per annum. Calculate a 99% confidence interval for the size of the percentage daily change in the variable.

18.12. Explain how an interest rate swap is mapped into a portfolio of zero-coupon bonds with standard maturities for the purposes of a VaR calculation.

18.13. Explain why the linear model can provide only approximate estimates of VaR for a portfolio containing options.

18.14. Verify that the 0.3-year zero-coupon bond in the cash-flow mapping example in the Appendix at the end of this chapter is mapped into a \$37,397 position in a three-month bond and a \$11,793 position in a six-month bond.

18.15. Suppose the 5-year and 7-year rates are 6% and 7%, respectively (both with annual compounding), the daily volatility of a 5-year zero-coupon bond is 0.5%, and the daily volatility of a 7-year zero-coupon bond is 0.58%. The correlation between daily returns on the two bonds is 0.6. Map a cash flow of \$1,000 received at 6.5 years into a position in a 5-year bond and a position in a 7-year bond using the approach in the Appendix at the end of this chapter. What cash flows in 5 and 7 years are equivalent to the 6.5-year cash flow?

18.16. Some time ago a company entered into a forward contract to buy £1 million for \$1.5 million. The contract now has six months to maturity. The daily volatility of a six-month zero-coupon sterling bond (when its price is translated to dollars) is 0.06% and the daily volatility of a six-month zero-coupon dollar bond is 0.05%. The correlation between returns from the two bonds is 0.8. The current exchange rate is 1.53. Calculate the standard deviation of the change in the dollar value of the forward contract in one day. What is the 10-day 99% VaR? Assume that the six-month interest rate in both sterling and dollars is 5% per annum with continuous compounding.

18.17. The most recent estimate of the daily volatility of the U.S. dollar–sterling exchange rate is 0.6%, and the exchange rate at 4 p.m. yesterday was 1.5000. The parameter λ in the EWMA model is 0.9. Suppose that the exchange rate at 4 p.m. today proves to be 1.4950. How would the estimate of the daily volatility be updated?

18.18. Suppose that the daily volatilities of asset A and asset B calculated at close of trading yesterday are 1.6% and 2.5%, respectively. The prices of the assets at close of trading yesterday were \$20 and \$40, and the estimate of the coefficient of correlation between the returns on the two assets made at the close of trading yesterday was 0.25. The parameter λ used in the EWMA model is 0.95.

a. Calculate the current estimate of the covariance between the assets.
b. On the assumption that the prices of the assets at close of trading today are \$20.5 and \$40.5, update the correlation estimate.

18.19. Suppose that the daily volatility of the FT-SE 100 stock index (measured in pounds sterling) is 1.8% and the daily volatility of the dollar/sterling exchange rate is 0.9%. Suppose further that the correlation between the FT-SE 100 and the dollar–sterling exchange rate is 0.4. What is the volatility of the FT-SE 100 when it is translated to U.S. dollars? Assume that the dollar–sterling exchange rate is expressed as the number of U.S. dollars per pound sterling. (*Hint*: When $Z = XY$, the percentage daily change in Z is approximately equal to the percentage daily change in X plus the percentage daily change in Y.)

18.20. Suppose that in Problem 18.19 the correlation between the S&P 500 index (measured in dollars) and the FT-SE 100 index (measured in sterling) is 0.7, the correlation between the S&P 500 index (measured in dollars) and the dollar–sterling exchange rate is 0.3, and the daily volatility of the S&P 500 index is 1.6%. What is the correlation between the S&P 500 index (measured in dollars) and the FT-SE 100 index when it is translated to dollars? (*Hint*: For three variables X, Y, and Z, the covariance between $X + Y$ and Z equals the covariance between X and Z plus the covariance between Y and Z.)

Assignment Questions

18.21. Consider a position consisting of a \$300,000 investment in gold and a \$500,000 investment in silver. Suppose that the daily volatilities of these two assets are 1.8% and 1.2%, respectively, and that the coefficient of correlation between their returns is 0.6. What is the 10-day 97.5% value at risk for the portfolio? By how much does diversification reduce the VaR?

18.22. Consider a portfolio of options on a single asset. Suppose that the delta of the portfolio is 12, the value of the asset is \$10, and the daily volatility of the asset is 2%. Estimate the one-day 95% VaR for the portfolio. Suppose that the gamma of the portfolio is −2.6. Derive a quadratic relationship between the change in the portfolio value and the percentage change in the underlying asset price in one day.

18.23. A bank has written a call option on one stock and a put option on another stock. For the first option, the stock price is 50, the strike price is 51, the volatility is 28% per annum, and the time to maturity is nine months. For the second option, the stock price is 20, the strike price is 19, the volatility is 25% per annum, and the time to maturity is one year. Neither stock pays a dividend, the risk-free rate is 6% per annum, and the correlation between stock price returns is 0.4. Calculate a 10-day 99% VaR using DerivaGem and the linear model.

18.24. Suppose that the current price of gold at close of trading yesterday was \$300, and its volatility was estimated as 1.3% per day. The price at the close of trading today is \$298. Update the volatility estimate using the EWMA model with $\lambda = 0.94$.

18.25. Suppose that in Problem 18.24 the price of silver at the close of trading yesterday was \$8, its volatility was estimated as 1.5% per day, and its correlation with gold was estimated as 0.8. The price of silver at the close of trading today is unchanged at \$8. Update the volatility of silver and the correlation between silver and gold using the EWMA model with $\lambda = 0.94$.

18.26. An Excel spreadsheet containing daily data on a number of different exchange rates and stock indices can be downloaded from the author's website:

`http://www.rotman.utoronto.ca/~hull/data`

Choose one exchange rate and one stock index. Estimate the value of λ in the EWMA model that minimizes the value of

$$\sum_i (v_i - \beta_i)^2$$

where v_i is the variance forecast made at the end of day $i - 1$ and β_i is the variance calculated from data between day i and $i + 25$. Use Excel's Solver tool. Set the variance forecast at the end of the first day equal to the square of the return on that day to start the EWMA calculations.

18.27. A common complaint of risk managers is that the model-building approach (either linear or quadratic) does not work well when delta is close to zero. Test what happens when delta is close to zero in using Sample Application E in the DerivaGem Application Builder software. (You can do this by experimenting with different option positions and adjusting the position in the underlying to give a delta of zero.) Explain the results you get.

APPENDIX

Cash-Flow Mapping

In this appendix we explain one procedure for mapping cash flows to standard maturity dates. We will illustrate the procedure by considering a simple example of a portfolio consisting of a long position in a single Treasury bond with a principal of $1 million maturing in 0.8 years. We suppose that the bond provides a coupon of 10% per annum payable semiannually. This means that the bond provides coupon payments of $50,000 in 0.3 years and 0.8 years. It also provides a principal payment of $1 million in 0.8 years. The Treasury bond can therefore be regarded as a position in a 0.3-year zero-coupon bond with a principal of $50,000 and a position in a 0.8-year zero-coupon bond with a principal of $1,050,000.

The position in the 0.3-year zero-coupon bond is mapped into an equivalent position in 3-month and 6-month zero-coupon bonds. The position in the 0.8-year zero-coupon bond is mapped into an equivalent position in 6-month and 1-year zero-coupon bonds. The result is that the position in the 0.8-year coupon-bearing bond is, for VaR purposes, regarded as a position in zero-coupon bonds having maturities of three months, six months, and one year.

The Mapping Procedure

Consider the $1,050,000 that will be received in 0.8 years. We suppose that zero rates, daily bond price volatilities, and correlations between bond returns are as given in Table 18.3. The first stage is to interpolate between the 6-month rate of 6.0% and the 1-year rate of 7.0% to obtain a 0.8-year rate of 6.6% (annual compounding is assumed for all rates). The present value of the $1,050,000 cash flow to be received in 0.8 years is

$$\frac{1{,}050{,}000}{1.066^{0.8}} = 997{,}662$$

We also interpolate between the 0.1% volatility for the 6-month bond and the 0.2% volatility for the 1-year bond to get a 0.16% volatility for the 0.8-year bond.

Table 18.3 Data to illustrate mapping procedure

Maturity	*3-Month*	*6-Month*	*1-Year*
Zero rate (% with annual compounding)	5.50	6.00	7.00
Bond price volatility (% per day)	0.06	0.10	0.20

Correlation between daily returns	*3-Month bond*	*6-Month bond*	*1-Year bond*
3-Month bond	1.0	0.9	0.6
6-Month bond	0.9	1.0	0.7
1-Year bond	0.6	0.7	1.0

Table 18.4 The cash-flow mapping result

	\$50,000 received in 0.3 years	*\$1,050,000 received in 0.8 years*	*Total*
Position in 3-month bond (\$)	37,397		37,397
Position in 6-month bond (\$)	11,793	319,589	331,382
Position in 1-year bond (\$)		678,074	678,074

Suppose we allocate w of the present value to the 6-month bond and $1 - w$ of the present value to the 1-year bond. Using equation (18.2) and matching variances, we obtain

$$0.0016^2 = 0.001^2 w^2 + 0.002^2(1 - w)^2 + 2 \times 0.7 \times 0.001 \times 0.002w(1 - w)$$

This is a quadratic equation that can be solved in the usual way to give $w = 0.320337$. This means that 32.0337% of the value should be allocated to a 6-month zero-coupon bond and 67.9663% of the value should be allocated to a 1-year zero coupon bond. The 0.8-year bond worth \$997,662 is therefore replaced by a 6-month bond worth

$$997{,}662 \times 0.320337 = \$319{,}589$$

and a 1-year bond worth

$$997{,}662 \times 0.679663 = \$678{,}074$$

This cash-flow mapping scheme has the advantage that it preserves both the value and the variance of the cash flow. Also, it can be shown that the weights assigned to the two adjacent zero-coupon bonds are always positive.

For the \$50,000 cash flow received at time 0.3 years, we can carry out similar calculations (see Problem 18.14). It turns out that the present value of the cash flow is \$49,189. It can be mapped into a position worth \$37,397 in a three-month bond and a position worth \$11,793 in a six-month bond.

The results of the calculations are summarized in Table 18.4. The 0.8-year coupon-bearing bond is mapped into a position worth \$37,397 in a three-month bond, a position worth \$331,382 in a six-month bond, and a position worth \$678,074 in a one-year bond. Using the volatilities and correlations in Table 18.3, equation (18.2) gives the variance of the change in the price of the 0.8-year bond with $n = 3$, $w_1 = 37{,}397$, $w_2 = 331{,}382$, $w_3 = 678{,}074$, $\sigma_1 = 0.0006$, $\sigma_2 = 0.001$ and $\sigma_3 = 0.002$, $\rho_{12} = 0.9$, $\rho_{13} = 0.6$, and $\rho_{23} = 0.7$. This variance is 2,628,518. The standard deviation of the change in the price of the bond is therefore $\sqrt{2{,}628{,}518} = 1{,}621.3$. Because we are assuming that the bond is the only instrument in the portfolio, the 10-day 99% VaR is

$$1621.3 \times \sqrt{10} \times 2.33 = 11{,}946$$

or about \$11,950.

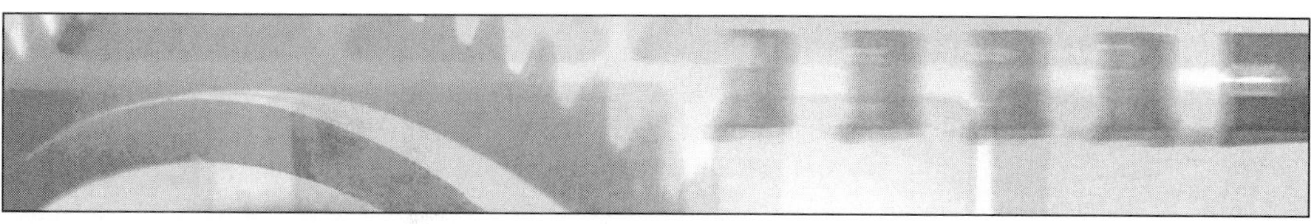

CHAPTER 19

Interest Rate Options

Interest rate options are options whose payoffs are dependent in some way on the level of interest rates. In recent years they have become increasingly popular. Many different types of interest rate options now trade very actively both in the over-the-counter market and on exchanges. This chapter discusses some of the products and how they are used. It describes in some detail the standard market models that are used for pricing three popular over-the-counter instruments: European bond options, interest rate caps and floors, and European swap options. These models are in the spirit of the original Black–Scholes model for European stock options and are based on the assumption that a key market variable will be lognormally distributed at a future time.

19.1 EXCHANGE-TRADED INTEREST RATE OPTIONS

Among the most actively traded interest rate options offered by exchanges in the United States are those on Treasury bond futures, Treasury note futures, and Eurodollar futures. Table 14.1 shows the closing prices for these instruments on February 4, 2004.

A Treasury bond futures option is an option to enter a Treasury bond futures contract. As mentioned in Chapter 6, one Treasury bond futures contract is for the delivery of \$100,000 of Treasury bonds. The price of a Treasury bond futures option is quoted as a percentage of the face value of the underlying Treasury bonds to the nearest sixty-fourth of 1%. Table 14.1 gives the price of the March call futures option on a Treasury bond on February 4, 2004, as 2-06, or $2\frac{6}{64}$% of the bond principal, when the strike price is 110. This means that one contract costs \$2,093.75. The quotes for options on Treasury notes are similar.

An option on Eurodollar futures is an option to enter into a Eurodollar futures contract. As explained in Chapter 6, when the Eurodollar futures quote changes by one basis point, or 0.01, there is a gain or loss on a Eurodollar futures contract of \$25. Similarly, in the pricing of options on Eurodollar futures, one basis point represents \$25. The *Wall Street Journal* quote for the CME Eurodollar futures contract in Table 14.1 should be multiplied by 10 to get the CME quote in basis points. For example, the 5.90 quote for the CME March call futures option when the strike price is 98.25 in Table 14.1 indicates that the CME quote is 59.0 basis points and one contract costs $59.0 \times \$25 = \$1,475.00$.

Interest rate futures option contracts work in the same way as the other futures options contracts discussed in Chapter 14. For example, the payoff from a call is $\max(F - K, 0)$, where F is the futures price at the time of exercise and K is the strike price. In addition to the cash payoff, the option holder obtains a long position in the futures contract when the option is exercised and the option writer obtains a corresponding short position.

Interest rate futures prices increase when bond prices increase (i.e., when interest rates fall). They decrease when bond prices decrease (i.e., when interest rates rise). An investor who thinks that short-term interest rates will rise can speculate by buying put options on Eurodollar futures, whereas an investor who thinks the rates will fall can speculate by buying call options on Eurodollar futures. An investor who thinks that long-term interest rates will rise can speculate by buying put options on Treasury note futures or Treasury bond futures, whereas an investor who thinks the rates will fall can speculate by buying call options on these instruments.

Example 1

It is February and the futures price for the June Eurodollar contract is 93.82. (This corresponds to a three-month Eurodollar interest rate of 6.18% per annum.) The price of a call option on the contract with a strike price of 94.00 is quoted at the CME as 0.20, or 20 basis points. This option could be attractive to an investor who thinks interest rates will decline. Suppose that short-term interest rates do drop by about 100 basis points and the investor exercises the call when the Eurodollar futures price is 94.78. (This corresponds to a three-month Eurodollar interest rate of 5.22% per annum.) The payoff is $25 \times (94.78 - 94.00) = \$1{,}950$. The cost of the contract is $20 \times 25 = \$500$. The investor's profit is therefore $1,450.

Example 2

It is August and the futures price for the December Treasury bond contract traded on the CBOT is 96-09 (or $96\frac{9}{32} = 96.28125$). The yield on long-term government bonds is about 6.4% per annum. An investor who feels that this yield will fall by December might choose to buy December calls with a strike price of 98. Assume that the price of these calls is 1-04 (or $1\frac{4}{64} = 1.0625\%$ of the principal). If long-term rates fall to 6% per annum and the Treasury bond futures price rises to 100-00, the investor will make a net profit per $100 of bond futures of

$$100.00 - 98.00 - 1.0625 = 0.9375$$

Because one option contract is for the purchase or sale of instruments with a face value of $100,000, the investor would make a profit of $937.50 per option contract bought.

Bond futures options and Eurodollar futures options are American. The easiest valuation approach is to use a binomial tree in the way described in Chapters 11, 14, and 16. When bond futures options are valued, the bond futures price is modeled by the tree and the volatility parameter used is the volatility of the bond futures price. In the case of Eurodollar futures, analysts often use the tree to model 100 minus the futures price. A call Eurodollar futures option with a strike price of 96 is then regarded as a put option on 100 minus the Eurodollar futures price with a strike price of 4, and the volatility used is the volatility of 100 minus the futures price.

19.2 EMBEDDED BOND OPTIONS

Some bonds contain embedded call and put options. For example, a *callable bond* contains provisions that allow the issuing firm to buy back the bond at a predetermined price at certain times in the future. The holder of such a bond has sold a call option to the issuer. The strike price or call price in the option is the predetermined price that must be paid by the issuer to the holder to buy back the bond. Callable bonds usually cannot be called for the first few years of their life. (This is known as a *lock-out period.*) After that the call price is usually a decreasing function of time. For example, a ten-year callable bond might have no call privileges for the first two years. After that the issuer might have the right to buy the bond back at a price of \$110.00 in years 3 and 4 of its life, at a price of \$107.50 in years 5 and 6, at a price of \$106.00 in years 7 and 8, and at a price of \$103.00 in years 9 and 10. The value of the call option is reflected in the quoted yields on bonds. Bonds with call features generally offer higher yields than bonds with no call features.

A *puttable bond* contains provisions that allow the holder to demand early redemption at a predetermined price at certain times in the future. The holder of such a bond has purchased a put option on the bond as well as the bond itself. Because the put option increases the value of the bond to the holder, bonds with put features provide lower yields than bonds with no put features. A simple example of a puttable bond is a 10-year retractable bond in which the holder has the right to be repaid at the end of five years.

A number of instruments other than bonds have embedded interest rate options. Sometimes the options are bond options. For example, the early redemption privileges on fixed-rate deposits are a put option on a bond. The prepayment privileges on a fixed-rate loan are a call option on a bond. Also, a loan commitment made by a bank or other financial institution is a put option on a bond. Suppose, for example, that a bank quotes a five-year interest rate of 10% per annum to a potential borrower and states that the rate is good for the next two months. The client has in effect obtained the right to sell a five-year bond with a 10% coupon to the financial institution for its face value any time within the next two months.

19.3 BLACK'S MODEL

Since the Black–Scholes model was first published in 1973, it has become a very popular tool. As explained in Chapters 13 and 14, the model has been extended so that it can be used to value options on foreign exchange, options on indices, and options on futures contracts. As outlined in Chapter 17, traders have found flexible ways of using the model to reflect their beliefs. It is not surprising, therefore, that the model has been extended so that it covers interest rate derivatives.

The extension of the Black–Scholes model that is most widely used in the interest rate area is known as Black's model.[1] As discussed in Section 14.8, this was originally developed for valuing options on commodity futures. In this chapter we explain how it is used to value a number of different types of over-the-counter interest rate derivatives.

---

[1] See F. Black "The Pricing of Commodity Contracts," *Journal of Financial Economics*, 3 (March 1976): 167–79.

Using Black's Model to Price European Options

Consider a European call option on a variable V. We define:

T: Time to maturity of the option
F: Futures price of V for a contract maturing at time T
F_0: Value of F at time zero
F_T: Value of F at time T
K: Strike price of the option
r: Interest rate for maturity T
σ: Volatility of F
V_T: Value of V at time T

The option pays off $\max(V_T - K, 0)$ at time T. Because the futures contract matures at time T, we have $F_T = V_T$ and we can also regard the option as paying off $\max(F_T - K, 0)$ at time T. As shown in Chapter 14, Black's model gives the value, c, of the option at time zero as

$$c = e^{-rT}[F_0N(d_1) - KN(d_2)] \tag{19.1}$$

where

$$d_1 = \frac{\ln(F_0/K) + \sigma^2T/2}{\sigma\sqrt{T}}$$

$$d_2 = \frac{\ln(F_0/K) - \sigma^2T/2}{\sigma\sqrt{T}} = d_1 - \sigma\sqrt{T}$$

The value, p, of the corresponding put option is given by

$$p = e^{-rT}[KN(-d_2) - F_0N(-d_1)] \tag{19.2}$$

Extension of Black's Model

We can extend Black's model by allowing the time when the payoff is made to be different from T. Assume that the payoff on the option is calculated from the value of the variable V at time T, but that the payoff is delayed until time T^* where $T^* \geqslant T$. In this case, it is necessary to discount the payoff from time T^* instead of from time T. We define r^* as the interest rate for maturity T^*, and equations (19.1) and (19.2) become

$$c = e^{-r^*T^*}[F_0N(d_1) - KN(d_2)] \tag{19.3}$$

$$p = e^{-r^*T^*}[KN(-d_2) - F_0N(-d_1)] \tag{19.4}$$

where

$$d_1 = \frac{\ln(F_0/K) + \sigma^2T/2}{\sigma\sqrt{T}}$$

$$d_2 = \frac{\ln(F_0/K) - \sigma^2T/2}{\sigma\sqrt{T}} = d_1 - \sigma\sqrt{T}$$

How the Model Is Used

When Black's model is used to price European interest rate options trading in the over-the-counter market, the variable F_0 in equations (19.1) to (19.4) is usually set equal to the forward price of V rather than its futures price. Recall from Chapter 5 that futures prices and forward prices are equal when interest rates are assumed to be constant, but different when they are assumed to evolve unpredictably. When we are dealing with an option on an interest-rate-dependent variable, the assumption that F_0 is a forward price is therefore questionable. However, it turns out (at least for the products considered in this chapter) that this assumption exactly offsets another assumption that is usually made when Black's model is used. This is that interest rates are constant for the purposes of discounting. When used to value interest rate options, Black's model therefore has a stronger theoretical basis than is sometimes supposed.[2]

19.4 EUROPEAN BOND OPTIONS

A European bond option is an option to buy or sell a bond for a certain price, K, at a certain time, T. A common assumption in valuing bond options is that the bond price is lognormal at time T. Equations (19.1) and (19.2) can then be used with F_0 equal to the forward bond price. The variable σ is the volatility of F, so that $\sigma\sqrt{T}$ is the standard deviation of the logarithm of the bond price at time T.

As explained in Chapter 5, F_0 can be calculated from today's spot bond price, B, using the formula

$$F_0 = (B - I)e^{rT} \tag{19.5}$$

where I is the present value of the coupons that will be paid during the life of the option and r is the interest rate for a maturity T. In this formula both the spot bond price and the forward bond price are cash prices rather than quoted prices. (The relationship between cash and quoted bond prices is explained in Chapter 6; the cash price is the quoted price plus accrued interest.) Traders refer to the quoted price of a bond as the "clean price" and the cash price as the "dirty price."

The strike price, K, in equations (19.1) and (19.2) should be the dirty (i.e., cash) strike price. If a particular contract defines the strike price as the cash amount that is exchanged for the bond when the option is exercised, K should be put equal to this strike price. If, as is more common, the strike price is the clean price applicable when the option is exercised, K should be set equal to the strike price plus accrued interest at the expiration date of the option.

Example

Consider a 10-month European call option on a 9.75-year bond with a face value of \$1,000. (When the option matures, the bond will have 8 years and 11 months remaining.) Suppose that the current cash bond price is \$960, the strike price is \$1,000, the 10-month risk-free interest rate is 10% per annum, and the forward bond price volatility is 9% per annum. The bond pays a semiannual coupon of 10%, and coupon payments of \$50 are expected in 3 months and 9 months.

[2] For an explanation of this, see J. C. Hull, *Options, Futures, and Other Derivatives*, 5th edn. (Upper Saddle River, NJ: Prentice Hall, 2000), Chapter 21.

(This means that the accrued interest is \$25 and the quoted bond price is \$935.) We suppose that the 3-month and 9-month risk-free interest rates are 9.0% and 9.5% per annum, respectively. The present value of the coupon payments is therefore

$$50e^{-0.09\times 0.25} + 50e^{-0.095\times 0.75} = 95.45$$

or \$95.45. The bond forward price, from equation (19.5), is given by

$$F_0 = (960 - 95.45)e^{0.1\times 10/12} = 939.68$$

(a) If the strike price is the cash price that would be paid for the bond on exercise, the parameters for equation (19.1) are $F_0 = 939.68$, $K = 1000$, $r = 0.1$, $\sigma = 0.09$, and $T = 0.8333$. The price of the call option is \$9.49.

(b) If the strike price is the quoted price that would be paid for the bond on exercise, one-month's accrued interest must be added to K, because the maturity of the option is one month after a coupon date. This produces a value for K of

$$1{,}000 + 50 \times 0.16667 = 1{,}008.33$$

The values for the other parameters in equation (19.1) are unchanged ($F_0 = 939.68$, $r = 0.1$, $\sigma = 0.09$, and $T = 0.8333$). The price of the option is \$7.97.

Yield Volatilities

The volatilities that are quoted for bond options are often yield volatilities rather than price volatilities. The duration concept, introduced in Chapter 6, is used by the market to convert a quoted yield volatility into a price volatility. Suppose that D is the modified duration of the bond underlying the option at the option maturity, as defined in Section 6.5. The relationship between the change in the forward bond price, F, and its yield, y_F, at the maturity of the option is

$$\frac{\Delta F}{F} \approx -D\,\Delta y_F$$

or

$$\frac{\Delta F}{F} \approx -D y_F \frac{\Delta y_F}{y_F}$$

Volatility is a measure of the standard deviation of percentage changes in the value of a variable. This equation therefore suggests that the volatility of the forward bond price, σ, used in Black's model can be approximately related to the volatility of the forward bond yield, σ_y, by

$$\sigma = D y_0 \sigma_y \tag{19.6}$$

where y_0 is the initial value of y_F. When a yield volatility is quoted for a bond option, the implicit assumption is usually that it will be converted to a price volatility using equation (19.6), and that this volatility will then be used in conjunction with equation (19.1) or (19.2) to obtain a price. Suppose that the bond underlying a call option will have a modified duration of five years at option maturity, the forward yield is 8%, and the forward yield volatility quoted by a broker is 20%. This means that the market price of the option corresponding to the broker quote is the price given by equation (19.1) when the volatility variable, σ, is

$$5 \times 0.08 \times 0.2 = 0.08$$

or 8% per annum.

The Bond_Options worksheet of the DerivaGem software accompanying this book can be used to price European bond options using Black's model by selecting Black-European as the Pricing Model. The user inputs a yield volatility, which is handled in the way just described. The strike price can be the cash or quoted strike price.

Example

Consider a European put option on a 10-year bond with a principal of 100. The coupon is 8% per year payable semiannually. The life of the option is 2.25 years and the strike price of the option is 115. The forward yield volatility is 20%. The zero curve is flat at 5% with continuous compounding. DerivaGem shows that the quoted price of the bond is 122.055. The price of the option when the strike price is a quoted price is 2.613. When the strike price is a cash price, the price of the option is \$1.938. (Note that DerivaGem's prices may not exactly agree with manually calculated prices because DerivaGem assumes 365 days per year and rounds times to the nearest whole number of days.)

19.5 INTEREST RATE CAPS

A popular interest rate option offered by financial institutions in the over-the-counter market is an *interest rate cap*. Interest rate caps can best be understood by first considering a floating rate note where the interest rate is reset periodically equal to LIBOR. The time between resets is known as the *tenor*. Suppose the tenor is three months. The interest rate on the note for the first three months is the initial three-month LIBOR rate; the interest rate for the next three months is set equal to the three-month LIBOR rate prevailing in the market at the three-month point; and so on.

An interest rate cap is designed to provide insurance against the rate of interest on the floating-rate note rising above a certain level. This level is known as the *cap rate*. The operation of the cap is illustrated schematically in Figure 19.1. Suppose that the principal amount is \$10 million, the life of the cap is five years, and the cap rate is 8%. (Because the tenor is three months, this cap rate is expressed with quarterly compounding.) Suppose that on a particular reset date the three-month LIBOR interest rate is 9%. The floating rate note would require

$$0.25 \times 0.09 \times \$10{,}000{,}000 = \$225{,}000$$

of interest to be paid three months later. With a three-month LIBOR rate of 8% the interest payment would be

$$0.25 \times 0.08 \times \$10{,}000{,}000 = \$200{,}000$$

The cap therefore provides a payoff of \$25,000 (= \$225,000 – \$200,000).[3] Note that the payoff does not occur on the reset date when the 9% is observed. It occurs three months

[3] This calculation assumes exactly one quarter of a year between reset dates. In practice, the calculation takes account of the exact number of days between reset dates using a specified day count convention.

Figure 19.1 Effect of a cap in providing insurance against LIBOR rising above the cap rate

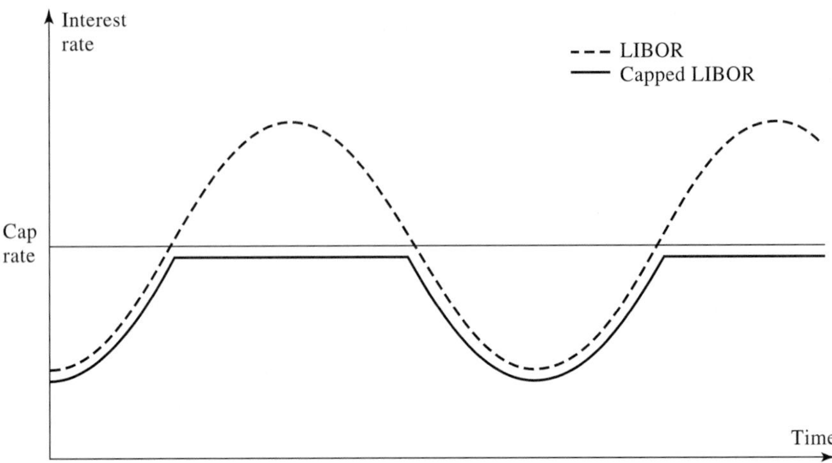

later. This reflects the usual time lag between an interest rate being observed and the corresponding payment being required.

If a corporation obtains a floating-rate loan where the rate of interest is linked to LIBOR, a cap can be used to limit the interest paid. For example, if the floating rate on a loan is LIBOR plus 30 basis points and the loan lasts for five years, the cap we have just considered would ensure that the rate paid is never higher than 8.30%. At each reset date during the life of the cap we observe LIBOR. If LIBOR is less than 8%, there is no payoff from the cap three months later. If LIBOR is greater than 8%, the payoff is one-quarter of the excess applied to the principal of $10 million. This example is summarized in Trading Note 19.1.

Note that caps are usually defined so that the initial LIBOR rate, even if it is greater than the cap rate, does not lead to a payoff on the first reset date. In our example, the cap lasts for five years. Therefore there is a total of 19 reset dates (at times 0.25, 0.50, 0.75, ..., 4.75 years) and 19 potential payoffs from the caps (at times 0.50, 0.75, 1.00, ..., 5.00 years).

Trading Note 19.1 Use of an interest rate cap

A company entering into a five-year $10 million floating-rate loan agreement is concerned about possible increases in interest rates. The rate on the loan is 3-month LIBOR plus 30 basis points.

The Strategy

The company buys a five-year interest rate cap with a cap rate of 8% per annum and a $10 million principal from a financial institution. This has the effect of ensuring that the interest rate paid by the company in any three-month period is never more than 8.3%.

The Cap as a Portfolio of Interest Rate Options

Consider a cap with a principal of L and a cap rate of R_K. Suppose that the reset dates are $t_1, t_2, \dots, t_n$ and the corresponding payment dates are $t_2, t_3, \dots, t_{n+1}$. Define R_k as the interest rate for the period between time t_k and t_{k+1} observed at time t_k ($1 \leqslant k \leqslant n$). The cap leads to a payoff at time t_{k+1} of

$$L\delta_k \max(R_k - R_K, 0) \tag{19.7}$$

where $\delta_k = t_{k+1} - t_k$.[4]

Equation (19.7) is a call option on the LIBOR rate observed at time t_k with the payoff occurring at time t_{k+1}. The cap is a portfolio of n such call options. These call options are known as *caplets*.

Floors and Collars

Interest rate floors are defined analogously to caps. A *floor* provides a payoff when the interest rate on the underlying floating-rate note falls below a certain rate. With the notation already introduced, a floor provides a payoff at time t_{k+1} ($k = 1, 2, \dots, n$) of

$$L\delta_k \max(R_K - R_k, 0)$$

Analogously to an interest rate cap, an interest rate floor is a portfolio of put options on interest rates. Each of the individual options comprising a floor is known as a *floorlet*.

An interest rate collar (sometimes called a floor–ceiling agreement) is an instrument designed to guarantee that the interest rate on the underlying floating-rate note always lies between two levels. A *collar* is a combination of a long position in a cap and a short position in a floor. It is usually constructed so that the price of the cap is initially equal to the price of the floor. The cost of entering into the collar is then zero.

As explained in Business Snapshot 19.1 there is a put–call parity relationship between caps and floors.

Valuation of Caps and Floors

As shown in equation (19.7), the caplet corresponding to the rate observed at time t_k provides a payoff at time t_{k+1} of

$$L\delta_k \max(R_k - R_K, 0)$$

If the rate R_k is assumed to be lognormal, equation (19.3) gives the value of this caplet as

$$L\delta_k e^{-r_{k+1}t_{k+1}}[F_k N(d_1) - R_K N(d_2)] \tag{19.8}$$

---

[4] In this equation both R_k and R_K are expressed with a compounding frequency equal to the frequency of resets. Also, it is assumed that they are measured on an actual/actual day count basis. In the United States LIBOR is quoted on an actual/360 basis. For the purposes of equation (19.7) and other equations in this chapter, we assume that LIBOR quotes have been multiplied by 365/360 or 366/360 to convert them to an actual/actual basis.

Business Snapshot 19.1 Put–call parity for caps and floors

There is a put–call parity relationship between the prices of caps and floors. This is

$$\text{Value of cap} = \text{Value of floor} + \text{Value of swap}$$

In this relationship, the cap and floor have the same strike price, R_K. The swap is an agreement to receive LIBOR and pay a fixed rate of R_K with no exchange of payments on the first reset date. All three instruments have the same life and the same frequency of payments.

To see that the result is true, consider a long position in the cap combined with a short position in the floor. The cap provides a cash flow of LIBOR − R_K for periods when LIBOR is greater than R_K. The short floor provides a cash flow of

$$-(R_K - \text{LIBOR}) = \text{LIBOR} - R_K$$

for periods when LIBOR is less than R_K. There is therefore a cash flow of LIBOR − R_K in all circumstances. This is the cash flow on the swap. It follows that the value of the cap minus the value of the floor must equal the value of the swap.

Note that swaps are usually structured so that LIBOR at time zero determines a payment on the first reset date. Caps and floors are usually structured so that there is no payoff on the first reset date. This is why the swap has to be defined as one with no payment on the first reset date.

where r_{k+1} is the continuously compounded rate for a maturity t_{k+1},

$$d_1 = \frac{\ln(F_k/R_K) + \sigma_k^2 t_k/2}{\sigma_k\sqrt{t_k}}$$

$$d_2 = \frac{\ln(F_k/R_K) - \sigma_k^2 t_k/2}{\sigma_k\sqrt{t_k}} = d_1 - \sigma_k\sqrt{t_k}$$

F_k is the forward rate for the period between time t_k and t_{k+1}, and σ_k is the volatility of F_k (so that $\sigma_k\sqrt{t_k}$ is the standard deviation of ln R_k). The value of the corresponding floorlet is, from equation (19.4),

$$L\delta_k e^{-r_{k+1}t_{k+1}}[R_K N(-d_2) - F_k N(-d_1)] \tag{19.9}$$

Note that R_K and F_k are expressed with a compounding frequency equal to the frequency of resets in these equations, while r_{k+1} is expressed with continuous compounding.

Example

Consider a contract that caps the interest rate on a \$10,000 loan at 8% per annum (with quarterly compounding) for three months starting in one year. This is a caplet and could be one element of a cap. Suppose that the zero curve is flat at 7% per annum with quarterly compounding and the volatility of the three-month forward rate underlying the caplet is 20% per annum. The continuously compounded zero rate for all maturities is 6.9394%. In equation (19.8), $F_k = 0.07$, $\delta_k = 0.25$, $L = 10{,}000$, $R_K = 0.08$, $r_{k+1} = 0.069394$, $\sigma_k = 0.20$, $t_k = 1.0$, and $t_{k+1} = 1.25$.

Also,

$$d_1 = \frac{\ln(0.07/0.08) + 0.2^2 \times 1/2}{0.20 \times 1} = -0.5677$$

$$d_2 = d_1 - 0.20 = -0.7677$$

so that the caplet price is

$$0.25 \times 10{,}000 \times e^{-0.069394 \times 1.25}[0.07N(-0.5677) - 0.08N(-0.7677)] = \$5.162$$

(Note that DerivaGem gives \$5.146 for the price of this caplet. This is because it assumes 365 days per year and rounds times to the nearest whole number of days.)

Each caplet of a cap must be valued separately using equation (19.8). One approach is to use a different volatility for each caplet. The volatilities are then referred to as *spot volatilities*.[5] An alternative approach is to use the same volatility for all the caplets comprising any particular cap, but to vary this volatility according to the life of the cap. The volatilities used are then referred to as *flat volatilities*. The volatilities quoted in the market are usually flat volatilities. However, many traders like to work with spot volatilities because this allows them to identify underpriced and overpriced caplets and floorlets. The options on Eurodollar futures that trade on the Chicago Mercantile Exchange are similar to caplets. The implied spot volatilities for caplets on three-month LIBOR are frequently compared with those calculated from the prices of Eurodollar futures options.

Figure 19.2 shows a typical pattern for spot volatilities and flat volatilities as a function of maturity. (In the case of a spot volatility, the maturity is the maturity of a caplet; in the case of a flat volatility, it is the maturity of a cap.) The flat volatilities are akin to cumulative averages of the spot volatilities and therefore exhibit less variability.

Figure 19.2 The volatility hump

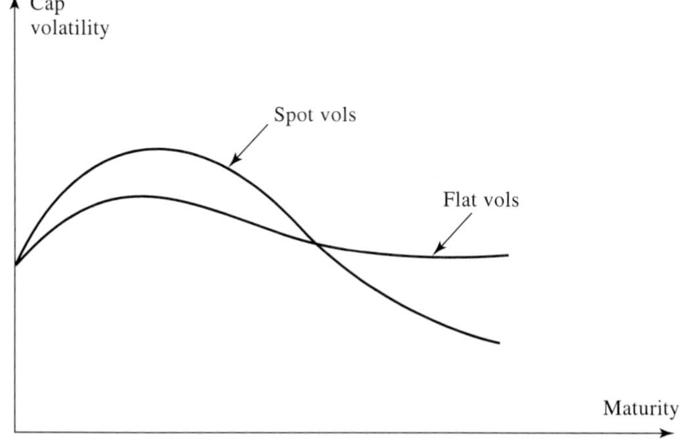

[5] The term *forward volatilities* is sometimes also used to describe these volatilities.

Table 19.1 Typical broker flat volatility quotes for U.S. dollar caps and floors (percent per annum)

Life (years)	*Cap bid*	*Cap offer*	*Floor bid*	*Floor offer*
1	18.00	20.00	18.00	20.00
2	23.25	24.25	23.75	24.75
3	24.00	25.00	24.50	25.50
4	23.75	24.75	24.25	25.25
5	23.50	24.50	24.00	25.00
7	21.75	22.75	22.00	23.00
10	20.00	21.00	20.25	21.25

As indicated by Figure 19.2, we usually observe a "hump" in the volatilities at about the two- to three-year point. This hump is observed both when the volatilities are implied from option prices and when they are calculated from historical data. There is no general agreement on the reason for the existence of the hump. One possible explanation is as follows. Rates at the short end of the zero curve are controlled by central banks. By contrast, two- and three-year interest rates are determined to a large extent by the activities of traders. These traders may be overreacting to the changes they observe in the short rate and causing the volatility of these rates to be higher than the volatility of short rates. For maturities beyond two to three years, the mean reversion of interest rates, which will be discussed later in this chapter, causes volatilities to decline.

Brokers provide tables of flat implied volatilities for caps and floors. The instruments underlying the quotes are usually at the money. This means that the cap/floor rate equals the swap rate for a swap that has the same payment dates as the cap. Table 19.1 shows typical broker quotes for the U.S. dollar market. The tenor of the cap is three months, and the cap life varies from one year to ten years. The volatilities are flat volatilities rather than spot volatilities. The data exhibits the type of "hump" shown in Figure 19.2.

Using DerivaGem

The DerivaGem software accompanying this book can be used to price interest rate caps and floors using Black's model. In the Cap_and_Swap_Option worksheet, select Cap/Floor as the Underlying Type and Black-European as the Pricing Model. The zero curve is input using continuously compounded rates. The inputs include the start date and the end date of the period covered by the cap, the flat volatility, and the cap settlement frequency (i.e., the tenor). The software calculates the payment dates by working back from the end of period covered by the cap to the beginning. The initial caplet/floorlet is assumed to cover a period of length between 0.5 and 1.5 times a regular period. Suppose, for example, that the period covered by the cap is 1.22 years to 2.80 years and the settlement frequency is quarterly. There are six caplets covering the periods 2.55 years to 2.80 years, 2.30 years to 2.55 years, 2.05 years to 2.30 years, 1.80 years to 2.05 years, 1.55 years to 1.80 years, and 1.22 years to 1.55 years.

Business Snapshot 19.2 Swaptions and bond options

As explained in Chapter 7, an interest rate swap can be regarded as an agreement to exchange a fixed-rate bond for a floating-rate bond. At the start of a swap, the value of the floating-rate bond always equals the principal amount of the swap. It follows that a swaption can be regarded as an option to exchange a fixed-rate bond for the principal amount of the swap.

A swaption is therefore a type of bond option. If a swaption gives the holder the right to pay fixed and receive floating, it is a put option on the fixed-rate bond with strike price equal to the principal. If a swaption gives the holder the right to pay floating and receive fixed, it is a call option on the fixed-rate bond with a strike price equal to the principal.

19.6 EUROPEAN SWAP OPTIONS

Swap options, or *swaptions*, are options on interest rate swaps and are an increasingly popular type of interest rate option. They give the holder the right, but not the obligation, to enter into a specified interest rate swap at a certain time in the future. Large financial institutions that offer interest rate swap contracts to their corporate clients are often also prepared to sell them swaptions or buy swaptions from them. As shown in Business Snapshot 19.2, a swaption can be viewed as a type of bond option.

To give an example of how a swaption might be used, consider a company that knows that in six months it will enter into a five-year floating-rate loan agreement and that it will wish to swap the floating-interest payments for fixed-interest payments to convert the loan into a fixed-rate loan. (See Chapter 7 for a discussion of how swaps can be used in this way.) At a cost, the company could enter into a swaption giving it the right to receive six-month LIBOR and pay a certain fixed rate of interest (say, 6% per annum) for a five-year period starting in six months. If the fixed rate on a regular five-year swap in six months turns out to be less than 6% per annum, the company will choose not to exercise the swaption and will enter into a swap agreement in the usual way. However, if the fixed rate turns out to be greater than 6% per annum, the company will choose to exercise the swaption and will obtain a swap at more favorable terms than those available in the market.

When used in the way just described, swaptions provide companies that are planning future borrowings with protection against interest rate increases. Swaptions are an alternative to forward swaps (sometimes called *deferred swaps*). Forward swaps involve no up-front cost, but have the disadvantage that they obligate the company to enter into a swap agreement. With a swaption, the company is able to benefit from favorable interest rate movements while acquiring protection from unfavorable interest rate movements. The difference between a swaption and a forward swap is analogous to the difference between an option on a foreign currency and a forward contract on the currency.

Valuation of European Swaptions

Consider a swaption where we have the right to pay a rate R_K and receive LIBOR on a swap that will last n years starting in T years. We suppose that there are m payments per year under the swap and that the principal is L.

As explained in Chapter 7, the *swap rate* for a particular maturity at a particular time is the fixed rate that would be exchanged for LIBOR in a newly issued swap with that maturity. Suppose that the swap rate for an n-year swap starting at time T is R. (Both R and R_K are expressed with a compounding frequency of m times per year.) By comparing the cash flows on a swap where the fixed rate is R to the cash flows on a swap where the fixed rate is R_K, we see that the payoff from the swaption consists of a series of cash flows equal to

$$\frac{L}{m}\max(R - R_K, 0)$$

The cash flows are received m times per year for the n years of the life of the swap. Suppose that the swap payment dates are $t_1, t_2, \dots, t_{mn}$, measured in years from today. (It is approximately true that $t_i = T + i/m$.) Each cash flow is the payoff from a call option on R with strike price R_K.

The standard market model for valuing swaptions assumes that R is lognormal. Using equation (19.3), the value of the cash flow received at time t_i is

$$\frac{L}{m}e^{-r_i t_i}[F_0 N(d_1) - R_K N(d_2)]$$

where

$$d_1 = \frac{\ln(F_0/R_K) + \sigma^2 T/2}{\sigma\sqrt{T}}$$

$$d_2 = \frac{\ln(F_0/R_K) - \sigma^2 T/2}{\sigma\sqrt{T}} = d_1 - \sigma\sqrt{T}$$

Here F_0 is the forward swap rate, r_i is the continuously compounded zero-coupon interest rate for a maturity of t_i, and σ is the volatility of the forward swap rate (so that $\sigma\sqrt{T}$ is the standard deviation of $\ln R$).

The total value of the swaption is

$$\sum_{i=1}^{mn} \frac{L}{m}e^{-r_i t_i}[F_0 N(d_1) - R_K N(d_2)]$$

If we define A as the value of a contract that pays $1/m$ at times t_i $(1 \leqslant i \leqslant mn)$ so that

$$A = \frac{1}{m}\sum_{i=1}^{mn} e^{-r_i t_i}$$

then the value of the swaption becomes

$$LA[F_0 N(d_1) - R_K N(d_2)] \qquad \textbf{(19.10)}$$

If the swaption gives the holder the right to receive a fixed rate of R_K instead of paying it, the payoff from the swaption is

$$\frac{L}{m}\max(R_K - R, 0)$$

This is a put option on R. As before, the payoffs are received at times t_i $(1 \leqslant i \leqslant mn)$.

Equation (19.4) gives the value of the swaption as

$$LA[R_K N(-d_2) - F_0 N(-d_1)] \tag{19.11}$$

The DerivaGem software provides an implementation of equations (19.10) and (19.11). In the Cap_and_Swap_Options worksheet select Swap Option as the Underlying Type and Black-European as the Pricing Model.

Example

Suppose that the LIBOR yield curve is flat at 6% per annum with continuous compounding. Consider a swaption that gives the holder the right to pay 6.2% in a 3-year swap starting in 5 years. The volatility of the forward swap rate is 20%. Payments are made semiannually and the principal is \$100. In this case,

$$A = \tfrac{1}{2}(e^{-0.06\times 5.5} + e^{-0.06\times 6} + e^{-0.06\times 6.5} + e^{-0.06\times 7} + e^{-0.06\times 7.5} + e^{-0.06\times 8}) = 2.0035$$

A rate of 6% per annum with continuous compounding translates into 6.09% with semiannual compounding. It follows that in this example $F_0 = 0.0609$, $R_K = 0.062$, $T = 5$, and $\sigma = 0.2$, so that

$$d_1 = \frac{\ln(0.0609/0.062) + 0.2^2 \times 5/2}{0.2\sqrt{5}} = 0.1836$$

$$d_2 = d_1 - 0.2\sqrt{5} = -0.2636$$

From equation (19.10) the value of the swaption is

$$100 \times 2.0035[0.0609 \times N(0.1836) - 0.062 \times N(-0.2636)] = 2.07$$

or \$2.07. (This is in agreement with the price given by DerivaGem.)

Brokers provide tables of implied volatilities for European swap options. The instruments underlying the quotes are usually at the money. This means that the strike swap rate equals the forward swap rate. Table 19.2 shows typical broker quotes provided for

Table 19.2 Typical broker quotes for U.S. European swap options (mid-market volatilities % per annum)

	Swap length (years)						
Expiration	*1*	*2*	*3*	*4*	*5*	*7*	*10*
1 month	17.75	17.75	17.75	17.50	17.00	17.00	16.00
3 months	19.50	19.00	19.00	18.00	17.50	17.00	16.00
6 months	20.00	20.00	19.25	18.50	18.75	17.75	16.75
1 year	22.50	21.75	20.50	20.00	19.50	18.25	16.75
2 years	22.00	22.00	20.75	19.50	19.75	18.25	16.75
3 years	21.50	21.00	20.00	19.25	19.00	17.75	16.50
4 years	20.75	20.25	19.25	18.50	18.25	17.50	16.00
5 years	20.00	19.50	18.50	17.75	17.50	17.00	15.50

the U.S. dollar market. The tenor of the underlying swaps (i.e., the frequency of resets on the floating rate) is six months. The life of the option is shown on the vertical scale. This varies from one month to five years. The life of the underlying swap at the maturity of the option is shown on the horizontal scale. This varies from one year to ten years. The volatilities in the extreme left column of the table correspond to instruments that are similar to caps. They exhibit the hump discussed earlier. As we move to the columns corresponding to options on longer-lived swaps, the hump persists, but it becomes less pronounced.

19.7 TERM STRUCTURE MODELS

The European bond option pricing model that we have presented assumes that a bond price at some future time is lognormally distributed; the cap pricing model assumes that an interest rate at some future time is lognormally distributed; the European swap option pricing model assumes that a swap rate at some future time is lognormally distributed. These assumptions are not consistent with each other. This makes it difficult for traders to compare the way the market prices different types of instruments.

A related disadvantage of the models is that they cannot easily be extended to value instruments other than those for which they were designed. For example, Black's model for valuing a European swap option cannot easily be extended to value American swap options. A more sophisticated approach to valuing interest rate derivative securities involves constructing a *term structure model*. This is a model that describes the probabilistic behavior of the term structure of interest rates. Term structure models are more complicated than those used to describe the movements of a stock price or currency. This is because they are concerned with movements in the whole zero-coupon yield curve, not with changes to a single variable. As time passes, all interest rates do

Figure 19.3 Mean reversion

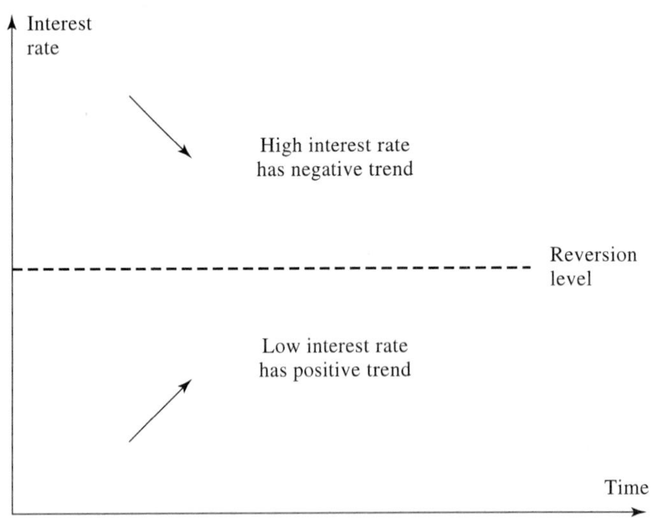

not necessarily change by the same amount so that the shape of the yield curve is liable to change.

Explaining how term structure models are constructed is beyond the scope of this book. But it is worth noting one property of an interest rate that distinguishes it from a stock price or an exchange rate—or indeed the price of any investment asset. A short-term interest rate (say, the three-month rate) appears to exhibit a property known as *mean reversion*. It tends to be pulled back to some long-run average level. When the short-term interest rate is very high, it tends to move down; when it is very low, it tends to move up. For example, if the three-month interest rate in the United States reaches 15%, the next movement is more likely to be down than up; if it reaches 1%, the next movement is more likely to be up than down. This is illustrated in Figure 19.3.

If a stock price exhibited mean reversion, there would be an obvious trading strategy: buy the stock when its price is at a historic low; sell the stock when its price is at a historic high. Mean-reverting three-month interest rates do not provide us with a similar trading strategy. This is because an interest rate is not the price of a security that can be traded. There is no traded instrument whose price is always equal to the three-month rate.

SUMMARY

Interest rate options arise in practice in many different ways. For example, options on Treasury bond futures, Treasury note futures, and Eurodollar futures are actively traded by exchanges. Many traded bonds include features that are options. The loans and deposit instruments offered by financial institutions often contain embedded options.

Three popular over-the-counter instruments are bond options, interest caps and floors, and swap options. A bond option is an option to buy or sell a particular bond. An interest rate cap (floor) provides a payoff when a floating rate of interest rises above (falls below) the strike rate. A swap option is an option to enter into a swap, where a specified fixed rate will be exchanged for floating, at a particular time in the future. Black's model is the model used by the market for valuing these instruments. In the case of bond options, the probability distribution of the underlying bond is assumed to be lognormal. In the case of caps and floors, the underlying interest rates are assumed to be lognormal. In the case of swap options, the underlying swap rate is assumed to be lognormal.

FURTHER READING

Black, F. "The Pricing of Commodity Contracts," *Journal of Financial Economics*, 3 (1976): 167–79.

Black, F., E. Derman, and W. Toy. "A One-Factor Model of Interest Rates and Its Application to Treasury Bond Options," Financial Analysts Journal, (January/February 1990): 33–39.

Black, F., and P. Karasinski. "Bond and Option Pricing When Short Rates Are Lognormal," *Financial Analysts Journal*, (July/August 1991): 52–59.

Brace A., D. Gatarek, and M. Musiela. "The Market Model of Interest Rate Dynamics," *Mathematical Finance*, 7, 2 (1997): 127–55.

Cox, J. C., J. E. Ingersoll, and S. A. Ross. "A Theory of the Term Structure of Interest Rates," *Econometrica*, 53 (1985): 385–407.

Heath, D., R. Jarrow, and A. Morton. "Bond Pricing and the Term Structure of Interest Rates: A New Methodology," *Econometrica*, 60 (1992): 77–105.

Ho, T. S. Y., and S. B. Lee. "Term Structure Movements and Pricing Interest Rate Contingent Claims," *Journal of Finance*, 41 (December 1986): 1011–29.

Hull, J. C. *Options, Futures, and Other Derivatives*. 5th edn. Upper Saddle River, NJ: Prentice-Hall, 2003.

Hull, J. C., and A. White. "Pricing Interest Rate Derivative Securities," *Review of Financial Studies*, 3, 4 (1990): 573–92.

Hull, J. C., and A. White. "Using Hull–White Interest Rate Trees," *Journal of Derivatives*, (Spring 1996): 26–36.

James, J., and N. Webber. *Interest Rate Modeling*. Chichester, UK: Wiley, 2000.

Jamshidian, F. "LIBOR and Swap Market Models and Measures," *Finance and Stochastics*, 1 (1997): 293–330.

Miltersen, K., K. Sandmann, and D. Sondermann, "Closed Form Solutions for Term Structure Derivatives with Lognormal Interest Rates," *Journal of Finance*, 52, 1 (March 1997): 409–30.

Rebonato, R. *Interest Rate Option Models*. 2nd edn. New York: Wiley, 1998.

Vasicek, O. A. "An Equilibrium Characterization of the Term Structure," *Journal of Financial Economics*, 5(1977): 177–88.

Quiz (Answers at End of Book)

19.1. A company caps three-month LIBOR at 10% per annum. The principal amount is $20 million. On a reset date three-month LIBOR is 12% per annum. What payment would this lead to under the cap? When would the payment be made?

19.2. Explain the features of (a) callable and (b) puttable bonds.

19.3. Explain why a swaption can be regarded as a type of bond option.

19.4. Use Black's model to value a 1-year European put option on a 10-year bond. Assume that the current value of the bond is $125, the strike price is $110, the 1-year interest rate is 10% per annum, the bond's forward price volatility is 8% per annum, and the present value of the coupons that will be paid during the life of the option is $10.

19.5. Suppose you buy a Eurodollar call futures option contract with a strike price of 97.25. You exercise when the underlying Eurodollar futures price is 98.12. What is the payoff?

19.6. Calculate the price of an option that caps the 3-month rate starting in 18 months' time at 13% (quoted with quarterly compounding) on a principal amount of $1,000. The forward interest rate for the period in question is 12% per annum (quoted with quarterly compounding), the 21-month risk-free interest rate (continuously compounded) is 11.5% per annum, and the volatility of the forward rate is 12% per annum.

19.7. What are the advantages of term structure models over Black's model for valuing interest rate derivatives?

Questions and Problems (Answers in Solutions Manual/Study Guide)

19.8. Suppose that the LIBOR yield curve is flat at 8% with annual compounding. A swaption gives the holder the right to receive 7.6% in a 5-year swap starting in 4 years. Payments are made annually. The volatility of the forward swap rate is 25% per annum and the principal is $1 million. Use Black's model to price the swaption.

19.9. A bank uses Black's model to price European bond options. Suppose that an implied price volatility for a 5-year option on a bond maturing in 10 years is used to price a 9-year option on the bond. Would you expect the resultant price to be too high or too low? Explain your answer.

19.10. Consider a 4-year European call option on a bond that will mature in 5 years. The 5-year bond price is \$105, the price of a 4-year bond with the same coupon as the 5-year bond is \$102, the strike price of the option is \$100, the 4-year risk-free interest rate is 10% per annum (continuously compounded), and the volatility of the forward price of the bond underlying the option is 2% per annum. What is the present value of the principal in the 4-year bond? What is the present value of the coupons in the 4-year bond? What is the forward price of the bond underlying the option? What is the value of the option?

19.11. If the yield volatility for a 5-year put option on a bond maturing in 10 years time is specified as 22%, how should the option be valued? Assume that, based on today's interest rates, the modified duration of the bond at the maturity of the option will be 4.2 years and the forward yield on the bond is 7%.

19.12. A corporation knows that in three months it will have \$5 million to invest for 90 days at LIBOR minus 50 basis points and wishes to ensure that the rate obtained will be at least 6.5%. What position in exchange-traded interest rate options should the corporation take?

19.13. Explain carefully how you would use (a) spot volatilities and (b) flat volatilities to value a 5-year cap.

19.14. What other instrument is the same as a 5-year zero-cost collar in which the strike price of the cap equals the strike price of the floor? What does the common strike price equal?

19.15. Suppose that the 1-year, 2-year, 3-year, 4-year and 5-year zero rates are 6%, 6.4%, 6.7%, 6.9%, and 7%. The price of a 5-year semiannual cap with a principal of \$100 at a cap rate of 8% is \$3. Use DerivaGem to determine:
a. The 5-year flat volatility for caps and floors
b. The floor rate in a zero-cost 5-year collar when the cap rate is 8%

19.16. Show that $V_1 + f = V_2$, where V_1 is the value of a swap option to pay a fixed rate of R_K and receive LIBOR between times T_1 and T_2, f is the value of a forward swap to receive a fixed rate of R_K and pay LIBOR between times T_1 and T_2, and V_2 is the value of a swap option to receive a fixed rate of R_K between times T_1 and T_2. Deduce that $V_1 = V_2$ when R_K equals the current forward swap rate.

19.17. Explain why there is an arbitrage opportunity if the implied Black (flat) volatility for a cap is different from that for a floor. Do the broker quotes in Table 19.1 present an arbitrage opportunity?

19.18. Suppose that zero rates are as in Problem 19.15. Use DerivaGem to determine the value of an option to pay a fixed rate of 6% and receive LIBOR on a five-year swap starting in one year. Assume that the principal is \$100 million, payments are exchanged semiannually, and the swap rate volatility is 21%.

Assignment Questions

19.19. Consider an eight-month European put option on a Treasury bond that currently has 14.25 years to maturity. The bond principal is \$1,000. The current cash bond price is \$910, the exercise price is \$900, and the volatility of the forward bond price is 10% per annum. A coupon of \$35 will be paid by the bond in three months. The risk-free interest rate is 8% for all maturities up to one year. Use Black's model to determine the price of the option. Consider both the case where the strike price corresponds to the cash price of the bond and the case where it corresponds to the quoted price.

19.20. Use the DerivaGem software to value a five-year collar that guarantees that the maximum and minimum interest rates on a LIBOR-based loan (with quarterly resets) are 5% and 7%, respectively. The LIBOR zero curve (continuously compounded) is currently flat at 6%. Use a flat volatility of 20%. Assume that the principal is \$100.

19.21. Suppose that the LIBOR yield curve is flat at 8% with annual compounding. A swaption gives the holder the right to receive 7.6% in a 5-year swap starting in 4 years. Payments are made annually. The volatility of the forward swap rate is 25% per annum and the principal is \$1 million. Use Black's model to price the swaption. Compare your answer to that given by DerivaGem.

19.22. Calculate the price of a cap on the 3-month LIBOR rate in 9 months' time for a principal amount of \$1,000. Use Black's model and the following information:

Quoted 9-month Eurodollar futures price = 92
Interest rate volatility implied by a 9-month Eurodollar option = 15% per annum
Current 12-month interest rate with continuous compounding = 7.5% per annum
Cap rate = 8% per annum

19.23. Use the DerivaGem software to value a European swap option that gives you the right in 2 years to enter into a 5-year swap in which you pay a fixed rate of 6% and receive floating. Cash flows are exchanged semiannually on the swap. The 1-year, 2-year, 5-year, and 10-year zero-coupon interest rates (continuously compounded) are 5%, 6%, 6.5%, and 7%, respectively. Assume a principal of \$100 and a volatility of 15% per annum. Give an example of how the swap option might be used by a corporation. What bond option is equivalent to the swap option?

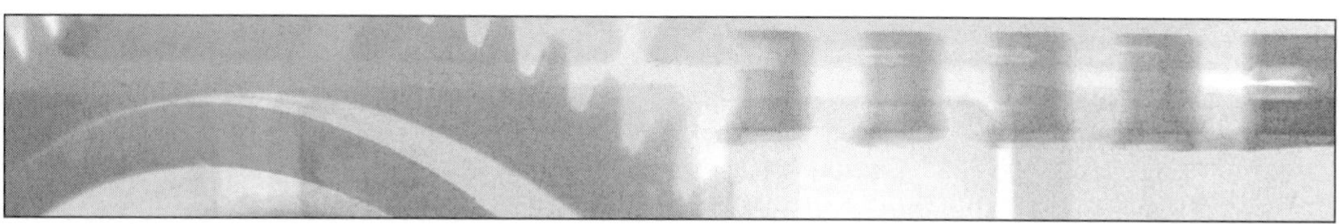

CHAPTER 20 Exotic Options and Other Nonstandard Products

The derivatives we have covered in the first 19 chapters of this book are what are termed *plain vanilla products*. They have standard well-defined properties and trade actively. Their prices or implied volatilities are quoted by exchanges or by brokers on a regular basis. One of the exciting features of the over-the-counter derivatives market is the number of nonstandard (or exotic) products that have been created by financial engineers. Although they are usually a relatively small part of its portfolio, these exotic products are important to an investment bank because they are generally much more profitable than plain vanilla products.

Exotic products are developed for a number of reasons. Sometimes they meet a genuine hedging need in the market; sometimes there are tax, accounting, legal, or regulatory reasons why corporate treasurers or fund managers find exotic products attractive; sometimes the products are designed to reflect a corporate treasurer's or fund manager's view on potential future movements in particular market variables; occasionally an exotic product is designed by an investment bank to appear more attractive than it is to an unwary corporate treasurer or fund manager.

We start by considering exotic options. These are variations on the standard call and put options that we have covered in Chapters 8 to 18. We then look at mortgage-backed securities, which have become an important feature of the U.S. interest rate derivatives market. Finally, we describe some nonstandard swap products. The objective of this chapter is to give a flavor for the range of instruments that have been developed. It does not provide a comprehensive list of all exotic products that exist.

20.1 EXOTIC OPTIONS

In this section we describe a number of different types of exotic options that large investment banks offer on underlying assets such as stocks, stock indices, and currencies. We use a categorization similar to that in an excellent series of articles written by Eric Reiner and Mark Rubinstein for *RISK* magazine in 1991 and 1992. Asian, barrier, binary, chooser, compound, and lookback options can be valued using DerivaGem.[1]

[1] The procedures used by the market to value all the options described in this section are covered in J. C. Hull, *Options, Futures, and Other Derivatives*, 5th edn. (Upper Saddle River, NJ: Prentice Hall, 2003), Chapter 19.

Packages

A *package* is a portfolio consisting of standard European calls, standard European puts, forward contracts, cash, and the underlying asset itself. We discussed a number of different types of packages in Chapter 10: bull spreads, bear spreads, butterfly spreads, calendar spreads, straddles, strangles, and so on.

Often a package is structured by traders so that it has zero cost initially. An example is a *range-forward contract*.[2] Figure 20.1 shows the payoff from short and long range-forward contracts. A short range-forward contract consists of a long position in a put with a low strike price, K_1, and a short position in a call with a high strike price, K_2. It guarantees that the underlying asset can be sold for a price between K_1 and K_2 at the maturity of the options. A long range-forward contract consists of a short position in a put with the low strike price, K_1, and a long position in a call with the high strike price, K_2. It guarantees that the underlying asset can be purchased for a price between K_1 and K_2 at the maturity of the options. The price of the call equals the price of the put when the contract is initiated. As K_1 and K_2 are moved closer to each other, the price that will be received or paid for the asset at maturity becomes more certain. In the limit when $K_1 = K_2$, the range-forward contract becomes a regular forward contract.

Nonstandard American Options

In a standard American option, exercise can take place at any time during the life of the option, and the exercise price is always the same. In practice, the American options that are traded in the over-the-counter market do not always have these features. For example:

1. Early exercise may be restricted to certain dates. The instrument is then known as a *Bermudan option*.
2. Early exercise may be allowed during only part of the life of the option.
3. The strike price may change during the life of the option.

Figure 20.1 Payoffs from (a) short and (b) long range-forward contract

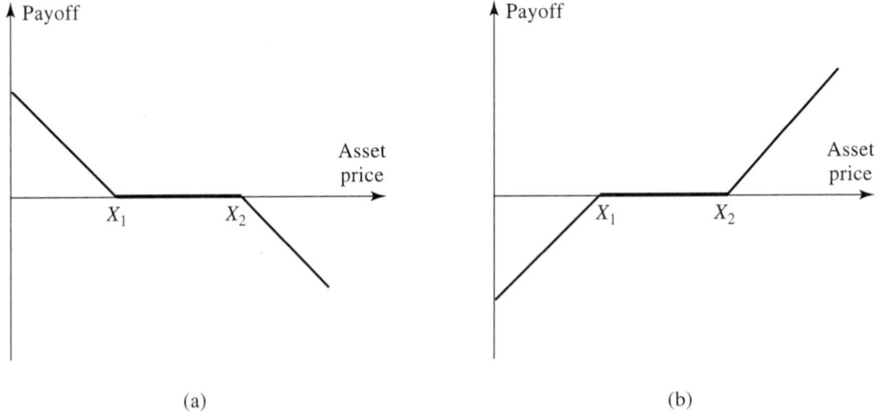

[2] Other names used for a range-forward contract are zero-cost collar, flexible forward, cylinder option, option fence, min–max, and forward band.

The warrants issued by corporations on their own stock often have some of these features. For example, in a seven-year warrant, exercise might be possible on particular dates during years 3 to 7, with the strike price being $30 during years 3 and 4, $32 during the next two years, and $33 during the final year.

Nonstandard American options can usually be valued using a binomial tree. At each node, the test (if any) for early exercise is adjusted to reflect the terms of the option.

Forward Start Options

Forward start options are options that will start at some time in the future. Executive stock options, which are discussed in Business Snapshot 8.3, can be viewed as a type of forward start option. In a typical stock option plan, a company promises that it will grant at-the-money options to executives at certain times in the future.

When the underlying asset provides no income, an at-the-money forward start option is (using the assumptions underlying Black–Scholes) worth the same as a regular at-the-money option with the same life. For example, an at-the-money option that will start in three years and mature in five years is worth the same as a two-year at-the-money option initiated today (see Problem 20.13).

Compound Options

Compound options are options on options. There are four main types of compound options: a call on a call, a put on a call, a call on a put, and a put on a put. Compound options have two strike prices and two exercise dates. Consider, for example, a call on a call. On the first exercise date, T_1, the holder of the compound option is entitled to pay the first strike price, K_1, and receive a call option. The call option gives the holder the right to buy the underlying asset for the second strike price, K_2, on the second exercise date, T_2. The compound option will be exercised on the first exercise date only if the value of the second option on that date is greater than the first strike price. A compound option is generally much more sensitive to volatility than a plain vanilla option.

Chooser Options

A *chooser* option (sometimes referred to as an *as you like it* option) has the feature that, after a specified period of time, the holder can choose whether the option is a call or a put. Suppose that the time when the choice is made is T_1. The value of the chooser option at this time is

$$\max(c, p)$$

where c is the value of the call underlying the option and p is the value of the put underlying the option.

If the options underlying the chooser option are both European and have the same strike price, put–call parity can be used to provide a valuation formula. Suppose that S_1 is the underlying asset price at time T_1, K is the strike price, T_2 is the maturity of the options, and r is the risk-free interest rate. Put–call parity implies that

$$\begin{aligned}\max(c, p) &= \max(c,\ c + Ke^{-r(T_2-T_1)} - S_1e^{-q(T_2-T_1)}) \\ &= c + e^{-q(T_2-T_1)}\max(0,\ Ke^{-(r-q)(T_2-T_1)} - S_1)\end{aligned}$$

This shows that the chooser option is a package consisting of:

1. A call option with strike price K and maturity T_2
2. $e^{-q(T_2-T_1)}$ put options with strike price $Ke^{-(r-q)(T_2-T_1)}$ and maturity T_1

As such, it can readily be valued.

Barrier Options

Barrier options are options where the payoff depends on whether the underlying asset's price reaches a certain level during a certain period of time. A number of different types of barrier options regularly trade in the over-the-counter market. They are attractive to some market participants because they are less expensive than the corresponding regular options. Barrier options can be classified as either *knock-out options* or *knock-in options*. A knock-out option ceases to exist when the underlying asset price reaches a certain level; a knock-in option comes into existence only when the underlying asset price reaches a certain level.

There are four types of knock-out options. An *up-and-out call* option is a regular European call option that ceases to exist as soon as the asset price reaches a barrier level. The barrier level is greater than the asset price at the time the option is initiated. A *down-and-out call* is defined similarly except that the barrier level is below the asset price at the time the option is initiated. An *up-and-out put* and *down-and-out put* are defined similarly.

There are similarly four types of knock-in options. An *up-and-in call* option is a regular European call option that starts to exist as soon as the asset price reaches a barrier level. The barrier level is greater than the asset price when the option is initiated. A *down-and-in call* is similar except that the barrier level is below the asset price when the option is initiated. An *up-and-in put* and a *down-and-in put* are defined analogously. There are relationships between the prices of barrier options and regular options. For example, the price of a down-and-out call option plus the price of a down-and-in call option must equal the price of a regular European option. Similarly, the price of a down-and-out put option plus the price of a down-and-in put option must equal the price of a regular European option.

Barrier options often have quite different properties from regular options. For example, sometimes vega is negative. Consider an up-and-out call option when the asset price is close to the barrier level. As volatility increases, the probability that the barrier will be hit increases. As a result, a volatility increase causes a price decrease.

In determining whether a barrier is hit, sometimes the price is observed on a more or less continuous basis.[3] On other occasions the terms on the contract state that the price is observed periodically (e.g., once a day at 12 noon).

Binary Options

Binary options are options with discontinuous payoffs. A simple example of a binary option is a *cash-or-nothing call*. This pays off nothing if the asset price ends up below the strike price at time T and pays a fixed amount, Q, if it ends up above the strike price. In a risk-neutral world, the probability of the asset price being above the strike price at the maturity of an option is, with our usual notation, $N(d_2)$. The value of a

[3] One way to track whether a barrier is reached from below (above) is to send a limit order to an exchange to sell (buy) the asset at the barrier price and see whether the order is filled.

cash-or-nothing call is therefore $Qe^{-rT}N(d_2)$. A *cash-or-nothing put* is defined analogously to a cash-or-nothing call. It pays off Q if the asset price is below the strike price and nothing if it is above the strike price. The value of a cash-or-nothing put is $Qe^{-rT}N(-d_2)$.

Another type of binary option is an *asset-or-nothing call*. This pays off nothing if the underlying asset price ends up below the strike price and pays an amount equal to the asset price itself if it ends up above the strike price. With our usual notation, the value of an asset-or-nothing call is $S_0e^{-qT}N(d_1)$. An *asset-or-nothing put* pays off nothing if the underlying asset price ends up above the strike price and an amount equal to the asset price if it ends up below the strike price. The value of an asset-or-nothing put is $S_0e^{-qT}N(-d_1)$.

A regular European call option is equivalent to a long position in an asset-or-nothing call and a short position in a cash-or-nothing call where the cash payoff on the cash-or-nothing call equals the strike price. Similarly, a regular European put option is equivalent to a long position in a cash-or-nothing put and a short position in an asset-or-nothing put where the cash payoff on the cash-or-nothing put equals the strike price.

Lookback Options

The payoffs from lookback options depend on the maximum or minimum asset price reached during the life of the option. The payoff from a European-style lookback call is the amount that the final asset price exceeds the minimum asset price achieved during the life of the option. The payoff from a European-style lookback put is the amount by which the maximum asset price achieved during the life of the option exceeds the final asset price.

A lookback call is a way that the holder can buy the underlying asset at the lowest price achieved during the life of the option. Similarly, a lookback put is a way that the holder can sell the underlying asset at the highest price achieved during the life of the option. The underlying asset in a lookback option is often a commodity. The frequency with which the asset price is observed for the purposes of computing the maximum or minimum is important and must be specified in the contract.

Shout Options

A *shout option* is a European option where the holder can "shout" to the writer at one time during its life. At the end of the life of the option, the option holder receives either the usual payoff from a European option or the intrinsic value at the time of the shout, whichever is greater. Suppose the strike price is \$50 and the holder of a call shouts when the price of the underlying asset is \$60. If the final asset price is less than \$60, the holder receives a payoff of \$10. If it is greater than \$60, the holder receives the excess of the final asset price over \$50.

A shout option has some of the same features as a lookback option, but is considerably less expensive. It can be valued by noting that, if the option is shouted at a time τ when the asset price is S_τ, the payoff from the option is

$$\max(0,\ S_T - S_\tau) + (S_\tau - K)$$

where, as usual, K is the strike price and S_T is the asset price at time T. The value at time τ if the option is shouted is therefore the present value of $S_\tau - K$ plus the value of a European option with strike price S_T. This allows a binomial tree to be used to value the option.

Asian Options

Asian options are options where the payoff depends on the average price of the underlying asset during at least some part of the life of the option. The payoff from an *average price call* is $\max(0, S_{ave} - K)$ and that from an *average price put* is $\max(0, K - S_{ave})$, where S_{ave} is the average value of the underlying asset calculated over a predetermined averaging period. Average price options are less expensive than regular options and are arguably more appropriate than regular options for meeting some of the needs of corporate treasurers. Suppose that a U.S. corporate treasurer expects to receive a cash flow of 100 million Australian dollars spread evenly over the next year from the company's Australian subsidiary. The treasurer is likely to be interested in an option that guarantees that the average exchange rate realized during the year is above some level. An average price put option can achieve this more effectively than regular put options. We discussed a way binomial trees can be used to value Asian options at the end of Chapter 16.

Another type of Asian option is an average strike option. An *average strike call* pays off $\max(0, S_T - S_{ave})$ and an *average strike put* pays off $\max(0, S_{ave} - S_T)$. Average strike options can guarantee that the average price paid for an asset in frequent trading over a period of time is not greater than the final price. Alternatively, it can guarantee that the average price received for an asset in frequent trading over a period of time is not less than the final price.

Options to Exchange One Asset for Another

Options to exchange one asset for another (sometimes referred to as *exchange options*) arise in various contexts. An option to buy yen with Australian dollars is, from the point of view of a U.S. investor, an option to exchange one foreign currency asset for another foreign currency asset. A stock tender offer is an option to exchange shares in one stock for shares in another stock.

An option to obtain the better or worse of two assets is closely related to an exchange option. It is a position in one of the assets combined with an option to exchange it for the other asset:

$$\min(U_T, V_T) = V_T - \max(V_T - U_T, 0)$$

$$\max(U_T, V_T) = U_T + \max(V_T - U_T, 0)$$

Options Involving Several Assets

Options involving two or more risky assets are sometimes referred to as *rainbow options*. One example is the bond futures contract traded on the CBOT described in Chapter 6. The party with the short position is allowed to choose between a large number of different bonds when making delivery.

Probably the most common example of an option involving several assets is a *basket option*. This is an option where the payoff is dependent on the value of a portfolio (or basket) of assets. The assets are usually either individual stocks or stock indices or currencies. Basket option prices depend on both the volatilities of the assets' prices and the correlations between them. The latter are usually estimated from historical data.

20.2 MORTGAGE-BACKED SECURITIES

One feature of the United States interest rate derivatives market is the active trading in *mortgage-backed securities*. A mortgage-backed security (MBS) is created when a financial institution decides to sell part of its residential mortgage portfolio to investors. The mortgages are put into a pool and investors acquire a stake in the pool by buying units. The units are known as mortgage-backed securities. A secondary market is usually created for the units so that investors can sell them to other investors as desired. An investor who owns units representing X percent of a certain pool is entitled to X percent of the principal and interest cash flows received from the mortgages in the pool.

The mortgages in a pool are generally guaranteed by a government-related agency such as the Government National Mortgage Association (GNMA) or the Federal National Mortgage Association (FNMA), so that investors are protected against defaults. This makes an MBS sound like a regular fixed-income security issued by the government. However, there is a critical difference between an MBS and a regular fixed-income investment. The mortgages in an MBS pool have prepayment privileges and these can be quite valuable to the householder. In the United States mortgages typically last for 25 years and can be prepaid at any time. This means that the householder has a 25-year American-style option to put the mortgage back to the lender at its face value.

In practice, prepayments on mortgages occur for a variety of reasons. Sometimes interest rates have fallen and the owner of the house decides to refinance at a lower rate of interest. On other occasions a mortgage is prepaid simply because the house is being sold. A critical element in valuing an MBS is the determination of the *prepayment function*. This function describes expected prepayments on the underlying pool of mortgages at a particular time in terms of interest rates and other relevant variables.

A prepayment function is very unreliable as a predictor of actual prepayment experience for an individual mortgage. When many similar mortgage loans are combined in the same pool, there is a "law of large numbers" effect at work, and prepayments can be predicted from an analysis of historical data more accurately. As already mentioned, prepayments are not always motivated by pure interest rate considerations. Nevertheless, prepayments tend to be more likely when interest rates are low than when they are high. This means that investors should require a higher rate of interest on an MBS than on other fixed-income securities because there is a tendency for the cash received from prepayments to be reinvested at low rates.

Collateralized Mortgage Obligations

The MBSs described so far are sometimes referred to as *pass-throughs*. All investors receive the same return and bear the same prepayment risk. Not all mortgage-backed securities work in this way. In a *collateralized mortgage obligation* (CMO) the investors are divided into a number of classes, and rules are developed for determining how principal repayments are channeled to different classes.

As an example of a CMO, consider an MBS with investors divided into three classes: class A, class B, and class C. All the principal repayments (both those that are scheduled and those that are prepayments) are channeled to class A investors until investors in this class have been completely paid off. Principal repayments are then channeled to class B investors until these investors have been completely paid off. Finally, principal repayments are channeled to class C investors. In this situation class A investors bear the most prepayment risk. The class A securities can be expected to last less long than the class B securities, which in turn can be expected to last less long than the class C securities.

The objective of this type of structure is to create classes of securities that are more attractive to institutional investors than those created by the simpler pass-through MBS. The prepayment risks assumed by the different classes depend on the par value in each class. For example, class C bears very little prepayment risk if the par values in classes A, B, and C are 400, 300, and 100, respectively. It bears rather more prepayment risk if the par values in the classes are 100, 200, and 500.

IOs and POs

In a *stripped MBS*, principal payments are separated from interest payments. All principal payments are channeled to one class of security, known as a *principal only* (PO). All interest payments are channeled to another class of security, known as an *interest only* (IO). Both IOs and POs are risky investments. As prepayment rates increase, a PO becomes more valuable and an IO becomes less valuable. As prepayment rates decrease, the reverse happens. In a PO, a fixed amount of principal is returned to the investor, but the timing is uncertain. A high rate of prepayments on the underlying pool leads to the principal being received early (which is, of course, good news for the holder of the PO). A low rate of prepayments on the underlying pool delays the return of the principal and reduces the yield provided by the PO. In an IO, the total of the cash flows received by the investor is not certain. The higher the rate of prepayments, the lower the total cash flows received by the investor, and vice versa.

20.3 NONSTANDARD SWAPS

We discussed plain vanilla interest rate swaps in Chapter 7. These are agreements to exchange interest at the LIBOR rate for interest at a fixed rate. Business Snapshot 7.1 in Chapter 7 gives a confirmation for a hypothetical plain vanilla swap. In this section we describe a number of nonstandard swap agreements.[4]

Variations on the Vanilla Deal

Many interest rate swaps involve relatively minor changes being made to the plain vanilla swaps we discussed in Chapter 7. In some swaps the notional principal changes with time in a predetermined way. Swaps where the notional principal is an increasing function of time are known as *step-up swaps*. Swaps where the notional principal is a decreasing function of time are known as *amortizing swaps*. Step-up swaps could be useful for a construction company that intends to borrow increasing amounts of money at floating

[4] The valuation of many of the swaps described here is described in J. C. Hull, *Options, Futures, and Other Derivatives*, 5th edn. (Upper Saddle River, NJ: Prentice Hall, 2003), Chapters 22–24.

Business Snapshot 20.1 Hypothetical confirmation for nonstandard swap

Trade date	5-January-2004
Effective date	11-January-2004
Business day convention (all dates)	Following business day
Holiday calendar	U.S.
Termination date	11-January-2009
Fixed Amounts	
Fixed-rate payer	Microsoft
Fixed-rate notional principal	USD 100 million
Fixed-rate	6% per annum
Fixed-rate day count convention	Actual/365
Fixed-rate payment dates	Each 11-July and 11-January, commencing 11-July, 2004, up to and including 11-January, 2009
Floating Amounts	
Floating-rate payer	Goldman Sachs
Floating-rate notional principal	USD 120 million
Floating rate	USD 1 month LIBOR
Floating-rate day count convention	Actual/360
Floating-rate payment dates	11-July, 2004, and the 11th of each month thereafter, up to and including 11-January, 2009

rates to finance a particular project and wants to swap it to fixed-rate funding. An amortizing swap could be used by a company that has fixed-rate borrowings with a certain prepayment schedule and wants to swap them to borrowings at a floating rate.

The principal can be different on the two sides of a swap. Also the frequency of payment can be different. This is illustrated by the hypothetical swap between Microsoft and Goldman Sachs in Business Snapshot 20.1 where the notional principal is \$120 million on the floating side and \$100 million on fixed side. Payments are made every month on the floating side and every six months on the fixed side.

The floating reference rate for a swap is not always LIBOR. In some swaps, for instance, it is the commercial paper (CP) rate. A *basis swap* involves exchanging cash flows calculated using one floating reference rate for those calculated using another floating reference rate, for example a swap where the three-month CP rate plus 10 basis points is exchanged for three-month LIBOR with both being applied to a principal of \$100 million. A basis swap could be used for risk management by a financial institution whose assets and liabilities are dependent on different floating reference rates.

Compounding Swaps

Another variation on the plain vanilla swap is a *compounding swap*. A confirmation for a compounding swap is in Business Snapshot 20.2. In this example there is only one payment date for both the floating-rate payments and the fixed-rate payments. This is at

Business Snapshot 20.2 Hypothetical confirmation for compounding swap

Trade date	5-January-2004
Effective date	11-January-2004
Holiday calendar	U.S.
Business day convention (all dates)	Following business day
Termination date	11-January-2009
Fixed Amounts	
Fixed-rate payer	Microsoft
Fixed-rate notional principal	USD 100 million
Fixed rate	6% per annum
Fixed-rate day count convention	Actual/365
Fixed-rate payment date	11-January, 2009
Fixed-rate compounding	Applicable at 6.3%
Fixed-rate compounding dates	Each 11-July and 11-January, commencing 11-July, 2004, up to and including 11-July, 2008
Floating Amounts	
Floating-rate payer	Goldman Sachs
Floating-rate notional principal	USD 100 million
Floating rate	USD 6 month LIBOR plus 20 basis points
Floating-rate day count convention	Actual/360
Floating-rate payment date	11-January, 2009
Floating-rate compounding	Applicable at LIBOR plus 10 basis points
Floating-rate compounding dates	Each 11-July and 11-January, commencing 11-July, 2004, up to and including 11-July, 2008

the end of the life of the swap. The floating rate of interest is LIBOR plus 20 basis points. Instead of being paid, the interest is compounded forward until the end of the life of the swap at a rate of LIBOR plus 10 basis points. The fixed rate of interest is 6%. Instead of being paid this interest is compounded forward at a fixed rate of interest of 6.3% until the end of the swap.

Currency Swaps

We introduced currency swaps in Chapter 7. They enable an interest rate exposure in one currency to be swapped for an interest rate exposure in another currency. Usually two principals are specified, one in each currency. The principals are exchanged at both the beginning and the end of the life of the swap, as described in Section 7.8.

Suppose that the currencies involved in a currency swap are U.S. dollars (USD) and British pounds (GBP). In a fixed-for-fixed currency swap, a fixed rate of interest is specified in each currency. The payments on one side are determined by applying the fixed rate of interest in USD to the USD principal; the payments on the other side are determined by applying the fixed rate of interest in GBP to the GBP principal.

Another popular type of currency swap is floating-for-floating. In this the payments on one side are determined by applying USD LIBOR (possibly with a spread added) to the USD principal; similarly the payments on the other side are determined by applying GBP LIBOR (possibly with a spread added) to the GBP principal. A third type of swap is a cross-currency interest rate swap where a floating rate in one currency is exchanged for a fixed rate in another currency.

Valuation and Convexity Adjustments

In Chapter 7 we explained that plain vanilla interest rate and currency swaps can be valued by assuming that interest rates in the future will equal the corresponding forward interest rates observed in the market today. The nonstandard swaps we have discussed so far can also be valued in this way. However, the next three types of swaps that we will discuss cannot. They are valued by assuming that interest rates in the future will equal the corresponding forward interest rates observed in the market today plus an adjustment. The adjustment is known as a *convexity adjustment*.[5]

LIBOR-in-Arrears Swap

A plain vanilla interest rate swap is designed so that the floating rate of interest observed on one payment date is paid on the next payment date. An alternative instrument that is sometimes traded is a *LIBOR-in-arrears swap*. In this, the floating rate paid on a payment date equals the rate observed on the payment date itself.

CMS and CMT Swaps

A constant maturity swap (CMS) is an interest rate swap where the floating rate equals the swap rate for a swap with a certain life. For example, the floating payments on a CMS swap might be made every six months at a rate equal to the five-year swap rate. Usually there is a lag so that the payment on a particular payment date is equal to the swap rate observed on the previous payment date. Suppose that rates are set at times $t_0, t_1, t_2, \ldots$, payments are made at times $t_1, t_2, t_3, \ldots$, and L is the notional principal. The floating payment at time t_{i+1} is

$$\delta_i L s_i$$

where $\delta_i = t_{i+1} - t_i$ and s_i is the five-year swap rate at time t_i.

Differential Swaps

A *differential swap*, sometimes referred to as a *diff swap*, is an interest rate swap where a floating interest rate is observed in one currency and applied to a principal in another currency. For example, a swap might involve the payments going one way being calculated as USD LIBOR applied to a USD principal and the payments going the other way being calculated as GBP LIBOR (plus or minus a spread) being applied to the same USD principal. Diff swaps are sometimes also referred to as *quantos*.

A diff swap is a "pure interest rate play." This distinguishes it from a regular floating-for-floating currency swap. The company paying GBP in our diff swap example gains if

---

[5] For a discussion of these types of convexity adjustments, see J.C. Hull, *Options, Futures, and Other Derivatives*, 5th edn. (Upper Saddle River, NJ: Prentice Hall, 2003), Chapter 22.

Business Snapshot 20.3 Hypothetical confirmation for an equity swap

Trade date	5-January-2004
Effective date	11-January-2004
Business day convention (all dates)	Following business day
Holiday calendar	U.S.
Termination date	11-January-2009
Equity Amounts	
Equity payer	Microsoft
Equity index	Total Return S&P 500 index
Equity payment	$100(I_1 - I_0)/I_0$, where I_1 is the index level on the payment date and I_0 is the index level on the immediately preceding payment date. In the case of the first payment date, I_0 is the index level on 11 January, 2004
Equity payment dates	Each 11-July and 11-January, commencing 11-July, 2004, up to and including 11-January, 200
Floating Amounts	
Floating-rate payer	Goldman Sachs
Floating-rate notional principal	USD 100 million
Floating-rate	USD 6 month LIBOR
Floating-rate day count convention	Actual/360
Floating-rate payment dates	Each 11-July and 11-January, commencing 11-July, 2004, up to and including 11-January, 2009

GBP LIBOR decreases relative to USD LIBOR and loses if the reverse happens. The payoff from a currency swap where GBP floating is exchanged for USD floating depends on exchange-rate movements as well as on interest rate movements in the two countries.

Equity Swaps

In an equity swap one party promises to pay the return on an equity index applied to a notional principal and the other promises to pay a fixed or floating return on the notional principal. Equity swaps enable fund managers to increase or reduce their exposure to an index without buying and selling stock. An equity swap is a convenient way of packaging a series of forward contracts on an index to meet the needs of the market.

The equity index is usually a total return index where dividends are reinvested in the stocks comprising the index. A confirmation for an equity swap is in Business Snapshot 20.3. In this, Microsoft pays the six-month return on the S&P 500 to Goldman Sachs and Goldman Sachs pays six-month LIBOR to Microsoft. The principal on either side of the swap is $100 million and payments are made every six months.

Accrual Swaps

Accrual swaps are swaps where the interest on one side accrues only when the floating reference rate is within a certain range. Sometimes the range remains fixed during the entire life of the swap; sometimes it is reset periodically.

As a simple example of an accrual swap, consider a deal where a fixed rate of 6% is exchanged for three-month LIBOR every quarter. The principal is \$10 million and the fixed rate accrues only on days when three-month LIBOR is below 8% per annum. Define n_1 as the number of days in a quarter that the three-month LIBOR is below 8% and n_2 is the number of days in the year. The payment made at the end of the quarter is

$$10{,}000{,}000 \times 0.06 \times \frac{n_1}{n_2}$$

For example, when $n_1 = 25$ and $n_2 = 365$, the payment is \$41,096. In a regular swap the payment would be about $0.25 \times 0.06 \times 10{,}000{,}000$ or \$150,000.

Compared with a regular swap, the fixed-rate payer saves $10{,}000{,}000 \times 0.06/365 =$ \$1,644 for each day interest rates are above 8%. The fixed-rate payer's position can therefore be considered equivalent to a regular swap plus a series of binary options, one for each day of the life of the swap.

Cancelable Swaps

A cancelable swap is a plain vanilla interest rate swap where one side has the option to terminate on one or more payment dates. Terminating a swap is the same as entering into the offsetting (opposite) swap. Consider a swap between Microsoft and Goldman Sachs. If Microsoft has the option to cancel, it can regard the swap as a regular swap plus a long position in an option to enter into the offsetting swap. If Goldman Sachs has the cancelation option, Microsoft has a regular swap plus a short position in an option to enter into the same swap.

If there is only one termination date, a cancelable swap is the same as a regular swap plus a position in a European swap option. Consider, for example, a ten-year swap where Microsoft will receive 6% and pay LIBOR. Suppose that Microsoft has the option to terminate at the end of six years. The swap is a regular ten-year swap to receive 6% and pay LIBOR plus long position in a six-year European option to enter into a four-year swap where 6% is paid and LIBOR is received. (The latter is referred to as a 6×4 European option.) The standard market model for valuing European swap options is described in Chapter 19.

When the swap can be terminated on a number of different payment dates, it is a regular swap option plus a Bermudan-style swap option. Consider, for example, the situation where Microsoft has entered into a five-year swap with semiannual payments where 6% is received and LIBOR is paid. Suppose that the counterparty has the option to terminate on the swap on payment dates between year 2 and year 5. The swap is regular swap plus a short position in a Bermudan-style swap option where the Bermudan style swap option is an option to enter into a swap that matures in five years and involves a fixed payment at 6% being received and a floating payment at LIBOR being paid. The swap can be exercised on any payment date between year 2 and year 5.

Sometimes compounding swaps are cancelable. Typically the confirmation agreement states that on termination the floating rate payer pays the compounded value of the floating amounts up to the termination date and the fixed rate payer pays the compounded value of the fixed payments up to the termination date.

Index Amortizing Swaps

A swap that was very popular in the United States in the mid-1990s is an *index amortizing rate swap* (sometimes also called an *indexed principal swap*). With this swap, the principal reduces in a way dependent on the level of interest rates. The lower the interest rate, the greater the reduction in the principal. The fixed side of an indexed amortizing swap was originally designed to mirror, at least approximately, the return obtained by an investor from a mortgage-backed security. To an investor, the swap then has the effect exchanging the return on a mortgage-backed security for a floating-rate return.

Commodity Swaps

Commodity swaps are now becoming increasingly popular. A company that consumes 100,000 barrels of oil per year could agree to pay $2 million each year for the next 10 years and to receive in return $100{,}000S$, where S is the current market price of oil per barrel. The agreement would in effect lock in the company's oil cost at $20 per barrel. An oil producer might agree to the opposite exchange, thereby locking in the price it realized for its oil at $20 per barrel.

Other Swaps

Swaps can be engineered in many other ways. A recent innovation in swap markets is a *volatility swap*. In this the payments depend on the volatility of a stock (or other asset). Suppose that the principal is L. On each payment date, one side pays $L\sigma$, where σ is the historical volatility calculated in the usual way by taking daily observations on the stock during the immediately preceding accrual period, and the other side pays $L\sigma_K$, where σ_K is a constant prespecified volatility level. Variance swaps, correlation swaps, and covariance swaps are defined similarly.

Some swaps have payoffs that are calculated in quite bizarre ways. An example is a deal entered into between Procter & Gamble and Bankers Trust in 1993 (see Business Snapshot 20.4). The details of this transaction are in the public domain because it later became the subject of litigation.[6]

SUMMARY

Exotic options are options with rules governing the payoffs that are not as straightforward as those for standard options. They provide corporate treasurers and fund managers with a wide range of alternatives for achieving their objectives. Some exotic options are nothing more than portfolios of regular European and American calls and puts. Others are much more complicated.

Mortgage-backed securities are created when a financial institution decides to sell part of its residential portfolio of mortgages to investors. The mortgages are put in a

[6] See D. J. Smith, "Aggressive Corporate Finance: A Close Look at the Procter and Gamble–Bankers Trust Leveraged Swap," *Journal of Derivatives* 4, No. 4 (Summer 1997): 67–79.

Business Snapshot 20.4 Procter & Gamble's bizarre deal

A particularly bizarre swap is the so-called "5/30" swap entered into between Bankers Trust (BT) and Procter & Gamble (P&G) on November 2, 1993. This was a five-year swap with semiannual payments. The notional principal was $200 million. BT paid P&G 5.30% per annum. P&G paid BT the average 30-day commercial paper (CP) rate minus 75 basis points plus a spread. The average CP rate was calculated by taking observations on the 30-day CP rate each day during the preceding accrual period and averaging them.

The spread was zero for the first payment date (May 2, 1994). For the remaining nine payment dates, it was

$$\max\left[0, \frac{98.5\left(\dfrac{5\,\text{yr CMT\%}}{5.78\%}\right) - (30\,\text{yr TSY price})}{100}\right]$$

In this expression, five-year CMT is the constant maturity Treasury yield (i.e., the yield on a five-year Treasury note, as reported by the Federal Reserve). The 30-year TSY price is the midpoint of the bid and offer cash bond prices for the 6.25% Treasury bond maturing on August 2023. Note that the spread calculated from the formula is a decimal interest rate. It is not measured in basis points. If the formula gives 0.1 and the CP rate is 6%, the rate paid by P&G is 15.25%.

P&G were hoping that the spread would be zero and the deal would enable them to exchange fixed-rate funding at 5.30% for funding at 75 basis points less than the commercial paper rate. In fact, interest rates rose sharply in early 1994, bond prices fell, and the swap proved very, very expensive. (See Problem 20.20.)

pool and investors acquire a stake in the pool by buying units. The mortgages are guaranteed against defaults by a government agency, but investors are subject to prepayment risk. Often the return from a pool of mortgages is split into a number of components with different properties in an attempt to meet the needs of different types of investors.

Swaps have proved to be very versatile financial instruments, and many variations on the plain vanilla fixed-for-floating deal now exist. Some such as step-up swaps, amortizing swaps, compounding swaps, LIBOR in arrears swaps, diff swaps, and CMS/CMT swaps involve changes to the way payments are calculated or their timing. Others such as accrual swaps and cancelable swaps have embedded options.

FURTHER READING

Boyle, P. P., and S. H. Lau. "Bumping Up against the Barrier with the Binomial Method," *Journal of Derivatives*, 1, 4 (Summer 1994): 6–14.

Broadie, M., P. Glasserman, and S. G. Kou. "A Continuity Correction for Discrete Barrier Options," *Mathematical Finance*, 7, 4 (October 1997): 325–49.

Broadie, M., P. Glasserman, and S. G. Kou. "Connecting Discrete and Continuous Path-Dependent Options," *Finance and Stochastics*, 2 (1998): 1–28.

Chance, D., and D. Rich. "The Pricing of Equity Swap and Swaptions," *Journal of Derivatives*, 5, 4 (Summer 1998): 19–31.

Clewlow, L., and C. Strickland. *Exotic Options: The State of the Art*. London: Thomson Business Press, 1997.

Conze, A., and S. Viswanathan. "Path Dependent Options: The Case of Lookback Options," *Journal of Finance*, 46 (1991): 1893–1907.

Demeterfi, K., E. Derman, M. Kamal, and J. Zou. "A Guide to Volatility and Variance Swaps," *Journal of Derivatives*, 6, 4 (Summer 1999): 9–32.

Forster, D. M. "The State of the Law after Procter & Gamble vs Bankers Trust," *Derivatives Quarterly*, 3, 2 (1996): 8–17.

Geske, R. "The Valuation of Compound Options," *Journal of Financial Economics*, 7 (1979): 63–81.

Goldman B., H. Sosin, and M. A. Gatto. "Path Dependent Options: Buy at the Low, Sell at the High," *Journal of Finance*, 34 (December 1979): 1111–27.

Hull, J. C. *Options, Futures, and Other Derivatives*, 5th edn., Upper Saddle River, NJ: Prentice Hall, 2003.

Hull, J. C., and A. White. "Efficient Procedures for Valuing European and American Path-Dependent Options," *Journal of Derivatives*, (Fall 1993): 21–31.

Laatch, F. E. "Tax Clienteles, Arbitrage, and the Pricing of Total Return Swaps," *Journal of Derivatives*, 8, 2 (Winter 2000): 37–46.

Margrabe, W. "The Value of an Option to Exchange One Asset for Another," *Journal of Finance*, 33 (March 1978): 177–86.

Rubinstein, M. "Pay Now, Choose Later," *RISK* (February 1991).

Rubinstein, M. "Options for the Undecided," *RISK* (April 1991).

Rubinstein, M. "Two in One," *RISK* (May 1991).

Rubinstein, M. "One for Another," *RISK* (July/August 1991).

Rubinstein, M. "Somewhere Over the Rainbow." *RISK* (November 1991).

Rubinstein, M. "Double Trouble," *RISK* (December 1991 / January 1992).

Rubinstein, M., and E. Reiner. "Breaking Down the Barriers," *RISK*, (September 1991).

Rubinstein, M., and E. Reiner. "Unscrambling the Binary Code," *RISK* (October 1991).

Smith D. J. "Aggressive Corporate Finance: A Close Look at the Procter and Gamble–Bankers Trust Leveraged Swap," *Journal of Derivatives*, 4, 4 (Summer 1997): 67–79.

Stulz, R. "Options on the Minimum or Maximum of Two Assets," *Journal of Financial Economics*, 10 (1982): 161–85.

Turnbull, S. M., and L. M. Wakeman. "A Quick Algorithm for Pricing European Average Options," *Journal of Financial and Quantitative Analysis*, 26 (September 1991): 377–89.

Zhang, P. G. Exotic Options: A Guide to Second Generation Options, 2nd edn., World Scientific, Singapore, 1998.

Quiz (Answers at End of Book)

20.1. Explain the difference between a forward start option and a chooser option.

20.2. What is the value of a cash-or-nothing call that promises to pay \$100 if the price of a non-dividend-paying stock is above \$50 in three months. The current stock price is \$50, the risk-free rate is 4%, and the stock price volatility is 20%.

20.3. List eight types of barrier options.

20.4. How does an equity swap work?

20.5. Explain why IOs and POs have opposite sensitivities to the rate of prepayments.

20.6. Explain the relationship between a cancelable swap and a swap option.

20.7. The Canadian dollar LIBOR rate is 2% higher than the U.S. LIBOR rate for all maturities. A trader thinks that the spread between three-month U.S. LIBOR and three-month Canadian LIBOR will widen, but is unsure about how the exchange rate between the U.S. dollar and Canadian dollar will move. Explain how the trader could use a diff swap. Why would the trader prefer a diff swap to a floating-for-floating currency swap?

Questions and Problems (Answers in Solutions Manual/Study Guide)

20.8. Describe the payoff from a portfolio consisting of a lookback call and a lookback put with the same maturity.

20.9. Consider a chooser option where the holder has the right to choose between a European call and a European put at any time during a two-year period. The maturity dates and strike prices for the calls and puts are the same regardless of when the choice is made. Is it ever optimal to make the choice before the end of the two-year period? Explain your answer.

20.10. Suppose that c_1 and p_1 are the prices of a European average price call and a European average price put with strike price K and maturity T, c_2 and p_2 are the prices of a European average strike call and European average strike put with maturity T, and c_3 and p_3 are the prices of a regular European call and a regular European put with strike price K and maturity T. Show that

$$c_1 + c_2 - c_3 = p_1 + p_2 - p_3$$

20.11. The text derives a decomposition of a particular type of chooser option into a call maturing at time t_2 and a put maturing at time t_1. By using put–call parity to obtain an expression for c instead of p, derive an alternative decomposition into a call maturing at time t_1 and a put maturing at time t_2.

20.12. Explain why a down-and-out put is worth zero when the barrier is greater than the strike price.

20.13. Prove that an at-the-money forward start option on a non-dividend-paying stock that will start in three years and mature in five years is worth the same as a two-year at-the-money option starting today.

20.14. Suppose that the strike price of an American call option on a non-dividend-paying stock grows at rate g. Show that if g is less than the risk-free rate, r, it is never optimal to exercise the call early.

20.15. Answer the following questions about compound options:

a. What put–call parity relationship exists between the price of a European call on a call and a European put on a call?

b. What put–call parity relationship exists between the price of a European call on a put and a European put on a put?

20.16. Does a lookback call become more valuable or less valuable as we increase the frequency with which we observe the asset price in calculating the minimum?

20.17. Does a down-and-out call become more valuable or less valuable as we increase the frequency with which we observe the asset price in determining whether the barrier has been crossed? What is the answer to the same question for a down-and-in call?

20.18. Explain why a regular European call option is the sum of a down-and-out European call and a down-and-in European call.

20.19. What is the value of a derivative that pays off $100 in six months if the S&P 500 index is greater than 1,000 and zero otherwise. Assume that the current level of the index is 960, the risk-free rate is 8% per annum, the dividend yield on the index is 3% per annum, and the volatility of the index is 20%.

20.20. Estimate the interest rate paid by P&G on the 5/30 swap in Business Snapshot 20.4 if (a) the CP rate is 6.5% and the Treasury yield curve is flat at 6% and (b) the CP rate is 7.5% and the Treasury yield curve is flat at 7%.

Assignment Questions

20.21. Use DerivaGem to calculate the value of:

a. A regular European call option on a non-dividend-paying stock where the stock price is $50, the strike price is $50, the risk-free rate is 5% per annum, the volatility is 30%, and the time to maturity is one year

b. A down-and-out European call which is as in (a) with the barrier at $45

c. A down-and-in European call which is as in (a) with the barrier at $45

Show that the option in (a) is worth the sum of the values of the options in (b) and (c).

20.22. What is the value in dollars of a derivative that pays off £10,000 in one year provided that the dollar–sterling exchange rate is greater than 1.5000 at that time? The current exchange rate is 1.4800. The dollar and sterling interest rates are 4% and 8% per annum, respectively. The volatility of the exchange rate is 12% per annum.

20.23. Consider an up-and-out barrier call option on a non-dividend-paying stock when the stock price is 50, the strike price is 50, the volatility is 30%, the risk-free rate is 5%, the time to maturity is one year, and the barrier is 80. Use DerivaGem to value the option and graph the relationship between (a) the option price and the stock price, (b) the option price and the time to maturity, and (c) the option price and the volatility. Provide an intuitive explanation for the results you get. Show that the delta, theta, and vega for an up-and-out barrier call option can be either positive or negative.

20.24. Suppose that the LIBOR zero rate is flat at 5% with annual compounding. In a five-year swap, company X pays a fixed rate of 6% and receives LIBOR annually on a principal of $100 million. The volatility of the two-year swap rate in three years is 20%.

a. What is the value of the swap?

b. Use DerivaGem to calculate the value of the swap if company X has the option to cancel after three years.

c. Use DerivaGem to calculate the value of the swap if the counterparty has the option to cancel after three years.

d. What is the value of the swap if either side can cancel at the end of three years?

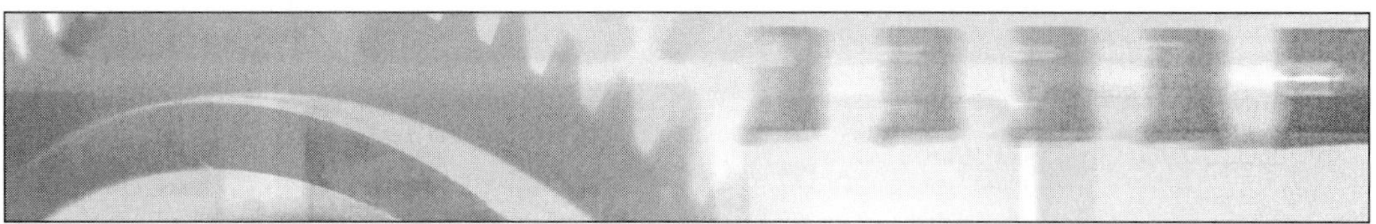

CHAPTER 21 Credit Derivatives

One of the most exciting developments in derivatives markets in recent years has been the growth of the credit derivatives market. In 2000 the total notional principal for outstanding credit derivatives contracts was about $800 billion. By 2002 this had grown to $2 trillion. Credit derivatives are contracts where the payoff depends on the creditworthiness of one or more commercial or sovereign entities. In this chapter we explain how credit derivatives work and discuss some valuation issues.

Credit derivatives allow companies to trade credit risks in much the same way that they trade market risks. Banks and other financial institutions used to be in the position where they could do little once they had assumed a credit risk except wait (and hope for the best). Now they can actively manage their portfolios of credit risks, keeping some and entering into credit derivatives contracts to protect themselves from others. Since the late 1990s banks have been the biggest buyers of credit protection and insurance companies have been the biggest sellers, as indicated in Business Snapshot 21.1.

21.1 CREDIT DEFAULT SWAPS

The most popular credit derivative is a *credit default swap* (CDS). This is a contract that provides insurance against the risk of a default by particular company. The company is known as the *reference entity* and a default by the company is known as a *credit event*. The buyer of the insurance obtains the right to sell bonds issued by the company for their face value when a credit event occurs and the seller of the insurance agrees to buy the bonds for their face value when a credit event occurs.[1] The total face value of the bonds that can be sold is known as the credit default swap's *notional principal*.

The buyer of the CDS makes periodic payments to the seller until the end of the life of the CDS or until a credit event occurs. These payments are typically made in arrears every quarter, every half year, or every year. The settlement in the event of a default involves either physical delivery of the bonds or a cash payment.

An example will help to illustrate how a typical deal is structured. Suppose that two parties enter into a five-year credit default swap on March 1, 2004. Assume that the

[1] The face value (or par value) of a bond is the principal amount that the issuer will repay at maturity if it does not default.

Business Snapshot 21.1 Who bears the credit risk?

Traditionally banks have been in the business of making loans and then bearing the credit risk that the borrower will default. But this is changing. Banks have for some time been reluctant to keep loans on their balance sheets. This is because, after the capital required by regulators has been accounted for, the average return earned on loans is often less attractive than that on other assets. During the 1990s banks created asset-backed securities (similar to the mortgage-backed securities discussed in Section 20.2) to pass loans (and their credit risk) on to investors. In the late 1990s and early 2000s banks have made extensive use of credit derivatives to shift the credit risk in their loans to other parts of the financial system.

If banks have been net buyers of credit protection, who have been net sellers? The answer is insurance companies. Insurance companies are not regulated in the same way as banks and tend to look at credit risks from an actuarial perspective rather than a capital markets perspective. As a result they are more willing to bear the risks than banks.

The result of all this is that the financial institution bearing the credit risk of a loan is often different from the financial institution that did the original credit checks. Whether this proves to be good for the overall health of the financial system remains to be seen.

notional principal is $100 million and the buyer agrees to pay 90 basis points annually for protection against default by the reference entity.

The CDS is shown in Figure 21.1. If the reference entity does not default (i.e., there is no credit event), the buyer receives no payoff and pays $900,000 on March 1 of each of the years 2005, 2006, 2007, 2008, and 2009. If there is a credit event a substantial payoff is likely. Suppose that the buyer notifies the seller of a credit event on June 1, 2007 (a quarter of the way into the fourth year). If the contract specifies physical settlement, the buyer has the right to sell bonds issued by the reference entity with a face value of $100 million for $100 million. If the contract requires cash settlement, an independent calculation agent will poll dealers to determine the mid-market value of the cheapest deliverable bond a predesignated number of days after the credit event. Suppose this bond is worth $35 per $100 of face value. The cash payoff would be $65 million.

The regular quarterly, semiannual, or annual payments from the buyer of protection to the seller of protection cease when there is a credit event. However, because these payments are made in arrears, a final accrual payment by the buyer is required. In our example, the buyer would be required to pay to the seller the amount of the annual payment accrued between March 1, 2007, and June 1, 2007 (approximately $225,000), but no further payments would be required.

Figure 21.1 Credit default swap

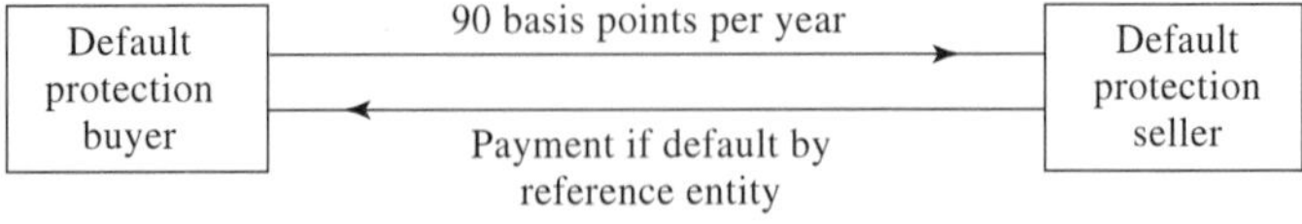

The total amount paid per year as a percentage of the notional principal to buy protection is known as the *CDS spread*. Several large banks are market makers in the credit default swap market. When quoting on a new five-year credit default swap on Ford Motor Credit, a market maker might bid 250 basis points and offer 270 basis points. This means that the market maker is prepared to buy protection on Ford by paying 250 basis points per year (i.e., 2.5% of the principal per year) and to sell protection on Ford for 270 basis points per year (i.e., 2.7% of the principal per year).

Recovery Rate

When a company goes bankrupt, those that are owed money by the company file claims against the assets of the company. Sometimes there is a reorganization in which these creditors agree to a partial payment of their claims. In other cases the assets are sold by the liquidator and the proceeds are used to meet the claims as far as possible. Some claims typically have priorities over other claims and are met more fully.

The recovery rate for a bond is normally defined as the bond's value immediately after a default, as a percent of its face value. Table 21.1 provides historical data on recovery rates for different categories of bonds in the United States. It shows that senior secured debtholders had an average recovery rate of 53.1 cents per dollar of face value while junior subordinated debtholders had an average recovery rate of only 23.6 cents per dollar of face value.

Given the way recovery rate is defined the payoff from a CDS can be expressed in terms of the recovery rate. It is $L(1 - R)$, where L is the notional principal and R is the recovery rate.

Credit Default Swaps and Bond Yields

A CDS can be used to hedge a position in a corporate bond. Suppose that an investor buys a five-year corporate bond yielding 7% per year for its face value and at the same time enters into a five-year CDS to buy protection against the issuer of the bond defaulting. Suppose that the CDS spread is 2% per annum. The effect of the CDS is to convert the corporate bond to a risk-free bond (at least approximately). If the bond issuer does not default the investor earns 5% per year (when the CDS spread is netted against the corporate bond yield). If the bond does default the investor earns 5% up to

Table 21.1 Recovery rates on corporate bonds as a percent of face value, 1982–2002 (*Source*: Moody's)

Class	*Average recovery rate (%)*
Senior secured	53.1
Senior unsecured	37.4
Senior subordinated	32.0
Subordinated	30.4
Junior subordinated	23.6

Table 21.2 Unconditional default probabilities and survival probabilities

Time (years)	*Default probability*	*Survival probability*
1	0.0200	0.9800
2	0.0196	0.9604
3	0.0192	0.9412
4	0.0188	0.9224
5	0.0184	0.9039

the time of the default. Under the terms of the CDS the investor is then able to exchange the bond for its face value. This face value can be invested at the risk-free rate for the remainder of the five years.

The n-year CDS spread should be approximately equal to the excess of the par yield on an n-year corporate bond over the par yield on an n-year risk-free bond. If it is markedly less than this, an investor can earn more than the risk-free rate by buying the corporate bond and buying protection. If it is markedly greater than this, an investor can borrow at less than the risk-free rate by shorting the corporate bond and selling CDS protection. These are not perfect arbitrages, but they do give a guide to the relationship between CDS spreads and bond yields. Note that the relevant risk-free rate is a LIBOR rate, not a Treasury rate.[2]

Determining CDS Spreads

Mid-market CDS spreads (i.e., the average of the bid and offer CDS spreads quoted by brokers) are in practice calculated from default probability estimates. We will illustrate how this is done with a simple example.

Table 21.3 Calculation of the present value of expected payments. Payment = s per annum

Time (years)	*Probability of survival*	*Expected payment*	*Discount factor*	*PV of expected payment*
1	0.9800	0.9800s	0.9512	0.9322s
2	0.9604	0.9604s	0.9048	0.8690s
3	0.9412	0.9412s	0.8607	0.8101s
4	0.9224	0.9224s	0.8187	0.7552s
5	0.9039	0.9039s	0.7788	0.7040s
Total				4.0704s

[2] For a discussion of this, see J. Hull, M. Predescu, and A. White, "The Relationship between Credit Default Swap Spreads, Bond Yields, and Credit Rating Announcements," *Journal of Banking and Finance*, forthcoming.

Table 21.4 Calculation of the present value of expected payoff. Notional principal = $1

Time (years)	*Probability of default*	*Recovery rate*	*Expected payoff ($)*	*Discount factor*	*PV of expected payoff ($)*
0.5	0.0200	0.4	0.0120	0.9753	0.0117
1.5	0.0196	0.4	0.0118	0.9277	0.0109
2.5	0.0192	0.4	0.0115	0.8825	0.0102
3.5	0.0188	0.4	0.0113	0.8395	0.0095
4.5	0.0184	0.4	0.0111	0.7985	0.0088
Total					0.0511

Suppose that the probability of a reference entity defaulting during a year conditional on no earlier default is 2%.[3] Table 21.2 shows survival probabilities and unconditional default probabilities (that is default probabilities as seen at time zero) for each of the five years. The probability of a default during the first year is 0.02 and the probability the reference entity will survive until the end of the first year is 0.98. The probability of a default during the second year is $0.02 \times 0.98 = 0.0196$ and the probability of survival until the end of the second year is $0.98 \times 0.98 = 0.9604$. The probability of default during the third year is $0.02 \times 0.9604 = 0.0192$, and so on.

We will assume that defaults always happen halfway through a year and that payments on the credit default swap are made once a year, at the end of each year. We also assume that the risk-free (LIBOR) interest rate is 5% per annum with continuous compounding and the recovery rate is 40%. There are three parts to the calculation. These are shown in Tables 21.3, 21.4, and 21.5.

Table 21.3 shows the calculation of the expected present value of the payments made on the CDS assuming that they are made at the rate of s per year and the notional principal is $1. For example, there is a 0.9412 probability that the third payment of s is made. The expected payment is therefore $0.9412s$ and its present value is $0.9412se^{-0.05\times 3} = 0.8101s$. The total present value of the expected payments is $4.0704s$.

Table 21.5 Calculation of the present value of accrual payment

Time (years)	*Probability of default*	*Expected accrual payment*	*Discount factor*	*PV of expected accrual payment*
0.5	0.0200	$0.0100s$	0.9753	$0.0097s$
1.5	0.0196	$0.0098s$	0.9277	$0.0091s$
2.5	0.0192	$0.0096s$	0.8825	$0.0085s$
3.5	0.0188	$0.0094s$	0.8395	$0.0079s$
4.5	0.0184	$0.0092s$	0.7985	$0.0074s$
Total				$0.0426s$

[3] Conditional default probabilities are known as hazard rates. The hazard rate is here expressed with annual compounding.

Table 21.4 shows the calculation of the expected present value of the payoff assuming a notional principal of \$1. As mentioned earlier, we are assuming that defaults always happen halfway through a year. For example, there is a 0.0192 probability of a payoff halfway through the third year. Given that the recovery rate is 40% the expected payoff at this time is $0.0192 \times 0.6 \times 1 = 0.0115$. The present value of the expected payoff is $0.0115e^{-0.05\times 2.5} = 0.0102$. The total present value of the expected payoffs is \$0.0511.

As a final step we evaluate in Table 21.5 the accrual payment made in the event of a default. For example, there is a 0.0192 probability that there will be a final accrual payment halfway through the third year. The accrual payment is $0.5s$. The expected accrual payment at this time is therefore $0.0192 \times 0.5s = 0.0096s$. Its present value is $0.0096se^{-0.05\times 2.5} = 0.0085s$. The total present value of the expected accrual payments is $0.0426s$.

From Tables 21.2 and 21.4 the present value of the expected payments is

$$4.0704s + 0.0426s = 4.1130s$$

From Table 21.3, the present value of the expected payoff is 0.0511. Equating the two, the CDS spread for a new CDS is given by

$$4.1130s = 0.0511$$

or $s = 0.0124$. The mid-market spread should be 0.0124 times the principal or 124 basis points per year. This example is designed to illustrate the method of calculation. In practice, we are likely to find that calculations are more extensive than those in Table 21.3 to 21.5 because (a) payments are often made more frequently than once a year and (b) we might want to assume that defaults can happen more frequently than once a year.

Valuing a CDS

If the credit default swap in our example had been negotiated some time ago for a spread of 150 basis points, the present value of the payments by the buyer would be $4.1130 \times 0.0150 = 0.0617$ and the present value of the payoff would be 0.0511, as above. The value of the swap to the seller would therefore be $0.0617 - 0.0511$, or 0.0106 times the principal. Similarly the value of the swap to the buyer of protection would be -0.0106 times the principal.

Default Probabilities

The key parameters necessary to value credit default swaps are default probabilities. In practice these are frequently implied from the prices of actively traded CDSs and then used to price less actively traded CDSs. They are also sometimes implied from bond prices.

Suppose that we change the example in Tables 21.3, 21.4 and 21.5 so that we do not know the default probabilities. Instead we know that the mid-market CDS spread for a newly issued five-year CDS is 100 basis points per year. We can reverse engineer our calculations to conclude that the implied default probability per year (conditional on no earlier default) is 1.61% per year.[4]

[4] Ideally we would like to estimate a different default probability for each year instead of a single hazard rate. We could do this if we had spreads for 1-, 2-, 3-, 4-, and 5-year CDS swaps or bond prices.

Using either quoted CDS spreads or quoted bond prices to estimate implied default probabilities requires an estimate of the recovery rate. The same recovery rate is typically used to (a) estimate implied default probabilities and (b) value credit default swaps. The net result of this is the value of a CDS (or the estimate of a CDS spread) is not very sensitive to the recovery rate. This is because implied probabilities of default are approximately proportional to $1/(1-R)$ and the payoffs from a CDS are proportional to $1-R$, so that the expected payoff is almost independent of R.

The default probabilities implied from CDS spreads or bond prices are *risk-neutral default probabilities*. These are the correct default probabilities to use when valuing a credit derivative.[5] It is tempting to estimate default probabilities from the historical data on defaults provided by rating agencies. However, the latter are *actuarial default probabilities* and are not correct for valuing derivatives. Risk-neutral default probabilities are markedly higher than actuarial default probabilities.[6]

Why are actuarial default probabilities inappropriate for valuing credit derivatives? A financial institution that sells credit protection is exposing itself to some systematic (nondiversifiable) risk. When the economy does badly more companies default and payoffs on CDSs increase. The financial institution needs to base its premiums on more than actuarial default probabilities in order to be adequately compensated for bearing this systematic risk.

Binary Credit Default Swaps

A binary credit default swap is structured similarly to a regular credit default swap except that the payoff is a fixed dollar amount. Suppose that, in the example we have considered in Tables 21.2 to 21.5, the payoff is \$1, instead of $1-R$ dollars and the swap spread is s. Tables 21.2, 21.3, and 21.5 are the same. Table 21.4 is replaced by Table 21.6. The CDS spread for a new binary CDS is given by

$$4.1130s = 0.0852$$

so that the CDS spread, s, is 0.0207 or 207 basis points.

Table 21.6 Calculation of the present value of expected payoff from a binary credit default swap. Principal = \$1

Time (years)	*Probability of default*	*Expected payoff (\$)*	*Discount factor*	*PV of expected payoff (\$)*
0.5	0.0200	0.0200	0.9753	0.0195
1.5	0.0196	0.0196	0.9277	0.0182
2.5	0.0192	0.0192	0.8825	0.0170
3.5	0.0188	0.0188	0.8395	0.0158
4.5	0.0184	0.0184	0.7985	0.0147
Total				0.0852

[5] This is because we are using risk-neutral valuation to value the CDS. We estimate expected cash flows in a risk-neutral world and discount them at the risk-free rate.

[6] As mentioned in Business Snapshot 21.1, this may be one reason why insurance companies, which are comfortable using actuarial probabilities, find it attractive to sell protection.

In the case of a regular CDS we pointed out that there is very little sensitivity to the recovery rate provided the same recovery rate is used to estimate default probabilities and to value the CDS. The same is not true of a binary CDS.

Basket Credit Default Swaps

In a *basket credit default swap*, there are a number of reference entities. An *add-up basket* CDS provides a payoff when any of the reference entities default. It is equivalent to a portfolio of credit default swaps, one on each reference entity. A *first-to-default* CDS provides a payoff only when the first default occurs. A *second-to-default* CDS provides a payoff only when the second default occurs. More generally, an *nth-to-default* CDS provides a payoff only when the nth default occurs. Payoffs are calculated in the same way as for a regular CDS. After the relevant default has occurred, there is a settlement. The swap then terminates and there are no further payments by either party.

The default correlation between two companies is a measure of their tendency to default at about the same time. An nth-to-default swaps is more complicated to value than a regular credit default swaps because it depends on the default correlation between the reference entities in the basket. For example, the higher the default correlation, the lower the CDS spread on a first-to-default swap.

The Future of the CDS Market

The market for credit default swaps has grown rapidly in the late 1990s and early 2000s. Credit default swaps account for about 70% of all credit derivatives. They have become important tools for managing credit risk. A financial institution can reduce its credit exposure to particular companies by buying protection. It can also use CDSs to diversify credit risk. For example, if a financial institution has too much credit exposure to a particular business sector, it can buy protection against defaults by companies in the sector and at the same time sell protection against default by companies in other unrelated sectors.

Some people think the CDS market's growth will continue and that it will be as big as the interest rate swap market by 2010. Others are less optimistic. As pointed out in Business Snapshot 21.2, there is a potential asymmetric information problem in the CDS market that is not present in other over-the-counter derivatives markets.

We now move on to consider other credit derivatives.

21.2 TOTAL RETURN SWAPS

A *total return swap* is an agreement to exchange the total return on a bond (or any portfolio of assets) for LIBOR plus a spread. The total return includes coupons, interest, and the gain or loss on the asset over the life of the swap.

An example of a total return swap is a five-year agreement with a notional principal of \$100 million to exchange the total return on a corporate bond for LIBOR plus 25 basis points. This is illustrated in Figure 21.2. On coupon payment dates the payer pays the coupons earned on an investment of \$100 million in the bond. The receiver pays interest at a rate of LIBOR plus 25 basis points on a principal of \$100 million. (LIBOR is set on one coupon date and paid on the next as in a plain vanilla interest rate

Business Snapshot 21.2 Is the CDS market a fair game?

There is one important difference between credit default swaps and the other over-the-counter derivatives that we have considered in this book. The other over-the-counter derivatives depend on interest rates, exchange rates, equity indices, commodity prices, and so on. There is no reason to assume that any one market participant has better information than other market participants about these variables.

Credit default swaps spreads depend on the probability that a particular company will default during a particular period of time. Arguably some market participants have more information to estimate this probability than others. A financial institution that works closely with a particular company by providing advice, making loans, and handling new issues of securities is likely to have more information about the creditworthiness of the company than another financial institution that has no dealings with the company. Economists refer to this as an *asymmetric information* problem.

Whether asymmetric information will curtail the expansion of the credit default swap market remains to be seen. Financial institutions emphasize that the decision to buy protection against the risk of default by a company is normally made by a risk manager and is not based on any special information that many exist elsewhere in the financial institution about the company.

swap.) At the end of the life of the swap, there is a payment reflecting the change in value of the bond. For example, if the bond increases in value by 10% over the life of the swap, the payer is required to pay $10 million (= 10% of $100 million) at the end of the five years. Similarly, if the bond decreases in value by 15%, the receiver is required to pay $15 million at the end of the five years. If there is a default on the bond, the swap is usually terminated and the receiver makes a final payment equal to the excess of $100 million over the market value of the bond.

If we add the notional principal to both sides at the end of the life of the swap, we can characterize the total return swap as follows. The payer pays the cash flows on an investment of $100 million in the 5% corporate bond. The receiver pays the cash flows on a $100 million bond paying LIBOR plus 25 basis points. If the payer owns the bond, the total return swap allows it to pass the credit risk on the bond to the receiver. If it does not own the bond the total return swap allows it to take a short position in the bond.

Total return swaps are often used as a financing tool. One scenario that could lead to the swap in Figure 21.2 is as follows. The receiver wants financing to invest $100 million in the reference bond. It approaches the payer (which is likely to be a financial institution) and agrees to the swap. The payer then invests $100 million in the

Figure 21.2 Total return swap

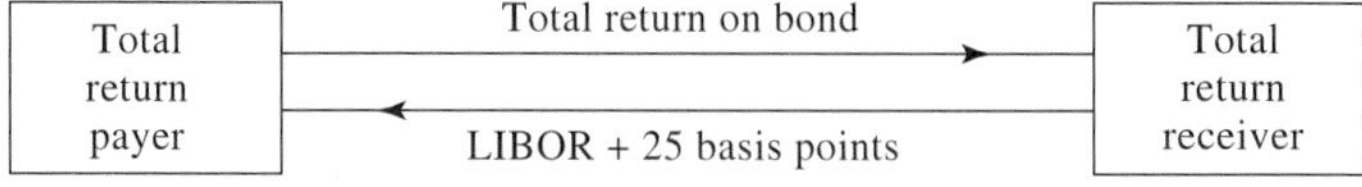

bond. This leaves the receiver in the same position as it would have been if it had borrowed money at LIBOR plus 25 basis points to buy the bond. The payer retains ownership of the bond for the life of the swap and faces less credit risk than it would have done if it had lent money to the receiver to finance the purchase of the bond, with the bond being used as collateral for the loan. If the receiver defaults, the payer does not have the legal problems of trying to realize on its collateral. Total return swaps are similar to repos (see Section 4.1) in that they are structured to minimize credit risk when securities are being financed.

The spread over LIBOR received by the payer is compensation for bearing the risk that the receiver will default. The payer will lose money if the receiver defaults at a time when the reference bond's price has declined. The spread therefore depends on the credit quality of the receiver, the credit quality of the bond issuer, and the default correlation between the two.

There are a number of variations on the standard deal we have described. Sometimes, instead of there being a cash payment for the change in value of the bond, there is physical settlement where the payer exchanges the underlying asset for the notional principal at the end of the life of the swap. Sometimes the change-in-value payments are made periodically rather than all at the end. The swap then has similarities to an equity swap (see Section 20.3).

21.3 CDS FORWARDS AND OPTIONS

A forward credit default swap is the obligation to buy or sell a particular credit default swap on a particular reference entity at a particular future time T. If the reference entity defaults before time T, the forward contract ceases to exist. Thus a bank could enter into a forward contract to sell five-year protection on Ford Motor Credit for 280 basis points starting in one year. If Ford defaults during the next year the bank's obligation under the forward contract ceases to exist.

A credit default swap option is an option to buy or sell a particular credit default swap on a particular reference entity at a particular future time T. For example, an investor could negotiate the right to buy five-year protection on Ford Motor Credit starting in one year for 280 basis points. This is a call option. If the five-year CDS spread for Ford in one year turns out to be more than 280 basis points the option will be exercised; otherwise it will not be exercised. The cost of the option would be paid up front. Similarly an investor might negotiate the right to sell five-year protection on Ford Motor Credit for 280 basis points starting in one year. This is a put option. If the five-year CDS spread for Ford in one year turns out to be less than 280 basis points the option will be exercised; otherwise it will not be exercised. Again the cost of the option would be paid up front. Like CDS forwards, CDS options are usually structured so that they will cease to exist if the reference entity defaults before option maturity.

An option contract that has become popular in the credit derivatives market is a call option on a basket of reference entities. If there are m reference entities in the basket that have not defaulted by the option maturity, the option gives the holder the right to buy a portfolio of CDSs on the names for mK basis points, where K is the strike price. In addition the holder gets the usual CDS payoff on any reference entities that do default during the life of the contract.

21.4 COLLATERALIZED DEBT OBLIGATIONS

A collateralized debt obligation (CDO) is a way of creating securities with widely different risk characteristics from a portfolio of debt instruments. An example is shown in Figure 21.3. In this example, four types of securities (or tranches) are created from a portfolio of bonds. The first tranche has 5% of the total bond principal and absorbs all credit losses from the portfolio during the life of the CDO until they have reached 5% of the total bond principal. The second tranche has 10% of the principal and absorbs all losses during the life of the CDO in excess of 5% of the principal up to a maximum of 15% of the principal. The third tranche has 10% of the principal and absorbs all losses in excess of 15% of the principal up to a maximum of 25% of the principal. The fourth tranche has 75% of the principal absorbs all losses in excess of 25% of the principal. The yields in Figure 21.3 are the rates of interest paid to tranche holders. These rates are paid on the balance of the principal remaining in the tranche after losses have been paid. Consider tranche 1. Initially the return of 35% is paid on the whole amount invested by the tranche 1 holders. But after losses equal to 1% of the total bond principal have been experienced, tranche 1 holders have lost 20% of their investment and the return is paid on only 80% of the original amount invested. Tranche 1 is sometimes referred to as toxic waste. A default loss of 2.5% on the bond portfolio translates into a loss of 50% of the tranche's principal. Tranche 4 by contrast is usually given an Aaa rating. Defaults on the bond portfolio must exceed 25% before the holders of this tranche are responsible for any credit losses.

The creator of the CDO normally retains tranche 1 and sells the remaining tranches in the market. A CDO provides a way of creating high quality debt from average quality (or even low quality) debt. The risk to the purchaser of tranches 2, 3, or 4 depends on

Figure 21.3 Collateralized debt obligation

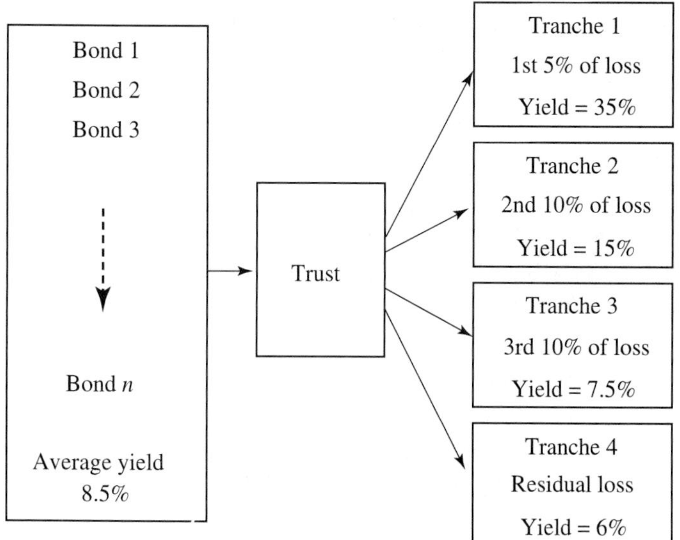

the default correlation between the issuers of the debt instruments in the portfolio. The lower the correlation the more highly tranches 2, 3, and 4 will be rated.

Synthetic CDOs

The CDO in Figure 21.3 is referred to as a cash CDO. An alternative structure is a synthetic CDO where the creator of the CDO sells a portfolio of credit default swaps to third parties. It then passes on the default risk to the synthetic CDO's tranche holders. Analogously to Figure 21.3 the first tranche might be responsible for the payoffs on the credit default swaps until they have reached 5% of the total notional principal; the second tranche might be responsible for the payoffs between 5% and 15% of the total notional principal; and so on. The income from the credit default swaps is distributed to the tranches in a way that reflects the risk they are bearing. For example, the first tranche might get 3,000 basis points; the second tranche 1,000 basis points, and so on. As in a cash CDO, this would be paid on a principal that declined as defaults for which the tranche is responsible occur.

An alternative structure for a synthetic CDO (or a cash CDO) is where the first tranche agrees to absorb losses from the first X% of companies that default (as opposed to the first X% of losses); the second tranche agrees to absorb the losses from the next Y% of defaulting companies, and so on. As in the other structure the principal on which the income is earned declines as there are defaults. For example, if a tranche is responsible for the sixth to fifteenth defaults, the principal on which income is earned is 50% of the original principal after there have been 10 defaults.

SUMMARY

Credit derivatives enable banks and other financial institutions to actively manage their credit risks. They can be used to transfer credit risk from one company to another and to diversify credit risk by swapping one type of exposure for another.

The most common credit derivative is a credit default swap. This is a contract where one company buys insurance against another company defaulting on its obligations. The payoff is usually the difference between the par value of a bond issued by the second company and its value immediately after a default. Credit default swaps can be analyzed by calculating the present value of the expected payments and the present value of the expected payoff.

A total return swap is an instrument where the total return on a portfolio of credit-sensitive assets is exchanged for LIBOR plus a spread. Total return swaps are often used as financing vehicles. A company wanting to purchase a portfolio of bonds will approach a financial institution, who will buy the bonds on its behalf. The financial institution will then enter into a total return swap where it pays the return on the bonds to the company and receives LIBOR. The advantage of this type of arrangement is that the financial institution reduces its exposure to defaults by the company.

A forward credit default swap is an obligation to enter into a particular credit default swap on the maturity date. A credit default swap option is the right to enter into a particular credit default swap on the maturity. Both instruments cease to exist if the reference entity defaults before the maturity date.

In collateralized debt obligations a number of different securities are created from a portfolio of corporate bonds or commercial loans. There are rules for determining how credit losses are allocated to the securities. The result of the rules is that securities with both very high and very low credit ratings are created from the portfolio. A synthetic collateralized debt obligation creates a similar set of securities from credit default swaps.

FURTHER READING

Das, S. *Credit Derivatives: Trading & Management of Credit & Default Risk*. Singapore: Wiley, 1998.

Hull, J. C., and A. White, "Valuing Credit Default Swaps I: No Counterparty Default Risk," *Journal of Derivatives*, 8, 1 (Fall 2000): 29–40.

Hull, J. C., and A. White, "The Valuation of Credit Default Swap Options," *Journal of Derivatives*, 10, 3 (Spring 2003): 40–50.

Tavakoli, J. M., *Credit Derivatives: A Guide to Instruments and Applications*. New York: Wiley, 1998.

Schonbucher, P. J. *Credit Derivatives Pricing Models*. Wiley, 2003.

Quiz (Answers at End of Book)

21.1. Explain the difference between a regular credit default swap and a binary credit default swap.

21.2. A credit default swap requires a semiannual payment at the rate of 60 basis points per year. The principal is \$300 million and the credit default swap is settled in cash. A default occurs after four years and two months, and the calculation agent estimates that the price of the cheapest deliverable bond is 40% of its face value shortly after the default. List the cash flows and their timing for the seller of the credit default swap.

21.3. Explain the two ways a credit default swap can be settled.

21.4. Explain how a CDO and a Synthetic CDO are created.

21.5. Explain what a first-to-default credit default swap is. Does its value increase or decrease as the default correlation between the companies in the basket increases? Explain why.

21.6. Explain the difference between risk-neutral and actuarial default probabilities.

21.7. Explain why a total return swap can be useful as a financing tool.

Questions and Problems (Answers in Solutions Manual/Study Guide)

21.8. Suppose that the risk-free zero curve is flat at 7% per annum with continuous compounding and that defaults can occur halfway through each year in a new five-year credit default swap. Suppose, further, that the recovery rate is 30% and the default probabilities each year conditional on no earlier default is 3%. Estimate the credit default swap spread. Assume payments are made annually.

21.9. What is the value of the swap in Problem 21.8 per dollar of notional principal to the protection buyer if the credit default swap spread is 150 basis points?

21.10. What is the credit default swap spread in Problem 21.8 if it is a binary CDS.

21.11. How does a five-year nth-to-default credit default swap work. Consider a basket of 100 reference entities where each reference entity has a probability of defaulting in each year of 1%. As the default correlation between the reference entities increases what would you expect to happen to the value of the swap when (a) $n = 1$ and (b) $n = 25$. Explain your answer.

21.12. How is the recovery rate of a bond usually defined?

21.13. Show that the spread for a new plain vanilla CDS should be $1 - R$ times the spread for a similar new binary CDS, where R is the recovery rate.

21.14. Verify that if the CDS spread for the example in Tables 21.2 to 21.5 is 100 basis points then the probability of default in a year (conditional on no earlier default) must be 1.61%. How does the probability of default change when the recovery rate is 20% instead of 40%. Verify that your answer is consistent with the implied probability of default being approximately proportional to $1/(1 - R)$, where R is the recovery rate.

21.15. A company enters into a total return swap where it receives the return on a corporate bond paying a coupon of 5% and pays LIBOR. Explain the difference between this and a regular swap where 5% is exchanged for LIBOR.

21.16. Explain how forward contracts and options on credit default swaps are structured.

21.17. "The position of a buyer of a credit default swap is similar to the position of someone who is long a risk-free bond and short a corporate bond." Explain this statement.

21.18. Why is there a potential asymmetric information problem in credit default swaps?

21.19. Does valuing a CDS using actuarial default probabilities rather than risk-neutral default probabilities overstate or understate its value? Explain your answer.

Assignment Questions

21.20. Suppose that the risk-free zero curve is flat at 6% per annum with continuous compounding and that defaults can occur at times 0.25, 0.75, 1.25, and 1.75 years in a two-year plain vanilla credit default swap with semiannual payments. Suppose, further, that the recovery rate is 20% and the unconditional probabilities of default (as seen at time zero) are 1% at times 0.25 years and 0.75 years, and 1.5% at times 1.25 years and 1.75 years. What is the credit default swap spread? What would the credit default spread be if the instrument were a binary credit default swap?

21.21. Assume that the default probability for a company in a year, conditional on no earlier defaults is λ and the recovery rate is R. The risk-free interest rate is 5% per annum. Default always occur halfway through a year. The spread for a five-year plain vanilla CDS where payments are made annually is 120 basis points and the spread for a five-year binary CDS where payments are made annually is 160 basis points. Estimate R and λ.

21.22. Explain how you would expect the yields offered on the various tranches in a CDO to change when the correlation between the bonds in the portfolio increases.

21.23. Suppose that (a) the yield on a five-year risk-free bond is 7%, (b) the yield on a five-year corporate bond issued by company X is 9.5%, and (c) a five-year credit default swap providing insurance against company X defaulting costs 150 basis points per year. What arbitrage opportunity is there in this situation? What arbitrage opportunity would there be if the credit default spread were 300 basis points instead of 150 basis points? Give two reasons why arbitrage opportunities such as those you identify are less than perfect.

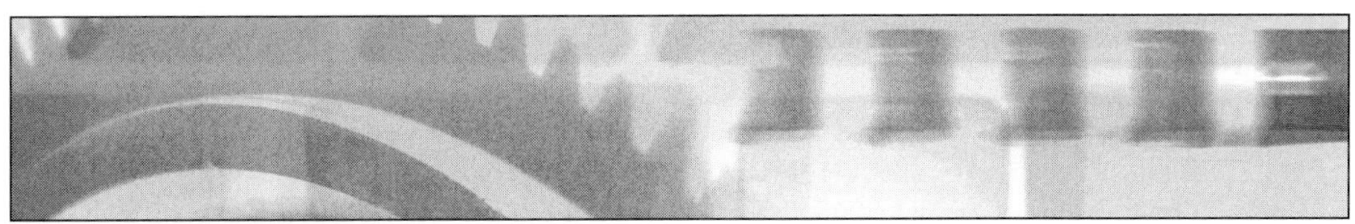

CHAPTER 22

Weather, Energy, and Insurance Derivatives

In this chapter we examine some recent innovations in derivatives markets. We explain the products that have been developed to manage weather risk, energy price risk, and the risks facing insurance companies. Some of the markets that we will talk about are in the early stages of their development. As they mature, we may well see significant changes in both the products that are offered and the ways they are used.

22.1 WEATHER DERIVATIVES

Many companies are in the position where their performance is liable to be adversely affected by the weather.[1] It makes sense for these companies to consider hedging their weather risk in much the same way as they hedge foreign exchange or interest rate risks.

The first over-the-counter weather derivatives were introduced in 1997. To understand how they work, we explain two variables:

HDD: Heating degree days

CDD: Cooling degree days

A day's HDD is defined as

$$\text{HDD} = \max(0, 65 - A)$$

and a day's CDD is defined as

$$\text{CDD} = \max(0, A - 65)$$

where A is the average of the highest and lowest temperature during the day at a specified weather station, measured in degrees Fahrenheit. For example, if the maximum temperature during a day (midnight to midnight) is 68° Fahrenheit and the minimum temperature is 44° Fahrenheit, $A = 56$. The daily HDD is then 9 and the daily CDD is 0.

A typical over-the-counter product is a forward or option contract providing a payoff

[1] The U.S. Department of Energy has estimated that one-seventh of the U.S. economy is subject to weather risk.

dependent on the cumulative HDD or CDD during a period. For example, an investment dealer could in January 2004 sell a client a call option on the cumulative HDD during February 2005 at the Chicago O'Hare Airport weather station with a strike price of 700 and a payment rate of \$10,000 per degree day. If the actual cumulative HDD is 820, the payoff is \$1.2 million. Often contracts include a payment cap. If the payment cap in our example is \$1.5 million, the contract is the equivalent of a bull spread. The client has a long call option on cumulative HDD with a strike price of 700 and a short call option with a strike price of 850.

A day's HDD is a measure of the volume of energy required for heating during the day. A day's CDD is a measure of the volume of energy required for cooling during the day. At the time of writing, most weather derivative contracts are entered into by energy producers and consumers. But retailers, supermarket chains, food and drink manufacturers, health service companies, agriculture companies, and companies in the leisure industry are also potential users of weather derivatives. The Weather Risk Management Association (www.wrma.org) has been formed to serve the interests of the weather risk management industry.

In September 1999 the Chicago Mercantile Exchange began trading weather futures and European options on weather futures. The contracts are on the cumulative HDD and CDD for a month observed at a weather station.[2] The contracts are settled in cash just after the end of the month once the HDD and CDD are known. One futures contract is on \$100 times the cumulative HDD or CDD. The HDD and CDD are calculated by a company, Earth Satellite Corporation, using automated data collection equipment.

In Section 21.1 we made the point that the payoffs from credit derivatives have systematic risk, and default probabilities calculated from historical data should not be used for valuation purposes. There is no systematic risk associated with the payoffs on weather derivatives. They can therefore be priced using historical data. Consider, for example, the call option on the February 2005 HDD at Chicago O'Hare airport mentioned earlier. We could collect 50 years of data and estimate a probability distribution for the HDD. This in turn could be used to provide a probability distribution for the option payoff. Our estimate of the value of the option would be the mean of this distribution discounted at the risk-free rate. We might want to adjust the probability distribution for temperature trends. For example, a linear regression might show that the cumulative February HDD is decreasing at a rate of 10 per year on average. The output from the regression could then be used to estimate a trend-adjusted probability distribution for the HDD in February 2005.

22.2 ENERGY DERIVATIVES

Energy companies are among the most active and sophisticated users of derivatives. Many energy products trade in both the over-the-counter market and on exchanges. In this section we will examine the trading in crude oil, natural gas, and electricity derivatives.

---

[2] The CME has introduced contracts for 10 different weather stations (Atlanta, Chicago, Cincinnati, Dallas, Des Moines, Las Vegas, New York, Philadelphia, Portland, and Tucson).

Crude Oil

Crude oil is one of the most important commodities in the world with global demand amounting to about 80 million barrels daily. Ten-year fixed-price supply contracts have been commonplace in the over-the-counter market for many years. These are swaps where oil at a fixed price is exchanged for oil at a floating price.

In the 1970s the price of oil was highly volatile. The 1973 war in the Middle East led to a tripling of oil prices. The fall of the Shah of Iran in the late 1970s again increased prices. These events led oil producers and users to a realization that they needed more sophisticated tools for managing oil price risk. In the 1980s both the over-the-counter market and the exchange-traded market developed products to meet this need.

In the over-the-counter market, virtually any derivative that is available on common stocks or stock indices is now available with oil as the underlying asset. Swaps, forward contracts, and options are popular. Contracts sometimes require settlement in cash and sometimes require settlement by physical delivery (i.e., by delivery of oil).

Exchange-traded contracts are also popular. The New York Mercantile Exchange (NYMEX) and the International Petroleum Exchange (IPE) trade a number of oil futures and oil futures options contracts. Some of the futures contracts are settled in cash; others are settled by physical delivery. For example, the Brent crude oil futures traded on the IPE has cash settlement based on the Brent index price; the light sweet crude oil futures traded on NYMEX requires physical delivery. In both cases the amount of oil underlying one contract is 1,000 barrels. NYMEX also trades popular contracts on two refined products: heating oil and gasoline. In both cases one contract is for the delivery of 42,000 gallons.

Natural Gas

The natural gas industry throughout the world has been going through a period of deregulation and the elimination of government monopolies. The supplier of natural gas is now not necessarily the same company as the producer of the gas. Suppliers are faced with the problem of meeting daily demand.

A typical over-the-counter contract is for the delivery of a specified amount of natural gas at a roughly uniform rate over a one-month period. Forward contracts, options, and swaps are available in the over-the-counter market. The seller of gas is usually responsible for moving the gas through pipelines to the specified location.

NYMEX trades a contract for the delivery of 10,000 million British thermal units of natural gas. The contract, if not closed out, requires physical delivery to be made during the delivery month at a roughly uniform rate to a particular hub in Louisiana. The IPE trades a similar contract in London.

Electricity

Electricity is an unusual commodity because it cannot easily be stored.[3] The maximum supply of electricity in a region at any moment is determined by the maximum capacity

[3] Electricity producers with spare capacity sometimes use it to pump water to the top of their hydroelectric plants so that it can be used to produce electricity at a later time. This is the closest they can get to storing this commodity.

of all the electricity-producing plants in the region. In the United States there are 140 regions known as *control areas*. Demand and supply are first matched within a control area, and any excess power is sold to other control areas. It is this excess power that constitutes the wholesale market for electricity. The ability of one control area to sell power to another control area depends on the transmission capacity of the lines between the two areas. Transmission from one area to another involves a transmission cost, charged by the owner of the line, and there are generally some transmission or energy losses.

A major use of electricity is for air-conditioning systems. As a result the demand for electricity, and therefore its price, is much greater in the summer months than in the winter months. The nonstorability of electricity causes occasional very large movements in the spot price. Heat waves have been known to increase the spot price by as much as 1000% for short periods of time.

Like natural gas, electricity has been going through a period of deregulation and the elimination of government monopolies. This has been accompanied by the development of an electricity derivatives market. NYMEX now trades a futures contract on the price of electricity, and there is an active over-the-counter market in forward contracts, options, and swaps. A typical contract (exchange-traded or over-the-counter) allows one side to receive a specified number of megawatt hours for a specified price at a specified location during a particular month. In a 5×8 contract, power is received for five days a week (Monday to Friday) during the off-peak period (11 p.m. to 7 a.m.) for the specified month. In a 5×16 contract, power is received five days a week during the on-peak period (7 a.m. to 11 p.m.) for the specified month. In a 7×24 contract, it is received around the clock every day during the month. Option contracts have either daily exercise or monthly exercise. In the case of daily exercise, the option holder can choose on each day of the month (by giving one day's notice) to receive the specified amount of power at the specified strike price. When there is monthly exercise a single decision on whether to receive power for the whole month at the specified strike price is made at the beginning of the month.

An interesting contract in electricity and natural gas markets is what is known as a *swing option* or *take-and-pay option*. In this contract a minimum and maximum for the amount of power that must be purchased at a certain price by the option holder is specified for each day during a month and for the month in total. The option holder can change (or swing) the rate at which the power is purchased during the month, but usually there is a limit on the total number of changes that can be made.

Characteristics of Energy Prices

Energy prices, like stock prices, exhibit volatility. Unlike stock prices, they also exhibit seasonality and mean reversion (see Section 19.7 for a discussion of mean reversion). The seasonality is created by the seasonal demand for energy and the difficulties in storing it. The mean reversion arises because short-term supply and demand imbalances cause prices to move away from their seasonal average, but once normal market conditions are restored they tend to be "pulled back" toward the seasonal average. For crude oil, volatility, seasonality, and mean reversion are all relatively low. For natural gas they are somewhat higher, and for electricity they are very much greater. A typical volatility for oil is 20% per annum, for natural gas it is 40% per annum, and for electricity it is often in the 100 to 200% per annum range.

How an Energy Producer Can Hedge Risks

There are two components to the risks facing an energy producer. One is the risk associated with the market price for the energy (the price risk); the other is risk associated with the amount of energy that will be bought (the volume risk). Although prices do adjust to reflect volumes, there is a less-than-perfect relationship between the two, and energy producers have to take both into account when developing a hedging strategy. The price risk can be hedged using the energy derivative contracts discussed in this section. The volume risks can be hedged using the weather derivatives discussed in the previous section. Define:

Y: Profit for a month

P: Average energy prices for the month

T: Relevant temperature variable (HDD or CDD) for the month

An energy producer can use historical data to obtain a best-fit linear regression relationship of the form

$$Y = a + bP + cT + \epsilon$$

where ϵ is the error term. The energy producer can then hedge risks for the month by taking a position of $-b$ in energy forwards or futures and a position of $-c$ in weather forwards or futures. The relationship can also be used to analyze the effectiveness of alternative option strategies.

22.3 INSURANCE DERIVATIVES

When derivative contracts are used for hedging purposes, they have many of the same characteristics as insurance contracts. Both types of contracts are designed to provide protection against adverse events. It is not surprising that many insurance companies have subsidiaries that trade derivatives and that many of the activities of insurance companies are becoming very similar to those of investment banks.

Traditionally the insurance industry has hedged its exposure to catastrophic (CAT) risks such as hurricanes and earthquakes using a practice known as reinsurance. Reinsurance contracts can take a number of forms. Suppose that an insurance company has an exposure of \$100 million to earthquakes in California and wants to limit this to \$30 million. One alternative is to enter into annual reinsurance contracts that cover on a pro rata basis 70% of its exposure. If California earthquake claims in a particular year total \$50 million, the costs to the company would then be only \$15 million. Another more popular alternative, involving lower reinsurance premiums, is to buy a series of reinsurance contracts covering what are known as *excess cost layers*. The first layer might provide indemnification for losses between \$30 million and \$40 million; the next layer might cover losses between \$40 million and \$50 million; and so on. Each reinsurance contract is known as an *excess-of-loss* reinsurance contract. The reinsurer has written a bull spread on the total losses. It is long a call option with a strike price equal to the lower end of the layer and short a call option with a strike price equal to the upper end of the layer.[4]

[4] Reinsurance is also sometimes offered in the form of a lump sum if a certain loss level is reached. The reinsurer is then writing a cash-or-nothing binary call option on the losses.

The principal providers of CAT reinsurance have traditionally been reinsurance companies and Lloyds syndicates (which are unlimited liability syndicates of wealthy individuals). In recent years the industry has come to the conclusion that its reinsurance needs have outstripped what can be provided from these traditional sources. It has searched for new ways in which capital markets can provide reinsurance. One of the events that caused the industry to rethink its practices was Hurricane Andrew in 1992, which caused about $15 billion of insurance costs in Florida. This exceeded the total of relevant insurance premiums received in Florida during the previous seven years. If Hurricane Andrew had hit Miami, it is estimated that insured losses would have exceeded $40 billion. Hurricane Andrew and other catastrophes have led to increases in insurance/reinsurance premiums.

Exchange-traded insurance futures contracts have been developed by the CBOT, but have not been highly successful. The over-the-counter market has come up with a number of products that are alternatives to traditional reinsurance. The most popular is a CAT bond. This is a bond issued by a subsidiary of an insurance company that pays a higher-than-normal interest rate. In exchange for the extra interest the holder of the bond agrees to provide an excess-of-cost reinsurance contract. Depending on the terms of the CAT bond, the interest or principal (or both) can be used to meet claims. In the example considered above where an insurance company wants protection for California earthquake losses between $30 million and $40 million, the insurance company could issue CAT bonds with a total principal of $10 million. In the event that the insurance company's California earthquake losses exceeded $30 million, bondholders would lose some or all of their principal. As an alternative the insurance company could cover this excess cost layer by making a much bigger bond issue where only the bondholders' interest is at risk.

CAT bonds typically give a high probability of an above-normal rate of interest and a low probability of a high loss. Why would investors be interested in such instruments? The answer is that there are no statistically significant correlations between CAT risks and market returns.[5] CAT bonds are therefore an attractive addition to an investor's portfolio. They have no systematic risk, so their total risk can be completely diversified away in a large portfolio. If a CAT bond's expected return is greater than the risk-free interest rate (and typically it is), it has the potential to improve risk–return tradeoffs.

SUMMARY

This chapter has shown that when there are risks to be managed, derivative markets have been very innovative in developing products to meet the needs of the market.

The market for weather derivatives is relatively new, but is already attracting a lot of attention. Two measures, HDD and CDD, have been developed to describe the temperature during a month. These are used to define the payoffs on both exchange-traded and over-the-counter derivatives. No doubt, as the weather derivatives market develops, we will see contracts on rainfall, snow, and similar variables become more commonplace.

---

[5] See R. H. Litzenberger, D. R. Beaglehole, and C. E. Reynolds, "Assessing Catastrophe Reinsurance-Linked Securities as a New Asset Class," *Journal of Portfolio Management* (Winter 1996): 76–86.

In energy markets, oil derivatives have been important for some time and play a key role in helping oil producers and oil consumers manage their price risk. Natural gas and electricity derivatives are relatively new. They became important for risk management when these markets were deregulated and government monopolies discontinued.

Insurance derivatives are now beginning to be an alternative to traditional reinsurance as a way for insurance companies to manage the risks of a catastrophic event such as a hurricane or an earthquake. We will doubtless see other sorts of insurance (e.g., life insurance and automobile insurance) being securitized in a similar way as this market develops.

FURTHER READING

On weather derivatives

Arditti, F., L. Cai, M. Cao, and R. McDonald. "Whether to Hedge," *RISK: Supplement on Weather Risk* (August 1999): 9–12.

Hunter, R. "Managing Mother Nature," *Derivatives Strategy* (February 1999).

On energy derivatives

Clewlow, L., and C. Strickland. *Energy Derivatives: Pricing and Risk Management*. Lacima Group, 2000.

Eydeland, A., and H. Geman. "Pricing Power Derivatives." *Risk* (October 1998): 71–73.

Joskow, P. "Electricity Sectors in Transition," *The Energy Journal*, 19 (1998): 25–52.

Kendall, R. "Crude Oil: Price Shocking," *Risk Supplement on Commodity Risk* (May 1999).

On insurance derivatives

Canter, M. S., J. B. Cole, and R. L. Sandor. "Insurance Derivatives: A New Asset Class for the Capital Markets and a New Hedging Tool for the Insurance Industry," *Journal of Applied Corporate Finance* (Autumn 1997): 69–83.

K. A. Froot. "The Market for Catastrophe Risk: A Clinical Examination," *Journal of Financial Economics*," 60 (2001): 529–571.

K. A. Froot. *The Financing of Catastrophe Risk*. Chicago: University of Chicago Press, 1999.

Geman, H. "CAT Calls," *Risk* (September 1994): 86–89.

Hanley, M. "A Catastrophe Too Far," *Risk Supplement on Insurance* (July 1998).

Litzenberger, R. H., D. R. Beaglehole, and C. E. Reynolds. "Assessing Catastrophe Reinsurance-Linked Securities as a New Asset Class," *Journal of Portfolio Management* (Winter 1996): 76–86.

Quiz (Answers at End of Book)

22.1. What is meant by HDD and CDD?

22.2. Suppose that each day during July the minimum temperature is 68° Fahrenheit and the maximum temperature is 82° Fahrenheit. What is the payoff from a call option on the cumulative CDD during July with a strike of 250 and a payment rate of $5,000 per degree day?

22.3. How is a typical natural gas forward contract structured.

22.4. Why is the price of electricity more volatile than that of other energy sources.

22.5. Why is an actuarial approach appropriate for pricing a weather derivatives contract and a CAT bond?

22.6. How can an energy producer user derivative markets to hedge risks?

22.7. Explain how CAT bonds work.

Questions and Problems (Answers in Solutions Manual/Study Guide)

22.8. "HDD and CDD can be regarded as payoffs from options on temperature." Explain this statement.

22.9. Suppose that you have 50 years of temperature data at your disposal. Explain the analysis you would you carry out to calculate the forward cumulative CDD for next July.

22.10. Would you expect mean reversion to cause the volatility of the three-month forward price of an energy source to be greater than or less than the volatility of the spot price? Explain your answer.

22.11. Explain how a 5×8 option contract for May 2005 on electricity with daily exercise works. Explain how a 5×8 option contract for May 2005 on electricity with monthly exercise works. Which is worth more?

22.12. Consider two bonds that have the same coupon, time to maturity, and price. One is a B-rated corporate bond. The other is a CAT bond. An analysis based on historical data shows that the expected losses on the two bonds in each year of their life is the same. Which bond would you advise a portfolio manager to buy and why?

Assignment Question

22.13. An insurance company's losses of a particular type are to a reasonable approximation normally distributed with a mean of \$150 million and a standard deviation of \$50 million. (Assume no difference between losses in a risk-neutral world and losses in the real world.) The one-year risk-free rate is 5%. Estimate the cost of the following:

a. A contract that will pay in one year's time 60% of the insurance company's costs on a pro rata basis

b. A contract that pays \$100 million in one year's time if losses exceed \$200 million

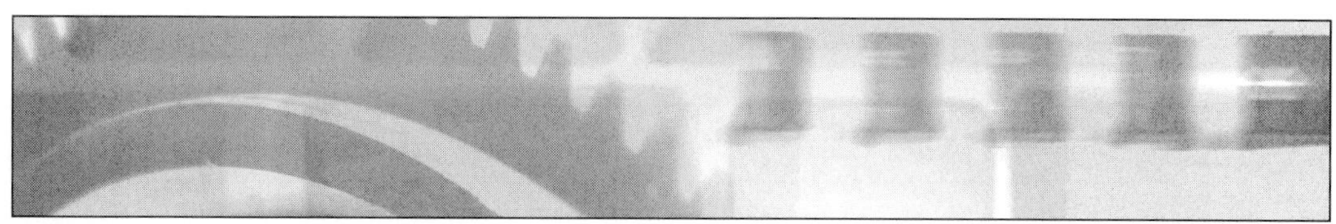

CHAPTER 23

Derivatives Mishaps and What We Can Learn from Them

Since the mid-1980s there have been some spectacular losses in derivatives markets. Some of the losses made by financial institutions are listed in Business Snapshot 23.1, and some of those made by nonfinancial organizations in Business Snapshot 23.2. What is remarkable about these lists is the number of situations where huge losses arose from the activities of a single employee. In 1995, Nick Leeson's trading brought a 200-year-old British bank, Barings, to its knees; in 1994, Robert Citron's trading led to Orange County, a municipality in California, losing about \$2 billion. Joseph Jett's trading for Kidder Peabody lost \$350 million. John Rusnak's losses of \$700 million for Allied Irish Bank came to light in 2002. The huge losses at Daiwa, Shell, and Sumitomo were also each the result of the activities of a single individual.

The losses should not be viewed as an indictment of the whole derivatives industry. The derivatives market is a vast multitrillion dollar market that by most measures has been outstandingly successful and has served the needs of its users well. The events listed represent a tiny proportion of the total trades (both in number and value). Nevertheless, it is worth considering carefully the lessons we can learn from them. This is what we will do in this final chapter.

23.1 LESSONS FOR ALL USERS OF DERIVATIVES

First, we consider the lessons appropriate to all users of derivatives, whether they are financial or nonfinancial companies.

Define Risk Limits

It is essential that all companies define in a clear and unambiguous way limits to the financial risks that can be taken. They should then set up procedures for ensuring that the limits are obeyed. Ideally, overall risk limits should be set at board level. These should then be converted to limits applicable to the individuals responsible for managing particular risks. Daily reports should indicate the gain or loss that will be

Business Snapshot 23.1 Big losses by financial institutions

Allied Irish bank
This bank lost about $700 million from speculative activities of one of its foreign exchange traders, John Rusnak, that lasted a number of years. Rusnak covered up his losses by creating fictitious option trades.

Barings (see page 16)
This 200-year-old British bank was wiped out in 1995 by the activities of one trader, Nick Leeson, in Singapore. The trader's mandate was to arbitrage between Nikkei 225 futures quotes in Singapore and Osaka. Instead, he made big bets on the future direction of the Nikkei 225 using futures and options. The total loss was close to $1 billion.

Daiwa Bank
A trader working in New York for this Japanese bank lost more than $1 billion in the 1990s.

Kidder Peabody (see page 102)
The activities of a single trader, Joseph Jett, led to this New York investment dealer losing $350 million trading U.S. government securities and their strips. (Strips are created when each of the cash flows underlying a bond is sold as a separate security.) The loss arose because of a mistake in the way the company's computer system calculated profits.

Long-Term Capital Management (see page 30)
This hedge fund lost about $4 billion in 1998. The strategy followed by the fund was convergence arbitrage. This involved attempting to identify two nearly identical securities whose prices were temporarily out of line with each other. The company would buy the less expensive security and short the more expensive one, hedging any residual risks. In mid-1998 the company was badly hurt by widening credit spreads resulting from defaults on Russian bonds. The hedge fund was considered too large to fail. The New York Federal Reserve organized a $3.5 billion bailout by encouraging 14 banks to invest in the fund.

Midland Bank
This British bank lost $500 million in the early 1990s largely because of a wrong bet on the direction of interest rates. It was later taken over by the Hong Kong and Shanghai bank.

National Westminster Bank
This British bank lost about $130 million from using an inappropriate model to value swap options in 1997.

experienced for particular movements in market variables. These should be checked against the actual losses that are experienced to ensure that the valuation procedures underlying the reports are accurate.

It is particularly important that companies monitor risks carefully when derivatives are used. This is because, as we saw in Chapter 1, derivatives can be used for hedging, speculation, and arbitrage. Without close monitoring, it is impossible to know whether

Business Snapshot 23.2 Big losses by nonfinancial organizations

Allied Lyons
The treasury department of this drinks and food company lost $150 million in 1991 selling call options on the US dollar–sterling exchange rate.

Gibson Greetings
The treasury department of this greeting card manufacturer in Cincinnati lost about $20 million in 1994 trading highly exotic interest rate derivatives contracts with Bankers Trust. They later sued Bankers Trust and settled out of court.

Hammersmith and Fulham *(see page 176)*
This British Local Authority lost about $600 million on sterling interest rate swaps and options in 1988. All its contracts were later declared null and void by the British courts, much to the annoyance of the banks on the other side of the transactions.

Metallgesellschaft *(see page 69)*
This German company entered into long-term contracts to supply oil and gasoline and hedged them by rolling over short-term futures contracts. It lost $1.8 billion when it was forced to discontinue this activity.

Orange County *(see page 86)*
The activities of the treasurer, Robert Citron, led to this California municipality losing about $2 billion in 1994. The treasurer was using derivatives to speculate that interest rates would not rise.

Procter & Gamble *(see page 445)*
The treasury department of this large U.S. company lost about $90 million in 1994 trading highly exotic interest rate derivatives contracts with Bankers Trust. They later sued Bankers Trust and settled out of court.

Shell
A single employee working in the Japanese subsidiary of this company lost $1 billion dollars in unauthorized trading of currency futures.

Sumitomo
A single trader working for this Japanese company lost about $2 billion in the copper spot, futures, and options market in the 1990s.

a derivatives trader has switched from being a hedger to a speculator or switched from being an arbitrageur to being a speculator. Barings is a classic example of what can go wrong. Nick Leeson's mandate was to carry out low-risk arbitrage between the Singapore and Osaka markets on Nikkei 225 futures. Unknown to his superiors in London, Leeson switched from being an arbitrageur to taking huge bets on the future direction of the Nikkei 225. Systems within Barings were so inadequate that nobody knew what he was doing.

The argument here is not that no risks should be taken. A treasurer working for a corporation, or a trader in a financial institution, or a fund manager should be allowed to take positions on the future direction of relevant market variables. What we are arguing is that the sizes of the positions that can be taken should be limited and the systems in place should accurately report the risks being taken.

Take the Risk Limits Seriously

What happens if an individual exceeds risk limits and makes a profit? This is a tricky issue for senior management. It is tempting to ignore violations of risk limits when profits result. However, this is shortsighted. It leads to a culture where risk limits are not taken seriously, and it paves the way for a disaster. In many of the situations listed in Business Snapshots 23.1 and 23.2, the companies had become complacent about the risks they were taking because they had taken similar risks in previous years and made profits.

The classic example here is Orange County. Robert Citron's activities in 1991–93 had been very profitable for Orange County, and the municipality had come to rely on his trading for additional funding. People chose to ignore the risks he was taking because he had produced profits. Unfortunately, the losses made in 1994 far exceeded the profits from previous years.

The penalties for exceeding risk limits should be just as great when profits result as when losses result. Otherwise, traders who make losses are liable to keep increasing their bets in the hope that eventually a profit will result and all will be forgiven.

Do Not Assume You Can Outguess the Market

Some traders are quite possibly better than others. But no trader gets it right all the time. A trader who correctly predicts the direction in which market variables will move 60% of the time is doing well. If a trader has an outstanding track record (as Robert Citron did in the early 1990s), it is likely to be a result of luck rather than superior trading skill.

Suppose that a financial institution employs 16 traders and one of those traders makes profits in every quarter of a year. Should the trader receive a good bonus? Should the trader's risk limits be increased? The answer to the first question is that inevitably the trader will receive a good bonus. The answer to the second question should be no. The chance of making a profit in four consecutive quarters from random trading is 0.5^4 or 1 in 16. This means that just by chance one of the 16 traders will "get it right" every single quarter of the year. We should not assume that the trader's luck will continue and we should not increase the trader's risk limits.

Do Not Underestimate the Benefits of Diversification

When a trader appears good at predicting a particular market variable, there is a tendency to increase the trader's limits. We have just argued that this is a bad idea because it is quite likely that the trader has been lucky rather than clever. However, let us suppose that we are really convinced that the trader has special talents. How undiversified should we allow ourselves to become in order to take advantage of the trader's special skills? The answer is that the benefits from diversification are huge, and it is unlikely that any trader is so good that it is worth foregoing these benefits to speculate heavily on just one market variable.

An example will illustrate the point here. Suppose that there are 20 stocks, each of which have an expected return of 10% per annum and a standard deviation of returns of 30%. The correlation between the returns from any two of the stocks is 0.2. By dividing an investment equally among the 20 stocks, an investor has an expected return of 10% per annum and standard deviation of returns of 14.7%. Diversification enables the investor to reduce risks by over half. Another way of expressing this is that diversification enables an investor to double the expected return per unit of risk taken. The investor would have to be extremely good at stock picking to get a better risk–return tradeoff by investing in just one stock.

Carry out Scenario Analyses and Stress Tests

The calculation of risk measures such as VaR should always be accompanied by scenario analyses and stress testing to obtain an understanding of what can go wrong. These techniques were mentioned in Chapter 18. They are very important. Human beings have an unfortunate tendency to anchor on one or two scenarios when evaluating decisions. In 1993 and 1994, for example, Procter & Gamble and Gibson Greetings were so convinced that interest rates would remain low that they ignored the possibility of a 100 basis point increase in their decision making.

It is important to be creative in the way scenarios are generated. One approach is to look at 10 or 20 years of data and choose the most extreme events as scenarios. Sometimes there is a shortage of data on a key variable. It is then sensible to choose a similar variable for which much more data is available and use historical daily percentage changes in that variable as a proxy for possible daily percentage changes in the key variable. For example, if there is little data on the prices of bonds issued by a particular country, we can look at historical data on prices of bonds issued by other similar countries to develop possible scenarios.

23.2 LESSONS FOR FINANCIAL INSTITUTIONS

We now move on to consider lessons that are primarily relevant to financial institutions.

Monitor Traders Carefully

In trading rooms there is a tendency to regard high-performing traders as "untouchable" and to not subject their activities to the same scrutiny as other traders. Apparently Joseph Jett, Kidder Peabody's star trader of Treasury instruments, was often "too busy" to answer questions and discuss his positions with the company's risk managers.

It is important that all traders—particularly those making high profits—be fully accountable. It is important for the financial institution to know whether the high profits are being made by taking unreasonably high risks. It is also important to check that the financial institution's computer systems and pricing models are correct and are not being manipulated in some way.

Separate the Front, Middle, and Back Office

The *front office* in a financial institution consists of the traders who are executing trades, taking positions, and so forth. The *middle office* consists of risk managers who are monitoring the risks being taken. The *back office* is where the record keeping and accounting takes place. Some of the worst derivatives disasters have occurred because these functions were not kept separate. Nick Leeson controlled both the front and back office for Barings in Singapore and was, as a result, able to conceal the disastrous nature of his trades from his superiors in London for some time. Although full details are not available, it appears that a lack of separation of the front and back office was at least partially responsible for the huge losses experienced by Sumitomo in copper trading.

Do Not Blindly Trust Models

Some of the large losses in by financial institutions arose because of the models and computer systems being used. We discussed how Kidder Peabody was misled by its own systems on page 102. Another example of an incorrect model leading to losses is provided by National Westminster Bank. This bank had an incorrect model for valuing swap options that led to significant losses.

If large profits are reported when relatively simple trading strategies are followed, there is a good chance that the models underlying the calculation of the profits are wrong. Similarly, if a financial institution appears to be particularly competitive on its quotes for a particular type of deal, there is a good chance that it is using a different model from other market participants, and it should analyze what is going on carefully. To the head of a trading room, getting too much business of a certain type can be just as worrisome as getting too little business of that type.

Be Conservative in Recognizing Inception Profits

When a financial institution sells a highly exotic instrument to a nonfinancial corporation, the valuation can be highly dependent on the underlying model. For example, instruments with long-dated embedded interest rate options can be highly dependent on the interest rate model used. In these circumstances, a phrase used to describe the daily marking to market of the deal is *marking to model*. This is because there are no market prices for similar deals that can be used as a benchmark.

Suppose that a financial institution manages to sell an instrument to a client for \$10 million more than it is worth—or at least \$10 million more than its model says it is worth. The \$10 million is known as an *inception profit*. When should it be recognized? There appears to be quite a variation in what different investment banks do. Some recognize the \$10 million immediately, whereas others are much more conservative and recognize it slowly over the life of the deal.

Recognizing inception profits immediately is very dangerous. It encourages traders to use aggressive models, take their bonuses, and leave before the model and the value of the deal come under close scrutiny. It is much better to recognize inception profits slowly, so that traders have the motivation to investigate the impact of several different models and several different sets of assumptions before committing themselves to a deal.

Do Not Sell Clients Inappropriate Products

It is tempting to sell corporate clients inappropriate products, particularly when they appear to have an appetite for the underlying risks. But this is shortsighted. The most dramatic example of this is the activities of Bankers Trust (BT) in the period leading up to the spring of 1994. Many of BT's clients were persuaded to buy high-risk and totally inappropriate products. A typical product (e.g., the 5/30 swap discussed on page 445) would give the client a good chance of saving a few basis points on its borrowings and a small chance of costing a large amount of money. The products worked well for BT's clients in 1992 and 1993, but blew up in 1994 when interest rates rose sharply. The bad publicity that followed hurt BT greatly. The years it had spent building up trust among corporate clients and developing an enviable reputation for innovation in derivatives were largely lost as a result of the activities of a few overly aggressive salesmen. BT was forced to pay large amounts of money to its clients to settle lawsuits out of court. It was taken over by Deutsche Bank in 1999.

Do Not Ignore Liquidity Risk

Financial engineers usually base the pricing of exotic instruments and instruments that trade relatively infrequently on the prices of actively traded instruments. For example:

1. A financial engineer often calculates a zero curve from actively traded government bonds (known as on-the-run bonds) and uses it to price bonds that trade less frequently (off-the-run bonds).
2. A financial engineer often implies the volatility of an asset from actively traded options and uses it to price less actively traded options.
3. A financial engineer often implies information about the behavior of interest rates from actively traded interest rate caps and swap options and uses it to price products that are highly structured.

These practices are not unreasonable. However, it is dangerous to assume that less actively traded instruments can always be traded at close to their theoretical price. When financial markets experience a shock of one sort or another there is often a "flight to quality." Liquidity becomes very important to investors, and illiquid instruments often sell at a big discount to their theoretical values. Trading strategies that assume large volumes of relatively illiquid instruments can be sold at short notice at close to their theoretical values are dangerous.

An example of liquidity risk is provided by Long-Term Capital Management (LTCM), which we discussed in Section 2.4. This hedge fund followed a strategy known as *convergence arbitrage*. It attempted to identify two securities (or portfolios of securities) that should in theory sell for the same price. If the market price of one security was less that of the other, it would buy that security and sell the other. The strategy is based on the idea that if two securities have the same theoretical price their market prices should eventually be the same.

In the summer of 1998 LTCM made a huge loss. This was largely because a default by Russia on its debt caused a flight to quality. LTCM tended to be long illiquid instruments and short the corresponding liquid instruments (for example, it was long off-the-run bonds and short on-the-run bonds). The spreads between the prices of illiquid instruments and the corresponding liquid instruments widened sharply after the Russian default. Credit spreads also increased. LTCM was highly leveraged. It experienced huge losses and there were margin calls on its positions that it was unable to meet.

The LTCM story reinforces the importance of carrying out scenario analyses and stress testing to look at what can happen in the worst of all worlds. LTCM could have tried to examine other times in history when there have been extreme flights to quality to quantify the liquidity risks it was facing.

Beware When Everyone Is Following the Same Trading Strategy

It sometimes happens that many market participants are following essentially the same trading strategy. This creates a dangerous environment where there are liable to be big market moves, unstable markets, and large losses for the market participants.

We gave one example of this in Chapter 15 when discussing portfolio insurance and the market crash of October 1987. In the months leading up to the crash, increasing numbers of portfolio managers were attempting to insure their portfolios by creating synthetic put options. They bought stocks or stock index futures after a rise in the market and sold them after a fall. This created an unstable market. A relatively small decline in stock prices could lead to a wave of selling by portfolio insurers. The latter would lead to a further decline in the market, which could give rise to another wave of selling, and so on. There is little doubt that without portfolio insurance the crash of October 1987 would have been much less severe.

Another example is provided by LTCM in 1998. Its position was made more difficult by the fact that many other hedge funds were following similar convergence arbitrage strategies. After the Russian default and the flight to quality, LTCM tried to liquidate part of its portfolio to meet margin calls. Unfortunately, other hedge funds were facing similar problems to LTCM and trying to do similar trades. This exacerbated the situation, causing liquidity spreads to be even higher than they would otherwise have been and reinforcing the flight to quality. Consider, for example, LTCM's position in U.S. Treasury bonds. It was long the illiquid off-the-run bonds and short the liquid on-the-run bonds. When a flight to quality caused spreads between yields on the two types of bonds to widen, LTCM had to liquidate its positions by selling off-the-run bonds and buying on-the-run bonds. Other large hedge funds were doing the same. As a result, the price of on-the-run bonds rose relative to off-the-run bonds and the spread between the two yields widened even more than it had done already.

A further example is provided by the activities of British insurance companies in the late 1990s. These insurance companies had entered into many contracts promising that the rate of interest applicable to an annuity received by an individual on retirement would be the greater of the market rate and a guaranteed rate. At about the same time, all insurance companies decided to hedge part of their risks on these contracts by buying long-dated swap options from financial institutions. The financial institutions they dealt with hedged their risks by buying huge numbers of long-dated sterling bonds. As a result, bond prices rose and long sterling rates declined. More bonds had to be bought to maintain the dynamic hedge, long sterling rates declined further, and so on. Financial institutions lost money and, because long rates declined, insurance companies found themselves in a worse position on the risks they had chosen not to hedge.

The chief lesson to be learned from these stories is that it is important to see the big picture of what is going on in financial markets and to understand the risks inherent in situations where many market participants are following the same trading strategy.

23.3 LESSONS FOR NONFINANCIAL CORPORATIONS

We now consider lessons primarily applicable to nonfinancial corporations.

Make Sure You Fully Understand the Trades You Are Doing

Corporations should never undertake a trade or a trading strategy that they do not fully understand. This is a somewhat obvious point, but it is surprising how often a trader working for a nonfinancial corporation will, after a big loss, admit to not knowing what was really going on and claim to have been misled by investment bankers. Robert Citron, the treasurer of Orange County did this. So did the traders working for Hammersmith and Fulham, who in spite of their huge positions were surprisingly uninformed about how the swaps and other interest rate derivatives they traded really worked.

If a senior manager in a corporation does not understand a trade proposed by a subordinate, the trade should not be approved. A simple rule of thumb is that if a trade and the rationale for entering into it are so complicated that they cannot be understood by the manager, it is almost certainly inappropriate for the corporation. The trades undertaken by Procter & Gamble and Gibson Greetings would have been vetoed using this criterion.

One way of ensuring that you fully understand a financial instrument is to value it. If a corporation does not have the in-house capability to value an instrument, it should not trade it. In practice, corporations often rely on their investment bankers for valuation advice. This is dangerous, as Procter & Gamble and Gibson Greetings found out. When they wanted to unwind their deals, they found they were facing prices produced by Bankers Trust's proprietary models, which they had no way of checking.

Make Sure a Hedger Does Not Become a Speculator

One of the unfortunate facts of life is that hedging is relatively dull, whereas speculation is exciting. When a company hires a trader to manage foreign exchange, commodity price, or interest rate risk, there is a danger that the following might happen. At first, the trader does the job diligently and earns the confidence of top management. He or she assesses the company's exposures and hedges them. As time goes by, the trader becomes convinced that he or she can outguess the market. Slowly the trader becomes a speculator. At first things go well, but then a loss is made. To recover the loss, the trader doubles up the bets. Further losses are made—and so on. The result is likely to be a disaster.

As mentioned earlier, clear limits to the risks that can be taken should be set by senior management. Controls should be put in place to ensure that the limits are obeyed. The trading strategy for a corporation should start with an analysis of the risks facing the corporation in foreign exchange, interest rate, commodity markets, and so on. A decision should then be taken on how the risks are to be reduced to acceptable levels. It is a clear sign that something is wrong within a corporation if the trading strategy is not derived in a very direct way from the company's exposures.

Be Cautious about Making the Treasury Department a Profit Center

In the last 20 years there has been a tendency to make the treasury department within a corporation a profit center. This appears to have much to recommend it. The treasurer is motivated to reduce financing costs and manage risks as profitably as possible. The problem is that the potential for the treasurer to make profits is limited. When raising funds and investing surplus cash, the treasurer is facing an efficient market. The treasurer can usually improve the bottom line only by taking additional risks. The company's hedging program gives the treasurer some scope for making shrewd decisions that increase profits. But it should be remembered that the goal of a hedging program is to reduce risks, not to increase expected profits. As pointed out in Chapter 3, the decision to hedge will lead to a worse outcome than the decision not to hedge roughly 50% of the time. The danger of making the treasury department a profit center is that the treasurer is motivated to become a speculator. This is liable to lead to the type of outcome experienced by Orange County, Procter & Gamble, or Gibson Greetings.

SUMMARY

The huge losses experienced from the use of derivatives have made many treasurers very wary. Since the spate of mishaps in 1994 and 1995, some nonfinancial corporations have announced plans to reduce or even eliminate their use of derivatives. This is unfortunate because derivatives provide treasurers with very efficient ways to manage risks.

The stories behind the losses emphasize the point, made as early as Chapter 1, that derivatives can be used for either hedging or speculation; that is, they can be used either to reduce risks or to take risks. Most losses occurred because derivatives were used inappropriately. Employees who had an implicit or explicit mandate to hedge their company's risks decided instead to speculate.

The key lesson to be learned from the losses is the importance of *internal controls*. Senior management within a company should issue a clear and unambiguous policy statement about how derivatives are to be used and the extent to which it is permissible for employees to take positions on movements in market variables. Management should then institute controls to ensure that the policy is carried out. It is a recipe for disaster to give individuals authority to trade derivatives without a close monitoring of the risks being taken.

FURTHER READING

Dunbar, N. *Inventing Money: The Story of Long-Term Capital Management and the Legends Behind It*. Chichester, U.K.: Wiley, 2000.

Jorion, P. *Big Bets Gone Bad: Derivatives and Bankruptcy in Orange County*. New York: Academic Press, 1995.

Jorion, P. "How Long-Term Lost Its Capital," *RISK* (September 1999).

Ju, X., and N. Pearson. "Using Value at Risk to Control Risk Taking: How Wrong Can You Be?" *Journal of Risk*, 1 (1999): 5–36.

Thomson, R. *Apocalypse Roulette: The Lethal World of Derivatives*. London: Macmillan, 1998.

Zhang, P. G. *Barings Bankruptcy and Financial Derivatives*. Singapore: World Scientific Publishing, 1995.

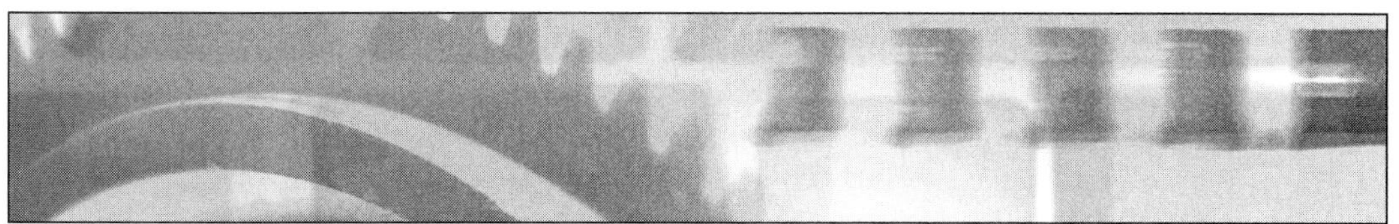

Answers to Quiz Questions

CHAPTER 1

1.1 A trader who enters into a long futures position is agreeing to *buy* the underlying asset for a certain price at a certain time in the future. A trader who enters into a short futures position is agreeing to *sell* the underlying asset for a certain price at a certain time in the future.

1.2 A company is *hedging* when it has an exposure to the price of an asset and takes a position in futures or options markets to offset the exposure. In a *speculation* the company has no exposure to offset. It is betting on the future movements in the price of the asset. *Arbitrage* involves taking a position in two or more different markets to lock in a profit.

1.3 In (a) the investor is obligated to buy the asset for \$50 and does not have a choice. In (b) the investor has the option to buy the asset for \$50 but does not have to exercise the option.

1.4 a. The investor is obligated to sell pounds for 1.5000 when they are worth 1.4900. The gain is $(1.5000 - 1.4900) \times 100{,}000 = \$1{,}000$.

b. The investor is obligated to sell pounds for 1.5000 when they are worth 1.5200. The loss is $(1.5200 - 1.5000) \times 100{,}000 = \$2{,}000$.

1.5 You have sold a put option. You have agreed to buy 100 shares for \$40 per share if the party on the other side of the contract chooses to exercise the right to sell for this price. The option will be exercised only when the price of stock is below \$40. Suppose, for example, that the option is exercised when the price is \$30. You have to buy at \$40 shares that are worth \$30; you lose \$10 per share, or \$1,000 in total. If the option is exercised when the price is \$20, you lose \$20 per share, or \$2,000 in total. The worst that can happen is that the price of the stock declines to almost zero during the three-month period. This highly unlikely event would cost you \$4,000. In return for the possible future losses, you receive the price of the option from the purchaser.

1.6 One strategy is to buy 200 shares. Another is to buy 2,000 options (20 contracts). If the share price does well, the second strategy will give rise to greater gains. For example, if the share price goes up to \$40, you gain $[2{,}000 \times (\$40 - \$30)] - \$5{,}800 = \$14{,}200$ from the second strategy and only $200 \times (\$40 - \$29) = \$2{,}200$ from the first strategy. However, if the share price does badly, the second strategy yields greater losses. For example, if the share price goes down to \$25, the first strategy leads to a loss of $200 \times (\$29 - \$25) = \$800$, whereas the second strategy leads to a loss of the entire \$5,800 investment.

1.7 The over-the-counter market is a telephone- and computer-linked network of financial institutions, fund managers, and corporate treasurers where two participants can enter into any mutually acceptable contract. An exchange-traded market is a market organized by an exchange where traders either meet physically or communicate electronically and the contracts that can be traded have been defined by the exchange. When a market maker quotes a bid and an offer, the bid is the price at which the market maker is prepared to buy and the offer is the price at which the market maker is prepared to sell.

CHAPTER 2

2.1 The *open interest* of a futures contract at a particular time is the total number of long positions outstanding. (Equivalently, it is the total number of short positions outstanding.) The *trading volume* during a certain period of time is the number of contracts traded during this period.

2.2 A *commission broker* trades on behalf of a client and charges a commission. A *local* trades on his or her own behalf.

2.3 There will be a margin call when \$1,000 has been lost from the margin account. This will occur when the price of silver increases by 1,000/5,000 = \$0.20. The price of silver must therefore rise to \$5.40 per ounce for there to be a margin call. If the margin call is not met, your broker closes out your position.

2.4 The total profit is (\$20.50 − \$18.30) × 1,000 = \$2,200. Of this, (\$19.10 − \$18.30) × 1,000 = \$800 is realized on a day-by-day basis between September 2004 and December 31, 2004. A further (\$20.50 − \$19.10) × 1,000 = \$1,400 is realized on a day-by-day basis between January 1, 2005, and March 2005. A hedger would be taxed on the whole profit of \$2,200 in 2005. A speculator would be taxed on \$800 in 2004 and \$1,400 in 2005.

2.5 A *stop order* to sell at \$2 is an order to sell at the best available price once a price of \$2 or less is reached. It could be used to limit the losses from an existing long position. A *limit order* to sell at \$2 is an order to sell at a price of \$2 or more. It could be used to instruct a broker that a short position should be taken, providing it can be done at a price more favorable than \$2.

2.6 The margin account administered by the clearinghouse is marked to market daily, and the clearinghouse member is required to bring the account back up to the prescribed level daily. The margin account administered by the broker is also marked to market daily. However, the account does not have to be brought up to the initial margin level on a daily basis. It has to be brought up to the initial margin level when the balance in the account falls below the maintenance margin level. The maintenance margin is usually about 75% of the initial margin.

2.7 In futures markets prices are quoted as the number of U.S. dollars per unit of foreign currency. Spot and forward rates are quoted in this way for the British pound, euro, Australian dollar, and New Zealand dollar. For other major currencies, spot and forward rates are quoted as the number of units of foreign currency per U.S. dollar.

CHAPTER 3

3.1 A *short hedge* is appropriate when a company owns an asset and expects to sell that asset in the future. It can also be used when the company does not currently own the asset but expects to do so at some time in the future. A *long hedge* is appropriate when a company knows it will have to purchase an asset in the future. It can also be used to offset the risk from an existing short position.

3.2 *Basis risk* arises from the hedger's uncertainty as to the difference between the spot price and futures price at the expiration of the hedge.

3.3 A *perfect hedge* is one that completely eliminates the hedger's risk. A perfect hedge does not always lead to a better outcome than an imperfect hedge. It just leads to a more certain outcome. Consider a company that hedges its exposure to the price of an asset. Suppose the asset's price movements prove to be favorable to the company. A perfect hedge totally neutralizes the company's gain from these favorable price movements. An imperfect hedge, which only partially neutralizes the gains, might well give a better outcome.

3.4 A minimum variance hedge leads to no hedging when the coefficient of correlation between changes in the futures price and changes in the price of the asset being hedged is zero.

3.5 a. If the company's competitors are not hedging, the treasurer might feel that the company will experience less risk if it does not hedge (see Table 3.1).

b. The shareholders might not want the company to hedge.

c. If there is a loss on the hedge and a gain from the company's exposure to the underlying asset, the treasurer might feel that he or she will have difficulty justifying the hedging to other executives within the organization.

3.6 The optimal hedge ratio is

$$0.8 \times \frac{0.65}{0.81} = 0.642$$

This means that the size of the futures position should be 64.2% of the size of the company's exposure in a three-month hedge.

3.7 The formula for the number of contracts that should be shorted gives

$$1.2 \times \frac{20{,}000{,}000}{1080 \times 250} = 88.9$$

Rounding to the nearest whole number, 89 contracts should be shorted. To reduce the beta to 0.6, half of this position, or a short position in 44 contracts, is required.

CHAPTER 4

4.1 a. The rate with continuous compounding is

$$4 \ln\left(1 + \frac{0.14}{4}\right) = 0.1376$$

or 13.76% per annum.

b. The rate with annual compounding is

$$\left(1 + \frac{0.14}{4}\right)^4 - 1 = 0.1475$$

or 14.75% per annum.

4.2 LIBOR is the London interbank offer rate. It is the rate a bank quotes for deposits it is prepared to place with other banks. LIBID is the London interbank bid rate. It is the rate a bank quotes for deposits from other banks. LIBOR is greater than LIBID.

4.3 Suppose the bond has a face value of \$100. Its price is obtained by discounting the cash flows at 10.4%. The price is

$$\frac{4}{1.052}+\frac{4}{1.052^2}+\frac{104}{1.052^3}=96.74$$

If the 18-month zero rate is R, we must have

$$\frac{4}{1.05}+\frac{4}{1.05^2}+\frac{104}{(1+R/2)^3}=96.74$$

which gives $R = 10.42\%$.

4.4 a. With annual compounding the return is

$$\frac{1100}{1000}-1=0.1$$

or 10% per annum.

b. With semiannual compounding the return is R, where

$$1000\left(1+\frac{R}{2}\right)^2=1100$$

that is,

$$1+\frac{R}{2}=\sqrt{1.1}=1.0488$$

so that $R = 0.0976$. The percentage return is therefore 9.76% per annum.

c. With monthly compounding the return is R, where

$$1000\left(1+\frac{R}{12}\right)^{12}=1100$$

that is,

$$\left(1+\frac{R}{12}\right)=\sqrt[12]{1.1}=1.00797$$

so that $R = 0.0957$. The percentage return is therefore 9.57% per annum.

d. With continuous compounding the return is R, where

$$1000e^R=1100$$

that is,

$$e^R=1.1$$

so that $R = \ln 1.1 = 0.0953$. The percentage return is therefore 9.53% per annum.

4.5 The forward rates with continuous compounding are as follows:

Qtr 2: 8.4%
Qtr 3: 8.8%
Qtr 4: 8.8%
Qtr 5: 9.0%
Qtr 6: 9.2%

4.6 The forward rate is 9.0% with continuous compounding or 9.102% with quarterly compounding. From equation (4.9), the value of the FRA is therefore

$$[1{,}000{,}000\times 0.25\times(0.095-0.09102)]e^{-0.086\times 1.25}=893.56$$

or \$893.56.

4.7 When the term structure is upward sloping, $c > a > b$. When it is downward sloping, $b > a > c$.

CHAPTER 5

5.1 The investor's broker borrows the shares from another client's account and sells them in the usual way. To close out the position, the investor must purchase the shares. The broker then replaces them in the account of the client from whom they were borrowed. The party with the short position must remit to the broker dividends and other income paid on the shares. The broker transfers these funds to the account of the client from whom the shares were borrowed. Occasionally the broker runs out of places from which to borrow the shares. The investor is then short squeezed and has to close out the position immediately.

5.2 The forward price of an asset today is the price at which you would agree to buy or sell the asset at a future time. The value of a forward contract is zero when you first enter into it. As time passes the underlying asset price changes and the value of the contract may become positive or negative.

5.3 The forward price is

$$30e^{0.12\times 0.5} = \$31.86$$

5.4 The futures price is

$$350e^{(0.08-0.04)\times 0.3333} = \$354.7$$

5.5 Gold is an investment asset. If the futures price is too high, investors will find it profitable to increase their holdings of gold and short futures contracts. If the futures price is too low, they will find it profitable to decrease their holdings of gold and go long in the futures market. Copper is a consumption asset. If the futures price is too high, a strategy of buy copper and short futures works. However, because investors do not in general hold the asset, the strategy of sell copper and buy futures is not available to them. There is therefore an upper bound, but no lower bound, to the futures price.

5.6 *Convenience yield* measures the extent to which there are benefits obtained from ownership of the physical asset that are not obtained by owners of long futures contracts. The *cost of carry* is the interest cost plus storage cost less the income earned. The futures price, F_0, and spot price, S_0, are related by

$$F_0 = S_0 e^{(c-y)T}$$

where c is the cost of carry, y is the convenience yield, and T is the time to maturity of the futures contract.

5.7 A foreign currency provides a known interest rate, but the interest is received in the foreign currency. The value in the domestic currency of the income provided by the foreign currency is therefore known as a percentage of the value of the foreign currency. This means that the income has the properties of a known yield.

CHAPTER 6

6.1 There are 33 calendar days between July 7, 2004, and August 9, 2004. There are 184 calendar days between July 7, 2004, and January 7, 2005. The interest earned per \$100 of principal is therefore $3.5 \times 33/184 = \$0.6277$. For a corporate bond we assume 32 days between July 7 and August 9, 2004, and 180 days between July 7, 2004, and January 7, 2005. The interest earned is $3.5 \times 32/180 = \$0.6222$.

6.2 There are 89 days between October 12, 2004, and January 9, 2005. There are 182 days between October 12, 2004, and April 12, 2005. The cash price of the bond is obtained by adding the accrued interest to the quoted price. The quoted price is $102\frac{7}{32}$ or 102.21875. The cash price is therefore

$$102.21875 + \frac{89}{182} \times 6 = \$105.15$$

6.3 The conversion factor for a bond is equal to the quoted price the bond would have per dollar of principal on the first day of the delivery month on the assumption that the interest rate for all maturities equals 6% per annum (with semiannual compounding). The bond maturity and the times to the coupon payment dates are rounded down to the nearest three months for the purposes of the calculation. The conversion factor defines how much an investor with a short bond futures contract receives when bonds are delivered. If the conversion factor is 1.2345, the amount the investor receives is calculated by multiplying 1.2345 by the most recent futures price and adding accrued interest.

6.4 The Eurodollar futures price has increased by 6 basis points. The investor makes a gain per contract of $25 \times 6 = \$150$, or \$300 in total.

6.5 Suppose that a Eurodollar futures quote is 95.00. This gives a futures rate of 5% for the three-month period covered by the contract. The convexity adjustment is the amount by which futures rate has to be reduced to give an estimate of the forward rate for the period. The convexity adjustment is necessary because the marking to market of a futures contract leads to the futures rate being greater than the forward rate.

6.6 Duration provides information about the effect of a small parallel shift in the yield curve on the value of a bond portfolio. The percentage decrease in the value of the portfolio equals the duration of the portfolio multiplied by the amount by which interest rates are increased in the small parallel shift. The duration measure has the following limitation. It applies only to parallel shifts in the yield curve that are small.

6.7 The value of a contract is $108\frac{15}{32} \times 1{,}000 = \$108{,}468.75$. The number of contracts that should be shorted is

$$\frac{6{,}000{,}000}{108{,}468.75} \times \frac{8.2}{7.6} = 59.7$$

Rounding to the nearest whole number, 60 contracts should be shorted. The position should be closed out at the end of July.

CHAPTER 7

7.1 A has an apparent comparative advantage in fixed-rate markets but wants to borrow floating. B has an apparent comparative advantage in floating-rate markets but wants to borrow fixed. This provides the basis for the swap. There is a 1.4% per annum differential between the fixed rates offered to the two companies and a 0.5% per annum differential between the floating rates offered to the two companies. The total gain to all parties from

Swap for Quiz 7.1

the swap is therefore $1.4 - 0.5 = 0.9\%$ per annum. Because the bank gets 0.1% per annum of this gain, the swap should make each of A and B 0.4% per annum better off. This means that it should lead to A borrowing at LIBOR − 0.3% and to B borrowing at 13%. The appropriate arrangement is therefore as shown in the diagram above.

7.2 X has a comparative advantage in yen markets but wants to borrow dollars. Y has a comparative advantage in dollar markets but wants to borrow yen. This provides the basis for the swap. There is a 1.5% per annum differential between the yen rates and a 0.4% per annum differential between the dollar rates. The total gain to all parties from the swap is therefore $1.5 - 0.4 = 1.1\%$ per annum. The bank requires 0.5% per annum, leaving 0.3% per annum for each of X and Y. The swap should lead to X borrowing dollars at $9.6 - 0.3 = 9.3\%$ per annum and to Y borrowing yen at $6.5 - 0.3 = 6.2\%$ per annum. The appropriate arrangement is therefore as shown in the diagram below. All foreign exchange risk is borne by the bank.

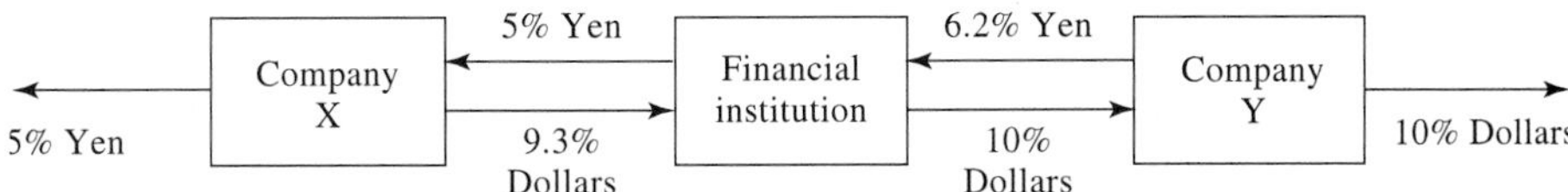

Swap for Quiz 7.2

7.3 In four months \$6 million ($= 0.5 \times 0.12 \times \$100$ million) will be received and \$4.8 million ($= 0.5 \times 0.096 \times \$100$ million) will be paid. (We ignore day count issues.) In 10 months \$6 million will be received, and the LIBOR rate prevailing in four months' time will be paid. The value of the fixed-rate bond underlying the swap is

$$6e^{-0.1\times 4/12} + 106e^{-0.1\times 10/12} = \$103.328 \text{ million}$$

The value of the floating-rate bond underlying the swap is

$$(100 + 4.8)e^{-0.1\times 4/12} = \$101.364 \text{ million}$$

The value of the swap to the party paying floating is $\$103.328 - \$101.364 = \$1.964$ million. The value of the swap to the party paying fixed is −\$1.964 million. These results can also be derived by decomposing the swap into forward contracts. Consider the party paying floating. The first forward contract involves paying \$4.8 million and receiving \$6 million in four months. It has a value of $1.2e^{-0.1\times 4/12} = \$1.161$ million. To value the second forward contract, we note that the forward interest rate is 10% per annum with continuous compounding, or 10.254% per annum with semiannual compounding. The value of the forward contract is

$$100 \times (0.12 \times 0.5 - 0.10254 \times 0.5)e^{-0.1\times 10/12} = \$0.803 \text{ million}$$

The total value of the forward contract is therefore $\$1.161 + \$0.803 = \$1.964$ million.

7.4 A swap rate for a particular maturity is the average of the bid and offer fixed rates that a market maker is prepared to exchange for LIBOR in a standard plain vanilla swap with that maturity. The frequency of payments and day count conventions in the standard swap that is considered vary from country to country. In the United States, payments on a standard swap are semiannual and the day count convention for quoting LIBOR is actual/360. The day count convention for quoting the fixed rate is usually actual/365. The swap rate for a particular maturity is the LIBOR rate for that maturity.

7.5 The swap involves exchanging the sterling interest of $20 \times 0.14 = 2.8$ million for the dollar interest of $30 \times 0.1 = \$3$ million. The principal amounts are also exchanged at the end of the life of the swap. The value of the sterling bond underlying the swap is

$$\frac{2.8}{(1.11)^{1/4}} + \frac{22.8}{(1.11)^{5/4}} = £22.739 \text{ million}$$

The value of the dollar bond underlying the swap is

$$\frac{3}{(1.08)^{1/4}} + \frac{33}{(1.08)^{5/4}} = \$32.916 \text{ million}$$

The value of the swap to the party paying sterling is therefore

$$32.916 - (22.739 \times 1.65) = -\$4.604 \text{ million}$$

The value of the swap to the party paying dollars is +\$4.604 million. The results can also be obtained by viewing the swap as a portfolio of forward contracts. The continuously compounded interest rates in sterling and dollars are 10.436% and 7.696% per annum, respectively. The 3-month and 15-month forward exchange rates are

$$1.65e^{-(0.10436-0.07696)\times 0.25} = 1.6387 \quad \text{and} \quad 1.65e^{-(0.10436-0.07696)\times 1.25} = 1.5944.$$

The values of the two forward contracts corresponding to the exchange of interest for the party paying sterling are therefore

$$(3 - 2.8 \times 1.6387)e^{-0.07696\times 0.25} = -\$1.558 \text{ million}$$

$$(3 - 2.8 \times 1.5944)e^{-0.07696\times 1.25} = -\$1.330 \text{ million}$$

The value of the forward contract corresponding to the exchange of principals is

$$(30 - 20 \times 1.5944)e^{-0.07696\times 1.25} = -\$1.716 \text{ million}$$

The total value of the swap is $-\$1.558 - \$1.330 - \$1.716 = -\$4.604$ million.

7.6 Credit risk arises from the possibility of a default by the counterparty. Market risk arises from movements in market variables such as interest rates and exchange rates. A complication is that the credit risk in a swap is contingent on the values of market variables. A company's position in a swap has credit risk only when the value of the swap to the company is positive.

7.7 The rate is not truly fixed because, if the company's credit rating declines, it will not be able to roll over its floating rate borrowings at LIBOR plus 150 basis points. The effective fixed borrowing rate then increases. Suppose for example that the treasurer's spread over LIBOR increases from 150 to 200 basis points. The borrowing rate increases from 5.2% to 5.7%.

CHAPTER 8

8.1 The investor makes a profit if the price of the stock on the expiration date is less than \$37. In these circumstances the gain from exercising the option is greater than \$3. The option will be exercised if the stock price is less than \$40 at the maturity of the option. The variation of the investor's profit with the stock price is as shown in the diagram below.

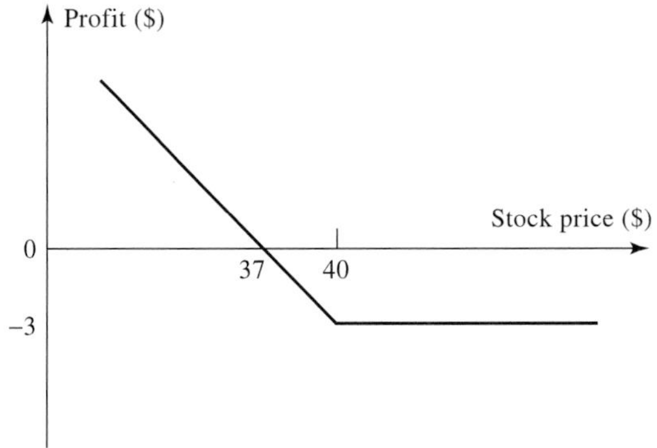

Investor's Profit in Quiz 8.1

8.2 The investor makes a profit if the price of the stock is below \$54 on the expiration date. If the stock price is below \$50, the option will not be exercised and the investor makes a profit of \$4. If the stock price is between \$50 and \$54, the option is exercised and the investor makes a profit between \$0 and \$4. The variation of the investor's profit with the stock price is as shown in the diagram below.

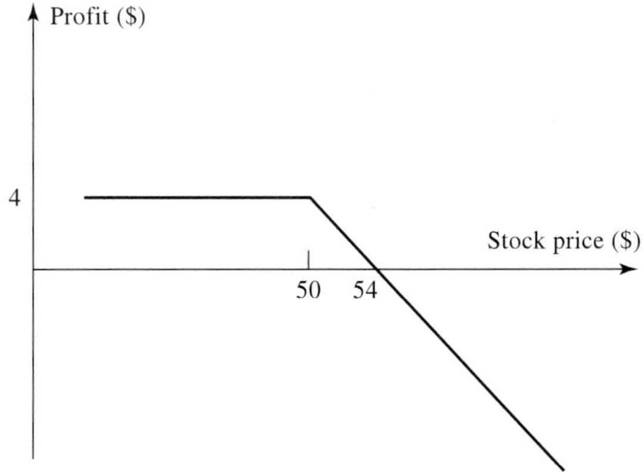

Investor's Profit in Quiz 8.2

8.3 The payoff to the investor is

$$-\max(S_T - K, 0) + \max(K - S_T, 0)$$

This is $K - S_T$ in all circumstances. The investor's position is the same as a short position in a forward contract with delivery price K.

8.4 When an investor buys an option, cash must be paid up front. There is no possibility of future liabilities and therefore no need for a margin account. When an investor sells an option, there are potential future liabilities. To protect against the risk of a default, margins are required.

8.5 On April 1, options trade with expiration months of April, May, August, and November. On May 30, options trade with expiration months of June, July, August, and November.

8.6 The strike price is reduced to \$30, and the option gives the holder the right to purchase twice as many shares.

8.7 Executive stock options last a long time (often 10 years or more). There is a vesting period during which the options cannot be exercised. If the executive leaves the company during the vesting period, the options are forfeited. If the executive leaves the company after the end of the vesting period, in-the-money options are exercised immediately while out-of-the-money options are forfeited. The options cannot be sold to another party by the executive.

CHAPTER 9

9.1 The six factors affecting stock option prices are the stock price, strike price, risk-free interest rate, volatility, time to maturity, and dividends.

9.2 The lower bound is

$$28 - 25e^{-0.08\times 0.3333} = \$3.66$$

9.3 The lower bound is

$$15e^{-0.06\times 0.08333} - 12 = \$2.93$$

9.4 Delaying exercise delays the payment of the strike price. This means that the option holder is able to earn interest on the strike price for a longer period of time. Delaying exercise also provides insurance against the stock price falling below the strike price by the expiration date. Assume that the option holder has an amount of cash K and that interest rates are zero. Exercising early means that the option holder's position will be worth S_T at expiration. Delaying exercise means that it will be worth $\max(K, S_T)$ at expiration.

9.5 An American put when held in conjunction with the underlying stock provides insurance. It guarantees that the stock can be sold for the strike price, K. If the put is exercised early, the insurance ceases. However, the option holder receives the strike price immediately and is able to earn interest on it between the time of the early exercise and the expiration date.

9.6 An American call option can be exercised at any time. If it is exercised, its holder gets the intrinsic value. It follows that an American call option must be worth at least its intrinsic value. A European call option can be worth less than its intrinsic value. Consider, for example, the situation where a stock is expected to provide a very high dividend during the life of an option. The price of the stock will decline as a result of the dividend. Because the European option can be exercised only after the dividend has been paid, its value may be less than the intrinsic value today.

9.7 In this case $c = 1$, $T = 0.25$, $S_0 = 19$, $K = 20$, and $r = 0.04$. From put–call parity,

$$p = c + Ke^{-rT} - S_0$$

or

$$p = 1 + 20e^{-0.04\times 0.25} - 19 = 1.80$$

so that the European put price is \$1.80.

CHAPTER 10

10.1 A protective put consists of a long position in a put option combined with a long position in the underlying shares. It is equivalent to a long position in a call option plus a certain amount of cash. This follows from put–call parity:

$$p + S_0 = c + Ke^{-rT} + D$$

10.2 A bear spread can be created using two call options with the same maturity and different strike prices. The investor shorts the call option with the lower strike price and buys the call option with the higher strike price. A bear spread can also be created using two put options with the same maturity and different strike prices. In this case, the investor shorts the put option with the lower strike price and buys the put option with the higher strike price.

10.3 A butterfly spread involves a position in options with three different strike prices (K_1, K_2, and K_3). A butterfly spread should be purchased when the investor considers that the price of the underlying stock is likely to stay close to the central strike price, K_2.

10.4 An investor can create a butterfly spread by buying call options with strike prices of \$15 and \$20 and selling two call options with strike prices of $\$17\frac{1}{2}$. The initial investment is $(4 + \frac{1}{2}) - (2 \times 2) = \$\frac{1}{2}$. The following table shows the variation of profit with the final stock price:

Stock price, S_T	Profit
$S_T < 15$	$-\frac{1}{2}$
$15 < S_T < 17\frac{1}{2}$	$(S_T - 15) - \frac{1}{2}$
$17\frac{1}{2} < S_T < 20$	$(20 - S_T) - \frac{1}{2}$
$S_T > 20$	$-\frac{1}{2}$

10.5 A reverse calendar spread is created by buying a short-maturity option and selling a long-maturity option, both with the same strike price.

10.6 Both a straddle and a strangle are created by combining a long position in a call with a long position in a put. In a straddle, the two have the same strike price and expiration date. In a strangle, they have different strike prices and the same expiration date.

10.7 A strangle is created by buying both options. The pattern of profits is as follows:

Stock price, S_T	Profit
$S_T < 45$	$(45 - S_T) - 5$
$45 < S_T < 50$	-5
$S_T > 50$	$(S_T - 50) - 5$

CHAPTER 11

11.1 Consider a portfolio consisting of:
-1: Call option
$+\Delta$: Shares
If the stock price rises to \$42, the portfolio is worth $42\Delta - 3$. If the stock price falls to \$38, it is worth 38Δ. These are the same when

$$42\Delta - 3 = 38\Delta$$

or $\Delta = 0.75$. The value of the portfolio in one month is 28.5 for both stock prices. Its value today must be the present value of 28.5, or $28.5e^{-0.08\times0.08333} = 28.31$. This means that

$$-f + 40\Delta = 28.31$$

where f is the call price. Because $\Delta = 0.75$, the call price is $40 \times 0.75 - 28.31 = \$1.69$. As an alternative approach, we can calculate the probability, p, of an up movement in a risk-neutral world. This must satisfy:

$$42p + 38(1 - p) = 40e^{0.08\times0.08333}$$

so that

$$4p = 40e^{0.08\times0.08333} - 38$$

or $p = 0.5669$. The value of the option is then its expected payoff discounted at the risk-free rate:

$$[3 \times 0.5669 + 0 \times 0.4331]e^{-0.08\times0.08333} = 1.69$$

or \$1.69. This agrees with the previous calculation.

11.2 In the no-arbitrage approach, we set up a riskless portfolio consisting of a position in the option and a position in the stock. By setting the return on the portfolio equal to the risk-free interest rate, we are able to value the option. When we use risk-neutral valuation, we first choose probabilities for the branches of the tree so that the expected return on the stock equals the risk-free interest rate. We then value the option by calculating its expected payoff and discounting this expected payoff at the risk-free interest rate.

11.3 The delta of a stock option measures the sensitivity of the option price to the price of the stock when small changes are considered. Specifically, it is the ratio of the change in the price of the stock option to the change in the price of the underlying stock.

11.4 Consider a portfolio consisting of:

-1: Put option
$+\Delta$: Shares

If the stock price rises to \$55, this is worth 55Δ. If the stock price falls to \$45, the portfolio is worth $45\Delta - 5$. These are the same when

$$45\Delta - 5 = 55\Delta$$

or $\Delta = -0.50$. The value of the portfolio in one month is -27.5 for both stock prices. Its value today must be the present value of -27.5, or $-27.5e^{-0.1\times0.5} = -26.16$. This means that

$$-f + 50\Delta = -26.16$$

where f is the put price. Because $\Delta = -0.50$, the put price is \$1.16. As an alternative approach, we can calculate the probability, p, of an up movement in a risk-neutral world. This must satisfy

$$55p + 45(1 - p) = 50e^{0.1\times0.5}$$

so that

$$10p = 50e^{0.1\times0.5} - 45$$

or $p = 0.7564$. The value of the option is then its expected payoff discounted at the risk-free rate:

$$[0 \times 0.7564 + 5 \times 0.2436]e^{-0.1\times0.5} = 1.16$$

or \$1.16. This agrees with the previous calculation.

11.5 In this case, $u = 1.10$, $d = 0.90$, $\Delta t = 0.5$, and $r = 0.08$, so that

$$p = \frac{e^{0.08\times0.5} - 0.90}{1.10 - 0.90} = 0.7041$$

The tree for stock price movements is shown in the diagram below.

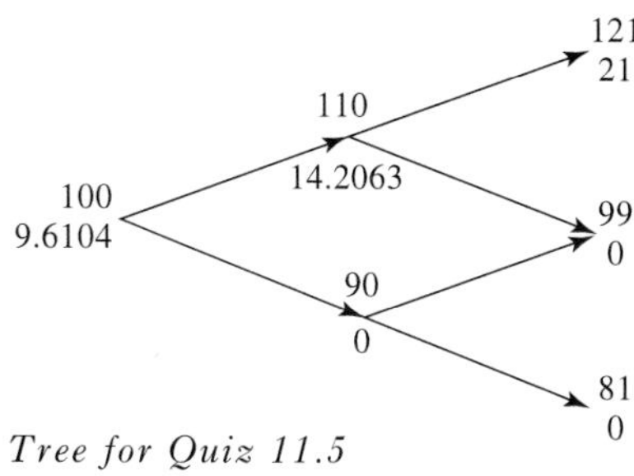

Tree for Quiz 11.5

We can work back from the end of the tree to the beginning, as indicated in the diagram, to give the value of the option as \$9.61. The option value can also be calculated directly from equation (11.10):

$$[0.7041^2 \times 21 + 2 \times 0.7041 \times 0.2959 \times 0 + 0.2959^2 \times 0]e^{-2\times0.08\times0.5} = 9.61$$

or \$9.61.

11.6 The diagram below shows how we can value the put option using the same tree as in Quiz 11.5. The value of the option is \$1.92. The option value can also be calculated directly from equation (11.10):

$$e^{-2\times0.08\times0.5}[0.7041^2 \times 0 + 2 \times 0.7041 \times 0.2959 \times 1 + 0.2959^2 \times 19] = 1.92$$

or \$1.92. The stock price plus the put price is $100 + 1.92 = \$101.92$. The present value of the strike price plus the call price is $100e^{-0.08\times1} + 9.61 = \$101.92$. These are the same, verifying that put–call parity holds.

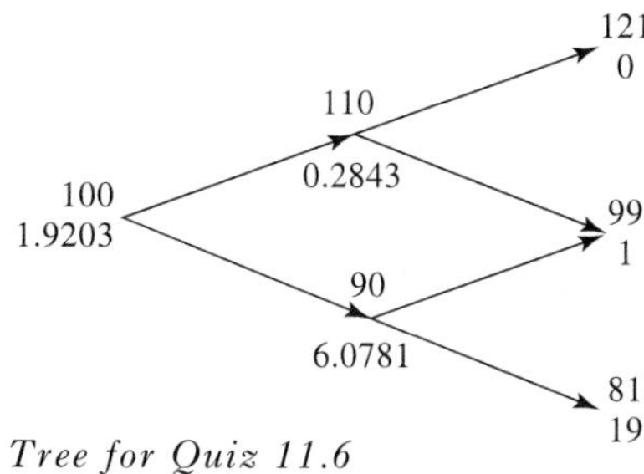

Tree for Quiz 11.6

11.7 $u = e^{\sigma\sqrt{\Delta t}}$ and $d = e^{-\sigma\sqrt{\Delta t}}$

CHAPTER 12

12.1 The Black–Scholes option pricing model assumes that the probability distribution of the stock price in one year (or at any other future time) is lognormal. Equivalently, it assumes that the continuously compounded rate of return on the stock is normally distributed.

12.2 The standard deviation of the percentage price change in time Δt is $\sigma\sqrt{\Delta t}$, where σ is the volatility. In this problem, $\sigma = 0.3$ and, assuming 252 trading days in one year, $\Delta t = 1/252 = 0.003968$, so that $\sigma\sqrt{\Delta t} = 0.3\sqrt{0.003968} = 0.019$ or 1.9%.

12.3 Assuming that the expected return from the stock is the risk-free rate, we calculate the expected payoff from a call option. We then discount this payoff from the end of the life of the option to the beginning at the risk-free interest rate.

12.4 In this case, $S_0 = 50$, $K = 50$, $r = 0.1$, $\sigma = 0.3$, $T = 0.25$, and

$$d_1 = \frac{\ln(50/50) + (0.1 + 0.09/2)0.25}{0.3\sqrt{0.25}} = 0.2417$$

$$d_2 = d_1 - 0.3\sqrt{0.25} = 0.0917$$

The European put price is

$$50N(-0.0917)e^{-0.1\times 0.25} - 50N(-0.2417) = 50 \times 0.4634e^{-0.1\times 0.25} - 50 \times 0.4045$$
$$= 2.37$$

or \$2.37.

12.5 In this case, we must subtract the present value of the dividend from the stock price before using Black–Scholes. Hence, the appropriate value of S_0 is

$$S_0 = 50 - 1.50e^{-0.1\times 0.1667} = 48.52$$

As before, $K = 50$, $r = 0.1$, $\sigma = 0.3$, and $T = 0.25$. In this case,

$$d_1 = \frac{\ln(48.52/50) + (0.1 + 0.09/2)0.25}{0.3\sqrt{0.25}} = 0.0414$$

$$d_2 = d_1 - 0.3\sqrt{0.25} = -0.1086$$

The European put price is

$$50N(0.1086)e^{-0.1\times 0.25} - 48.52N(-0.0414) = 50 \times 0.5432e^{-0.1\times 0.25} - 48.52 \times 0.4835$$
$$= 3.03$$

or \$3.03.

12.6 The implied volatility is the volatility that makes the Black–Scholes price of an option equal to its market price. It is calculated by trial and error. We test in a systematic way different volatilities until we find the one that gives the European put option price when it is substituted into the Black–Scholes formula.

12.7 In Black's approximation, we calculate the price of a European call option expiring at the same time as the American call option and the price of a European call option expiring just before the final ex-dividend date. We set the American call option price equal to the greater of the two.

CHAPTER 13

13.1 When the S&P 100 goes down to 700, the value of the portfolio can be expected to be $10 \times (700/800) =$ \$8.75 million. (This assumes that the dividend yield on the portfolio equals the dividend yield on the index.) Buying put options on $10{,}000{,}000/800 = 12{,}500$ times the index with a strike of 700 therefore provides protection against a drop in the value of the portfolio below \$8.75 million. Because each contract is on 100 times the index, a total of 125 contracts would be required.

13.2 A stock index is analogous to a stock paying a dividend yield, the dividend yield being the dividend yield on the index. A currency is analogous to a stock paying a dividend yield, the dividend yield being the foreign risk-free interest rate.

13.3 The lower bound is given by equation (13.1) as

$$300e^{-0.03\times0.5} - 290e^{-0.08\times0.5} = 16.90$$

13.4 The tree of exchange-rate movements is shown in the diagram below. In this case, $u = 1.02$ and $d = 0.98$. The probability of an up movement in a risk-neutral world is

$$p = \frac{e^{(0.06-0.08)\times0.08333} - 0.98}{1.02 - 0.98} = 0.4584$$

The tree shows that the value of an option to purchase one unit of the currency is \$0.0067.

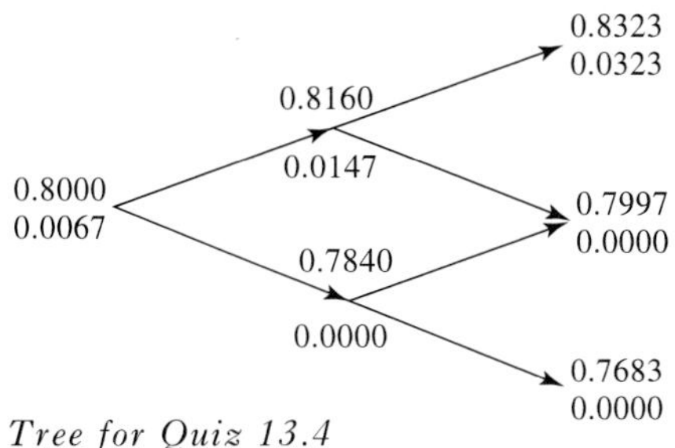

Tree for Quiz 13.4

13.5 A company that knows it is due to receive foreign currency at a certain time in the future can buy a put option. This guarantees that the price at which the currency will be sold will be at or above a certain level. A company that knows it is due to pay foreign currency at a certain time in the future can buy a call option. This guarantees that the price at which the currency will be purchased will be at or below a certain level.

13.6 In this case, $S_0 = 250$, $K = 250$, $r = 0.10$, $\sigma = 0.18$, $T = 0.25$, $q = 0.03$, and

$$d_1 = \frac{\ln(250/250) + (0.10 - 0.03 + 0.18^2/2)0.25}{0.18\sqrt{0.25}} = 0.2394$$

$$d_2 = d_1 - 0.18\sqrt{0.25} = 0.1494$$

and the call price is

$$\begin{aligned}250N(0.2394)e^{-0.03\times0.25} &- 250N(0.1494)e^{-0.10\times0.25}\\ &= 250 \times 0.5946e^{-0.03\times0.25} - 250 \times 0.5594e^{-0.10\times0.25}\\ &= 11.14\end{aligned}$$

13.7 In this case, $S_0 = 0.52$, $K = 0.50$, $r = 0.04$, $r_f = 0.08$, $\sigma = 0.12$, $T = 0.6667$, and

$$d_1 = \frac{\ln(0.52/0.50) + (0.04 - 0.08 + 0.12^2/2)0.6667}{0.12\sqrt{0.6667}} = 0.1771$$

$$d_2 = d_1 - 0.12\sqrt{0.6667} = 0.0791$$

and the put price is

$$\begin{aligned}0.50N(-0.0791)e^{-0.04\times0.6667} &- 0.52N(-0.1771)e^{-0.08\times0.6667}\\ &= 0.50 \times 0.4685e^{-0.04\times0.6667} - 0.52 \times 0.4297e^{-0.08\times0.6667}\\ &= 0.0162\end{aligned}$$

CHAPTER 14

14.1 A call option on yen gives the holder the right to buy yen in the spot market at an exchange rate equal to the strike price. A call option on yen futures gives the holder the right to receive the amount by which the futures price exceeds the strike price. If the yen futures option is exercised, the holder also obtains a long position in the yen futures contract.

14.2 The main reason is that a bond futures contract is a more liquid instrument than a bond. The price of a Treasury bond futures contract is known immediately from trading on CBOT. The price of a bond can be obtained only by contacting dealers.

14.3 A futures price behaves like a stock paying a dividend yield at the risk-free interest rate.

14.4 In this case, $u = 1.12$ and $d = 0.92$. The probability of an up movement in a risk-neutral world is

$$\frac{1 - 0.92}{1.12 - 0.92} = 0.4$$

From risk-neutral valuation, the value of the call is

$$e^{-0.06\times0.5}(0.4 \times 6 + 0.6 \times 0) = 2.33$$

14.5 The put–call parity formula for futures options is the same as the put–call parity formula for stock options except that the stock price is replaced by F_0e^{-rT}, where F_0 is the current futures price, r is the risk-free interest rate, and T is the life of the option.

14.6 The American futures call option is worth more than the corresponding American option on the underlying asset when the futures price is greater than the spot price prior to the maturity of the futures contract.

14.7 In this case, $F_0 = 19$, $K = 20$, $r = 0.12$, $\sigma = 0.20$, and $T = 0.4167$. The value of the European put futures option is

$$20N(-d_2)e^{-0.12\times0.4167} - 19N(-d_1)e^{-0.12\times0.4167}$$

where

$$d_1 = \frac{\ln(19/20) + (0.04/2)0.4167}{0.2\sqrt{0.4167}} = -0.3327$$

$$d_2 = d_1 - 0.2\sqrt{0.4167} = -0.4618$$

This is

$$e^{-0.12\times0.4167}[20N(0.4618) - 19N(0.3327)] = e^{-0.12\times0.4167}(20 \times 0.6778 - 19 \times 0.6303)$$
$$= 1.50$$

or \$1.50.

CHAPTER 15

15.1 A stop-loss scheme can be implemented by arranging to have a covered position when the option is in the money and a naked position when it is out of the money. When using the scheme, the writer of an out-of-the-money call would buy the underlying asset as soon as the price moved above the strike price, K, and sell the underlying asset as soon as the price moved below K. In practice, when the price of the underlying asset equals K, there is no way of knowing whether it will subsequently move above or below K. The asset will therefore be bought at $K + \epsilon$ and sold at $K - \epsilon$ for some small ϵ. The cost of hedging depends on the number of times the asset price equals K. The hedge is therefore relatively poor. It will cost nothing if the asset price never reaches K; on the other hand, it will be quite expensive if the asset price equals K many times. In a good hedge, the cost of hedging is known in advance to a reasonable level of accuracy.

15.2 A delta of 0.7 means that, when the price of the stock increases by a small amount, the price of the option increases by 70% of this amount. Similarly, when the price of the stock decreases by a small amount, the price of the option decreases by 70% of this amount. A short position in 1,000 options has a delta of −700 and can be made delta neutral with the purchase of 700 shares.

15.3 In this case, $S_0 = K$, $r = 0.1$, $\sigma = 0.25$, and $T = 0.5$. Also,

$$d_1 = \frac{\ln(S_0/K) + [(0.1 + 0.25^2)/2]0.5}{0.25\sqrt{0.5}} = 0.3712$$

The delta of the option is $N(d_1)$, or 0.64.

15.4 No. A long or short position in the underlying asset has zero vega. This is because its value does not change when volatility changes.

15.5 The gamma of an option position is the rate of change of the delta of the position with respect to the asset price. For example, a gamma of 0.1 indicates that, when the asset price increases by a certain small amount, delta increases by 0.1 times this amount. When the gamma of an option writer's position is large and negative and the delta is zero, the option writer will lose money if there is a large movement (either an increase or a decrease) in the asset price.

15.6 To hedge an option position, it is necessary to create the opposite option position synthetically. For example, to hedge a long position in a put, it is necessary to create a short position in a put synthetically. It follows that the procedure for creating an option position synthetically is the reverse of the procedure for hedging the option position.

15.7 Portfolio insurance by creating put options synthetically was popular in 1987. It works as follows. When a portfolio's value declines, the portfolio is rebalanced by (a) selling part of the portfolio or (b) selling some index futures. If enough portfolio managers are following this strategy, an unstable situation is created. A small decline leads to selling. This in turn causes a bigger decline and leads to more selling, etc. It is argued that this phenomenon played a role in the October, 1987, crash.

CHAPTER 16

16.1 Delta, gamma, and theta can be determined from a single binomial tree. Vega is determined by making a small change to the volatility and recomputing the option price using a new tree. Rho is calculated by making a small change to the interest rate and recomputing the option price using a new tree.

16.2 With our usual notation the answers are (a) $e^{r\Delta t}$, (b) $e^{(r-q)\Delta t}$, (c) $e^{(r-r_f)\Delta t}$, and (d) 1.

16.3 In this case, $S_0 = 60$, $K = 60$, $r = 0.1$, $\sigma = 0.45$, $T = 0.25$, and $\Delta t = 0.0833$. Also,

$$u = e^{\sigma\sqrt{\Delta t}} = e^{0.45\sqrt{0.0833}} = 1.1387, \quad d = \frac{1}{u} = 0.8782, \quad a = e^{r\Delta t} = e^{0.1\times 0.0833} = 1.0084,$$

$$p = \frac{a-d}{u-d} = 0.4998, \quad 1 - p = 0.5002$$

The tree is shown in the diagram below. The calculated price of the option is \$5.16.

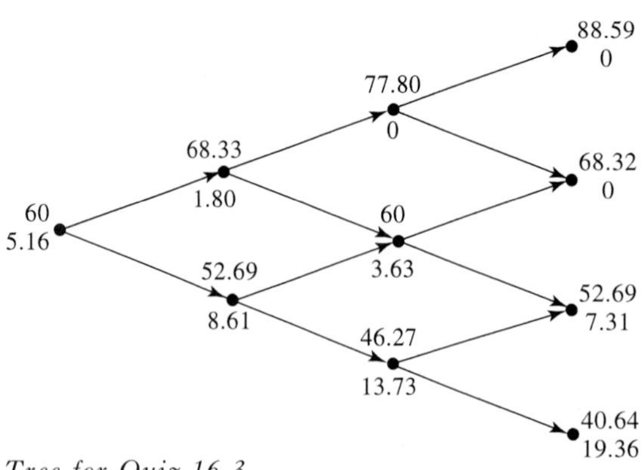

Tree for Quiz 16.3

16.4 The control variate technique is implemented by:

a. Valuing an American option using a binomial tree in the usual way (to get f_A)

b. Valuing the European option with the same parameters as the American option using the same tree (to get f_E)

c. Valuing the European option using Black–Scholes (to get f_{BS})

The price of the American option is estimated as $f_A + f_{BS} - f_E$.

16.5 In this case, $F_0 = 198$, $K = 200$, $r = 0.08$, $\sigma = 0.3$, $T = 0.75$, and $\Delta t = 0.25$. Also,

$$u = e^{0.3\sqrt{0.25}} = 1.1618, \quad d = \frac{1}{u} = 0.8607, \quad a = 1$$

$$p = \frac{a - d}{u - d} = 0.4626, \quad 1 - p = 0.5373$$

The tree is as shown in the diagram below. The calculated price of the option is 20.3 cents.

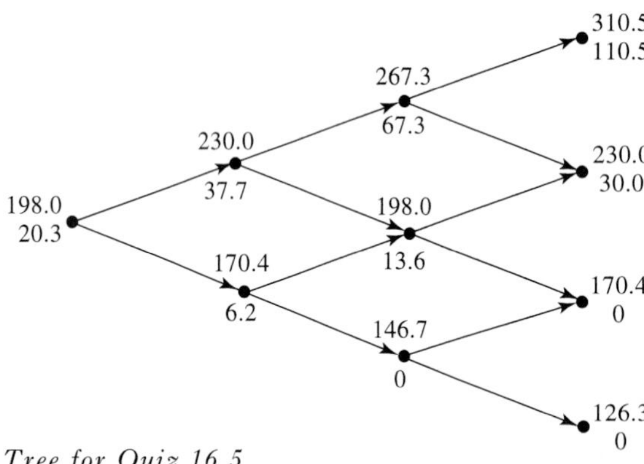

Tree for Quiz 16.5

16.6 Suppose a dividend equal to D is paid during a certain time interval. If S is the stock price at the beginning of the time interval, it will be either $Su - D$ or $Sd - D$ at the end of the time interval. At the end of the next time interval, it will be one of $(Su - D)u$, $(Su - D)d$, $(Sd - D)u$, or $(Sd - D)d$. Because $(Su - D)d$ does not equal $(Sd - D)u$, the tree does not recombine. If S is equal to the stock price less the present value of future dividends, this problem is avoided.

16.7 In Monte Carlo simulation, we sample paths through the tree, working from the beginning to the end. When a node is reached, we have no way of knowing whether early exercise is optimal.

CHAPTER 17

17.1 When both tails of the stock price distribution are less heavy than those of the lognormal distribution, Black–Scholes will tend to produce relatively high prices for options when they are either significantly out of the money or significantly in the money. This leads to an implied volatility pattern similar to that in Figure 17.7. When the right tail is heavier and the left tail is less heavy, Black–Scholes will tend to produce relatively low prices for out-of-the-money calls and in-the-money puts, and it will tend to produce relatively high prices for out-of-the-money puts and in-the-money calls. This leads to implied volatility being an increasing function of strike price.

17.2 A downward sloping volatility smile is usually observed for equities.

17.3 Jumps tend to make both tails of the stock price distribution heavier than those of the lognormal distribution. This creates a volatility smile similar to that in Figure 17.1. The volatility smile is likely to be more pronounced for the three-month option.

17.4 The put has a price that is too low relative to the call's price. The correct trading strategy is to buy the put, buy the stock, and sell the call.

17.5 The heavier left tail should lead to high prices, and therefore high implied volatilities, for out-of-the-money (low-strike-price) puts. Similarly, the less heavy right tail should lead to low prices, and therefore low volatilities for out-of-the-money (high-strike-price) calls. A volatility smile where volatility is a decreasing function of strike price results.

17.6 With the notation in the text,

$$c_{\text{bs}} + Ke^{-rT} = p_{\text{bs}} + Se^{-qT}$$

$$c_{\text{mkt}} + Ke^{-rT} = p_{\text{mkt}} + Se^{-qT}$$

It follows that

$$c_{\text{bs}} - c_{\text{mkt}} = p_{\text{bs}} - p_{\text{mkt}}$$

In this case, $c_{\text{mkt}} = 3.00$, $c_{\text{bs}} = 3.50$, and $p_{\text{bs}} = 1.00$. It follows that p_{mkt} should be 0.50.

17.7 The crashophobia argument is an attempt to explain the pronounced volatility skew in equity markets since 1987. (This was the year equity markets shocked everyone by crashing more than 20% in one day.) The argument is that traders are concerned about another crash and as a result increase the price of out-of-the-money puts. This creates the volatility skew.

CHAPTER 18

18.1 The historical simulation method involves constructing N scenarios of what might happen between today and tomorrow from N days of historical data. The first scenario assumes that the percentage change in all market variables will be the same as that between the first day (Day 0) and the second day (Day 1); the second scenario assumes that the percentage change in all market variables will be the same as that between the second day (Day 1) and the third day (Day 2); and so on. The final scenario assumes that the percentage change in all market variables will be the same as that between yesterday (Day $N-1$) and today (Day N). The portfolio is valued for each scenario and VaR is calculated from the probability distribution of portfolio value changes.

18.2 Define u_i as $(S_i - S_{i-1})/S_{i-1}$, where S_i is the value of a market variable on day i. In the EWMA model, the variance rate of the market variable (i.e., the square of its volatility) is a weighted average of the u_i^2. For some constant λ $(0 < \lambda < 1)$, the weight given to u_{i-1}^2 (which is calculated on day $i-1$) is λ times the weight given to u_i^2 (which is calculated on day i). The volatility σ_n estimated at the end of day $n-1$ is related to the volatility σ_{n-1} estimated at the end of day $n-2$ by

$$\sigma_n^2 = \lambda\sigma_{n-1}^2 + (1-\lambda)u_{n-1}^2$$

This formula shows that the EWMA model has one very attractive property. To calculate the volatility estimate for day n, it is sufficient to know the volatility estimate for day $n-1$ and u_{n-1}^2.

18.3 In this case, $\sigma_{n-1} = 0.015$ and $u_n = 0.5/30 = 0.01667$, so that equation (18.10) gives

$$\sigma_n^2 = 0.94 \times 0.015^2 + 0.06 \times 0.01667^2 = 0.0002282$$

The volatility estimate on day n is therefore $\sqrt{0.0002282}$ or 1.51%.

18.4 Measured in thousands of dollars, the variance of daily changes in the portfolio value is

$$300^2 \times 0.018^2 + 500^2 \times 0.012^2 + 2 \times 300 \times 500 \times 0.018 \times 0.012 \times 0.3 = 84.60$$

The standard deviation of daily changes in the portfolio is $\sqrt{84.60} = 9.20$. The standard deviation of changes over five days is $9.20\sqrt{5} = 20.57$. The 5-day 95% VaR for the portfolio is therefore $1.65 \times 20.57 = 33.94$, or \$33,940.

18.5 The approximate relationship between the daily change in the portfolio value, ΔP, and the daily change in the exchange rate, ΔS, is

$$\Delta P = 56\Delta S$$

The proportional daily change in the exchange rate, Δx, equals $\Delta S/1.5$. It follows that

$$\Delta P = 56 \times 1.5\Delta x$$

or

$$\Delta P = 84\Delta x$$

The standard deviation of Δx equals the daily volatility of the exchange rate, or 0.7%. The standard deviation of ΔP is therefore $84 \times 0.007 = 0.588$. It follows that the 10-day 99% VaR for the portfolio is

$$0.588 \times 2.33 \times \sqrt{10} = 4.33$$

18.6 From equation (18.5), the relationship is

$$\Delta P = 56 \times 1.5\Delta x + \tfrac{1}{2} \times 1.5^2 \times 16.2 \times \Delta x^2$$

or

$$\Delta P = 84\Delta x + 18.225\Delta x^2$$

18.7 The historical simulation method assumes that the joint probability distribution of the market variables is the distribution given by the historical data. The model building approach usually assumes that the market variables have a multivariate normal distribution. The volatilities of, and correlations between, market variables in the model building approach are usually calculated using an approach, such as the exponentially weighted moving average method, that applies more weight to recent data.

CHAPTER 19

19.1 An amount

$$\$20,000,000 \times (0.12 - 0.10) \times 0.25 = \$100,000$$

would be paid out three months later.

19.2 A callable bond is a bond where the issuer has the option to buy back the bond from the holder at certain times at prespecified prices. A puttable bond is a bond where the holder has the right to sell the bond back to the issuer at certain times at prespecified prices.

19.3 A swaption is an option to enter into an interest rate swap at a certain time in the future with a certain fixed rate being exchanged for floating. An interest rate swap can be regarded as the exchange of a fixed-rate bond for a floating-rate bond. Thus, a swaption is the option to exchange a fixed-rate bond for a floating-rate bond. The floating-rate bond will be worth its face value at the beginning of the life of the swap. The swaption is therefore an option on a fixed-rate bond with the strike price equal to the face value of the bond.

19.4 In this case, $F_0 = (125 - 10)e^{0.1\times 1} = 127.09$, $K = 110$, $r = 0.1$, $\sigma = 0.08$, $T = 1.0$, and

$$d_1 = \frac{\ln(127.09/110) + (0.08^2/2)}{0.08} = 1.8456$$

$$d_2 = d_1 - 0.08 = 1.7656$$

The value of the put option is

$$110e^{-0.1}N(-1.7656) - 115N(-1.8456) = 0.12$$

or \$0.12.

19.5 The payoff is $25 \times 87 = \$2,175$.

19.6 In this case, $L = 1,000$, $\delta_k = 0.25$, $F_k = 0.12$, $R_K = 0.13$, $\sigma_k = 0.12$, $t_k = 1.5$, $e^{-0.115\times 1.75} = 0.8177$, and

$$d_1 = \frac{\ln(0.12/0.13) + 0.12^2 \times 1.5/2}{0.12\sqrt{1.5}} = -0.4711$$

$$d_2 = -0.4711 - 0.12\sqrt{1.5} = -0.6181$$

The value of the option is

$$1000 \times 0.25 \times 0.8177[0.12N(-0.4711) - 0.13N(-0.6181)] = 0.69$$

or \$0.69.

19.7 There are two main advantages of yield curve models. First, they enable all interest rate derivative securities to be valued on a consistent basis. Second, they enable securities that cannot be handled using Black's model to be valued. An example of a security that cannot be valued using Black's model but can be valued using yield curve models is a long-dated American swap option.

CHAPTER 20

20.1 A forward start option is an option that is granted now but will start at some time in the future. The strike price is usually equal to the price of the asset at the time the option starts. A chooser option is an option where, at some time in the future, the holder chooses whether the option is a call or a put.

20.2 With the usual notation, the value is $100e^{-0.04\times 0.25}N(d_2)$. In this case,

$$d_2 = \frac{\ln(50/50) + (0.04 - 0.2^2/2)0.25}{0.2\sqrt{0.25}} = 0.05$$

and

$$N(d_2) = 0.5199$$

and the value of the option is $100e^{-0.04\times 0.25} \times 0.5199 = \$51.48$

20.3 Up-and-in call, up-and-out call, up-and-in put, up-and-out put, down-and-in call, down-and-out call, down-and-in put, and down-and-out put.

20.4 In an equity swap, one party promises to pay the return on an equity index applied to a notional principal and the other promises to pay a fixed or floating return on the notional principal.

20.5 When prepayments increase, the principal is received sooner. This increases the value of a PO. When prepayments increase, less interest is received. This decreases the value of an IO.

20.6 A cancelable swap gives company X the option to terminate the swap early. Suppose that the swap lasts until time T and company X terminates at time t. This is equivalent to company X entering into a new swap at time t. This new swap lasts until time T and has the opposite cash flows to the original swap. The termination option therefore gives company X the right to enter into a swap, that is, it gives company X a swap option.

20.7 The trader could enter into a diff swap where interest is paid on a U.S. dollar principal at the three-month U.S. dollar LIBOR rate and interest is received on the same U.S. dollar principal at the three-month Canadian LIBOR rate minus a 2% spread. This is better than a regular floating-for-floating swap where the Canadian dollar LIBOR is applied to a Canadian dollar principal because it avoids any exposure to the Canadian dollar/U.S. dollar exchange rate.

CHAPTER 21

21.1 Both provide insurance against a particular company defaulting during a period of time. In a credit default swap the payoff is the notional principal amount multiplied by one minus the recovery rate. In a binary swap the payoff is the notional principal.

21.2 The seller receives

$$300{,}000{,}000 \times 0.0060 \times 0.5 = \$900{,}000$$

at times 0.5, 1.0, 1.5, 2.0, 2.5, 3.0, 3.5, and 4.0 years. The seller also receives a final accrual payment of about \$300,000 (= \$300,000,000 × 0.060 × 2/12) at the time of the default (4 years and 2 months). The seller pays

$$300{,}000{,}000 \times 0.6 = \$180{,}000{,}000$$

at the time of the default.

21.3 Sometimes there is physical settlement and sometimes there is cash settlement. In the event of a default when there is physical settlement, the buyer of protection sells bonds issued by the reference entity for their face value. Bonds with a total face value equal to the notional principal can be sold. In the event of a default when there is cash settlement, a calculation agent estimates the value of the cheapest-to-deliver bonds issued by the reference entity a specified number of days after the default event. The cash payoff is then based on the excess of the face value of these bonds over the estimated value.

21.4 A CDO is created from a bond portfolio. The returns from the bond portfolio flow to a number of tranches (i.e., different categories of investors). The tranches differ as far as the credit risk they assume. The first tranche might have an investment in 5% of the bond portfolio and be responsible for the first 5% of losses. The next tranche might have an investment in 10% of the portfolio and be responsible for the next 10% of the losses, and so on. In a synthetic CDO, there is no bond portfolio. Instead a portfolio of credit default swaps is sold and the resulting credit risks are allocated to tranches in a similar way to that just described.

21.5 In a first-to-default basket CDS, there are a number of reference entities. When the first one defaults, there is a payoff (calculated in the usual way for a CDS) and basket CDS terminates. The value of a first-to-default basket CDS decreases as the correlation between the reference entities in the basket increases.

21.6 Risk-neutral default probabilities are backed out from credit default swaps or bond prices. Actuarial default probabilities are calculated from historical data.

21.7 Suppose a company wants to buy some assets. If a total return swap is used, a financial institution buys the assets and enters into a swap with the company where it pays the company the return on the assets and receives from the company LIBOR plus a spread. The financial institution has less risk than it would have if it lent the company money and used the assets as collateral. This is because, in the event of a default by the company, it owns the assets.

CHAPTER 22

22.1 A day's HDD is max(0, 65 – A) and a day's CDD is max(0, A – 65), where A is the average of the highest and lowest temperature during the day at a specified weather station, measured in degrees Fahrenheit.

22.2 The average temperature each day is 75°. The CDD each day is therefore 10 and the cumulative CDD for the month is $10 \times 31 = 310$. The payoff from the call option is therefore $(310 - 250) \times 5{,}000 = \$300{,}000$.

22.3 It is an agreement by one side to delivery a specified amount of gas at a roughly uniform rate during a month to a particular hub for a specified price.

22.4 Unlike most commodities electricity cannot be stored easily. If the demand for electricity exceeds the supply, as it sometimes does during the air-conditioning season, the price of electricity in a deregulated environment will skyrocket. When supply and demand become matched again, the price will return to former levels.

22.5 There is no systematic risk (i.e., risk that is priced by the market) in weather derivatives and CAT bonds.

22.6 The energy producer faces quantity risks and price risks. It can use weather derivatives to hedge the quantity risks and energy derivatives to hedge against the price risks.

22.7 CAT bonds (catastrophe bonds) are an alternative to reinsurance for an insurance company that has taken on a certain catastrophic risk (e.g., the risk of a hurricane or an earthquake) and wants to get rid of it. CAT bonds are issued by the insurance company. They provide a higher rate of interest than government bonds. However, the bondholders agree to forego interest, and possibly principal, to meet any claims against the insurance company that are within a prespecified range.

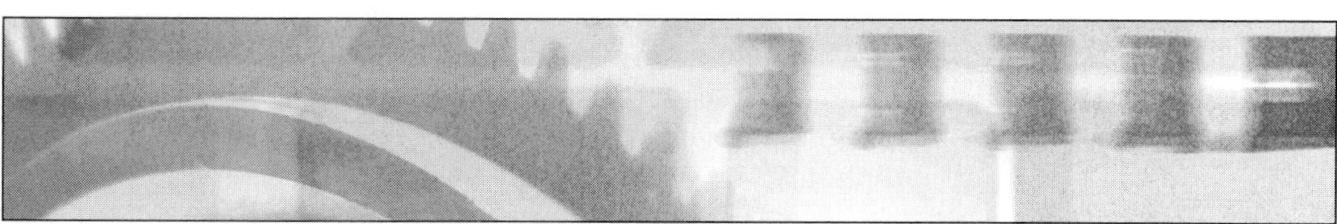

Glossary of Terms

Accrual Swap An interest rate swap where interest on one side accrues only when a certain condition is met.

Accrued Interest The interest earned on a bond since the last coupon payment date.

American Option An option that can be exercised at any time during its life.

Amortizing Swap A swap where the notional principal decreases in a predetermined way as time passes.

Analytic Result Result where the answer is in the form of an equation.

Arbitrage A trading strategy that takes advantage of two or more securities being mispriced relative to each other.

Arbitrageur An individual engaging in arbitrage.

Asian Option An option with a payoff dependent on the average price of the underlying asset during a specified period.

Ask Price *See* Offer price.

Asked Price *See* Offer price.

Asset-or-nothing Call Option An option that provides a payoff equal to the asset price if the asset price is above the strike price and zero otherwise.

Asset-or-nothing Put Option An option that provides a payoff equal to the asset price if the asset price is below the strike price and zero otherwise.

As-you-like-it Option *See* Chooser option.

At-the-money Option An option in which the strike price equals the price of the underlying asset.

Average Price Call Option An option giving a payoff equal to the greater of zero and the amount by which the average price of the asset exceeds the strike price.

Average Price Put Option An option giving a payoff equal to the greater of zero and the amount by which the strike price exceeds the average price of the asset.

Average Strike Option An option that provides a payoff dependent on the difference between the final asset price and the average asset price.

Back Testing Testing a value-at-risk or other model using historical data.

Backwards Induction A procedure for working from the end of a tree to its beginning in order to value an option.

Barrier Option An option whose payoff depends on whether the path of the underlying asset has reached a barrier (i.e., a certain predetermined level).

Basis The difference between the spot price and the futures price of a commodity.

Basis Point When used to describe an interest rate, a basis point is one hundredth of one percent (= 0.01 percent).

Basis Risk The risk to a hedger arising from uncertainty about the basis at a future time.

Basis Swap A swap where cash flows determined by one floating reference rate are exchanged for cash flows determined by another floating reference rate.

Basket Credit Default Swap Credit default swap where there are several reference entities.

Basket Option An option that provides a payoff dependent on the value of a portfolio of assets.

Bear Spread A short position in a put option with strike price X_1 combined with a long position in a put option with strike price X_2, where $X_2 > X_1$. (A bear spread can also be created with call options.)

Bermudan Option An option that can be exercised on specified dates during its life.

Beta A measure of the systematic risk of an asset.

Bid–Ask Spread *See* Bid–Offer spread.

Bid–Offer Spread The amount by which the offer price exceeds the bid price.

Bid Price The price that a dealer is prepared to pay for an asset.

Binary Option Option with a discontinuous payoff, e.g. a cash-or-nothing option or an asset-or-nothing option.

Binomial Model A model where the price of an asset is monitored over successive short periods of time. In each short period, it is assumed that only two price movements are possible.

Binomial Tree A tree that represents how an asset price can evolve under the binomial model.

Black's Approximation An approximate procedure developed by Fischer Black for valuing a call option on a dividend-paying stock.

Black's Model An extension of the Black–Scholes model for valuing European options on futures contracts.

Black–Scholes Model A model for pricing European options on stocks, developed by Fischer Black, Myron Scholes, and Robert Merton.

Board Broker The individual who handles limit orders in some exchanges. The board broker makes information on outstanding limit orders available to other traders.

Bond Option An option where a bond is the underlying asset.

Bond Yield Discount rate which, when applied to all the cash flows of a bond, causes the present value of the cash flows to equal the bond's market price.

Bootstrap Method A procedure for calculating the zero-coupon yield curve from market data.

Boston Option *See* Deferred payment option.

Break Forward *See* Deferred payment option.

Bull Spread A long position in a call with strike price X_1 combined with a short position in a call with strike price X_2, where $X_2 > X_1$. (A bull spread can also be created with put options.)

Butterfly Spread A position that is created by taking a long position in a call with strike price X_1, a long position in a call with strike price X_3, and a short position in two calls with strike price X_2, where $X_3 > X_2 > X_1$ and $X_2 = 0.5(X_1 + X_3)$. (A butterfly spread can also be created with put options.)

Calendar Spread A position that is created by taking a long position in a call option that matures at one time and a short position in a similar call option that matures at a different time. (A calendar spread can also be created using put options.)

Callable bond A bond containing provisions that allow the issuer to buy it back at a predetermined price at certain times during its life.

Call Option An option to buy an asset at a certain price by a certain date.

Cancelable Swap A swap that can be canceled by one side on prespecified dates.

Cap *See* Interest-rate cap.

Capital Asset Pricing Model A model relating the expected return on an asset to its beta.

Caplet One component of an interest-rate cap.

Cap Rate The rate determining payoffs in an interest-rate cap.

Cash Flow Mapping A procedure for representing an instrument as a portfolio of zero-coupon bonds for the purpose of calculating value at risk.

Cash-or-nothing Call Option An option that provides a fixed predetermined payoff if the final asset price is above the strike price and zero otherwise.

Cash-or-nothing Put Option An option that provides a fixed predetermined payoff if the final asset price is below the strike price and zero otherwise.

Cash Settlement Procedure for settling a futures contract in cash rather than by delivering the underlying asset.

CAT Bond Bond where the interest and, possibly, the principal paid are reduced if a particular category of "catastrophic" insurance claims exceed a certain amount.

CDD (Cooling degree days) The maximum of zero and the amount by which the daily average temperature is greater than 65° Fahrenheit. The average temperature is the average of the highest and lowest temperatures (midnight to midnight).

Cheapest-to-deliver Bond The bond that is cheapest to deliver in the Chicago Board of Trade bond futures contract.

Chooser Option An option where the holder has the right to choose whether it is a call or a put at some point during its life.

Class of Options *See* Option class.

Clean Price of Bond The quoted price of a bond. The cash price paid for the bond (or dirty price) is calculated by adding the accrued interest to the clean price.

Clearinghouse A firm that guarantees the performance of the parties in an exchange-traded derivatives transaction. Also referred to as a *clearing corporation*.

Clearing margin A margin posted by a member of a clearinghouse.

CMO (Collateralized mortgage obligation) A mortgage-backed security where investors are divided into classes and there are rules for determining how principal repayments are channeled to the classes.

Collar *See* Interest rate collar

Collateralized Debt Obligation A way of packaging credit risk. Several classes of securities are created from a portfolio of bonds and there are rules for determining how defaults are allocated to classes.

Combination A position involving both calls and puts on the same underlying asset.

Commission Brokers Individuals who execute trades for other people and charge a commission for doing so.

Commodity Futures Trading Commission A body that regulates trading in futures contracts in the United States.

Commodity Swap A swap where cash flows depend on the price of a commodity.

Compounding Frequency This defines how an interest rate is measured.

Compounding Swap A swap where interest compounds instead of being paid.

Compound Option An option on an option.

Conditional Value at Risk (C-VaR) Expected loss during N days conditional on being in the $(100 - X)\%$ tail of the distribution of profits/losses. The variable N days is the time horizon and $X\%$ is the confidence level.

Confirmation Contract confirming verbal agreement between two parties to a trade in the over-the-counter market.

Constant Maturity Swap A swap where a swap rate is exchanged for either a fixed rate or a floating rate on each payment date.

Constant Maturity Treasury Swap A swap where the yield on a Treasury bond is exchanged for either a fixed rate or a floating rate on each payment date.

Consumption Asset An asset held for consumption rather than investment.

Contango A situation where the futures price is above the expected future spot price.

Continuous Compounding A way of quoting interest rates. It is the limit as the assumed compounding interval is made smaller and smaller.

Control Variate Technique A technique that can sometimes be used for improving the accuracy of a numerical procedure.

Convenience Yield A measure of the benefits from ownership of an asset that are not obtained by the holder of a long futures contract on the asset.

Conversion Factor A factor used to determine the number of bonds that must be delivered in the Chicago Board of Trade bond futures contract.

Convertible Bond A corporate bond that can be converted into a predetermined amount of the company's equity at certain times during its life.

Convexity A measure of the curvature in the relationship between bond prices and bond yields.

Convexity Adjustment An overworked term. It can refer to the adjustment necessary to convert a futures interest rate to a forward interest rate.

Cost of Carry The storage costs plus the cost of financing an asset minus the income earned on the asset.

Counterparty The opposite side in a financial transaction.

Coupon Interest payment made on a bond.

Covered Call A short position in a call option on an asset combined with a long position in the asset.

Credit Default Swap An instrument that gives the holder the right to sell a bond for its face value in the event of a default by the issuer.

Credit Derivative A derivative whose payoff depends on the creditworthiness of one or more entities.

Credit Rating A measure of the creditworthiness of a bond issue.

Credit Risk The risk that a loss will be experienced because of a default by the counterparty in a derivatives transaction.

Credit Spread Option Option whose payoff depends on the spread between the yields earned on two assets.

Cumulative Distribution Function The probability that a variable will be less than x as a function of x.

Currency Swap A swap where interest and principal in one currency are exchanged for interest and principal in another currency.

Day Count A convention for quoting interest rates.

Day Trade A trade that is entered into and closed out on the same day.

Default Correlation Measures the tendency of two companies to default at about the same time.

Default Probability Density Measures the unconditional probability of default in a future short period of time.

Deferred Payment Option An option where the price paid is deferred until the end of the option's life.

Deferred Swap An agreement to enter into a swap at some time in the future. Also called a *forward swap*.

Delivery Price Price agreed to (possibly some time in the past) in a forward contract.

Delta The rate of change of the price of a derivative with the price of the underlying asset.

Delta Hedging A hedging scheme that is designed to make the price of a portfolio of derivatives insensitive to small changes in the price of the underlying asset.

Delta-neutral Portfolio A portfolio with a delta of zero so that there is no sensitivity to small changes in the price of the underlying asset.

DerivaGem The software accompanying this book.

Derivative An instrument whose price depends on, or is derived from, the price of another asset.

Deterministic Variable A variable whose future value is known.

Diagonal Spread A position in two calls where both the strike prices and times to maturity are different. (A diagonal spread can also be created with put options.)

Differential Swap A swap where a floating rate in one currency is exchanged for a floating rate in another currency and both rates are applied to the same principal.

Discount Bond *See* Zero-coupon bond.

Discount Instrument An instrument, such as a Treasury bill, that provides no coupons.

Discount Rate The annualized dollar return on a Treasury bill or similar instrument expressed as a percentage of the final face value.

Dividend A cash payment made to the owner of a stock.

Dividend Yield The dividend as a percentage of the stock price.

Down-and-in Option An option that comes into existence when the price of the underlying asset declines to a prespecified level.

Down-and-out Option An option that ceases to exist when the price of the underlying asset declines to a prespecified level.

Duration A measure of the average life of a bond. It is also an approximation to the ratio of the proportional change in the bond price to the absolute change in its yield.

Duration Matching A procedure for matching the durations of assets and liabilities in a financial institution.

Dynamic Hedging A procedure for hedging an option position by periodically changing the position held in the underlying assets. The objective is usually to maintain a delta-neutral position.

Early Exercise Exercise prior to the maturity date.

Efficient Market Hypothesis A hypothesis that asset prices reflect relevant information.

Electronic Trading System of trading where a computer is used to match buyers and sellers.

Embedded Option An option that is an inseparable part of another instrument.

Empirical Research Research based on historical market data.

Equity Swap A swap where the return on an equity portfolio is exchanged for either a fixed or a floating rate of interest.

Eurocurrency A currency that is outside the formal control of the issuing country's monetary authorities.

Eurodollar A dollar held in a bank outside the United States.

Eurodollar Futures Contract A futures contract written on a Eurodollar deposit.

Eurodollar Interest Rate The interest rate on a Eurodollar deposit.

European Option An option that can be exercised only at the end of its life.

EWMA Exponentially weighted moving average.

Exchange Option An option to exchange one asset for another.

Ex-dividend Date When a dividend is declared, an ex-dividend date is specified. Investors who own shares of the stock immediately before the ex-dividend date receive the dividend.

Executive Stock Option A stock option issued by a company on its own stock and given to its executives as part of their remuneration.

Exercise Price The price at which the underlying asset may be bought or sold in an option contract. Also called the *strike price*.

Exotic Option A nonstandard option.

Expectations Theory The theory that forward interest rates equal expected future spot interest rates.

Expected Value of a Variable The average value of the variable obtained by weighting the alternative values by their probabilities.

Expiration Date The end of the life of a contract.

Exponentially Weighted Moving Average Model A model where exponential weighting is used to provide forecasts for a variable from historical data. It is sometimes applied to the variance per day in value at risk calculations.

Exponential Weighting A weighting scheme where the weight given to an observation depends on how recent it is. The weight given to an observation i time periods ago is λ times the weight given to an observation $i-1$ time periods ago, where $\lambda < 1$.

Exposure The maximum loss from default by a counterparty.

Extendable Bond A bond whose life can be extended at the option of the holder.

Extendable Swap A swap whose life can be extended at the option of one side to the contract.

FAS Financial Accounting Standard.

FASB Financial Accounting Standards Board.

Financial Intermediary A bank or other financial institution that facilitates the flow of funds between different entities in the economy.

Fixed Rate A rate that is fixed through time.

Flat Volatility The name given to volatility used to price a cap when the same volatility is used for each caplet.

Flex Option An option traded on an exchange with terms that are different from the standard options traded by the exchange.

Floating Rate A rate that changes through time.

Floor *See* Interest rate floor.

Floor–Ceiling Agreement *See* Interest rate collar.

Floorlet One component of a floor.

Floor Rate The rate in an interest rate floor agreement.

Foreign Currency Option An option on a foreign exchange rate.

Forward Contract A contract that obligates the holder to buy or sell an asset for a predetermined delivery price at a predetermined future time.

Forward Exchange Rate The forward price of one unit of a foreign currency.

Forward Interest Rate The interest rate for a future period of time implied by the rates prevailing in the market today.

Forward Price The delivery price in a forward contract that causes the contract to be worth zero.

Forward Rate Rate of interest for a period of time in the future implied by today's zero rates.

Forward Rate Agreement (FRA) Agreement that a certain interest rate will apply to a certain principal amount for a certain time period in the future.

Forward Start Option An option designed so that it will be at the money at some time in the future.

Forward Swap *See* Deferred swap.

Futures Contract A contract that obligates the holder to buy or sell an asset at a predetermined delivery price during a specified future time period. The contract is marked to market daily.

Futures Option An option on a futures contract.

Futures Price The delivery price currently applicable to a futures contract.

Gamma The rate of change of delta with respect to the asset price.

Gamma-neutral portfolio A portfolio with a gamma of zero.

Geometric Mean The nth root of the product of n numbers.

Greeks Hedge parameters such as delta, gamma, vega, theta, and rho.

Hazard Rate Measures probability of default in a short period of time conditional on no earlier default.

HDD (Heating degree days) The maximum of zero and the amount by which the daily average temperature is less than 65° Fahrenheit. The average temperature is the average of the highest and lowest temperatures (midnight to midnight).

Hedge A trade designed to reduce risk.

Hedger An individual who enters into hedging trades.

Hedge Ratio The ratio of the size of a position in a hedging instrument to the size of the position being hedged.

Historical Simulation A simulation based on historical data.

Historic Volatility A volatility estimated from historical data.

Holiday Calendar Calendar defining which days are holidays for the purposes of determining payment dates in a swap.

Implied Distribution A distribution for a future asset price implied from option prices.

Implied Volatility Volatility implied from an option price using the Black–Scholes or a similar model.

Index Amortizing Swap *See* Indexed principal swap.

Index Arbitrage An arbitrage involving a position in the stocks comprising a stock index and a position in a futures contract on the stock index.

Indexed Principal Swap A swap where the principal declines over time. The reduction in the principal on a payment date depends on the level of interest rates.

Index Futures A futures contract on a stock index or other index.

Index Option An option contract on a stock index or other index.

Initial Margin The cash required from a futures trader at the time of the trade.

Interest Rate Cap An option that provides a payoff when a specified interest rate is above a certain level. The interest rate is a floating rate that is reset periodically.

Interest Rate Collar A combination of an interest rate cap and an interest rate floor.

Interest Rate Derivative A derivative whose payoffs are dependent on future interest rates.

Interest Rate Floor An option that provides a payoff when an interest rate is below a certain level. The interest rate is a floating rate that is reset periodically.

Interest Rate Option An option where the payoff is dependent on the level of interest rates.

Interest Rate Swap An exchange of a fixed rate of interest on a certain notional principal for a floating rate of interest on the same notional principal.

In-the-money Option Either (a) a call option where the asset price is greater than the strike price or (b) a put option where the asset price is less than the strike price.

Intrinsic Value For a call option, this is the greater of the excess of the asset price over the strike price and zero. For a put option, it is the greater of the excess of the strike price over the asset price and zero.

Inverted Market A market where futures prices decrease with maturity.

Investment Asset An asset held by at least some individuals for investment purposes.

IO (Interest only) A mortgage-backed security where the holder receives only interest cash flows on the underlying mortgage pool.

Kappa *See* Vega.

Kurtosis A measure of the fatness of the tails of a distribution.

Lambda *See* Vega.

LEAPS (Long-term equity anticipation securities) These are relatively long-term options on individual stocks or stock indices.

LIBID (London interbank bid rate) The rate bid by banks on Eurocurrency deposits (i.e., the rate at which a bank is willing to borrow from other banks).

LIBOR (London interbank offer rate) The rate offered by banks on Eurocurrency deposits (i.e., the rate at which a bank is willing to lend to other banks).

LIBOR Curve LIBOR zero-coupon interest rates as a function of maturity.

LIBOR-in-arrears Swap Swap where the LIBOR rate observed on a date is paid on that date rather than one accrual period later.

Limit Move The maximum price move permitted by the exchange in a single trading session.

Limit Order An order that can be executed only at a specified price or one more favorable to the investor.

Liquidity Preference Theory A theory leading to the conclusion that forward interest rates are above expected future spot interest rates.

Liquidity Premium The amount that forward interest rates exceed expected future spot interest rates.

Liquidity Risk Risk that it will not be possible to sell a holding of a particular instrument at its theoretical price.

Locals Individuals on the floor of an exchange who trade for their own account rather than for someone else.

Lognormal Distribution A variable has a lognormal distribution when the logarithm of the variable has a normal distribution.

Long Hedge A hedge involving a long futures position.

Long Position A position involving the purchase of an asset.

Lookback Option An option whose payoff is dependent on the maximum or minimum of the asset price achieved during a certain period.

Maintenance Margin When the balance in a trader's margin account falls below the maintenance margin level, the trader receives a margin call requiring the account to be topped up to the initial margin level.

Margin The cash balance (or security deposit) required from a futures or options trader.

Margin Call A request for extra margin when the balance in the margin account falls below the maintenance margin level.

Market Maker A trader who is willing to quote both bid and offer prices for an asset.

Market Model A model most commonly used by traders.

Market Segmentation Theory A theory that short interest rates are determined independently of long interest rates by the market.

Marking to Market The practice of revaluing an instrument to reflect the current values of the relevant market variables.

Maturity Date The end of the life of a contract.

Mean Reversion The tendency of a market variable (such as an interest rate) to revert back to some long-run average level.

Modified Duration A modification to the standard duration measure so that it more accurately describes the relationship between proportional changes in a bond price and absolute changes in its yield. The modification takes account of the compounding frequency with which the yield is quoted.

Monte Carlo Simulation A procedure for randomly sampling changes in market variables in order to value a derivative.

Mortgage-backed Security A security that entitles the owner to a share in the cash flows realized from a pool of mortgages.

Naked Position A short position in a call option that is not combined with a long position in the underlying asset.

No-arbitrage Assumption The assumption that there are no arbitrage opportunities in market prices.

Nonsystematic risk Risk that can be diversified away.

Normal Backwardation A situation where the futures price is below the expected future spot price.

Normal Distribution The standard bell-shaped distribution of statistics.

Normal Market A market where futures prices increase with maturity.

Notional Principal The principal used to calculate payments in an interest rate swap. The principal is "notional" because it is neither paid nor received.

Numerical Procedure A method of valuing an option when no formula is available.

OCC (Options Clearing Corporation) *See* Clearinghouse.

Offer Price The price that a dealer is offering to sell an asset.

Open Interest The total number of long positions outstanding in a futures contract (equals the total number of short positions).

Open Outcry System of trading where traders meet on the floor of the exchange.

Option The right to buy or sell an asset.

Option-adjusted Spread The spread over the Treasury curve that makes the theoretical price of an interest rate derivative equal to the market price.

Option Class All options of the same type (call or put) on a particular stock.

Option Series All options of a certain class with the same strike price and expiration date.

Order Book Official *See* Board broker.

Out-of-the-money Option Either (a) a call option where the asset price is less than the strike price or (b) a put option where the asset price is greater than the strike price.

Over-the-counter Market A market where traders deal by phone. The traders are usually financial institutions, corporations, and fund managers.

Package A derivative that is a portfolio of standard calls and puts, possibly combined with a position in forward contracts and the asset itself.

Parallel Shift A movement in the yield curve where each point on the curve changes by the same amount.

Par Value The principal amount of a bond.

Par Yield The coupon on a bond that makes its price equal the principal.

Path-dependent Option An option whose payoff depends on the whole path followed by the underlying variable—not just its final value.

Payoff The cash realized by the holder of an option or other derivative at the end of its life.

Plain Vanilla A term used to describe a standard deal.

PO (Principal only) A mortgage-backed security where the holder receives only principal cash flows on the underlying mortgage pool.

Portfolio Immunization Making a portfolio relatively insensitive to interest rates.

Portfolio Insurance Entering into trades to ensure that the value of a portfolio will not fall below a certain level.

Position Limit The maximum position a trader (or group of traders acting together) is allowed to hold.

Premium The price of an option.

Prepayment function A function estimating the prepayment of principal on a portfolio of mortgages in terms of other variables.

Principal The par or face value of a debt instrument.

Program Trading A procedure where trades are automatically generated by a computer and transmitted to the trading floor of an exchange.

Protective Put A put option combined with a long position in the underlying asset.

Put–Call Parity The relationship between the price of a European call option and the price of a European put option when they have the same strike price and maturity date.

Put Option An option to sell an asset for a certain price by a certain date.

Puttable Bond A bond where the holder has the right to sell it back to the issuer at certain predetermined times for a predetermined price.

Puttable Swap A swap where one side has the right to terminate early.

Quanto A derivative where the payoff is defined by variables associated with one currency but is paid in another currency.

Rainbow Option An option whose payoff is dependent on two or more underlying variables.

Range-forward Contract The combination of a long call and short put or the combination of a short call and long put.

Real Option Option involving real (as opposed to financial) assets. Real assets include land, plant, and machinery.

Rebalancing The process of adjusting a trading position periodically. Usually the purpose is to maintain delta neutrality.

Repo (Repurchase agreement) A procedure for borrowing money by selling securities to a counterparty and agreeing to buy them back later at a slightly higher price.

Repo Rate The rate of interest in a repo transaction.

Reset Date The date in a swap or cap or floor when the floating rate for the next period is set.

Reversion Level The level to which the value of a market variable (e.g., an interest rate) tends to revert.

Rho Rate of change of the price of a derivative with the interest rate.

Rights Issue An issue to existing shareholders of a security giving them the right to buy new shares at a certain price.

Risk-free Rate The rate of interest that can be earned without assuming any risks.

Risk-neutral Valuation The valuation of an option or other derivative assuming the world is risk neutral. Risk-neutral valuation gives the correct price for a derivative in all worlds, not just in a risk-neutral world.

Risk-neutral World A world where investors are assumed to require no extra return on average for bearing risks.

Roll Back *See* Backwards induction.

Scalper A trader who holds positions for a very short period of time.

Scenario Analysis An analysis of the effects of possible alternative future movements in market variables on the value of a portfolio.

SEC Securities and Exchange Commission.

Settlement Price The average of the prices that a futures contract trades for immediately before the bell signaling the close of trading for a day. It is used in mark-to-market calculations.

Short Hedge A hedge where a short futures position is taken.

Short Position A position involving the sale of an asset.

Short Rate The interest rate applying for a very short period of time.

Short Selling Selling in the market shares that have been borrowed from another investor.

Short-term Risk-free Rate *See* Short rate.

Shout Option An option where the holder has the right to lock in a minimum value for the payoff at one time during its life.

Simulation *See* Monte Carlo simulation.

Specialist An individual responsible for managing limit orders on some exchanges. The specialist does not make the information on outstanding limit orders available to other traders.

Speculator An individual who is taking a position in the market. Usually the individual is betting that the price of an asset will go up or that the price of an asset will go down.

Spot Interest Rate *See* Zero-coupon interest rate.

Spot Price The price for immediate delivery.

Spot Volatilities The volatilities used to price a cap when a different volatility is used for each caplet.

Spread Transaction A position in two or more options of the same type.

Static Hedge A hedge that does not have to be changed once it is initiated.

Step-up Swap A swap where the principal increases over time in a predetermined way.

Stochastic Variable A variable whose future value is uncertain.

Stock Dividend A dividend paid in the form of additional shares.

Stock Index An index monitoring the value of a portfolio of stocks.

Stock Index Futures Futures on a stock index.

Stock Index Option An option on a stock index.

Stock Option Option on a stock.

Stock Split The conversion of each existing share into more than one new share.

Storage Costs The costs of storing a commodity.

Straddle A long position in a call and a put with the same strike price.

Strangle A long position in a call and a put with different strike prices.

Strap A long position in two call options and one put option with the same strike price.

Stress Testing Testing of the impact of extreme market moves on the value of a portfolio.

Strike Price The price at which the asset may be bought or sold in an option contract. Also called the *exercise price*.

Strip A long position in one call option and two put options with the same strike price.

Swap An agreement to exchange cash flows in the future according to a prearranged formula.

Swap Rate The fixed rate in an interest rate swap that causes the swap to have a value of zero.

Swaption An option to enter into an interest rate swap where a specified fixed rate is exchanged for floating.

Swing Option Energy option in which the rate of consumption must be between a minimum and maximum level. There is usually a limit on the number of times the option holder can change the rate at which the energy is consumed.

Synthetic Option An option created by trading the underlying asset.

Systematic Risk Risk that cannot be diversified away.

Take-and-pay Option *See* Swing option.

Term Structure of Interest Rates The relationship between interest rates and their maturities.

Terminal Value The value at maturity.

Theta The rate of change of the price of an option or other derivative with the passage of time.

Time Decay *See* Theta.

Time Value The value of an option arising from the time left to maturity (equals an option's price minus its intrinsic value).

Total Return Swap A swap where the return on an asset such as a bond is exchanged for LIBOR plus a spread. The return on the asset includes income such as coupons and the change in value of the asset.

Transactions Costs The cost of carrying out a trade (commissions plus the difference between the price obtained and the midpoint of the bid–offer spread).

Treasury Bill A short-term, non-coupon-bearing instrument issued by the government to finance its debt.

Treasury Bond A long-term, coupon-bearing instrument issued by the government to finance its debt.

Treasury Bond Futures A futures contract on Treasury bonds.

Treasury Note *See* Treasury bond. (Treasury notes have maturities of less than 10 years.)

Treasury Note Futures A futures contract on Treasury notes.

Tree A representation of the evolution of the value of a market variable for the purposes of valuing an option or other derivative.

Underlying Variable A variable on which the price of an option or other derivative depends.

Unsystematic risk *See* Nonsystematic risk.

Up-and-in Option An option that comes into existence when the price of the underlying asset increases to a prespecified level.

Up-and-out Option An option that ceases to exist when the price of the underlying asset increases to a prespecified level.

Uptick An increase in price.

Value at Risk A loss that will not be exceeded at some specified confidence level.

Variance–Covariance Matrix A matrix showing variances of, and covariances between, a number of different market variables.

Variance Rate The square of volatility.

Variation Margin An extra margin required to bring the balance in a margin account up to the initial margin when there is a margin call.

Vega The rate of change in the price of an option or other derivative with volatility.

Vega-neutral Portfolio A portfolio with a vega of zero.

Volatility A measure of the uncertainty of the return realized on an asset.

Volatility Matrix A table showing the variation of implied volatilities with strike price and time to maturity.

Volatility Skew A term used to describe the volatility smile when it is nonsymmetrical.

Volatility Smile The variation of implied volatility with strike price.

Volatility Surface Variation of implied volatility with strike price and time to maturity.

Volatility Swap Swap where the realized volatility during an accrual period is exchanged for a fixed volatility. Both percentage volatilities are applied to a notional principal.

Volatility Term Structure The variation of implied volatility with time to maturity.

Warrant An option issued by a company or a financial institution. Call warrants are frequently issued by companies on their own stock.

Weather Derivative Derivative where the payoff depends on the weather.

Wild Card Play The right to deliver on a futures contract at the closing price for a period of time after the close of trading.

Writing an Option Selling an option.

Yield A return provided by an instrument.

Yield Curve *See* Term structure of interest rates.

Zero-coupon Bond A bond that provides no coupons.

Zero-coupon Interest Rate The interest rate that would be earned on a bond that provides no coupons.

Zero-coupon Yield Curve A plot of the zero-coupon interest rate against time to maturity.

Zero Curve *See* Zero-coupon yield curve.

Zero Rate *See* Zero-coupon interest rate.

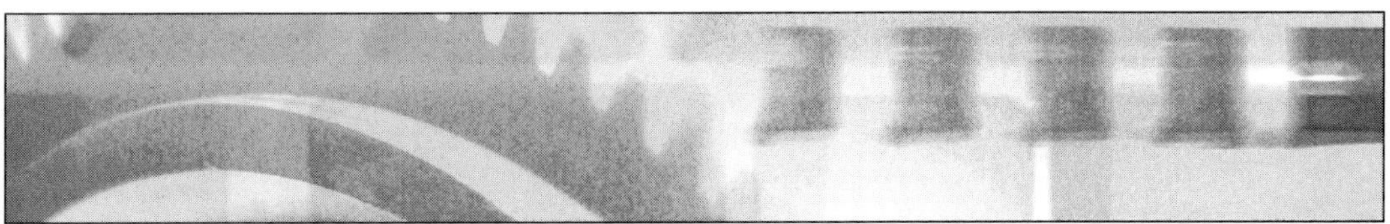

DerivaGem Software

The software accompanying this book is DerivaGem for Excel, Version 1.51. It requires Excel Version 7.0 or later. The software consists of three files: dg151.dll, DG151.xls, and DG151functions.xls To install the software, you should create a directory with the name DerivaGem (or some other name of your own choosing) and load DG151.xls and DG151functions.xls into the directory. You should load dg151.dll into the Windows\System directory (Windows 95 and 98 users) or the WINNT\System32 directory (Windows 2000 and Windows NT users).[1]

Excel 2000 users should ensure that Security for Macros is set at *Medium* or *Low*. Check *Tools* followed by *Macros* in Excel to change this. While using the software, you may be asked whether you want to enable macros. You should click *Enable Macros*.

Updates to the software can be downloaded from the author's website:

http://www.rotman.utoronto.ca/~hull

There are two parts to the software: the Options Calculator (DG151.xls) and the Applications Builder (DG151functions.xls). Both parts require dg151.dll to be loaded into the Windows\System or WINNT\System32 directory.

New users are advised to start with The Options Calculator.

THE OPTIONS CALCULATOR

DG151.xls is a user-friendly options calculator. It consists of three worksheets. The first worksheet is used to carry out computations for stock options, currency options, index options, and futures options; the second is used for European and American bond options; the third is used for caps, floors, and European swap options.

The software produces prices, Greek letters, and implied volatilities for a wide range of different instruments. It displays charts showing the way that option prices and the

[1] Note that it is not uncommon for Windows Explorer to be set up so that *.dll files are not displayed. To change the setting so that the *.dll file can be seen, proceed as follows. In Windows 95, click *View*, followed by *Options*, followed by *Show All Files*. In Windows 98 click *View*, followed by *Folder Options*, followed by *View*, followed by *Show All Files*. In Windows 2000, click *Tools*, followed by *Folder Options*, followed by *View*, followed by *Show Hidden Files and Folders*.

Greek letters depend on inputs. It also displays binomial and trinomial trees, showing how the computations are carried out.

General Operation

To use the options calculator, you should choose a worksheet and click on the appropriate buttons to select Option Type, Underlying Type, and so on. You should then enter the parameters for the option you are considering, hit *Enter* on your keyboard, and click on *Calculate*. DerivaGem will then display the price or implied volatility for the option you are considering, together with Greek letters. If the price has been calculated from a tree, and you are using the first or second worksheet, you can then click on *Display Tree* to see the tree. Sample displays of the tree are shown in Chapters 11 and 16. Many different charts can be displayed in all three worksheets. To display a chart, you must first choose the variable you require on the vertical axis, the variable you require on the horizontal axis, and the range of values to be considered on the horizontal axis. Following that you should hit *Enter* on your keyboard and click on *Draw Graph*. Note that, whenever the values in one or more cells are changed, it is necessary to hit *Enter* on your keyboard before clicking on one of the buttons.

If your version of Excel is later than 7.0, you will be asked whether you want to update to the new version when you first save the software. You should choose the *Yes* button.

Options on Stocks, Currencies, Indices, and Futures

The first worksheet (Equity_FX_Index_Futures) is used for options on stocks, currencies, indices, and futures. To use it you should first select the Underlying Type (Equity, Currency, Index, or Futures). You should then select the Option Type (Analytic European, Binomial European, Binomial American, Asian, Barrier Up and In, Barrier Up and Out, Barrier Down and In, Barrier Down and Out, Binary Cash or Nothing, Binary Asset or Nothing, Chooser, Compound Option on Call, Compound Option on Put, or Lookback). You should then enter the data on the underlying asset and data on the option. Note that all interest rates are expressed with continuous compounding.

In the case of European and American equity options, a table pops up allowing you to enter dividends. Enter the time of each ex-dividend date (in years) in the first column and the amount of the dividend in the second column. Dividends must be entered in chronological order.

You must click on buttons to choose whether the option is a call or a put and whether you wish to calculate an implied volatility. If you do wish to calculate an implied volatility, the option price should be entered in the cell labeled Price.

Once all the data has been entered you should hit *Enter* on your keyboard and click on *Calculate*. If Implied Volatility was selected, DerivaGem displays the implied volatility in the Volatility (% per year) cell. If Implied Volatility was not selected, it uses the volatility you entered in this cell and displays the option price in the Price cell.

Once the calculations have been completed, the tree (if used) can be inspected and charts can be displayed.

When Analytic European is selected, DerivaGem uses the equations in Chapters 12, 13, and 14 to calculate prices, and the equations in Chapter 15 to calculate Greek letters. When Binomial European or Binomial American is selected, a binomial tree is constructed as described in Chapter 16. Up to 500 time steps can be used.

The input data are largely self-explanatory. In the case of an Asian option, the Current Average is the average price since inception. If the Asian option is new (Time since Inception equals zero), then the Current Average cell is irrelevant and can be left blank. In the case of a Lookback Option, the Minimum to Date is used when a Call is valued and the Maximum to Date is used when a Put is valued. For a new deal, these should be set equal to the current price of the underlying asset.

Bond Options

The second worksheet (Bond_Options) is used for European and American options on bonds. You should first select a pricing model (Black European, Normal-Analytic European, Normal-Tree European, Normal American, Lognormal European, or Lognormal American). You should then enter the Bond Data and the Option Data. The coupon is the rate paid per year and the frequency of payments can be selected as Quarterly, Semi-Annual, or Annual. The zero-coupon yield curve is entered in the table labeled Term Structure. Enter maturities (measured in years) in the first column and the corresponding continuously compounded rates in the second column. The maturities should be entered in chronological order. DerivaGem assumes a piecewise linear zero curve similar to that in Figure 4.1. Note that, when valuing interest rate derivatives, DerivaGem rounds all times to the nearest whole number of days.

When all data have been entered, hit *Enter* on your keyboard. The quoted bond price per $100 of Principal, calculated from the zero curve, is displayed when the calculations are complete. You should indicate whether the option is a call or a put and whether the strike price is a quoted (clean) strike price or a cash (dirty) strike price. (See the discussion and example in Section 19.4 to understand the difference between the two.) Note that the strike price is entered as the price per $100 of principal. You should indicate whether you are considering a call or a put option and whether you wish to calculate an implied volatility. If you select implied volatility and the normal model or lognormal model is used, DerivaGem implies the short-rate volatility, keeping the reversion rate fixed.

Once all the inputs are complete, you should hit *Enter* on your keyboard and click *Calculate*. After that the tree (if used) can be inspected and charts can be displayed. Note that the tree displayed lasts until the end of the life of the option. DerivaGem uses a much larger tree in its computations to value the underlying bond.

Note that, when Black's model is selected, DerivaGem uses the equations in Section 19.3. Also, the procedure in Section 19.4 is used for converting the input yield volatility into a price volatility.

Caps and Swap Options

The third worksheet (Caps_and_Swap_Options) is used for caps and swap options. You should first select the Option Type (Swap Option or Cap/Floor) and Pricing Model (Black, Normal European, or Normal American). You should then enter data on the option you are considering. The Settlement Frequency indicates the frequency of payments and can be Annual, Semi-Annual, Quarterly, or Monthly. The software calculates payment dates by working backward from the end of the life of the cap or swap option. The initial accrual period may be a nonstandard length between 0.5 and 1.5 times a normal accrual period. The software can be used to imply either a volatility or a cap rate/swap rate from the price. When a normal model or a lognormal model is used, DerivaGem implies the short rate volatility keeping the reversion rate fixed. The zero-coupon yield curve is entered in the table labeled Term Structure. Enter maturities (measured in years) in the first column and the corresponding continuously compounded rates in the second column. The maturities should be entered in chronological order. DerivaGem assumes a piecewise linear zero curve similar to that in Figure 4.1.

Once all the inputs are complete, you should click *Calculate*. After that, charts can be displayed.

Note that, when Black's model is used, DerivaGem uses the equations in Sections 19.5 and 19.6.

Greek Letters

In the Equity_FX_Index_Futures worksheet, the Greek letters are calculated as follows.

Delta: Change in option price per dollar increase in underlying asset.

Gamma: Change in delta per dollar increase in underlying asset.

Vega: Change in option price per 1% increase in volatility (e.g., volatility increases from 20% to 21%).

Rho: Change in option price per 1% increase in interest rate (e.g., interest increases from 5% to 6%).

Theta: Change in option price per calendar day passing.

In the Bond_Options and Caps_and_Swap_Options worksheets, the Greek letters are calculated as follows:

DV01: Change in option price per one basis point upward parallel shift in the zero curve.

Gamma01: Change in DV01 per one basis point upward parallel shift in the zero curve, multiplied by 100.

Vega: Change in option price when volatility parameter increases by 1% (e.g., volatility increases from 20% to 21%)

THE APPLICATIONS BUILDER

The Applications Builder is DG151functions.xls. It is a set of 21 functions and seven sample applications from which users can build their own applications.

The Functions

The following is a list of the 21 functions included in the Applications Builder. Full details are on the first worksheet (FunctionSpecs).

1. Black_Scholes. This carries out Black–Scholes calculations for a European option on a stock, stock index, currency, or futures contract.

2. TreeEquityOpt. This carries out binomial tree calculations for a European or American option on a stock, stock index, currency, or futures contract.
3. BinaryOption. This carries out calculations for a binary option on a stock, stock index, currency, or futures contract.
4. BarrierOption. This carries out calculations for a barrier option on a non-dividend-paying stock, stock index, currency, or futures contract.
5. AverageOption. This carries out calculations for an Asian option on a non-dividend-paying stock, stock index, currency, or futures contract.
6. ChooserOption. This carries out calculations for a chooser option on a non-dividend-paying stock, stock index, currency, or futures contract.
7. CompoundOption. This carries out calculations for compound options on non-dividend-paying stocks, stock indices, currencies, and futures.
8. LookbackOption. This carries out calculations for a lookback option on a non-dividend-paying stock, stock index, currency, or futures contract.
9. EPortfolio. This carries out calculations for a portfolio of options on a stock, stock index, currency, or futures contract.
10. BlackCap. This carries out calculations for a cap or floor using Black's model.
11. HullWhiteCap. This carries out calculations for a cap or floor using the Hull–White model.
12. TreeCap. This carries out calculations for a cap or floor using a trinomial tree.
13. BlackSwapOption. This carries out calculations for a swap option using Black's model.
14. HullWhiteSwap. This carries out calculations for a swap option using the Hull–White model.
15. TreeSwapOption. This carries out calculations for a swap option using a trinomial tree.
16. BlackBondOption. This carries out calculations for a bond option using Black's model.
17. HullWhiteBondOption. This carries out calculations for a bond option using the Hull–White model.
18. TreeBondOption. This carries out calculations for a bond option using a trinomial tree.
19. BondPrice. This values a bond.
20. SwapPrice. This values a plain vanilla interest rate swap. Note that it ignores cash flows arising from reset dates prior to start time.
21. IPortfolio. This carries out calculations for a portfolio of interest rate derivatives.

Sample Applications

DG151functions.xls includes seven worksheets with sample applications:

A. Binomial Convergence. This investigates the convergence of the binomial model in Chapters 11 and 16.

B. GreekLetters. This provides charts showing the Greek letters in Chapter 15.

C. Delta Hedge. This investigates the performance of delta hedging as in Tables 15.2 and 15.3.

D. Delta and Gamma Hedge. This investigates the performance of delta plus gamma hedging for a position in a binary option.

E. Value and Risk. This calculates Value at Risk for a portfolio consisting of three options on a single stock using three different approaches.

F. Barrier Replication. This carries out calculations for static options replication (not covered in this book).

G. Trinomial Convergence. This investigates the convergence of a trinomial tree (not covered in this book).

Major Exchanges Trading Futures and Options

American Stock Exchange	AMEX	www.amex.com
Australian Stock Exchange	ASX	www.asx.com.au
Bolsa de Mercadorias y Futuros, Brazil	BM&F	www.bmf.com.br
Chicago Board of Trade	CBOT	www.cbot.com
Chicago Board Options Exchange	CBOE	www.cboe.com
Chicago Mercantile Exchange	CME	www.cme.com
Coffee, Sugar & Cocoa Exchange, New York	CSCE	www.csce.com
Commodity Exchange, New York	COMEX	www.nymex.com
Copenhagen Stock Exchange	FUTOP	www.xcse.dk
Deutsche Termin Börse, Germany	DTB	www.exchange.de
Eurex	EUREX	www.eurexchange.com
Euronext	EURONEXT	www.euronext.com
Hong Kong Futures Exchange	HKFE	www.hkfe.com
International Petroleum Exchange, London	IPE	www.ipe.uk.com
International Securities Exchange	ISE	www.iseoptions.com
Kansas City Board of Trade	KCBT	www.kcbt.com
London International Financial Futures & Options Exchange	LIFFE	www.liffe.com
London Metal Exchange	LME	www.lme.co.uk
Malaysian Derivatives Exchange	MDEX	www.mdex.com.my
Marché à Terme International de France	MATIF	www.matif.fr
Marché des Options Négociables de Paris	MONEP	www.monep.fr
MEFF Renta Fija and Variable, Spain	MEFF	www.meff.es
Mexican Derivatives Exchange	MEXDER	www.mexder.com
Minneapolis Grain Exchange	MGE	www.mgex.com
Montreal Exchange	ME	www.me.org
New York Board of Trade	NYBOT	www.nybot.com
New York Cotton Exchange	NYCE	www.nyce.com
New York Futures Exchange	NYFE	www.nyce.com
New York Mercantile Exchange	NYMEX	www.nymex.com
New York Stock Exchange	NYSE	www.nyse.com
OMHEX	MHEX	www.omhex.com
Osaka Securities Exchange	OSA	www.ose.or.jp
Pacific Exchange	PXS	www.pacificex.com
Philadelphia Stock Exchange	PHLX	www.phlx.com
Singapore International Monetary Exchange	SIMEX	www.simex.com.sg
Sydney Futures Exchange	SFE	www.sfe.com.au
Swiss Exchange	SWX	www.swx.com
Tokyo Grain Exchange	TGE	www.tge.or.jp
Tokyo International Financial Futures Exchange	TIFFE	www.tiffe.or.jp
Winnipeg Commodity Exchange	WCE	www.wce.ca

A number of exchanges have merged or formed alliances. For example, Eurex is jointly operated by DTB and SWX, and Euronext owns LIFFE, MATIF, and MONEP.

Table for $N(x)$ When $x \leqslant 0$

This table shows values of $N(x)$ for $x \leqslant 0$. The table should be used with interpolation. For example,

$$\begin{aligned} N(-0.1234) &= N(-0.12) - 0.34[N(-0.12) - N(-0.13)] \\ &= 0.4522 - 0.34 \times (0.4522 - 0.4483) \\ &= 0.4509 \end{aligned}$$

x	.00	.01	.02	.03	.04	.05	.06	.07	.08	.09
−0.0	0.5000	0.4960	0.4920	0.4880	0.4840	0.4801	0.4761	0.4721	0.4681	0.4641
−0.1	0.4602	0.4562	0.4522	0.4483	0.4443	0.4404	0.4364	0.4325	0.4286	0.4247
−0.2	0.4207	0.4168	0.4129	0.4090	0.4052	0.4013	0.3974	0.3936	0.3897	0.3859
−0.3	0.3821	0.3783	0.3745	0.3707	0.3669	0.3632	0.3594	0.3557	0.3520	0.3483
−0.4	0.3446	0.3409	0.3372	0.3336	0.3300	0.3264	0.3228	0.3192	0.3156	0.3121
−0.5	0.3085	0.3050	0.3015	0.2981	0.2946	0.2912	0.2877	0.2843	0.2810	0.2776
−0.6	0.2743	0.2709	0.2676	0.2643	0.2611	0.2578	0.2546	0.2514	0.2483	0.2451
−0.7	0.2420	0.2389	0.2358	0.2327	0.2296	0.2266	0.2236	0.2206	0.2177	0.2148
−0.8	0.2119	0.2090	0.2061	0.2033	0.2005	0.1977	0.1949	0.1922	0.1894	0.1867
−0.9	0.1841	0.1814	0.1788	0.1762	0.1736	0.1711	0.1685	0.1660	0.1635	0.1611
−1.0	0.1587	0.1562	0.1539	0.1515	0.1492	0.1469	0.1446	0.1423	0.1401	0.1379
−1.1	0.1357	0.1335	0.1314	0.1292	0.1271	0.1251	0.1230	0.1210	0.1190	0.1170
−1.2	0.1151	0.1131	0.1112	0.1093	0.1075	0.1056	0.1038	0.1020	0.1003	0.0985
−1.3	0.0968	0.0951	0.0934	0.0918	0.0901	0.0885	0.0869	0.0853	0.0838	0.0823
−1.4	0.0808	0.0793	0.0778	0.0764	0.0749	0.0735	0.0721	0.0708	0.0694	0.0681
−1.5	0.0668	0.0655	0.0643	0.0630	0.0618	0.0606	0.0594	0.0582	0.0571	0.0559
−1.6	0.0548	0.0537	0.0526	0.0516	0.0505	0.0495	0.0485	0.0475	0.0465	0.0455
−1.7	0.0446	0.0436	0.0427	0.0418	0.0409	0.0401	0.0392	0.0384	0.0375	0.0367
−1.8	0.0359	0.0351	0.0344	0.0336	0.0329	0.0322	0.0314	0.0307	0.0301	0.0294
−1.9	0.0287	0.0281	0.0274	0.0268	0.0262	0.0256	0.0250	0.0244	0.0239	0.0233
−2.0	0.0228	0.0222	0.0217	0.0212	0.0207	0.0202	0.0197	0.0192	0.0188	0.0183
−2.1	0.0179	0.0174	0.0170	0.0166	0.0162	0.0158	0.0154	0.0150	0.0146	0.0143
−2.2	0.0139	0.0136	0.0132	0.0129	0.0125	0.0122	0.0119	0.0116	0.0113	0.0110
−2.3	0.0107	0.0104	0.0102	0.0099	0.0096	0.0094	0.0091	0.0089	0.0087	0.0084
−2.4	0.0082	0.0080	0.0078	0.0075	0.0073	0.0071	0.0069	0.0068	0.0066	0.0064
−2.5	0.0062	0.0060	0.0059	0.0057	0.0055	0.0054	0.0052	0.0051	0.0049	0.0048
−2.6	0.0047	0.0045	0.0044	0.0043	0.0041	0.0040	0.0039	0.0038	0.0037	0.0036
−2.7	0.0035	0.0034	0.0033	0.0032	0.0031	0.0030	0.0029	0.0028	0.0027	0.0026
−2.8	0.0026	0.0025	0.0024	0.0023	0.0023	0.0022	0.0021	0.0021	0.0020	0.0019
−2.9	0.0019	0.0018	0.0018	0.0017	0.0016	0.0016	0.0015	0.0015	0.0014	0.0014
−3.0	0.0014	0.0013	0.0013	0.0012	0.0012	0.0011	0.0011	0.0011	0.0010	0.0010
−3.1	0.0010	0.0009	0.0009	0.0009	0.0008	0.0008	0.0008	0.0008	0.0007	0.0007
−3.2	0.0007	0.0007	0.0006	0.0006	0.0006	0.0006	0.0006	0.0005	0.0005	0.0005
−3.3	0.0005	0.0005	0.0005	0.0004	0.0004	0.0004	0.0004	0.0004	0.0004	0.0003
−3.4	0.0003	0.0003	0.0003	0.0003	0.0003	0.0003	0.0003	0.0003	0.0003	0.0002
−3.5	0.0002	0.0002	0.0002	0.0002	0.0002	0.0002	0.0002	0.0002	0.0002	0.0002
−3.6	0.0002	0.0002	0.0001	0.0001	0.0001	0.0001	0.0001	0.0001	0.0001	0.0001
−3.7	0.0001	0.0001	0.0001	0.0001	0.0001	0.0001	0.0001	0.0001	0.0001	0.0001
−3.8	0.0001	0.0001	0.0001	0.0001	0.0001	0.0001	0.0001	0.0001	0.0001	0.0001
−3.9	0.0000	0.0000	0.0000	0.0000	0.0000	0.0000	0.0000	0.0000	0.0000	0.0000
−4.0	0.0000	0.0000	0.0000	0.0000	0.0000	0.0000	0.0000	0.0000	0.0000	0.0000

Table for $N(x)$ When $x \geqslant 0$

This table shows values of $N(x)$ for $x \geqslant 0$. The table should be used with interpolation. For example,

$$\begin{aligned} N(0.6278) &= N(0.62) + 0.78[N(0.63) - N(0.62)] \\ &= 0.7324 + 0.78 \times (0.7357 - 0.7324) \\ &= 0.7350 \end{aligned}$$

x	.00	.01	.02	.03	.04	.05	.06	.07	.08	.09
0.0	0.5000	0.5040	0.5080	0.5120	0.5160	0.5199	0.5239	0.5279	0.5319	0.5359
0.1	0.5398	0.5438	0.5478	0.5517	0.5557	0.5596	0.5636	0.5675	0.5714	0.5753
0.2	0.5793	0.5832	0.5871	0.5910	0.5948	0.5987	0.6026	0.6064	0.6103	0.6141
0.3	0.6179	0.6217	0.6255	0.6293	0.6331	0.6368	0.6406	0.6443	0.6480	0.6517
0.4	0.6554	0.6591	0.6628	0.6664	0.6700	0.6736	0.6772	0.6808	0.6844	0.6879
0.5	0.6915	0.6950	0.6985	0.7019	0.7054	0.7088	0.7123	0.7157	0.7190	0.7224
0.6	0.7257	0.7291	0.7324	0.7357	0.7389	0.7422	0.7454	0.7486	0.7517	0.7549
0.7	0.7580	0.7611	0.7642	0.7673	0.7704	0.7734	0.7764	0.7794	0.7823	0.7852
0.8	0.7881	0.7910	0.7939	0.7967	0.7995	0.8023	0.8051	0.8078	0.8106	0.8133
0.9	0.8159	0.8186	0.8212	0.8238	0.8264	0.8289	0.8315	0.8340	0.8365	0.8389
1.0	0.8413	0.8438	0.8461	0.8485	0.8508	0.8531	0.8554	0.8577	0.8599	0.8621
1.1	0.8643	0.8665	0.8686	0.8708	0.8729	0.8749	0.8770	0.8790	0.8810	0.8830
1.2	0.8849	0.8869	0.8888	0.8907	0.8925	0.8944	0.8962	0.8980	0.8997	0.9015
1.3	0.9032	0.9049	0.9066	0.9082	0.9099	0.9115	0.9131	0.9147	0.9162	0.9177
1.4	0.9192	0.9207	0.9222	0.9236	0.9251	0.9265	0.9279	0.9292	0.9306	0.9319
1.5	0.9332	0.9345	0.9357	0.9370	0.9382	0.9394	0.9406	0.9418	0.9429	0.9441
1.6	0.9452	0.9463	0.9474	0.9484	0.9495	0.9505	0.9515	0.9525	0.9535	0.9545
1.7	0.9554	0.9564	0.9573	0.9582	0.9591	0.9599	0.9608	0.9616	0.9625	0.9633
1.8	0.9641	0.9649	0.9656	0.9664	0.9671	0.9678	0.9686	0.9693	0.9699	0.9706
1.9	0.9713	0.9719	0.9726	0.9732	0.9738	0.9744	0.9750	0.9756	0.9761	0.9767
2.0	0.9772	0.9778	0.9783	0.9788	0.9793	0.9798	0.9803	0.9808	0.9812	0.9817
2.1	0.9821	0.9826	0.9830	0.9834	0.9838	0.9842	0.9846	0.9850	0.9854	0.9857
2.2	0.9861	0.9864	0.9868	0.9871	0.9875	0.9878	0.9881	0.9884	0.9887	0.9890
2.3	0.9893	0.9896	0.9898	0.9901	0.9904	0.9906	0.9909	0.9911	0.9913	0.9916
2.4	0.9918	0.9920	0.9922	0.9925	0.9927	0.9929	0.9931	0.9932	0.9934	0.9936
2.5	0.9938	0.9940	0.9941	0.9943	0.9945	0.9946	0.9948	0.9949	0.9951	0.9952
2.6	0.9953	0.9955	0.9956	0.9957	0.9959	0.9960	0.9961	0.9962	0.9963	0.9964
2.7	0.9965	0.9966	0.9967	0.9968	0.9969	0.9970	0.9971	0.9972	0.9973	0.9974
2.8	0.9974	0.9975	0.9976	0.9977	0.9977	0.9978	0.9979	0.9979	0.9980	0.9981
2.9	0.9981	0.9982	0.9982	0.9983	0.9984	0.9984	0.9985	0.9985	0.9986	0.9986
3.0	0.9986	0.9987	0.9987	0.9988	0.9988	0.9989	0.9989	0.9989	0.9990	0.9990
3.1	0.9990	0.9991	0.9991	0.9991	0.9992	0.9992	0.9992	0.9992	0.9993	0.9993
3.2	0.9993	0.9993	0.9994	0.9994	0.9994	0.9994	0.9994	0.9995	0.9995	0.9995
3.3	0.9995	0.9995	0.9995	0.9996	0.9996	0.9996	0.9996	0.9996	0.9996	0.9997
3.4	0.9997	0.9997	0.9997	0.9997	0.9997	0.9997	0.9997	0.9997	0.9997	0.9998
3.5	0.9998	0.9998	0.9998	0.9998	0.9998	0.9998	0.9998	0.9998	0.9998	0.9998
3.6	0.9998	0.9998	0.9999	0.9999	0.9999	0.9999	0.9999	0.9999	0.9999	0.9999
3.7	0.9999	0.9999	0.9999	0.9999	0.9999	0.9999	0.9999	0.9999	0.9999	0.9999
3.8	0.9999	0.9999	0.9999	0.9999	0.9999	0.9999	0.9999	0.9999	0.9999	0.9999
3.9	1.0000	1.0000	1.0000	1.0000	1.0000	1.0000	1.0000	1.0000	1.0000	1.0000
4.0	1.0000	1.0000	1.0000	1.0000	1.0000	1.0000	1.0000	1.0000	1.0000	1.0000

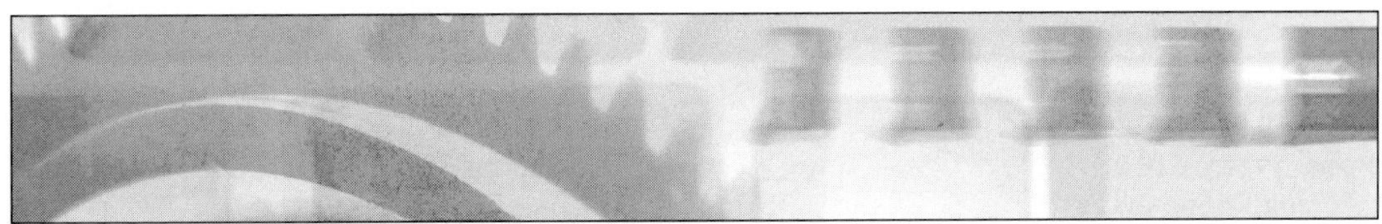

Index

References to items in the Glossary of Terms are **bolded**.

C

D

E

R

S

Y

Z

DATA DISK LICENSE AGREEMENT AND LIMITED WARRANTY

READ THIS LICENSE CAREFULLY BEFORE USING THIS PACKAGE. BY USING THIS PACKAGE, YOU ARE AGREEING TO THE TERMS AND CONDITIONS OF THIS LICENSE. IF YOU DO NOT AGREE, DO NOT USE THE PACKAGE. PROMPTLY RETURN THE UNUSED PACKAGE AND ALL ACCOMPANYING ITEMS TO THE PLACE YOU OBTAINED THEM. *THESE TERMS APPLY TO ALL LICENSED SOFTWARE ON THE DISK EXCEPT THAT THE TERMS FOR USE OF ANY SHAREWARE OR FREEWARE ON THE DISKETTES ARE AS SET FORTH IN THE ELECTRONIC LICENSE LOCATED ON THE DISK:*

1. GRANT OF LICENSE and OWNERSHIP: The enclosed data disk ("Software") is licensed, not sold, to you by Pearson Education, Inc., publishing as Prentice Hall ("We" or the "Company") for academic purposes and in consideration of your purchase or adoption of the accompanying Company textbooks and/or other materials, and your agreement to these terms. This license allows instructors and students enrolled in the course using the Company textbook that accompanies this Software (the "Course") to use, display and manipulate the data for academic use only, so long as you comply with the terms of this Agreement. We reserve any rights not granted to you. You own only the disk(s) but we and our licensors own the Software itself.

2. RESTRICTIONS ON USE AND TRANSFER: You may not transfer, distribute or make available the Software or the Documentation, except to instructors and students in your school in connection with the Course. You may not reverse engineer, disassemble, decompile, modify, adapt, translate or create derivative works based on the Software or the Documentation. You may be held legally responsible for any copying or copyright infringement that is caused by your failure to abide by the terms of these restrictions.

3. TERMINATION: This license is effective until terminated. This license will terminate automatically without notice from the Company if you fail to comply with any provisions or limitations of this license. Upon termination, you shall destroy the Documentation and all copies of the Software. All provisions of this Agreement as to limitation and disclaimer of warranties, limitation of liability, remedies or damages, and our ownership rights shall survive termination.

4. DISCLAIMER OF WARRANTY: THE COMPANY AND ITS LICENSORS MAKE NO WARRANTIES ABOUT THE SOFTWARE, WHICH IS PROVIDED "AS-IS." IF THE DISK IS DEFECTIVE IN MATERIALS OR WORKMANSHIP, YOUR ONLY REMEDY IS TO RETURN IT TO THE COMPANY WITHIN 30 DAYS FOR REPLACEMENT UNLESS THE COMPANY DETERMINES IN GOOD FAITH THAT THE DISK HAS BEEN MISUSED OR IMPROPERLY INSTALLED, REPAIRED, ALTERED OR DAMAGED. THE COMPANY DISCLAIMS ALL WARRANTIES, EXPRESS OR IMPLIED, INCLUDING WITHOUT LIMITATION, THE IMPLIED WARRANTIES OF MERCHANTABILITY AND FITNESS FOR A PARTICULAR PURPOSE. THE COMPANY DOES NOT WARRANT, GUARANTEE OR MAKE ANY REPRESENTATION REGARDING THE ACCURACY, RELIABILITY, CURRENTNESS, USE, OR RESULTS OF USE, OF THE SOFTWARE.

5. LIMITATION OF REMEDIES AND DAMAGES: IN NO EVENT, SHALL THE COMPANY OR ITS EMPLOYEES, AGENTS, LICENSORS OR CONTRACTORS BE LIABLE FOR ANY INCIDENTAL, INDIRECT, SPECIAL OR CONSEQUENTIAL DAMAGES ARISING OUT OF OR IN CONNECTION WITH THIS LICENSE OR THE SOFTWARE, INCLUDING, WITHOUT LIMITATION, LOSS OF USE, LOSS OF DATA, LOSS OF INCOME OR PROFIT, OR OTHER LOSSES SUSTAINED AS A RESULT OF INJURY TO ANY PERSON, OR LOSS OF OR DAMAGE TO PROPERTY, OR CLAIMS OF THIRD PARTIES, EVEN IF THE COMPANY OR AN AUTHORIZED REPRESENTATIVE OF THE COMPANY HAS BEEN ADVISED OF THE POSSIBILITY OF SUCH DAMAGES. SOME JURISDICTIONS DO NOT ALLOW THE LIMITATION OF DAMAGES IN CERTAIN CIRCUMSTANCES, SO THE ABOVE LIMITATIONS MAY NOT ALWAYS APPLY.

6. GENERAL: THIS AGREEMENT SHALL BE CONSTRUED IN ACCORDANCE WITH THE LAWS OF THE UNITED STATES OF AMERICA AND THE STATE OF NEW YORK, APPLICABLE TO CONTRACTS MADE IN NEW YORK, AND SHALL BENEFIT THE COMPANY, ITS AFFILIATES AND ASSIGNEES. This Agreement is the complete and exclusive statement of the agreement between you and the Company and supersedes all proposals, prior agreements, oral or written, and any other communications between you and the company or any of its representatives relating to the subject matter. If you are a U.S. Government user, this Software is licensed with "restricted rights" as set forth in subparagraphs (a)–(d) of the Commercial Computer-Restricted Rights clause at FAR 52.227-19 or in subparagraphs (c)(1)(ii) of the Rights in Technical Data and Computer Software clause at DFARS 252.227-7013, and similar clauses, as applicable.

Should you have any questions concerning this agreement or if you wish to contact the Company for any reason, please contact in writing:

Director, Media Production
Prentice Hall
1 Lake Street
Upper Saddle River, NJ 07458